O9-CFS-735

Cambridge
BUSINESS PUBLISHERS
Series in Accounting

Computerized Accounting
- **QuickBooks Online:** *2019 Update*, by Williams & Johnson
- **Computerized Accounting with QuickBooks® 2019** *(Desktop version)*, by Williams

Financial Accounting
- **Financial Accounting for Undergraduates, 4e** by Wallace, Nelson, and Christensen
- **Financial Accounting for Decision Makers, 2e** by DeFond
- **Financial Accounting, 6e** by Hanlon, Magee, Pfeiffer, and Dyckman
- **Financial Accounting for MBAs, 7e** by Easton, Wild, Halsey, and McAnally
- **Financial Accounting for Executives & MBAs, 4e** by Simko, Ferris, and Wallace
- **Financial Accounting Using IFRS, 2e** by Wong, Dyckman, Hanlon, Magee, and Pfeiffer

Managerial Accounting
- **Managerial Accounting for Undergraduates, 2e** by Christensen, Hobson, Wallace, and Matthews
- **Managerial Accounting, 8e** by Hartgraves & Morse

Combined Financial & Managerial Accounting
- **Financial & Managerial Accounting for Undergraduates, 2e** by Wallace, Nelson, Christensen, Hobson, and Matthews
- **Financial & Managerial Accounting for Decision Makers, 3e** by Dyckman, Hanlon, Magee, Pfeiffer, Hartgraves, and Morse
- **Financial & Managerial Accounting for MBAs, 5e** by Easton, Halsey, McAnally, Hartgraves, and Morse

Intermediate Accounting
- **Intermediate Accounting, 2e** by Hanlon, Hodder, Nelson, Roulstone, and Dragoo
- **Guide to Intermediate Accounting Research, 2e** by Collins

Cost Accounting
- **Cost Accounting: Foundations and Evolutions, 10e** by Kinney & Raiborn **(COMING 2020)**

Auditing
- **Alpine Cupcakes: An Audit Case with Data Analytics, 2e** by Dee, Durtschi, and Mindak

Financial Statement Analysis & Valuation
- **Financial Statement Analysis & Valuation, 5e** by Easton, McAnally, Sommers, and Zhang
- **Corporate Valuation, 2e** by Holthausen & Zmijewski
- **Valuation Using Financial Statements, 1e** by Sommers & Easton

Advanced Accounting
- **Advanced Accounting, 4e** by Hamlen
- **Advanced Accounting, 4e** by Hopkins & Halsey

Taxation
- **Scholes & Wolfson's Taxes and Business Strategy, 6e** by Erickson, Hanlon, Maydew, and Shevlin

Governmental and Not-For-Profit Accounting
- **Accounting for Governmental and Nonprofit Organizations, 1e** by Patton, Patton, and Ives
- **Governmental and Not-for-Profit Accounting: An Active Learning Workbook, 2e** by Convery

FASB Codification and eIFRS
- **Skills for Accounting Research: Text & Cases, 4e** by Collins

Casebooks
- **Cases in Financial Reporting, 8e** by Drake, Engel, Hirst, and McAnally
- **Cases in Managerial and Cost Accounting, 1e** by Allen, Brownlee, Haskins, and Lynch

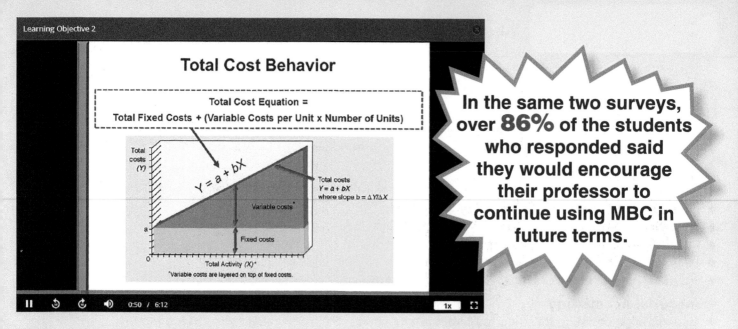

Make Instruction Needs-Based

◆ Identify where your students are struggling and customize your instruction to address their needs.
◆ Gauge how your entire class or individual students are performing by viewing the easy-to-use gradebook.
◆ Ensure your students are getting the additional reinforcement and direction they need between class meetings.

Provide Instruction and Practice 24/7

◆ Assign homework from your Cambridge Business Publishers' textbook and have myBusinessCourse grade it for you automatically.
◆ With our eLectures, your students can revisit accounting topics as often as they like or until they master the topic.
◆ Guided Examples show students how to solve select problems.
◆ Make homework due before class to ensure students enter your classroom prepared.
◆ For an additional fee, upgrade MBC to include the eBook and you have all the tools needed for an online course.

LMS Integration

 integrates with many learning management systems, including **Canvas**, **Blackboard**, **Moodle**, **D2L**, **Schoology**, and **Sakai**. Your gradebooks sync automatically.

Getting Started is as EASY as 1, 2, 3 . . . 4!

1. Sign Up	**2.** Setup Your Course	**3.** Invite Your Students	**4.** Manage Your Course
Instructors register with myBusinessCourse.com	Add your class details and additional materials.	Students register using your unique course code.	Study, test, and grade assignments. It's simple!

Want to learn more about myBusinessCourse?

Contact your sales representative or visit www.mybusinesscourse.com.

Financial Accounting for Executives & MBAs

Text & Cases

Fourth Edition

PAUL J. SIMKO
Darden School of Business
University of Virginia

KENNETH R. FERRIS
W.P. Carey School of Business
Arizona State University

JAMES S. WALLACE
The Peter F. Drucker and Masatoshi Ito
Graduate School of Management
Claremont Graduate University

Cambridge
BUSINESS PUBLISHERS

Photo Credits
Chapter 1: Getty Images
Chapter 2: iStock Photo
Chapter 3: iStock Photo
Chapter 4: iStock Photo
Chapter 5: iStock Photo
Chapter 6: iStock Photo
Chapter 7: iStock Photo
Chapter 8: iStock Photo
Chapter 9: iStock Photo
Chapter 10: Getty Images
Chapter 11: iStock Photo
Chapter 12: Getty Images

FINANCIAL ACCOUNTING FOR EXECUTIVES & MBAs, Fourth Edition, by Paul Simko, Kenneth Ferris, and James Wallace

Student ISBN: 978-1-61853-198-8

Bookstores & Faculty: to order this book, contact the company via email **customerservice@cambridgepub.com** or call 800-619-6473.

Students: to order this book, please visit the book's website and order directly online.

Printed in the United States of America.
10 9 8 7 6 5 4 3 2

About the Authors

Paul J. Simko is Associate Dean of the MBA for Executives Program and Associate Professor of Business at the University of Virginia's Darden School. He received Bachelor of Science and Master in Accountancy degrees from the University of Florida, and a Ph.D. from the University of Texas at Austin. Professor Simko was previously on the faculty at Emory University, and has served as a visiting professor at Indiana, INSEAD, the Helsinki School of Economics, and the Indian School of Business. He was a Senior Analyst with Citicorp and is a Certified Public Accountant, and he remains a frequent consultant to government agencies and public and private corporations. Professor Simko has received numerous recognitions for his research and teaching. His research has appeared in such journals as *The Accounting Review, Journal of Accounting Research, Financial Analysts Journal*, and the *Stanford Journal of Law, Business and Finance*.

Kenneth R. Ferris is a Professor in the W.P. Carey School of Business at Arizona State University. He received a B.B.A. and an M.B.A. from The George Washington University and an M.A. and a Ph.D. from The Ohio State University. He previously served on the faculties of Northwestern University, The Claremont Graduate University, Southern Methodist University, and Thunderbird School of Global Management, In addition, he has taught at numerous academic institutions in Australia, Hong Kong, Japan, and New Zealand. Professor Ferris is the author or co-author of eleven books, over fifty academic and professional publications, and over eighty case studies. He previously served as a director of several NYSE listed companies and is active in executive education programs around the world.

James S. Wallace is an Associate Professor at The Peter F. Drucker and Masatoshi Ito Graduate School of Management at The Claremont Graduate University. He received his B.A. from the University of California, Santa Barbara, his M.B.A. from the University of California, Davis, and his Ph.D. from the University of Washington. Professor Wallace also holds a CPA certification from the state of California. He previously served on the faculty of the University of California, Irvine and has served as a visiting professor at the University of California, San Diego. Professor Wallace's work has appeared in leading academic journals including the *Journal of Accounting and Economics*, the *Journal of Corporate Finance*, and *Information Systems Research*, along with leading applied journals such as the *Journal of Applied Corporate Finance*, the *Journal of Accountancy*, *Issues in Accounting Education* and *Accounting Horizons*. Prior to his career in academics, Professor Wallace worked in public accounting and in industry with a Fortune 500 company. He has done consulting work with numerous companies in multiple industries.

Preface

Welcome to the fourth edition of *Financial Accounting for Executives & MBAs*. If you have prior business experience, either working for a company or managing your own business, then you know firsthand that an understanding of financial accounting is essential to achieve your full potential on the job. Although business decisions certainly involve a careful analysis of non-financial factors, they also almost always require analysis of financial accounting information. Initiating a marketing campaign, restructuring a subsidiary, determining the sale price of a new product, or assessing whether to acquire another company (and at what price) are just a few of the business decisions that require an understanding of financial accounting. This textbook is written to facilitate that understanding and to facilitate the reader's personal goal of gaining a more complete understanding of financial accounting and its use in business decisions.

Target Audience

Financial Accounting for Executives & MBAs is written specifically for the Executive MBA and MBA markets. This concise text can be used in a wide variety of course formats, ranging from brief executive programs lasting only a few weekends to more traditional 15-week courses.

> "I've been teaching 10 years, and this is the BEST text I've seen for introducing financial accounting to a layperson. My major problem with texts has been that they are either too broad or too detailed. This book is the perfect mix of breadth and depth for a layperson, be they an executive who has had some exposure to accounting or a student who is just entering the study of accounting. This book is excellent."
>
> — **Catherine Eason, *Queens University of Charlotte***

Book Organization

A flexible 12-chapter structure that fits all varieties of MBA programs: full-time, part-time, and executive. This book provides students with the tools and insights necessary to make informed business decisions ranging from performance evaluation to firm valuation. The chapters are organized around a decision-focused structure. The first three chapters introduce the basic structure of financial accounting. This includes a focus on the role of accounting for the firm and the financial markets, as well as a detailed review of the primary financial statements. This is followed by a chapter focused exclusively on the financial analysis techniques and key ratios used to evaluate firm performance, solvency, and capital structure.

I. The Foundations of Accounting and the Financial Statements (Chapters 1–3)

II. Financial Statement Analysis (Chapter 4)

The next six chapters provide additional structure around these opening themes, with each chapter including a section that discusses how the chapter's content should be analyzed and how that analysis will impact firm value:

III. Operating Resources and Decisions (Chapters 5–6)

IV. Investing Resources and Decisions (Chapters 7–8)

V. Financing Resources and Decisions (Chapters 9–11)

The book concludes with an introduction to various methodologies to assess the value of a company:

VI. Equity Valuation (Chapter 12)

What is the Unique Approach to Illustrating Financial Accounting Concepts?

Both the traditional and executive MBA markets tend to be more analytical and decision-focused than the undergraduate market. Because of this, financial accounting needs be introduced in an accessible and highly relevant, manner. Unlike many graduate and undergraduate textbooks in accounting that use the classic debit and credit paradigm to explain key concepts, this textbook explains the fundamentals of financial accounting using a template approach that mirrors what is found in practice. It also is easily adaptable to spreadsheet applications. Not only is this approach more user-friendly (because most managers routinely use spreadsheets in their daily professional lives), but it is also far less labor- and time-intensive than the classic debit/credit paradigm.

The unique approach to recording transactions taken in this textbook emphasizes user analysis and deemphasizes bookkeeping. It builds upon the basic accounting equation to demonstrate how business events are processed and ultimately recorded. Both executive and MBA students praise the approach for its simplicity and intuitive appeal, as well as for its link back to how they observe accounting information in their professional lives. More specifically, it presents a vertical format to the balance sheet equation, functionally following the form and presentation of the balance sheet most often observed in practice and annual reports. The format is also used to illustrate income statement accounts as inputs directly into the retained earnings account, reinforcing this important concept to students in a way that helps them more clearly understand the relation between the balance sheet and income statement. Below is an example of the financial statement spreadsheet approach used in the context of a long-term fixed asset acquisition and sale:

	Acquire Machine	Depreciate Machine	Sell Machine	End. Bal. (summary)	
Assets					
Cash........................	(60,000)		15,000	(45,000)	
::					
Property, plant and equipment.....	60,000		(60,000)	—	
Accumulated depreciation........		(50,000)	50,000	—	
Shareholders' Equity					
Retained earnings				(45,000)	
Depreciation expense..........		(50,000)			} Retained earnings = ($45,000)
Gain on sale			5,000		

Decision-Relevant Focus

A key skill set for all investment professionals, lenders, managers, analysts, and shareholders is the ability to use accounting information for decision-making purposes. In this book, we link the discussion of topics to the following two business decisions:

1. Should I extend credit, and at what terms, to this company?
2. Should I invest in this company, and if so, at what price?

Thus, the analysis of financial statements is a key organizational theme that extends throughout the book.

> "I believe that the concise and clear writing is a major strength of this book. The authors should also be complimented on being able to use a good number of examples while still keeping the chapters concise."
>
> — **Charles Leflar**, *University of Arkansas*

Grounded in the Context of Corporate Decisions

Accounting information is an integral part of decision making at every level in business. Consequently, the book's discussion of important accounting concepts is grounded in the context of actual corporate decisions. To this end, the book contains an abundance of excerpts and illustrations from actual corporate financial reports and disclosures that highlight the role and impact of accounting information, and financial statements specifically, in business decision making. Following is one example in the context of comprehensive income disclosures:

EXHIBIT 11.3	Other Comprehensive Income Disclosures			
GENERAL ELECTRIC COMPANY				
December 31 ($ millions)		2014	2013	Change
Accumulated other comprehensive income, net				
Investment securities		$ 708	$ (374)	$ 1,082
Currency translation adjustments		(2,729)	(308)	(2,421)
Cash flow hedges		234	467	(233)
Benefit plans		(7,279)	11,300	(18,579)
Total accumulated other comprehensive income, net		$(9,066)	$11,085	$(20,151)

Does the Book Reflect Contemporary Knowledge?

In our experience, EMBAs and MBAs frequently seem interested in exploring empirical questions such as: "How do the capital markets respond to accounting policy changes?" and "Which EPS measure—Basic EPS or Diluted EPS—is used by the capital market to value a company's stock?" Where appropriate, we have made reference to, and discussion of, the existing research in accounting and finance to address some of these empirically-based questions. By doing so, we enable the interested reader to further her/his knowledge of these questions.

BUSINESS PERSPECTIVE

IPOs Around the World

Historically, the U.S. stock exchanges have attracted the vast majority of the world's initial public offerings (IPOs). Recently, however, as world economies and financial markets have grown, stock exchanges around the world have become attractive alternatives. The tables below from a recent Ernst & Young study confirm this fact; they summarize the top 12 worldwide IPOs for 2013 by the number of deals and by cumulative size. While the New York Stock Exchange (NYSE) still led the way in terms of total dollars of new capital, the NASDAQ and stock exchanges in Asia, Europe, Australia and South America were also very active. Hong Kong, in fact, raised the second highest total of IPO capital in 2013. The NYSE and NASDAQ combined had just over 25 percent of the world's 2013 IPOs.

2013 Global IPOs by Stock Exchange

Top 12 Exchanges by Number of Deals			Top 12 Exchanges by Capital Raised		
Exchange	No. of Deals	% of Global Total	Exchange	Capital Raised ($ mill.)	% of Global Total
New York (NYSE)	114	13.2%	New York (NYSE)	$ 44,081	27.0%
NASDAQ	108	12.5%	Hong Kong (HKEx)	16,548	10.2%
Hong Kong (HKEx)	68	7.9%	NASDAQ	15,560	9.5%
Australia (ASX)	52	6.0%	London (LSE)	13,306	8.2%
London (AIM)	49	5.7%	Tokyo (TSE)	9,249	5.7%
KOSDAQ	37	4.3%	Sao Paulo (BM&F BOVESPA)	8,479	5.2%
Bombay SME	30	3.5%	Australia (ASX)	5,854	3.6%
Indonesia (IDX)	29	3.4%	Thailand (SET)	5,195	3.2%
Tokyo MOTHERS	29	3.4%	Mexican (BMV)	4,805	2.9%
Hong Kong GEM	21	2.4%	Singapore (SGX)	4,647	2.9%
Thailand (SET)	21	2.4%	New Zealand (NZX)	3,893	2.4%
London (LSE)	20	2.3%	Deutsche Borse	3,288	2.0%
All other exchanges	285	33.0%	All other exchanges	28,110	17.2%
Total	863	100.00%	Global total	$163,015	100.00%

Source: "EY Global IPO Trends Q4 2013," Ernst & Young

Important Pedagogical Elements

The book applies several pedagogical elements to help readers further understand the ramifications of accounting for business.

Global Perspective boxed inserts emphasize the similarity of U.S. GAAP and IFRS, but they also identify key differences. Exposure to similarities and differences is important as the pressure mounts to harmonize accounting standards globally.

GLOBAL PERSPECTIVE

In some countries, when common shares carry a letter class designation, it is in reference to who may purchase the shares (a citizen of the country or a noncitizen). For instance, in China for many years, Class A shares could only be purchased by Chinese citizens whereas (until 2001) only noncitizens could purchase Class B shares. In 2003, as China began liberalizing its capital markets to facilitate increased foreign investment, its securities laws were relaxed to permit the sale of H shares in Hong Kong, L shares in London, N shares in New York, and S shares in Singapore.

Ethics Perspective boxed inserts emphasize ethical decision making, as well as the importance of ethics in accounting. In today's environment post-implementation of Sarbanes-Oxley, this information is pertinent to business students and accounting students alike.

ETHICS PERSPECTIVE

Numerous reasons were cited in this chapter as to why some firms use leasing as a financing approach for acquiring capital assets. One reason is the managerial desire to avoid disclosing the operating lease liability on a company's balance sheet. It can be argued that there should not be any difference to financial statement users whether a lease obligation appears on the face of the balance sheet or is disclosed in the footnotes to the financial statements. As demonstrated in this chapter, it is a simple procedure for financial statement users to adjust the balance sheet for this type of off-balance-sheet debt. Nonetheless, many managers behave as if they believe that financial statement users will not undertake the necessary financial statement adjustments to develop a complete assessment of a firm's debt exposure. Available evidence, however, indicates that financial markets are not fooled by off-balance-sheet financing, and instead, market participants appear to incorporate this information in their assessments of the risk premium associated with public companies utilizing off-balance-sheet financing. Even so, the FASB has now taken steps to close this form of off-balance-sheet financing with proposed new lease accounting standards.

Business Perspective boxed inserts illustrate key chapter topics using real-world examples and financial statements.

BUSINESS PERSPECTIVE

Airline Ticket Revenue Recognition at Delta Air Lines

Delta Air Lines is the largest airline in the world when measured by almost any metric: total revenue, fleet size, passenger miles flown, and number of passengers. The company is based in Atlanta, Georgia, the location of its primary hub, and it has helped make Atlanta's Hartsfield-Jackson International Airport the busiest in the world.

The sale of an airline ticket may seem straightforward from the consumer-perspective: buy a ticket, sometimes months in advance, then take the flight. But from Delta's perspective the sale involves other factors to consider regarding how much and when to record revenue. According to the company's footnotes to its financial statements, when tickets are sold a portion is initially recorded as a component of "air traffic liability," a current liability on the balance sheet (equivalent to deferred revenue or unearned revenue); and, if the passenger has a frequent flyer account, a portion is allocated to "frequent flyer deferred revenue." Delta's 2014 annual 10-K report filing with the U.S. Securities and Exchange Commission reports the amount of recognized revenue and deferred revenue for 2014 and 2013 was as follows:

(in millions)	December 31 2014	December 31 2013
Income Statement		
Revenues	$40,462	$37,773
Balance Sheet (liabilities)		
Air traffic liability	$4,296	$ 4,122
Frequent flyer deferred revenue—current	1,580	1,861
Frequent flyer deferred revenue—noncurrent	2,602	2,559

These deferred revenue liability accounts are quite significant to Delta, approximating 21% and

---

Tax Perspective boxed inserts highlight select aspects of U.S. tax law and how they differ from generally accepted accounting principles. Executives and MBAs very often are interested in understanding how their decisions affect both financial accounting earnings and the cash flows related to the tax treatment of those same decisions. While this text is clearly focused on the former, high-level overviews of some key tax reporting differences are offered throughout the text. Below is an example related to investments:

TAX PERSPECTIVE

Zero-coupon Bonds and Taxes

In general, the tax treatment of zero-coupon bonds and notes follows the GAAP accounting treatment—that is, the accrued interest on the debt is tax-deductible in the period incurred, not when paid at maturity. Thus, zero-coupon bonds have two cash flow advantages: (1) the periodic interest cost remains unpaid until maturity, and (2) the unpaid periodic interest cost is currently tax-deductible, providing an immediate interest tax shield to the issuing company.

From the perspective of the IRS, the tax effect of zero-coupon bonds is essentially tax-neutral. The unpaid interest expense is tax-deductible to the issuing firm but is taxable income to the buyer of the bonds in the period in which the interest is effectively earned, not the period when it is received.

In Practice boxed inserts help bridge the gap between the classroom and what students encounter in the real world. "In Practice" illustrations document situations a reader is likely to encounter and present the choices that companies make in reporting financial results.

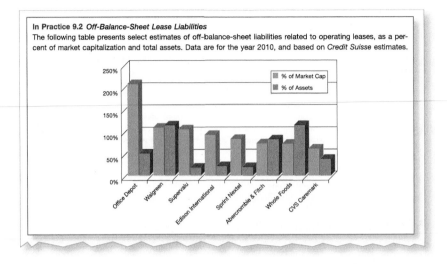

Tools that Reinforce Reader Comprehension

Each chapter includes many tools that reinforce an understanding of the chapter contents. These tools include:

- **Review Problem**, with solution
- **Executive Summary**
- **Key Concepts and Terms**, with page references
- **Discussion Questions**
- **Exercises**
- **Problems**
- **Corporate Analysis**
- **Check figures** to accompany select exercises and problems, denoted by CHECK FIGURE

"The discussion questions are great for an Executive MBA or MBA audience because they are targeted at a more sophisticated student than the typical introductory financial accounting text. They should help a professor stimulate interesting discussions in the classroom."

— **Jeffrey Wong,** *University of Nevada, Reno*

NEW IN THE FOURTH EDITION

This edition of *Financial Accounting for Executives & MBAs* includes a number of important new features. These include:

- Updated reference to recent changes in accounting principles, including the new standards and guidelines for revenue recognition, leases, and extraordinary items.
- Extensive reference to timely accounting treatments facing high-profile companies.
- Revisions and updates to many of the end of chapter questions, exercises, and problems.
- An expanded appendix focused on key financial statement metrics and ratios.
- Expanded the number of Review problems per chapter with corresponding Guided Example videos for students.
- Revised Takeaways to ensure coverage of all topics.
- New Appendix on Working Capital Management.

- Refinements and more precision to time value of money illustrations throughout the text including a spreadsheet and financial calculator demonstration in Appendix A.
- Changes and updates to the tax perspectives boxes and to international accounting standards.
- The addition of cases to select chapters' end of chapter sections with solutions and case notes for instructors.
- BusinessCourse (MBC) is a complete learning and assessment program that accompanies the textbook and contributes to student success in this course. With the fourth edition, MBC has been enhanced to include new questions and improvements to existing questions and functionality. The Chapter Takeaways are now denoted with an icon in the margin, indicating availability of eLecture videos for students.

Companion Casebook for Case-Based Instruction

Cases in Financial Reporting, 8th edition by Michael Drake (Brigham Young University), Ellen Engel (University of Chicago), D. Eric Hirst (University of Texas–Austin), and Mary Lea McAnally (Texas A&M University). This book comprises 27 cases and is a perfect companion book for faculty interested in exposing students to a wide range of real financial statements. The cases are current and cover companies from Canada, France, Austria, the Netherlands, the UK, India, as well as from the U.S. Many of the U.S. companies are major multinationals. Each case deals with a specific financial accounting topic within the context of one (or more) company's financial statements. Each case contains financial statement information and a set of directed questions pertaining to one or two specific financial accounting issues. This is a separate, saleable casebook (**ISBN 978-1-61853-122-3**). Contact your sales representative to receive a desk copy or email customerservice@cambridgepub.com.

SUPPLEMENTAL MATERIALS

For Instructors

Solutions Manual: Written by the textbook authors, the Solutions Manual provides suggestions for classroom use and suggested solutions for the end-of-chapter questions, exercises, and problems.

Test Bank: The Test Bank provides a full range of mechanical, analytical, and critical thinking problems for each chapter of the book.

PowerPoint Presentations: PowerPoint presentations illustrate chapter concepts and help formulate classroom lectures and presentations.

BusinessCourse: A web-based learning and assessment program intended to complement your textbook and classroom instruction. This easy-to-use course management system grades homework automatically and provide students with additional help when you are not available. In addition, detailed diagnostic tools assess class and individual performance. myBusinessCourse is ideal for online courses or traditional face-to-face courses for which you want to offer students more resources to succeed. Assignments with the MBC in the margin are available in myBusinessCourse. eLecture videos are available for the Chapter Takeaways, and Guided Examples are available for you to assign to students.

For Students

Check Figures: Exercises and problems with check figures are identified with CHECK FIGURE in the margin. Check figures are located at the text Website.

eLectures: Each chapter's takeaway includes an eLecture video available in our online learning management system, myBusinessCourse (see below for more information.)

Guided Examples: Guided Example problems are available for student review.

BusinessCourse is a web-based learning and assessment program intended to complement your textbook and faculty instruction. eLecture videos and Guided Example videos are available to you along with practice quizzes. This easy-to-use program provides you with additional help when your instructor is not available. With Instructor-Led MBC courses, assignments with MBC in the margin are also available and are automatically graded. Access to MBC is free with new copies of this textbook (look for page containing the access code towards the front of the book). If you buy a used copy of the book, you can purchase access at www.mybusinesscourse.com.

ACKNOWLEDGEMENTS

The development of this textbook and the accompanying Solutions Manual has benefited from the assistance of Ms. Torrey Mann. Our special thanks for her help. We also thank George Werthman, Debbie McQuade, Terry McQuade, Katie Jones-Aiello, Jill Fischer, Jocelyn Mousel, Lorraine Gleeson, Beth Gilgen Nodus, Jill Sternard, and the rest of the staff at Cambridge Business Publishers for their help. A special thank you to Eric Jourdan for his help checking the accuracy of our work. Professor Graeme Rankine made a significant academic contribution to the development of this book; and, our thanks are extended to him for his involvement. Finally, we extend our gratitude to the following colleagues, who provided detailed chapter feedback and insightful advice on the first and second editions:

Peter Aghimien, *University of Indiana-South Bend*
Robert Allen, *University of Utah*
Alicia Amaral, *Tufts University*
Paul Bahnson, *Boise State University*
Andrew Borchers, *Lipscomb University*
Jeff Brothers, *Regis University*
Marvin Bouillon, *Iowa State University*
Louis Braiotta, *SUNY-Binghamton*
Philip Brown, *Harding University*
Steve Buchheit, *Texas Tech University*
Thomas Buchman, *University of Colorado-Boulder*
Catherine Byrne, *Boston College*
James Cannon, *Iowa State University*
Jack Cathey, *University of North Carolina-Charlotte*
Robert Churchman, *Harding University*
Paul Clikeman, *University of Richmond*
Jane Cote, *Washington State University*
David Cottrell, *Brigham Young University*
Kelvie Crabb, *University of Kansas*
Shirley J. Daniel, *University of Hawaii-Manoa*
Somnath Das, *University of Illinois at Chicago*
Mark Dawkins, *University of Georgia*
Mark DeFond, *University of Southern California*
David Donnelly, *University of Missouri-Kansas City*
Catherine Eason, *Queens University*
Laurel Franzen, *University of Texas-Dallas*
George Geiss, *UCLA*
Hubert Glover, *Drexel University*
Julia Grant, *Case Western Reserve University*
Carla Hayn, *UCLA*
Michele C. Henderson, *Queens University*
Maggie Houston, *Wright State University*
Henry Huang, *Prairie View A&M University*
Lijyun Angela Hwang, *Eastern Michigan University*
Gun Joh, *San Diego State University*
Jeff Jones, *Auburn University*
Richard C. Jones, *Hofstra University*
Thomas Kelley, *Seattle University*
Michael Kimbrough, *University of Maryland*
Alison Kirby-Jones, *Boston University*
Mehmet Kocakulah, *University of Southern Indiana*
SP Kothari, *Massachusetts Institute of Technology*
Gopal Krishnan, *Lehigh University*
Claire Latham, *Washington State University*

Charles Leflar, *University of Arkansas*
David Lemoine, *Boston College*
Margarita Lenk, *Colorado State University*
Xu Li, *Lehigh University*
Barbara Lougee, *University of San Diego*
Anna Lusher, *Slippery Rock University*
Robert Magee, *Northwestern University*
Michel Magnan, *Concordia University*
Ajay Maindiratta, *New York University*
Nancy Mangold, *California State University, East Bay*
Paul Mason, *University of Kansas*
Lorie Milam, *University of Texas-San Antonio*
John J. Morris, *Kansas State University*
Mark Myring, *Ball State University*
Sandeep Nabar, *Oklahoma State University*
Bruce Neumann, *University of Colorado-Denver*
Michelle Nickla, *Ivy Tech Community College*
Sarah Nutter, *George Mason University*
Leslie Oakes, *New Mexico State University*
Derek Oler, *Texas Tech University*
Deborah Pavelka, *Roosevelt University*
Sy Pearlman, *California State University, Long Beach*
Aaron Pennington, *University of Cincinnati*
Suresh Radhakrishnan, *University of Texas-Dallas*
Timothy Redmer, *Regent University*
Laura Rickett, *Kent State University*
Debra Salbador, *Virginia Tech University*
Elaine Sanders, *University of Texas-San Antonio*
Hadley Schaefer, *University of Florida*
Adina Scruggs, *Bryan College*
Sandy Simon, *University of Denver*
Charles Stanley, *Baylor University*
Jan Taylor, *Sam Houston State University*
Robin Thomas, *North Carolina University*
Samuel Tiras, *Louisiana State University*
Thomas Tyson, *St. John Fisher College*
Mark Vargus, *University of Texas-Dallas*
Marcia Vorholt, *Xavier University*
Robert Walsh, *University of Dallas*
Charles Wasley, *University of Rochester*
Raymond Wilson, *Boston University*
Jeffrey A. Wong, *University of Nevada-Reno*
Lee Yao, *Loyola University-New Orleans*

Paul J. Simko
Kenneth R. Ferris
James S. Wallace
October 2016

Brief Contents

CHAPTER 1   The Economic Environment of Accounting Information   3

CHAPTER 2   From Business Events to Financial Statements   39

CHAPTER 3   Measuring Performance: Cash Flow and Net Income   85

CHAPTER 4   Using Financial Statements for Investing and Credit Decisions   129

CHAPTER 5   Operating Cycle, Revenue Recognition, and Receivable Valuation   175

CHAPTER 6   Operating Expenses, Inventory Valuation, and Accounts Payable   219

CHAPTER 7   Long-Lived Fixed Assets, Intangible Assets, and Natural Resources   261

CHAPTER 8   Investing In Other Entities   297

CHAPTER 9   Debt Financing: Bonds, Notes, and Leases   339

CHAPTER 10 Commitments and Contingent Liabilities, Deferred Tax Liabilities, and Retirement Obligations   379

CHAPTER 11 Equity Financing and Shareholders' Equity   413

CHAPTER 12 Using Accounting Information in Equity Valuation   457

Appendix A: The Time Value of Money   506

Appendix B: Financial Statement Ratios and Metrics   522

Appendix C: IFRS Illustrated: LVMH Moët Hennessey-Louis Vuitton S.A.   526

Appendix D: Accounting Mechanics: T-Accounts and Journal Entries   532

Appendix E: Working Capital Management   554

Index   560

Table of Contents

CHAPTER **1**

**The Economic Environment
of Accounting Information   3**

Financial Accounting and Its Relevance   **4**
   Why Accounting Information Is Important   **5**
   Financial Accounting: What Is It?   **5**
Financial Statements   **7**
Review Problem 1.1   13
   Qualitative Attributes of Accounting Information   **13**
   Amazon's Accounting Methods and the Role of the
     Independent Auditor   **14**
Generally Accepted Accounting Principles   **16**
Role of Financial Accounting in
  Investment Decisions: An Overview   **19**
Review Problem 1.2   21
Changing Economic Landscape   **21**
Seven Accounting Myths   **22**
Executive Summary   **23**
Key Concepts and Terms   **23**
Appendix 1A: Agency Costs and the Separation
           of Management and Capital
           Providers   **24**
   Conflicts Between Managers and Shareholders   **25**
   Conflicts Between Debtholders and Shareholders   **25**
Appendix 1B: Generally Accepted Accounting
           Principles: Purpose, Concepts, and
           Elements   **26**
Questions   **27**
Exercises   **29**
Problems   **31**
Corporate Analysis   **35**
Solutions to Review Problems   **36**

CHAPTER **2**

**From Business Events to
Financial Statements   39**

Balance Sheet Equation   **40**
   Defining Some Accounting Terms   **42**
Review Problem 2.1   43
Preparing Financial Statements from Business
  Events   **43**

The Russian River Valley Winery   **44**
   Projected Business Events   **47**
   Preparing the Financial Statements   **57**
   Articulation of the Financial Statements   **60**
   Accounting Policy Decisions at Russian River Valley
     Winery   **62**
Review Problem 2.2   63
Evaluating Business Performance and Making
  Financial Decisions   **63**
   Evaluating Firm Profitability   **64**
   Return on Equity Analysis   **65**
   Evaluating Financial Risk   **67**
Review Problem 2.3   67
Managerial Discretion and Accounting Methods   **68**
   Operating Revenues at B.J.'s Wholesale Club   **68**
   Operating Expenses at America Online   **69**
Executive Summary   **70**
Key Concepts and Terms   **70**
Questions   **71**
Exercises   **72**
Problems   **74**
Corporate Analysis   **80**
Solutions to Review ProblemS   **81**

CHAPTER **3**

**Measuring Performance:
Cash Flow and Net
Income   85**

Analyzing and Computing Cash Flow
  Information   **86**
   Statement of Cash Flow   **86**
   Presenting Cash Flow Information   **87**
   Computing Cash Flow Under the Indirect Method   **88**
Review Problem 3.1   96
Analysis of the Statement of Cash Flow   **96**
   Cash Flow Ratios   **98**
   Alternative Measures of Cash Flow   **99**
Review Problem 3.2   102
Identifying and Understanding
  Sustainable Earnings   **102**
   Special Items and Extraordinary Items   **103**
   Discontinued Operations   **105**

Earnings per Share **105**
Review Problem 3.3 107
Pro Forma Earnings **108**
Executive Summary **110**
Key Concepts and Terms **110**
Appendix 3A: Converting Indirect Method Cash Flows to Direct Method Cash Flows **111**
Questions **112**
Exercises **114**
Problems **117**
Corporate Analysis **124**
Case **125**
Solutions to Review Problems **127**

CHAPTER **4**
Using Financial Statements for Investing and Credit Decisions 129

Analyzing Financial Performance **130**
Fundamentals of Financial Statement Analysis **130**
Percentage Change and Common-Size Financial Statements **132**
Review Problem 4.1 135
Financial Ratios **136**
Review Problem 4.2 140
Credit Risk Analysis **141**
Benchmarking: Comparisons with Similar Companies **141**
ROE Model Framework **143**
Estimating Sustainable Growth **144**
Review Problem 4.3 146
Limitations of Financial Statement Analysis **146**
Executive Summary **148**
Key Concepts and Terms **148**
Appendix 4A: Unlevering Financial Ratios **148**
Appendix 4B: Pro Forma Financial Statements **149**
Appendix 4C: Calculating the Cost of Equity Financing **150**
Questions **151**
Exercises **153**
Problems **157**
Corporate Analysis **164**
Case **165**
Solutions to Review Problems **172**

CHAPTER **5**
Operating Cycle, Revenue Recognition, and Receivable Valuation 175

Operating Cycle of a Business **176**
Fundamentals of Revenue Recognition **177**
Revenue Recognition by Retail and Service Companies **180**
Review Problem 5.1 180
Revenue Recognition by Manufacturing Companies **181**
Review Problem 5.2 186
Valuing and Reporting Accounts Receivable **186**
Percentage-of-Credit-Sales Method **187**
Aging Method **189**
Review Problem 5.3 193
Managing a Company's Investment in Receivables **194**
Sales Discounts **194**
Sales Returns **196**
Review Problem 5.4 196
Monetizing Accounts Receivable to Manage Operating Cash Flow **196**
Factoring **196**
Pledging **197**
Securitization **197**
Analyzing Operating Revenue and Receivables **198**
Revenue Recognition Policy **198**
Receivable Valuation Policy **198**
Executive Summary **200**
Key Concepts and Terms **201**
Appendix 5A: Revenue Recognition: SAB No. 101 **201**
General Guidance on Revenue Recognition **201**
Persuasive Evidence of a Sales Arrangement **201**
Delivery and Performance **202**
Fixed or Determinable Sales Price **202**
Other Issues **202**
Appendix 5B: New Revenue Recognition Standards: Revenue from Contracts with Customers **202**
A Five-Step Process **203**
Questions **205**
Exercises **206**
Problems **208**
Corporate Analysis **212**
Case **213**
Solutions to Review Problems **216**

CHAPTER **6**

Operating Expenses, Inventory Valuation, and Accounts Payable   219

Operating Cycle of a manufacturer   220
Measuring Cost of Goods Sold
and Ending Inventory   221
   Case Illustration: How Much are Earnings?   222
   Inventory Management Systems   223
   The Inventory Count   224
Valuing Inventory Using FIFO, LIFO, and Weighted-
average—A Closer Look   225
   Choosing an Inventory Method   228
Review Problem 6.1   230
   Lower-of-Cost-or-Market (LCM)   230
Review Problem 6.2   232
   Inventory Accounting Under International Financial
     Reporting Standards   232
LIFO Layers and the LIFO Inventory Reserve   232
   Liquidating LIFO Layers   235
Managing a Company's Investment
in Inventories   237
Accounts Payable and a company's Operating
Cycle   237
Review Problem 6.3   238
Analyzing Inventory and Cost of Goods Sold   240
Executive Summary   241
Key Concepts and Terms   242
Questions   242
Exercises   243
Problems   246
Corporate Analysis   253
Case   254
Solutions to Review Problems   257

CHAPTER **7**

Long-Lived Fixed Assets, Intangible Assets, and Natural Resources   261

Acquisition Cost of a Long-Lived Asset   262
   Betterment Versus Maintenance Expenditures   263
Matching: The Allocation of costs to future
periods   264
   Straight-Line Method   264
   Accelerated Methods   266
   Units-of-Production Method   267
   Choosing a Depreciation Method   269
Review Problem 7.1   271
   Accounting Policy Changes   271
Revaluing Long-Lived Assets   273
Sale or Retirement of Long-Lived Assets   274

Review Problem 7.2   275
   Distortion Caused by Aging Assets   275
Intangible Assets   276
   Research and Development Costs, Patents, and
     Copyrights   277
   Goodwill   277
   Marketing Costs   278
Natural Resources   278
Review Problem 7.3   279
Long-Term Fixed Asset Accounting Under
  International Financial Reporting Standards   279
Analyzing Capital Investments   280
Executive Summary   282
Key Concepts and Terms   282
Review Problem 7.4   282
Questions   283
Exercises   284
Problems   286
Corporate Analysis   289
Case   291
Solutions to Review Problems   294

CHAPTER **8**

Investing In Other Entities   297

Investments in Other Entities   298
   Overview of Accounting for Debt and Equity
     Securities   299
Accounting for Marketable Debt and Equity
  Securities—Passive investments   301
   Valuation Adjustments   302
   Recording the Sale of Investment Securities   302
Review Problem 8.1   304
   Managerial Discretion   305
Equity Method and Consolidation Accounting   307
Review Problem 8.2   314
   Deconsolidation   314
   Accounting for Joint Ventures   315
   Accounting for Special Purpose Entities   316
Accounting for Investments in Foreign Entities   318
   Currency Exchange Rate Fluctuations   318
   Illustration of Current Rate Method   319
Review Problem 8.3   321
Analyzing Intercorporate Investments   321
Executive Summary   322
Key Concepts and Terms   323
Questions   323
Exercises   325
Problems   327
Corporate Analysis   333
Solutions to Review Problems   336

CHAPTER **9**

Debt Financing: Bonds, Notes, and Leases   339

Financing Operations and Assets with Debt: Bonds and Notes   340
    Credit Ratings and the Cost of Debt   341
Valuing Bonds and Notes   342
    Interest Expense   344
    Market Rates of Interest and the Book Value of Debt   346
    Early Debt Retirement   346
    Zero-Coupon Bonds and Notes   348
Review Problem 9.1   350
Lease Financing   350
    Accounting for Leases   350
    Lease Accounting, Disclosures and Security Prices   355
    New Lease Accounting Guidelines   356
Calculating the Weighted-average Cost of Debt   357
Managing Reported Debt   357
Analyzing a Company's Use of Leverage   358
Review Problem 9.2   361
Executive Summary   362
Key Concepts and Terms   362
Questions   363
Exercises   365
Problems   367
Corporate Analysis   371
Case   372
Solutions to Review Problems   376

CHAPTER **10**

Commitments and Contingent Liabilities, Deferred Tax Liabilities, and Retirement Obligations   379

Commitments and Contingent Liabilities   380
Deferred Income Tax Liabilities   382
    Analyzing Deferred Income Taxes   387
Review Problem 10.1   392
Employee Retirement Obligations   392
    Estimating Retirement Obligations and Their Cost   393
    Retirement Benefit Disclosures   394
    Managing Retirement Obligations   396
Review Problem 10.2   397
Analyzing Other Potential Liabilities   397
Executive Summary   398
Key Concepts and Terms   398
Appendix 10A: Financial Instruments and Derivatives   399
Questions   400

Exercises   402
Problems   404
Corporate Analysis   409
Solutions to Review Problems   410

CHAPTER **11**

Equity Financing and Shareholders' Equity   413

Equity financing   414
    Going Public   414
    Issuances and Repurchases of Equity   416
Review Problem 11.1   421
Dividends   421
    Cash Dividends   421
    Free Share Distributions   424
    Stock Dividends   425
    Stock Splits   425
Review Problem 11.2   428
Other Comprehensive Income   428
Employee Stock Options   430
Analyzing Equity Financing and Shareholders' Equity   435
Executive Summary   437
Key Concepts and Terms   437
Review Problem 11.3   437
Questions   438
Exercises   439
Problems   443
Corporate Analysis   448
Case   449
Solutions to Review Problems   454

CHAPTER **12**

Using Accounting Information in Equity Valuation   457

Pro Forma Financial Statements   458
Review Problem 12.1   462
    Introduction to Equity Valuation   463
Using Cash Flow Data to Value a Company   464
    Developing Cash Flow Data   464
Valuation using the Discounted Cash Flow Model   467
    The Operating Value of a Firm   467
    Free Cash Flow   468
    Valuing a Firm's Equity   469
    Valuing the Russian River Valley Winery Shares   470
Review Problem 12.2   472
Valuation using the Residual Income Model   473
    Valuing the Russian River Valley Winery Shares   474

Review Problem 12.3 *475*
Valuation using Price-Earnings Multiples **475**
Executive Summary **477**
Review Problem 12.4 *477*
Key Concepts and Terms **478**
Questions **478**
Exercises **479**
Problems **482**

Corporate Analysis 501

Solutions to Review Problems 502

Appendix A: The Time Value of Money **506**

Appendix B: Financial Statement Ratios and
                Metrics **522**

Appendix C: IFRS Illustrated: LVMH Moët
                Hennessey-Louis Vuitton S.A. **526**

Appendix D: Accounting Mechanics: T-Accounts and
                Journal Entries **532**

Appendix E: Working Capital Management **554**

Index 560

When you complete this chapter you should be able to:

1. Describe the role of financial accounting in facilitating a properly functioning capital market. (page 4)

2. Identify the basic financial statements—the income statement, the balance sheet, the statement of cash flow, and the statement of shareholders' equity. (page 7)

3. Explain how companies acquire capital from investors, who purchase debt and equity securities to obtain an expected return commensurate with the risk they assume. (page 8)

4. Describe the accounting principles and the role of institutions that establish financial accounting regulations. (page 16)

5. Identify the most common myths about financial accounting. (page 22)

6. Explain the conflicts of interest that can arise between managers and investors, and the costs associated with the divergent incentives that can arise when management and ownership of a company are separated. (page 24)

7. Understand the purpose of GAAP and identify the ten elements that form the basic building blocks of the financial statements. (page 26)

The Economic Environment of Accounting Information

1

Amazon.com, Inc. was one of the first, and became perhaps the best known, internet-based reseller of retail goods. The company was one of the high-flying internet stocks that became a favorite of equity investors during the stock market bubble period of the late 1990s. But eventually, like many dot.com companies that lacked a history of proven earnings, investors began to question the sustainability of Amazon's business model following the U.S. stock market decline of 2001–2002. The way the stock market valued companies during this period of so-called "irrational exuberance" was too often detached from the underlying basic business fundamentals. As a consequence, there eventually occurred a shift back to firm valuations based on such standards as strong operating earnings and a solid balance sheet.

AMAZON.COM

Amazon.com was founded by Jeff Bezos in 1995 under the name Cadabra.com as an online bookstore to compete with traditional "brick-and-mortar" bookstores and mail-order catalogs. Bezos renamed the company "Amazon" after the world's largest river and took the company public in 1997. Like the South American river, Amazon.com was huge in scale, offering many times the selection of products of even its largest competitors. Amazon has since greatly expanded its product offerings to include DVDs, CDs, computer software, video games, electronics, clothing, furniture, food, toys and much more. All of these offerings are designed to leverage the company's massive distribution network. As recent examples, with the launch of the *Kindle* in 2007 the company became the pioneer in the burgeoning e-book and e-reader markets. In 2011 Amazon entered the tablet computer market with the *Kindle Fire*, enabling it to further capitalize on the growth in electronic media. In 2014 the company expanded its consumer electronics again with the launch of *Amazon Fire TV Stick* and the *Amazon Echo*. Amazon has also always been a constant innovative internet force that makes it difficult for other companies to compete. For instance, for all of its electronic media sales (e.g., music and movies) it offers cloud based storage accessible from anywhere and on any device. And to get physical products ordered in the hands of customers as quickly as possible, in 2015 the company announced it was looking into using drones for automated package delivery.

From the start, Bezos believed in the long-term prospects for his company, although he did not expect the business to produce a profit for many years. As history has since demonstrated, Bezos' business strategy proved successful. Unlike many internet companies, Amazon grew at a steady pace and focused on such business fundamentals as revenue growth, cash flows, and attaining profitability. The bursting of the dot.com bubble in the early 2000s forced many e-companies out of business. Amazon, however, persevered and eventually reported its first profit in the fourth quarter of 2002. Amazon.com has reported choppy earnings performance in recent years as it continues to invest for and builds its market share. It reported income of $274 million in 2013 and a loss of $241 million in 2014. In fact, Amazon's cumulative profit had only turned positive for the first time in 2008, largely as a consequence of its early history of operating losses. Today, Amazon.com trades on the NASDAQ stock exchange under the symbol AMZN and is a member of the prestigious Standard & Poor's 500 Index, an index of the shares of the 500 largest companies traded on U.S. stock exchanges.

In this chapter, we examine the financial statements of Amazon, as well as consider the generally accepted accounting principles that have been established to ensure a level of comparability among the many public companies, like Amazon, that produce financial statements for use by investors, lenders, and shareholders.

FINANCIAL ACCOUNTING AND ITS RELEVANCE

Takeaway 1
Describe the
role of financial
accounting
in facilitating
a properly
functioning capital
market.

Most individuals are familiar with the game of baseball and its many rules. Most know, for instance, that according to the rules of baseball, the team with the most runs scored at the completion of play is considered the winner. Of course the rules do much more than decide the measure by which we are able to determine which team won and which team lost; they also provide a framework within which to play and define how players should interact depending on their different roles. Imagine the chaos that might ensue if there were no mutually accepted rules for baseball. How would it be determined, for instance, if a base runner was out or was safe, if a pitch was a ball or a strike, and so on? Without an accepted set of rules governing the game, it would be impossible to play the sport, ensure a consistent set of outcomes, and ultimately determine the winner.

Keeping score with an accepted set of rules applies to more activities than just baseball; it also applies to the financial accounting rules that relate to running a business like Amazon.com. In fact, the similarities between the two are probably closer than you might imagine. Understanding the "rules of the game" helps us do more than simply declare the winner of a game or calculate the annual profit of a business; it enables us to keep track of various measures that can be used to determine the quality of a team's play and likewise the quality of a business's operations. Our knowledge of the rules and how both teams and businesses have performed—for example, team batting averages, pitching records, and fielding percentages for baseball teams, and assorted financial ratios such as the return on assets, return on equity, or return on sales for a business—can, in turn, help us to predict how those teams and businesses will perform in the future. This knowledge, as you will see in subsequent chapters, is invaluable when attempting to assess the value of a sports franchise or of a business enterprise.

Simply reading a rule book, however, may not be sufficient to obtain a complete understanding as to how a game is played and scored. It is also critical to understand the limitations regarding how the rules are applied, along with what is not covered by the rules. This caveat especially applies to financial accounting. Imagine the difficulty that would occur if each baseball team was able to decide the distance from home plate to first base in its own stadium. Or imagine the confusion if, with the bases loaded, a team could choose which direction to run toward home plate, scoring either from first base or from third base. As we will see in the following chapters of this textbook, however, financial accounting permits considerable flexibility in determining the applicability of its "rules" to individual business enterprises. As a consequence, the rules governing financial accounting will often be seen to involve considerable managerial judgment. In baseball, for example, while general guidelines exist as to whether a pitch should be called a ball or a strike, it is up to an umpire's judgment to make the exact call. In a similar fashion, while general accounting guidelines exist as to what is considered revenue for a business, financial accounting often requires that corporate managers exercise judgment in assessing just how much revenue a business earned in a given fiscal period. In addition to the obvious analytical challenges that can result from this flexibility in the application of the rules of the game, business analysis is also often hampered by a lack of certain key information. Many of the factors that are critical to a business's operating success, for example the quality of its workforce or a well-recognized brand name, are not measured and reported under current financial accounting rules.

Why Accounting Information Is Important

If you have prior business experience, either working for a company or managing your own business, then you have personal experience that a working knowledge of accounting is essential to do just about any job successfully. Although business decisions may involve a careful analysis of nonfinancial factors, they almost always involve a significant consideration of financial information. Initiating a multimillion-dollar marketing campaign, restructuring a subsidiary, acquiring another company, deciding on the sales price for a product—these are just some of the business decisions that require at least a basic knowledge of accounting. That's why, for instance, Anne Mulcahy, Chief Executive Officer of Xerox Corporation had to learn about accounting and finance when she took over at Xerox in 2001. As *Fortune* magazine explained,

> She knew she had to get to the bottom of Xerox's problems quickly. She cast about for someone, anyone, who could teach her Balance Sheet 101. The guy she found, Joe Mancini Jr., director of corporate financial analysis . . . became her tour guide in deciphering the company's $30 billion balance sheet. He taught her about debt structure, inventory trends, and the impact of taxes and currency moves so that she could understand what would generate cash and how each of her decisions would affect the balance sheet. (*Fortune*, June 9, 2003).

Executives, such as Anne Mulcahy, are also getting up to speed on accounting issues because now, more than ever, the post-Enron corporate environment in the United States puts these individuals at risk for civil and criminal lawsuits.[1] Under the **Sarbanes-Oxley Act**, passed into law by the United States Congress in 2002, the Chief Executive Officer (CEO) and Chief Financial Officer (CFO) of each company (foreign or domestic) with public debt or equity sold in the United States must certify in writing that the information contained in the company's publicly disseminated financial statements presents, in all material respects, the company's financial condition and results of operations. Section 906 of the Sarbanes-Oxley Act provides for both financial penalties (up to $5 million) and incarceration (up to 20 years) for executives who falsely certify their company's financial data. Excerpts from paragraphs (a) and (b) of Section 906 are provided below.

> **(a) CERTIFICATION OF PERIODIC FINANCIAL REPORTS.** Each periodic report containing financial statements filed by an issuer with the Securities Exchange Commission pursuant to section 13(a) or 15(d) of the Securities Exchange Act of 1934 shall be accompanied by a written statement by the chief executive officer and chief financial officer of the issuer.
>
> **(b) CONTENT.** The statement required under subsection (a) shall certify that the periodic report containing the financial statements fully complies with the requirements of section 13(a) or 15(d) of the Securities Exchange Act of 1934 and that information contained in the periodic report fairly presents, in all material respects, the financial condition and results of operations of the issuer.

Note that the language used in the Act requires that the CEO and CFO certify that the financial reports "fairly present . . . the financial condition and results . . . ." This standard raises the stake, and implies that these executives must consider *all* relevant financial material and avoid misleading those reading those reports.

In sum, a theme that will be repeated throughout this textbook is that accounting information is useful not only for keeping score of a business's past operating performance and financial health, but also for predicting its future performance and financial well-being, and ultimately, for helping to assess firm value. However, to be a good scorekeeper and a good analyst, and ultimately a great leader, one needs to know not only the rules of the game, but also how to interpret the data resulting from the application of the rules, the limitations of the rules, and when to make adjustments to the information to aid in its use for decision-making.

Financial Accounting: What Is It?

Financial accounting concerns the preparation and use of the accounting information provided in a company's financial statements. To appreciate the importance of financial accounting information one must

---

[1] *The Wall Street Journal* (July 22, 2003) reported that 70 percent of the executives who took a test of basic accounting principles shortly after the passage of the Sarbanes-Oxley Act failed to earn a passing score. A survey of executives taken two years following the passage of the legislation indicates that executive understanding of accounting and finance issues has substantially improved since the legislation's enactment (*CFO Magazine*, May 2005).

first recognize the foundation for the need. At its most fundamental level, financial accounting is necessary from one overriding activity: capital has been exchanged with the intent of earning a return. As an organization grows, its need for outside sources of capital grows, often at a rapid pace. With this growth comes the demand by those willing to provide capital for some objective evidence of the company's ability to provide a return. Without financial accounting there would be no basis upon which to evaluate their investment. In other words, there would be no basis upon which one could keep "score."

The overarching objective of the financial accounting process is to provide a basis upon which to evaluate the financial position and performance of a company for those that have invested in that company, but for whom such information would not otherwise be available in a succinct, reliable and timely basis. By providing financial accounting information to the shareholders of a company, those who actually own the company through the shares they purchase, they can now adequately assess the risk and potential returns related to their investments. Although shareholders are the primary user group for which the financial accounting process is centered, they are not the only group of stakeholders that have motivations for understanding the present and current prospects of a company. Bankers, a subset of the general investing group who loan money to a company for a fixed return, will want information about the financial status of the firm to help them assess their lending risk. Suppliers, competitors and customers all stand to be influenced in their own activities by the company's relative success or failure. Many governmental entities, such as the Federal Trade Commission, base regulatory decisions on information disclosed in annual reports. Public utilities, in fact, will frequently base their energy rates on the financial accounting based net income that it can generate. Taxing authorities, such as the IRS, will review financial accounting information in their reconciliations of taxable income. Labor unions might look to financial reporting performance to argue for greater benefits. Internally, the board of directors is known to use financial accounting information in decisions about dividend payments, compensation decisions, and other company policies. In sum, the financial accounting process provides information to a variety and diverse set of users, each with their own unique needs.

A financial accounting perspective can be distinguished from two other common processes that generate accounting information: managerial accounting and tax accounting. Unlike the external focus of financial accounting, **managerial accounting** focuses on the production of accounting information internal to a firm for deciding such operational questions as how much inventory to produce, what price to charge customers, and for measuring and rewarding the performance of a firm's employees. Managerial accounting information is rarely provided to anyone other than a firm's board of directors, managers, and employees, to avoid revealing proprietary information that might adversely affect a firm's competitive position. **Tax accounting** refers to the system of measurement used by tax authorities to determine the amount of taxes to levy on a company. Because this objective is quite distinct from that required by investors, these measurement rules can differ dramatically from financial accounting. The focus of this textbook is on financial accounting, and how financial advisors, investors, lenders, managers, and shareholders use this information for decision-making purposes. However, because tax accounting considerations often drive many real decisions faced by management, where appropriate throughout the text we highlight key high-level differences between financial and tax accounting.

Before getting into the details of how financial accounting information is prepared and analyzed, it is useful to first discuss the end result of the financial accounting process—the four primary financial statements. For the moment, don't worry about the numerous details that you will see, because these details will be explored in later chapters. Also don't worry about the numerous other supporting documents that often accompany the financial statements. Company financial reports include many items besides the basic financial statements, such as explanatory footnotes, a chairman's statement, and a management discussion and analysis of recent events and company performance. For simplicity, these latter items have been omitted from our discussion here as they will be considered in subsequent chapters.

To begin, it is useful to obtain a "big picture" view of a company by reading the introductory information about a company's business and its business strategy—that is, management's view of where the company is going based on the resources it has available (e.g., human, physical, intangible and financial). Reading the financial statements will help you determine whether a company has the necessary financial resources, or can acquire them, to get where it wants to be.

Consider, for example, the corporate mission of Amazon.com:

We seek to be Earth's most customer-centric company for four primary customer sets: consumers, sellers, enterprises, and content creators.

No small thinking here! Amazon truly aims to capture the world, virtually the entirety of the retail market space as their "customers"—buyers, sellers, and product developers. If Amazon can attract the millions of customers that the company has the capacity to handle, its future sales will be enormous.

Investment professionals who track the performance of companies like Amazon formalize sales and sales growth projections by gathering data regarding consumer demand, product shipments, product prices and sales discounts. These

> Access to corporate financial statements has increased greatly in recent years thanks to various internet sources. Companies such as Amazon routinely provide financial statements on their corporate website.

projections are integral to the analytical reports developed by investment professionals concerning a company's current financial health, and hence, its fair market value. Your review of Amazon's financial statements is likely to be enhanced by obtaining and reviewing a copy of a reputable analyst's report from any one of a variety of financial websites such as Yahoo.com or MSN.com or from a financial services company like Merrill Lynch or Wells Fargo. As to the stated mission that the company is "customer-centric" and that it meets the needs of four distinct sets of customers, you can verify for yourself whether it meets these objectives by logging on to Amazon's website (www.Amazon.com) if you haven't done so already.

FINANCIAL STATEMENTS

The basic financial statements for Amazon.com, Inc.—the balance sheet, the income statement, and the statement of cash flow—are provided in Exhibits 1.1, 1.2, and 1.3. (A fourth financial statement, the

Takeaway 2
Identify the basic financial statements—the income statement, the balance sheet, the statement of cash flow, and the statement of shareholders' equity.

EXHIBIT 1.1	Consolidated Balance Sheet

AMAZON.COM, INC. Consolidated Balance Sheet		
	Year Ended December 31,	
(in millions, except par value)	**2014**	**2013**
Assets		
Current assets		
Cash and cash equivalents.	$14,557	$ 8,658
Marketable securities	2,859	3,789
Inventories	8,299	7,411
Accounts receivable, net and other	5,612	4,767
Total current assets.	31,327	24,625
Property and equipment, net	16,967	10,949
Goodwill	3,319	2,655
Other assets	2,892	1,930
Total assets	$54,505	$40,159
Liabilities and Stockholders' Equity		
Current liabilities		
Accounts payable.	$16,459	$15,133
Accrued expenses and other	9,807	6,688
Unearned revenue	1,823	1,159
Total current liabilities	28,089	22,980
Long-term debt	8,265	3,191
Other long-term liabilities	7,410	4,242
Stockholders' equity		
Common stock, $0.01 par value:		
Authorized shares— 5,000		
Issued shares—488 and 483		
Outstanding shares—465 and 459	5	5
Treasury stock, at cost	(1,837)	(1,837)
Additional paid-in-capital	11,135	9,573
Accumulated other comprehensive loss	(511)	(185)
Retained earnings.	1,949	2,190
Total stockholders' equity	10,741	9,746
Total liabilities and stockholders' equity	**$54,505**	**$40,159**

| EXHIBIT 1.2 | Consolidated Income Statement |

AMAZON.COM, INC.
Consolidated Income Statement

(in millions, except earnings per share data)	Year Ended December 31, 2014	2013	2012
Net product sales..	$70,080	$60,903	$51,733
Net services sales	18,908	13,549	9,360
Total net sales	88,988	74,452	61,093
Operating expenses			
Cost of sales...	62,752	54,181	45,971
Fulfillment	10,766	8,585	6,419
Marketing	4,332	3,133	2,408
Technology and content.......................................	9,275	6,565	4,564
General and administrative....................................	1,552	1,129	896
Other operating expense (income), net	133	114	159
Total operating expenses	88,810	73,707	60,417
Income from operations.......................................	178	745	676
Interest income..	39	38	40
Interest expense...	(210)	(141)	(92)
Other income (expense), net	(118)	(136)	(80)
Total non-operating income (expense)....................	(289)	(239)	(132)
Income before income taxes	(111)	506	544
Provision for income taxes....................................	(167)	(161)	(428)
Equity-method investment activity, net of tax	37	(71)	(155)
Net income	$(241)	$274	$(39)
Basic earnings per share	$(0.52)	$0.60	$(0.09)
Diluted earnings per share	$(0.52)	$0.59	$(0.09)
Weighted average shares used in earnings per share:			
Basic...	462	457	453
Diluted	462	465	453

eLectures
MBC

Takeaway 3

Explain how companies acquire capital from investors, who purchase debt and equity securities to obtain an expected return commensurate with the risk they assume.

statement of shareholders' equity, will be discussed later in this chapter.) The **balance sheet** in Exhibit 1.1 shows what resources the company currently has and who provided the financing to acquire the various resources—debtholders or shareholders. Specifically, Amazon's balance sheet reveals the amount and type of assets owned, the liabilities owed, and the shareholders' equity investment in the company. **Assets** refer to the resources of a company that are expected to provide future economic benefit. **Liabilities** represent the value of the company's obligations to repay monies loaned to it, to pay for goods or services received by it, or to fulfill commitments made by it. **Shareholders' equity**, the difference between a company's assets and liabilities, represents the shareholders' (owners') financial stake in a company. In essence, two investment constituencies provided the necessary financing for Amazon's assets—the shareholders who own the company as a consequence of their share purchases, and debtholders who have loaned money and other assets to the company. The basic accounting equation, Assets = Liabilities + Shareholders' equity, provides the foundation not for only the balance sheet, but more importantly for the entire methodology underpinning the recording of all accounting transactions. In various ways we will repeat this important facet of the balance sheet numerous times in the coming chapters.[2]

An alternative to the accrual basis of accounting is the **cash basis of accounting**. Under the cash basis, the financial effects of a business event are recorded in the financial statements *only* when the cash effect of the transaction occurs. Thus, a company records revenue from a sales transaction *only* after cash has been collected from the customer; similarly, expenses are recorded *only* when they are paid. For simplicity many small companies will prepare their financial statements using cash basis accounting. But note that cash basis accounting is not an acceptable method of presentation under U.S. GAAP.

Amazon's balance sheet is based on this foundation. By the end of 2014, Amazon's bal-

---

[2] Each transaction that is recorded must be done so such that the equation remains in balance. For this reason, the term "double-entry" accounting is often used to describe this method of recording transactions.

ance sheet reveals that it had acquired $54.505 billion in assets while the company's liabilities stood at $43.764 billion ($28.089 plus $8.265 plus $7.410). Notice that shareholders had a residual interest valued at $10.741 billion, and of that $1.949 billion has been earned and retained by the company. To evaluate how Amazon generates its earnings, we will need to explore the income statement, which we consider shortly.

A few other features of Amazon's balance sheet are noteworthy at this point. The presence of various accounts on Amazon's balance sheet such as **accounts receivable**, the amount that Amazon expects to receive from its customers for prior online purchases, and **accounts payable**, the amount that Amazon expects to pay to its suppliers for prior credit purchases of inventory, indicates that this financial statement was prepared using the **accrual basis of accounting**. This approach requires Amazon to record the financial effects of a business transaction even though the timing of the cash effects of the event takes place at a different time. That is, Amazon records the revenue from each sales transaction when it occurs, regardless of whether the customer has paid for the ordered goods or not. Similarly, Amazon records the cost of doing business when such costs are incurred, regardless of whether those costs have yet to be paid. The balance sheets and income statements of most companies are prepared using the accrual basis of accounting, as this approach is widely recognized as being superior to all other approaches for measuring the financial performance and health of a company. In fact, financial statements that follow U.S. GAAP must be prepared under the accrual basis.

Amazon's **income statement** in Exhibit 1.2 reports how much merchandise the company sold and how much profit, if any, it made from those sales. Amazon's consolidated statement of income reveals that the company's sales grew to almost $89 billion by 2014. The "bottom line" of the income statement indicates that Amazon had a net loss in 2014 of $241 million, reversing a profit of $274 million from a year earlier. What is surprising for all the success of Amazon is that in its history it has not generated consistent and sustained profits. Prior to 2008, the company had racked up cumulative losses of just over $1.3 billion. In fact, a review of Amazon's historical financial statements (not presented here) reveals that from 1996 until 2002, Amazon failed to earn a profit in any of

> Exhibit 1.2 presents Amazon's **consolidated income statement**. But just what was "consolidated" and what remains "unconsolidated"? Under the accounting rules of most countries, when one company obtains a majority of the voting shares of another company, the financial results of the two companies are combined and reported on a "consolidated" basis. Thus, in the case of Amazon, the consolidated income statement includes the complete financial results of Amazon's majority-owned subsidiaries, but only summary results of its subsidiaries in which its ownership interest is less than a majority. We will provide greater detail on this accounting treatment in Chapter 8.

the seven years since it became a public company! This history of operating losses during the early years of the company's existence explains the relatively modest size of retained earnings on the 2014 balance sheet.

To appreciate this, consider that both the balance sheet and income statement are prepared under an important tenet underlying the accrual basis of accounting—the **going concern assumption**. This notion specifies that the financial statements are prepared assuming that a business will continue operating in the future unless there is substantial evidence to the contrary. When a business has reached a steady state and is expected to continue operating in the future, investors tend to focus on revenues and net income from the income statement in order to forecast a firm's future operating performance. If, on the other hand, a business is expected to cease operations, investors are likely to focus their attention more closely on shareholders' equity on the balance sheet to determine what an investor might receive if, and when, the company is liquidated. Academic research consistent with the going concern assumption indicates that in setting share prices, investors place relatively more weight on shareholders' equity on the balance sheet when a business is facing financial distress than when a business is financially healthy.[3]

Even though Amazon is currently highly profitable, you may have wondered how it can sustain multiple years of operating losses and still remain in business. The answers to these types of questions typically reside in a review of a company's statement of cash flow, to which we now turn.

Exhibit 1.3 presents Amazon's statement of cash flow. The **statement of cash flow** tells us how much cash Amazon.com generated from its core business operations versus received from

> There exists substantial empirical evidence that investors who buy and sell shares use information about the past, especially financial statement information, to help make predictions about a company's future. Financial analysts, individual investors, bankers, and many other interested parties spend considerable time and resources predicting a company's future earnings and cash flows to help assess what a company's share price should currently be worth. We will have more to say about how to value a company's shares in Chapter 12; however, let it suffice for the moment that the value of a share of stock today is thought to be a function of a company's *future* earnings and cash flow.

---

[3] See M. Barth and W. Landsman, "Relative Valuation Roles of Equity Book Value and Net Income as a Function of Financial Health," *Journal of Accounting and Economics* (February 1998).

| EXHIBIT 1.3 | Consolidated Statement of Cash Flow |

AMAZON.COM, INC.
Consolidated Statement of Cash Flow

($ millions)	Year Ended December 31,		
	2014	2013	2012
Cash and cash equivalents, beginning of period.	$ 8,658	$8,084	$5,269
Operating activities			
Net income	(241)	274	(39)
Adjustments to reconcile net income to net cash provided by operating activities:			
Depreciation of fixed assets, including internal-use software and website			
development, and other amortization	4,746	3,253	2,159
Stock-based compensation.	1,497	1,134	833
Other operating expenses (income), net	129	114	154
Losses (gains) on sales of marketable securities, net	(3)	1	(9)
Other expense (income), net	62	166	253
Deferred income taxes.	(316)	(156)	(265)
Excess tax benefits from stock-based compensation	(6)	(78)	(429)
Changes in operating assets and liabilities:			
Inventories	(1,193)	(1,410)	(999)
Accounts receivable, net and other.	(1,039)	(846)	(861)
Accounts payable	1,759	1,888	2,070
Accrued expenses and other.	706	736	1,038
Additions to unearned revenue	4,433	2,691	1,796
Amortization of previously unearned revenue	(3,692)	(2,292)	(1,521)
Net cash provided by operating activities	6,842	5,475	4,180
Investing activities			
Purchases of fixed assets, including internal-use software			
and website development.	(4,893)	(3,444)	(3,785)
Acquisitions, net of cash acquired, and other	(979)	(312)	(745)
Sales and maturities of marketable securities and other investments.	3,349	2,306	4,237
Purchases of marketable securities and other investments.	(2,542)	(2,826)	(3,302)
Net cash used in investing activities	(5,065)	(4,276)	(3,595)
Financing activities			
Excess tax benefits from stock-based compensation.	6	78	429
Common stock repurchased	—	—	(960)
Proceeds from long-term debt and other.	6,359	394	3,378
Repayments of long-term debt, capital lease, and finance lease obligations	(1,933)	(1,011)	(588)
Net cash provided by (used in) financing activities	4,432	(539)	2,259
Foreign-currency effect on cash and cash equivalents	(310)	(86)	(29)
Net increase in cash and cash equivalents	5,899	574	2,815
Cash and cash equivalents, end of period.	$14,557	$8,658	$8,084

its shareholders and debtholders, and how much it spent to buy software and equipment. Investors are usually very interested in the statement of cash flow because it provides insight into a business beyond that provided by a balance sheet, which reflects a firm's current financial health, or an income statement, which depicts a firm's recent operating performance. Amazon's statement of cash flow shows, for instance, that its operating activities generated $6.842 billion in cash in 2014 despite reporting a net loss of $241 million. Amazon's total cash and cash equivalents increased by a whopping $5.899 billion in 2014, and the company's cash holdings on the balance sheet were in excess of $14.5 billion! Thus, Amazon has substantial cash on hand despite reporting many early years of operating losses on the income statement. These seemingly conflicting financial results are possible because of Amazon's use of the accrual basis of accounting in the preparation of its income statement and its balance sheet.

Without proper context, you might think that Amazon.com, which only began to earn an operating profit in 2003 and with liabilities representing over 80 percent of its assets, would have a share price that

EXHIBIT 1.4	Stock Price Performance of Amazon.com: May 1997 (IPO) to December 2015.

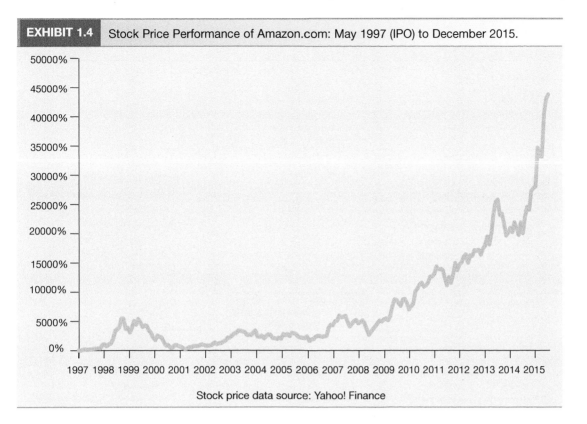

Stock price data source: Yahoo! Finance

was floundering. Yet Exhibit 1.4 shows that Amazon's share price soared by over 40,000 percent since its initial public offering. The much broader Standard & Poor's 500 Index was relatively stable over the same period, returning a cumulative 137 percent. Amazon's share price at its initial public offering was just over $1.50 per share, but by July 2015, its share price was over $530 per share, giving the company a market value of about $246 billion (shares outstanding × share price). This illustrates an important distinction between a company's financial statements and its share price—the former is concerned with the past while the latter is concerned with the future. Financial statements are a description of the historical financial performance of a company, whereas share prices reflect investor *expectations* regarding a firm's future financial health and performance. The fact that Amazon's market value is $246 billion versus a balance sheet value of just $10.741 billion for shareholders' equity suggests that the stock market is extremely optimistic that Amazon's future is going to be much brighter than its past.

To summarize then, companies like Amazon.com who obtain capital from external sources such as debtholders and shareholders are expected to periodically provide these interested stakeholders with financial accounting information. This information includes an income statement, a balance sheet, and a statement of cash flow. The relation between these three financial statements is illustrated in Exhibit 1.5. A fourth statement—the statement of shareholders' equity—is also typically provided and is discussed in greater detail in Chapter 2.

> Publicly listed companies in the United States are required to file a quarterly financial report (Form 10-Q) and an annual set of financial statements (Form 10-K) with the U.S. Securities and Exchange Commission. This information is also typically available on company websites, and is often mailed or e-mailed to shareholders and debtholders.

From Exhibit 1.5 a number of important points can be made about the basic financial statements. First, a balance sheet is a description of a business's assets, liabilities, and shareholders' equity as of a particular point in time, usually the end of the fiscal year or the end of a quarter. The balance sheet is represented by the basic accounting equation: total assets equal total liabilities plus shareholders' equity. Second, the income statement describes a firm's performance over the fiscal period; it summarizes all of the company's revenues less expenses, the total equating to that period's net income. Note that the net income earned by a business may be either distributed to shareholders as a dividend or retained in the business to provide financing for future operations. The **statement of shareholders' equity** captures this decision by summarizing the detailed reason for the change in each shareholders' equity account. It reveals how the shareholders' investment in a business grew by the amount of any net income retained in the business or declined as a consequence of any dividend distributions to shareholders or any losses

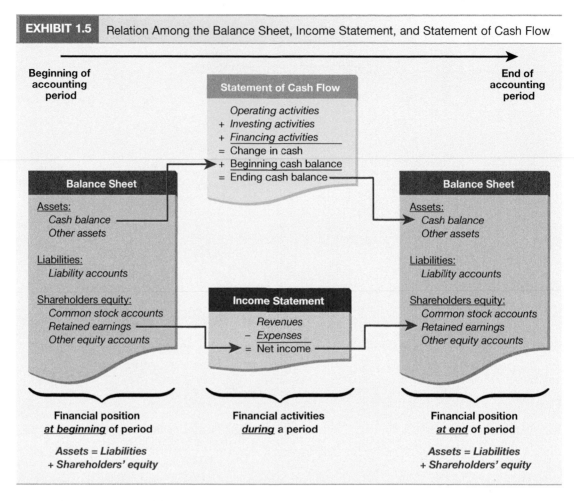

EXHIBIT 1.5   Relation Among the Balance Sheet, Income Statement, and Statement of Cash Flow

sustained by a business. This statement also reveals whether the shareholders' investment in a business increased by any new share sales or declined by any share repurchases. The statement of shareholders' equity is discussed in greater detail in subsequent chapters. Third, the statement of cash flow reports the cash flow from operations, the cash flow from investing, and the cash flow from financing for a firm. The net cash flow for a fiscal period equals the change in the cash account on the balance sheet from the beginning of the period to the end of the period. Finally, note that the financial statements are not independent, but rather they are interrelated. (The interrelationship of the basic financial statements is referred to in accounting jargon as "articulation;" that is, the basic financial statements are said to articulate, or link, with one another.) As you will see in subsequent chapters, there is unique, but interrelated information in each of the financial statements that is of interest to lenders, managers, shareholders, and investment professionals, among others.

EXHIBIT 1.6   Balance Sheets and Income Statements: "Stocks" and "Flows"

Exhibit 1.6 illustrates another example of the interrelationship of the basic financial statements, in this case between the income statement and the balance sheet, using an analogy of a river and a lake. An income statement, like a river, measures activity over a period of time—a flow concept. On the income statement, activity is measured in terms of earnings in dollars, and with a river, activity can be measured in terms of the flow of water in cubic feet or meters. Balance sheets and lakes, in contrast, measure levels—a stock concept. Balance sheets measure the level of net assets (assets − liabilities) and lakes can be measured as a level of water, both at a point in time. Just as a lake's level of water rises and falls because of the inflow and outflow of water from a river, the level of net assets on the balance sheet rises and falls as a consequence of the operating earnings or losses generated by a business and reported on its income statement. A similar analogy could be used between the cash balance on the balance sheet and the statement of cash flow. The cash account on the balance sheet reports the level of cash currently available to a business, whereas the statement of cash flow reports the inflows and outflows of cash that occurred over the fiscal period. To repeat, the balance sheet discloses the available "stocks" of various assets, while the income statement and the statement of cash flow reveal the various "flows" of those assets and claims on those assets.

REVIEW PROBLEM 1.1

Compute the missing amounts (in millions) in the following table. The ending balance in retained earnings in Year 3 was $7.30.

	Year 1	Year 2	Year 3
Retained earnings (beginning)	$ 0.0	$3.3	$?
Revenues	10.2	?	10.7
Expenses	4.1	4.5	4.7
Dividends	?	2.2	2.3

The solution is on page 36.

Qualitative Attributes of Accounting Information

It is generally agreed that accounting information is valuable because it contributes to the making of important economic decisions. For instance, managers often use accounting information to decide the price that they must charge for their company's products; bank credit analysts use accounting information to decide whether to extend a loan to a business; and, investors use accounting information to decide whether to invest in the shares of a company and at what price. Thus, accounting information is said to have **decision usefulness**.

There are two important attributes that underlie accounting information that help make it decision useful—relevance and faithful representation. **Relevance** refers to the capacity of accounting information to influence a decision. Relevant information is timely and possesses feedback value, predictive value, or both. Timeliness alone does not make accounting information relevant, but a lack of timeliness can render accounting information irrelevant. By preparing periodic financial statements it is possible for companies to provide analysts, managers, and investors with timely information. **Feedback value** pertains to decisions and actions already taken. Accounting information allows financial statement users to measure those actions and evaluate their success. **Predictive value**, on the other hand, suggests that accounting information helps financial statement

In Practice 1.1 *Fiscal Year-End: A Glimpse of a Sample of Fortune 1000 Companies* The following table identifies the month selected as a firm's fiscal year-end based on a survey of 600 Fortune 1000 companies. As can be seen, December was selected by nearly two-thirds of the sampled firms, although every month is represented:

Source: Accounting Trends & Techniques

users form predictions about future outcomes. Investment professionals and shareholders use the historical financial statements to help predict a firm's future operating performance, and hence, its market value.

Because too much information can overwhelm financial statement users (i.e., the problem of "information overload"), **materiality** is a disclosure criterion used worldwide by companies to decide what, and how much, information to provide in their financial statements. Information that is immaterial is unlikely to be relevant to a decision maker. Although the definition of materiality varies from firm to firm, and often between external auditors, a common threshold for the income statement is five percent of revenues. Hence, any income statement item that equals or exceeds five percent of revenues presumably merits disclosure on a firm's income statement as such items are numerically large enough to potentially influence an investor's assessment of firm performance.

The decision usefulness of accounting information is also influenced by the degree to which it faithfully represents events that occur during a period. **Faithful representation** refers to the fact that accounting information is, or should be, free from error or bias; accounting rules, therefore, tend to be written in such a way that the accounts are both objective and verifiable. This is a trade-off, however, and unfortunately the attributes of relevance and faithful representation are often in conflict with one another. As one example, the fair value of long-term fixed assets, while clearly relevant information, is typically not recorded under U.S. accounting rules because it cannot be objectively measured. And for those values that are recorded, a major role of the independent auditor, to which we now turn, is to review a company's publicly available accounting information to ensure that it is largely error free.

Amazon's Accounting Methods and the Role of the Independent Auditor

By now, one question that you have probably considered about Amazon's financial statements is: Could the proper application of financial accounting by Amazon have led to accounting results computed in more than one way? The answer is yes. Nearly every country around the world maintains a set of formal accounting standards. In the U.S. these are Generally Accepted Accounting Principles—or GAAP—that provide guidance to companies regarding the preferred way to measure and report their performance. The confusing aspect about these standards, however, is their flexibility. For example, consider the depreciation on a building. Instead of having just one approach to calculate depreciation on a building, most countries allow for multiple methods, all of which are considered "generally accepted." As you will see in Chapter 7, just which depreciation method is selected can have a dramatic effect on a firm's reported performance.

Consider, for instance, the $8.299 billion reported by Amazon.com for inventory on its 2014 balance sheet in Exhibit 1.1. Was this the amount that Amazon paid for the inventory? Or, was it what the inventory could be sold for at the end of the year? Or, was it what the same inventory would cost to replace if it were purchased at the end of 2014? Companies provide details about their accounting methods and how the various accounts are measured in the **footnotes** to their financial statements. For example, the footnotes to Amazon's 2014 financial statements report that:

Inventories, consisting of products available for sale, are primarily accounted for using the first-in, first-out ("FIFO") method, and are valued at the lower of cost or market value. This valuation requires us to *make judgments* (emphasis added), based on currently-available information, about the likely method of disposition, such as through sales to individual customers, returns to product vendors, or liquidations, and expected recoverable values of each disposition category.

There are several points to observe here. First, Amazon's financial statements are prepared by the company itself, raising the concern that the company might be tempted to boost its inventory value to make it appear that Amazon has more assets than it really does. Second, Amazon's top management and financial staff "make judgments" in deciding what inventory values to report. But since the financial statements provided by Amazon's management are potentially affected by these judgments, investors might skeptically discount the reported information and reduce their estimate of what the company is presumably worth. This issue is known as the **lemons problem**.[4]

---

[4] G.A. Ackerlof, "The Market for Lemons: Quality Uncertainty and the Market Mechanism," *The Quarterly Journal of Economics*, (1970). In markets where buyers are uncertain about the quality of goods offered for sale, markets may break down because buyers reduce the price that they are willing to pay, causing sellers with high-quality products to withdraw from the market. The downward price spiral continues as products of continually decreasing quality become the only products available for sale, and eventually, market breakdowns can occur.

One solution to the lemons problem is for a credible, independent party to provide a "warranty" as to the quality of the product offered. For example, in the used car market, an auto dealer might promise to take a vehicle back if the buyer experiences any problems. In the "accounting market," independent audit firms such as Deloitte & Touche, Ernst & Young, KPMG, and PricewaterhouseCoopers provide assurance of the faithful representation of the financial statements of the companies they audit in an **audit report** that accompanies the financial statements. Audit firms work hard to provide this assurance because errors in detecting defective financial statements can result in a significant loss of investor capital. A failure to adequately provide assurance can result in the loss of an audit firm's valuable reputation, and ultimately, as illustrated by the demise of Arthur Andersen in 2002, the collapse of an entire audit firm. Audit firms may also bear civil and criminal penalties from lawsuits brought by shareholders, debtholders, and/or governmental agencies like the U.S. Securities and Exchange Commission (SEC) if their work is found to be negligent.

In Practice 1.2 *Financial Statement Rounding: A Glimpse of a Sample of Fortune 1000 Companies*   The following table identifies the degree of rounding in financial statements in a survey of 600 Fortune 1000 companies. Nearly all of the sampled firms rounded their reported numbers, with rounding to the nearest thousand dollars the most commonly used choice:

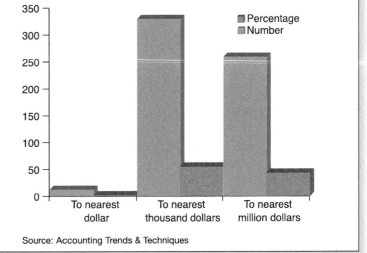

Source: Accounting Trends & Techniques

The independent auditors' report by Ernst & Young for Amazon's financial statements is provided in Exhibit 1.7. Note first to whom the report is written—the directors and shareholders of Amazon. This is no accident, as it is to them that the financial reports are targeted and it is their capital at risk.

EXHIBIT 1.7 Independent Auditors' Report

Report of Independent Registered Public Accounting Firm

The Board of Directors and Shareholders
Amazon.com, Inc.

We have audited the accompanying consolidated balance sheets of Amazon.com, Inc. as of December 31, 2014 and 2013, and the related consolidated statements of operations, comprehensive income, stockholders' equity, and cash flows for each of the three years in the period ended December 31, 2014. These financial statements are the responsibility of the Company's management. Our responsibility is to express an opinion on these financial statements based on our audits.

We conducted our audits in accordance with the standards of the Public Company Accounting Oversight Board (United States). Those standards require that we plan and perform the audit to obtain reasonable assurance about whether the financial statements are free of material misstatement. An audit includes examining, on a test basis, evidence supporting the amounts and disclosures in the financial statements. An audit also includes assessing the accounting principles used and significant estimates made by management, as well as evaluating the overall financial statement presentation. We believe that our audits provide a reasonable basis for our opinion.

In our opinion, the financial statements referred to above present fairly, in all material respects, the consolidated financial position of Amazon.com, Inc. at December 31, 2014 and 2013, and the consolidated results of its operations and its cash flows for each of the three years in the period ended December 31, 2014, in conformity with U.S. generally accepted accounting principles.

We also have audited, in accordance with the standards of the Public Company Accounting Oversight Board (United States), Amazon.com, Inc.'s internal control over financial reporting as of December 31, 2014, based on criteria established in Internal Control—Integrated Framework issued by the Committee of Sponsoring Organizations of the Treadway Commission (2013 framework) and our report dated January 29, 2015 expressed an unqualified opinion thereon.

/s/ Ernst & Young LLP
Seattle, Washington
January 29, 2015

The expected **return** on an investment refers to the expected income to be earned on the investment, whereas the **riskiness** of an investment refers to the uncertainty associated with the expected return. In general, risk and expected return are positively correlated; that is, investments with higher risk are generally expected to earn a higher rate of return.

The first paragraph of the report indicates that the scope of Ernst & Young's audit includes Amazon's balance sheet, income statement, statement of shareholders' equity, statement of cash flow, and other financial items. This paragraph also highlights the fact that the auditors' responsibility is only to provide an opinion, whereas the responsibility for the preparation of the statements themselves lies with Amazon's management. The second paragraph discloses that the audit firm's procedures used in the review of Amazon's financial data were in accordance with **U.S. generally accepted auditing standards** as prescribed by the Public Company Accounting Oversight Board, but that accepted auditing procedures do not consider every business transaction and instead rely only on a set of sampled transactions to form an opinion. An audit of a company like Amazon would be prohibitively expensive if every single business transaction was examined to reach an opinion.

The third paragraph provides Ernst & Young's opinion that Amazon has prepared its financial statements in accordance with generally accepted accounting principles and that there are no important (material) errors in representing the firm's accounting information. The final paragraph indicates that, in addition to its audit of the financial statements, Ernst & Young performed an audit of the effectiveness of Amazon's internal controls over its financial reporting.

Amazon's audit opinion refers to **U.S. generally accepted accounting principles**, or GAAP. But what principles are generally accepted, who accepted them, how did they get accepted, and why were they accepted?

GENERALLY ACCEPTED ACCOUNTING PRINCIPLES

eLectures
MBC

Takeaway 4
Describe the accounting principles and the role of institutions that establish financial accounting regulations.

Generally accepted accounting principles arose to benefit the capital market participants who use financial statements to evaluate a security's **expected return** and **risk**. The standardized conditions provided by the use of GAAP give market participants confidence that the investment decisions they make using accounting reports will be greatly enhanced by that information. In the United States, the ultimate power to set accounting standards rests with the U.S. Congress, which in 1934 established the **Securities and Exchange Commission (SEC)** by giving it the power to regulate securities markets and establish and enforce the accounting rules used by companies issuing those securities. At the time only state-by-state "blue sky"[5] laws existed that regulated disclosures made by firms offering public securities. The oversight role of the SEC is depicted in Exhibit 1.8. The stock market crash of 1929 and the Great Depression of the early 1930s brought turbulent times to the U.S. financial markets. The scandalous behavior of corporate executives in the downfall of some companies and the specter of ordinary citizens who had lost all of their savings were all that the U.S. Congress needed to step in and establish the SEC.

Similar events occurred again 70 years later. Calls for action in the aftermath of the Enron, World-Com, and Global Crossing debacles resulted in the passage of the Sarbanes-Oxley Act in 2002, bringing greater regulation of the accounting profession by a new organization called the **Public Company Accounting Oversight Board (PCAOB)**, which became responsible for overhauling auditing standards, inspecting accounting firms, and disciplining wayward auditors. The PCAOB supplanted a system of self-regulation in which accountants at the **American Institute of Certified Public Accountants (AICPA)** oversaw their peers.

Although the SEC has the final authority over the form and content of financial statements, it has delegated the responsibility for establishing U.S. GAAP to a private sector organization called the **Financial Accounting Standards Board (FASB)**. The FASB's position under the oversight of the SEC is depicted in Exhibit 1.8. The FASB was established in 1973 after the Accounting Principles Board (APB), the predecessor to the FASB, was discontinued. The APB was abandoned after losing public confidence and support for its role in setting accounting standards. The FASB is administered by the **Financial Accounting Foundation (FAF)**, whose trustees are drawn from several different groups including the American Accounting Association, the American Institute of Certified Public Accountants, the Association for

---

[5] The term "blue sky" is commonly attributed to Supreme Court Justice McKenna who noted that many speculative schemes have "no more basis than so many feet of blue sky" (*Hall v. Geiger-Jones Co. 1917*). Others attribute the phrase to a Kansas legislator who observed that some investors in his state owned nothing more than a piece of the "blue sky." As of today, the authority of states to review the registration of securities offered nationally is limited by federal legislation.

EXHIBIT 1.8   Economic Environment of Accounting Information

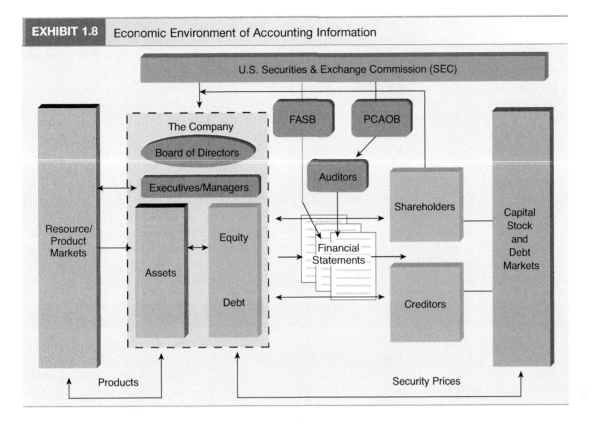

Investment Management and Research, the Financial Executives Institute, and the Securities Industry Association.

The FASB has seven full-time members who must relinquish all ties to their former employers and accept no other paid employment during their five-year terms. Beginning in 2009, U.S. GAAP was streamlined into roughly 90 topics under the FASB's Codification Project. The FASB now updates and clarifies U.S. GAAP through the issuance of Accounting Standards Updates. The adoption of an Update requires the support of a simple majority of the board members.[6]

The FASB accomplishes its mission through a comprehensive and independent process that includes wide participation from those who would be most affected by a proposed new rule. To the layperson, the notion that accounting rules generate heated debates is almost laughable. But in the late 1990s, the FASB issued a proposed accounting rule that required companies to charge the cost of executive stock options against corporate net earnings. Many technology companies feared that the decline in their reported income after implementation of this proposed accounting rule would cause their company's share price to materially decline. The debate over stock option accounting even reached the floor of the U.S. Congress. Senator Joseph Lieberman of Connecticut proposed a law prohibiting the SEC from requiring that executive stock options be expensed. The FASB, under intense political pressure, ultimately backed down, giving firms a choice of deducting the cost of stock options against net income or disclosing in their footnotes what a firm's net income would have been if the options had been charged against its income.

Stock option accounting resurfaced as a controversial topic in the aftermath of the Enron, WorldCom, and Global Crossing scandals as critics attributed the collapse of these companies, at least in part, to the incentive that option-holding executives had to drive share prices higher by inflating reported corporate earnings. Numerous companies began to voluntarily charge the cost of employee stock options against earnings while other companies (such as Microsoft) abandoned stock options in favor of other compensation arrangements. The FASB now requires that firms charge the expense of employee stock options against corporate earnings. (We will have more to say about employee stock options in Chapter 11.)

A more recent example of a hotly debated and controversial accounting topic relates to the required use of fair value accounting for most of a company's financial contracts. In 2006, the FASB implemented a standard (FAS 157) that clarified how and when to use fair values for these contracts, particularly those that

---

[6] For a list of projects currently on the FASB's agenda, see www.fasb.org.

were complex and those that did not have clearly defined inputs that could be used in the determination of fair values. The coincident timing of this rule could not have been worse, as just a year later the financial crisis began. At the same time many banks had to openly report the valuation of contracts such as **mortgage backed securities (MBS)** and **credit default swaps (CDS)**. The underlying problem many had with the accounting rules was that fair value could not be determined when financial markets were not functioning in an orderly manner. As homeowner defaults accelerated and the financial crisis picked up steam, the MBS and CDS paper was becoming "worthless," as there were no willing buyers of such contracts. Because the accounting required that these contracts be valued at prices between a willing buyer and willing seller, banks were technically deemed insolvent. The accounting rule itself was exacerbating the financial crisis.

The U.S. House Capital Markets Subcommittee, led by chairman Barney Frank of Massachusetts, demanded that the FASB modify fair value accounting rules in the face of financial crisis. In response, in early 2008 the FASB issued clarifying rules that now dictate how to apply fair value rules to illiquid markets. Interestingly, The Emergency Stabilization Act of 2008 also charged the SEC to conduct a detailed study of "mark-to-market" and its impact on financial institutions. The conclusion reached was that fair values are an important source of information to investors, and these rules did not play a meaningful role in bank failures during the crisis. We will have more to say about fair value accounting for financial contracts in Chapter 8.

GLOBAL PERSPECTIVE

Accounting standards have traditionally been established on a country-by-country basis. Unfortunately, this situation made the comparability and transparency of financial information across national borders difficult at best. To overcome the diversity in transnational GAAP, the **International Accounting Standards Board (IASB)** was established in 2001 to "harmonize" global accounting practice. The IASB replaced the International Accounting Standards Committee which had been established in 1973 with the goal of harmonizing world accounting standards. Many countries (Bulgaria, Estonia, Jamaica, New Zealand, Russia, Tanzania, and the Ukraine) have replaced their national GAAP with the **International Financial Reporting Standards (IFRS)** issued by the IASB. Beginning in 2005, the European Union (EU) required that all publicly-held companies in EU-member states and EU-applicant states use IFRS in their consolidated financial statements. Until recently, foreign companies that wanted to raise debt or equity capital in the U.S. were required to prepare their financial statements for U.S. investors using U.S. GAAP or, if their financial statements were prepared using some other form of GAAP, to present a reconciliation of their net income and shareholders' equity under the foreign GAAP and U.S. GAAP. In late 2007, however, the U.S. Securities and Exchange Commission voted to allow foreign registrants to file their financial statements with the SEC using IFRS. If some other form of foreign GAAP is used, a reconciliation statement is still required. Many accounting and finance professionals hailed the SEC decision as the first step in a process that could later give U.S. companies the choice of filing their quarterly and annual financial data with the SEC using U.S. GAAP or IFRS. However, almost a decade later, that reciprocity appeared to be at a standstill. In a 2015 speech in New York City, the Chief Accountant of the SEC, James Schnurr, indicated he would not be recommending that U.S. companies have the choice of preparing the financial statements under foreign standards of any type. The financial statements of LVMH Moet Hennessey-Louis Vuitton S.A. illustrating the use of IFRS are presented in Appendix C to this book.

(Note: For convenience, we use "IFRS" to refer to both the International Accounting Standards (IAS) issued by the International Accounting Standards Committee (IASC) and the International Financial Reporting Standards (IFRS) issued by the IASC's successor, the International Accounting Standards Board (IASB).)

As a concluding observation, it is helpful to understand that, in most countries, accounting standards are used only to prepare the financial statements distributed to such external parties as financial analysts, shareholders, and debtholders. It is rare that the same rules are used to prepare a company's income tax statements because income tax regulations are customarily set by elected legislators or governmental agencies, not accounting professionals. The internal financial statements used by managers to run a company may also differ from those statements issued to shareholders and debtholders. In short, it is not unusual for a company to maintain three (or more) sets of financial data—for managers, for the taxation authorities, and for analysts, shareholders, and debtholders. The focus of this textbook is on those financial statements prepared using GAAP for such external constituencies as financial advisors, lenders, investors, and shareholders. However, because of the importance of tax rules to managers and executives when they gauge the financial reporting effects of certain transactions, throughout the text we will highlight critical differences between financial reporting rules and tax rules.

ROLE OF FINANCIAL ACCOUNTING IN INVESTMENT DECISIONS: AN OVERVIEW

In very simplified terms, the lifetime profile of an individual consists of 12 to 16 years of education, 35 years of employment, and 15 to 20 years of retirement. During the first few years of employment, individuals spend most of their earnings acquiring assets like a car, a house, and taking the occasional vacation. After the basics are acquired, most individuals begin to consider the possibility that they will need substantial funds to maintain a lifestyle in retirement that they will have grown accustomed to in their working life. That means developing a retirement plan. The basic retirement plan consists of decisions about how long to work, the amount of funds to set aside over the employment period, and how to allocate those funds across different types of investments.

Individuals typically invest some of their retirement funds in the shares of companies or in a portfolio of companies to diversify their holdings. The old adage *Don't put all your eggs in one basket!* is good advice since a diversified portfolio reduces risk. Over the last decade, more and more individuals have begun simplifying the process of diversifying their equity investments by buying shares in mutual funds. By investing in a spectrum of companies, the value of mutual fund shares is not unduly influenced by the share price performance of a single company, but instead by the broad movement of stock prices in general. Stock market indices such as the Dow Jones Industrial Average (DJIA) and the Standard & Poor's 500 Index (S&P 500) are examples of indexes of a large portfolio of stocks that mutual funds often try to mimic.

Individuals also typically put a sizeable portion of their retirement funds in tax deferred, company-sponsored pension plans. Some individuals dislike risk so they put more of their funds in government debt securities that provide interest payments and repayment of principal. Securities issued by the United States government, and the governments of most other developed countries, are considered to be risk-free because of the very low probability that these entities will fail to pay the interest and principal on their debt securities.

The portfolio decisions of millions of individuals and businesses in allocating funds across different investment opportunities can be thought of as the **supply of capital**. At the same time, there are companies that have opportunities to invest in assets that far exceed their ability to generate the needed investment funds. These unfunded investment opportunities of millions of businesses can be thought of as the **demand for capital**. The **capital market**, on the other hand, can be thought of as the marketplace in which funds are traded between the suppliers of capital and those firms in search of capital. The financial statements provided by the multitude of firms seeking capital are used by the various suppliers of capital to evaluate the investment alternatives. Equilibrium prices for equity and debt securities result when millions of buyers and sellers agree to exchange capital on mutually acceptable terms.

Individual companies raise funds—that is, obtain capital—by issuing shares to shareholders and/or by borrowing from creditors such as financial institutions and bond investors. For shareholders, the return on their investment is derived from dividend payments and any appreciation (or

> Companies "go public"—that is, sell ownership shares in the public capital market—as a means to gain access to capital to grow, to provide the original investors with "liquidity" (the ability to sell their ownership interests), and to have shares to be used to facilitate future mergers and acquisitions.

depreciation) experienced from changes in a company's share price. In general, the return (r) for an equity security over a given period, such as a month or a year, is a function of its price at the end of the period (P_t), any dividends received during the period (D_t), and its price at the beginning of the period (P_{t-1}). That is,

$$r_t = (P_t + D_t - P_{t-1})/P_{t-1}$$

For lenders, a return is generated by the interest payments paid by borrowers and the full and timely repayment of their initial capital investment.

In Practice 1.3 provides data on the average annual return for various types of securities sold in the United States over the 86-year period of 1926 to 2011. The In Practice also shows the standard deviation of the annual returns, a measure of the variation around the average return, which is often used as an indication of the riskiness of a given investment. According to the data, large company shares earned an average return of 9.8 percent per year compared to a return of 5.7 percent for long-term government bonds, but the standard deviation of the returns for large company stocks was much higher, 20.2 percent versus 9.7 percent. Small company shares have done even better than large company shares, having earned an average annual return of 11.9 percent, but the standard deviation of 32.3 percent is also considerably higher. The high standard deviation for small company shares means that the actual return in any year will vary considerably more than for large company shares. In short, when small company share prices fall (rise), they tend to fall (rise) farther than large company share prices; and thus, small company shares are considered to be a riskier investment than large company shares.

In Practice 1.3 *Average Annual Rate of Return by Type of Security: 1926–2011*

Security Classification	Average Return	Standard Deviation
Large company stocks....................	9.8%	20.2%
Small company stocks....................	11.9%	32.3%
Long-term corporate bonds................	6.1%	8.7%
Long-term government bonds..............	5.7%	9.7%
U.S. Treasury bills.......................	3.6%	3.1%
Inflation................................	3.0%	4.4%

Source: Ibbotson Associates, Morningstar

The data in In Practice 1.3 indicate that investments in shares have provided higher average annual returns than investments in government bonds. If the standard deviation of the return is a reasonable measure of risk, the data indicate that shares have higher risk than government bonds, supporting the intuitive notion that higher returns come at the price of bearing higher risk. Investors in common shares can lose all of their investment whereas an investment in government bonds is considered to be risk-free (which means, an investor will receive all interest payments when due and will receive a full return of invested capital). The data also provide support for the notion that shareholders of large firms bear more risk than corporate bondholders since the standard deviation of corporate bonds is only 8.7 percent versus 20.2 percent for stocks. Yet, shareholders are compensated for this additional risk by earning higher returns, 9.8 percent versus 6.1 percent for bondholders.

What is the role of accounting information in the capital markets? For investors who follow an active investment strategy, one very important role for financial statement information is to provide better assessments of the expected return and risk of a firm's securities. This is called the **information role** of financial statements. In essence, financial statements help convey information about a firm's future prospects, namely its earnings power and expected persistence of earnings. Because stock prices correlate so strongly to these measures, any insights that can be gleaned from the trends, ratios, and accounts that embody the financial statements is of great value to these investors. However, for other investors who might follow a long-term buy-and-hold strategy, accounting information may have less value since these investors implicitly operate under the premise that security prices reflect all information that is publicly available. Many of these investors believe that it is not possible to find mispriced securities because capital markets quickly impound all financial information. A market in which security prices correctly reflect all publicly available information (for example, the information contained in financial statements) is referred to as an **efficient market**. But even though the market may indeed be efficient, on average, at the individual security level both anecdotal evidence and formal academic research refuting the market's efficiency abounds. One only need look to the size and growth of Wall Street's financial analyst community as testament to that fact. Opportunities to use historical financial statement information to enhance investment returns clearly exist.

Unlike those investing in stock, debtholders use financial statement and other accounting information for the sole purpose of assessing and monitoring financial risk—that is, the risk that a firm may not pay its debt service charges and principal payments on a timely basis. When debtholders determine that financial risk is high, they will demand commensurately higher returns (by charging higher interest rates) to compensate them for the additional risk assumed by lending to such a firm. They also frequently place formal restrictions on the dollar value and ratios derived from the financial statements, taking the form of contractually defined **debt covenants**.

REVIEW PROBLEM 1.2

Presented below are the beginning-of-year common share price (P_{t-1}), the end-of-year common share price (P_t), and the annual dividend (D_t) for two competitors—Minaret Company and Owens Company.

	P_{t-1}	P_t	D_t
Minaret Company	27.50	28.50	1.20
Owens Company	36.20	35.50	4.50

Required

Calculate the annual return (r_t) for each of the two individual securities.

The solution is on page 36.

CHANGING ECONOMIC LANDSCAPE

Enron, WorldCom, and Global Crossing are now household names synonymous with the most egregious corporate wrongdoing in the United States. These financial scandals brought about significant changes in U.S. corporate regulation. To demonstrate that it was responsive to the public's demand for action, numerous corporate executives and employees from Arthur Andersen, auditor for all three failed companies, were questioned on the floor of the U.S. Congress. In response to their findings, the U.S. Congress quickly enacted the Sarbanes-Oxley Act, establishing the Public Company Accounting Oversight Board to regulate the accounting profession.

Some observers believe, however, that the enacted changes didn't go to the root cause of the financial scandals, the seeds of which were sown in regulation changes made 30 years ago. They cite changes made in the 1970s to increase competition in audit markets by permitting accountants to advertise and solicit clients and to changes in the law that permitted auditors to be sued more easily for financial statement errors as causes of the "race to the bottom."[7] With decreasing fees from competition and increased legal costs, accounting firms introduced changes in auditing methodologies to reduce audit costs and lobbied for more precise standards to better defend themselves in lawsuits. Accounting firms also diversified into corporate consulting to reduce their dependence on auditing fees, the less profitable side of the business, and, by rewarding partners on the basis of client retention and new client acquisition, encouraged a compliant attitude to financial reporting disagreements. Observers also cite regulatory changes that abolished fixed brokerage commissions as another root-cause of the scandals. With the profitability of the securities business reduced, the research side of the securities industry focused more on pleasing clients that brought in underwriting and investment-banking business by releasing favorable earnings forecasts and recommendations. Thus, analysts lost their objectivity and failed to perform hard-nosed fundamental analysis that previously provided value to investors.[8]

Over the years, generally accepted accounting rules have become increasingly complicated, often requiring detailed manuals to guide companies in their implementation. The Sarbanes-Oxley Act of 2002 mandated, among other things, an investigation of the possibility of using "principles" rather than increasingly detailed "rules" as a basis for U.S. accounting standards. Whether principles become the guiding influence in setting future accounting standards remains to be seen.

What many now believe will drive the outcome of this debate is the potential wholesale replacement of U.S. GAAP by International Financial Reporting Standards (IFRS). In 2007, the U.S. SEC concluded that foreign registrants should be permitted to issue their financial reports to U.S. investors using IFRS without the need to perform a reconciliation to U.S. GAAP. There is strong sentiment among many that U.S. firms should also be given this option, although as of 2015 the SEC remains committed to requiring U.S. firms to continue following U.S. GAAP. The consensus among most in the U.S. financial community is not whether IFRS GAAP will be allowed, but whether IFRS will completely supplant U.S. GAAP

---

[7] P.M. Healy and K.G. Palepu, "How the Quest for Efficiency Corroded the Market," *Harvard Business Review* (July 2003).
[8] Ibid.

or whether the two sets of accounting principles will coexist and firms will be permitted to elect to use either set of principles.

ETHICS PERSPECTIVE

There is an intense debate within the U.S. accounting standard-setting community as to whether accounting principles should be rules-based, as is the case with U.S. GAAP, or principles-based, as is the standard with international GAAP. The fundamental difference between these approaches is that principles-based accounting provides a conceptual basis for accountants to follow instead of a list of detailed rules. The landmark Sarbanes-Oxley legislation called for the U.S. Securities and Exchange Commission to study the adoption of principles-based standards for U.S. GAAP. The subsequent SEC staff report recommended that U.S. GAAP move toward a principles-based approach. In fact, the auditing firm of PricewaterhouseCoopers placed a full-page advertisement in the *Wall Street Journal*. Joining the debate over whether GAAP should be more principles—versus rules—based, the audit firm wrote: "Rules-based systems encourage creativity (and not the good kind) in financial reporting. They allow some to stretch the limits of what is permissible under the law, even though it may not be ethically or morally acceptable. A principles-based system requires companies to report, and auditors to audit, the substance or business purpose of transactions, not merely whether they can qualify as acceptable under incredibly complex or overly technical rules." The accounting firm advertisement further stated: "A rules-based system allows managers to ignore the substance and, instead ask, 'Where in the rules does it say I can't do this?'"

---

eLectures

MBC

Takeaway 5
Identify the most common myths about financial accounting.

SEVEN ACCOUNTING MYTHS

It is rare that someone starting an introductory course in financial accounting begins the experience with a blank mental slate. Rather, most individuals bring with them a set of expectations. Almost everyone has had experience with some aspect of accounting, from balancing a checkbook or filling out a credit card application, to reading a set of financial statements. Through these experiences, and from discussions with others, a certain accounting mystery develops along with the formation of certain myths and misconceptions. It is the goal of this textbook to take you on a journey through the world of financial accounting, and along the way, attempt to solve many of the mysteries and debunk many of the myths and misconceptions.

The first two myths about accounting relate to the underlying rules that govern how accounting numbers are calculated and reported. This set of rules is known as **generally accepted accounting principles**, or GAAP. Perhaps the most widely held myth that we explore is the belief that:

1. Generally accepted accounting principles are a set of rigid rules that, if followed correctly, will lead to a unique, "correct" representation of the financial performance and health of a firm.

Closely related to myth number one is the belief that:

2. GAAP is created from a comprehensive analytical process, which is free from political influence.

The following four myths relate to the basic financial statements that are the output of the accounting process:

3. The basic financial statements, consisting of a balance sheet, an income statement, a statement of shareholders' equity, and a statement of cash flow, reflect a complete, accurate, and timely portrayal of the financial performance and well-being of a firm.

4. All of a firm's identifiable assets and liabilities appear on the balance sheet, and the difference between a firm's assets and its liabilities represents the value of the firm.

5. Each of the financial statements is independent, with each reflecting a different aspect of a firm's performance and financial health.

6. Cash flow is ultimately what matters to a firm and its investors; therefore, it is not really necessary to worry about the definition of earnings used in the preparation of the income statement. Rather, one need only consider the sources and uses of cash as reflected on a firm's statement of cash flow.

Lastly, and what we feel is perhaps the biggest myth of all is:

7. A knowledge of accounting is necessary only for someone who wants to be an accountant.

Some of the terminology from the above list of myths may be unfamiliar to you at this point. One thing that is certainly not a myth is that a major challenge associated with learning accounting is to simply understand all of the jargon. Perhaps we should have added an additional myth: Accounting is hard! While this is certainly a subjective assessment that each student will make, we believe that the approach followed in this textbook will go a long way to turning this challenge into a myth as well.

While most individuals reading this book do not plan to pursue a career in accounting, we believe that it is critical for anyone planning a career in management to understand the fundamentals of accounting, for it is the language of business. To use an analogy from sports, you don't have to be a great baseball player to enjoy the game of baseball. Stated alternatively, it is not critical to be trained as an accountant but you must understand how the game is played and scored.

Accounting, as noted above, has its own language. Two of the words that seem to strike fear into new accounting students are "debit" and "credit." Debits and credits represent a mechanism for accountants to record business transactions, in other words to keep score of the game. For those executives planning to continue their accounting studies to a more advanced level, we have included details on using debits and credits in Appendix D of this text. Sometimes, however, it is difficult to see the forest through all of the trees. Therefore, we utilize a spreadsheet approach to recording transactions within the chapters to explain the accounting process in a more straightforward, intuitive manner.

EXECUTIVE SUMMARY

In this chapter we considered the basic financial statements of Amazon.com, an online retailer of products. We examined how the financial statements can be used by debtholders and shareholders to predict the expected return and risk of individual securities. We also considered the role of the FASB, the IASB, and the SEC in setting accounting rules and the role of auditors in monitoring compliance with those rules.

As a validation of your understanding of the content of this chapter, you should now be able to:

- Understand the role of accounting rules in facilitating a properly functioning capital market.
- Identify the basic financial statements—the income statement, the balance sheet, the statement of shareholders' equity, and the statement of cash flow.
- Understand that companies acquire capital from investors who purchase the debt and equity securities, issued by such firms, to obtain an expected return commensurate with the risk the investors assume.
- Understand the conflicts of interest that may arise between the executives, shareholders, and debtholders of a corporation, and the costs associated with the divergent incentives that can arise when the ownership and management of a company are separated (see appendix).
- Describe the accounting principles and the role of institutions that establish financial accounting regulations.
- Identify the most common myths about financial accounting.
- Understand the purpose of GAAP and identify the ten elements that form the basic building blocks of the financial statements

In Chapter 2, we consider how the basic financial statements are developed from accounting events.

KEY CONCEPTS AND TERMS

Accounts payable, 9
Accounts receivable, 9
Accrual basis of accounting, 9
Agency costs, 25
American Institute of Certified
   Public Accountants (AICPA), 16
Assets, 8, 26
Audit report, 15
Balance sheet, 8
Capital market, 19
Cash basis of accounting, 8
Comparability, 26
Comprehensive income, 27

Conservatism, 26
Consolidated income statement, 9
Contracting role, 25
Corporate charter, 24
Corporate governance, 24
Corporations, 24
Covenants, 26
Credit default swaps (CDS), 18
Debt covenants, 20, 25
Decision usefulness, 13
Demand for capital, 19
Distributions to owners, 27
Economic entity, 26

Efficient market, 20
Equity, 26
Expected return, 16
Expenses, 27
Faithful representation, 14, 26
Feedback value, 13
Financial accounting, 5
Financial Accounting Foundation
   (FAF), 16
Financial Accounting Standards
   Board (FASB), 16
Fiscal period, 26
Footnotes, 14

Gains, 27
Generally accepted accounting
      principles, 22
Going concern, 26
Going concern assumption, 9
Income statement, 9
Information role, 20
International Accounting Standards
      Board (IASB), 18
International Financial Reporting
      Standards (IFRS), 18
Investments by owners, 27
Lemons problem, 14
Liabilities, 8, 26

Limited liability, 24
Losses, 27
Managerial accounting, 6
Materiality, 14, 26
Monetary unit, 26
Mortgage backed securities
      (MBS), 18
Predictive value, 13
Public Company Accounting
      Oversight Board (PCAOB), 16
Relevance, 13, 26
Return, 16
Revenues, 26
Risk, 16

Riskiness, 16
Sarbanes-Oxley Act, 5
Securities and Exchange
      Commission (SEC), 16
Shareholders' equity, 8
Statement of cash flow, 9
Statement of shareholders' equity, 11
Supply of capital, 19
Tax accounting, 6
U.S. generally accepted accounting
      principles, 16
U.S. generally accepted auditing
      standards, 16

APPENDIX 1A: Agency Costs and the Separation of Management and Capital Providers

eLectures

MBC

Takeaway 6
Explain the conflicts of interest that can arise between managers and investors, and the costs associated with the divergent incentives that can arise when management and ownership of a company are separated.

Today, businesses are often organized as **corporations** owned by shareholders under the laws of the state or province in which a company is incorporated. State incorporation laws require a company to have a **corporate charter**—a set of bylaws governing the rights and responsibilities of the board of directors to a firm's shareholders and covering such topics as annual meetings, the election of directors, the type and quantity of shares to be sold, and shareholder voting rights. Shareholders usually delegate the task of running a business on their behalf to a board of directors who are elected by shareholders at the annual shareholders' meeting. The board of directors, on the other hand, has oversight responsibility for the company, but the day-to-day management of the firm is directed by the chief executive officer (CEO) who appoints the senior management team including the president, the chief operating officer (COO), and the chief financial officer (CFO). With the assistance of top management, the board of directors recommends a firm's independent auditors to shareholders. The shareholders vote on audit firm appointment (and reappointment) at the annual meeting. These arrangements are collectively referred to as a company's **corporate governance**, a topic much debated since the collapse of Enron, WorldCom, Global Crossing, and a host of other trouble-ridden firms.

A noteworthy characteristic of the corporate form of organization is the principle of **limited liability**, a feature that limits the liability of a business's shareholders for the debts incurred by the business. Thus, if a corporation's assets are insufficient to pay off a business's liabilities when they mature, the lenders are unable to satisfy their claims against the company by attempting to gain control of the personal assets of the company's shareholders.

BUSINESS PERSPECTIVE

The corporate form of business is one of the two primary organizational forms of companies. The other form is a partnership, also known as a sole proprietorship when there is only one partner. There are several key differences between these alternative organizational forms, the principal ones being limited liability, tax status, and ease of ownership transferability. The primary advantage of the corporate form of business is the limited liability provision in which shareholders are only liable for the debts of a business to the extent of their investment in the business. Partners in a partnership, in contrast, face joint and severable liability wherein each partner is liable for not only their own acts, but also for the acts of the other partners. In addition, a partner's liability is not limited to just his/her partnership investment, but liability extends to his/her personal assets as well. The limited liability attribute of corporations is essential to their ability to raise large amounts of capital because shareholders can invest in a corporation without risking their entire personal wealth. This attribute also facilitates the transferability of ownership interests in a corporation relative to a partnership.

Corporations are not without negatives, however, and the principal one is tax status. Corporations face a corporate income tax on their earnings, which may lead to a situation of "double taxation" when any previously taxed corporate income is taxed again to the shareholders when they receive a dividend distribution. Partnerships are not taxed separately; instead, the partnership income is taxed only once at the individual-partner level. In addition to these two primary organizational forms, several hybrid forms exist that have attributes of both corporations and partnerships. These hybrid forms include limited partnerships, limited liability partnerships, sub-chapter S corporations, and limited liability corporations.

The development of the concept of limited liability was significant because it enabled the ownership of a firm to be separated from the day-to-day management of the firm; and, consequently, permitted the segmentation of risk bearing by shareholders from the operational control of a business by its team of managers. Unfortunately, the separation of the ownership of a business from the management of a business often leads to a conflict of interest between the preferences of shareholders for greater wealth and the preferences of managers for increased leisure and on-the-job "perks" such as a company-financed jet. The separation of ownership and the provision of debt financing can also potentially create a conflict of interest between shareholders with preferences for higher-valued shares and debtholders with preferences for timely debt servicing and loan repayment. The costs associated with these divergent self-interests are referred to as **agency costs**.

Since conflicts of interest are likely to arise among the various constituencies that comprise a corporation (i.e., shareholders, managers, and creditors), the agency costs associated with these conflicts must be born by the company's shareholders by virtue of their ownership of the firm. Consequently, it is normally in the shareholders' interest to engage in various "monitoring" and "contracting" activities to help control or reduce these conflicts. For example, financial statement information is often used in employment contracts between managers and shareholders to measure, monitor, and control managerial behavior. This is referred to as the **contracting role** of accounting information.

Conflicts Between Managers and Shareholders

Since shareholders must bear the agency costs associated with the conflicting self-interests that result from the separation of management and ownership of a corporation, they are incentivized to develop contracts with corporate management that direct or control managerial behavior. For example, the shareholders of a business often develop and institute incentive contracts with a business's executives that tie an executive's compensation to the company's share price, via stock options or a restricted stock plan, or to the company's accounting earnings which have been shown to be correlated with a company's share price. Thus, incentive contracts work to align the financial interests of managers with those of a company's shareholders, thereby encouraging the managers to simultaneously work to maximize their own wealth as well as that of the shareholders. Amazon.com, for example, reported that the company granted bonus opportunities to various executive officers payable upon the achievement of *certain performance goals*. Undoubtedly, some of the performance goals were measured in terms of such accounting numbers as sales, cash flow or profits. By linking executive compensation to measurable accounting variables, management is more likely to take appropriate actions to see that the performance goals are met or exceeded, thereby increasing the wealth of the shareholders, and that of their own.

Conflicts Between Debtholders and Shareholders

Agency costs can also arise from conflicts between debtholders and shareholders. An extreme example of such behavior would occur in the case of a firm whose shareholders borrow a large amount of money from debtholders only to pay the borrowed funds out as a dividend. In effect, the shareholders redistribute the borrowed wealth from the debtholders to themselves, potentially leaving the debtholders with a worthless corporate shell and no resources to repay the loan. By virtue of their ownership of the firm, shareholders bear the agency costs of this conflict via higher interest rates because debtholders can anticipate these potentially unconstrained actions by shareholders. A solution to this conflict is for shareholders to agree to be bound by a legally enforceable loan contract containing provisions that restrict the shareholders' behavior. These contract provisions are called **debt covenants**, and may, for example, restrict the amount of dividends that may be paid.

To illustrate, the following disclosure is from the 2014 annual report of Arch Coal, a coal mining company headquartered in St. Louis:

Debt Covenants

Financial covenant requirements may restrict the amount of unused capacity available to the Company for borrowings and letters of credit under credit facilities. The credit facility amendment on December 17, 2013 amended financial maintenance covenants to include only a minimum liquidity test until June, 2015, at which time a maximum secured leverage ratio test takes effect. The amendment also limits dividends to one cent per share per fiscal year.

Terms of the Company's credit facilities and leases also contain covenants that limit the ability of the Company to, among other things, acquire, dispose, merge or consolidate assets; incur additional debt; pay dividends and make distributions or repurchase stock; make investments; create liens; issue and sell capital stock of subsidiaries; enter into restrictions affecting the ability of restricted subsidiaries to make distributions, loans or advances to the Company; engage in transactions with affiliates and enter into sale and leaseback transactions. Failure by the Company to comply with such covenants could result in an event of default, which, if not cured or waived, could have a material adverse effect on the Company.

Another example of a corporate action creating agency costs is the issuance of new debt with repayment priority over existing debt. In this situation, there is a redistribution of wealth from the initial debtholders to the shareholders. A solution to this conflict is for the shareholders to agree to a legally enforceable contract that limits the firm's ability

When a company borrows funds, the terms of the loan agreement are formalized in a legal contract. Typically, these loan contracts contain provisions, called **covenants**, which restrict the actions of the borrower. For example, a common debt covenant limits the amount of dividends that can be paid to shareholders. Covenants are used by lenders to reduce financial risk and increase the likelihood that borrowers pay their interest and principal repayments in a timely manner.

to issue new debt with priority over the old debt. For example, in the mid 2000s Amazon had covenants restricting the company's ability to borrow by requiring that the ratio of aggregate indebtedness divided by pre-tax operating earnings be less than 6 to 1. Under the terms of this covenant, Amazon was required to periodically provide debtholders with audited financial statements from which measures of aggregate indebtedness and pre-tax operating earnings could be taken and used to evaluate the firm's compliance with the covenant. How does this help Amazon? By agreeing to the restrictions imposed by the covenant, Amazon.com was able to obtain a loan that it might not otherwise gain access to.

APPENDIX 1B: Generally Accepted Accounting Principles: Purpose, Concepts, and Elements

Takeaway 7
Understand the purpose of GAAP and identify the ten elements that form the basic building blocks of the financial statements.

Generally accepted accounting principles (GAAP) have as their purpose the measurement of economic activity by a business enterprise and the reporting of this activity in the form of financial statements, along with disclosures to aid users in the interpretation of the financial statements. The primary promulgator of U.S. GAAP is the Financial Accounting Standards Board (FASB). Prior to its codification project in 2009, the FASB issued a series of pronouncements, called Statements of Financial Accounting Concepts (SFAC), that served to create a foundation for U.S. GAAP.

The first SFAC identifies the three principal objectives of financial reporting: (1) the creation of information useful in making economic decisions; (2) providing information to aid in predicting cash flows; and (3) providing relevant information regarding a business's economic resources. These objectives facilitate the measurement and reporting of business activity during a **fiscal period** by an **economic entity** that is assumed to be a **going concern**. The economic entity assumption implies that the business activity to be measured can be identified with a particular unit of accountability and requires that the activity of the entity be assessed separately from the activities of its owners. It is further assumed that the entity will remain a going concern for the foreseeable future; in other words, that the enterprise will have a long life. Because the entity will exist for an extended period of time, it is necessary to segment its operational life into reporting periods, known as fiscal periods, so as to provide interested parties with timely, relevant information about its various activities. Public corporations that report to the Securities and Exchange Commission (SEC) file quarterly financial statements, called a 10-Q, and annual financial statements, called a 10-K. An additional **monetary unit** assumption implies that only those items that can be expressed in terms of a monetary unit, the U.S. dollar in the United States, are included in the financial statements. Because inflation is relatively mild in the United States, price-level changes are ignored and the U.S. dollar is assumed to remain stable over time.

Another SFAC discusses the qualities that make accounting information useful. The primary qualities are **relevance** and **faithful representation**. For information to be relevant, it should be timely and should either assist in predicting future cash flows or provide feedback value regarding past events. For information to be faithfully represented, it should be verifiable and faithfully represent the observed economic activity. Finally, information should also be comparable, consistent, and understandable. **Comparability** refers to comparisons made between different business entities, whereas consistency refers to comparisons made across time for a particular business entity.

The above qualities are subject to a **materiality** constraint. The materiality constraint is not explicitly defined and consequently requires some judgment in its application. In general, only economic events that are significant enough to affect a user's decisions are required to be accounted for in a manner consistent with GAAP.

Not all of these qualities are compatible, however; for example, there is often a conflict between relevance and faithful representation. When trade-offs between the qualities are necessary, GAAP tends to place more weight on the role of **conservatism**. Conservatism is a reaction to the uncertainty inherent in many financial events. Conservatism dictates that, when in doubt, the financial statements should understate assets, overstate liabilities, delay the recognition of revenues, and accelerate the recognition of expenses.

A third concept statement defines ten elements that form the basic building blocks of the financial statements. The first three elements relate to the balance sheet, which portrays an entity's net resources as of a particular point in time:

1. **Assets**—Probable future economic benefits obtained or controlled by a particular entity as a result of past transactions or events.
2. **Liabilities**—Probable future sacrifices of economic benefits arising from present obligations of a particular entity to transfer assets or provide services to other entities in the future as a result of past transactions.
3. **Equity** (net assets)—The residual interest in the assets that remain after deducting its liabilities.

The next five elements relate to the income statement, which measures an entity's performance over a given period of time:

4. **Revenues**—Inflows or other enhancements of assets of an entity or settlement of its liabilities (or a combination of both) from delivering or producing goods, rendering services, or carrying out other activities that constitute the entity's ongoing major and central purpose.

5. **Expenses**—Outflows or other using up of assets or incurrences of liabilities (or a combination of both) from delivering or producing goods, rendering services, or carrying out other activities that constitute the entity's ongoing major and central purpose.

6. **Gains**—Increases in equity (net assets) from peripheral or incidental transactions of an entity and from all other transactions and other events and circumstances affecting the entity except those that result from revenues or investments by owners.

7. **Losses**—Decreases in equity (net assets) from peripheral or incidental transactions of an entity and from all other transactions and other events and circumstances affecting the entity except those that result from revenues or investments by owners.

8. **Comprehensive income**—The change in equity of a business enterprise during a period from transactions and other events and circumstances from sources other than investments by owners or distribution to owners.

The final two elements relate to transfers between a business enterprise and its owners:

9. **Investments by owners**—Increases in equity of a particular business enterprise resulting from transfers to it for the purpose of increasing ownership interests.

10. **Distributions to owners**—Decreases in the equity of a particular business enterprise resulting from transferring assets, rendering services, or incurring liabilities to owners.

QUESTIONS

Q1.1   **Financial Statement Data Users.**   Financial statement data is utilized by a variety of user-groups to include a company's board of directors, bondholders, corporate employees and executives, customers, investment advisors, labor unions, loan officers and credit analysts, shareholders and suppliers. For each user-group, discuss how financial statement data might be used in their decision-making process.

Q1.2   **GAAP.**   Discuss why generally accepted accounting principles are important to investors and to a properly functioning, efficient capital market. How do accounting rules help capital markets be (or become) "efficient"?

Q1.3   **Corporate Governance.**   Discuss what "corporate governance" is and why it is important to shareholders.

Q1.4   **Risk, Return, and Accounting Information.**   Discuss the relationship between investment risk and the expected rate of return on an investment. Explain why accounting information is useful in evaluating the risk/return trade-off inherent in all investments.

Q1.5   **Global GAAP.**   Discuss the major impediments to the acceptance of a global set of generally accepted accounting principles. Prepare a list of those key impediments. Of the items on your list, which do you think will be the most difficult to overcome? Why? Why is having a global set of GAAP desirable?

Q1.6   **Asymmetric U.S. GAAP.**   Under U.S. GAAP, long-lived assets such as real estate are carried on the balance sheet at the original purchase price of the asset. In the event that the value of a real estate asset becomes "impaired"—that is, the current value of the real estate falls below its original purchase price and is unlikely to recover the lost value in the foreseeable future—the asset's book value is written down to the lower current value and a loss is recorded on the firm's income statement. Under no circumstances, however, can a firm write up the value of its real estate assets in the event that current value exceeds original purchase price. Discuss whether U.S. GAAP should be changed to allow a symmetric treatment of asset value increases and decreases. What are the implications of this asymmetry in the accounting treatment of assets (such as real estate) for current U.S. financial statement users?

Q1.7   **Human Assets.**   The balance sheet allegedly reports all of the assets of a business. But one of the most important assets of any business is its employees, and this asset is omitted from the balance sheet of every company in every country in the world. Thus, it can be concluded that the balance sheet of any company understates the true value of its assets. Discuss what types of companies and which industries are most likely to be impacted by this situation. Prepare a list of the companies that you feel are most adversely affected by this accounting practice. Why did you select these companies?

Q1.8   **Key Performance Indicators: Amazon.com.**   Based upon your reading of the chapter, specifically a review of the financial statements of Amazon.com, identify five key indicators of performance (KPIs) for Amazon.com. Explain why you selected the five KPIs. Identify five KPIs that are _not_ present in Amazon's financial statements but that you believe are important to consider when making a decision about whether to invest in Amazon.com.

Q1.9   **Audit Reports.**   Review Amazon.com's audit report in Exhibit 1.7 and discuss what the report tells you about Amazon's financial statements. Is there anything in the audit report that causes you concern? Why or why not? According to the independent auditors, who has ultimate responsibility for the preparation of and fairness of the company's financial statements?

Q1.10   **Accounting Assumptions and Concepts.**   Discuss the following accounting assumptions and concepts:
- Accrual basis of accounting
- Cash basis of accounting
- Going concern assumption
- Materiality concept
- Information role of accounting
- Contracting role of accounting

Why are the assumptions and concepts important?

Q1.11   **The Basic Financial Statements.**   Describe or define the four basic financial statements:
- Income statement
- Balance sheet
- Statement of shareholders' equity
- Statement of cash flow

Discuss how the four statements are interconnected.

Q1.12   **Debt Covenants.**   American Airlines has outstanding lines of credit and various loan agreements with a number of financial institutions. Under the terms of these debt contracts, American is required to (a) maintain a minimum balance of $1.25 billion of unrestricted cash and short-term investments, (b) maintain a ratio of operating cash flow to interest expense of at least 1.3 to 1.0, and (c) restrict any dividend payments to American shareholders to not more than 25 percent of net income. Discuss why American's lenders would impose these financial and operating restrictions on the airline. Discuss why American would agree to the restrictions.

Q1.13   **Debt Covenants.**   Titanium Metals Corporation (TIMET) is one of the world's leading producers of titanium products. In November 2012, it was announced the company was being purchased by Precision Castparts, a diversified manufacturer of complex metal components and products. In TIMET's annual report, prior to its acquisition by Precision Castparts, the company disclosed the following:

> Under the terms of the company's U.S. asset-based revolving credit agreement, borrowings are limited to the lesser of $105 million or a formula-determined borrowing-base. . . . Borrowings are collateralized by substantially all of the company's U.S. assets.
>
> The U.S. credit agreement prohibits . . . the payment of dividends on the company's common stock . . . , limits additional indebtedness, requires compliance with certain financial covenants including a minimum net worth covenant and a fixed charge ratio covenant . . . .

Discuss why TIMET's U.S. lenders would impose such restrictions on the company. Discuss why TIMET would agree to such restrictions.

Q1.14   **(Appendix 1A) Separation of Ownership and Management.**   Describe a conflict that may arise between the shareholders of a company and the managers of the company. Discuss what the shareholders might do to overcome that conflict and explain why you feel that your solution to the conflict would be effective.

Q1.15   **(Appendix 1A) Conflicts Between Shareholders and Debtholders.**   Describe a conflict that may arise between the shareholders of a company and the debtholders of the company. Discuss what the debtholders might do to resolve that conflict and explain why you feel that your solution to the conflict would be effective.

Q1.16   **The Going Concern Assumption.**   Ernst & Young, LLP is the independent public accountant for AMR Corporation, the parent company of American Airlines and American Eagle. In February 2013 AMR and US Airways Group announced the two companies would merge to form the largest airline in the world. In AMR's 2012 annual report, Ernst & Young gave AMR a "clean opinion," indicating that its financial statements were fairly presented. In the 2012 auditors' report for AMR, however, Ernst & Young notes:

> The accompanying consolidated financial statements have been prepared assuming that the Company will continue as a going concern. As discussed in Note 1 to the consolidated financial statements, the Company's bankruptcy filing raises substantial doubt about the Company's ability to continue as a going concern. Management's plans concerning these matters are described in Note 1. The consolidated financial statements do not include adjustments that might result from the outcome of this uncertainty.

Discuss why Ernst & Young would issue a "clean opinion" on the financial statements of AMR Corporation given its many doubts about the firm's ability to "continue as a going concern."

Q1.17   **Is the Sarbanes-Oxley Act Effective?**   In 2006, *BusinessWeek* magazine (April 17, 2006) carried an opinion piece which questioned the effectiveness of the Sarbanes-Oxley Act of 2002. According to the author, Professor D. Moore, "key business failures that cost investors and employees tens of billions of dollars are all but sure to happen again. The calamitous scandals of Enron and many other companies were possible only because of breaches in a bulwark of our free market system—auditor independence." Professor Moore states that the Sarbanes-Oxley Act will be ineffective in preventing future corporate scandals because the act fails to address the real underlying problem, namely the lack of auditor objectivity. Do you agree with Professor Moore? If so, why? If not, why not?

Q1.18   **Should the Sarbanes-Oxley Act Be Revised?**   In late 2006, *BusinessWeek* magazine (December 18, 2006) carried a report on the aftermath of the passage of the Sarbanes-Oxley Act. According to the piece, "the intentions were good, but in the two years since its passing, the Sarbanes-Oxley Act has collapsed into a glob of regulatory confusion costing U.S. businesses billions of dollars a year in compliance costs." The article further noted that "(T)he act never got the vetting it deserved because of the race to approve it after the Enron and WorldCom meltdowns. . ." Nevertheless, one direct consequence of the Act was that a record number of U.S.-listed firms—1,300 companies, or over 8 percent of the total—restated their earnings in 2005. Discuss whether the criticisms of the Act noted in the *BusinessWeek* article are justified given the large number of firms that found it necessary to restate their reported earnings following the passage of the Act.

Q1.19   **(Ethics Perspective) Rules-based Versus Principles-based Accounting.**   Do you believe that rules-based accounting leads to unethical managerial behavior? If so, why? Do you think that rules-based GAAP allows businesses to design their financial reporting so as to stay within the letter of the accounting standards even if they clearly violate the spirit of the standards?

Q1.20   **(Appendix 1B)**   Financial statements must contain objective and verifiable data if they are to be useful. Yet, many estimates and subjective assumptions are required to facilitate the preparation of these reports. Please reconcile these apparent inconsistencies in the preparation of the basic financial statements.

Q1.21   **(Appendix 1B)**   Much of the information contained in the balance sheet is reported on a historical cost basis. This means that such assets as land are reported at the amount that was originally paid for the item when purchased. Alternative possible reporting methods include current value, what a similar item would currently cost to acquire, and liquidation value, the amount an entity would receive if it was forced to sell the item. Discuss how the concepts of relevance, faithful representation, and going concern influence the choice of historical cost as a reporting method.

Assignments with the ⓂⒷⒸ logo in the margin are available in ᵐʸBusinessCourse.
See the Preface of the book for details.
CHECK FIGURE indicates that check figures are available on the book's Website.

EXERCISES

E1.22   **Account Identification.**   Presented below is a list of financial statement accounts. Using the letter A for assets, L for liabilities, SE for shareholders' equity, R for revenue, E for expenses, and N/A for not applicable, identify (a) whether the listed accounts appear on the balance sheet (B/S) or income statement (I/S), and if so, (b) the nature of the account (A, L, SE, R, E, or N/A).

TA 2

MBC

1. Accounts receivable
2. Common stock
3. Sales
4. Land
5. Retained earnings
6. Notes payable
7. Dividends paid
8. Inventory

9. Depreciation expense
10. Accounts payable
11. Cash flow from operating activities
12. Cash
13. Cost of goods sold
14. Equipment
15. Selling expense
16. Interest income

E1.23   **The Balance Sheet Equation.**   The Arcadia Company reported the following financial results during its first two years of operations:

TA 2

MBC

Year End	Assets	=	Liabilities	+	Shareholders' Equity
Year 1 ...	$80,000	=	$60,000	+	$20,000
Year 2 ...	70,000	=	40,000	+	30,000

Assuming that no dividends were declared and that no additional capital was invested in Year 2, determine Arcadia's net income (or loss) for Year 2.

TA 2
CHECK
FIGURE

E1.24 **The Balance Sheet Equation.** The Claremont Company reported the following financial results during its first two years of operations.

Year End	Assets	=	Liabilities	+	Shareholders' Equity
Year 1 . . .	$110,000	=	$60,000	+	$50,000
Year 2 . . .	125,000	=	80,000	+	45,000

Assuming that no dividends were declared and that no additional capital was invested in Year 2, determine the net income (loss) for the Claremont Company in Year 2.

TA 2
CHECK
FIGURE

E1.25 **Key Relations: Revenues, Expenses, Dividends, and Retained Earnings.** Compute the missing amounts (in millions) in the following table. (The balance in retained earnings at year-end 2015 was $2.2.) Comment on the firm's performance over the three-year period after calculating the level of expenses as a percentage of total revenues and net income as a percentage of total revenues. What advice would you give to this company in regards to its dividend policy?

	2013	2014	2015
Retained earnings (beginning)	$1.2	$ 2.0	?
Revenues	8.8	11.8	11.8
Expenses	7.4	?	11.0
Dividends	?	.6	.6

TA 2, 3

E1.26 **Key Relations: Revenues, Expenses, Dividends, and Retained Earnings.** Compute the missing amounts in the following table. (At the end of 2015, retained earnings had a balance of negative $2,086.) Comment on the company's performance over the three-year period after calculating the relationship of expenses as a percentage of revenues and net income as a percentage of revenues. Do you agree with the company's dividend policy? Why?

	2013	2014	2015
Retained earnings (beginning)	$(1,746.5)	$(1,830.5)	$(2,653.0)
Revenues	4,840.5	5,327.0	?
Expenses	?	5,628.0	5,425.0
Dividends	-0-	?	17.5

TA 2, 3 **E1.27** **Financial Statement Results.** In its 2014 annual report to shareholders, General Electric reported the following financial results:

- Revenues increased from $146.0 to $148.5 billion.
- Net income increased from $13.1 to $15.2 billion.
- Total assets decreased from $656.6 to $648.3 billion.
- Shareholders' equity decreased from $130.6 to $128.1 billion.
- For the year, the cash flow from operating activities was $27.1 billion, the cash flow from investing activities was negative $17.0 billion, and the cash flow from financing activities was negative $5.0 million.

Discuss the possible explanations for the financial results of General Electric.

TA 2, 3 **E1.28** **Financial Statement Results.** In its 2014 annual report to shareholders, Johnson & Johnson, a consumer-products company, reported the following financial results:

- Revenues increased from $71.3 to $74.3 billion.
- Net income increased from $13.8 to $16.3 billion.
- Total assets decreased from $132.6 to $131.6 billion.
- Shareholders' equity decreased from $74.0 to $69.7 billion.
- For the year, the cash flow from operating activities amounted to $18.4 billion, the cash flow from investing activities amounted to negative $12.3 billion, and the cash flow from financing activities amounted to $14.5 billion.

Discuss the possible explanations for the financial results of Johnson & Johnson.

E1.29 **Calculating Security Returns.** Presented below are the beginning-of-year common share price (P_{t-1}), the   TA 4
end-of-year common share price (P_t), and the annual dividend (D_t) for three competitors—General Electric,   CHECK
Philips Electronics NV, and Siemens AG.   FIGURE

	P_{t-1}	P_t	D_t
General Electric Co.	$32.01	$34.50	$0.86
Philips Electronics NV	72.52	72.90	1.28
Siemens AG	27.20	25.36	0.52

Calculate the annual return for each of the three individual securities. Which security provided the greatest
return over the one-year period? What other information would you need to assess the return/risk trade-off on
each of these individual securities?

PROBLEMS

P1.30 **Key Financial Statement Relations: Balance Sheet, Income Statement, and Statement of Cash Flow.**   TA 2, 3
Compute the missing amounts in the following financial statements. You may assume that accounts receivable   CHECK
relate only to credit sales and that accounts payable relate only to credit purchases of inventory. There were no   FIGURE
sales of property and equipment during 2015 and any purchases of property and equipment were made using
cash. What is your assessment of the company's financial performance in 2015?

Balance Sheet at	December 31, 2014	December 31, 2015
Current assets		
Cash	$?	$ 25,000
Marketable securities	3,000	5,000
Accounts receivable	12,000	37,000
Merchandise inventory	52,000	23,000
Prepaid advertising	15,000	18,000
Total current assets	92,000	108,000
Property, plant, and equipment, (net)	?	223,000
Land	15,000	?
Intangible assets	?	7,000
Total assets	$258,000	$342,000
Current liabilities		
Accounts payable	$ 12,000	$ 23,000
Wages payable	?	18,000
Interest payable	6,000	5,000
Dividends payable	3,000	?
Taxes payable	17,000	12,000
Total current liabilities	43,000	60,000
Long-term debt	?	86,000
Shareholders' equity		
Common stock	150,000	172,000
Retained earnings	23,000	32,000
Treasury stock	(10,000)	?
Total liabilities and shareholders' equity	$258,000	$342,000

Income Statement for Year Ending	December 31, 2015
Sales revenue.	$?
Cost of sales.	123,000
Gross profit.	162,000
Expenses:	
Wages.	15,000
Advertising	18,000
Depreciation	28,000
Amortization	4,000
Total expenses	65,000
Operating profit	97,000
Interest	?
Income (loss) before taxes	88,000
Tax expense	?
Net income	$ 53,000

Statement of Cash Flow for Year Ended	December 31, 2015
Cash flow from operating activities	
Cash collections from customers.	$ 260,000
Cash payments for:	
Inventory.	(83,000)
Wages.	(2,000)
Taxes	(40,000)
Interest	(10,000)
Advertising	?
Net cash provided by operations	104,000
Cash flow from investing activities	
(Purchases) sale of property, plant and equipment	(111,000)
(Purchase) sale of marketable securities	?
(Purchase) sale of land	11,000
Net cash provided by investing activities.	(102,000)
Cash flow from financing activities	
Issuance (repayment) of long-term debt	34,000
Payment of dividend	(45,000)
Issuance (repurchase) of common stock	?
(Purchase) sale of treasury stock	2,000
Net cash provided by financing activities.	13,000
Change in cash.	$?

TA 2, 3 **P1.31** **Key Financial Statement Relations: Balance Sheet, Income Statement, and Statement of Cash Flow.**
Compute the missing amounts in the following financial statements. You may assume that accounts receivable relate only to credit sales and that accounts payable relate only to credit purchases of inventory. There were no sales of property and equipment during 2015 and any purchases of property and equipment were made using cash. What is your assessment of the company's financial performance in 2015?

Balance Sheet at	December 31, 2014	December 31, 2015
Current assets		
Cash.	$ 18,000	$?
Marketable securities	2,000	5,000
Accounts receivable.	8,000	10,000
Merchandise inventory	41,000	58,000
Prepaid advertising.	13,000	16,000
Total current assets	82,000	104,000
Property, plant and equipment (cost).	?	201,000
Accumulated depreciation	(41,000)	(52,000)
Land	12,000	19,000
Intangible assets	12,000	?
Total assets.	$227,000	$282,000
Current liabilities		
Accounts payable.	$ 18,000	$?
Wages payable.	15,000	18,000
Interest payable	?	6,000
Dividends payable	2,000	4,000
Taxes payable.	5,000	1,000
Total current liabilities.	48,000	50,000
Long-term debt	46,000	?
Shareholders' equity		
Common stock.	121,000	160,000
Retained earnings	22,000	32,000
Treasury stock	?	(12,000)
Total liabilities and shareholders' equity.	$227,000	$282,000

Income Statement for Year Ending	December 31, 2015
Sales revenue.	$140,000
Cost of sales.	87,000
Gross profit.	53,000
Expenses	
Wages.	?
Advertising	5,000
Depreciation	?
Amortization	2,000
Total expenses	24,000
Operating profit	29,000
Interest	3,000
Income (loss) before taxes	26,000
Tax expense	?
Net income.	$ 18,000

Statement of Cash Flow for Year Ended	December 31, 2015
Cash flow from operating activities	
Cash collections from customers.	$?
Cash payments for:	
Inventory.	(101,000)
Wages.	(3,000)
Taxes	(12,000)
Interest	(5,000)
Advertising	(8,000)
Net cash provided by operations.	9,000
Cash flow from investing activities	
(Purchases) sale of property, plant and equipment	(39,000)
(Purchase) sale of marketable securities	(3,000)
(Purchase) sale of land.	?
Net cash provided by investing activities.	(49,000)
Cash flow from financing activities	
Issuance (repayment) of long-term debt	6,000
Payment of dividend	(6,000)
Issuance (repurchase) of common stock.	39,000
(Purchase) sale of treasury stock	(2,000)
Net cash provided by financing activities.	37,000
Net cash flow	$ (3,000)

TA 2   **P1.32**   **Creating Balance Sheets and Income Statements.**   Using the information in the below table, prepare a classified balance sheet for Arrow Company as of December 31, 2014 and December 31, 2015, along with multi-step income statements for the years then ended.

Account	December 31, 2014	December 31, 2015
Property, plant, and equipment (net)	$ 650	$ 735
Long-term debt	490	690
Depreciation expense.	50	60
Retained earnings	130	295
Sales revenue.	1,000	1,500
Income taxes	50	70
Current portion of long-term debt	50	70
Total current liabilities.	130	160
Inventory.	125	300
Cost of goods sold.	600	900
Cash.	100	140
Selling, general, and administrative expenses.	175	290
Other current assets.	40	40
Accounts receivable.	135	230
Interest expense.	25	50
Dividends	20	25
Accounts payable.	80	90
Common stock.	300	300

CORPORATE ANALYSIS

CA1.33 **The Procter & Gamble Company.**   The 2015 annual report of The Procter & Gamble Company (P&G)   TA 2, 3, 4
is available at www.pginvestor.com. After reviewing P&G's annual report, respond to the following questions:

    a. Prepare a list of some of the products produced by P&G. In what industry does P&G operate? Who are some of P&G's key competitors? (To identify the key competitors for P&G, you will need to access the internet [e.g., http://finance.yahoo.com] or obtain a copy of a recent research report for P&G.)

    b. How much net income did P&G earn in 2013, 2014 and 2015? How much operating revenue did P&G report in 2013, 2014 and 2015? Are the trends in operating revenue and net income consistent and positive (i.e., increasing)?

    c. How much cash flow from operations was generated by P&G in 2013, 2014 and 2015? Is the trend in the cash flow from operations consistent with the trend in operating revenue and net income? Calculate the ratio of the cash flow from operations divided by net income for 2013, 2014 and 2015. (Note: The ratio of cash flow from operations divided by net income is called the "operating funds ratio.") What does this ratio tell you?

    d. Calculate the ratio of total liabilities divided by total assets for 2014 and 2015. What does this ratio tell you? Is P&G principally debt-financed or principally equity-financed? Is the form of P&G's financing changing over time?

    e. Consider the audit report for P&G. Who are P&G's auditors? What does P&G's audit report say about the firm's financial statements? Is there anything in P&G's audit report that causes you any concern? If so, what?

CA1.34 **Internet-based Analysis.**   Consider a publicly held company whose products you are familiar with. Some   TA 2, 4, 6, 7
examples might include:

Company	Product	Corporate Website
• Johnson & Johnson.............	• Band-Aids	• www.jnj.com
• Microsoft Corporation...........	• Windows software	• www.microsoft.com
• Intel Corporation	• Pentium processors	• www.intel.com
• Kimberly-Clark Corporation.......	• Kleenex	• www.kimberly-clark.com

Access the company's public website and search for its most recent annual report. (Some companies will provide access to their financial data through an "investor relations" link, while others will provide a direct link to their "annual reports.") After locating your company's most recent annual report, open the file and review its contents. After reviewing the annual report for your selected company, prepare answers to the following questions:

    1. Prepare a list of the company's products.

    2. Identify which accounting firm audited the company's financial data. Briefly describe the contents of the audit report.

    3. How much net income did the company earn in each of the past two years?

    4. How much cash flow from operations did the company generate in each of the last two years?

    5. Explain why the amount of net income and the cash flow from operations differed.

    6. Comment on the company's performance and financial health over the last two years. Is the company's performance and financial health improving or declining? Why?

CA1.35 **IFRS Financial Statements.**   The 2014 financial statements of LVMH Moet Hennessey-Louis Vuitton   TA 2, 4
S.A. are presented in Appendix C at the end of this book. LVMH is a Paris-based holding company and one of the world's largest and best-known luxury goods companies. As a member-nation of the European Union, French companies are required to prepare their consolidated (group) financial statements using International Financial Reporting Standards (IFRS). After reviewing LVMH's consolidated balance sheet in Appendix C, prepare answers to the following questions:

    a. Under U.S. GAAP, the balance sheet equation is defined as Assets = Liabilities + Shareholders' Equity. Describe how the balance sheet equation is defined under IFRS. Does the IFRS definition of the balance sheet equation change the informational content of the consolidated sheet?

    b. Under U.S. GAAP, current assets and current liabilities are listed before noncurrent assets and noncurrent liabilities. Describe the listing sequence of LVMH's assets and liabilities. Does the listing sequence impact the informational content of the consolidated balance sheet?

    c. Under U.S. GAAP, current assets are listed according to their expected liquidity, with the most liquid current assets listed first and the least liquid current assets listed last. How would you describe the listing sequence of current assets for LVMH?

    d. Under U.S. GAAP, the balance sheet equation is defined as A = L + SE. LVMH replaces the label "shareholders' equity" with just "equity." What might explain this difference in labeling of this section of the consolidated balance sheet?

SOLUTIONS TO REVIEW PROBLEMS

Solution 1.1

	Year 1	Year 2	Year 3
Retained earnings (beginning)	$ 0.0	$3.3	$ 3.6
Revenues	10.2	7.0	10.7
Expenses	4.1	4.5	4.7
Dividends	2.80	2.2	2.3

Solution 1.2

Minaret Company	8.0%
Owens Company	10.5%

Annual Return $= r_t = (P_t - P_{t-1} + D_t)/P_{t-1}$

When you complete this chapter you should be able to:

1. Understand the balance sheet equation. (page 40)

2. Explain the accounting meaning behind the terms *asset*, *liability*, *shareholders' equity*, *revenue and expense*, and *matching*. (page 42)

3. Apply the balance sheet equation in the preparation of financial statements from business events. (page 43)

4. Apply selected financial ratios to evaluate a company's financial performance. (page 63)

5. Understand the managerial motives for selecting between alternative accounting methods. (page 68)

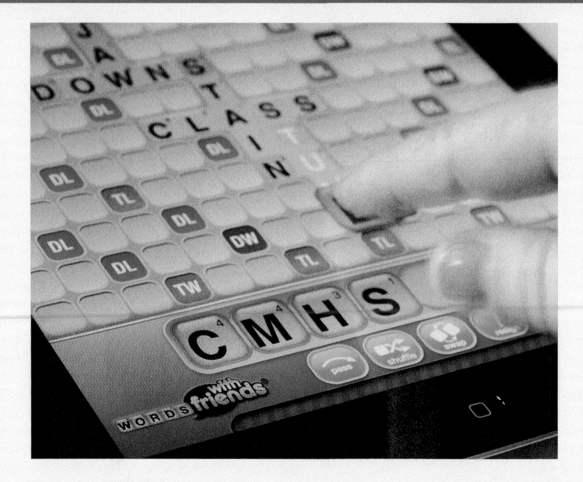

From Business Events to Financial Statements

Zynga Inc., headquartered in San Francisco, is a social game developer with some of the most widely used games in the world. The company's games can be found on most social networking sites and mobile platforms, such as Facebook, and are

ZYNGA

accessible on the iOS and Android platforms. As of January 2015, Zynga's games had over 108 million monthly active users, and its games were the most widely used on Facebook. The most popular (and most addictive) titles were *FarmVille*, *Words with Friends*, and *Zynga Poker*. With all of the company's success, Zynga is less than a decade old, founded in 2007 by Marc Pincus.

In July of 2011 Zynga filed a prospectus with the U.S. Securities and Exchange Commission (SEC) to raise approximately $1 billion in an initial public offering (IPO). One motive for the IPO was no doubt related to the desire to quickly raise large amounts of cash as a way to capitalize on the enormous growth potential of its products, both existing and proposed. The company issued 100 million shares valued at $10 per share, but this represented only 15 percent of the total outstanding shares. The total company, after the IPO, was valued at approximately $7 billion. Not bad for what was, a few years earlier, just an idea.

In the prospectus filed by the company, management provided three years of historical financial statements, figures that prior to that date had not before been previously published. From that data, numerous Wall Street analysts went to work forecasting the company's future prospects, beginning with forecasts of earnings and cash flows. Behind these calculations were full forecasts of Zynga's financial statements, direct from anticipated sales, costs, and investing and financing expectations.

The analyst forecasts were driven in large part by the financial prospects and product launches provided in various company disclosures. Zynga's topline was driven by two factors: the number of daily active users (DAUs) and the average amount that users pay per day to play the games. Zynga games were generally free to play, with the company generating revenue through in-game sales of virtual goods and advertising revenues. Forecasting growth expectations for sales was further complicated by the fact that DAU levels for each game could erode quickly, so the company's total DAU count had to be supported by the release of even more popular titles even more frequently.

Unlike other blockbuster tech IPOs (e.g., Netflix and Alibaba), Zynga's IPO received only a lukewarm reception on Wall Street, perhaps due to these difficult-to-meet growth expectations or perhaps because the offering was too large and too many shares were made available to yield a boost in the stock. By the end of 2014, the stock price had fallen to under $3 per share, valuing Zynga at just over $2.5 billion.

In this and subsequent chapters, we will learn the techniques needed to understand how financial statements, and components in those statements such as earnings, cash flow, and net assets, can be derived from business events such as Zynga's stock issue and product sales. The balance sheet approach we take in this text provides a convenient way to record events in a format that facilitates the preparation and analysis of financial statements.

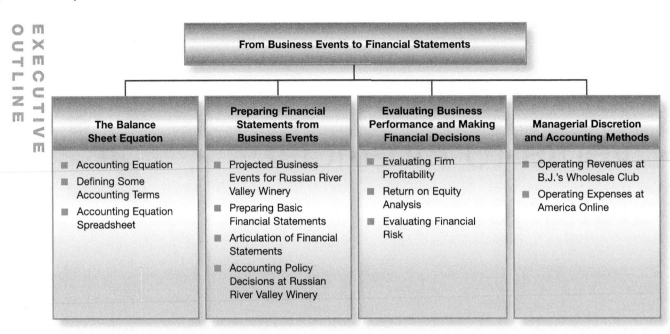

From Business Events to Financial Statements

The Balance Sheet Equation	Preparing Financial Statements from Business Events	Evaluating Business Performance and Making Financial Decisions	Managerial Discretion and Accounting Methods
■ Accounting Equation ■ Defining Some Accounting Terms ■ Accounting Equation Spreadsheet	■ Projected Business Events for Russian River Valley Winery ■ Preparing Basic Financial Statements ■ Articulation of Financial Statements ■ Accounting Policy Decisions at Russian River Valley Winery	■ Evaluating Firm Profitability ■ Return on Equity Analysis ■ Evaluating Financial Risk	■ Operating Revenues at B.J.'s Wholesale Club ■ Operating Expenses at America Online

BALANCE SHEET EQUATION

eLectures
MBC

Takeaway 1
Understand the balance sheet equation.

Most individuals outside of the professional financial fields think of accounting as something that others do, or that others are responsible for, or that only others need to understand. The truth is, however, that most of us apply the basic principles that comprise the framework of financial accounting in our everyday lives. When we balance our checkbook, decide whether to finance a new car purchase, or even think about what we might do with a raise, we are implicitly applying the principles that form the basis of financial accounting. Recognizing and appreciating this basic premise might save you some frustration when, later, you might be struggling with how a specific transaction is recorded in financial statements. As a means to introduce this notion, consider an event that most of us experience at some point in our lives—the process of securing a mortgage on a home.

The purchase of a personal residence is the single largest financial transaction entered into by most individuals. This purchase generally requires the individual to take out a loan, typically called a mortgage. Before lending any money, however, a financial institution will request certain information to assess whether the borrower represents a good credit risk. Exhibit 2.1 presents an example form that would need to be completed in order to have a loan application considered. If you have never completed one of these forms, now is a good time to try it out. As you review the form, pay close attention to its format, the level of detail requested, and some of the judgments that must be made by the preparer. You might consider the following questions: Why is this structure helpful to both the borrower and the lender? Why are certain categories required, while others are not? What estimates must be made, and what are the implications of providing estimates instead of precise values?

Let's focus on the left side of the form—your assets. The caption "cash or market value" indicates that the numbers that you are requested to insert should be your assets' current value. The top part of the form asks for the balance of your cash and checking/savings accounts, with the names and addresses of the institutions where you keep these accounts so that the lender can verify the reported amounts. The section below cash and checking/savings accounts asks for the value of all your stocks and bonds. To fill in this information, you will need to know the number of stocks and bonds that you own of each company and the current price for each security. If the stocks and bonds are traded on an exchange such as the New York Stock Exchange, the London Stock Exchange, or even the Tokyo Stock Exchange, you can simply access a financial internet site to find the current price for each of the securities. Next, you will have to get the cash surrender value of any life insurance policies. If you have a life insurance policy, your insurance agent would provide that information.

The section below life insurance asks for the market value of any real estate owned, such as a rental house or a vacation home. Where do you get the market value for your real estate properties? It is harder to get this type of information because real estate does not have an actively traded market like a stock exchange. You may have to hire an appraiser who will estimate the value of your house by considering comparable properties—that is, houses with the same number of bedrooms, bathrooms, and in the same

EXHIBIT 2.1   A Typical Loan Application

VI. ASSETS AND LIABILITIES

This statement and any applicable supporting schedules may be completed jointly by both married and unmarried Co-borrowers if their assets and liabilities are sufficiently joined so that the Statement can be meaningfully and fairly presented on a combined basis; otherwise separate Statements and Schedules are required. If the Co-Borrower section was completed about a spouse, this Statement and supporting schedules must be completed about that spouse also.

Completed ☐ Jointly ☐ Not Jointly

ASSETS Description	Cash or Market Value	Liabilities and Pledged Assets. List the creditor's name, address and account number for all outstanding debts, including automobile loans, revolving charge accounts, real estate loans, alimony, child support, stock pledges, etc. Use continuation sheet, if necessary. Indicate by (*) those liabilities which will be satisfied upon sale of real estate owned or upon refinancing of the subject property. LIABILITIES	Monthly Payt. & Mos. Left to Pay	Unpaid Balance
Cash deposit toward purchase held by:	$	Name and address of Company	$ Payt./Mos.	$
List checking and savings accounts below Name and address of Bank, S&L, or Credit Union				
		Acct. no.		
		Name and address of Company	$ Payt./Mos.	$
Acct. no.	$			
Name and address of Bank, S&L, or Credit Union				
		Acct. no.		
		Name and address of Company	$ Payt./Mos.	$
Acct. no.	$			
Name and address of Bank, S&L, or Credit Union				
		Acct. no.		
		Name and address of Company	$ Payt./Mos.	$
Acct. no.	$			
Name and address of Bank, S&L, or Credit Union				
		Acct. no.		
		Name and address of Company	$ Payt./Mos.	$
Acct. no.	$			
Stocks & Bonds (Company name/ number & description)	$			
		Acct. no.		
		Name and address of Company	$ Payt./Mos.	$
Life insurance net cash value				
Face amount: $	$			
Subtotal Liquid Assets	$			
Real estate owned (enter market value from schedule of real estate owned)	$	Acct. no.		
Vested interest in retirement fund	$	Name and address of Company	$ Payt./Mos.	$
Net worth of business(es) owned (attach financial statement)	$			
Automobiles owned (make and year)	$			
		Acct. no.		
		Alimony/Child Support/Separate Maintenance Payments Owed to:	$	
Other Assets (itemize)	$	Job Related Expense (child care, union dues, etc.)	$	
		Total Monthly Payments	$	
Total Assets a.	$	Net Worth (a-b) $	Total Liabilities b.	$

neighborhood. So determining the market value for your real estate holdings is considerably more subjective than coming up with a value for your stocks, bonds, or life insurance. If you hired three different appraisers, you would probably get three different estimates. This is the first indication that accounting for your assets is not a precise exercise. After you have included any remaining assets that you own, such as a car or a business, you can then total them all up and put a number in the box for "Total Assets a."

Now turn to the far right column where you are asked to insert amounts for the unpaid balances on all of your outstanding loans, including credit cards, student loans, and real estate or automobile loans. For each of these loans you must also disclose the names and addresses of the people you owe money to so that the lender can verify your reported amounts. The sum of all of these items can be put in the box labeled "Total Liabilities b."

Finally, the form asks you to come up with your "Net Worth (a-b)." Thus, your **net worth** is simply the difference between what you have and what you owe, or your total assets less your total liabilities. This is an important relationship so let's write it out:

$$A - L = NW$$

This expression says that your personal net worth (NW) is equal to the amount left over from your assets (A) after paying off all of your liabilities (L). Notice that this expression implicitly suggests that your creditors have a claim on your listed assets and you get to keep what remains. Since the lenders have a first claim before yours, they are in a less risky position.[1]

We can rearrange the relationship as follows:

$$A = L + NW$$

> In some countries, the balance sheet equation is formatted as:
>
> $$A - L = NW$$
>
> This format emphasizes the measurement of net worth. Regardless of which format is adopted, the information contained in a balance sheet is exactly the same.

We call this new expression the **balance sheet equation**. It shows that the total assets on the left side must exactly equal the sum of the claims on those assets on the right side. There are two types of claims: (1) the lenders who have first claim over your assets, and (2) you, the person who gets what is left over. It should now be clear why the balance sheet equation always balances—NW is just a balancing (or plug) figure! As you will see through numerous examples in this text, the balance sheet equation represents not only the basic structure of the balance sheet itself, but it also provides a basic structure that can be used at the individual transaction level. More on this later.

If we think about a company instead of an individual, shareholders (those that purchase ownership shares in the business) have the last claim on the corporate assets listed on the balance sheet. In the case of a business, the term NW can be replaced by the term SE, an acronym for shareholders' equity, to better represent this claim. Thus, the balance sheet equation that we will use to refer to a business is virtually identical to that of an individual:

$$A = L + SE$$

Refer back to the Amazon.com balance sheet that is presented in Exhibit 1.1 in Chapter 1. While the presentation and placement of the items in a loan application may be different, the similarities in the two documents should be readily apparent. The balance sheets are as of a specific reporting date in the life of the company. The list of accounts provided by Amazon is those relevant to that unique entity, and the sum of all the assets is equal to (*balanced with*) the sum of all the liability and stockholder equity claims. The balance sheet equation is represented in a different form by Amazon, which is typical of virtually all public company balance sheets, but you should clearly see the parallel with the formula listed above. Here we represent the balance sheet values for Amazon in the balance sheet equation:

$$\$54,505 = \$43,764 + \$10,741$$

In a nutshell, the bottom half of the corporate balance sheet (i.e., the right side of the balance sheet equation), tells us that a business obtains cash and/or other assets (A) from shareholders by issuing shares (SE) and from lenders by promising to pay interest on any debt and repay any borrowed funds (L). As you will see in subsequent chapters, some companies borrow sparingly and thus are financed principally by shareholders. Other companies borrow extensively, and these companies are referred to as being **leveraged**. The relative mix of funding between shareholders and lenders is an important **financing decision** that can have a dramatic effect on a firm's financial performance.

The top half of the balance sheet (i.e., the left hand side of the balance sheet equation) shows how a business allocates its resources in various assets (A)—this is known as the **investment decision**. Who makes the investment decision? Technically, the shareholders have the right to make such decisions, but they usually delegate these decisions to a management team. Not surprisingly, shareholders are preoccupied with maintaining and growing their wealth; thus, they expect the management team to make investment decisions that increase SE over time.

Takeaway 2
Explain the accounting meaning behind the terms *asset, liability, shareholders' equity, revenue and expense,* and *matching.*

Defining Some Accounting Terms

We have used the terms "asset," "liability," and "shareholders' equity" without precisely defining these terms. From the loan application shown in Exhibit 2.1, it is clear that assets include cash, stocks, bonds,

---

[1] As we observed in Chapter 1, there is a positive relationship between the amount of assumed risk and the expected return on an investment; that is, greater (less) assumed risk implies a higher (lower) expected return.

and real estate, among other things. For now, we will define an **asset** as an economic resource that is expected to generate future benefits for a business. As we will see, assets for companies may comprise a variety of economic resources to include those mentioned above, as well as inventory, property and equipment, and various intangible assets such as copyrights and patents, among others.

From the loan application shown in Exhibit 2.1, liabilities include car loans, credit card debt, student loans, and mortgages. But as you will soon see, a company's liabilities may include many types of obligations. For now, we define a **liability** simply as an obligation to make future payments. This definition implies that if a business is obliged to make payments in the future, then the obligation qualifies as a liability. In subsequent chapters, however, we will see that some liabilities that satisfy this definition need not be (and often are not) reported on the balance sheet. These unreported obligations are referred to as **off-balance-sheet liabilities**. (Subsequent chapters will reveal that many of a firm's economic assets also fail to appear on the balance sheet!) Finally, we define **shareholders' equity** as the residual value of a business—that is, the value of any assets remaining after all liabilities have been satisfied. Shortly, we will see that shareholders' equity has two key components—the value of the shareholders' direct investment in a business, called **contributed capital** or **common stock** (CS), and the amount of any profits retained in the business to support future operations, called **retained earnings** (RE). Incorporating these two components of SE into the balance sheet equation yields the following:

$$A = L + (CS + RE)$$

REVIEW PROBLEM 2.1

Use the balance sheet equation to determine the missing values below.

Assets	Liabilities	Common Stock	Retained Earnings
320,000	150,000	45,000	?
?	75,000	30,000	40,000
250,000	90,000	?	120,000
540,000	?	200,000	150,000

The solution is on page 81.

PREPARING FINANCIAL STATEMENTS FROM BUSINESS EVENTS

Recording Transactions.   You may feel that there is little reason why you should be subjected to the rigors of learning how to record transactions since you probably have little, if any, desire to become an accountant. In fact, most executives and managers are apt to hire an accountant to perform these tasks. But having some knowledge of the recording process can be invaluable, and this can be illustrated by way of an analogy.

It is doubtful that the readers of this book will ever go on to a career in auto repair. Many readers, in fact, may never even look under the hood of a car. Each of you, however, likely drives a car; and, many of you likely have experienced mechanical problems at one time or another. When this invariably occurs, it would certainly be helpful to the mechanic who is be responsible for repairing your car if you have the ability to provide detailed information regarding what is wrong. It could also prove financially beneficial to your wallet if you have some understanding of what the mechanic plans to charge for repairs. You certainly do not want to be completely at his or her mercy. The same applies for business transactions. While you may not be responsible for the actual recording of a transaction, as a manager you are responsible for understanding the reported financial statements. At a minimum, you would want to understand the financial statement implications, both in the past and in the future, of any transaction that affects your company. Wouldn't you want to be able to intelligently discuss with your accountant or controller what *needs to be* recorded and

Takeaway 3
Apply the balance sheet equation in the preparation of financial statements from business events.

Because the balance sheet measures account values as of a specific date, liabilities are recorded initially at the amount of principal owed. Under the **accrual** basis of accounting, any interest owed but not paid will be recorded as necessary at future balance sheet dates, with an appropriate charge to earnings (and retained earnings).

Russian River Valley Winery Transaction Summary (all amounts in thousands)	
	(3)
Cash...........................	4,800
Buildings	
Land	
Intangible assets	
Total assets	
Loan payable	4,800
Total liabilities	
Common stock	
Total shareholders' equity	

4. Kate and Matt concluded that since the Russian River Valley Winery was a new business venture, with no existing brand recognition or customer base, it would be wise to acquire an existing brand name from one of the established wine makers. After some research, they concluded that an established label would likely cost $100,000. This transaction would decrease the company's cash (A) account and increase its intangible assets by $100,000.

Most recorded assets such as buildings have an actual physical presence and are referred to as **tangible assets**. However, some recorded assets lack a physical presence, but still provide future benefits to the organization. These **intangible assets** include such items as patents, copyrights, and brand names.

Russian River Valley Winery Transaction Summary (all amounts in thousands)	
	(4)
Cash....................	(100)
Buildings	
Land	
Intangible assets	100
Total assets	
Loan payable	
Total liabilities	
Common stock	
Total shareholders' equity	

Note that for each of the four individual transactions the integrity of the balance sheet transactions was maintained. That is, any change in assets always equaled the change in liabilities plus shareholders' equity. Thus, because the individual transactions balance, the sum of the individual transactions must balance as well. Following the four pre-opening events identified by Kate and Matt, the winery's complete transaction summary would appear as follows:

Russian River Valley Winery Transaction Summary (all amounts in thousands)					
	(1)	(2)	(3)	(4)	Totals
Cash.......................			4,800	(100)	4,700
Buildings...................		2,000			2,000
Land.......................	4,000				4,000
Intangible assets				100	100
Total assets					**10,800**
Loan payable				4,800	4,800
Total liabilities					**4,800**
Common stock...............	4,000	2,000			6,000
Total shareholders' equity ...					**6,000**

$$A = L + SE$$

Utilizing the column totals from the spreadsheet facilitates the construction of the winery's pre-opening balance sheet:

RUSSIAN RIVER VALLEY WINERY, INC. Pre-Opening Balance Sheet			
($ thousands)			
Assets		**Liabilities**	
Cash...................	$ 4,700	Loan payable	$ 4,800
Buildings................	2,000		
Land....................	4,000	**Shareholders' equity**	
Intangible assets	100	Common stock...................	6,000
Total assets..............	**$10,800**	**Liabilities and shareholders' equity** ..	**$10,800**

As expected, the winery's pre-opening total assets of $10.8 million equal the sum of the winery's liabilities plus shareholders' equity, also $10.8 million.

Projected Business Events

To comply with the bank's request for **forecasted financial statements**—that is, financial statements prepared on an "as if" basis using assumptions about what might happen in the future—Matt and Kate compiled a list of the important events that would likely occur during the first year of operations. These events appear below as business event numbers 1 through 14. Matt and Kate's analyses of how each of the events would affect the winery's balance sheet equation appear as bullet items. Observe that the analysis of each event leads to the identification of (at least) two financial effects on the balance sheet equation; and, that the financial effects of each transaction are recorded in the appropriate columns of the winery's spreadsheet. Further, notice in the Russian River Valley spreadsheet that after each event is analyzed, the balance sheet equation remains in balance, with total assets equal to the sum of total liabilities and shareholders' equity. To help understand how the balance sheet equation is affected by the various events, each asset account is labeled with an A, each liability account with an L, and each shareholders' equity account as SE. Finally, notice that the account balances from the winery's pre-opening balance sheet have been entered into the spreadsheet in the column labeled "beginning balance."

1. The winery would purchase $380,000 of inventory (grapes, corks, bottles, labels). All purchases would initially be on credit and would subsequently require payment within 30 days of the initial purchase transaction. It was estimated that the unpaid balance of this credit purchase would be $20,000 at the end of the year.

In competitive business environments, it is often necessary to permit customers to buy goods and services on credit, allowing them to pay for the purchased goods over 30, 60, or even 90 days without incurring any interest charges. Extending credit to customers, however, carries a hidden cost to a business, called an **opportunity cost**. This opportunity cost is equal to the cost of borrowing over the time period during which the purchase price remains unpaid. We will have more to say about opportunity costs in Chapter 5. You may also want to read Appendix A at the end of this book for insights about the time value of money.

Russian River Valley Winery Transaction Summary (all amounts in thousands)				
	Beg. Bal.	(1a)	(1b)	Thru (1)
Cash........................	4,700		(360)	4,340
Inventory....................		380		380
Buildings....................	2,000			2,000
Land........................	4,000			4,000
Intangible assets	100			100
Total assets	**10,800**			**10,820**
Accounts payable............		380	(360)	20
Loan payable	4,800			4,800
Total liabilities	**4,800**			**4,820**
Common stock...............	6,000			6,000
Total shareholders' equity ...	**6,000**			**6,000**

- In 4(b), customers are expected to owe the winery $800,000 at year-end; hence, they must have paid $720,000 in cash during the year. Thus, cash (A) is increased by $720,000 and accounts receivable (A) is decreased by $720,000.

5. Payroll expenses for employees were estimated to require cash payments of $100,000 during the year. Selling and administrative expenses of $300,000 were also expected to be paid.

Russian River Valley Winery Transaction Summary (all amounts in thousands)				
	Thru (4)	(5a)	(5b)	Thru (5)
Cash..........................	1,940	(100)	(300)	1,540
Accounts receivable................	800			800
Inventory.........................	380			380
Equipment	3,500			3,500
Buildings........................	2,000			2,000
Land............................	4,000			4,000
Intangible assets	100			100
Total assets....................	12,720			12,320
Accounts payable.................	20			20
Loan payable	4,800			4,800
Total liabilities	4,820			4,820
Common stock....................	6,000			6,000
Retained earnings	1,900			1,500
Wages and salaries............		(100)		
Selling and administrative			(300)	
Total shareholders' equity	7,900			7,500

Expenses (E) represent the using up of goods and services associated with the production of revenues by a business. Since expenses reduce assets or increase liabilities, expenses are a wealth-reducing event. The cost of the goods and services consumed in generating revenues is said to be matched with the revenues they generate; as a consequence, within a given accounting period, a business is able to convey its accomplishments (revenue) with its effort (expenses). This important concept is known as the **matching concept** of accounting.

- In 5(a), the winery pays $100,000 in cash for employee wage expenses; thus, cash (A) decreases by $100,000 and shareholders' equity (specifically, expenses, a component of retained earnings) decreases by $100,000.

- In 5(b), the winery reduces cash (A) by $300,000 for the payment of selling and administrative expenses. Since these services are consumed in the process of generating revenues from wine sales, the cost of these used-up resources is matched with revenues, thus reducing retained earnings (SE) by $300,000.

6. The loan agreement will require payment of principal and interest at the end of the year.

Russian River Valley Winery Transaction Summary (all amounts in thousands)				
	Thru (5)	(6a)	(6b)	Thru (6)
Cash.	1,540	(480)	(288)	772
Accounts receivable.	800			800
Inventory.	380			380
Equipment	3,500			3,500
Buildings.	2,000			2,000
Land	4,000			4,000
Intangible assets	100			100
Total assets	**12,320**			**11,552**
Accounts payable.	20			20
Loan payable	4,800	(480)		4,320
Total liabilities	**4,820**			**4,340**
Common stock.	6,000			6,000
Retained earnings	1,500			1,212
Interest expense			(288)	
Total shareholders' equity . . .	**7,500**			**7,212**

- In 6(a), cash (A) is reduced by $480,000, the first of 10 annual loan repayments ($4.8 million divided by 10), and the loan payable (L) account is reduced by the same amount.
- In 6(b), cash (A) is reduced by $288,000 (6 percent of $4.8 million) for the first year's interest payment. Interest is the cost of borrowing funds from a financial institution and is a financing expense of the business. Hence, retained earnings (SE) is also reduced by $288,000 as this business expense must be matched with the enterprise's revenues.
- We have separated transactions 6(a) and 6(b) for pedagogical reasons. However, in practice the payment of a loan would entail a single check that would be allocated across both principal and interest. Much like when an individual pays an auto loan or a home mortgage, the monthly check is written to cover a partial pay-down of the loan balance in addition to a monthly charge for interest.

7. The winery's policy was to order only as much inventory as would be needed for the current year's sales. Thus, it was estimated that the ending inventory would be zero.

Russian River Valley Winery Transaction Summary (all amounts in thousands)			
	Thru (6)	(7)	Thru (7)
Cash.	772		772
Accounts receivable.	800		800
Inventory.	380	(380)	—
Equipment	3,500		3,500
Buildings.	2,000		2,000
Land	4,000		4,000
Intangible assets	100		100
Total assets	**11,552**		**11,172**
Accounts payable.	20		20
Loan payable	4,320		4,320
Total liabilities	**4,340**		**4,340**
Common stock.	6,000		6,000
Retained earnings	1,212		832
Cost of goods sold		(380)	
Total shareholders' equity . . .	**7,212**		**6,832**

- The entire available inventory is assumed to have been used up in the production and sale of wine. Thus, inventory (A) decreases by $380,000, as does retained earnings (SE). The cost of inventory sold is an expense to be matched with revenues. Notice that inventory is first classified as an asset since it is assumed to provide future benefit to the enterprise in the form of future cash inflows. When the inventory is sold, and therefore used up, the asset is removed from the balance sheet and an expense, called cost of goods sold, is reported on the income statement, and ultimately as a reduction in shareholders' equity. This is another example of the matching concept in which the cost of goods sold (an expense account) is matched with the revenues from the sale of the goods, all recognized in the same accounting period. Without this alignment of expenses with revenues, net income reported would be artificially skewed upwards in some periods and downwards in others. The matching principle helps ensure that net income represents the actual earning process within the proper accounting period.

  Notice that if a company's inventory is overstated, the amount removed from inventory and transferred to cost of goods sold will be understated. This will result in net income and retained earnings both being overstated. We will have more to say about the effects of inventory errors in Chapter 6.

8. Depreciation for the year was estimated as follows: $175,000 for equipment, based on an expected useful life of 20 years, and $50,000 for buildings, based on an expected useful life of 40 years.

Russian River Valley Winery Transaction Summary (all amounts in thousands)				
	Thru (7)	(8a)	(8b)	Thru (8)
Cash.	772			772
Accounts receivable.	800			800
Inventory.	—			—
Equipment	3,500			3,500
Buildings.	2,000			2,000
Accumulated depreciation		(175)	(50)	(225)
Land	4,000			4,000
Intangible assets	100			100
Total assets	**11,172**			**10,947**
Accounts payable.	20			20
Loan payable	4,320			4,320
Total liabilities	**4,340**			**4,340**
Common stock.	6,000			6,000
Retained earnings	832			607
Depreciation		(175)	(50)	
Total shareholders' equity . . .	**6,832**			**6,607**

Balance sheet accounts that are subtracted from other accounts (such as accumulated depreciation) are known as **contra-accounts** (CA). The difference between the cost of an asset (e.g. equipment) and its accumulated depreciation is called the **net book value** of the asset. Other common contra-account examples include the allowance for uncollectible accounts and discounts on bonds payable.

- Depreciation refers to the systematic expensing of an asset as a consequence of the passage of time. Accountants often estimate the amount of depreciation to be taken on an asset by estimating the expected useful life of the asset and then allocating its cost equally across all years of the asset's expected useful life, a method called straight-line depreciation. In 8(a), the expected life of the equipment is 20 years so depreciation expense (E) is $175,000 ($3.5 million divided by 20 years). Hence, retained earnings (SE) is decreased by $175,000. Of course, the asset must also be decreased, but by convention, the equipment account is not decreased directly. Another account—called accumulated depreciation—is increased, and thus, reflects the negative $175,000. The accumulated depreciation account is then subtracted from the equipment account. We show an increase in accumulated depreciation as a negative number under the assets section of the spreadsheet. This is because accumulated depreciation is actually a contra-asset, where by convention it maintains a balance of the opposite sign as a regular asset. We will have much more to say about both depreciation expense and accumulated depreciation in Chapter 7. Another important point to note is that the purpose of depreciation is not to reduce the asset's value in an attempt to equate its balance sheet value with its market value. Rather, the purpose of depreciation is to allocate the cost of the asset over time in an attempt to match the asset's original cost with the revenue it generates in each future period, an application again of the matching concept.

- In 8(b), the depreciation expense associated with using the buildings for a year is estimated to be $50,000 ($2 million divided by 40 years); hence, retained earnings (SE) is decreased by $50,000. As in 8(a), accumulated depreciation (CA) is increased by $50,000 and deducted from the buildings account.

9. Kate and Matt decide that the acquired brand name of the business should be expensed over two years.

Russian River Valley Winery Transaction Summary (all amounts in thousands)			
	Thru (8)	(9)	Thru (9)
Cash	772		772
Accounts receivable	800		800
Inventory	—		—
Equipment	3,500		3,500
Buildings	2,000		2,000
Accumulated depreciation	(225)		(225)
Land	4,000		4,000
Intangible assets	100	(50)	50
Total assets	**10,947**		**10,897**
Accounts payable	20		20
Loan payable	4,320		4,320
Total liabilities	**4,340**		**4,340**
Common stock	6,000		6,000
Retained earnings	607		557
Amortization		(50)	
Total shareholders' equity . . .	**6,607**		**6,557**

- The write-off of the the purchased brand name, called amortization, is an expense of the business. Thus, the intangible asset account (A) is reduced by $50,000 ($100,000 divided by 2 years), as is retained earnings (SE). If Matt and Kate had estimated a five-year expected life for the brand name instead of just two years, the amortization expense would have been only $20,000 per year ($100,000 divided by five years). Estimating the expected useful life of equipment, buildings, and such intangible assets as brand names is an important managerial activity. An incorrect estimate of an asset's expected useful life can have a dramatic positive (or negative) effect on a firm's reported performance. As you will see, many accounting numbers, like amortization expense, are just estimates, and as such, can be quite imprecise.

10. Matt and Kate issue 200,000 additional shares to an outside investor for $2 per share to finance future expansion plans.

Russian River Valley Winery Transaction Summary (all amounts in thousands)			
	Thru (9)	(10)	Thru (10)
Cash	772	400	1,172
Accounts receivable	800		800
Inventory	—		—
Equipment	3,500		3,500
Buildings	2,000		2,000
Accumulated depreciation	(225)		(225)
Land	4,000		4,000
Intangible assets	50		50
Total assets	10,897		11,297
Accounts payable	20		20
Loan payable	4,320		4,320
Total liabilities	4,340		4,340
Common stock	6,000	400	6,400
Retained earnings	557		557
Total shareholders' equity	6,557		6,957

- The issuance of additional common shares increases common stock (SE) by $400,000 and increases cash (A) by the same amount. As a consequence of selling shares to the outside investor, Matt and Kate must now share control of the business and its profits with the investor who has become a co-owner of the winery. Kate and Matt must have forecasted that they would need the extra cash badly enough to relinquish some control of the business. If you look at the cash row you can see why—there is a large quantity of cash outflows.

> Brand names are not reported in the balance sheet unless purchased from other entities; in some countries (such as France), however, estimating the value of a brand name and placing that asset on the balance sheet is permitted.

11. Matt and Kate intend to buy grapes from the most respected local growers; and thus, they expect that their wines will be well received by their customers. As a consequence, Matt and Kate believe that their ownership shares in the business will be worth considerably more by the end of the year and that this should be reflected in the projected financial statements.

- The winery records no transaction for this information. Although a good business reputation is a valuable business asset, typically resulting in significant customer loyalty, higher sales revenue and increased profitability, an increase in a company's market value as a consequence of a strong reputation is not directly recorded in a company's financial statements. There are two reasons for this. First, there is no generally accepted approach to assessing the value of a company and the recorded amounts could vary wildly. Second, under U.S. GAAP, financial statements are generally premised on the historical cost concept discussed earlier, and not the fair value of a business's assets. Zynga, Inc., introduced at the beginning of this chapter, is an example of a company with a brand that may be quite valuable but will not be recorded on the company's balance sheet.

12. Federal income taxes were estimated to be $240,000 with 60 percent being paid by year-end.

Russian River Valley Winery Transaction Summary (all amounts in thousands)			
	Thru (11)	(12)	Thru (12)
Cash......................	1,172	(144)	1,028
Accounts receivable...........	800		800
Inventory....................	—		—
Equipment	3,500		3,500
Buildings...................	2,000		2,000
Accumulated depreciation......	(225)		(225)
Land......................	4,000		4,000
Intangible assets	50		50
Total assets	**11,297**		**11,153**
Accounts payable............	20		20
Taxes payable...............		96	96
Loan payable	4,320		4,320
Total liabilities	**4,340**		**4,436**
Common stock...............	6,400		6,400
Retained earnings	557		317
Income taxes.............		(240)	
Total shareholders' equity ...	**6,957**		**6,717**

- Income taxes are a cost of doing business, and consequently, this expense must be matched with the winery's revenue; hence, retained earnings (SE) is reduced by $240,000. Since the winery expects to pay $144,000 (60 percent of $240,000), cash (A) is reduced by $144,000 and the remaining amount of $96,000 is still owed; thus, taxes payable (L) increases by $96,000.

13. On the last day of the year, Kate and Matt expect to acquire $60,000 of new grape inventory in anticipation of the following year's production. The purchase would be on credit, with payment terms of 30 days.

Russian River Valley Winery Transaction Summary (all amounts in thousands)			
	Thru (12)	(13)	Thru (13)
Cash......................	1,028		1,028
Accounts receivable...........	800		800
Inventory....................	—	60	60
Equipment	3,500		3,500
Buildings...................	2,000		2,000
Accumulated depreciation......	(225)		(225)
Land......................	4,000		4,000
Intangible assets	50		50
Total assets	**11,153**		**11,213**
Accounts payable............	20	60	80
Taxes payable...............	96		96
Loan payable	4,320		4,320
Total liabilities	**4,436**		**4,496**
Common stock...............	6,400		6,400
Retained earnings	317		317
Total shareholders' equity ...	**6,717**		**6,717**

- Inventory (A) increases by $60,000 and, since this purchase is not immediately paid for, accounts payable (L) increases by an equivalent amount.

14. Matt and Kate expect to declare and pay cash dividends of $260,000.
   - The dividend that Matt and Kate expect to pay is a distribution of the winery's earned profit; hence, it reduces cash (A) by $260,000 and retained earnings (SE) by $260,000. A dividend is considered to be a distribution of a company's earnings to its owners and not a cost of doing business; consequently, dividends are not considered in the calculation of net income on the income statement, although they are reflected in the calculation of retained earnings.

Russian River Valley Winery Transaction Summary (all amounts in thousands)			
	Thru (13)	(14)	Thru (14)
Cash	1,028	(260)	768
Accounts receivable	800		800
Inventory	60		60
Equipment	3,500		3,500
Buildings	2,000		2,000
Accumulated depreciation	(225)		(225)
Land	4,000		4,000
Intangible assets	50		50
Total assets	**11,213**		**10,953**
Accounts payable	80		80
Taxes payable	96		96
Loan payable	4,320		4,320
Total liabilities	**4,496**		**4,496**
Common stock	6,400		6,400
Retained earnings	317		57
Dividends		(260)	
Total shareholders' equity	**6,717**		**6,457**

Following the analysis of the 14 projected transactions identified by Kate and Matt, the winery's summary spreadsheet will appear as follows:

Russian River Valley Winery Transaction Summary (all amounts in thousands)																					
	Beg. Bal.	(1a)	(1b)	(2)	(3)	(4a)	(4b)	(5a)	(5b)	(6a)	(6b)	(7)	(8a)	(8b)	(9)	(10)	(11)	(12)	(13)	(14)	End Bal.
Cash	4,700		(360)	(1,500)	(2,000)	380	720	(100)	(300)	(480)	(288)					400		(144)		(260)	768
Accounts receivable						1,520	(720)														800
Inventory		380										(380)							60		60
Equipment				1,500	2,000																3,500
Buildings	2,000																				2,000
Accumulated depreciation													(175)	(50)							(225)
Land	4,000																				4,000
Intangible assets	100														(50)						50
Total assets	**10,800**																				**10,953**
Accounts payable		380	(360)																60		80
Taxes payable																	96				96
Loan payable	4,800									(480)											4,320
Total liabilities	**4,800**																				**4,496**
Common stock	6,000															400					6,400
Retained earnings																					57
Revenues						1,900															
Cost of goods sold												(380)									
Wages and salaries								(100)													
Selling and administrative									(300)												
Depreciation													(175)	(50)							
Amortization															(50)						
Interest expense											(288)										
Income taxes																		(240)			
Dividends																				(260)	
Total shareholders' equity	**6,000**																				**6,457**

Income Statement accounts

Preparing the Financial Statements

Since all of the projected financial events for the first year of operations for the winery have been analyzed and the financial effects entered into the spreadsheet, it is now possible to complete the spreadsheet by summing up the various values in each of the rows. These final balances are entered in the final column labeled "ending balance." The completed spreadsheet for the Russian River Valley Winery thus becomes the basis for preparing the company's basic financial statements. The ending balance column of the spreadsheet, in particular, provides the necessary inputs (the ending account balances) for the winery's balance sheet as of the end of the first year of operations. This statement is presented in Exhibit 2.2.

Exhibit 2.2 reveals that the winery's total assets are projected to grow from $10.800 million at the beginning of the year to $10.953 million by year-end. By comparing the various account balances at the beginning of the year with those at the end of the year, it is possible to identify both the significance and the trends in each account. One of the objectives in reviewing a company's balance sheet is not only to understand what assets and liabilities a company has, but also how the changes in those accounts reflect the management of the business.

Russian River Valley's balance sheets in Exhibit 2.2 also provide information beyond just a listing of the company's assets, liabilities, shareholders' equity, and whether their balances changed over the fiscal period. The balance sheet provides information, for example, about when a company's noncash assets are likely to be converted into cash and when they are expected to be consumed as part of the company's regular operations, as well as information about when its liabilities are likely to require payment. This information is evident from the classification of the assets and liabilities into the categories of "current" and

In Practice 2.1 *Balance Sheet Title: A Glimpse of a Sample of Fortune 1000 Companies*   The following table identifies the title used on the balance sheet by a sample of 600 Fortune 1000 companies. The title preferred by over 96 percent of the surveyed firms is "balance sheet":

- Balance Sheet 96.1%
- Statement of Financial Position 3.7%
- Statement of Financial Condition 0.2%

Source: Accounting Trends & Techniques

EXHIBIT 2.2 Illustrative Balance Sheets

RUSSIAN RIVER VALLEY WINERY, INC.
Balance Sheets

($ thousands)	Pre-Opening	End of Year 1		Pre-Opening	End of Year 1
Assets			**Liabilities and shareholders' equity**		
Current assets			*Current liabilities*		
Cash.....................	$ 4,700	$ 768	Accounts payable.........	$ 0	$ 80
Accounts receivable...........	0	800	Taxes payable...........	0	96
Inventory....................	0	60	Loan payable—current.....	0	480
Total current assets	4,700	1,628	Total current liabilities......	0	656
Noncurrent assets			*Noncurrent liabilities*		
Property, plant & equipment			Loan payable—noncurrent..	4,800	3,840
Equipment	0	3,500	**Total liabilities...........	4,800	4,496**
Buildings....................	2,000	2,000			
Land.......................	4,000	4,000	*Shareholders' equity*		
	6,000	9,500	Common stock..........	6,000	6,400
Accumulated depreciation	0	(225)	Retained earnings	0	57
Property, plant & equipment (net)..	6,000	9,275	**Total shareholders' equity .	6,000	6,457**
Intangible assets	100	50	**Total liabilities &**		
Total noncurrent assets	6,100	9,325	**shareholders' equity......	$10,800	$10,953**
**Total assets.................	$10,800	$10,953**			

In Practice 2.2 *Income Statement Title: A Glimpse of a Sample of Fortune 1000 Companies* The following table identifies the title used on the income statement by a sample of 600 Fortune 1000 companies. The survey shows that "income statement" and "statement of operations" are almost equally preferred by the surveyed firms:

Income Statement 42.5%
Statement of Operations 42.3%
Statement of Earnings 14.4%
Other 0.8%

Source: Accounting Trends & Techniques

"noncurrent." (In accounting jargon, the balance sheet in Exhibit 2.2 is known as a *classified balance sheet*.) **Current assets** are those assets that are expected to be converted into cash or used to support operations during the next 12 months, while **noncurrent assets** are those assets expected to be available to support the continuing operations of a business beyond 12 months. **Current liabilities** are those liabilities that are expected to require payment within the next 12 months, whereas **noncurrent liabilities** are obligations that are not expected to require payment for more than one year. The phrase "long-term" is often used instead of "noncurrent."

Notice in Exhibit 2.2 that since the second annual principal payment of $480,000 on the winery's outstanding bank loan is due within 12 months of the date when the balance sheet is prepared, this amount is reclassified from the noncurrent liabilities section of the balance sheet to the current liabilities section of the winery's balance sheet. This reclassification is important because it will enable anyone reviewing the balance sheet to fully understand just how much cash will be needed to satisfy the various claims against the business in the coming year.

Can other information be obtained from the Russian River Valley Winery spreadsheet? Recall that the retained earnings rows of the spreadsheet contained all of the revenue and expenses of the business. Thus, an income statement can be readily prepared from data contained in the retained earnings rows of the spreadsheet. The income statement for the first year of operations for the winery is presented in Exhibit 2.3.

Like the balance sheet, the Russian River Valley income statement provides a number of useful pieces of information. For instance, the income statement highlights several key measures of firm performance: revenues, gross profit, operating income, and net income. **Revenues** measure the inflow of cash and other assets (such as, accounts receivable) from a firm's primary business activity. **Gross profit**, on the other hand, measures the amount of cash and assets remaining after deducting the cost of sales, or what is often called the cost of goods sold. **Operating income** refers to a firm's net income before deducting such items as interest expense and income taxes; and, **net income** is the firm's bottom-line performance—the company's net income after all expenses are deducted, both operating and nonoperating, recurring and non-recurring.

EXHIBIT 2.3 An Illustrative Income Statement	
RUSSIAN RIVER VALLEY WINERY, INC. **Income Statement**	
($ thousands)	**Year 1**
Revenues.	$1,900
Cost of goods sold.	380
Gross profit.	1,520
Operating expenses	
Wages and salaries	100
Selling & administrative	300
Depreciation.	225
Amortization.	50
Total operating expenses	675
Operating income.	845
Interest expense.	288
Income before income taxes	557
Income taxes	240
Net income	$ 317

Observe that the top section of the income statement, through operating income, reflects the results of the company's primary business activities—that is, the winery's core business of producing and selling wine, which is often referred to as its **recurring operations**. The section below operating income reflects the financing activities of the business and any non-recurring operations. The winery doesn't expect to have any non-recurring activities for the year but it does expect to have costs associated with financing its business, namely interest expense on the outstanding bank loan. The winery's net income of $317,000 is the "bottom line" profit available to shareholders. The management of a business must decide whether to reinvest these earnings in the business or to distribute them to shareholders as a dividend, and this decision is reflected in the statement of shareholders' equity.

Recall from Chapter 1 that the remaining two financial statements relate directly to the activity captured in changes in balance sheet accounts. The statement of shareholders' equity reveals how the shareholders' direct investment in a business increased (decreased) due to the company's sale (repurchase) of its own common stock and how the retained earnings of a business was increased by net income and decreased by any net losses or dividends paid to shareholders. A statement of shareholders' equity for the Russian River Valley Winery is presented in Exhibit 2.4. Like the income statement, the information needed to prepare a statement of shareholders' equity is available from the shareholders' equity rows of the winery's spreadsheet. Exhibit 2.4 shows that the winery begins the year with a zero balance in retained earnings but is expected to end the year with a balance of $57,000, and that the winery begins the year with $6 million in common stock but is expected to end the year with a balance of $6.4 million. Notice how these figures reconcile with the data reported for retained earnings and common stock on the winery's balance sheet in Exhibit 2.2. In accounting jargon, we say that the data from the statement of shareholders' equity "articulates" with the data from the winery's balance sheet.

EXHIBIT 2.4	An Illustrative Statement of Shareholders' Equity		
RUSSIAN RIVER VALLEY WINERY, INC. **Statement of Shareholders' Equity**			
($ thousands)	Common Stock	Retained Earnings	Total
Balance at beginning of Year 1..................	$6,000	$ 0	$6,000
Net income.....................................		317	317
Dividends paid		(260)	(260)
Sale of common stock..........................	400		400
Balance at end of Year 1	$6,400	$ 57	$6,457

In addition to generating profits, a business must make sure that its profits translate into cash so that expenses and obligations can be paid as they come due. The information about a company's available cash flow can be obtained from its final required financial statement, the statement of cash flow, which can be prepared from the cash inflows and outflows reported in the cash row of the completed spreadsheet. Exhibit 2.5 presents a statement of cash flow for the Russian River Valley Winery. Notice that all of the cash inflows and outflows from the cash row of the spreadsheet are summarized in this statement.

The statement of cash flow classifies a company's cash flow into the three activity categories of operating, investing, and financing, which correspond to the main activities of any business. The **operating activities** section provides information about the day-to-day cash inflow and outflow from core business operations. The **investing activities** section contains information about the purchase and sale of long-term assets by the firm. This section provides insights about a company's investment strategy. Finally, the **financing activities** section provides information regarding how a business was financed during the period, for example whether the company raised cash from issuing debt or equity or used cash to repay debt or buy back its shares. This section provides insight about a firm's financing strategy. Notice that the cash dividend paid to shareholders is included in the financing section, yet the cash paid for interest on the bank loan is listed in the operating section. Under the accounting rules of most countries, interest expense is an operating cash outflow, whereas dividends are a financing cash outflow. Finally, notice that the "bottom line" of the statement of cash flow—the net cash flow for the period—equals the change in the cash account from a company's balance sheet. In the case of the

EXHIBIT 2.5	An Illustrative Statement of Cash Flow

RUSSIAN RIVER VALLEY WINERY, INC.
Statement of Cash Flow

($ thousands)	Year 1
Operating activities	
Cash receipts	
Cash sales	$ 380
Cash collections on account	720
Total cash receipts	1,100
Cash disbursements	
Cash payments for inventory	(360)
Cash payments for interest	(288)
Cash payments for wages & salaries	(100)
Cash payments for selling & administrative	(300)
Cash payments for taxes	(144)
Total cash disbursements	(1,192)
Cash flow from operations	**(92)**
Investing activities	
Purchases of property, plant & equipment	(3,500)
Cash flow from investing	**(3,500)**
Financing activities	
Sale of common stock	400
Repayment of loan	(480)
Payment of common stock dividends	(260)
Cash flow from financing	**(340)**
Change in cash	(3,932)
Cash balance, beginning of year	4,700
Cash balance, end of year	$ 768

Russian River Valley Winery, the change in cash as reported in Exhibit 2.5 is negative $3,932 ($768 − $4,700 = −$3,932). In essence, a statement of cash flow provides the detailed information to explain how and why the cash account on the balance sheet changed from the beginning of the fiscal period to the end. We will have more to say about the statement of cash flow in Chapter 3.

At this point, anyone reviewing the four financial statements can see a complete financial picture of how the business is anticipated to perform during the first year of operations. Kate and Matt are likely to be pleased with the projected net income of $317,000; however, they are also likely to be concerned about the large outflow of cash as shown on the statement of cash flow. Kate and Matt can explain most of the decrease in their cash balance as a necessary consequence of purchasing property, plant, and equipment, investments that are necessary for a young, growing company. They should be concerned, however, that they are also spending more cash on normal operating activities than they are taking in from these activities. As a consequence, Kate and Matt may wish to examine some alternative strategies for their business plan, such as the way that they price their products for sale or their policies regarding extending credit to, and collecting from, their customers.

Articulation of the Financial Statements

It should be apparent at this point that the basic financial statements of the Russian River Valley Winery are highly interconnected and are not independent from one another. In accounting parlance, we refer to this interconnectedness as **articulation**. Using the schematic from Exhibit 1.5 in Chapter 1, the articulation of the Russian River Valley Winery's basic financial statements can be illustrated as follows:

As a review, notice that:

- The change in the cash account (−$3,932) on the balance sheet from the beginning of the year to the end of the year equals the sum of the cash flow from operations (−$92), the cash flow from investing (−$3,500), and the cash flow from financing (−$340) on the statement of cash flow.

> The divergent treatment of interest, the cost of debt financing, and dividends, the cost of equity financing, in the statement of cash flow is attributable to the fact that a statement of cash flow is prepared from the perspective of shareholders, reporting the residual cash flows from operations accruing to the owners after all expenses have been paid but *before* any cash distributions for dividends have been made.

- The change in retained earnings ($57) on the balance sheet equals the sum of the beginning balance ($0) in retained earnings plus net income ($317) from the income statement less any dividends (−$260) paid to shareholders.

- The change in shareholders' equity ($457) on the balance sheet equals the change in retained earnings ($57) plus the change in common stock ($400) as reported on the statement of shareholders' equity.

Although the basic financial statements articulate with one another, they present different types of information about a business. The income statement, for example, describes a firm's operating performance for the current fiscal period, whereas the balance sheet describes the firm's financial condition as of the beginning or end of the fiscal period. The statement of shareholders' equity, on the other hand, describes how the shareholders' investment changed over the period, and the statement of cash flow explains why (and how) one very important business asset—cash—increased or decreased over the fiscal period. Like the income statement, the statement of cash flow also describes the firm's operating performance for the current period. The difference between these statements, however, relates to the definition of "firm operating performance." The income statement defines firm performance in terms of accrual net earnings whereas the statement of cash flow defines performance in terms of operating cash flow. Thus, although interconnected, the financial statements each depict a different aspect of a business's financial information. It is also important to note once again that the balance sheet is *at a period in time,* sometimes referred to as a snapshot. In contrast, the other statements are reported *for a period of time,* such as a year.

Accounting Policy Decisions at Russian River Valley Winery

While identifying the expected future events for the winery, Matt and Kate were required to implicitly make a number of accounting policy decisions that affected the forecasted financial statements of the winery, and thus, its likelihood of getting the bank loan. For example, by assuming that all of the $800,000 of outstanding accounts receivable at year-end was reasonably assured of collection, the winery's net income is potentially overstated. For most businesses, the existence of unpaid accounts receivable will usually mean that some future losses can be anticipated for uncollectible accounts. By not estimating what these losses might be, and by not matching those potential losses with the related operating revenue, Kate and Matt may have allowed the winery's projected performance for the first year of operations to be overstated.

Further, depreciation on the equipment and buildings was estimated by Matt and Kate based on expected useful lives of 20 and 40 years, respectively. If Kate and Matt overestimate the length of the useful lives of these assets, the annual depreciation expense on the income statement will be understated and projected net income overstated. Finally, the expected life chosen to amortize the purchased brand name was estimated to be two years. If Kate and Matt underestimate this expected life, the amortization expense will be overstated and the winery's net income understated.

These policy choices illustrate a little appreciated fact about accounting: Financial statements require managers to make many estimates and assumptions which may prove incorrect, and consequently, cause the financial statements to incorrectly characterize a company's performance. Because of the many estimates and assumptions inherent in preparing financial statements, it is wise to remember that accounting data, and hence, the financial statements themselves, are not precise descriptions of a business's financial performance.

To illustrate this point, consider the following statement from the General Motors Corporation 2014 annual report to shareholders:

> The consolidated financial statements are prepared in conformity with U.S. GAAP, which require the use of estimates, judgments and assumptions . . . . we believe that the accounting estimates employed are appropriate and resulting balances are reasonable; however, due to inherent uncertainties in making estimates actual results could differ from the original estimates, requiring adjustments to these balances in future periods.

GLOBAL PERSPECTIVE

The mechanical preparation of financial statements around the world proceeds in exactly the same fashion. Not surprisingly, however, some differences in the actual format of the financial statements and in the labels used to describe various financial statement accounts do arise. For example, in North America, the labels "revenue" and "sales" are used to describe the value of the goods sold by a company as reported on its income statement. In the United Kingdom, however, the label "turnover" is used instead to represent the sales of a business. These labeling differences are superficial and in no way alter the content or purpose of the basic financial statements. In essence, worldwide, an income statement is an income statement; and, a balance sheet is a balance sheet!

REVIEW PROBLEM 2.2

The Arcadia Company was founded by Thomas Smith and began operations in July 2015 as a neighborhood hardware store, selling branded lawn and garden supplies, household products, and small tools. The following transactions occurred during the second half of 2015:

1. Smith established The Arcadia Company by contributing $250,000 of his personal funds and receiving all of the company's capital stock in return for his equity investment.
2. The company purchased a small shop in a strip mall for $150,000 cash.
3. Needing working capital to purchase inventory, the company borrowed $120,000 cash from a local bank, using the recently purchased store as collateral for the loan. Interest on the loan was set at six percent per year, payable every six months. The loan could be repaid at any time, but full loan repayment was required within three years.
4. Smith used the entire loan amount of $120,000 to purchase inventory. In addition, he purchased $30,000 of inventory on credit. By the end of 2015, all but $6,000 of the credit purchase had been repaid.
5. Smith decided to use a simple rule-of-thumb for pricing his inventory for sale—all goods would be marked up 100 percent above their cost. By year-end, Smith noted that he had sold inventory with a cost basis of $80,000. All sales were for cash or on a debit/credit card.
6. Smith decided to depreciate his shop on a straight-line basis, using an expected useful life of 20 years.
7. During the latter half of 2015, Smith withdrew $20,000 in cash from the business as his salary.

Ignore all taxes when answering the following questions. Note: If treated as a corporation, the business would owe payroll taxes on the wages paid to the owner unless the money is paid as a dividend.

Required

1. Prepare a spreadsheet for The Arcadia Company using the balance sheet equation, reflecting the financial effects of the above transactions.
2. Prepare an income statement, balance sheet, and statement of cash flow for The Arcadia Company at the end of the first year of operations.

The solution is on page 82.

EVALUATING BUSINESS PERFORMANCE AND MAKING FINANCIAL DECISIONS

Producing financial statements about a business is important, particularly if those statements are useful in decision-making. Matt and Kate would certainly be interested in using the financial statement information in Exhibits 2.2, 2.3, 2.4, and 2.5 to decide whether they should proceed with their proposed winery. Similarly, Bob Buck of Hap eLoan Corporation will find the data in the forecasted financial statements invaluable in helping to decide whether lending money to Russian River Valley is a prudent idea. While a business's owners are primarily interested in the profitability of the business, a financial institution is primarily interested in assessing the financial risk that it will be exposed to when lending to a business. But how can the financial statements help us learn about business profitability and the risks inherent in lending to a business? Stated alternatively, how can financial statements help us make investment and lending decisions?

Takeaway 4
Apply selected financial ratios to evaluate a company's financial performance.

> **Financial ratios** are frequently used to evaluate firm performance. They permit valid comparisons of performance over time or between competitors. By dividing one accounting measure (such as, net income) by a second accounting measure (such as, net sales), the resulting ratio is standardized, thereby enabling an "apples-to-apples" comparison of firm performance.

Evaluating Firm Profitability

To evaluate the profitability of a business, it is often useful to consider various performance indicators from the financial statements. To illustrate, let's consider the most basic measure of firm performance—whether a business made a profit. The income statement in Exhibit 2.3 shows that net income for the Russian River Valley Winery is indeed expected to be positive—net income is projected to be $317,000 for its first year of operations. That's good news! But just looking at the absolute level of profits ignores how much investment it took to generate those profits. In addition, it is hard to compare the performance of firms of different sizes or of a company over time by just comparing the level of their profits. For example, one would certainly expect a firm such as General Electric, with over $670 billion in reported assets, to have a higher level of profit than a small winery. With far greater levels of sales and investments, it is only natural for General Electric to show a higher level of profit. Consequently, the use of financial ratios provides one approach to making useful comparisons of performance between firms of differing size and for a given firm over various time periods.

One profitability measure that considers relative firm size is the **return on sales** ratio (ROS), or net income divided by sales revenue:[2]

Ratio	Financial Variables	Computation	Result
Return on sales (ROS)	$\dfrac{\text{Net income}}{\text{Sales revenue}}$	$\dfrac{\$317}{\$1,900}$	16.7%

The ROS ratio, which is also referred to as the **profit margin ratio**, for the Russian River Valley Winery is forecasted to be 16.7 percent, which indicates that for every dollar of sales revenue, the winery is expected to generate nearly 17 cents of bottom-line profit. You don't have to know much about wineries to recognize that a 16.7 percent return on sales is quite high. But to be certain, it would be wise to compare the Russian River Valley Winery's ROS against the ROS for other small wineries or against the average ROS for the wine industry. By making such inter-firm and industry comparisons, it is possible to more clearly benchmark the winery's performance and to determine how successfully the business is expected to perform.

Another measure of profitability that considers relative firm size is the **return on assets** (ROA) ratio, or net income plus after-tax interest expense divided by total assets:

Ratio	Financial Variables	Computation	Result
Return on assets (ROA)	$\dfrac{\text{Net income} + [\text{Interest expense} \times (1 - \text{Tax rate})]}{\text{Total assets}}$	$\dfrac{\$317 + [\$288 \times (1 - (\$240/\$557))]}{\$10,953}$	4.4%

The return on assets ratio represents the amount of earnings available to a business's capital providers, to include both its lenders and its shareholders. Since lenders obtain their return in the form of interest payments, and since this expense is subtracted in the calculation of net income, it is necessary to add the interest expense back to net income to produce a measure of the total return available to a firm's capital providers.[3] Interest expense, however, is tax deductible by the business, and therefore, effectively reduces a firm's total income tax expense. The positive impact of interest expense on a firm's income tax expense is referred to as a "tax shield." In order to correctly account for the **tax shield**, the amount of interest added back to net income should be reduced by the amount of the tax shield which is already reflected in a firm's income tax provision, and hence, in its net income. The income tax rate used in this calculation is the company's **effective tax rate**, or a firm's tax expense divided by its income before income taxes. Note that no such adjustment is needed for dividends paid to shareholders since dividends are not tax deductible and are not subtracted in the calculation of net income, and consequently, do not need to be added back.

Russian River Valley's expected ROA, also referred to as the **return on investment**, is 4.4 percent, indicating that it takes about $1 of assets to generate about four and a half cents of net income. Is that good?

---

[2] Some investment professionals calculate the ROS ratio on an "unlevered" basis as follows:

$$\text{Unlevered ROS} = \frac{\text{Net income} + [\text{Interest expense} \times (1 - \text{Tax rate})]}{\text{Net sales}}$$

Unlevering the ROS ratio–that is, adding the interest expense paid by a company net of the tax benefit of the interest expense back to net income–creates a measure of net income as if the company were all equity financed. This alternative measure of ROS allows the analyst to focus on the efficacy of management's operating decisions independent of management's financing decisions. We will have more to say about unlevered ROS in Chapter 4.

[3] Many analysts will exclude the numerator adjustment for interest in the ROA calculation. This modification is done either (i) for simplicity, or (ii) because interest expense is not readily available.

One benchmark—the six percent interest rate (but only 3.4 percent after considering the interest tax shield) to be charged by Hap eLoan Corporation on the proposed bank loan—suggests that the winery's expected ROA is quite low. While the winery will earn slightly more than its 3.4 percent after-tax cost of borrowed funds, this is not a very large margin.[4] The low projected ROA for Russian River Valley may indicate several things—that the wine business is highly competitive, producing only marginal returns, or alternatively, that the winery's business model needs more work to enable the business to be more profitable.

From a shareholder perspective, the size of a business's profit relative to the shareholders' investment in the business is an important measure of profitability, and this can be evaluated by the **return on shareholders' equity** (ROE) ratio, or net income divided by shareholders' equity.[5] This ratio indicates how much profit was generated given the shareholders' investment in a business:

Ratio	Financial Variables	Computation	Result
Return on equity (ROE)	$\dfrac{\text{Net income}}{\text{Shareholder' equity}}$	$\dfrac{\$317}{\$6,457}$	4.9%

The Russian River Valley Winery's expected ROE is 4.9 percent, which indicates that for every dollar of shareholders' equity invested in the winery, the business is expected to generate less than five cents of profit for its shareholders. This is a little higher than the after-tax 3.4 percent interest rate to be charged by Hap eLoan Corporation on the bank loan, yet Matt and Kate bear much more risk than the lender. (Recall that assuming higher risk should result in higher returns.) We can tentatively conclude that this expected return is high enough to justify the investment that Kate and Matt will have to make. But, the two entrepreneurs will certainly want to focus on ways of improving the profitability of the business and its ROE.

Return on Equity Analysis

Investment professionals have devised an ingenious way of analyzing the profitability of a business by breaking the return on shareholders' equity (ROE) ratio into three component financial ratios—the return on sales, asset turnover, and financial leverage:

This paradigm reveals that there are four ways to improve a company's ROE, and hence, a firm's profitability: 1) improve a business's return on sales; 2) improve a business's asset turnover; 3) improve a business's use of financial leverage; or, 4) some combination of items 1, 2, and 3. **Asset turnover** is a measure of how effectively a business's assets are being used by the management team to generate sales

---

[4] Russian River Valley's after-tax cost of borrowed funds is calculated as follows:

$$\text{After-tax cost of borrowing} = \text{Before-tax cost of borrowing} \times (1 - \text{Tax rate})$$

In the case of Russian River Valley, the effective tax rate is 43 percent ($240/$557); hence, the after-tax cost of borrowing is:

$$3.4\% = 6.0\% \times (1 - 0.43)$$

[5] Many investment professionals define the return on shareholders' equity (ROE) ratio as:

$$\text{ROE} = \frac{\text{Net income} - \text{Preferred stock dividends}}{\text{Common shareholders' equity}}$$

This ratio definition reflects the widely held view that preferred stock is a quasi-form of debt, and hence, the cost of preferred stock (preferred stock dividends) should be subtracted from net income just as the cost of debt financing (interest expense) is subtracted from net income. Common shareholders' equity is then defined as total shareholders' equity less preferred stock equity. Since many firms do not issue preferred shares, the ROE ratio collapses to just net income divided by shareholders' equity. In addition, some ratios, like ROE, include a metric in the numerator that is measured over time (such as net income) and a metric in the denominator that is measured at a point in time (such as shareholders' equity). Because of this mismatch of the time dimension of a ratio's components, some analysts use averages, rather than ending balances, for the denominator of these ratios.

Financial leverage refers to the use of debt to finance a business's assets and/ or its operations. The cost of debt financing is defined as the rate of interest specified in a debt contract. If a firm is able to earn a return on its borrowed assets greater than its after-tax cost of borrowing, the excess return accrues to the firm's shareholders. And, as a consequence, a company's ROE will exceed its ROA—for example, 4.9 percent versus 4.4 percent for the Russian River Valley Winery. Thus, when we observe that a firm's ROE exceeds its ROA, we can conclude that the firm has been able to successfully utilize financial leverage. When a firm is all equity financed, ROE and ROA will be equivalent.

revenue. This ratio is calculated as sales revenue divided by total assets. This metric is an important indicator of firm performance since the principal objective of any business is to generate income, and that is only possible after the business first generates sales revenue. **Financial leverage**, on the other hand, refers to the relative mix of debt versus equity financing used by a business and is calculated as total assets divided by shareholders' equity. For a firm that is all equity financed, the financial leverage ratio will equal one and will increase in value as debt financing is added. Since the after-tax interest rate on the winery's debt is only 3.4 percent, financing some of the Russian River Valley's assets with debt takes advantage of this cheaper source of financing.[6] We can apply ROE analysis to the winery's forecasted financial data as follows:

Return on Equity	=	Return on Sales	×	Asset Turnover	×	Financial Leverage
$\dfrac{\text{Net income}}{\text{Shareholder' equity}}$	=	$\dfrac{\text{Net income}}{\text{Sales revenue}}$	×	$\dfrac{\text{Sales revenue}}{\text{Total assets}}$	×	$\dfrac{\text{Total assets}}{\text{Shareholders' equity}}$
$\dfrac{\$317}{\$6,457}$	=	$\dfrac{\$317}{\$1,900}$	×	$\dfrac{\$1,900}{\$10,953}$	×	$\dfrac{\$10,953}{\$6,457}$
4.9%	=	16.7%	×	0.173	×	1.70

The ROE analysis for the Russian River Valley Winery reveals why the winery's expected return on equity (4.9 percent) is low. Although the winery's expected ROS is a healthy 16.7 percent, Russian River Valley's expected asset turnover is only 0.173, which indicates that each dollar invested in the business's assets is expected to generate less than 18 cents in sales. Further, the winery has a financial leverage ratio of 1.70, indicating that the winery's assets are forecasted to be about 1.7 times the amount of shareholders' equity invested in the business. Put another way, the Russian River Valley Winery assets are financed with relatively more equity ($6,457) than debt ($4,496). Since the winery is able to earn a slightly higher return on its borrowed funds than the after-tax cost that the business will be charged for the use of these funds, the winery's expected ROE is enhanced by its use of financial leverage.

To enable us to benchmark the expected performance of the winery, Exhibit 2.6 presents an ROE analysis for ten wine companies over a recent five-year period. The data confirm the assessment that Russian River Valley has a low expected return on equity and asset turnover but a relatively high expected return on sales, as compared to the average of the other ten wineries. Observe, for instance, that while the expected ROS for Russian River Valley is 16.7 percent, it averages only about 6.3 percent for the ten wineries; and, while Russian River Valley's expected asset turnover is only 0.173, it averages 0.59 for the ten wineries, or more than three times higher than the turnover forecasted by the winery. This kind of information can be very useful to Kate and Matt in that it highlights the various financial strengths and weaknesses of their proposed business, and thus, highlights those areas in which Matt and Kate should try to improve their business plan. As ROE increases and decreases across accounting periods, this component analysis of ROE can also shed light on which aspect of the business might be contributing to the change. We will have more to say about ROE analysis in Chapter 4.

EXHIBIT 2.6	ROE Analysis: Median Values for 10 Firms in the Wine Industry					
Return on Equity	=	Return on Sales	×	Asset Turnover	×	Financial Leverage
7.97%	=	6.28%	×	0.59	×	2.15

Source: *Compustat*

---

[6] For all businesses, the cost of debt financing is cheaper than the cost of equity financing. Recall that since buying shares in a business is riskier than lending to a business, the returns expected by shareholders should be higher than the returns expected by lenders–lenders have first claim on the assets of a business and shareholders get what is left over.

Evaluating Financial Risk

The concerns that the Russian River Valley Winery may have insufficient cash to pay its annual interest payments and repay the principal on its proposed bank loan on a timely basis are the types of financial risk that financial institutions must consider when lending to a business. Two financial ratios that assess this form of risk include the **long-term debt-to-equity ratio** and the **interest coverage ratio**:

Ratio	Financial Variables	Computation	Result
Long-term debt-to-equity	$\dfrac{\text{Long-term debt}}{\text{Shareholders' equity}}$	$\dfrac{\$4,320}{\$6,457}$	0.67
Interest coverage	$\dfrac{\text{Operating income}}{\text{Interest expense}}$	$\dfrac{\$845}{\$288}$	2.93

The long-term debt-to-equity ratio reveals the relative investment of long-term lenders versus that of the shareholders in the Russian River Valley Winery. A high debt-to-equity ratio, for example, indicates a financing strategy heavily dependent on borrowed versus shareholder-invested funds. The interest coverage ratio, on the other hand, reveals the extent to which current operating earnings "cover" current debt service charges (interest expense). A high interest coverage ratio, also referred to as the **times-interest-earned ratio**, indicates that a business has strong operating earnings (or low interest charges), and thus, has the capacity to take on additional debt and additional debt service costs, as well as to easily service its existing debt.

The Russian River Valley Winery's expected long-term debt-to-equity ratio is 0.67, indicating that its long-term debt of $4,320 ($3,840 + $480) is about two-thirds the amount of its shareholders' equity of $6,457. The winery's expected interest coverage ratio is 2.93, suggesting that the winery's operating income is projected to be almost three times the expected interest expense for the period. Both ratios indicate that there is a fair amount of cushion for the business's lenders. Overall, with a reasonable debt-to-equity ratio and interest coverage ratio, the winery should have a good chance of getting the proposed $4.8 million loan because it appears to have a good chance of paying both the annual interest charge and principal repayments in a timely manner.

REVIEW PROBLEM 2.3

The following data were obtained from the year-end financial statements of The Arcadia Company:

Cash.	$212,400
Net income.	52,650
Sales revenue.	160,000
Interest expense.	3,600
Tax rate.	0%
Total shareholders' equity	302,650
Common stock.	250,000
Long-term debt	120,000
Operating income.	56,250
Total assets.	428,650

Required

Compute the following ratios for The Arcadia Company: (1) Return on Sales, (2) Return on Assets, (3) Return on Equity, (4) Long-Term Debt-to-Equity, and (5) Interest Coverage.

The solution is on page 83.

Takeaway 5
Understand
the managerial
motives for
selecting between
alternative
accounting
methods.

MANAGERIAL DISCRETION AND ACCOUNTING METHODS

The balance sheet equation used for analyzing the various accounting events of a business can be helpful in understanding the accounting method choices that a company makes and how those choices affect a business's financial statements. To illustrate, we use the balance sheet equation to examine how B.J.'s Wholesale Club accounted for the membership fees it charges its customers and how America Online accounted for the cost of computer diskettes it used to attract new internet customers.

Operating Revenues at B.J.'s Wholesale Club

B.J.'s Wholesale Club Inc. is a wholesale membership club in the United States. Customers pay an annual fee of $50 for the right to shop at any of B.J.'s outlets, which offer its customers lower prices on goods that it buys in very large quantities. B.J.'s accounts for the $50 membership fee as operating revenue when it is received. To illustrate the financial effects associated with this practice, assume that a customer paid the $50 fee on July 1, halfway through B.J.'s fiscal year, which ends on December 31. B.J.'s would report the event by increasing cash (A) by $50 and increasing operating revenue and retained earnings (SE) by $50 (see Panel A, Exhibit 2.7).

EXHIBIT 2.7	B.J.'s: Accounting for Membership Fees		
Panel A			
	Cash	**Liabilities**	**Retained Earnings**
July 1	$50		$50
Ending Balance	$50		$50
Panel B			
	Cash	**Liabilities**	**Retained Earnings**
July 1	$50	$ 50	
December 31		$(25)	$25
Ending balance.	$50	$ 25	$25

B.J.'s accounting for membership fees, however, came under criticism from the U.S. Securities and Exchange Commission which required that the company abandon the practice and instead recognize the fee ratably over the 12-month membership period.[7] Under the new accounting policy, on July 1, B.J.'s would show an increase in cash of $50 and an increase in a liability account (called "unearned revenue") of $50 to recognize B.J.'s obligation to provide member services to its customer for the coming year (see Panel B). By December 31, B.J.'s has satisfied six months (or one-half) of its obligation and thus, would recognize $25 of operating revenues and a reduction in the liability for future services of $25. At the end of the year, B.J.'s has a remaining liability of $25 for services it has agreed to provide for the next six months.

Let's compare B.J.'s former accounting policy with its new policy by contrasting the account balances in Panels A and B in Exhibit 2.7. The former policy increases earnings by $25 for the year, reduces liabilities by $25, and increases shareholders' equity by $25. Thus, under the old policy, the performance of the company appears superior. Yet, the cash flows under both accounting policies are identical.

An astute observer might notice that with no new customers next year, the old accounting policy will result in zero earnings in Year Two. This observation highlights a fundamental difference between accrual accounting and cash accounting. Accrual accounting, with its adherence to revenue recognition and expense matching, creates timing differences between earnings recognition and cash flows. Over the two-year period, there will be no difference in cumulative net income; but, under B.J.'s new accounting policy, earnings will be $25 in the second year. Thus, the new policy shifts some revenues and earnings from the current year to the following year but does not change the total revenues or earnings over the two-year period. But suppose that there are more customers in each succeeding year—then current earn-

---

[7] Some investment professionals refer to B.J.'s original accounting treatment of its membership fees as **front-end loading of revenues**. Under this practice, the cash flows from the sale of a membership are immediately recognized as revenue even though some portion of the revenue may relate to services to be delivered in a future period.

ings will be higher under the old accounting policy than under the new accounting policy—and B.J.'s management team will appear to be doing a better job.

Operating Expenses at America Online

America Online (AOL) was a pioneer internet service provider that blanketed the United States with promotional materials (e.g., computer diskettes and CDs) to entice customers to sign up for the company's service. For accounting purposes, AOL accounted for the cost of these promotional materials as an asset on the balance sheet, called "deferred marketing costs," and expensed the resulting asset over a two-year period.[8] To see the effect of this accounting policy on AOL's balance sheet, assume that it costs $2 to produce and distribute each set of materials and that they are shipped on January 1. (AOL's fiscal year ends on December 31.) On January 1, AOL reduces cash (A) by $2 and increases intangible assets (A) by the same amount. On December 31, AOL expenses $1 by reducing intangible assets by $1 and reducing retained earnings (SE) by $1. These events are illustrated in Panel A of Exhibit 2.8.

EXHIBIT 2.8	AOL: Accounting for Advertising Costs		
Panel A			
	Cash	**Intangible Asset**	**Retained Earnings**
January 1	$(2.00)	$ 2.00	
December 31		$(1.00)	$(1.00)
Ending balance.	$(2.00)	$ 1.00	$(1.00)
Panel B			
	Cash	**Intangible Asset**	**Retained Earnings**
January 1	$(2.00)		$(2.00)
Ending balance.	$(2.00)		$(2.00)

After repeated criticism from Wall Street analysts regarding this policy, AOL switched to immediately expensing the cost of the promotional materials. Under immediate expensing, AOL would reduce cash (A) by $2 and reduce retained earnings (SE) by the same amount. The event would be recorded as shown in Panel B of Exhibit 2.8.

Contrasting the account balances from Panels A and B of Exhibit 2.8 reveals the effect of AOL's decision to change its accounting policy. Immediately expensing the cost of the promotional materials reduces assets on the balance sheet by $1 at December 31 and reduces earnings for the year by $1. Yet, there is no cash flow effect associated with the change since cash is initially reduced by $2 under both methods. Over a two-year period, there is no difference in AOL's performance under the two policies; however, under the old policy, net income is higher in Year One.

In both examples—B.J.'s and AOL—the selection of a firm's accounting policies can materially impact reported firm performance, in many instances making the operating performance look better than it really was. A theme throughout each of the following chapters is that informed financial statement users must look beyond the reported numbers and also consider the accounting policy choices made by a company's management. Evaluating a company's profits without knowledge of how that number is derived is like reporting the temperature on a given day without understanding what temperature scale was used—Celsius or Fahrenheit (32 degrees Fahrenheit is quite cold while 32 degrees Celsius is quite pleasant). As we will see from actual corporate examples, some managers will make judicious accounting policy choices in an attempt to manage the level of reported firm performance, and consequently, to influence the perceived value of a firm.

---

[8] Some investment professionals refer to AOL's treatment of deferred marketing costs as **rear-end loading of expenses**. Under this practice, the cash outflows for advertising and marketing are capitalized to the balance sheet as an asset even though some (or all) of the expenditure should be currently recognized on the income statement as an expense.

ETHICS PERSPECTIVE

B.J.'s Wholesale Club Inc. and America Online represent two examples of how managers can use their discretion to manage the reported earnings of a firm. Much of this discretion is within the flexible guidelines that are part of the institutional setting of accounting; however, sometimes managers cross the line of acceptable accounting practice and engage in fraudulent reporting. Very often the line between the two is quite grey, where it is difficult to separate aggressive financial reporting from fraudulent financial reporting. In either case, it can be argued that the intent of some corporate managers is to deceive the investing public by misrepresenting a firm's financial performance.

In the post-Enron environment, and with the enactment of the Sarbanes-Oxley Act, many firms are proactively portraying themselves as being "ethical." Ethical behavior is, for example, part of the Corporate Social Responsibility movement. This behavior includes many dimensions, including the ethical treatment of employees and the environment, as well as ethical financial reporting. Academic research has found a positive correlation between a firm's reputation and its financial performance. Do you feel that strong ethics makes good business sense?

EXECUTIVE SUMMARY

In this chapter we examined the balance sheet equation and how financial statements are derived from a set of accounting events that affect a business. We also considered some of the estimates and assumptions inherent in the financial statement preparation process, observing that since estimates and assumptions can be incorrect, financial statements should never be considered to be a precise representation of a company's financial performance. Finally, we investigated how to use financial statement data to evaluate a business's operating performance and its financial risk.

As a validation of your understanding of the content of this chapter, you should now be able to:

- Understand the balance sheet equation.
- Explain the accounting meaning behind the terms asset, liability, shareholders' equity, revenue, expense, and matching.
- Prepare financial statements from business events.
- Use selected financial ratios to evaluate a company's financial performance.
- Use the balance sheet equation to understand the managerial motives for selecting between alternative accounting methods.

In the next chapter, we examine the various components of the income statement and also learn how to prepare a statement of cash flow from just an income statement and a set of balance sheets.

KEY CONCEPTS AND TERMS

Accrual, 44
Articulation, 58
Asset, 41
Asset turnover, 63
Balance sheet equation, 40
Common stock, 41
Contra-accounts, 50
Contributed capital, 41
Current assets, 56
Current liabilities, 56
Effective tax rate, 62
Entity principle, 43
Expenses, 47
Financial leverage, 64
Financial ratios, 61
Financing activities, 57
Financing decision, 40
Forecasted financial statements, 45

Front-end loading of revenues, 66
Gross profit, 56
Historical cost principle, 46
Intangible assets, 44
Interest coverage ratio, 65
Investing activities, 57
Investment decision, 40
Leveraged, 40
Liability, 41
Long-term debt-to-equity ratio, 65
Matching concept, 48
Net book value, 50
Net income, 56
Net worth, 39
Noncurrent assets, 56
Noncurrent liabilities, 56
Off-balance-sheet liabilities, 41
Operating activities, 57

Operating income, 56
Opportunity cost, 45
Profit margin ratio, 62
Rear-end loading of expenses, 67
Recurring operations, 57
Retained earnings, 41
Return on assets, 62
Return on investment, 62
Return on sales, 62
Return on shareholders' equity, 63
Revenue recognition principle, 47
Revenues, 47, 56
Shareholders' equity, 41
Tangible assets, 44
Tax shield, 62
Times-interest-earned ratio, 65

QUESTIONS

Q2.1 **Accounting Terminology.** Describe or define the following terms:

- Asset
- Liability
- Shareholders' equity
- Revenue
- Expense

Discuss how the five terms relate to one another.

Q2.2 **Historical Versus Forecasted Financial Statements.** Discuss the difference between historical and fore-casted (or pro forma) financial statements. How are these different sets of financial statements used by managers and shareholders for decision-making purposes?

Q2.3 **Accounting Principles.** Consider the following accounting principles:

- Entity principle
- Revenue recognition principle
- Matching concept

Define these accounting principles. Discuss how these principles relate to one another.

Q2.4 **Balance Sheet Classifications.** Most balance sheets are defined as "classified balance sheets" in that both the assets and liabilities are dichotomized into the categories of current and noncurrent. [Note: In those industries in which the business operating cycle is longer than one year (such as the wine industry, the real estate industry, the financial services industry), classified balance sheets are not required under U.S. GAAP.] How do you think the balance sheet classifications of current versus noncurrent convey important information about a firm's financial condition to managers and shareholders?

Q2.5 **Key Performance Indicators: The Income Statement.** Describe or define the following key performance indicators (KPIs) from the income statement:

- Operating revenue
- Gross profit
- Operating income
- Net income

Discuss how each of these measures depicts a firm's performance.

Q2.6 **Key Performance Indicators: The Statement of Cash Flow.** Describe or define the following key performance indicators (KPIs) from the statement of cash flow:

- Cash flow from operating activities
- Cash flow from investing activities
- Cash flow from financing activities

Discuss how each of these measures conveys important information about firm performance to managers and shareholders.

Q2.7 **Return on Shareholders' Equity.** The return on shareholders' equity ratio can be decomposed into three separate financial ratios—the return on sales, asset turnover, and financial leverage. Define each of the ratios assuming the firm is all equity financed and discuss what actions a manager might take to increase a firm's return on shareholders' equity.

Q2.8 **Evaluating Financial Risk.** Investment professionals use a variety of financial ratios to evaluate a company's financial risk. Two popular financial risk ratios include:

- Long-term debt-to-equity ratio
- Interest coverage ratio

Define each ratio and discuss what actions a manager might take to reduce a firm's financial riskiness.

Q2.9 **Managing Operating Revenues.** Some corporate executives have reportedly attempted to manage their firm's operating revenues through such actions as "front-end loading" or "rear-end loading" of operating revenues. Explain the concepts of front-end loading and rear-end loading of operating revenues. Discuss why some managers might undertake these actions. Discuss how you might be able to identify that a manager is managing a firm's operating revenues.

Q2.10 **Net Income, Cash Flow from Operations, and Dividend Policy.** The Arizona Corporation reported positive net income but negative cash flow from operations. Further, despite the negative cash flow from operations, the company continued to pay its regular dividend on its common shares. Discuss why it is possible for a company to report positive net income when the cash flow from operations is negative. Do you agree with the firm's strategy of maintaining its regular dividend? Why or why not?

Q2.11 **Debt Covenants.** Bristol-Myers Squibb (BMS) Company reports that it maintains a $2 billion, five-year revolving line of credit with a syndicate of lenders. The company disclosed in its annual report that:

> The availability of the line of credit is subject to the Company's ability . . . to meet certain conditions, including a financial covenant in which net debt-to-capital cannot exceed 50 percent.

Discuss why BMS would agree to the above financial covenant. Discuss why the syndicate of lenders would impose such a constraint on BMS. How would you calculate the "net debt-to-capital" ratio? What does the ratio reveal about a company?

Q2.12 **Managing Operating Expenses.** Some corporate executives have reportedly attempted to manage their firm's operating expenses through such actions as "front-end loading" or "rear-end loading" of their operating expenses. Explain the concepts of front-end loading and rear-end loading of operating expenses. Discuss why some managers might undertake these actions. Discuss how you might be able to identify that a manager is managing a firm's operating expenses.

Q2.13 **Net Loss, Cash Flow from Operations, and Dividend Policy.** The Phoenix Corporation reported a net loss but a positive cash flow from operations. Further, despite the net loss, the company continued to pay its regular dividend. Discuss why it is possible for a company to report a net loss while also reporting a positive cash flow from operations. Do you agree with the company's decision to continue the payment of its regular dividend? Why or why not?

Q2.14 **(Ethical Perspective) Corporate Social Responsibility and Ethics.** In the post-Enron environment, and with the enactment of the Sarbanes-Oxley legislation, many firms are proactively portraying themselves as being "ethical." Ethical behavior is, for example, part of the Corporate Social Responsibility movement. This behavior includes many dimensions, from the ethical treatment of employees and the environment, to ethical financial reporting. Academic research has found a positive correlation between a firm's reputation and its financial performance. Why do you think that there is a positive correlation between ethical behavior and successful corporate financial performance?

Assignments with the ⓜⓑⓒ logo in the margin are available in BusinessCourse.
See the Preface of the book for details.
CHECK FIGURE indicates that check figures are available on the book's Website.

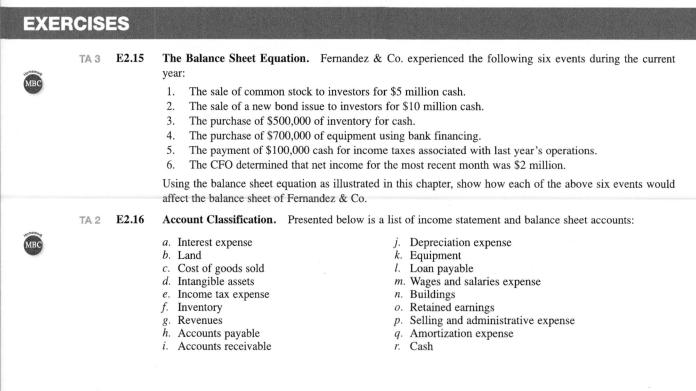

EXERCISES

TA 3   **E2.15**   **The Balance Sheet Equation.**   Fernandez & Co. experienced the following six events during the current year:

1.   The sale of common stock to investors for $5 million cash.
2.   The sale of a new bond issue to investors for $10 million cash.
3.   The purchase of $500,000 of inventory for cash.
4.   The purchase of $700,000 of equipment using bank financing.
5.   The payment of $100,000 cash for income taxes associated with last year's operations.
6.   The CFO determined that net income for the most recent month was $2 million.

Using the balance sheet equation as illustrated in this chapter, show how each of the above six events would affect the balance sheet of Fernandez & Co.

TA 2   **E2.16**   **Account Classification.**   Presented below is a list of income statement and balance sheet accounts:

a. Interest expense
b. Land
c. Cost of goods sold
d. Intangible assets
e. Income tax expense
f. Inventory
g. Revenues
h. Accounts payable
i. Accounts receivable

j. Depreciation expense
k. Equipment
l. Loan payable
m. Wages and salaries expense
n. Buildings
o. Retained earnings
p. Selling and administrative expense
q. Amortization expense
r. Cash

For each account, indicate whether it would appear on the balance sheet (B/S) or the income statement (I/S). For those accounts appearing on the balance sheet, indicate whether the account is an asset (A), liability (L), or shareholders' equity (SE) account. For those accounts appearing on the income statement, indicate whether the account is a revenue (R) account or an expense (E) account.

E2.17 **Asset or Expense.** The Rankine Corporation reported net income of $10 million in 2016, and it appears that net income for 2017 will be the same. During 2017, the company made the following expenditures: TA 2, 5

1. $250,000 was spent to resurface the company parking lot. The resurfacing has to be done about every five years.
2. $500,000 was spent to upgrade the company's air filtration system in the plating department. The system worked satisfactorily, but the U.S. Department of Labor recently promulgated new rules (effective three years from today) that would have required the changes the company made voluntarily.
3. $900,000 was paid to a consultant for the design of a new manufacturing facility. The new plant was the dream of the prior CEO but had been shelved because the current CEO was uncertain about the firm's future.
4. $600,000 was spent on the development of a new inventory control system. The system was designed to allow salespeople in the field to electronically enter orders into the system so that they could be shipped the next day. The system appeared to be on track, but another $200,000 would have to be spent before it could be demonstrated that it would function as planned.
5. The company's Arizona plant was shut down for three months because of the slow economy. The company struggled to find ways to keep its employees busy so they could retain as many as possible. Some employees agreed to accept half pay while the company found maintenance work and training for the other employees. At the end of three months, about 85 percent of the workforce was still on the payroll when the company resumed normal production. The maintenance work done by the employees during this time cost about $1 million; the training cost the company another $800,000.

Indicate whether the above expenditures should be considered as an asset or as an expense. Be prepared to justify your answer.

E2.18 **The Statement of Cash Flow.** The following cash flow information was taken from the 2015 annual report for Johnson & Johnson. Compute the missing values in the table (amounts are in millions). Based on this data, how does the company finance its ongoing operations and asset purchases? TA 3

	2015	2014	2013
Cash, beginning balance	$14,523	$?	$14,911
Cash flow from operating activities	19,279	?	17,414
Cash flow from investing activities.	(7,735)	(12,305)	?
Cash flow from financing activities.	?	(12,570)	(6,295)
Cash, ending balance.	$13,732	$?	$20,927

E2.19 **The Statement of Cash Flow.** The following cash flow information was taken from the 2015 annual report for General Electric. Compute the missing values in the table (amounts are in millions). Based on this data, describe GE's cash flow performance for the three-year period. TA 3 CHECK FIGURE

	2015	2014	2013
Cash, beginning balance	$?	$88,792	$?
Cash flow from operating activities	19,891	27,709	28,510
Cash flow from investing activities.	?	(5,034)	29,117
Cash flow from financing activities.	(79,517)	?	(46,368)
Cash, ending balance.	$90,879	$91,017	$?

E2.20 **Preparing the Basic Financial Statements.** Marilyn Miller opened a floral shop using $5,000 of her own cash savings and with $15,000 in cash borrowed from her parents. She signed a lease on a small store for one year, agreeing to pay $350 per month in rent. During the first year of operations, Marilyn purchased fresh flowers from a local nursery for $2,500, paid $1,200 for utilities, and generated floral sales totaling $12,000. (Assume all transactions were cash transactions.) Marilyn was hoping to be able to repay her parents one-half of the borrowed money at the end of the first year of operations. TA 3

Prepare an income statement, balance sheet, and statement of cash flow for the floral shop. Can Marilyn achieve her goal of repaying one-half of the $15,000 loan at the end of the first year of operations?

E2.21   **Preparing Cash Flow Data.**   Marilyn Miller began the second year of her floral business with $12,000 in cash in her bank account. Using the information below, all of which occurred during Year 2, prepare a statement of cash flow for Marilyn. Evaluate her cash management strategy during Year 2.

1. Sold an equity interest in the business for $13,000 cash.
2. Generated revenue from floral sales of $20,000, collecting all but $5,000.
3. Incurred operating expenses totaling $9,000, of which $2,000 remained unpaid at the end of Year 2.
4. Purchased new store equipment for $5,000, with a down payment of $2,500 cash and signing a note payable for $2,500.
5. Paid shareholders a cash dividend of $2,800.

PROBLEMS

P2.22   **Accounting Event Analysis and Financial Statement Preparation.**   Smith & Co. experienced the following six events in its first year of operations:

1. Shareholders contributed $60,000 cash.
2. Purchased land for $40,000 cash.
3. Borrowed $18,000 in cash from a bank.
4. Provided services for $16,000, which will be paid to Smith & Co. next year.
5. Paid $11,000 cash for miscellaneous operating expenses.
6. Paid a $1,000 cash dividend to shareholders.

Required

Using the balance sheet equation as illustrated in this chapter, identify how each of the above six events affected the various accounts involved. Prepare an income statement, a statement of shareholders' equity, a balance sheet, and a statement of cash flow for the first year of operations. What is your assessment of the company's financial performance in its first year of operations?

P2.23   **Accounting Event Analysis and Financial Statement Preparation.**   Wilmot Real Estate Company experienced the following events during its first year of operations:

1. Received $50,000 in cash from investors as an equity investment.
2. Borrowed $40,000 in cash from a bank.
3. Purchased two parcels of land, each costing $15,000, for a total of $30,000 cash. The land was purchased for investment purposes.
4. Paid $10,000 cash to rent office equipment for the year.
5. Provided real estate appraisal services valued at $25,000, receiving $20,000 in cash and an account receivable for an additional $5,000.
6. Paid miscellaneous expenses totaling $11,000 in cash.
7. Sold one parcel of land, costing $15,000, for $22,000 cash.
8. Paid a $5,000 cash dividend to shareholders.

Required

Using the balance sheet equation as illustrated in this chapter, identify how each of the above events affect the balance sheet equation of A = L + SE. Prepare an income statement, a statement of shareholders' equity, a balance sheet, and a statement of cash flow for the first year of operations. Evaluate the company's financial performance during its first year of operations.

P2.24   **Accounting Event Analysis and the Balance Sheet.**   Presented below are the balance sheet accounts of the Mayfair Company as of December 1, 2017. The accounts are listed in random order.

Machinery & equipment (net)	$15,000	Cash	$10,000
Accounts payable	10,000	Notes payable	9,500
Note receivable	2,000	Accounts receivable	15,000
Inventory	3,000	Long-term investments	8,000
Bank loan	10,500	Additional paid-in capital	76,000
Building (net)	30,000	Land	40,000
Common stock ($1 par value)	5,000	Retained earnings	12,000

During the month of December 2017, the following events occurred:

1. Purchased inventory on credit that cost $3,000.
2. Issued common stock at par value in exchange for machinery and equipment valued at $12,000.
3. The building was appraised at a value of $45,000 by a certified real estate appraiser.

4. The note receivable of $2,000 was collected.
5. $8,000 cash was paid on the outstanding accounts payable.
6. Purchased land valued at $25,000, paying $3,000 in cash and signing a five-year note for the remaining amount.

Required
1. Prepare the balance sheet as of December 1, 2017, for the Mayfair Company.
2. Prepare a spreadsheet using the balance sheet equation as illustrated in this chapter for the December events.
3. Prepare the balance sheet as of December 31, 2017, for the Mayfair Company.
4. Evaluate the company's financial leverage at year-end 2017.

P2.25   Preparing a Balance Sheet. The following financial information is known about Pfizer, Inc. for the year ended December 31, 2015. (all amounts in millions):   TA 3, 4
  a. The balance of cash and cash equivalents was $3,641.
  b. Short-term investments have a fair market value of $19,649.
  c. Gross accounts receivable total $8,560, which includes $384 that is not expected to be collected.
  d. Inventory has a cost basis of $7,513.
  e. Current tax assets total $2,662; other current assets total $2,163, and long-term investments total $15,999.
  f. Property, plant and equipment have a cost basis of $27,268 and accumulated depreciation of $13,502.
  g. Intangible assets have a cost basis of $89,396 and accumulated amortization of $49,040.
  h. Noncurrent deferred tax assets, other taxes assets, and other noncurrent assets total $5,293 and Goodwill totals $48,242.
  i. Accounts payable total $3,620; accrued expenses payable total $15,619; and, short-term borrowings total $10,160.
  j. Long-term debt totals $28,818, and pension and post-retirement benefit obligations total $8,119.
  k. Noncurrent deferred tax liabilities $26,877, and other taxes payable and noncurrent liabilities of $9,249.
  l. Shareholders' equity totals $64,720, composed of retained earnings of $71,993, other comprehensive income (loss) of $(9,522), treasury stock of negative $79,252, and contributed capital of $81,501. Equity attributable to noncontrolling interests totals $278.

Required
Prepare a balance sheet for Pfizer, Inc. as of December 31, 2015. Calculate Pfizer's total debt to total assets ratio and long-term debt-to-equity ratio and evaluate the results.

P2.26   Analysis of Financial Statement Data. The following data were taken from the financial statements of The Amphlett Corporation, which is all equity financed.   TA 4 CHECK FIGURE

	2016	2017
Net sales.	$145,860	$161,585
Net income.	24,765	28,340
Total assets.	171,225	192,440
Shareholders' equity	101,975	121,165

Required
1. Calculate the following ratios for 2016 and 2017:
   a. Return on equity
   b. Return on assets
   c. Return on sales
   d. Total assets to shareholders' equity (financial leverage)
   e. Asset turnover
2. Comment on the financial performance of The Amphlett Corporation based on your ratio calculations.

P2.27   Analysis of Financial Statement Data. The following data were taken from the financial statements of The Mann Corporation, which is all equity financed.   TA 4

	2016	2017
Net sales.	$1,300,000	$2,320,000
Net income.	100,000	220,000
Total assets.	558,659	894,309
Shareholders' equity	303,030	371,622

Required

1. Calculate the following ratios for 2016 and 2017:
    a. Return on equity
    b. Return on assets
    c. Return on sales
    d. Total assets to shareholders' equity (financial leverage)
    e. Asset turnover
2. Comment on the financial performance of The Mann Corporation based on your ratio calculations.

TA 4   **P2.28**   **Analyzing Financial Statement Information.**   The Thunderbird Corporation has applied to the Biltmore National Bank for a $100,000 loan to purchase new equipment for its manufacturing operations. As part of the loan application, the chief financial officer of Thunderbird submitted the following financial statement information:

	2017	2016
Balance sheet		
Current assets	$ 49,000	$ 42,000
Noncurrent assets	175,000	150,500
Total assets	224,000	192,500
Current liabilities	24,500	21,000
Noncurrent liabilities	91,000	73,500
Shareholders' equity	108,500	98,000
Income statement		
Operating revenues	$122,500	$112,000
Operating expenses.	(80,500)	(91,000)
Net income.	$ 42,000	$ 21,000
Statement of cash flow		
Cash flow from operating activities	$ 52,500	$ 31,500
Cash flow from investing activities	(49,000)	(42,000)
Cash flow from financing activities	24,500	17,500
Change in cash	$ 28,000	$ 7,000

Required

Analyze the financial statement information of The Thunderbird Corporation and indicate whether you believe that the firm's loan application should be approved. And, if so, why?

TA 1, 3, 4   **P2.29**   **The Operating Cycle and Financial Statements.**   Presented below is the year-end 2016 balance sheet for The Little Corporation.

CHECK FIGURE

THE LITTLE CORPORATION				
Balance Sheet				
December 31, 2016				
Assets			**Liabilities & Shareholders' Equity**	
Current			Current liabilities	
Cash.		$ 510,000	Accounts payable	$ 650,000
Accounts receivable (net). . . .		564,000	Wages payable	173,000
Inventory		720,000	Interest payable.	56,000
Prepaid rent		222,000	Total current liabilities	879,000
Total current assets		2,016,000	Noncurrent liabilities	
Noncurrent			Bank loan.	450,000
Long-term investments		496,500	Bonds payable.	1,950,000
Equipment	$1,440,000		Total liabilities.	3,279,000
Less Accum. depreciation . . .	(288,000)			
		1,152,000	Shareholders' equity	
Machinery	2,850,000		Common stock	1,200,000
Less Accum. depreciation . . .	(712,500)		Retained earnings	1,548,000
		2,137,500	Total shareholders' equity	2,748,000
Intangible assets (net)		225,000	**Total liabilities &**	
Total assets		**$6,027,000**	**shareholders' equity . . . .**	**$6,027,000**

During 2017, the company entered into the following events:

1. Sales to customers totaled $2 million, of which $1.6 million were on credit and the remainder was cash sales. The cost of goods sold totaled $800,000.
2. Purchased $700,000 of inventory on credit.
3. Paid $620,000 cash to employees as wages. (This amount includes the wages payable at December 31, 2016.)
4. Collected $1.75 million cash from customers as payment on outstanding accounts receivable.
5. Paid $1.2 million cash to suppliers on outstanding accounts payable.
6. Sold machinery for $120,000 cash on January 1, 2017. The machinery had cost $370,000 and at the time of sale it had a net book value of $160,000.
7. Paid miscellaneous expenses totaling $98,000 cash.
8. Sold common stock for $450,000 cash.
9. Invested $200,000 of excess cash in short-term marketable securities.
10. Declared and paid a cash dividend of $100,000.

As part of the year-end audit, the internal audit staff identified the following additional information:

a. $180,000 of prepaid rent was consumed during the year.
b. The equipment had a useful life of 10 years and the machinery of 20 years. The company uses straight-line depreciation. (No depreciation should be recorded for machinery in Item 6 above.)
c. The intangible assets had a remaining useful life of 10 years.
d. Interest on the bank loan and bonds payable was 10 percent. During the year, interest payments totaling $260,000 had been paid in cash.

Required
1. Using the balance sheet equation as illustrated in this chapter, prepare a spreadsheet reflecting the events of The Little Corporation during 2017.
2. Prepare the income statement for 2017.
3. Prepare the statement of shareholders' equity, balance sheet, and statement of cash flow for 2017.
4. How has the company's use of leverage changed from 2016 to 2017?

P2.30   **Preparing Financial Statements from Accounting Events.** Photovoltaics, Inc. is an Arizona-based   TA 1, 3, 4
manufacturer and distributor of photovoltaic solar energy units. The company was founded in 2015 by Arthur Manelas and Harry Linn. Manelas, formerly a research scientist with NASA, had been operating a small photovoltaic manufacturing company in Massachusetts when Linn, a marketing consultant to the industry and himself an owner of a solar energy company in Oregon, proposed the joint venture.

Convinced that excellent market opportunities for the solar arrays existed, Linn began preparing a pro-spectus that could be used to help raise capital to significantly expand Manelas's current operations. The two founders had located a manufacturing facility in Tucson, Arizona, that would cost approximately $8 million to acquire and equip with updated production equipment. Based on his prior experience, Linn knew that prospective venture capital investors would expect to see the following:

- A balance sheet identifying the company's assets and equities as they would appear at the start of operations.
- A pro forma income statement for the first year of operations.
- A pro forma balance sheet as it would appear at the end of the first year of operations.
- A pro forma statement of cash flow for the first year of operations.

In anticipation of preparing these reports, Linn collected the following information and arrived at the following projections for the first year of operations:

Data related to pre-opening events
1. Ten million shares of common stock (par value $1) were authorized for sale by the company's charter of incorporation. Manelas received 500,000 shares in exchange for the rights to the photovoltaic patent, and Linn received an equal number of shares after contributing $500,000 in personal funds to the firm.
2. Incorporation and attorney's fees (start-up costs) amounted to $27,000 and would be paid in cash. (*Hint:* Start-up costs are generally expensed as incurred; however, Linn decided to capitalize these costs as assets on the balance sheet.)
3. Sales of common stock to venture capitalists would total 2.5 million shares. A selling price of $3.25 per share was set, and transaction costs of 1.5 percent of the stock proceeds were projected (to be paid in cash). (*Hint:* Stock issuance fees are accounted for as start-up costs.)
4. The $8 million purchase price of the manufacturing facility, paid in cash, was to be allocated as follows: building—$4.5 million; land—$750,000; and, equipment—$2.75 million. In addition, raw materials and partially completed solar units would be purchased on credit from Manelas's original manufacturing

company at a cost of $1.3 million. A note, secured by the inventory itself and accruing interest at a rate of 10 percent per year on the unpaid balance, would be issued to Manelas.

Projected events

5. Revenues from the sale of solar arrays for the first year were projected to be $480,000, with 20 percent of this amount estimated to be uncollected at year-end. The company had decided to follow a particularly rigid credit-granting policy until operations were well established; hence, no provision for bad debts would be established because no uncollectible accounts were anticipated.
6. Cash purchases of inventory were estimated at $70,000; the cost of inventory sold was projected to be $215,000.
7. Insurance on the building, equipment, and inventory was expected to cost $2,700 per year.
8. Employee wages were estimated at $72,000; selling and administrative costs were projected at 2 percent of gross sales.
9. The useful life of the acquired assets was estimated as follows:

Building	20 years
Equipment	10 years

Linn decided to amortize the patent over its remaining legal life of 17 years and amortize the start-up costs over five years.

10. Salaries to Linn and Manelas were set at $20,000 each for the first year.
11. Interest payments, but no principal repayments, would be made on the ten-percent notes issued to Manelas during the first year of operations.
12. Income taxes were estimated at 22 percent of pre-tax net income.
13. A cash dividend of $100,000 would be paid at the end of the first year to the equity investors.

Required

1. Using the balance sheet equation as illustrated in this chapter, prepare the following financial statements:
    a. Opening balance sheet as of the start of operations (i.e., after pre-opening events).
    b. Income statement for the first year.
    c. Balance sheet at the end of the first year.
    d. Statement of cash flow for the first year.
2. As a prospective investor in the company, what factors would you look for in the financial statements to help you decide whether to invest in the venture? Do you agree with the decision to pay a $100,000 cash dividend at the end of the first year of operations? Why?

TA 3, 4   **P2.31**   **Preparing Financial Statements from Accounting Events.**   In January 2017, Susan and Clark Shipley, co-owners of Island Foods, Inc. began discussing the possibility of expanding their restaurant business from a single location in Glendale, Arizona, to two additional locations—one in Scottsdale and a second in Phoenix. Although the Glendale restaurant had only been open for about two years, it had attracted a loyal customer base from neighborhood businesses and schools. Despite the success of the Glendale restaurant in its first two years of operations, the Shipleys would still need to borrow money to finance the two new restaurants. Susan and Clark knew that they would be expected to present a set of recent financial statements as part of any loan proposal. So, the co-owners spent an afternoon compiling data regarding the key transactions of the two preceding years.

Background

In early 2015, Clark and Susan Shipley moved from the damp, gray environment of Seattle, Washington, to the dry, sunny climate of Phoenix, Arizona. After some reflection on their life in Seattle, as well as an analysis of the local business environment in the Phoenix area, they concluded that they would like to own and manage a restaurant. Glendale was Arizona's third largest city, but it was not noted for a plethora of eating establishments, and those that did exist were principally Italian, Mexican, or fast food. The Shipleys concluded that their restaurant would feature Japanese rice bowls and operate under the name "Island Teriyaki."

With that decision made, Clark and Susan began the long and difficult process of setting up their restaurant. In March 2015, they formed Island Foods, Inc. by contributing $10,000 in cash in exchange for all of the company's 1,000 shares of stock. Clark convinced his parents to loan the new venture $120,000 in cash, with principal payable at the rate of $12,000 per year over ten years and interest payable at a rate of 7.5 percent on the outstanding balance as of the beginning of the loan's year. The loan agreement was signed on March 31, 2015, and provided that both principal and interest would be paid only once a year on March 31.

During March, the Shipleys searched for a suitable location for the restaurant. Clark negotiated a lease for approximately 2,000 square feet of retail space at a rate of $1,400 per month. The lease agreement ran for five years, with an option to renew for five more years. The landlord agreed to give the Shipleys three months of free rent on the front end of the lease in order to help the new business survive the critical start-up period.

Also during the month of March, Clark arranged to buy a commercial refrigerator, range, and grill for $26,000 in cash, to be delivered and installed on March 31. Discussions with the seller indicated that the kitchen equipment should last for five years. Clark and Susan also purchased a computer system, with restaurant-specific software already installed, at a cost of $12,000 cash. While the system could last indefinitely, Susan suggested that it be depreciated over six years. Other purchases included food preparation equipment at a cost of $1,200 cash and various restaurant furniture and fixtures at a cost of $2,700 in cash; the equipment, furniture, and fixtures were expected to have a useful life of three years.

To enable the restaurant to be fully operational on April 1, the landlord allowed the Shipleys' carpenter, electrician, painters, and plumbers to begin renovations to the leased store on March 30 and 31. Working round-the-clock, the workers completed all necessary improvements and renovations to the leased space at a cost of $68,000 in cash.

- The improvements and renovations would be depreciated over five years.

On March 31, the purchased kitchen equipment was delivered and "Island Teriyaki" opened for business as planned on April 1, 2015.

First Two Years of Operations

Although Susan and Clark had prepared a timely U.S. income tax return in April of 2016 (for 2015 income taxes), they had not bothered to prepare a full set of financial statements using the accrual method of accounting. Since Clark had "backed up" the hard drive on their computer system on a weekly basis, he had a CD containing all of the 2015 and 2016 transactions. Working from the CD, Clark generated the necessary accounting information regarding the first two years of operations; he assembled the cash flow information in columnar form (see below) and relevant accrual information by each income statement account:

	2015	2016
• **Revenues** In general, all restaurant sales were cash transactions; however, the Shipleys had developed a personal relationship with the general manager of one of Glendale's local businesses. As a courtesy to him, they had agreed to cater the company's New Year's Eve party each year and to bill the company directly. The billings totaled $3,000 in 2015 and $5,000 in 2016, and were paid by the company within 15 days of the following month.	$212,000	$327,000
• **Expenses**		
○ **Food costs** Susan usually sat down once a week to write checks for any recent bills. Consequently, by year-end, only one week of food costs remained unpaid, totaling $9,000 in 2015 and $12,000 in 2016.	$60,000	$105,000
○ **Supply costs** Since payment on delivery was required for these miscellaneous restaurant supplies (such as ice, napkins, etc.), Susan usually paid this bill directly out of petty cash.	$4,800	$6,200
○ **Utility charges** At year-end one month's payment for electricity, telephone, and water remained due.	$8,000	$12,000
○ **Employee wages** Because Clark did much of the cooking himself while Susan worked on food and sauce preparation, the Shipleys were able to keep their labor costs fairly low. They also made a conscious decision to hire local high school and college students. At year-end, Clark determined that one week of wages, amounting to $1,100 in 2015 and $1,400 in 2016, were due to the employees.	$44,000	$76,000
○ **Licenses** Clark paid the one-time Glendale "new business license" fee at 9 a.m. on April 1, 2015, to enable the business to immediately begin operations.	$900	—

continued

Solution 2.2

1.

	(1)	(2)	(3a)	(3b)*	(4a)	(4b)	(4c)	(5a)**	(5b)	(6)***	(7)	Balance Sheet
THE ARCADIA COMPANY — Spreadsheet												
Cash.....................	250,000	(150,000)	120,000	(3,600)	(120,000)		(24,000)	160,000			(20,000)	212,400
Inventory.................					120,000	30,000				(80,000)		70,000
Buildings.................		150,000										150,000
Accumulated depreciation										(3,750)		(3,750)
Total assets												428,650
Accounts payable...........						30,000	(24,000)					6,000
Loan payable			120,000									120,000
Total liabilities												126,000
Capital stock	250,000											250,000
Retained earnings												52,650
Revenues								160,000				
Cost of goods sold										(80,000)		
Depreciation										(3,750)		
Wages and salaries											(20,000)	
Interest expense				(3,600)								
Total shareholders' equity ...												302,650

Income Statement accounts (Revenues, Cost of goods sold, Depreciation, Wages and salaries, Interest expense)

* ($120,000 × 0.06)/2 = $3,600
** $80,000 × 2 = $160,000
*** ($150,000/20)/2 = $3,750

2.

THE ARCADIA COMPANY
Income Statement

Revenues	$160,000
Less: Cost of goods sold...........	80,000
Depreciation expense	3,750
Wages expense	20,000
Interest expense.............	3,600
Net income.....................	$ 52,650

THE ARCADIA COMPANY
Balance Sheet

Assets		Liabilities	
Cash...................	$212,400	Accounts payable........	$ 6,000
Inventory..............	70,000	Loan payable	120,000
Total current assets	282,400	Total liabilities	126,000
Building	150,000	**Shareholders' equity**	
Less Accum. deprec......	(3,750)	Capital stock	250,000
	146,250	Retained earnings	52,650
		Total	302,650
		Total liabilities &	
Total assets............	$428,650	**shareholders' equity**...	$428,650

THE ARCADIA COMPANY	
Statement of Cash Flow	
Operating Activities	
Cash sales	$ 160,000
Payments for inventory	(144,000)*
Cash wages	(20,000)
Interest payment	(3,600)
Cash flow from operations.	(7,600)
Investing Activities	
Purchase of building	(150,000)
Cash flow from investing	(150,000)
Financing Activities	
Sale of capital stock	250,000
Bank loan	120,000
Cash flow from financing	370,000
Cash, beginning	-0-
Cash, ending	212,400
Change in cash.	$212,400

*($120,000 + ($30,000 − $6,000)) = $144,000

Solution 2.3

ROS = 52,650/160,000 = 32.9%
ROA = (52,650 + 3,600*(1 − 0%))/428,650 = 13.1%
ROE = 52,650/302,650 = 17.4%
Long-Term Debt-to-Equity = 120,000/302,650 = 39.6%
Interest Coverage = 56,250/3,600 = 15.625

When you complete this chapter you should be able to:

1. Interpret a statement of cash flow to explain a company's operating, financing, and investing strategies. (page 86)

2. Prepare a statement of cash flow using the indirect method. (page 88)

3. Compute and apply ratios based on operating cash flows. (page 98)

4. Explain the difference between earnings, EBITDA, free cash flow, and discretionary cash flow. (page 99)

5. Interpret the components of net income to evaluate a company's sustainable earnings. (page 102)

6. Understand the steps needed to convert an indirect method statement of cash flow to the direct method. (page 111)

Measuring Performance: Cash Flow and Net Income

The Bristol-Myers Squibb Company was formed in 1989 with the merger of pharmaceutical companies Bristol-Myers Company and the Squibb Corporation. It is headquartered in New York City. The company has as its mission "to discover, develop and deliver innovative medicines that help patients prevail over serious diseases." To that end, the company manufactures prescription pharmaceuticals in several therapeutic areas, including cancer (YERVOY), cardiovascular disease (PLAVIX), hepatitis (BARACLUDE), and diabetes (ONGLYZA). The company has long been rumored to be an acquisition target for other large pharmaceutical companies, such as Novartis AG and Eli Lilly.

BRISTOL-MYERS SQUIBB COMPANY

In 2002, Bristol-Myers Squibb agreed to pay $150 million to the U.S. Department of Justice and the U.S. Securities and Exchange Commission in settlement of a lawsuit alleging improper recording of $2.5 billion in revenue between 1999 and 2001. According to the government allegation, the company engaged in "channel stuffing" in order to report higher product sales on its income statement, presumably to meet Wall Street earnings' expectations. Channel stuffing refers to the practice of shipping unordered goods to retailers, usually with a guarantee to allow the retailers to return any unsold merchandise. When products are physically small but very expensive, like pharmaceuticals, this practice can lead to recording a boost to profits earlier than would otherwise occur, because the retailer would seldom return the goods.

Bristol-Myers Squibb apparently felt it was more important to report strong results on its income statement than it was to follow the "rules of the game." For those reading the financial statements, however, there was one telltale sign that something was suspect with the company's reported results: While the company was reporting inflated earnings on the unordered product it shipped to its customers, its operating cash flow failed to keep pace with the increase in sales. The end-user pharmacies had yet to pay for the unordered goods. So where would this information appear in the company's financial statements?

In addition to the income statement that included the inflated sales, Bristol-Myers Squibb was also required to provide a statement of cash flow to its shareholders. This statement includes a reconciliation of a firm's reported net income and its corresponding cash flow from operations. In 2001, the year prior to the alleged channel stuffing, Bristol-Myers reported net earnings in excess of $2 billion and cash flow from operations in excess of $5 billion. The company had in prior years consistently reported cash flow from operations that equaled or exceeded its reported net income. This changed in 2002, however, when the company reported net income in excess of $2 billion, but cash flow from operations of less than $1 billion. This shift in trend led the astute users of Bristol-Myers financial reports to search for the cause.

In this chapter, we examine how firm performance is measured. Both the income statement and the statement of cash flow contain important indicators of a company's operating performance. Public companies like Bristol-Myers Squibb are required to include both financial statements in their filings with the U.S. Securities and Exchange Commission and in their annual report to shareholders. To be fully informed, financial statement users must understand the information that each statement conveys about a company's operating performance.

Takeaway 1
Interpret a statement of cash flow to explain a company's operating, financing, and investing strategies.

ANALYZING AND COMPUTING CASH FLOW INFORMATION

Recall from Chapter 2 that the accounting process can be thought of as beginning with one balance sheet and ending with another. The other financial statements, specifically the income statement, the statement of cash flow and the statement of shareholders' equity, are designed to summarize various aspects of a company's performance that occur *during* that period of time. In the minds of most investment professionals, lenders, and managers, the two most important measures of a firm's performance come directly from these two statements—operating cash flow and net income. In this chapter, we explore these two measures in greater detail, examining their similarities and differences, and how they are interrelated. We will see that the accrual accounting process imbeds estimates of future cash flow into current net income, and as a consequence, that current period net income is often a very good predictor of future operating cash flow.

We begin this chapter by considering the various ways that cash flow data can be presented. We then consider how cash flow information can be extracted from balance sheets and income statements. Finally, we consider the important concept of sustainable earnings and the various alternative measures of cash flow used by investment professionals.

Statement of Cash Flow

The purpose of the statement of cash flow is to provide a user of the financial statements with important information about how the company manages its cash. It does this by summarizing a firm's inflows and outflows of cash by segmenting into three activity categories:

- Cash flow from *operating* activities
- Cash flow from *investing* activities
- Cash flow from *financing* activities

These three categories represent the three key activities undertaken by all businesses—providing a good or service (operating activities), obtaining the assets necessary to provide a good or service (investing activities), and financing both the basic operations of a business and the investment in assets required to produce a product or provide a service (financing activities). Consider these three basic activities with a simple illustration of a pizza delivery business. Before the business can start delivering pizzas, it must first obtain the necessary funds to buy a delivery van. Taking out a loan at a bank to acquire the van would be an example of a financing activity. When the borrowed cash is used to buy the van, this would represent an investing activity. Having purchased the van, the business can then begin using it to make deliveries and collecting cash from customers, an operating activity. Of course most companies are not this simple, but no matter how complex a company becomes, anything that it does can be reflected in these three activities.

Analyzing and understanding the contents of the statement of cash flow provide financial statement users with critical insights about a company's operating, investing, and financing strategies. Exhibit 3.1, for example, provides an illustration of a typical statement of cash flow. This exhibit reveals that the

cash flow from operations represents the aggregate of the cash received from the sale of goods and services less the cash spent on operating expenses. The **cash flow from investing**, on the other hand, is the aggregate of the cash received from the sale of investments, property and equipment, and intangible assets less the cash spent to acquire these various types of assets. Finally, the **cash flow from financing** represents the aggregate of the cash received from the sale of debt and equity securities less the cash paid to retire debt, repurchase equity securities, or pay dividends to shareholders.

The statement of cash flow can be presented in two alternative formats—the direct and indirect method—to which we now turn.

EXHIBIT 3.1 An Illustrative Statement of Cash Flow

Operating Activities
Cash received from the sale of goods and services
− Cash spent on operating expenses
} Operating Strategy

Cash Flow from Operations (CFFO)

Investing Activities
Cash received from the sale of investments, property and equipment, or intangible assets
− Cash invested in investments, property and equipment, or intangible assets
} Investing Strategy

Cash Flow from Investing (CFFI)

Financing Activities
Cash received from the sale of debt or equity securities
− Cash paid to retire debt or equity securities and to pay dividends
} Financing Strategy

Cash Flow from Financing (CFFF)

Presenting Cash Flow Information

There are two formats available under GAAP to present the statement of cash flow—the direct method format and the indirect method format. Importantly, note that these approaches differ only in how the cash flow from operations detail is presented. The cash flow from investing and the cash flow from financing are identical under the two formats.

As we will see, the indirect format provides information critical to understanding why net income differs from cash actually received. Because this information is so critical, GAAP requires that firms choosing to use the direct method format also provide the indirect format as a supplemental disclosure. Therefore, the practical reality is that the vast majority of publicly held companies (about 99 percent) utilize solely the indirect method format. Because of this we will principally focus our discussion on this format. Appendix 3A at the end of this chapter illustrates how to construct a **direct method** statement of cash flow for those interested. You will see that under the direct method statement of cash flow, cash flow from operations is computed directly from the company's cash transactions, the critical difference between the two methods.

Under the **indirect method** a company computes its cash flow from operations by making various adjustments to convert its accrual-based net income to its cash flow from operations. While this at first may seem odd, the objective of this approach is to provide the user of the statement with critical information about why the firm's net income did or did not translate into cash generation. By starting with net income and ending with a cash flow figure, the detail in between is a valuable source of information for analysis. Exhibit 3.2 presents an indirect method statement of cash flow for Texas Instruments, Inc. (TI).

Exhibit 3.2 reveals that TI's cash flow from operations begins with the company's 2014 net income of $2,821 million, and then reports the various adjustments needed to convert its net income under the accrual basis of accounting to its cash flow from operations of $3,892 million. Thus, these accrual accounting adjustments illustrate how it is possible for a company like TI to report cash flows from operating activities over one-third larger than earnings. TI's statement of cash flow reveals that the largest positive adjustments to its net income from operations were depreciation expense ($805 million), amortization of intangible assets ($380 million), and stock based compensation ($277 million).

| EXHIBIT 3.2 | Illustration of the Indirect Method for Statement of Cash Flow | | | |

TEXAS INSTRUMENTS INC.
Consolidated Statement of Cash Flow

For Fiscal Years Ending December 31 [millions of dollars]	2014	2013	2012
Cash flow from operating activities			
Net income	$2,821	$2,162	$1,759
Adjustments to net income:			
Depreciation	850	879	957
Amortization of intangibles and software	380	418	444
Stock-based compensation	277	287	263
Gain on sales of assets	(73)	(6)	—
Deferred income taxes	(61)	50	130
Increase (decrease) from changes in:			
Accounts receivable	(49)	16	311
Inventories	(53)	26	5
Prepaid expenses and other current assets	65	(136)	162
Accounts payable and accrued expenses	(194)	(284)	99
Accrued compensation	89	18	(82)
Income taxes payable	(81)	78	(229)
Other	(79)	(124)	(405)
Net cash provided by operating activities	3,892	3,384	3,414
Cash flow from investing activities			
Capital expenditures	(385)	(412)	(495)
Proceeds from asset sales	142	21	—
Purchases of short-term investments	(3,107)	(3,907)	(2,802)
Proceeds from short-term investments	2,966	4,249	2,198
Other	7	46	60
Net cash used in investing activities	(377)	(3)	(1,039)
Cash flow from financing activities			
Proceeds from issuance of long-term debt	498	986	1,492
Repayment of debt and commercial paper borrowings	(1,000)	(1,500)	(1,375)
Dividends paid	(1,323)	(1,175)	(819)
Stock repurchases	(2,831)	(2,868)	(1,800)
Proceeds from common stock transactions	616	1,314	523
Excess tax benefit from share-based payments	100	80	38
Other	(3)	(7)	(10)
Net cash provided by (used in) financing activities	(3,943)	(3,170)	(1,951)
Net (decrease) increase in cash and cash equivalents	(428)	211	424
Cash and cash equivalents at beginning of year	1,627	1,416	992
Cash and cash equivalents at end of year	$1,199	$1,627	$1,416

TI's statement of cash flow also reveals the company's investing and financing strategies. In 2014, for example, the company used its available cash flow to acquire property, plant and equipment ($385 million), and a significant amount for purchases ($3,107) and sales ($2,966) of investments. The company used its excess cash flow from operations to significantly pay down its debt ($1,000 million) and pay dividends ($1,323 million). Interestingly the company was also an active buyer of its own stock in 2014, with stock repurchases totaling $2,831 million. Notice that the sum of TI's operating cash flow ($3,892 million) plus its financing cash flow (−$3,943 million) was insufficient to cover its net capital investment of $377 million in 2014, forcing the company to draw down on its existing cash balance by a net $428 million.

Computing Cash Flow Under the Indirect Method

Takeaway 2
Prepare a statement of cash flow using the indirect method.

The statement of cash flow is a required corporate disclosure for public companies in their annual (10-K) and quarterly (10-Q) reports to shareholders filed with the U.S. Securities and Exchange Commission. There are many instances, however, where an important skill for investors, investment professionals, and managers to have is the ability to estimate a company's cash flow using only those statements that are more routinely available, namely income statements and balance sheets. (This skill is also important in the construction of forecasted financial statements, which are discussed in Chapters 4 and 12.)

In this section, we illustrate how to prepare an indirect method statement of cash flow using only two balance sheets and an income statement. To begin, it is important to revisit exactly what we are attempting to accomplish with the statement of cash flow. This statement details a firm's cash flow activity during a given fiscal period. It reveals how and why the cash balance on the balance sheet increased or decreased from the beginning of the period to the end of the period (i.e., the change in cash). The principal events that cause a firm's cash balance to change are summarized. These include the sale of goods, the purchase of inventory, the payment of operating expenses, the payment of dividends, the purchase or sale of property and equipment, and the sale or repurchase of stock, among other things. Importantly, you should recognize that all of the financial events that result in a change in the cash account are reported in some form on the firm's income statement or balance sheet. And, as a consequence, a statement of cash flow can be prepared using only a company's income statement and the changes in its balance sheet accounts. This can be seen by reference to the balance sheet equation:

$$\textbf{Assets (A) = Liabilities (L) + Shareholders' Equity (SE)} \tag{1}$$

Separation and expansion of a firm's assets into its cash assets (Cash) and its noncash assets (NCA):

$$\textbf{Cash + NCA = L + SE} \tag{2}$$

Rewriting the balance sheet equation as the difference (Δ) between two balance sheets yields:

$$\Delta\textbf{Cash} + \Delta\textbf{NCA} = \Delta\textbf{L} + \Delta\textbf{SE} \tag{3}$$

Finally, rearranging the components of the balance sheet equation shows that the change in cash, the ultimate objective of the statement of cash flow, can be computed from the change in all of the other balance sheet accounts:

$$\Delta\textbf{Cash} = \Delta\textbf{L} - \Delta\textbf{NCA} + \Delta\textbf{SE} \tag{4}$$

The importance of equation (4) rests with appreciating that the statement of cash flow will, by definition, summarize the changes in all the balance sheet accounts other than cash. Unfortunately, however, it is not as simple as merely computing differences in each balance sheet account in the construction of the statement. We will apply this as a first step, but later see that some accounts require more detailed analysis to determine more specifically how a change in an account can influence the firm's operating, investing, or financing activities. Below we illustrate the full preparation of the statement of cash flow in five steps.

Five Steps to Cash Flow.

Since you are already familiar with the financial affairs of the Russian River Valley Winery from Chapter 2, we will use this data for purposes of illustrating an approach for generating cash flow data from balance sheets and income statements. The process involves five steps, resulting in the preparation of an indirect method statement of cash flow. Our goal is to summarize the observed balance sheet change in cash for the company, a $3,932 decrease, using the required format under the indirect method. The approach we will use to get there, however, begins by focusing initially only on the balance sheet, and then proceeds to integrate a business's income statement through a series of systematic adjustments to a preliminary statement of cash flow derived solely from balance sheet data. Exhibit 3.3 presents the beginning of year (column 1) and end of year (column 2) balance sheets for the Russian River Valley Winery.

Step One: Calculate the change in all balance sheet accounts

Using just the beginning and ending balance sheets (see Columns 1 and 2 in Exhibit 3.3), calculate the change in each balance sheet account by subtracting the beginning balance sheet amount from the ending amount. The results of this step for Russian River Valley are presented in Column 3 of Exhibit 3.3. To simplify this step, the change in the property, plant, and equipment accounts is calculated as an aggregate amount after deducting any accumulated depreciation (on a net-of-accumulated-depreciation basis).

To verify the accuracy of the Step One calculations, simply compare the sum of the changes in the asset accounts ($153) to the sum of the changes in the liability and shareholders' equity accounts ($153). These totals must be equal. If the totals are not equal, it indicates the presence of a subtraction error that must be identified and corrected before progressing to Step Two.

Again to reemphasize, an important figure identified during Step One is the final result of the statement of cash flow, namely the change in the cash account. The bolded area in Exhibit 3.3 reveals that the cash account of the Russian River Valley Winery declined by $3,932 from the beginning of the year to the end of the year. Hence, all of the various cash inflows and outflows for the winery must aggregate to this figure.

EXHIBIT 3.3	Preparing a Statement of Cash Flow: The Indirect Method

RUSSIAN RIVER VALLEY WINERY, INC.
Balance Sheet

($ thousands)	(1) Beginning of Year 1	(2) End of Year 1	(3) Change For Year	(4) Cash Flow Classification
Current assets				
Cash....................................	$ 4,700	$ 768	$(3,932)	Net cash flow
Accounts receivable......................	0	800	800	Operating
Inventory...............................	0	60	60	Operating
Total current assets	4,700	1,628		
Noncurrent assets				
Equipment	0	3,500		
Buildings...............................	2,000	2,000		
Land...................................	4,000	4,000		
	6,000	9,500		
Accumulated depreciation................	0	(225)		
Property, plant & equipment, net...........	6,000	9,275	3,275	Investing/Operating
Intangible assets, net....................	100	50	(50)	Investing/Operating
Total assets...........................	$10,800	$10,953	$ 153	
Current liabilities				
Accounts payable........................	$ 0	$ 80	$ 80	Operating
Taxes payable..........................	0	96	96	Operating
Notes payable, current...................	0	480	480	Financing
Total current liabilities...................	0	656		
Notes payable, noncurrent...............	4,800	3,840	(960)	Financing
Shareholders' equity				
Common stock, $1 par..................	6,000	6,400	400	Financing
Retained earnings	0	57	57	Financing/Operating
Shareholders' equity	6,000	6,457		
Liabilities & shareholders' equity	$10,800	$10,953	$ 153	

Step Two: Classify each account into one of the three cash flow categories

This step involves identifying the appropriate cash-flow activity category—operating, investing, or financing—for each balance sheet account, and this is illustrated in Column 4 of Exhibit 3.3. Although measuring the change in the balance sheet accounts in Step One is straightforward, there can sometimes be confusion over the correct activity classification for some of the balance sheet accounts in Step Two. Learning the proper classifications often comes with some thought and practice. Accounts receivable, inventory, accounts payable and taxes payable are all easily identified as operating activity items because they are associated with the day-to-day operations of a business. Changes in the notes payable (current and noncurrent) and common stock accounts, on the other hand, are financing activity items because they are associated with raising capital to finance a business. Changes in net property, plant and equipment (PPE), however, can be both an investing activity item and an operating activity item.

In Practice 3.1 *Balance Sheet Caption: A Glimpse of a Sample of Fortune 1000 Companies* The following table identifies the caption used by a sample of 600 Fortune 1000 companies on their balance sheets to describe the cash account. The overwhelming majority of firms utilize the caption "cash and cash equivalents."

Balance Sheet Captions	Number	Percentage
Cash............................	22	3.7
Cash and cash equivalents	528	88.0
Cash and equivalents...............	34	5.6
Cash combined with marketable securities......................	13	2.2
Other...........................	3	0.5
Total	600	100.0

Source: Accounting Trends & Techniques

Purchases and sales of PPE are associated with the capital investment needed to run a business, and thus, are an investing activity item; but, the change in PPE associated with depreciation expense is related to operations since the depreciation of PPE is deducted as an operating expense in the calculation of accrual net income. Similarly, changes in intangible assets can be both an investing activity item and an operating activity item because the acquisition or sale of intangibles is an investment in the business, whereas the amortization of intangibles is an operating expense deducted in the calculation of accrual net income, and hence, an operating activity item. Finally, changes in retained earnings can be both an operating activity item and a financing activity item because retained earnings is increased by net income, an operating activity item, but decreased by the payment of dividends, a transaction with shareholders that is classifiable as a financing activity item.

As a general rule, the following cash flow activity classifications apply, although exceptions will exist:

Balance Sheet Account	Cash Flow Activity Category
Current assets	Operating
Noncurrent assets	Investing/Operating
Current liabilities.	Operating
Noncurrent liabilities.	Financing
Capital stock	Financing
Retained earnings	Operating/Financing

Examples of exceptions to the above general activity classifications include the following:

- Marketable securities, a current asset, are an investing activity item.

- Current maturities of long-term debt, a current liability, are a financing activity item.

- Employee pension obligations, a noncurrent liability, are an operating activity item.

In sum, the classification of the change in each balance sheet into operating, investing, or financing activities is necessary to provide detail to the user of the statement of cash flow regarding why cash has changed along these three broad dimensions. Try not to memorize these classifications, but rather recognize that each resulting classification is due to the underlying reason as to why the account likely changed. Accounts receivable, for instance, relates to the sale on credit to customers and the payments on those accounts by customers. Both of these are operating activities, and thus the entire change in the accounts receivable account is classifiable as operating. This logic can be applied to almost all current assets and current liability accounts. But for other accounts it is not so simple. Because some accounts have changes that relate to multiple activities, we are forced to split the change (e.g., retained earnings into both operations and financing).

Step Three: Prepare a preliminary statement of cash flow

Having completed Steps One and Two, you are now ready to build a preliminary statement of cash flow using the calculated increases or decreases in the various balance sheet accounts from Step One and the identified activity classifications from Step Two. The preliminary statement of cash flow for the Russian River Valley Winery, using the values from Column 3 of Exhibit 3.3 and the cash flow activity categories from Column 4, is presented in Exhibit 3.4.

Since a statement of cash flow measures the inflows and outflows of cash for a business, it is important to note that the sign of the asset account changes (but not the liabilities or shareholders' equity accounts) calculated in Step One must be reversed for purposes of preparing the preliminary statement of cash flow in Exhibit 3.4. This can be seen in equation (4) on page 89 in which the change in noncash assets has a negative sign. For instance, Exhibit 3.3 shows that the change in accounts receivable was an increase of $800, whereas the change in intangible assets was a decrease of $50. When preparing the indirect method cash flow statement, an $800 increase in accounts receivables represents a subtraction from net income (a cash outflow), and a decline in intangible assets of $50 represents an addition to net income (a cash inflow), to arrive at the cash flow from operations. To understand why an increase in accounts receivable must be subtracted from net income to arrive at operating cash flow, you first must recognize that net income is included in its entirety (i.e., $57 of retained earnings), but net income doesn't all represent the actual cash received by the company. Assume that a $2,000 sale is paid for by the customer with $1,200 in cash and the remaining $800 recorded as an increase in accounts receivable. In this example, net income would have increased by $2,000 but cash by only $1,200. Therefore, net income, relative to cash, was overstated—we must therefore reduce net income by the $800 increase in accounts receivable to yield the correct cash flow from operations. Similar logic explains why it is necessary to add back the decrease in intangible assets to net income to arrive at the correct cash flow from operations. Intangible assets were reduced by amortizing the cost of the asset by $50. This $50 expense reduced net income; however, no cash outflow was involved. Therefore, it is necessary to add $50 back to net income to yield the correct change in cash. Hence, when preparing the *preliminary* statement of cash flow in Step Three, it is important to remember to reverse the sign of the change values for the asset accounts. This reversal in sign is unnecessary for the liability and shareholders' equity accounts as can be seen from equation (4) on page 89.

EXHIBIT 3.4	An Illustration of a Preliminary Statement of Cash Flow: Balance Sheet Account Changes

RUSSIAN RIVER VALLEY WINERY, INC.
Preliminary Statement of Cash Flow

($ thousands)	Year 1
Operating activities	
Retained earnings	$ 57
Accounts receivable	(800)
Inventory	(60)
Accounts payable	80
Taxes payable	96
Preliminary CFFO	(627)
Investing activities	
Property, plant & equipment (net)	(3,275)
Intangible assets (net)	50
Preliminary CFFI	(3,225)
Financing activities	
Notes payable, current	480
Notes payable, noncurrent	(960)
Common stock	400
Preliminary CFFF	(80)
Change in cash (from balance sheet)	$(3,932)

Exhibit 3.4 presents the preliminary statement of cash flow for the Russian River Valley Winery. This preliminary statement suggests that the firm's cash flow from operating activities (CFFO) for the period was negative $627, the cash flow from investing activities (CFFI) was negative $3,225, and the cash flow from financing activities (CFFF) negative $80. As required, the cash inflows and outflows aggregate to the change in the cash account from the balance sheet of a decrease of $3,932. Worth noting, these subtotals for CFFO, CFFI, and CFFF are not final and will be changed as we include the income statement data in Steps Four and Five.

Step Four: Integrate the income statement data

To this point we have used the balance sheet exclusively to provide the needed inputs to our statement of cash flow. For most companies, however, cash flow will be generated by the firm's ongoing operations and not just by various events affecting the balance sheet accounts. Hence, it is now appropriate to introduce the operations-related data found on the winery's income statement. Exhibit 3.5 summarizes that income statement.

In Step Four, we will accomplish two important actions involving our preliminary statement of cash flow in Exhibit 3.4. First, we will replace the change in retained earnings from the balance sheet with net income from the income statement. In the event that the change in retained earnings does not equal net income, usually this difference represents cash dividends paid to shareholders. For the Russian River Valley Winery, net income is $317 and the change in retained earnings is $57. Thus, it is necessary to gross up the change in retained earnings by $260 to equal the current net income ($57 + $260 = $317) under the operating activities section; and, to keep the statement of cash flow in balance with the decrease in cash of $3,932, insert the cash outflow for dividends ($260) under the financing activities section.

| EXHIBIT 3.5 | Income Statement |

RUSSIAN RIVER VALLEY WINERY, INC.
Income Statement

($ thousands)	Year 1
Revenue	$1,900
Cost of goods sold	380
Gross profit	1,520
Operating expenses	
Wages & salaries	100
Selling, general & administrative	300
Depreciation	225
Amortization	50
Total operating expenses	675
Operating income	845
Interest expense	288
Income before income taxes	557
Income tax expense	240
Net income	$ 317

Second, we will adjust Russian River Valley's net income for any **noncash expenses** such as the depreciation of plant and equipment and the amortization of intangibles that were deducted in the process of calculating the firm's accrual net income. These noncash expenses must be added back to net income in the operating activities section to correctly measure the firm's operating cash flow. Without such adjustments we would be understating actual operating cash flow. However, to keep the preliminary statement of cash flow in balance with the check figure of a decrease in cash of $3,932, it is also necessary to subtract equivalent amounts in the investing activities section, where the changes in PPE and intangibles currently reside.

Depreciation expense and amortization expense are called **noncash expenses** because these expenses do not involve any current period cash outflow. Depreciation expense, for example, represents the allocation of the purchase price of plant and equipment over the many periods that these assets produce revenues for a business. The matching concept requires that the cost of plant and equipment be matched with the revenues produced by these assets, and this is accomplished on the income statement by the inclusion of the periodic depreciation expense.

To summarize, the adjustments to the Russian River Valley Winery preliminary statement of cash flow in Exhibit 3.4 are as follows:

1. Net income of $317 replaces the change in retained earnings of $57 in the operating activities section. This action added $260 to the CFFO. To keep the statement of cash flow in balance with the check figure of negative $3,932 (the decrease in cash), it is necessary to subtract $260 elsewhere on the statement. Since retained earnings is calculated as follows:

Retained earnings (beginning)	$ 0
+ Net income for the period	317
− Dividends paid	(260)
Retained earnings (ending)	$ 57

the outflow of $260 is reflected as a cash dividend paid to shareholders under the financing activities section.

2. Depreciation expense of $225, a noncash deduction from net income, is added back to net income to avoid understating the cash flow from operations. However, to keep the statement of cash flow in balance with the change in cash of negative $3,932, a similar amount must be subtracted from property and equipment under the investing activities section. Note that this has the effect of properly treating the remaining change ($3,500) as the purchase of property and equipment.

In Practice 3.2 *Method of Reporting the Cash Flow from Operations: A Glimpse of a Sample of Fortune 1000 Companies* The following table identifies the method of reporting the cash flow from operations as used by a sample of 600 Fortune 1000 companies. Over 98 percent of all companies surveyed used the indirect method:

Method of Reporting	Number	Percentage
Indirect method	592	98.7
Direct method	8	1.3
Total	600	100.0

Source: Accounting Trends & Techniques

3. Amortization expense of $50, another noncash deduction from net income, is added back to net income to avoid understating the cash flow from operations. To ensure that the statement is in balance with the check figure of negative $3,932, an equivalent amount is subtracted from intangible assets under the investing activities section.

The results of these adjustments are displayed in Exhibit 3.6, which presents the final statement of cash flow for the Russian River Valley Winery. Note that the winery's statement of cash flow remains in balance with the change in the cash account of negative $3,932 after the three adjustments. This result is possible because whatever amount was added to (or subtracted from) net income under the CFFO, an equal amount was subtracted from (or added to) CFFI or CFFF.

EXHIBIT 3.6	Statement of Cash Flow: Indirect Method

RUSSIAN RIVER VALLEY WINERY, INC. **Statement of Cash Flow**	
($ thousands)	**Year 1**
Operating activities	
Net income.	$ 317
Depreciation.	225
Amortization.	50
(Increase) decrease in accounts receivable	(800)
(Increase) decrease in inventory.	(60)
Increase (decrease) in accounts payable.	80
Increase (decrease) in taxes payable	96
Cash flow from operations	(92)
Investing activities	
Purchase of property, plant & equipment.	(3,500)
Cash flow from investing.	(3,500)
Financing activities	
Sale of common stock	400
Payment of notes payable (current)	(480)
Payment of cash dividends	(260)
Cash flow from financing.	(340)
Change in cash (on balance sheet).	(3,932)
Beginning cash.	4,700
Ending cash	$ 768

Step Five: Remove nonrecurring and/or nonoperating effects from net income

To provide the most useful cash flow data, a final step is required: make any appropriate adjustments to CFFO to calculate the recurring or sustainable CFFO. As noted above, the CFFO subtotal should include only the cash flow from operating activities. Recall also that the operating activities section of the indirect format of the statement of cash flow is a reconciliation of net income to CFFO. That is, the format requires the section begins with net income and ends with CFFO. Consequently, to calculate the CFFO of a company, it is necessary to review the income statement to identify and remove the financial effects of any nonoperating and/or nonrecurring transactions.[1]

To illustrate this point, assume that the Russian River Valley Winery sold property and equipment during the year at a loss of $25 and that the loss was included in its net income. This event is an investing

---

[1] An exception to this general rule is the treatment of interest expense, which many investment professionals view as a financing activity item. Interest payments are required to be included in CFFO (under U.S. GAAP). Another example of a noncash/nonoperating item that will need to be removed from net income when calculating the CFFO is any "income (loss) from equity investments." We will have more to say about this adjustment and the accounting for equity investments in Chapter 8.

activity and therefore properly belongs under CFFI. To correctly calculate the winery's CFFO, it is necessary to remove this loss from net income in the operating activity section and adjust the property and equipment under the investing activities section. These actions allow us to correctly measure the company's CFFO, as well as to correctly assess its cash flow for purchases of property and equipment. We will have more to say about this type of operating cash flow adjustment in subsequent chapters.

Exhibit 3.6 presents the final indirect method statement of cash flow for Russian River Valley and includes not only the adjustments from Step Four, but also, if needed, any adjustments to remove any nonoperating or nonrecurring gains and losses from the CFFO (Step Five). Russian River Valley's cash flow statement in Exhibit 3.6 using the indirect method reveals that the cash flow from operating activities is negative $92, the cash flow from investing activities is negative $3,500, and the cash flow from financing activities is negative $340. The resulting net cash flow of negative $3,932 exactly equals the decrease in cash on the balance sheet of $3,932, as required.

The following illustration summarizes the five-step process to preparing an indirect method statement of cash flow:

REVIEW PROBLEM 3.1

The following balance sheet and income statement data were taken from the financial records of The Arcadia Company.

THE ARCADIA COMPANY Balance Sheets						
	2015	**2014**			**2015**	**2014**
Assets			**Liabilities & Shareholders' Equity**			
Cash....................	$ 30,000	$ 7,000	Accounts payable.........		$ 63,000	$ 65,500
Marketable securities......	60,000	67,500	Wages payable...........		47,500	37,000
Inventory................	22,500	49,000	Total current liabilities......		110,500	102,500
Prepaid insurance.........	4,500	6,000	Bank loan payable		85,000	83,000
Total current assets	117,000	129,500	Capital stock		75,000	75,000
Building (net).............	190,000	187,500	Retained earnings		36,500	56,500
Totals	$307,000	$317,000	Totals		$307,000	$317,000

THE ARCADIA COMPANY Income Statement For Year Ended December 31, 2015	
Revenues	$ 480,000
Less	
Cost of goods sold	320,000
Depreciation expense	28,500
Wage expense.....................................	93,000
Insurance expense.................................	46,000
Interest expense	10,500
Net loss	$ (18,000)

Required

Prepare an indirect method statement of cash flow for The Arcadia Company for 2015.

The solution is on page 127.

ANALYSIS OF THE STATEMENT OF CASH FLOW

Like the income statement, the statement of cash flow portrays another aspect of a company's performance over a period of time. The major difference between these two financial statements concerns how "performance" is defined. The income statement defines performance in terms of a company's accrual net income, where earned revenues are matched against the expenses associated with generating that revenue whether or not associated with cash. The statement of cash flow, by contrast, defines performance in terms of a company's actual operating cash flow, with the statement showing sources and uses of cash. Rather than debating which statement is more important, it is better to understand what each statement tells us and how they complement each other.

As mentioned earlier in the chapter, the statement of cash flow can be prepared in two alternate formats, the indirect method as shown in Exhibit 3.6, and the direct method, as previously shown in Chapter 2 (Exhibit 2.5). Notice that each format provides identical totals for each of the three sections of the statement. The only difference between the two formats is in the presentation of the cash flow data in the operating activities section. As can be seen in Exhibit 2.5, the direct method format is prepared directly from the cash account and simply displays the sources and uses of operating cash flows. The indirect method, by contrast, comes to the same total operating cash flow in an indirect approach by starting with net income and then adjusting net income for the various noncash effects included in the measurement of net income under the accrual method. Net income, as we have seen, is computed by matching the earned revenues of a business, whether received in cash or not, with the related business expenses, regardless of whether those expenses have been paid in cash or not. Quite often, the revenues and expenses are recognized on a company's income statement in a different period than the corresponding cash inflow or outflow associated with those revenues and expenses. Consequently, it is necessary to adjust net income for these timing differences when calculating a company's operating cash flow using the indirect approach. For this reason the operating activities section of the statement of cash flow is often referred to as a "reconciliation between net income and changes in cash."

By partitioning a company's cash flow into the three categories of operating, investing, and financing activities, the statement of cash flow tells the reader much more than just how much its cash balance increased or decreased during the period; it also provides an explanation as to *why*. For instance, the statement of cash flow enables a financial statement user to understand whether a company's cash balance increased because the cash was earned from operations or because of an increase in bank borrowings. Similarly, statement users need to understand whether cash declined as a consequence of capital investments in new productive capacity or because the business is losing money from its operations. A review of each line in the statement of cash flow facilitates this type of understanding.

Most statement users agree that the more important component of the statement of cash flow is the cash flow from operating activities. This figure reflects the lifeblood of a company and is the principal source of financing for long-term survival. Regardless of the industry or life-stage of a business, it is always better for a company to generate a positive cash flow from operations. It should be noted, though, that many early-stage companies will show negative operating cash flow as a result of such normal business activities as building up inventory to service a growing customer base, or from significant research and development as it internally builds its product base.

While it is unambiguous that a company's cash flow from operating activities is better to be positive, the same cannot be said of the other two activity categories, investing and financing. A negative balance in the cash flow from investing activities, for example, will result when a firm spends more cash to purchase new equipment than it receives from the sale of old equipment. For many growth-oriented companies, a negative cash flow from investing activities is the norm, since investing in new productive capacity will ultimately result in future positive operating cash inflows. Most financial statement users expect to see a negative cash flow from investing activities since it indicates that a firm is maintaining itself as a going concern. In fact, a positive cash flow from investing activities may in some instances be a sign of concern since it may indicate that a business is liquidating its long-term, revenue-producing assets like plant and equipment.

Similar to the cash flows from investing activities, one cannot unambiguously say whether a positive or negative balance in financing activities is good or bad. A negative cash flow from financing activities will result when a company repays its loans and pays dividends to its shareholders, two activities that are usually considered positive by shareholders. A positive balance, on the other hand, could result from new business financing, perhaps from additional loans or the sale of capital stock. These activities may be necessary to finance new business growth, especially if a company's cash flow from operating activities is insufficient to finance this growth, which is often the case for early-stage companies.

As this discussion implies, the statement of cash flow provides a great deal of important information, but it also requires the user to have a solid understanding of what the statement is reporting. At the simplest level, the statement of cash flow merely tells the reader how much the company's cash balance changed during the period, reconciling the beginning and ending cash balances appearing on a company's balance sheet. At a more sophisticated level, the statement reveals just where a business's cash came from and how it was used. Such information is critical to those desiring to understand in greater detail how the company is being managed, and further, whether there are liquidity and solvency risks that might be of concern.

Exhibit 3.7 provides a summary of the typical sources and uses of cash in each of the three cash flow categories as a business progresses through its life cycle from a young start-up, through maturity, and later decline. As noted above, it is always the case that the cash flow from operating activities should be positive; however, for start-up companies, this is rarely the case. Likewise for start-up businesses, the cash flow from investing activities is often negative as the firm uses its available cash to invest in its future. As a firm matures, this category of cash flow tends to even out, as the firm's investing activities are generally for replacement of assets rather than growth. In the later, declining stage of a firm, the cash flow from investing may be positive as the firm sells off its assets as it exits certain markets. Finally, the cash flow from financing activities is likely to be positive for young companies as they require external financing to fund their growth. As the firm matures, its cash flow from financing tends to stabilize as the firm repays debt and begins paying dividends. Finally, in the declining stage, a firm is less likely to secure external financing and more likely to repay obligations or liquidate capital to retain its equity investors, leading to a negative cash flow from financing activities.

EXHIBIT 3.7	Cash Flow and a Company's Life Cycle		
Activity Section of the Statement of Cash Flow	**Life Cycle of the Firm**		
	Young/Start-Up	**Mature**	**Declining**
Operating	Likely negative	Likely positive	Uncertain
Investing.	Likely negative	Uncertain, but likely negative	Likely positive
Financing	Likely positive	Uncertain, but likely negative	Likely negative

The opening vignette to this chapter observed that an analysis of the statement of cash flow could have alerted a financial statement user about the problems at Bristol-Myers Squibb. The practice of "channel stuffing," in which large amounts of unordered goods are sent to retailers, is illustrated in the spreadsheet below. Assume for this illustration a company begins period 1 with a simple balance sheet consisting of only $1,000 of cash and $800 of inventory. Towards the end of period 1 the company liquidates its inventory and ships unordered products to a retailer, with an assumed selling price of $1,500, with later payment by the retailer expected in period 2. The gross profit on this sale is $700 ($1,500 less $800).

	Financial Statement Effects Channel Stuffing						
	Beg. Bal.	**(1)**	**(2)**	**Period 1**	**(3)**	**Period 2**
Cash.	1,000			1,000	1,500	2,500
Account receivable.		1,500		1,500	(1,500)	—
Inventory.	800		(800)	—		—
Total assets.	1,800			2,500		2,500
Total liabilities	—			—		—
Common stock.	1,800			1,800		1,800
Retained earnings				700		700
Sales		1,500				
Cost of goods sold			(800)			
Total shareholders' equity.	1,800			2,500		2,500

(1) Record sales of product sent to retailer in period 1
(2) Remove inventory value of product sent to retailer in period 1
(3) Customer pays receivable during period 2

When a company "stuffs its sales channel," it recognizes revenue for the shipped-but-unordered inventory, which in turn leads to an increase in net earnings; however, as can be seen in the spreadsheet, this also leads to an increase in accounts receivable during period 1 but not an increase in cash, unless and until the sales channel is able to absorb the additional product, sell the product to the end user, and make payment (period 2). These financial effects would be revealed in the operating activities section of the statement of cash flow *during period 1* as an unusual spike in earnings without the receipt of cash. Thus, the statement of cash flow helps highlight unusual shifts in balance sheet accounts that yield net income and cash flow differences.

Cash Flow Ratios

Takeaway 3
Compute and apply ratios based on operating cash flows.

Investment professionals frequently use components of the statement of cash flow to compute financial ratios that help highlight certain aspects of a firm's operating performance that might otherwise be obscured from financial statement users. For example, the **operating funds ratio** indicates the portion of a company's earnings supported by operating cash flow and is calculated as follows:

$$\text{Operating funds ratio} = \frac{\text{Cash flow from operations}}{\text{Net income}}$$

This ratio frequently approximates one for most firms, although during a period of business expansion (contraction), the ratio may decrease (increase) to less (more) than one. The operating funds ratio is not meaningful for the Russian River Valley Winery since cash flow from operations is negative; however, for Texas Instruments, the ratio is 1.38 (see Exhibit 3.2), indicating that Texas Instruments' operating cash flows are much greater than its net income.

Another cash-flow-based ratio is the **operating cash flow to current liabilities ratio**, which is calculated as follows:

$$\text{Operating cash flow to current liabilities ratio} = \frac{\text{Cash flow from operations}}{\text{Current liabilities}}$$

This ratio provides insights about a firm's liquidity, specifically the extent to which a company's current obligations can be satisfied by operating cash flow. This ratio highlights the fact that business liquidity is available not only from a firm's existing liquid assets and its ability to borrow or refinance, but also from its ongoing operations.

A final important cash-flow-based ratio is the **cash conversion ratio**, calculated as follows:

$$\text{Cash conversion ratio} = \frac{\text{Cash from sales}}{\text{Net sales}}$$

This ratio reveals the extent to which the sales reported on the income statement are converted into cash during the same accounting period.

> **Cash from sales** is calculated as net sales minus the increase in accounts receivable plus the increase in unearned (or deferred) revenue.

Like the operating funds ratio, this ratio typically approximates one, although smaller (or larger) ratio values are possible depending upon the growth (or decline) in a firm's accounts receivable and its deferred or unearned revenue. The cash conversion ratio for the Russian River Valley Winery is 0.58, indicating that the winery is projected to collect only $0.58 for each dollar of reported revenue during its first year of operations. (Can you verify the calculation of this ratio? Hint: Read Appendix 3A at the end of this chapter.)

Alternative Measures of Cash Flow

Although the statement of cash flow highlights the three cash flow measures of CFFO, CFFI, and CFFF, investment professionals often use other cash flow measures depending upon the purpose of their analysis. Three widely used alternatives are EBITDA, free cash flow, and discretionary cash flow.

EBITDA, or earnings before interest, taxes, depreciation and amortization, is often used as an alternative estimate of a firm's operating cash flow in those industries commonly identifiable as **capital intensive**—that is, in those industries characterized by large capital investments in property, plant and equipment and/or intangible assets. The financial statements of such firms typically include large non-cash expenses for amortization and depreciation. As a consequence, the net income of companies in these industries may be substantially burdened by these charges, particularly as compared to companies in non-capital-intensive industries. EBITDA is thought to provide an easily calculated alternative to operating cash flow as both measures begin with net income and both measures adjust for the noncash operating expenses of depreciation and amortization.

To make more effective performance comparisons between companies from different industries,

> **Takeaway 4**
> Explain the difference between earnings, EBITDA, free cash flow, and discretionary cash flow.

> **In Practice 3.3** *Average Dollar Amount of the Adjustments to Net Income when Computing the Cash Flow from Operations Using the Indirect Method Format.* The largest adjustment to net income is the depreciation and amortization expense, which averaged 83 percent of net income.
>
> | Operating activities (in millions) | |
> | --- | --- |
> | Net income . . . . | $171.9 |
> | Depreciation and amortization . . . . | 142.7 |
> | Gain on sale of assets . . . . | (12.8) |
> | Earnings from subsidiaries. . . . . . . | (2.3) |
> | Funds from operations—other . . . . | 59.8 |
> | Increase in accounts receivable. . . | (28.8) |
> | Increase in inventory . . . . | (56.8) |
> | Increase in accounts payable. . . . . | 18.4 |
> | Increase in taxes payable. . . . . | 2.2 |
> | Sources of funds—other . . . . | 16.9 |
> | Cash flow from operations . . . . | $311.2 |
>
> Source: Standard & Poor's Compustat, based on 6,316 firms reporting cash flow from operations.

and even within the same industry, some analysts rely on such metrics as EBITDA to level "the performance playing field." Because the metrics are not required GAAP disclosures, variants on EBITDA also exist and some are reported directly by management. For example, to help financial statement users better understand performance measures critical to the company, O'Reilly Automotive, Inc., an automotive parts retailer, reports a metric called "EBITDAR." For O'Reilly, EBITDAR represents an important alternative to net income that is used in debt contracting and is itself a modified version of EBITDA. Below is the excerpt of the calculation taken directly from O'Reilly's 2014 10-K filed with the SEC (in thousands):

	For the Year Ended December 31,	
	2014	**2013**
GAAP net income...	$ 778,182	$ 670,292
Add: Interest expense	53,290	49,074
Rent expense...	263,028	254,892
Provision for income taxes.................................	444,000	388,650
Depreciation expense.....................................	193,418	183,220
Amortization expense (benefit).............................	787	(40)
Non-cash share-based compensation.........................	23,095	21,722
Non-GAAP EBITDAR	$1,755,800	$1,567,810

You will note that the calculation starts with GAAP net income, and then a series of adjustments are made for expense related items. Conventional EBITDA would adjust for only interest, depreciation, taxes, and amortization. In the EBITDAR calculation, two additional expense items are used as adjustments: rent expense and non-cash share-based compensation. The bottom line—$1,755.8 million in EBITDAR arguably is a performance measure more closely aligned with the ability of O'Reilly to meet funding obligations from ongoing operations.

Another cash flow measure, **free cash flow** (FCF), is often used by analysts to evaluate a company's cash-flow strength. For instance, Acxiom Corporation, a company that integrates data, services and technology, reported that it generated free cash flow of $190.9 million in fiscal 2009, compared to operating cash flow of $268.8 million. The company noted that:

> . . . free cash flow provides investors with a useful alternative measure of operating performance by allowing an assessment of the amount of cash available for general corporate and strategic purposes after funding operating activities and capital expenditures, capitalized software expenses and deferred costs.

Stated differently, FCF is the amount of cash that could be "freely" distributed to the owners of the company, or used for general corporate purposes, without affecting the ongoing operations and required investments. FCF is an important performance reference point for many investment professionals because it is less subject to the accounting discretion and judgment that often characterizes accrual net income. Free cash flow is estimated as follows:

$$FCF = CFFO - CapEx$$

where CapEx is **capital expenditures**, the required reinvestment in the assets of a business necessary to enable the firm to maintain itself as a going concern.[2] It should be clear that a firm with strong free cash

[2] A company's CapEx is frequently segmented into maintenance CapEx and incremental CapEx. Maintenance CapEx is the amount of capital investment required to leave a going concern as well off at the end of a fiscal period as it was at the start of the fiscal period. Maintenance CapEx is frequently estimated by the amount of depreciation expense taken in a given period. Incremental CapEx, on the other hand, is any capital investment in excess of maintenance CapEx and is usually associated with an expansion in the productive capacity of a business.

flow will carry a higher firm value than one with weak (or no) free cash flow. Some investment professionals incorporate the construct of free cash flow into a ratio called the free cash flow yield to facilitate interfirm comparisons of cash flow strength. A firm's **free cash flow yield** is defined as its free cash flow divided by its market capitalization (market price per share times the number of shares outstanding). Companies with high free cash flow yields are frequently seen as attractive additions to a portfolio of investment securities. We will have more to say about FCF in Chapter 12.

While FCF addresses the issue of, "How much cash is available for general corporate use or distribution?" the concept of **discretionary cash flow** addresses the question, "How much internally-generated operating cash flow is available to permit a company's management to undertake a discretionary, value-creating action?" A business's discretionary cash flow (DisCF) is estimated as follows:

$$\text{DisCF} = \text{CFFO} - \text{Required debt payments} - \text{Dividend payments}$$

This expression reveals that DisCF is a company's internally-generated operating cash flow less any required payments to debtholders and any expected dividend payments to shareholders. Thus, DisCF is a measure of the excess internally-generated operating cash flow available to a business enterprise to undertake a discretionary project, for example investing in a new plant or acquiring a company. When DisCF is large, it indicates that a firm's internally-generated cash flow is strong relative to existing claims on those flows. When DisCF is small, it indicates that a firm will need additional external funding to facilitate a plant expansion, merger or acquisition, or debt retirement. Some analysts look to a business's discretionary cash flow as another indication of a business's cash flow health.

> **Market capitalization** refers to a firm's current fair market value, calculated as its market price per share times the number of shares outstanding. Market capitalization reflects the capital market's outlook regarding the company's future operating performance and differs from book value (i.e., the value of its shareholders' equity), which is based on past performance and accounting measurement rules.

GLOBAL PERSPECTIVE

Like U.S. GAAP, International Financial Reporting Standards (IFRS) require companies to report a statement of cash flow as one of the primary financial statements. The basic structure and objective of the statement is the same across the two reporting regimes, but a number of key differences do exist. First, IFRS allows companies to use either the direct or the indirect method of presentation. While this is true in the U.S. as well, GAAP requires firms using the direct method to also disclose as a supplement the indirect reconciliation of net income to cash from operations. No such requirement exists internationally. With respect to the format of the statement, under U.S. GAAP the statement of cash flow has three major activity categories—operating, investing, and financing—that reflect the three key activities that characterize all business enterprises. Under current IFRS, however, the cash flow statement is segmented into five activity categories: operating, investing, transactions relating to equity, financing, and the effect of exchange rate changes. While on the surface it may appear that the cash flow statement under IFRS, with its greater number of activities, is more encompassing than under U.S. GAAP, in reality the statements contain the same basic information since both must reconcile to the change in the cash account on the balance sheet.

Within these categories there are some classification differences as well. For instance, under GAAP interest paid and dividends received are treated as operating activities, while under IFRS the preparer has the choice of including these as either operating or financing. Taxes paid must be clearly delineated under IFRS (in the operating section), and is not so required in the U.S. The fifth IFRS section, the effect of exchange rate changes, is typically subsumed in the operating and investing activities under U.S. GAAP. Finally, even the definition of "cash" contains a subtle difference: IFRS requires bank overdrafts be treated as offsets to the cash balance and are thus treated as if they are simply negative cash, while under GAAP these are treated as loans in the financing section.

REVIEW PROBLEM 3.2

The following data was obtained from the year-end financial statements of The Monrovia Company:

Cash flow from operations.	$ 46,500
Net sales.	480,000
Net income.	32,500
Current liabilities.	110,500
Total liabilities.	195,500
Total assets.	307,000
Cash from sales	432,000
Capital expenditures	31,000
Dividend payments.	2,000
Debt payments.	2,000

Required

a. Compute the following cash flow ratios for The Monrovia Company: (1) Operating funds ratio, (2) Operating cash flow to current liabilities ratio, and (3) Cash conversion ratio.

b. Compute the following alternative measures of cash flow for The Monrovia Company; (1) Free cash flow, and (2) Discretionary cash flow.

The solution is on page 127.

IDENTIFYING AND UNDERSTANDING SUSTAINABLE EARNINGS

Takeaway 5
Interpret the components of net income to evaluate a company's sustainable earnings.

Net income, or earnings, is the "bottom line" measure of firm performance. It is a measure that depends on the accrual accounting framework under the revenue recognition and expense matching policies selected by a firm's management. Generally, users of financial accounting information have historically emphasized the importance of accounting earnings because past accounting earnings have been found to be a good predictor of a firm's future operating cash flow. In Chapter 12, we will see that in earnings-based valuation models, the value of a company's share price largely depends on a firm's expected future earnings. Thus, an important role for historical accounting numbers is their use in forecasting a company's future earnings, and hence, a firm's value.

One of the determinants of the ability of historical earnings to predict future earnings is the extent to which earnings recur over time, or what is known as **earnings persistence**. Since the value of a share of stock today is a function of a firm's ability to consistently generate earnings year in and year out, the sustainability or persistence of operating earnings is closely linked to value. **Sustainable earnings** are also sometimes referred to as **permanent earnings**, whereas non-sustainable earnings are often referred to as **transitory earnings**. In general, transitory earnings include such single-period items as extraordinary gains/losses (described later in this chapter), special items, restructuring charges, changes in accounting principle, and discontinued operations.

> **Intrinsic value** refers to the underlying economic value of a business as a going concern; that is, the value that a business could be sold for in an efficient market.

To assist investors in their assessment of a company's sustainable earnings, and hence in assessing a firm's **intrinsic value**, companies are required under GAAP to classify income statement accounts in a manner that aids the user in assessing a firm's sustainable earnings. Exhibit 3.8 illustrates the basic format of the income statement for a hypothetical company, Savanna Company. Notice that the income statement is organized in such a way that items with greater persistence are reported higher in the income statement, whereas items considered more transitory are reported further down in the statement. Thus, accounts representing financial events that are both usual and frequent are reported first. *Usual* refers to whether an item is central to a firm's core operations, whereas **unusual items** display a high degree of abnormality and/or are unrelated, and/or only incidentally related to the ordinary and typical activities of the enterprise. *Frequent* refers to how often an item is expected to occur, with infrequent items not reasonably expected to recur in the foreseeable future.

Usual and frequent items typically consist of such income statement accounts as sales, cost of goods sold, and other operating expenses. Just below these usual and frequent items are items that are either

EXHIBIT 3.8	The Income Statement: Potential Transitory Earnings Items

SAVANNA COMPANY
Income Statement
For Year Ended December 31

Sales.		$ 500
Cost of goods sold.		200
Gross profit.		300
Operating expenses.	$200	
Special items.	50	250
Net operating income.		50
Other income and expense		
Interest income.	25	
Interest expense.	(35)	
Gain on sale of equipment.	15	5
Net income from continuing operations before tax		55
Income tax.		20
Net income from continuing operations.		35
Gain (loss) on disposal of segment, net of tax		10
Net income before extraordinary item		45
Extraordinary gain (loss), net of tax		(15)
Net income		**$ 30**
Earnings per share (100 shares outstanding)		
Net income from continuing operations.		$0.35
Disposal of business segment		0.10
Extraordinary item.		(0.15)
Total earnings per share		**$0.30**

unusual or infrequent, but not both. Examples of these special items include such financial events as asset write-downs and restructuring charges. While these items are not expected to occur regularly, they are not considered unusual in nature. Income statement accounts such as interest expense, interest income, and gains on sales of equipment are often frequently recurring items; however, they are not considered part of a firm's central operations and therefore are considered unusual. Each of the above items is reported as part of continuing operations and is shown before any tax expense. GAAP, however, requires two single-period items, or one-time events, to be reported on an after-tax basis. These two items, discontinued operations and extraordinary items, are each shown net of any applicable income taxes. Reporting these items on a net-of-tax basis allows the income tax expense reported on the income statement to reflect only the income taxes associated with a firm's continuing operations, consequently enabling financial statement users to more readily predict a firm's future expected effective income tax rate.

Special Items and Extraordinary Items

There is no generally accepted definition as to what constitutes a **special item**; therefore, there is some variation in what firms will classify as "special." Special items often include gains or losses that are outside a firm's normal operations. For example, litigation settlements, impairment charges for long-lived assets, and the gains or losses associated with the sale of property, plant and equipment are typically classified as special items. The income statements for CSK Auto Corporation presented in Exhibit 3.9 reveal several special items, including investigation and restatement costs of $12.348 million and securities class action settlement of $11.7 million in 2008, and a loss on debt retirement of $19.45 million in 2007.

A controversial type of special item that some companies include in their income statement involves **restructuring charges** associated with changing a business's operations. Restructuring—also sometimes referred to as right-sizing or down-sizing—usually involves employee layoffs, closing facilities, and changing the company's financial structure by paying down debt with the issuance of new equity. For example, in Exhibit 3.9, CSK Auto Corporation reports "store closing costs" in each year from 2006 to 2008 associated with the closure of CSK stores that overlapped with better-situated, acquired stores, and the operating losses of acquired automotive service centers that were closed.

EXHIBIT 3.9	An Illustration of Extraordinary and Special Items

CSK AUTO CORPORATION and Subsidiaries
Consolidated Statements of Operations

(in thousands except per share data)	February 3, 2008	February 4, 2007	January 29, 2006
Net sales.	$ 1,851,647	$ 1,907,776	$ 1,651,285
Cost of sales.	984,649	1,011,712	864,674
Gross profit.	866,998	896,064	786,611
Other costs & expenses:			
Operating & administrative	804,265	788,400	653,471
Investigation and restatement costs	12,348	25,739	—
Securities class action settlement.	11,700	—	—
Store closing costs	1,983	1,487	2,903
Operating profit	36,702	80,438	130,237
Interest expense.	54,163	48,767	33,599
Loss on debt retirement.	—	19,450	1,600
Income (loss) before income taxes and cumulative effect of			
change in accounting principle.	(17,461)	12,221	95,038
Income tax expense (benefit)	(6,309)	4,991	37,248
Income (loss) before cumulative effect of change in accounting principle . . .	(11,152)	7,230	57,790
Cumulative effect of change in accounting principle, net of tax	—	(966)	—
Net income (loss)	$ **(11,152)**	$ **6,264**	$ **57,790**
Basic earnings (loss) per share:			
Income (loss) before cumulative effect of change in accounting principle . . .	$ (0.25)	$ 0.16	$ 1.30
Cumulative effect of change in accounting principle	—	(0.02)	—
Net income (loss) per share	$ (0.25)	$ 0.14	$ 1.30
Shares used in computing per share amounts.	43,971,417	43,876,533	44,465,409
Diluted earnings (loss) per share:			
Income (loss) before cumulative effect of change in accounting principle . . .	$ (0.25)	$ 0.16	$ 1.29
Cumulative effect of change in accounting principle	—	(0.02)	—
Net income (loss) per share.	$ **(0.25)**	$ **0.14**	$ **1.29**
Shares used in computing per share amounts.	43,971,417	44,129,278	44,812,302

In recent years, there has been increasing criticism of companies that report annual restructuring charges because it is believed that these write-offs have become a device for managing earnings. For example, Eastman Kodak Company had taken "one-time restructuring charges" every year for twenty-one consecutive years, from 1992 to 2012. By taking recurring write-downs of property and equipment, management may attempt to convey the impression to investors, shareholders, and investment professionals that the resulting restructuring charges are one-time events—that is, that they are transitory in nature and consequently should be ignored for purposes of valuing the firm.[3] It should be observed, however, that these charges effectively reduce the regular depreciation expense on the income statement, and thus improve future operating income on an annual basis. Critics of this practice also note that restructuring charges are often taken in a "bad year" in which operating earnings are unusually weak. Lumping restructuring charges in years characterized by poor operating results to enhance the probability of improved performance in future years has become known as "taking a bath." Available evidence suggests that restructuring charges are often reversed in subsequent periods to enable a firm to beat analysts' earnings forecasts, to avoid reporting losses, or to avoid a decline in earnings from a prior year.[4]

Another one-time item is the additional income or charges that result from the implementation of a voluntary or mandatory **change in accounting principle**. Mandatory accounting changes occur when an accounting regulatory body, such as the FASB or IASB, changes the generally accepted accounting practice that is applicable to all audited companies. For example, in Exhibit 3.9, CSK Auto Corporation discloses that

---

[3] Eastman Kodak filed for bankruptcy in 2012 as an attempt to survive a liquidity crisis after many years of declining film business sales. One might speculatively associate Kodak's frequent use of restructuring charges as indicative of its attempts to adapt to the fast changing photography industry.

[4] S.R. Moehrle, "Do Firms Use Restructuring Charge Reversals to Meet Earnings Targets?" *The Accounting Review* (April 2002).

in 2007 it implemented a mandatory change in its method of accounting for share-based compensation. This accounting policy change resulted in a reduction in CSK's net income of $966,000, net of income tax savings.

A basic principle within U.S. GAAP is the **consistency principle**. Consistency requires that a firm use the same accounting measurement principles from one fiscal period to the next. This is not to be confused with uniformity, where all firms would need to report their financial results using the same set of principles and methods. Instead, consistency allows different firms to use different reporting methods; however, the same firm is expected to report its performance on a consistent basis from one year to the next. The consistent use of accounting policies enables financial statement users to make valid, and hence useful, comparisons of performance across multiple time periods. Voluntary accounting policy changes do occur, however, when the management of a company and its independent auditor decide that an alternative accounting method better reflects a firm's operations. Fortunately, voluntary changes in accounting methods don't happen very often—on average, less than two accounting policy changes per firm over a 20-year period. The capital market generally regards voluntary accounting policy changes suspiciously, often penalizing the share price of companies that make such changes. We will have more to say about voluntary accounting policy changes in Chapter 7.

As reflected in Exhibit 3.9, firms like CSK Auto Corporation were required in the past to separately show the cumulative financial effect of an accounting policy change, net of any income tax effect, as a separate line item on the income statement following the income from continuing operations. Under a current GAAP rule, however, the financial effect of a change in a company's accounting policies is now applied retrospectively to all prior periods to which the change can be estimated, with the financial effect of the change reported as an adjustment to retained earnings on the statement of shareholders' equity rather than on the income statement.

For financial statements filed before December 15, 2015, there was one additional one-time item that had to be separately reported by companies—**extraordinary gains (losses)**. These were gains (losses) that were both *unusual* and *infrequent* in nature. Extraordinary items were reported in the income statement *net* of any applicable income taxes and after income from continuing operations—that is, the unusual and infrequent nature of these items was highlighted by prominently displaying them near the bottom of the income statement. Just what constitutes an extraordinary item, however, was confusing. Consider, for example, a company whose uninsured building in California was destroyed in an earthquake. The firm would not be able to classify the loss as extraordinary because although the occurrence of earthquakes in California is infrequent, it would not be considered unusual since it is part of the business risk of operating in California. Extraordinary items tended to include such items as a gain or loss resulting from a natural disaster when such events are unusual and infrequent (such as a hurricane) or a gain or loss resulting from new government regulations, such as an asset expropriation by a foreign government (e.g., Venezuela's 2007 expropriation of international oil company assets). Recognizing the difficulty of determining when an item should be classified as extraordinary, in 2015 the FASB eliminated the requirement to report such items.

Discontinued Operations

When a company discontinues a separately identifiable business unit, such as an existing division, to focus on other activities, it will generally incur costs to lay off employees, liquidate inventory, and shutter facilities. These costs and the profits (or losses) from operating the business unit until it can be disposed of are categorized as **discontinued operations** on the income statement. GAAP requires that companies separate the results of their continuing operations from their discontinued operations to facilitate shareholder assessment of sustainable earnings. As shown in Exhibit 3.10, General Electric's income from discontinued operations, after applicable income taxes, totaled a loss of $112 million in 2014. This amount is further partitioned into two components—a loss from discontinued operations ($127 million) and a disposal gain on discontinued operations ($15 million). These same components were much larger in 2013. Whereas the first component represents the net earnings for the operations that will be discontinued for the period, the second component represents the difference between the proceeds from the sale and the depreciated cost of the net assets disposed of.

Earnings per Share

Since investors own shares whose prices are customarily quoted in terms of a price per share, public companies are required to provide earnings numbers that are scaled by the number of shares held by their shareholders. For example, **basic earnings per share** (EPS) is net income (less preferred stock dividends)

EXHIBIT 3.10	Illustration of Discontinued Operations

GENERAL ELECTRIC
Notes to the 2014 Financial Statements
Note 2. Assets and Liabilities of Businesses Held for Sale and Discontinued Operations

Discontinued Operations

Discontinued operations primarily comprised GE Money Japan (our Japanese personal loan business, Lake, and our Japanese mortgage and card businesses, excluding our investment in GE Nissen Credit Co., Ltd.), our U.S. mortgage business (WMC), our Commercial Lending and Leasing (CLL) trailer services business in Europe (CLL Trailer Services), our Consumer banking business in Russia (Consumer Russia) and our Consumer mortgage lending business in Ireland (Consumer Ireland). Results of operations, financial position and cash flows for these businesses are separately reported as discontinued operations for all periods presented.

Financial Information for Discontinued Operations			
(In millions)	**2014**	**2013**	**2012**
Operations			
Total revenues and other income (loss)	$ 268	$ 186	$ 191
Earnings (loss) from discontinued operations, before income taxes	$(351)	$ (494)	$(586)
Benefit (provision) for income taxes	224	155	198
Earnings (loss) from discontinued operations, net of taxes	**$(127)**	**$ (339)**	**$(388)**
Disposal			
Gain (loss) on disposal before income taxes	$ 14	$(2,027)	$(792)
Benefit (provision) for income taxes	1	246	197
Gain (loss) on disposal, net of taxes	$ 15	$(1,781)	$(595)
Earnings (loss) from discontinued operations, net of taxes[a]	**$(112)**	**$(2,120)**	**$(983)**

[a] The sum of GE industrial earnings (loss) from discontinued operations, net of taxes, and GECC earnings (loss) from discontinued operations, net of taxes, is reported as GE industrial earnings (loss) from discontinued operations, net of taxes, on the Consolidated Statement of Earnings.

divided by the actual number of common shares outstanding—that is, the number of shares held by a company's shareholders. **Diluted earnings per share**, on the other hand, is basic earnings per share adjusted for the possibility that some existing claims against the business might be converted into additional shares of common stock, thus increasing the number of shares outstanding. Claims against a firm that can be satisfied by the issuance of additional shares of common stock are called **dilutive claims** because the issuance of shares to satisfy these claims will lower, or dilute, basic EPS. There are two adjustments to basic EPS for dilutive securities: (1) increasing the denominator shares outstanding for the additional shares, and (2) removing from net income in the numerator any earnings effects associated with those dilutive securities. Examples of dilutive claims include convertible bonds (which is discussed in Chapter 9) and employee stock options and convertible preferred shares (which are discussed in Chapter 11).

Since Kohl's diluted EPS for the year ending January 31, 2015, was $4.24 versus a basic EPS of $4.28 (see Business Perspective: Kohl's Corporation), the company must have had some dilutive claims outstanding. Does the capital market consider the impact of these dilutive claims by relying more heavily on diluted EPS than on basic EPS when assessing a company's intrinsic value? Available evidence that diluted EPS explains more of the variation in share prices than basic EPS does suggest that investors do indeed focus more closely on diluted EPS in setting share prices.[5] However, available evidence also suggests that alternative EPS measures that better capture the potential dilutive effect of employee stock options explain more of the variation in share prices than does even diluted EPS.[6] This is consistent with the notion that investors make additional adjustments to diluted EPS when assessing the performance of firms that issue employee stock options.

[5] R. Jennings, M.J. LeClere and R.B. Thompson, "Evidence on the Usefulness of Alternative Earnings per Share Measures," *Financial Analysts Journal* (November/December 1997).
[6] J.E. Core, W.R. Guay and S.P. Kothari, "The Economic Dilution of Employee Stock Options: Diluted EPS for Valuation and Financial Reporting," *The Accounting Review* (July 2002).

BUSINESS PERSPECTIVE

Which statement better predicts future performance?

Which statement, the income statement or the statement of cash flows is a better predictor of future performance? Many will likely guess the statement of cash flows because it is less susceptible to manipulation. After all, cash is cash, you can't fake it, right? You may be surprised to learn that numerous research studies have shown that the income statement is far better at predicting future performance, even if performance is based on cash flows. How can this be?

Keep in mind that accrual accounting is nothing more than an attempt to match performance to the proper accounting period. The differences between cash flows and accrual earnings are simply a matter of timing—totals will always be the same in the end. This is perhaps best illustrated with a stylized example.

Assume Kismet Company produces and sells magazines selling for $900 under a three-year subscription. Further assume it costs Kismet one-half of the selling price to produce and distribute the magazine. Magazines are all sold with the entire amount of $900 collected up front, while the magazines are produced and delivered over the three-year period.

First consider cash flows:

Year	1	2	3	Totals
Cash received.	$900	$ 0	$ 0	$900
Cash out.	(150)	(150)	(150)	(450)
Total	$750	$(150)	$(150)	$450

All the cash is received in the first year, however the cost of production and distribution occur in each year. Using cash flows we have a very "lumpy" distribution with any particular year being a poor predictor of an "average" year.

Now consider accrual accounting where revenue is only recorded as it is earned and expenses are then matched to these recorded revenues.

Year	1	2	3	Totals
Revenue	$300	$300	$300	$900
Cash out.	(150)	(150)	(150)	(450)
Total	$150	$150	$150	$450

As this example demonstrates, in the end both cash flows and accrual earnings total the exact same amount, the differences are only a matter of timing. But look how much better accrual earnings does of reporting actual period-by-period performance and how much better it does at predicting future performance.

REVIEW PROBLEM 3.3

Mary Company had the following outstanding stock securities held by its shareholders during the year:

1. 300,000 shares of common stock carrying an average market price during the year of $42.00

2. 6.0% convertible preferred, which had been sold at its par value of $200. The preferred stock is convertible into two shares of common stock and 4,000 preferred shares are currently outstanding.

During the year, Mary Company earned net income after taxes of 6.2 million.

Required
Compute (*a*) basic earnings per share and (*b*) diluted earnings per share for Mary Company as of the end of the year. Ignore taxes.

The solution is on page 127.

Pro Forma Earnings

In recent years, companies have begun reporting a variety of alternative measures of earnings that *exclude* certain expenses or write-offs, jokingly referred to by investment professionals as EBBS or "earnings before bad stuff." One such measure is **pro forma earnings**. While there is no generally accepted definition for the calculation of pro forma earnings, a commonly used calculation is net income before discontinued operations, restructuring charges, extraordinary and special items, and the effect of any mandatory or voluntary accounting policy changes.

Under the requirements of the Sarbanes-Oxley Act passed in 2002, companies that include a non-GAAP financial measure such as pro forma earnings with their audited financial statements must also provide the most directly comparable GAAP numbers. These firms must also provide a reconciliation between the two sets of numbers. For example, using GAAP Abercrombie & Fitch reported earnings of $0.71 per diluted share for the fiscal year ending January 31, 2015. Yet, on a pro forma basis, the company announced "adjusted non-GAAP earnings" of $1.54 per share, a swing of 217%, or $0.83 per share from GAAP EPS. The company justified its use of such adjustments in its annual report as follows:

> The Company believes that the non-GAAP financial measures discussed above are useful to investors as they provide the ability to measure the Company's operating performance and compare it against that of prior periods without reference to the impact of charges related to asset impairment, store closures, restructuring of the Gilly Hicks brand, CEO transition costs, the Company's profit improvement initiative, and corporate governance matters.

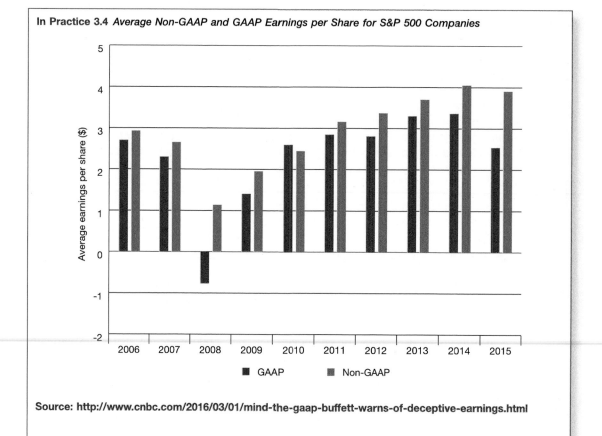

In Practice 3.4 *Average Non-GAAP and GAAP Earnings per Share for S&P 500 Companies*

Source: http://www.cnbc.com/2016/03/01/mind-the-gaap-buffett-warns-of-deceptive-earnings.html

Skeptics would point out, however, that each of the prior three years Abercrombie & Fitch had similarly reported boosts to reported GAAP earnings per share for the impact of periodic charges. For January 31, 2014 non-GAAP earnings disclosed by the company exceeded GAAP earnings by a whopping 177%.

The divergence between the generally higher pro forma earnings and GAAP earnings has increased over time. For example, In Practice 3.4 presents GAAP EPS and pro forma EPS for all S&P 500 firms from 2006 to 2015. Notably since 2011, the disparity between the two measures has been steadily increasing over time, with 2015 reported GAAP values about 36 percent lower than non-GAAP pro forma values. Unfortunately, the capital market's reliance on pro forma earnings as a performance metric has been well established, with evidence strongly suggesting that share prices track pro forma earnings more closely than GAAP earnings.[7] To ensure that investors consider GAAP EPS, the U.S. Securities and Exchange Commission adopted **Regulation G (Reg G)** in 2003, which requires that firms put GAAP-based earnings first in their public earnings announcements, as well as to reconcile any non-GAAP earnings numbers (e.g., pro forma earnings) with their GAAP-based earnings. The intent of Reg G is to ensure transparency regarding the differences between GAAP earnings and any non-GAAP earnings reported by companies.

BUSINESS PERSPECTIVE

Kohl's Corporation: Operating versus Nonoperating Earnings

The income statement for Kohl's Corporation is presented below. Kohl's consolidated income statement discloses such operating expenses as the cost of merchandise sold, depreciation and amortization on property and equipment, and selling and administrative expenses (see bolded areas). Kohl's separates the results of its core retailing business from the financing of its business by reporting interest expense as a nonoperating item. The underlying logic of this distinction is that Kohl's could relatively quickly change the way it finances its business and hence, these items are more transitory, but that exiting its core retailing business would require a longer period of time.

KOHL'S CORPORATION
Consolidated Statements of Income

($ millions, except per share data)	Fiscal Year Ended		
	January 31, 2015	February 1, 2014	February 2, 2013
Net sales.	$19,023	$19,031	$19,279
Cost of merchandise sold	12,098	12,087	12,289
Gross margin	6,925	6,944	6,990
Operating expenses			
Selling, general and administrative	4,350	4,313	4,267
Depreciation and amortization	886	889	833
Operating income.	1,689	1,742	1,890
Interest expense, net	340	338	329
Income before income taxes	1,349	1,404	1,561
Provision for income taxes	482	515	575
Net income.	$ 867	$ 889	$ 986
Net income per share			
Basic	$4.28	$4.08	$4.19
Diluted	$4.24	$4.05	$4.17

---

[7] M.T. Bradshaw and R.G. Sloan, "GAAP versus The Street: An Empirical Assessment of Two Alternative Definitions of Earnings," *Journal of Accounting Research* (March 2002).

ETHICS PERSPECTIVE

One of the potential problems associated with the corporate form of business is the agency costs that can result from the separation of the ownership of a corporation from those that manage the corporation. One mechanism used to mitigate these potential agency costs is employment compensation contracts. The theory underlying this mechanism is that if a compensation contract is properly structured, goal congruence between the manager and the corporation's shareholders will result. Thus, properly structured employment contracts provide performance incentives that result in larger amounts of compensation being paid when managers achieve better financial performance.

A potential unintended consequence of executive compensation contracts is that managers may also have an incentive to "cook the books" in order to report higher firm performance, and therefore, achieve higher personal compensation. In other words, rather than achieving goal congruence by working hard to sell more goods or to produce goods more efficiently, higher performance may be achieved through accounting trickery. Clearly, earnings management for purely personal gain can be argued to be an ethical breach of an executive's job.

EXECUTIVE SUMMARY

In this chapter, we examined the components of a company's net income in an effort to identify its sustainable earnings. Sustainable earnings are those operating and nonoperating income flows that are expected to persist over many fiscal periods; they are the permanent earnings of a business. Sustainable earnings are important to managers and investors because they are a key determinant of firm value.

We also illustrated how a company's statement of cash flow can be prepared from its income statement and balance sheets. Finally, we examined the various alternative measures of cash flow that investors and investment professionals use to evaluate a firm's financial health: EBITDA, free cash flow, and discretionary cash flow.

As a validation of your understanding of the content of this chapter, you should now be able to:

- Use a statement of cash flow to explain a business's operating, financing, and investing strategies.
- Prepare a statement of cash flow using the indirect method.
- Compute and apply ratios based on operating cash flows.
- Explain the difference between EBITDA, free cash flow, and discretionary cash flow.
- Understand the components of net income to evaluate a company's sustainable earnings.
- Understand the steps needed to convert an indirect method statement of cash flow to the direct method.

KEY CONCEPTS AND TERMS

Basic earnings per share, 105
Capital expenditures, 100
Capital intensive, 99
Cash conversion ratio, 99
Cash flow from financing, 87
Cash flow from investing, 87
Cash flow from operations, 87
Cash from sales, 99
Change in accounting principle, 104
Consistency principle, 105
Diluted earnings per share, 106
Dilutive claims, 106
Direct method, 87

Discontinued operations, 105
Discretionary cash flow, 101
Earnings persistence, 102
EBITDA, 99
Extraordinary gains (losses), 105
Free cash flow, 100
Free cash flow yield, 101
Indirect method, 87
Intrinsic value, 102
Market capitalization, 101
Noncash expenses, 93
Operating cash flow to current
    liabilities ratio, 99

Operating funds ratio, 98
Permanent earnings, 102
Pro forma earnings, 108
Regulation G (Reg G), 109
Restructuring charges, 103
Special item, 103
Sustainable earnings, 102
Taking a bath, 104
Transitory earnings, 102
Unusual items, 102

APPENDIX 3A: Converting Indirect Method Cash Flows to Direct Method Cash Flows

Although it is quite straightforward to create a direct method statement of cash flow given access to a company's internal accounting records, such access is rarely available to anyone except a company's management team. The Russian River Valley cash flow statement that appears in Exhibit 2.5 in the previous chapter, for example, is simply a compilation of the cash inflows and outflows reported in the cash column from the Russian River Valley spreadsheet. All that is necessary is to pull the numbers directly off the spreadsheet and place them in the appropriate section of the cash flow statement. This is why, in fact, the direct method is referred to as "direct"—the cash flow from operations is taken directly from the company's accounting records rather than being indirectly computed from net income. Unfortunately, investors and lenders rarely have access to such proprietary internal data. Thus, it is necessary to be able to create direct method cash flow information using only such publicly available data as the indirect method statement of cash flow.

Takeaway 6
Understand the steps needed to convert an indirect method statement of cash flow to the direct method.

The process of converting an indirect method statement of cash flow to the direct method requires two steps. First, replace net income (the first line item under the operating activities section of the indirect method statement format) with the key line items appearing on a firm's income statement. For instance, Russian River Valley's income statement in Exhibit 3.5 contains the following key line items (in thousands):

Revenue	$1,900
Cost of goods sold	(380)
Operating expenses	(675)
Interest	(288)
Income taxes	(240)
Net income	$ 317

Thus, for the winery, we begin by replacing the net income of $317 under the operating activities section in Exhibit 3.6 with the five key income statement line items shown above, which aggregate to $317.

The second step involves adjusting the key income statement line items identified in Step One with the remaining line items from the operating activities section of the indirect method statement of cash flow. Using Russian River Valley's data in Exhibit 3.6, those adjustments would appear as follows:

Income Statement Line Items		Operating Activities Line Items		Direct Method Cash Flow	
Revenues	$1,900	Less	$800 Accounts receivable	Cash collections from customers	$1,100
Cost of goods sold	(380)	Less Add	$60 Inventory $80 Accounts payable	Cash paid for inventory	(360)
Operating expenses	(675)	Add Add	$225 Depreciation $50 Amortization	Cash paid for operating expenses	(400)
Interest	(288)		(no adjustment required)	Cash paid for interest	(288)
Income taxes	(240)	Add	$96 Taxes payable	Cash paid for income taxes	(144)
Net income	$ 317			Cash flow from operations	$ (92)

Exhibit 3A.1 presents the winery's direct method statement of cash flow after undertaking the above two steps. As expected, the direct method CFFO of negative $92 is exactly equivalent to the indirect method CFFO of negative $92 as reported in Exhibit 3.6. Note that the CFFI and CFFF are exactly the same in both Exhibit 3.6 and Exhibit 3A.1. The only difference between the two exhibits is the manner in which the CFFO is calculated. In Exhibit 3.6, the CFFO is calculated by beginning with net income and then adjusting for various noncash expenses (e.g., depreciation and amortization), as well as adjusting for the changes in the various working capital accounts (e.g., accounts receivable, inventory, accounts payable, and taxes payable). In Exhibit 3A.1, net income is replaced with the key income statement line items and the noncash expenses and working capital adjustments are disaggregated to the individual line items. But in each case, the CFFO total remains the same.

EXHIBIT 3A.1	Statement of Cash Flow: The Direct Method

RUSSIAN RIVER VALLEY WINERY, INC.
Statement of Cash Flow

($ thousands)	Year 1
Operating activities	
Cash from customer collections	$ 1,100
Cash paid for inventory	(360)
Cash paid for operating expenses.	(400)
Cash paid for interest.	(288)
Cash paid for income taxes.	(144)
Cash flow from operations	**(92)**
Investing activities	
Purchase of property, plant & equipment	(3,500)
Cash flow from investing.	**(3,500)**
Financing activities	
Sale of common stock.	400
Payment of notes payable (current).	(480)
Payment of common stock dividends	(260)
Cash flow from financing.	**(340)**
Net cash flow	(3,932)
Beginning cash.	4,700
Ending cash	$ 768

QUESTIONS

Q3.1 **Building Shareholder Value.** Describe at least three ways that corporate managers can build shareholder value (increase their firm's share price). Rank-order the various managerial actions you identified according to their effectiveness in building shareholder value. Be prepared to justify your rank-ordering.

Q3.2 **Litigation, Reported Income, and Share Price.** In early 2006, Merck AG, a global pharmaceutical company, saw its share price decline dramatically after a jury in the United States found the company guilty of failing to warn consumers about safety issues surrounding one of the company's products, a painkilling drug called *Vioxx*. Although Merck was found not guilty in one case involving a plaintiff who died while taking the drug, the company was found guilty in a second case, with the court awarding the survivors of the deceased plaintiff $4.5 million in compensatory damages. At the time of the trial, over 5,000 separate *Vioxx*-related lawsuits had been filed against Merck. Discuss how Merck should disclose the $4.5 million lawsuit award in its 2006 annual report. How should Merck disclose the 5,000 pending lawsuits in its 2005 financial statements before the court case was decided against the company? How should Merck report the pending *Vioxx*-related lawsuits in its 2006 annual report?

Q3.3 **Basic Versus Diluted Earnings per Share.** In its 2014 annual report, Merck & Co., Inc., reported that its basic earnings per share were $4.12 per share while its diluted earnings per share were $4.07 per share. Discuss the factors that might cause the number of shares used in the calculation of earnings per share to increase, and thus, cause diluted earnings per share (EPS) to be less than basic earnings per share. Which measure do you feel is more important to shareholders—basic EPS or diluted EPS? Why?

Q3.4 **Assessing the Quality of Reported Earnings Using Cash Flow Data.** Although much of the work of an equity analyst involves quantitative analysis, some analysts also engage in various qualitative analyses to help them assess the persistence of a firm's current earnings. Consider, for example, the case of Blockbuster Entertainment Corporation. Prior to the dominance of Netflix, Blockbuster was the leading movie rental company in the U.S. In 1989, Lee J. Seidler, a senior analyst with Bear, Stearns & Co., issued a research report critical of Blockbuster's earnings. Mr. Seidler observed that although Blockbuster's 1988 net income was $15.5 million and its cash flow from operating activities $48.4 million, his review of the firm's cash flow data revealed that Blockbuster's purchases of new videocassette rental inventory had been classified as an "investing activity" rather than as an "operating activity" on the company's statement of cash flow. Presented below is selected financial statement information for Blockbuster:

(in millions)	1988	1987
Net income	$15.5	$4.09
Cash flow from operations	48.3	10.3
Purchases of videocassette rental inventory	(51.3)	(14.3)

Discuss how the statement of cash flow can be used to help evaluate the quality of a company's reported earnings. Describe how Blockbuster's cash flow data can be used to illustrate this. Do you agree with Blockbuster's decision to classify its videocassette inventory purchases as an "investing activity"? Why or why not? How does Blockbuster's cash flow classification of its video inventory purchases affect its cash flow from operations?

Q3.5   **Earnings Announcements and Share Prices.**   It is common to see share prices of a company increase with the announcement of good news from the company. It is also the case that record earnings qualify as very good news. The behavior of stock price increases with record earnings announcements is not always the case, however. For example, in January of 2013 Apple Inc., the maker of the iPhone and Mac computers, announced record earnings of over $41.7 billion for 2012. Apple's stock dropped nearly 10 percent following the earnings announcement. Discuss why a record earnings announcement may lead to a share price increase, but may also lead to a share price decline as experienced by Apple.

Q3.6   **Managing Earnings.**   Some members of the financial community allege that corporate managers "manage" their company's reported accounting results. Discuss the possible motivations behind this behavior. Can you envision a situation where a manager might manage a company's earnings downward? If so, why?

Q3.7   **Goodwill Impairment and Sustainable Earnings.**   In 2002, the FASB concluded that the amortization of goodwill should no longer be required, and instead that goodwill be subject to an annual impairment test to verify that its value had not materially declined. If a decline in value is observed, the goodwill account is written down and an "impairment loss" is recorded on the income statement.

In a 2012 study of goodwill impairment, Duff & Phelps found that Bank of America and AT&T had among the highest impairment charges in 2011. Discuss how Bank of America and AT&T will account for the goodwill write-down in their financial statements. How will the impairment charge affect the firm's book value? How will the impairment charge impact the firm's sustainable earnings?

Q3.8   **Special Charges.**   On September 11, 2001, two American Airlines aircraft were hijacked and destroyed in terrorist attacks on The World Trade Center in New York City and the Pentagon in northern Virginia. As a consequence of these actions, AMR Corporation, the parent company of American Airlines, concluded that its fleet of aircraft had become impaired, and consequently, took a special charge of $718 million against 2001 net income and an additional $1,466 million charge against 2002 net income.

Discuss how these special charges will be reflected in AMR's financial statements. Given the unusual circumstances associated with these charges, could they be considered extraordinary? Why or why not? Will these charges be included in the company's sustainable earnings? Why or why not? How will these items be treated after 2015?

Q3.9   **New Accounting Standard.**   In 2002, following its adoption of a new accounting standard issued by the FASB for the impairment of goodwill accounting, AMR Corporation, the parent company of American Airlines, conducted an impairment test of its existing goodwill which had largely arisen in conjunction with American's acquisition of TWA in 2001. Based on this test, AMR Corporation concluded that its entire balance of $1.4 billion of goodwill had been impaired. Consequently, at year-end 2002, the company recorded a one-time, noncash charge to write off all of its goodwill. The charge-off of AMR's goodwill was reported as a "cumulative effect of accounting change" in the amount of $988 million, net of the related income tax effect of $412 million, on its consolidated statement of earnings.

Discuss AMR's treatment of its goodwill impairment charge. Do you agree with the disclosure adopted by the company? Why or why not? How will the impairment affect the firm's future sustainable earnings?

Q3.10   **Market Capitalization, Book Value, and Intrinsic Value.**   Discuss the concepts of book value, intrinsic value, and market capitalization. Using a financial website such as YahooFinance or MSNMoney, identify the market capitalization and book value of The Procter & Gamble Company. Calculate the difference between these values. Why do these measures differ in value?

Q3.11   **Accounting Statement Restatements.**   The chart below summarizes the U.S. exchange traded companies that issued corrections to their financial statements during the years 2001 through 2014. The data was compiled by *Audit Analytics* and published in April, 2015.

Year	# of Unique Firms	# of Restatements
2001	589	625
2002	653	701
2003	735	789
2004	859	937
2005	1,426	1,573
2006	1,615	1,842
2007	1,146	1,271
2008	834	930
2009	707	761
2010	789	836
2011	774	848
2012	796	851
2013	782	867
2014	746	831

Why do you think the number of financial statement restatements increased so dramatically from 2004 to 2006, dropping off in later years? Discuss how you think the capital markets respond to financial statement restatements.

Q3.12   **(Ethics Perspective) Earnings Management to Prevent Technical Defaults.**   Earnings management may be used to avoid a technical default of a covenant under a loan agreement. Loan covenants are written into loan agreements in order to protect a lender from various actions that a borrower might undertake. These covenants often require attainment of certain target financial ratios calculated using reported GAAP numbers. Failing to achieve these minimum target ratios, and hence falling into technical default, can be very costly to a firm. Earnings management to prevent a technical default will likely save a corporation and its shareholders from experiencing a large loss in market value, without necessarily providing any direct personal benefit to the company's managers. Is earnings management to avoid a loan covenant violation an ethical breach by management?

Assignments with the 🔵 logo in the margin are available in BusinessCourse.
See the Preface of the book for details.
CHECK FIGURE indicates that check figures are available on the book's Website.

EXERCISES

TA 1   **E3.13**   **Classifying Accounting Events.**   Presented below is a list of accounting events for the Longo Corporation. Classify each of the events as an operating (O) activity event, an investing (I) activity event, a financing (F) activity event, or as none-of-the-above (N).
1. Sale of common stock for cash
2. Collection of cash on accounts receivable
3. Purchase of equipment for cash
4. Sale of inventory on credit
5. Borrowed cash from a bank
6. Payment of a cash dividend
7. Payment of utility expense using cash
8. Purchase of land using bank financing
9. Repurchase of previously issued stock using cash
10. Cash payment of interest on a bank loan

TA 1   **E3.14**   **Classifying Accounting Transactions.**   Presented below is a list of accounting transactions for the Davis
CHECK   Company. Classify each of the transactions as an operating (O) activity transaction, an investing (I) activity
FIGURE   transaction, a financing (F) activity transaction, or as none-of-the-above (N).
1. Purchase of machinery for cash
2. Cash payment on loan principal
3. Collection of cash on outstanding accounts receivable
4. Payment of a stock dividend
5. Sale of preferred stock for cash
6. Prepaid the office rent for six months
7. Cash payment of income tax expense
8. Sale of land held as an investment for cash
9. Declared (but did not pay) a cash dividend
10. Purchased treasury stock using cash

E3.15 **Analyzing Cash Flow Data.**   Presented below is cash flow information for two competitors—The Longo   TA 1, 2
Corporation and The Davis Company (amounts in thousands):

Company	Operating Profit	Cash Flow From		
		Operations	Investing	Financing
Longo Corporation.................	$(6,050)	$(1,320)	$ (693)	$ 415
Davis Company	(2,980)	(3,260)	1,502	1,809

Describe the cash management strategy of each company by identifying the key sources and uses of cash by
each firm. Explain why the cash flow from operations of The Longo Corporation differs from the company's
operating loss of $6,050. Calculate the change in the cash balance for The Davis Company.

E3.16 **Analyzing Cash Flow Data.**   Presented below is cash flow information for two competitors for 2015—   TA 1, 2
Pfizer, Inc., and Johnson & Johnson (amounts in millions):

Company	Operating Profit	Cash Flow From		
		Operations	Investing	Financing
Pfizer, Inc......................	$ 6,986	$14,512	$(2,980)	$(11,233)
Johnson & Johnson	15,409	19,279	(7,735)	(12,335)

Describe the cash management strategy of each company by identifying the key sources and uses of cash by
each firm. Calculate the change in the cash balance for each firm. Explain why cash flow from operations is
greater than operating profit for both firms.

E3.17 **Calculating Earnings per Share.**   During 2016, Mayfair Company had the following securities outstanding: TA 5

1.   250,000 shares of common stock with an average market price of $25 per share.
2.   9.5% convertible preferred, which had been sold at its par value of $100. The preferred stock is convert-
ible into three shares of common stock and 3,000 preferred shares are currently outstanding.

During 2016, Mayfair earned net income after income taxes of $3.2 million. Calculate the (*a*) basic earnings
per share and (*b*) diluted earnings per share for Mayfair Company for 2016.

E3.18 **Calculating Earnings per Share.**   Little, Inc., reported earnings of $159,000 for 2016, and at the end of the   TA 5
year, had the following securities outstanding: CHECK FIGURE

1.   60,000 shares of common stock. (The year-end share price was $25 per share.)
2.   Employee stock options for the purchase of 8,000 common shares at an exercise price of $22 per share.
(The options are fully vested.)

Calculate the (*a*) basic earnings per share and (*b*) diluted earnings per share for Little, Inc. for 2016.

E3.19 **Permanent Versus Transitory Earnings.**   Entrust, Inc., is a global provider of security software; it oper-   TA 5
ates in one business segment involving the design, production, and sale of software products for securing
digital identities and information. The consolidated statements of operations for a three-year period (all values
in thousands) follows. On January 1, Year 1, the Entrust common shares traded at $10.40 per share; by year-
end Year 3, the shares traded at $3.80 per share. The company's cash flow from operations was $(27,411),
$(20,908), and $9,606, for Year 1, Year 2, and Year 3, respectively.

Calculate the sustainable earnings of Entrust, Inc., for each of the three years. Compare the company's
reported net income (loss) with its sustainable earnings. Does Entrust's share price at year-end Year 3 reflect
the firm's apparent turn-around? Why or why not?

ENTRUST, INC. Consolidated Statements of Operations			
Year Ended December 31 ($ thousands)	Year 3	Year 2	Year 1
Revenues			
Product	$29,295	$ 30,974	$ 44,734
Services and maintenance.........................	61,662	56,920	58,013
Total revenues	90,957	87,894	102,747

continued

continued from previous page

As of Year-End ($ thousands)	2016	2015
Shareholders' equity		
Common stock, $10 par value............................	$ 775,000	$ 675,000
Additional paid-in-capital................................	380,000	300,000
Retained earnings	865,000	415,000
Total shareholders' equity	2,020,000	1,390,000
Total liabilities & shareholders' equity	$3,110,000	$2,240,000

AMPHLETT CORPORATION Consolidated Income Statement		
For Year Ended ($ thousands)	**2016**	**2015**
Revenues	$1,430,000	$1,200,000
Less: Cost of goods sold.............................	500,000	420,000
Gross margin	930,000	780,000
Less: Selling, general & administrative expenses	150,000	120,000
Operating income....................................	780,000	660,000
Gain on sale of investments...........................	70,000	—
Net income before taxes	850,000	660,000
Less: Income taxes	50,000	11,000
Net income after taxes...............................	$ 800,000	$ 649,000

The footnotes to the Amphlett Corporation's financial statements revealed the following additional information:

1. Property and equipment costing $450 million was sold for its book value of $200 million.
2. Long-term investments were sold for $150 million, which included a gain of $70 million.

Required

Using the above financial data for the Amphlett Corporation, prepare the firm's statement of cash flow for 2016 using the indirect method. What does the company's statement of cash flow reveal about the business's financial health?

TA 1, 2, 3   **P3.23**   **Statement of Cash Flow.** Presented below are the consolidated financial statements of The Mann Corpora-
CHECK   tion as of year-end 2016 and 2015.
FIGURE

THE MANN CORPORATION Consolidated Balance Sheets		
As of Year-End ($ thousands)	**2016**	**2015**
Assets		
Current assets		
Cash.......................................	$ 400,000	$ 250,000
Accounts receivable (net)........................	990,000	760,000
Inventory	710,000	400,000
Prepaid expenses	100,000	100,000
Total current assets	2,200,000	1,510,000
Investments in affiliate companies.....................	100,000	—
Property and equipment...........................	1,310,000	800,000
Less: Accumulated depreciation	(110,000)	(80,000)
Property & equipment (net).......................	1,200,000	720,000
Total assets......................................	$3,500,000	$2,230,000

continued

As of Year-End ($ thousands)	2016	2015
Liabilities & Shareholders' Equity		
Current liabilities		
Accounts payable	$ 570,000	$ 500,000
Accrued expenses payable	200,000	220,000
Dividends payable	70,000	—
Total current liabilities	840,000	720,000
Note payable—due in ten years	500,000	—
Total liabilities	1,340,000	720,000
Shareholders' equity		
Common stock ($5 par value)	300,000	200,000
Additional paid-in-capital	1,200,000	1,160,000
Retained earnings	660,000	150,000
Total shareholders' equity	2,160,000	1,510,000
Total liabilities & shareholders' equity	$3,500,000	$2,230,000

THE MANN CORPORATION Consolidated Income Statement		
For Year Ended ($ thousands)	2016	2015
Sales	$16,800,000	$12,000,000
Cost of goods sold	14,000,000	10,400,000
Gross margin	2,800,000	1,600,000
Selling & administrative expenses	1,930,000	1,048,000
Depreciation expense	30,000	20,000
Income tax expense	240,000	152,000
Net Income	$ 600,000	$ 380,000

Required

Using the above financial data, prepare the statement of cash flow for 2016 using the indirect method. What does the company's statement of cash flow reveal about the business's financial health?

P3.24   **Statement of Cash Flow.**   Presented below are the consolidated financial statements of Casual Clothing, Inc.   TA 1, 2 CHECK FIGURE

CASUAL CLOTHING INC. Consolidated Balance Sheet		
	12/31/17	12/31/16
Assets		
Current Assets		
Cash and cash equivalents	$ 8,794	$ 7,352
Merchandise inventory	94,153	42,045
Accounts receivable (net)	25,700	17,800
Other current assets	35,103	25,393
Total current assets	163,750	92,590
Noncurrent Assets		
Buildings, furniture & equipment (net)	1,826,863	1,658,990
Land	2,279,946	1,458,832
Construction-in-process	615,722	414,725
Intangibles (net)	9,780	6,700
Total assets	$4,896,061	$3,631,837

continued

continued from previous page

	12/31/17	12/31/16
Liabilities & Shareholders' Equity		
Current liabilities		
Notes payable	$ 779,904	$ 176,884
Current maturities of long-term debt	250,000	350,000
Accounts payable	167,207	185,945
Accrued expenses & other liabilities	384,209	351,710
Income taxes payable	17,824	26,263
Total current liabilities.	1,599,144	1,090,802
Long-term liabilities		
Long-term debt	880,216	780,925
Total liabilities.	2,479,360	1,871,727
Shareholders' equity		
Common stock ($.05 par value).	146,961	146,961
Additional paid-in-capital.	1,294,967	1,294,967
Retained earnings	974,773	318,182
Total shareholders' equity	2,416,701	1,760,110
Total liabilities & shareholders' equity	$4,896,061	$3,631,837

CASUAL CLOTHING, INC. Consolidated Statement of Earnings For Year Ended 12/31/17	
Net sales.	$13,673,460
Costs & expenses	
Costs of goods sold.	8,599,442
Operating expenses.	3,629,257
Interest expense (net).	62,876
	12,291,575
Earnings before income taxes	1,381,885
Income taxes	504,388
Net earnings.	$ 877,497

Note: In 2017, amortization expense for intangibles was $2,700 and depreciation expense for buildings, furniture & equipment was $123,000.

Required

Using the above financial data, prepare the statement of cash flow for 2017 for Casual Clothing, Inc. using the indirect method. What does the company's statement of cash flow reveal about the business's financial health?

TA 1, 2 **P3.25** **Statement of Cash Flow.** The following financial data were taken from the Catalina Divers Supply Company for the year ended December 31, 2017.

CATALINA DIVERS SUPPLY COMPANY Balance Sheet Data		
	12/31/17	12/31/16
Assets		
Cash.	$ 12,000	$ 10,800
Accounts receivable (net).	22,400	18,000
Inventory	30,000	31,200
Prepaid rent	2,400	3,600
Total current assets	66,800	63,600
Equipment (net)	116,000	104,000
Total assets.	$182,800	$167,600

continued

	12/31/17	12/31/16
Liabilities & Shareholders' Equity		
Accounts payable	$ 22,400	$ 29,200
Wages payable	18,000	13,600
Interest payable	3,000	4,400
Deferred revenue	13,000	9,400
Total current liabilities	56,400	56,600
Bank loan	56,000	56,800
Total liabilities	112,400	113,400
Capital stock	20,000	20,000
Retained earnings	50,400	34,200
Total shareholders' equity	70,400	54,200
Total liabilities & shareholders' equity	$182,800	$167,600

CATALINA DIVERS SUPPLY COMPANY
Income Statement
For the Year Ended December 31, 2017

Revenues	$218,200
Cost of goods sold	112,000
Gross margin	106,200
Wage expense	30,400
Rent expense	18,000
Interest expense	5,800
Depreciation expense	12,400
Loss on sale of equipment	8,400
Net income before income taxes	31,200
Income tax expense	8,800
Net income	$ 22,400

Required

Using the above data, prepare the 2017 statement of cash flow for Catalina Divers Supply Company using the indirect method. What does the company's statement of cash flow reveal about the business's financial health?

P3.26   **Analyzing and Interpreting Cash Flow Data: A Growing Enterprise.**   Presented below are cash flow data   TA 1, 2
for L.A. Gear Inc. During this period of time, the manufacturer of athletic shoes and sportswear experienced
a 1200 percent growth in net income.

L.A. GEAR INC.
Statement of Cash Flow
For Year Ended 12/31

(in thousands)	Year 3	Year 2	Year 1
Cash flow from operations			
Net income	$55,059	$22,030	$ 4,371
Depreciation	1,199	446	133
Noncash compensation to employees	558	—	—
Increase in accounts receivable	(51,223)	(34,378)	(12,410)
Increase in inventories	(72,960)	(50,743)	(1,990)
Increase in prepayments	(8,624)	(2,432)	(599)
Increase in accounts payable	17,871	7,197	1,656
Increase (decrease) in other current liabilities	10,587	11,193	(537)
Cash flow from operations	(47,533)	(46,687)	(9,376)

continued

continued from previous page

(in thousands)	Year 3	Year 2	Year 1
Cash flow from investing			
Sale of marketable securities	—	—	5,661
Acquisition of property, plant & equipment.	(6,168)	(2,546)	(874)
Acquisition of other noncurrent assets.	(246)	(406)	(241)
Cash flow from investing	(6,414)	(2,952)	4,546
Cash flow from financing			
Increase (decrease) in short-term borrowing	(19,830)	50,104	4,566
Issue of common stock	69,925	495	—
Cash flow from financing	50,095	50,599	4,566
Change in cash.	$ (3,852)	$ 960	$ (264)

Required

1. Explain why the cash flow from operations is negative.
2. How did the company finance its operations during the three-year period? Explain the logic of this strategy.
3. Depreciation expense as a percent of net income is only two to three percent during this period. What might explain this?

TA 1   **P3.27**   **Analyzing and Interpreting Cash Flow Data: A Failing Enterprise.**   L.A. Gear, a manufacturer of sports shoes and sportswear, began operations in the early 1980s. By late 1996, however, the company was in bankruptcy. Following are cash flow data for the company for the period 1995–1996.

L.A. GEAR INC.
Consolidated Statements of Cash Flow
For Year Ended 12/31

($ thousands)	1996	1995
Operating activities		
Net loss	$(61,689)	$(51,397)
Adjustments to reconcile net loss to net cash provided by (used in) operating activities		
Depreciation and amortization	4,555	7,266
Minority interest in net loss of joint venture	(6,986)	(1,324)
Loss on sale or abandonment of property and equipment . .	77	417
Increase in reserve for unused barter credits.	—	4,568
Write-off of goodwill.	8,324	1,012
Unrealized foreign exchange gain	—	(570)
(Increase) decrease, net of effects of acquisitions, in		
Accounts receivable, net	20,581	30,603
Inventories	18,095	6,100
Prepaid expenses & other current assets.	1,507	3,320
Other assets	(12)	1,624
Increase (decrease), net of effects of acquisitions, in		
Accounts payable & accrued liabilities.	16,166	(12,831)
Net cash provided by (used in) operating activities	618	(11,212)
Investing activities		
Capital expenditures	(710)	(3,256)
Net cash used in investing activities	(710)	(3,256)
Financing activities		
Costs related to issuance of Series B Shares	(661)	—
Net (repayments) borrowings under international credit facilities	(1,216)	622
Net cash (used in) provided by financing activities	(1,877)	622
Effect of exchange rate changes on cash & cash equivalents. . . .	252	92
Net (decrease) increase in cash & cash equivalents	(1,717)	(13,754)
Cash & cash equivalents at beginning of year	35,956	49,710
Cash & cash equivalents at end of year.	$ 34,239	$ 35,956

Required

Explain how L.A. Gear generated cash to sustain its operations during the period prior to its bankruptcy filing. What other financing options were available to the company?

P3.28   Statement of Cash Flow: International.   Recent financial statements for The Hoechst Group, a German   TA 1, 2
conglomerate with operations in agriculture, chemicals, pharmaceuticals, and veterinary products are presented as follows:

THE HOECHST GROUP Consolidated Balance Sheet (in millions of Euros) As of 12/31	Year 2	Year 1
Intangible assets	€15,077	€15,200
Property, plant & equipment	12,958	15,861
Investments	7,336	7,562
Noncurrent assets	35,371	38,623
Inventories	5,507	6,739
Receivables & prepaid items	14,630	14,908
Liquid assets	391	635
Current assets	20,528	22,282
Total assets	€55,899	€60,905
Equity of Hoechst AG stockholders	€16,599	€16,012
Minority interests	2,580	3,097
Stockholders' equity	19,179	19,109
Provisions for pensions & similar obligations	6,883	6,910
Other provisions	8,751	9,476
Provisions	15,634	16,386
Corporate debt	12,509	16,615
Liabilities & deferred income	8,577	8,795
Total stockholders' equity & liabilities	€55,899	€60,905

THE HOECHST GROUP Consolidated Statement of Profit & Loss (in millions of Euros) For Year Ended 12/31	Year 2	Year 1
Net sales	€43,704	€52,100
Cost of goods sold	(25,533)	(31,533)
Gross profit	18,171	20,567
Distribution & selling costs	(8,940)	(10,206)
Research & development costs	(3,820)	(3,990)
General & administrative costs	(2,680)	(2,808)
Other operating income	2,331	1,834
Other operating expense	(1,891)	(1,744)
Operating profit	3,171	3,653
Result on sale & transfer of business	64	304
Investment income, net	1,062	309
Interest expense, net	(1,037)	(1,019)
Other financial expense, net	(157)	(90)
Profit before taxes on income	3,103	3,157
Taxes on income	(944)	(1,383)
Income before minority interests	2,159	1,774
Minority interests	(264)	(431)
Net income	€ 1,895	€ 1,343

The following additional information was contained in the company's footnotes:

1. Depreciation expense of €2,190 in Year 2 was included in the cost of goods sold.
2. Amortization of intangible assets totaled €1,000 in Year 2 and was included in "General and Administrative Costs."
3. A gain on the sale of investments of €300 in Year 2 was included in "Investment income, net."
4. There were no sales or repurchases of Hoechst capital stock during Year 2.

Required

Prepare a statement of cash flow for The Hoechst Group for Year 2 using the indirect method. What does the company's statement of cash flow reveal about the business's financial health?

TA 1, 2, 4   **P3.29**   **Creating a Statement of Cash Flow from existing Balance Sheets and Income Statements.** Create a statement of cash flow for the Arrow Company for the years ended December 31, 2014 and December 31, 2015 from the balance sheets and income statement created in problem P1.32 from Chapter 1. Comment on your assessment of Arrow Company's financial statements, based only on the company's return on assets (levered). [Use end-of-year assets to compute return on assets.] Now, with the addition of Arrow's statement of cash flow, comment on any financial concern you might now have that did not show up with only access to the balance sheet and income statement. Arrow's first year of operations was 2014.

CORPORATE ANALYSIS

TA 3, 4, 5   **CA3.30**   **The Procter & Gamble Company.** The 2015 annual report of The Procter & Gamble Company (P&G) is available at www.pginvestor.com. After reviewing P&G's annual report, respond to the following questions:

    a. P&G's 2015 statement of cash flow is presented using the indirect method format. Calculate P&G's cash conversion ratio for 2015. What does the cash conversion ratio tell you about P&G's operating revenues? Is this good news or bad news? Why?

    b. Calculate P&G's EBITDA, free cash flow, and discretionary cash flow for 2013, 2014, and 2015. What can you conclude about P&G's cash position from these measures?

    c. Calculate P&G's sustainable earnings before taxes for 2013, 2014, and 2015. What can you conclude about the persistence of P&G's earnings?

TA 1, 4, 5, 6   **CA3.31**   **Internet-based Analysis.** Consider a publicly-held company whose products you are familiar with. Some examples might include:

Company	Product	Corporate Website
• Johnson & Johnson...............	• Band-Aids	• www.jnj.com
• Microsoft Corporation...............	• Windows software	• www.microsoft.com
• Apple, Inc..........................	• Cellular phones	• www.apple.com
• Intel Corporation	• Pentium processors	• www.intel.com
• Kimberly-Clark Corporation..........	• Kleenex	• www.kimberly-clark.com

Access the company's public website and search for its most recent annual report. (Note: Some companies will provide access to their financial data through an "investor relations" link, while others will provide a direct link to their "annual reports.") After locating your company's most recent annual report, open the file and review its contents. After reviewing the annual report for your selected company, prepare answers to the following questions:

    a. Identify the company's basic and diluted earnings per share (EPS) for the past two years. Is there a difference between these EPS numbers? If so, what dilutive claims are responsible for the decline in basic earnings per share?

    b. Review the company's income statement. Are there any extraordinary or special items, restructuring charges, changes in accounting principles, or discontinued operations in either of the last two years? If so, calculate the company's sustainable earnings for each year.

    c. Consider the company's statement of cash flow. What format—indirect or direct—is used to present the cash flow from operations? Convert the company's cash flow from operations from the indirect (direct) format to the direct (indirect) format (see Appendix 3A).

    d. Calculate the company's EBITDA, free cash flow, and discretionary cash flow for each of the past two years. Comment on the company's cash flow health.

CA3.32 IFRS Financial Statements. The 2014 financial statements of **LVMH Moet Hennessey-Louis Vuitton** TA 1, 4
S.A. are presented in Appendix C of this book. LVMH is a Paris-based holding company and one of the world's largest and best-known luxury goods companies. As a member-nation of the European Union, French companies are required to prepare their consolidated (group) financial statements using International Financial Reporting Standards (IFRS). After reviewing LVMH's consolidated income statement and consolidated cash flow statement in Appendix C, prepare answers to the following questions:

a. What differences (if any) do you observe between the format of LVMH's consolidated income statement under IFRS and what you would expect to see if the company had been using U.S. GAAP to prepare its income statement?

b. What differences (if any) do you observe between the format of LVMH's consolidated cash flow statement under IFRS and the statement of cash flow for Texas Instruments presented in Exhibit 3.2?

CASE

DOUBLE G WESTERN WEAR

Gerta Franklin's trip to buy a pair of cowboy boots had been frustrating—the 30-mile drive had yielded no boots. The selection available in her size was sparse, but, more important she had been unable to find her desired red boots. Strange, she thought, how life took a turn that day. On the drive home, she realized that many others living in her hometown had probably had a similar experience. Gerta began to think that she had discovered a fantastic business opportunity.

Gerta Franklin and her husband, George, had recently been married and were living in the heart of Central Florida's farm and horse country. George was temporarily between jobs and was currently looking for work on one of the many small farms that dotted the countryside. Gerta worked as a bookkeeper for a successful land developer but had always dreamed of running her own business. The timing was perfect. After three months of careful planning, on November 16, 2016, Gerta and George opened Double G Western Wear for business. Their store specialized in all forms of western equestrian clothing and shoes and was located just off a main business thoroughfare. Although open for only 45 days, the store managed to earn a small profit during

2016. A summary of Double G's 2016 financial information revealed the following:

- Gerta and George contributed $25,000 and a five-year-old truck valued at $5,000.
- Both agreed to take an annual salary of $36,000 ($3,000 a month each, starting at opening), reinvesting any annual profits back into the business.
- Leased space downtown was secured at $5,000 a month. One month's rent plus a $3,000 security deposit was required up front. The lease term began October 1, 2016, and all rent payments were due on the first of each month.
- Remodeling and improvements were made to the leased space. These included shelving materials ($10,000), four ceiling fans ($800), and contract labor ($3,000).
- A cash register was purchased for $2,000.
- Other operating expenses totaled $28,000.
- Inventory was acquired from two western-wear distributors. It included boots, hats, belts, scarves, vests, and knick-knacks. The total purchase price was $30,000.
- On November 1, $12,000 was borrowed from a local bank. Terms were 10% per annum required, with interest-only payments due for the first three years.
- A $15,000 line of credit was also established. Terms allowed for the first $1,000 to be interest-free, with a rate of 12% per annum for any amounts over $1,000.
- Sales of $82,000 were made through the end of the year. No credit was offered, although 40% of sales were made with credit cards. Credit-card processors charged a 2.5% fee.
- Inventory was replenished before year-end. During the year, inventory was priced to yield a 70% gross margin.
- Useful lives for all property and equipment were five years, starting in the month placed in service.

Exhibits 1 and 2 present the balance sheet and income statement for Double G Western Wear as of the end of 2016.

The Christmas season had helped Double G earn the 2016 profit, but sales returns early in 2017 had dampened the couple's enthusiasm. Contrary to the zero returns experienced in December, post-New Year's returns had totaled $5,100. In mid-January, Gerta realized she needed to plan for the year. She and George projected Double G's 2017 financial statements under what they believed were very conservative assumptions. They assumed that sales would continue at their present rate of approximately $52,000 a month. Sales returns would run at 3%, gross margins would hold at 70%, and the store would end the year with $35,000 of inventory on hand. Operating expenses—other than owners' salaries, rent, depreciation, and interest—would be approximately $19,000 a month. Finally, they would need a new truck, which, after trade-in, would cost $20,000.

Required

1. Reconstruct the 2016 transactions that led to the balance sheet and income statement presented in Exhibits 1 and 2.
2. Prepare a forecasted balance sheet as of December 31, 2017 and a forecasted income statement for the year 2017.
3. Using the data provided, prepare a statement of cash flow for the year 2017.

Exhibit 1		
DOUBLE G WESTERN WEAR		
Balance Sheet: 12-31-16		
Assets		
Cash	$ 6,280	
Inventory	16,400	
Prepaid assets	5,000	
Deposits	3,000	
Property and equipment (net)	20,107	
Total assets		$50,787
Liabilities		
Interest payable	100	
Taxes payable	553	
Accrued expenses	5,000	
Loan	12,000	
Total liabilities		17,653
Equity		
Common stock	30,000	
Retained earnings	3,134	
Total equity		$33,134

Exhibit 2		
DOUBLE G WESTERN WEAR		
Income Statement: 2016		
Sales	$82,000	
Cost of goods sold	24,600	
Gross margin		$57,400
Owners' salaries	9,000	
Operating expenses	28,000	
Rent	15,000	
Depreciation	693	
Interest	200	
Credit-card fees	820	
		53,713
Tax expense		553
Net income		$ 3,134

SOLUTIONS TO REVIEW PROBLEMS

Solution 3.1

THE ARCADIA COMPANY
Statement of Cash Flow
For Year Ended 12/31/15

(Indirect Method)

Operating activities	
Net loss	$(18,000)
Depreciation expense	28,500
Inventory	26,500
Prepaid insurance	1,500
Accounts payable	(2,500)
Wages payable	10,500
Cash flow from operations.	46,500
Investing activities	
Marketable securities.	7,500
Building, net.	(31,000)*
Cash flow from investing	(23,500)
Financing activities	
Bank loan.	2,000
Dividends paid	(2,000)**
Cash flow from investing	-0-
Net increase in cash.	23,000
Cash, beginning of year	7,000
Cash, end of year	$ 30,000
Change in cash (from balance sheet).	$ 23,000

*($190,000 − $187,500) + $28,500 = $31,000
**$56,500 + ($18,000) − $36,500 = $2,000

Solution 3.2

a. Operating funds ratio $46,500/$32,500 =   1.43
    Operating cash flow to current liabilities ratio $46,500/$110,500 =   0.42
    Cash conversion ratio $432,000/$480,000 =   0.90
b. Free cash flow $46,500 − $31,000 = $15,500
    Discretionary cash flow $46,500 − $2,000 − $2,000 = $42,500

Solution 3.3

a. $6,200,000 − (0.06 × $200 × 4,000)/300,000 shares = $20.51
b. $6,200,000/(300,000 + (2 × 4,000)) = $20.13

continued from previous page

THE DANA POINT COMPANY
Income Statements

	2016	2015
Revenues	$480,000	$430,000
Less: Cost of goods sold	250,000	240,000
Gross margin	230,000	190,000
Less: Depreciation expense	22,000	22,000
Wage expense	90,000	86,000
Insurance expense	16,000	16,000
Interest expense	6,600	6,800
Net income before taxes	95,400	59,200
Less: Tax expense (30%)	28,600	17,800
Net income.	$ 66,800	$ 41,400

Required

Prepare percentage change and common-sized balance sheets and income statements for The Dana Point Company for 2016.

The solution is on page 172.

Financial Ratios

Another technique for analyzing a company's financial performance is the calculation of **ratios** of relevant accounting variables—that is, dividing (or standardizing) one accounting measure by another economically relevant measure. A company may, for instance, report a numerically large net income, but the reason for the firm's success in generating a large net income may simply be a function of its size and not that the business is well run. To address this analytical issue, it is useful to compute such ratios as the return on assets (ROA), which provides an assessment of whether net income is large relative to a firm's size, as defined by its investment in assets. Financial ratios enable financial statement users to make valid comparisons of firm operating performance, over time for the same firm and between comparable companies.

When analyzing a firm's financial health, investment professionals, lenders, managers, and shareholders are usually interested in gaining insights about a firm's profitability, asset management, and financial risk. **Profitability** refers to how much income was generated by a business, particularly relative to the amount of total assets invested in the business or relative to the amount of assets specifically invested by a company's shareholders. **Asset management**, on the other hand, refers to how effectively the invested assets were used in the business by the company's management team. Finally, **financial risk** refers to a firm's ability to repay its borrowings in a timely manner and may be evaluated both in terms of a firm's short-term debt repayment capability and its long-term debt repayment capacity. **Liquidity** refers to the ability of a company to generate cash and is often considered a good indication of a company's ability to pay its outstanding *short-term* obligations. Short-term sources of liquidity include existing current assets, ongoing operations, and available lines of credit. **Solvency**, on the other hand, generally refers to the ability of a company to repay its outstanding *long-term* obligations. Liquidity and solvency are related concepts since a company must have sufficient liquidity to remain solvent. Firms that borrow extensively are said to be highly leveraged and carry greater financial risk; they are also said to be less solvent. **Leverage** refers to the use of borrowed funds to finance operations and/or asset purchases. Solvency and leverage are inversely related—that is, all else equal, a highly leveraged firm is less solvent than a firm that uses little or no debt to finance its business.

Some of the financial ratios that are commonly calculated by investment professionals, lenders, and managers are presented and explained in Exhibit 4.6. The application and interpretation of these ratios can be illustrated using the financial data of Under Armour, to which we now turn.

Financial ratios assessing the profitability, asset management, liquidity and solvency for Under Armour are shown in Exhibit 4.7. You may wish to replicate these calculations using Under Armour's financial statements in Exhibits 4.1, 4.2, 4.3, and the ratio definitions in Exhibit 4.6.

EXHIBIT 4.6	Key Financial Ratios	
Ratio	**Definition**	**Explanation**
Profitability		
• Return on shareholders' equity (ROE)	$$\frac{\text{Net income} - \text{Preferred stock dividends}}{\text{Shareholders' equity}}$$	Rate of return generated by a business for its common shareholders.
• Return on assets (ROA)	$$\frac{\text{Net income} + [\text{Interest expense} (1 - \text{Tax rate})]}{\text{Total assets}}$$	Rate of return generated on a company's investment in assets from all sources.
• Return on sales (ROS)	$$\frac{\text{Net income}}{\text{Net sales}}$$	Percentage of net income remaining from a dollar of sales after subtracting all expenses. Often this ratio is referred to as "net profit margin."
• Gross profit margin ratio	$$\frac{(\text{Net sales} - \text{Cost of goods sold})}{\text{Net sales}}$$	Percentage of income generated from sales after deducting the cost of goods sold.
Asset Management		
• Receivable turnover	$$\frac{\text{Net sales}}{\text{Accounts receivable}}$$	Number of sales/collection cycles experienced by a firm.
• Receivable collection period	$$\frac{365}{(\text{Net sales/Accounts receivable})}$$	Number of days required, on average, to collect an outstanding account receivable.
• Inventory turnover	$$\frac{\text{Cost of goods sold}}{\text{Inventory}}$$	Number of production/sales cycles experienced by a firm.
• Inventory-on-hand period	$$\frac{365}{(\text{Cost of goods sold/Inventory})}$$	Number of days, on average, required to sell the inventory currently on hand.
• Asset turnover	$$\frac{\text{Net sales}}{\text{Total assets}}$$	Amount of sales generated from each dollar invested in assets.
Liquidity		
• Cash and marketable securities to total assets	$$\frac{(\text{Cash} + \text{Marketable securities})}{\text{Total assets}}$$	Percentage of total assets held as highly liquid assets.
• Quick ratio	$$\frac{(\text{Cash} + \text{Marketable securities} + \text{Accounts receivable})}{\text{Current liabilities}}$$	Amount of liquid assets available to pay short-term liabilities.
• Current ratio	$$\frac{\text{Current assets}}{\text{Current liabilities}}$$	Amount of current assets available to service current liabilities.
• Accounts payable turnover	$$\frac{\text{Cost of goods sold}}{\text{Accounts payable}}$$	Number of account payment cycles experienced by a firm.
• Days' payable period	$$\frac{365}{\text{Cost of goods sold/Accounts payable}}$$	Number of days, on average, required to pay an outstanding account payable.
Solvency		
• Long-term debt to total assets	$$\frac{(\text{Long-term debt} + \text{Current portion of long-term debt})}{\text{Total assets}}$$	Percentage of total assets provided by creditors.
• Long-term debt to shareholders' equity	$$\frac{(\text{Long-term debt} + \text{Current portion of long-term debt})}{\text{Shareholders' equity}}$$	Relative investment of long-term creditors versus shareholders in a business.
• Interest coverage ratio	$$\frac{\text{Net income before taxes} + \text{Interest expense}}{\text{Interest expense}}$$	Extent to which current operating income covers current debt service charges.

There is no generally accepted definition for most of the financial ratios presented in Exhibit 4.6, and consequently, the ratios may be calculated in a variety of ways. For example, to calculate the return on assets ratio, some analysts use an average of the beginning and ending total assets as the denominator, while others use only the ending or beginning balance of total assets. This is done to match the numerator (i.e., net income), which is computed over a period of time, with the denominator (i.e., total assets), which is computed at a point in time. In general, unless there has been a large movement in the level of the denominator over the time period being analyzed, the definition used to define a ratio's calculation won't make much difference when ranking companies from best to worst. What is important is to define ratios consistently over time and between companies so that any performance comparisons are "apples to apples" and not "apples to oranges."

EXHIBIT 4.7	Financial Ratios: Under Armour, Inc.		
Fiscal year ending		**2014**	**2013**
Ratio			
Profitability			
Gross profit margin ratio		49.0%	48.7%
Return on sales (ROS)		6.7%	7.0%
Return on assets (ROA)		10.1%	10.4%
Return on equity (ROE)		15.4%	15.4%
Asset Management			
Receivable turnover (# times)		11.0	11.1
Receivable collection in days		33.1	32.9
Inventory turnover (# times)		2.9	2.5
Inventory-on-hand in days		124.6	143.2
Asset turnover		1.5	1.5
Liquidity			
Cash & marketable securities to total assets		28.3%	22.0%
Quick ratio		2.07	1.31
Current ratio		3.67	2.65
Accounts payable turnover (# times)		7.5	7.2
Days' payable in days		48.9	50.5
Solvency			
Long-term debt to total assets		13.6%	3.4%
Long-term debt to shareholders' equity		21.0%	5.0%
Interest coverage ratio (# times)		65.1	90.0

With respect to corporate profitability, Under Armour's cost of goods sold decreased slightly relative to net sales over the two-year period 2013 to 2014 (see Exhibit 4.4), allowing the company to incur a small increase in its **gross profit margin ratio** from 48.7 percent of net revenues in 2013 to 49.0 percent in 2014. However, Under Armour generated a slightly worse **return on sales** (ROS) of 6.7 percent in 2014, down from 7.0 percent in 2013.[1] This means that for every dollar of sales in 2014, Under Armour earned 6.7 cents after subtracting all expenses. An ROS of this magnitude may seem low, although it should be noted that the apparel industry is extremely competitive, requiring significant manufacturing and marketing expenditures. Under Armour's **return on assets** (ROA) of 10.1 percent in 2014 was also down from the company's 2013 level of 10.4 percent. The company's **return on equity** (ROE) however remained constant at 15.4 percent in 2014 and 2013, 5.3 percentage points over its 2014 ROA and 7.4 percentage points above its cost of equity. (See Appendix 4C for a discussion of how to calculate a company's cost of equity financing.)

One measure of how well a company utilizes its borrowed funds involves a comparison of the company's ROE with its ROA. Since the ROA represents the return to all capital contributors while ROE is the return to just the company's shareholders, an ROE in excess of ROA indicates that a firm is earning more on its borrowed funds than its cost to borrow those funds. For example, if a firm borrows funds at an interest rate of five percent and subsequently earns eight percent from the use of those funds, the excess earnings accrue to the company's shareholders. Since Under Armour reported an ROE that was 5.3 percentage points greater than its ROA, the company can be described as being able to effectively utilize financial leverage. We will discuss **financial leverage** in greater detail shortly.

With respect to asset management, Under Armour's **inventory-on-hand** period—that is, the average number of days that a business's inventory remains on hand before being sold—indicates that Under Armour keeps high amounts of inventory on hand (i.e., 124.6 days in 2014). This ratio indicates a very slow moving inventory that may carry with it inventory holding and storage costs as well as obsolescence risk, and is consistent with the high inventory levels observed in our review of the company's balance sheet. It should be

---

[1] Many investment professionals use an alternative calculation of the return of sales (ROS) ratio, called the unlevered ROS ratio, calculated as follows:

$$\text{Unlevered ROS} = \frac{\text{Net income} + [\text{Interest } (1 - \text{tax rate})]}{\text{Net sales}}$$

The unlevered ROS ratio enables the analyst to evaluate the effectiveness of a company's operating strategy independent of its financing strategy; that is, unlevering ROS restates a firm's net income as if the firm were all equity financed. A discussion of unlevering ratios is presented in Appendix 4A to this chapter.

noted, however, that Under Armour was able to reduce its inventory-on-hand from 143.2 days in 2013. The **receivable collection period**—that is, the average number of days that customers take to pay their bills—is a much more reasonable 33.1 days in 2014 (about one month). The company's **asset turnover** ratio indicates that, in both 2013 and 2014, every dollar invested in the business's assets generated $1.50 in sales. All else equal, the stability of this ratio indicates that as Under Armour has grown in size, it has not become more efficient at converting assets used in the business into sales to its customers.

GLOBAL PERSPECTIVE

Financial statement analysis is executed, worldwide, in exactly the same fashion. Common-size financial statements and financial ratios, for example, are currency-neutral and can be effectively utilized anywhere in the world. Not all ratios are relevant, however, in all countries. For example, in lesser-developed countries, which lack the infrastructure to support a credit system, ratios involving accounts receivable (such as receivable turnover and the receivable collection period) or accounts payable (such as accounts payable turnover and the days' payable period) are likely to be not as relevant for purposes of financial statement analysis.

Our review thus far of Under Armour indicates that inventory purchases and sales are critical operational drivers for the company. Ultimately purchases and sales of inventory must result in cash generation, and therefore analysts often combine the inventory-on-hand period with the receivable collection period to estimate the length of a company's **cash collection period**. This measure identifies the amount of time, on average, needed from the outlay of cash for inventory, through the sale of that inventory, until the ultimate collection of cash from the sale. In other words, the cash collection period represents the cash-to-cash cycle of a business. Since companies often acquire inventory on credit, without the necessity of paying interest on the credit purchase, an amount representing the average time taken to pay a company's accounts payable is often subtracted when estimating the cash collection period. The number of days needed to pay a firm's accounts payable is calculated as 365/(cost of goods sold/accounts payable) and is referred to as the **days' payable period**. Thus, a firm's cash collection period can be estimated as follows:

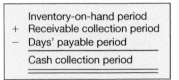

In the case of Under Armour, the cash collection period for 2014 was 108.8 days (33.1 + 124.6 − 48.9). Since Under Armour's business is inventory intensive and its inventory turnover very slow, the company is less able to finance its business operating cycle using interest-free trade credit from its suppliers. This business attribute may significantly impact Under Armour's profitability from year-to-year, as not only does the company bear certain inventory holding costs, but it is not able to leverage its suppliers to help finance that inventory. It is worth noting that accounts payable represent interest-free loans provided by one business to another business, and as such, need to be carefully monitored and managed through such financial indicators as the cash collection period and the days' payable period. It is also noteworthy that such interest-free debt as accounts payable are considered separately from a business's interest-bearing debt—its bank loans, bonds, and notes payable—when performing credit risk analysis, the focus of the next section.

The financial ratios in Exhibit 4.7 also indicate that Under Armour is relatively liquid—that is, it has liquid resources in the form of current assets to pay its current obligations as they come due. Under Armour's **current ratio**—the ratio of current assets to current liabilities—is well above one in both years. Hence, if all of the company's current assets were converted to cash, there would be sufficient cash to pay off all of Under Armour's current obligations. The **quick ratio**, which excludes Under Armour's potentially illiquid inventory, is 2.07 in 2014 and indicates that

> A company's **liquid assets** include cash, cash equivalents, marketable securities and accounts receivable, but exclude inventory and prepaid expenses, which are often illiquid. **Cash equivalents** are very short-term (90 days or less) investments in highly liquid, risk-free certificates of deposit or government securities.

Under Armour's highly **liquid assets**, such as cash, marketable securities, and accounts receivable, are over two times as large as the total of the obligations due within one year. Use of these ratios to analyze liquidity implicitly assumes that these assets can be converted into cash at a rate sufficient to match the timing of when the current obligations become due. Investment professionals often couple their analysis of the current and quick ratios with additional ratios such as the receivable collection period and the inventory-on-hand period, which indicate how quickly cash can be generated. Even though the cash collection period of 108.8 days for Under Armour may appear to be slow, the reality is that the company has solid liquidity in the short term, especially when coupled with its positive operating cash flow. Because of its liquid position and its high growth prospects, the relatively slow cash collection period for Under Armour is not as much of a concern as it otherwise might be.

REVIEW PROBLEM 4.2

The following balance sheet and income statement data were taken from the financial records of The Dana Point Company:

THE DANA POINT COMPANY Balance Sheets					
	2016	**2015**		**2016**	**2015**
Assets			**Liabilities & Shareholders' Equity**		
Cash..................	$ 7,000	$ 30,000	Accounts payable........	$ 65,500	$ 63,000
Accounts receivable.....	67,500	60,000	Wages payable..........	37,000	47,500
Inventory..............	49,000	22,500	Total current liabilities.....	102,500	110,500
Prepaid insurance.......	6,000	4,500	Bank loan payable	83,000	85,000
Total current assets	129,500	117,000	Capital stock	75,000	75,000
Building (net)..........	187,500	190,000	Retained earnings	56,500	36,500
Total	$317,000	$307,000	Total	$317,000	$307,000

THE DANA POINT COMPANY Income Statements		
	2016	**2015**
Revenues	$480,000	$430,000
Less: Cost of goods sold	250,000	240,000
Gross margin	230,000	190,000
Less: Depreciation expense.............................	22,000	22,000
Wage expense	90,000	86,000
Insurance expense	16,000	16,000
Interest expense	6,600	6,800
Net income before taxes	95,400	59,200
Less: Tax expense (30%)	28,600	17,800
Net income...	$ 66,800	$ 41,400

Required

1. Calculate the following ratios for The Dana Point Company for 2015 and 2016:

   - Return on equity
   - Return on sales
   - Asset turnover
   - Financial leverage
   - Receivable collection period
   - Inventory-on-hand period
   - Days' payable period

   - Long-term debt to total assets
   - Long-term debt to shareholders' equity
   - Interest coverage ratio
   - Quick ratio
   - Current ratio
   - Gross profit margin ratio

2. Comment on the trends in profitability, asset management, and financial risk for The Dana Point Company from 2015 to 2016.

The solution is on page 173.

Credit Risk Analysis

Current shareholders, investment advisors, and top management are vitally interested in a company's profitability and asset management because these factors are closely linked to future increases and decreases in a company's share price. Lenders, on the other hand, are less interested in these factors because creditors generally don't share in the upside potential of a firm when its share price appreciates. Creditors are more concerned with downside risk—that is, not getting paid the interest and principal they were promised. But what factors affect credit risk?

In general, the more indebtedness a firm has, the more likely it is that an unforeseen decline in sales and/or an increase in expenses will reduce a firm's capacity to meet its loan servicing commitments. The ratios of long-term debt, including the current portion of long-term debt, to total assets and to shareholders' equity are two ratios that measure the relative amount of a company's outstanding debt, and thus, its solvency. Similarly, the more operating income a company generates relative to the amount of its annual interest expense—the **interest coverage ratio**—the more likely it is that a company will be able to make timely interest payments from operating cash flow.

At the end of 2014, Under Armour's long-term debt was only 21.0 percent of its outstanding shareholders' equity. Further, Under Armour's interest coverage ratio—the ratio of operating income to interest expense—was a massive 65.1 times in 2014 and 90.0 times in 2013, respectively. On both counts, Under Armour's ability to take on additional debt with little risk to its lenders seems substantial. That puts the company in an excellent position to negotiate favorable credit terms such as a large loan with a low interest rate. With the company's strong historical operating cash flow averaging about $179.6 million per year over the period 2012–2014, the company should have little difficulty paying its interest charges or principal payments in a timely manner.

But how can you be sure that Under Armour has reported all of its outstanding debt on its balance sheet? Following the Enron Corporation scandal, it is likely that many more investors will carefully read the footnotes that accompany a company's financial statements, and in the case of Under Armour, such **due diligence** would be revealing. Under Armour's footnotes indicate that the company leases a number of its store locations through operating leases. Under an **operating lease** agreement, the value of the leased asset and the related lease liability do **not** appear on the company's balance sheet. Under Armour's footnotes reveal that the company has minimum future lease payments under operating leases of $472.6 million due in the future. That means that Under Armour's debt ratios measured using only the debt listed on Under Armour's balance sheet *understate* the total level of corporate debt! Even if those **off-balance-sheet liabilities** were considered, however, Under Armour appears to be an excellent credit risk.

> Because of complex accounting standards, some obligations (such as operating leases) do not appear on the face of the balance sheet, and thus, understate a firm's true debt position. These unreported liabilities are often referred to as **off-balance-sheet liabilities** and are described in detail in Chapters 9 and 10.

Benchmarking: Comparisons with Similar Companies

Assessing the significance of financial ratios can be substantially enhanced by comparing a company's financial ratios with those of competing companies in the same industry or the same line of business. This process is called **benchmarking** or **cross-sectional analysis**. Under Armour is classified as being in **Standard Industrial Classification (SIC)** code 2300—The Apparel/Accessories Industry. Nike is a direct competitor to Under Armour and also operates in this industry. The company's trademark "swoosh" is an easily recognized logo across the globe, and Nike has translated this advantage into over $24 billion in annual sales. Shoe sales represent about 56 percent of this total, but the company has a diversified athletic product line across multiple apparel categories.

Comparison ratios for Under Armour and Nike are reported in Exhibit 4.8. First observe that Nike has a fiscal year ending in the month of May, five months after Under Armour's fiscal year end of December. While the values used in both sets of ratios are still measured on an annual basis for both companies, the analyst should be aware that there is a five-month lag between the two, during which time economic and market conditions may differ. Our comparisons for each company will be made with respect to their most recent year.

> A **Standard Industrial Classification (SIC)** code is a categorization tool for all industries and services. The code itself is a unique number that corresponds to a text definition of a given industry. SIC codes are reported by companies on tax returns, U.S. Census Bureau reports, and other government filings.

EXHIBIT 4.8	Financial Ratios: Under Armour Versus Nike			
		Under Armour Year Ended Dec. 31		Nike Year Ended May 31
Fiscal Year Ending		2014	2013	2014	2013

Fiscal Year Ending	2014	2013	2014	2013
Profitability				
Gross profit margin ratio.	49.0%	48.7%	44.8%	43.6%
Return on sales (ROS)	6.7%	7.0%	9.7%	9.8%
Return on assets (ROA)	10.1%	10.4%	14.5%	14.1%
Return on equity (ROE).	15.4%	15.4%	24.9%	22.3%
Asset Management				
Receivable collection in days.	33.1	32.9	45.1	44.9
Inventory-on-hand in days.	124.6	143.2	93.8	89.1
Asset turnover	1.5	1.5	1.5	1.4
Liquidity				
Quick ratio	2.07	1.31	1.71	2.29
Current ratio.	3.67	2.65	2.72	3.44
Days' payable in days	48.9	50.5	45.9	42.7
Solvency				
Long-term debt to total assets.	13.6%	3.4%	6.5%	7.2%
Long-term debt to shareholders' equity.	21.0%	5.0%	11.1%	11.4%

With regard to firm profitability, Nike reported a lower gross profit margin, 44.8 percent versus Under Armour's 49.0 percent, but had a return on sales three percentage points higher than Under Armour's—9.7 percent versus 6.7 percent. This suggests that Nike does a better job than Under Armour in controlling its overall total costs, but Under Armour has a lower relative cost of sales. This latter difference may be due in part to the company's product mix and pricing, as well as where their products are sold. Compared to Nike, Under Armour currently has a greater proportion of its sales in the U.S. and a much lower overall proportion of shoe sales. Depending on the pricing and manufacturing costs associated with these items in these markets, differences in gross margins do not come as a surprise. Nike's return on assets of 14.5 percent was also higher than Under Armour's ROA of 10.1 percent, with the same relation found for return on equity—24.9 percent versus 15.4 percent. Overall, it is difficult to avoid the conclusion that Nike is more profitable than Under Armour.

In Practice 4.1 *Financial Ratio Benchmarks by Industry*   The following table presents industry median benchmarks for a set of selected financial ratios:

Industry	ROE	ROA	ROS	A/R Turnover	Inventory Turnover	Current Ratio	Debt-to-Equity
Agriculture Crops	10.2	4.4	2.8	12.3	9.3	1.6	72.6
Oil Gas Extraction.	14.4	6.9	7.3	5.4	34.2	1.4	82.1
Food, Kindred Product.	11.2	5.0	2.5	13.3	13.0	1.7	105.3
Apparel Related Products	10.9	5.1	2.5	9.6	7.8	2.4	74.8
Printing, Publishing	15.0	5.9	3.2	8.5	26.7	1.9	95.1
Rubber & Plastics.	12.7	5.5	2.6	8.0	10.3	2.1	96.7
Fabricated Metal Products.	14.6	6.7	3.3	8.0	11.1	2.2	85.3
Electrical Equipment	9.2	4.3	2.9	6.9	7.2	2.6	57.5
Trucking & Warehousing.	19.9	7.4	2.6	10.5	168.4	1.7	121.7
Transportation Services	21.9	8.1	2.0	9.8	43.3	1.5	138.3
Communication	8.3	1.8	1.9	8.9	36.7	1.4	95.2
Wholesale Trade.	12.9	5.2	1.9	9.6	8.5	1.9	113.8
Eating Drinking Places	13.6	6.2	2.9	82.9	83.8	1.0	102.9
Miscellaneous Retail Stores	8.8	4.1	1.5	22.7	8.2	2.1	80.9
Real Estate	13.2	4.3	7.1	20.2	20.5	1.9	86.7
Personal Services.	10.7	5.6	2.9	11.5	38.2	1.7	97.3
Misc. Business Services.	17.6	7.0	3.0	7.6	37.0	1.7	93.9
Health Services	9.1	4.4	3.7	7.7	60.4	2.0	83.8
Educational Services	6.9	3.6	5.0	16.7	163.1	2.1	68.2

Source: Dunn & Bradstreet Industry Norms & Key Business Ratios

In terms of asset management, Nike holds less inventory than Under Armour—93.8 days versus 124.6 days for Under Armour—which may reflect the different supply chain arrangements between the two companies, different strategies for product flexibility, or even possibly the effect of different inventory valuation methods (a topic that will be considered in Chapter 6). The two companies have similar asset turnover ratios at 1.5 each. In terms of liquidity, no conclusions can be reached other than Nike is carrying slightly less current assets (i.e., likely lower inventory levels), although both companies would be considered highly liquid as current ratios are strong. Quick ratios for each company also exceed 1.7, indicating highly liquid assets that can easily cover all liabilities that will come due in the next year. On both measures of solvency evaluated, it is apparent that Nike carries a much lower level of long-term debt—11.1 percent of equity versus 21.0 percent for Under Armour. However, given that both companies have overall little debt, coupled with the strong profitability measures of each, there appears to be a low likelihood of either company being unable to meet its debt service obligations. Even with this said, however, one could reasonably conclude that Under Armour has a slightly higher degree of financial risk than Nike.

To summarize, although Under Armour is profitable, Nike overall has been able to generate higher levels of profitability while at the same time taking on lower levels of leverage. Both companies arguably produced strong levels of profitability during an otherwise sluggish worldwide economy during this time period.

ROE MODEL FRAMEWORK

Takeaway 2
Explain the return on equity model of financial analysis.

The Return on Equity (ROE) Model introduced in Chapter 2 actually encompasses a second model known as the **DuPont Model**. The DuPont Model was developed by the controllers' department of the DuPont Chemical Company in the 1960s as a means to evaluate the performance of the company's many operating divisions and division-level managers. Under the DuPont Model, divisional performance is evaluated in terms of the return on assets (ROA), which can be shown to be a function of the return on sales (ROS) and asset turnover (AT). The DuPont Model does not include a component for financial leverage since most division-level managers have no control over how their division is financed. Consequently, as the level of financial analysis or performance evaluation shifts from a division to an entire company, it is important to move from the DuPont Model, which ignores leverage, to the ROE model, which includes leverage. The cornerstone of the ROE Model is the return on equity and reveals that a firm's ROE can be decomposed into the three component ratios of return on sales, asset turnover, and financial leverage:[2]

```
                    ┌─────────────────┐
                    │   Return on     │
                    │    Equity       │
                    │    (ROE)        │
                    └─────────────────┘
          ┌───────────────┬───────────────┐
  ┌───────────────┐ ┌───────────────┐ ┌───────────────┐
  │  Return on    │ │    Asset      │ │   Financial   │
  │    Sales    × │ │  Turnover   × │ │   Leverage    │
  │    (ROS)      │ │    (AT)       │ │    (LEV)      │
  └───────────────┘ └───────────────┘ └───────────────┘
```

The framework shows that, all else equal, a business can increase its return on equity by increasing one or more of the following factors:

■ Return on sales (such as by increasing the price of products sold and/or by reducing operating expenses).

■ Asset turnover (such as by using the key operating assets of accounts receivables, inventory and property and equipment more efficiently, for example by generating the same volume of sales with a smaller investment in these assets or generating greater sales volume with the same level of investment in these assets).

■ Financial leverage (such as by financing the business with debt to leverage the use of high-return assets with a lower after-tax cost of funds).

---

[2] Appendix 4A to this chapter presents a reformulation of the ROE Model using unlevered ratios.

The framework allows an analyst to better determine why ROE may change from one year to the next. While knowing that this ratio has changed is certainly important, it is far better to understand the cause of the change. Is it because the company has done a better job of controlling costs as indicated by the first component (ROS)? Or perhaps the company has increased its efficiency of assets and is able to generate more sales per dollar of assets as indicated by the second component (AT). Finally, the change may be the result of a change in the company's use of financial leverage, the third component (LEV).

We can illustrate how these components work together to generate ROE by considering a hypothetical for The Mammoth Company. Suppose The Mammoth Company reports net income of $100 on sales of $2,000. The company's total assets are $1,000. Total liabilities are $250 and stockholders' equity is $750. Therefore ROS computes to be 5 percent, indicating The Mammoth Company was able to generate 5 cents of net income for every dollar of sales after subtracting all expenses. Asset turnover computes to be 2.0, indicating The Mammoth Company is able to generate $2 of sales for every dollar of assets invested in the company. Together these two ratios indicate The Mammoth Company has a ROA of 10 percent, meaning the company is able to generate $0.10 of net income for every dollar of assets invested in the company. Finally, suppose we see The Mammoth Company has financed part of its operation with debt and has a financial leverage ratio (LEV) of 1.33. Multiplying this LEV by the company's ROA shows The Mammoth Company reported an ROE of 13.3 percent. We will see in a later chapter how the use of leverage can increase a company's profitability with ROE exceeding ROA as long as the company can earn more on its debt than the cost of that debt.

Data for computing an ROE analysis for Under Armour, Inc. is presented in Exhibit 4.9. In 2014, Under Armour's ROE remained constant relative to the preceding year at 15.4 percent, although in 2012 the company's ROE was at a high of 15.8 percent (see **bolded** area in Exhibit 4.9). As mentioned above, it is reasonable to conclude that based on the recent level of its ROE, Under Armour is a profitable company.

EXHIBIT 4.9	ROE Model Analysis: Under Armour, Inc.				
($ thousands)	2014	2013	2012	2011	2010
Financial statement values					
Total revenue	$3,084,370	$2,332,051	$1,834,921	$1,472,684	$1,063,927
Net income	208,042	162,330	128,778	96,919	68,477
Total assets	2,095,083	1,577,741	1,157,083	919,210	675,378
Stockholders' equity	1,350,300	1,053,354	816,922	636,432	496,966
ROE analysis					
ROE (NI/Shareholders' equity)	15.4%	15.4%	15.8%	15.2%	13.8%
=					
ROS (NI/Revenues)	6.7%	7.0%	7.0%	6.6%	6.4%
× AT (Revenues/Total assets)	1.47	1.48	1.59	1.60	1.58
× LEV (Total assets/SE)	1.55	1.50	1.42	1.44	1.36

But just what factors contributed to the decline in Under Armour's ROE to its current level from its high in 2012? The decline was due to a drop in ROS from 7.0 percent in 2012 to 6.7 percent in 2014, and a drop in asset turnover from 1.59 in 2012 to 1.47 in 2014. These decreases were partially offset by an increase in leverage from 1.42 in 2012 to 1.55 in 2014. Thus we can conclude that in 2014, relative to 2012, Under Armour is not controlling its costs per dollar of sales and its asset efficiency as well as it previously had.

In summary, Under Armour experienced a slight decline in its ROE from 2012 to 2013, and then held steady in 2014. It should also be noted that Under Armour reported an increasing trend since 2010. Finally, the company's share price increased almost ten-fold over the five-year period ending December 31, 2014, largely due to its steady and profitable growth and bright prospects to gain further market share. While Under Armour is able to earn returns well above its cost of borrowing, management has been reluctant until recently to utilize more than a minimum amount of leverage. The fact that Under Armour's return on assets of 10.1 percent in 2014 likely far exceeds its after-tax cost of borrowing suggests that the firm is foregoing the opportunity to maximize shareholder value by growing the company through additional leverage.

Estimating Sustainable Growth

Sales growth is one of the key factors of interest to all financial statement users, in part because of the high correlation between sales growth and growth in share price. Many investment professionals believe, for example, that the key driver of share price is the rate of growth in business revenue. In the case of Under Armour, Exhibit 4.1 revealed that revenues grew from $1,834.9 million in 2012 to over $3 billion in 2014, an average annual growth rate of nearly 30 percent. But revenue growth comes at a cost, namely the related growth in a firm's investment in such operating assets as accounts receivable, inventory, and property, plant and equipment. This was particularly the case with Under Armour and its recent spike in inventory. And, an increase in a firm's investment in operating assets presents a secondary problem—the need to finance the required investment in new operating assets.

As previously discussed, firms may finance their asset purchases with debt, new equity, or with internally-generated funds. In general, financing new capital investments with the sale of equity is the least desirable financing option as equity is the most expensive form of financing. (See Appendix 4C for a discussion of how to estimate a firm's cost of equity.) Hence, financing a firm's growth in operating assets with debt and/or internally generated funds are the options preferred by most managers.

Although sales growth is desirable, excessively rapid growth can strain the financial resources of a business, even to the point of destroying a business by inducing bankruptcy. To help managers avoid this situation, investment professionals have developed an approach to estimate a firm's maximum desired rate of growth, called the **sustainable growth rate** (SGR), which is calculated as follows:

Sustainable growth rate = Return on equity × Dividend retention rate

The **dividend retention rate** (DRR) is equal to the percentage of net income **not** paid to shareholders in the form of dividends, and consequently, which is retained in a business.[3] Thus, a business's SGR is the rate of return on shareholders' equity available to be reinvested in the business. Since a firm's ROE can be decomposed into its three component ratios of return on sales (ROS), asset turnover (AT), and financial leverage (LEV), we can identify the key drivers of a firm's SGR as follows:

SGR = ROS × AT × LEV × DRR

Thus, a firm can increase its SGR by increasing any of its key components—the return on sales, asset turnover, financial leverage, or the dividend retention rate.

To illustrate the use of SGR, let's apply the concept to Under Armour. To help you understand the concept of SGR, consider two extremes: a company that pays all of its earnings to shareholders as dividends (DRR = 0 percent), and a company that pays none of its earnings as dividends (DRR = 100 percent). For the former, the SGR is zero (ROE × 0%), because none of the returns on equity are reinvested in the business. Consequently, any sales growth experienced during the year that yielded earnings would not be sustainable to future periods, all else equal. The company that retains all of its earnings, by way of contrast, would have an SGR equal to its ROE, and would therefore be expected to be able to sustain its sales growth at a rate equivalent to its ROE. That is, a company that earns 10 percent and retains all of its earnings would be expected to sustain a 10 percent rate of growth. Under Armour, like many companies, does not pay a dividend, and thus the dividend retention rate for the period 2011 through 2014 would be 100 percent. Exhibit 4.10 reports Under Armour's ROE for this period and illustrates the SGR calculation:

EXHIBIT 4.10	Sales Growth, ROE and SGR: Under Armour 2011–2014			
	2014	2013	2012	2011
Sales Growth.	32.3%	27.1%	24.6%	38.4%
ROE	15.4%	15.4%	15.8%	15.2%
× DRR	100.0%	100.0%	100.0%	100.0%
= SGR	15.4%	15.4%	15.8%	15.2%
Sales Growth less SGR	16.9%	11.7%	8.8%	23.2%

[3] The dividend payout ratio (discussed in Chapter 11) is the percentage of net income paid out to shareholders in the form of dividends (Dividends paid/Net income). Thus, the dividend retention ratio can be calculated as 1 minus the dividend payout ratio. The dividend retention ratio is also sometimes referred to as the "plow-back percentage."

For each year presented the sales growth for Under Armour exceeded its SGR, with each year reporting a difference between 15.2 and 15.8 percent. These results indicate that Under Armour's high growth strategy is on a collision course with its financing strategy—that is, the company's past rate of growth is not sustainable given its current financial structure. The company's ROE generation would have to be much higher to sustain its present rate of sales growth.

REVIEW PROBLEM 4.3

The following selected balance sheet and income statement data were taken from the financial records of The Ventura Company:

	2016	2015	2014	2013
Total revenue	2,650	2,525	2,400	2,250
Net income	175	160	160	130
Total assets	2,000	1,900	1,750	1,700
Stockholders' equity	1,300	1,225	1,150	1,050
Dividend retention rate	40.0%	40.0%	40.0%	40.0%

Required

1. Use the Dupont Model to compute the 2013 through 2016 return on equity. Show the value of each component for The Ventura Company.
2. Compute the Ventura Company's sustainable growth rate for the years 2013–2016 and compare it to the company's revenue growth rate. Assume revenue in 2012 was $2,175.

The solution is on page 173.

LIMITATIONS OF FINANCIAL STATEMENT ANALYSIS

Takeaway 3
Recognize the limitations of financial statement analysis.

It is important to understand not only what can be learned about a company by using the financial statement analysis techniques illustrated in this chapter, but also to understand that there are limitations to these techniques. One limitation is the ratios themselves. There is no GAAP that prescribes which ratios should be used in any given analysis, nor even how the ratios that are used should be calculated. As such, it is critical that a manager or an investment professional either compute the ratios directly or be sure to learn how any provided ratio has been computed. For example, it is entirely possible to obtain the same ratio, such as the return on assets, from two different data sources that have calculated them differently. Without knowing this, it is possible to make incorrect inferences when comparing the performance of different companies.

Just knowing how a ratio has been computed, however, does not ensure the validity of the analysis. It is also quite possible that the numbers from which a ratio is calculated contain problems. Some of the potential problems that may exist with the underlying financial statement data include:

1. **Measurement concerns.** Arguably, the most relevant method of measurement for a company's assets and liabilities is their market value. After all, for valuation purposes you would expect to pay what something is currently worth, not what it was worth at some point in the past. Unfortunately, market values are often much more subjective than what accounting standard setters consider acceptable for use in the basic financial statements, and therefore, the more reliable historical cost concept pervades financial statement measurement. Thus, while the price paid for land in Manhattan, New York, forty years ago may be a reliable number, it is not terribly relevant to today's valuation of a business operating in New York City.

2. **Incomplete data.** Although the historical cost concept does help ensure that the reported financial statement numbers are reliable, the relevance of many of the reported assets and liabilities values on the balance sheet are lessened, and many are not even reported at all. One accounting construct that impedes the relevance of financial statement data is that of conservatism. **Conservatism** dictates that, when in doubt, a company should report its accounts such that assets are understated, liabilities are overstated, the recognition of losses is accelerated, while the recognition of gains is delayed. Many important assets such as a company's trained workforce, management talent, internal processes, and brand go unreported on the balance sheet. For example, while GAAP requires the firm to record salary expense, no effort is

made to record the value of those employees. In addition, money spent on public relations and advertising to enhance a company's brand image, or research and development expenditures to create future products, are expensed as incurred even though these expenditures arguably generate future benefits for a business. Conservatism dictates that these items not be capitalized as assets on the balance sheet because their future value is uncertain and because they cannot be reliably measured. In an apparent contradiction to conservatism, some liabilities are also excluded from the balance sheet. These so called off-balance-sheet liabilities include some leases and certain contingencies.

3. **Differing accounting methods.** GAAP is not a one-size-fits-all set of rules. Instead, management is allowed significant flexibility in choosing the accounting methods that are used to report a firm's performance. Choices among alternative depreciation methods, alternative inventory cost flow assumptions, and alternative revenue recognition approaches are but a small sample of the policy choices that can dramatically alter reported income in any given year. This flexibility creates difficulties when performing benchmarking if the comparison companies use different accounting methods.

4. **Biased data.** GAAP allows not only the flexibility to choose different accounting methods, but also significant discretion in the various accrual estimates used in the preparation of the income statement and the balance sheet. A partial list of estimates that impact reported earnings includes estimates for uncollectible accounts, warranty expense, and sales returns, along with estimates for such things as asset write-downs, pension expense, and asset lives. Because many employment contracts are written using reported accounting numbers, managers often have a perverse incentive to bias the estimates used in financial statements as a means to favorably influence the outcome of such contracts.

5. **Lack of timeliness.** The expression "old news is no news" was probably not written about accounting data, but it certainly applies to some extent. Security markets react nearly instantly to any news deemed valuation-relevant. Certainly company performance is valuation-relevant; however, the performance reported in a company's financial statements is not timely. The annual 10-K report containing a company's financial statements, for example, is often filed with the U.S. Securities and Exchange Commission over two months after a company's fiscal year-end. As a consequence, much of the information contained in the report is already known by the time the 10-K becomes public information. Further, the accounting reports are, by definition, backward-looking reports, reporting on what has already occurred. Investment professionals, in contrast, want timely information that helps them predict what the future holds.

ETHICS PERSPECTIVE

Financial analysts are one of the primary user-groups of the financial information considered in this chapter. There are two principal types of financial analysts—buy-side analysts and sell-side analysts. **Buy-side analysts** work primarily for investment management companies such as Fidelity Investments or The Vanguard Group. The job of these analysts is to provide unbiased research that helps the portfolio managers of these mutual fund companies select securities for inclusion in their mutual fund portfolios. A second type of analyst, the **sell-side analyst**, works primarily for large financial services/investment banking companies such as Merrill Lynch or Morgan Stanley. Unlike buy-side analysts who do their research for a company's internal use, sell-side analysts provide their research for sale and use by their company's customers.

It has been argued that sell-side analysts are sometimes put under unreasonable pressure to be less than completely objective in their recommendations. Several apparent lapses in ethical behavior by sell-side analysts have come to light in recent years, eventually leading to mandated changes prescribed in the Sarbanes-Oxley Act. The purpose of these changes was to eliminate many of the conflicts of interest that sell-side analysts were exposed to and included:

- A prohibition of the solicitation of investment banking business by sell-side analysts.
- The creation of separate organizational structures for sell-side analysts and investment bankers.
- Restrictions placed on the interactions between, and contact with, sell-side analysts and investment bankers.
- Imposition of policies designed to prevent investment bankers from influencing the content of analysts' research reports.
- Creation of analyst compensation packages in which a significant portion of a sell-side analyst's compensation is linked to the quality and accuracy of the analyst's research.

EXECUTIVE SUMMARY

In this chapter, we considered a variety of financial analysis techniques: ocular regression (or trend analysis), common-size financial statements, and financial ratios. These analytical techniques are used to gain an understanding of a company's historical financial performance. The performance areas of interest include profitability, asset management, and financial risk. As a validation of your understanding of the content of this chapter, you should now be able to:

- Analyze a company's financial statements to evaluate its profitability, asset management, and financial risk.
- Explain the Return on Equity model of financial analysis.
- Recognize the limitations of financial statement analysis.
- Apply unlevering adjustments to ROA and ROS. (See Appendix 4A.)
- Construct pro forma income statements, balance sheets, and statements of cash flow. (See Appendix 4B.)
- Understand a common approach to calculating the cost of equity financing. (See Appendix 4C.)

KEY CONCEPTS AND TERMS

Asset management, 136
Asset turnover, 139
Benchmarking, 141
Beta, 151
Buy-side analyst, 147
Capital asset pricing model, 150
Capital-intensive business, 131
Cash collection period, 139
Cash equivalents, 139
Common equity share of operating
    earnings, 149
Common-size balance sheet, 134
Common-size financial
    statements, 133
Common-size income statement, 133
Conservatism, 146
Cost of equity financing, 150
Cross-sectional analysis, 141
Current ratio, 139
Days' payable period, 139

Dividend retention rate, 145
Due diligence, 141
DuPont Model, 143
Equity risk premium, 151
Financial leverage, 138
Financial risk, 136
Gross profit margin ratio, 138
Interest coverage ratio, 141
Inventory-on-hand, 138
Leverage, 136
Liquid assets, 139
Liquidity, 136
Longitudinal analysis, 131
Net revenues, 134
Non-systematic risk, 151
Off-balance-sheet liabilities, 141
Operating lease, 141
Percentage change, 133
Percentage change income
    statement, 133

Profitability, 136
Pro forma statements, 149
Quick ratio, 139
Ratios, 136
Receivable collection period, 139
Return on assets, 138
Return on equity, 138
Return on sales, 134, 138
Sales discounts, 134
Sales returns, 134
Sell-side analyst, 147
Solvency, 136
Standard Industrial Classification
    (SIC), 141
Sustainable growth rate, 145
Systematic risk, 151
Trend analysis, 131

Takeaway 4
Apply
unlevering
adjustments to
ROA and ROS.

APPENDIX 4A: Unlevering Financial Ratios

In Chapter 4, the return on equity (ROE) model was introduced as an approach to organize the analysis of a company's financial performance and health. The ROE of a company was shown to be composed of three component ratios, as follows:

> **Return on equity = Return on sales × Asset turnover × Financial leverage**

Further, since the return on assets (ROA) ratio was revealed to be a function of the return on sales (ROS) ratio and asset turnover (AT), the ROE ratio could also be expressed as:

> **Return on equity = Return on assets × Financial leverage**

Because ROA is a measure of the return generated by a business's total investment in assets, to include those assets contributed by shareholders as well as those assets loaned to the business by its creditors, many investment professionals "unlever" the ROA ratio by adding the current-period interest expense paid to creditors back to the business's net income. Unlevering the ROA ratio grosses up net income for a business's cost of debt, yielding a measure of net income before any returns are distributed to either debtholders or shareholders. The resultant unlevered ROA is calculated as follows:

$$\text{Return on assets} = \frac{\text{Net income} + [\text{Interest} \, (1 - \text{Tax rate})]}{\text{Total assets}}$$

The interest expense added back to net income is multiplied by (1 − Tax rate), or one minus a firm's effective tax rate (Income tax expense/Net income before taxes). As a consequence, the amount of the interest expense added back to net income is reduced by the income tax savings associated with the tax deductibility of interest expense. These tax savings are referred to as the interest tax shield and must be removed to avoid double-counting their positive impact on net income (it is already reflected in the provision for income taxes used in the calculation of net income).

Some investment professionals believe that a similar unlevering adjustment should be made to the ROS ratio, as follows:

$$\text{Return on sales} = \frac{\text{Net income} - [\text{Interest}\,(1 - \text{Tax rate})]}{\text{Net sales}}$$

Unlevering ROS allows the financial analyst to focus on the effectiveness of a company's operating decisions, independent of the effectiveness of its financing decisions. Incorporating the unlevered ROS ratio into the calculation of ROA yields the following formulation:

$$\begin{matrix} \text{Unlevered return} \\ \text{on assets} \end{matrix} = \begin{matrix} \text{Unlevered return} \\ \text{on sales} \end{matrix} \times \begin{matrix} \text{Total asset} \\ \text{turnover} \end{matrix}$$

$$\text{ROA} = \frac{\text{Net income} + [\text{Interest}\,(1 - \text{Tax rate})]}{\text{Net sales}} \times \frac{\text{Net sales}}{\text{Total assets}}$$

$$= \frac{\text{Net income} + [\text{Interest}\,(1 - \text{Tax rate})]}{\text{Total assets}}$$

Unlevering ROS also facilitates a reformulation of the ROE Model, as follows:[4]

$$\text{ROE} = \begin{matrix} \text{Unlevered} \\ \text{ROS} \end{matrix} \times \begin{matrix} \text{Asset} \\ \text{turnover} \end{matrix} \times \begin{matrix} \text{Financial} \\ \text{leverage} \end{matrix} \times \begin{matrix} \text{Common equity share} \\ \text{of operating earnings} \end{matrix}$$

where the **common equity share of operating earnings** (CSOE) is defined as:

$$\text{CSOE} = \frac{\text{Net income}}{\text{Net income} + \text{Interest}\,(1 - \text{Tax rate})}$$

and represents the portion of a company's operating earnings allocable to the common shareholders.

Incorporating CSOE into the ROE model yields the following:

$$\text{ROE} = \frac{\text{Net income} + [\text{Interest}\,(1 - \text{Tax rate})]}{\text{Net sales}} \times \frac{\text{Net sales}}{\text{Total assets}} \times \frac{\text{Total assets}}{\text{Shareholders' equity}} \times \frac{\text{Net income}}{\text{Net income} + [\text{Interest}\,(1 - \text{Tax rate})]}$$

When a company is all (or substantially) equity financed, the unlevered ROA and ROS ratios collapse to their familiar levered form, as does the ROE Model:

Return on equity = Return on sales × Asset turnover × Financial leverage

APPENDIX 4B: Pro Forma Financial Statements

Takeaway 5
Construct pro forma financial statements to evaluate a company's ability to generate future earnings and cash flows.

Lenders, managers, investment professionals, and shareholders are often interested in how a firm might perform in the future under various economic scenarios. For example, lenders might be interested in assessing whether Under Armour's business can generate sufficient cash in the future to make the principal payments on a proposed bank loan. But how can you forecast the future, and especially, how can you forecast a firm's ability to repay debt? The past is often an excellent guide to the future because many financial variables remain relatively constant from one year to the next and many financial variables maintain a relatively stable relationship with sales or total assets over time.

Forecasted financial statements are called **pro forma statements**—that is, financial statements prepared on an "as if" basis using assumptions about what might happen in the future. Excel™ spreadsheets are handy devices for preparing pro forma financial statements because it is possible to build a spreadsheet in such a manner as to easily change the underlying assumptions to see what will happen under alternative operating scenarios.

The process of preparing pro forma financial statements typically involves five steps:

1. Forecast sales, cost of goods sold, gross profit, and other operating expenses on the income statement, and the cash balance on the balance sheet.

---

[4] The development of the ROE Model using unlevered ratios is generally attributed to C. Stickney and T. Selling, "The Effects of Business Environment and Strategy on a Firm's Rate of Return on Assets," *Financial Analysts' Journal* (1989).

2. Forecast accounts receivables, inventory, accounts payable, property and equipment, long-term debt, and short-term loans payable on the balance sheet.
3. Forecast depreciation expense and interest expense on the income statement.
4. Forecast any remaining items on the income statement, expected dividend payments, and then, the statement of shareholders' equity and the balance sheet.
5. Prepare the pro forma statement of cash flow from the forecasted income statement and forecasted balance sheets using the indirect method format.

When developing pro forma data, it is often the case that a plug figure will be needed to balance the pro forma balance sheet. If a plug figure is needed to balance the asset side of the pro forma balance sheet, most investment professionals use the current asset account "marketable securities" as their plug figure. When a firm is producing excess cash flow from its operations, that excess will usually be invested in short-term marketable securities to enable the firm to earn a higher rate of return than would be possible if the excess funds were invested in a lower-yielding cash account. Similarly, when additional cash is needed to support operations, the first source of that cash is likely to be the liquidation of any available short-term marketable securities. If, on the other hand, a plug figure is needed to balance the liability side of the pro forma balance sheet, most professionals use a short-term interest-bearing line of credit as the plug. A short-term line of credit is used as a plug figure because this form of financing is cheaper than financing with long-term debt, which of course, is cheaper than financing with equity, and therefore, likely to be the first choice of new financing by management.

The principal challenge to preparing pro forma statements is to determine how to forecast each of the income statement and balance sheet accounts. (It is unnecessary to forecast the pro forma statement of cash flow because the data for this statement can be indirectly derived from the pro forma income statements and balance sheets using the process described in Chapter 3.) The first account to be forecasted is revenue on the income statement, and this forecast is usually arrived at after a careful assessment of the expected external demand for a company's products. Most expenses on the income statement can be forecasted by reference to the common-size income statement percentages generated while developing the historical financial statement analysis of a company's past performance. Some expenses, however, must be forecasted by reference to items on the pro forma balance sheet. For example, depreciation expense is a function of a company's past and current investment in property, plant and equipment. Similarly, interest expense is a function of a company's past and current borrowings. And, income tax expense is a function of a firm's pre-tax net income and its expected effective tax rate. To forecast these expenses using historical common-size income statement percentages would mistakenly link the change in these expenses to the change in revenues.

On the balance sheet, many accounts are forecasted by reference to ratios that link the balance sheet account to a firm's operations. For example, here is a list of typical balance sheet accounts and the ratios that are commonly used to forecast them once a pro forma income statement has been prepared:

Balance Sheet Account	Ratio
Accounts receivable........	Receivable turnover
Inventory.................	Inventory turnover
Fixed assets..............	Fixed asset turnover
Total assets..............	Asset turnover
Accounts payable.........	Accounts payable turnover

For many income statement and balance sheet accounts that are immaterial in amount, investment professionals often forecast the account balance as a constant on grounds of immateriality. And, in the case of some balance sheet accounts (such as the cumulative foreign currency translation adjustment), whose future value is not readily forecasted, the investment professional will often merely assume a constant future value. The key to well-constructed pro forma financial statements is to thoughtfully forecast the key income statement accounts (such as operating revenue and expenses) and the key balance sheet accounts (such as operating assets and liabilities).

It is important to recognize that forecasting income statements and balance sheets is not a hard-and-fast science. There are many different approaches used by investment professionals, and for this reason, forecasting is referred to as "an art and not a science." We will have more to say about developing and using pro forma financial statements in Chapter 12.

Takeaway 6
Understand a common approach to calculating the cost of equity financing.

APPENDIX 4C: Calculating the Cost of Equity Financing

Shareholders buy shares in a company because they expect a return, either in the form of dividends or in the form of share price appreciation, or both. Since shareholders assume more risk than creditors, they are entitled to a higher rate of return. But how can the rate of return expected by shareholders be estimated? Stated alternatively, how can we calculate the expected **cost of equity financing** for a company?

A widely accepted approach to estimating the cost of equity financing—that is, the rate of return expected by shareholders—is through the **capital asset pricing model**, or CAPM.[5] The CAPM posits that there is a linear relation-

---

[5] W.F. Sharpe, "Capital Asset Prices: A Theory of Market Equilibrium," *Journal of Finance*, 1964.

ship between a company's systematic risk (β) and the expected return required by investors (r_e). The model states that if investors can earn the risk-free rate of return (r_f) by investing in government securities, then the expected return on a risky investment (such as common stock) should equal the risk-free rate of return plus an incremental return proportional to the company's risk. The incremental return associated with investing in equity securities versus risk-free securities is called the **equity risk premium**. The formula for the CAPM is given as follows:

$$r_e = r_f + [\beta \times (\textbf{Equity risk premium})]$$

where

r_e = Cost of equity financing.

r_f = Risk-free rate of return, often proxied by the current yield to maturity of the U.S. ten-year Treasury bond.

β = Measure of the systematic risk of a business, proxied by a firm's equity **beta** (available from any financial internet website).

The equity risk premium is estimated as follows:

$$\textbf{Equity risk premium} = r_m - r_f$$

where

r_m = Market rate of return for a diversified portfolio of equity securities, often proxied by the rate of return on the Standard & Poor's 500 Index.

The equity risk premium expected by investors on a diversified portfolio of equity securities is often assumed to be 7.0 percent, which is the average risk premium observed in the U.S. capital market over the past 85 years.

To illustrate the use of the CAPM, assume that our goal is to estimate the cost of equity financing for Under Armour. Yahoo!Finance reports Under Armour's beta (β) to be 0.86, suggesting that if the U.S. stock market increases by $1, Under Armour's share price will increase by $0.86; that is, there is a strong positive correlation between movements of the U.S. equity market and Under Armour's share price. Beta is a reflection of the **systematic risk** associated with a company's share price. Systematic risk is the risk that a company's share price will fall (rise) in some proportion to a fall (rise) in the overall stock market—that is, a rising tide lifts all ships. **Non-systematic risk** is the risk that a company's share price will fall (rise) as a consequence of firm-specific and industry-specific information. Thus, Under Armour's share price will fall (rise) as a consequence of overall market movements (systematic risk) or as a consequence of new information about the company's performance or about the apparel industry in general (non-systematic risk).

If the current yield on the U.S. ten-year Treasury bill is assumed to be 2 percent, and if we assume that the equity risk premium—that is, the incremental risk of investing in equity securities rather than in risk-free government bonds—is 7.0 percent, Under Armour's cost of equity can be estimated using the CAPM as follows:

$$r_e = 2.0\% + (0.86 \times 7.0\%) = 8.0\%$$

As a basis of comparison, if Under Armour had been a less well established company (more risky), investors would have expected a higher rate of return on their investment. Private equity investors, for example, who invest in nonpublic companies often expect a 20 to 40 percent return on their investments because these investments are less liquid than investments in publicly-traded companies like Under Armour—a reduced ability to sell shares (lower liquidity) implies higher risk for an investor. Similarly, venture capital investors who invest in high-risk new business ventures expect returns ranging from 40 to 100 percent, or more. As previously noted, the assumption of greater risk is typically associated with an expectation of higher returns.

In Chapter 4, our ratio analysis of Under Armour revealed that the company's return on equity (ROE) was a healthy 15.4 percent in 2014. Thus, Under Armour is able to earn a return on its equity that exceeds the cost of its equity funds (15.4% − 8.0% = 7.4%), and as a consequence, Under Armour is presently able to build value for its shareholders.

QUESTIONS

Q4.1 **Using Financial Ratios to Evaluate Firm Performance.**   Financial statement analysis is a process whereby the basic financial statements are reviewed and evaluated to assess a firm's financial health and/or performance. Calculating financial ratios is an integral part of financial statement analysis. Discuss what a ratio is and why the use of ratios is helpful in assessing firm performance and financial condition.

Q4.2 **Using Financial Leverage Effectively.**   Many corporations finance at least a part of their operations and asset purchases using debt, principally because the cost of debt financing is cheaper than equity financing. Moreover, some firms are able to use leverage more effectively than others—that is, the returns to shareholders as a result of financing with debt are higher for some firms than for other firms. Using the ROE model, discuss when the use of financial leverage is most effective and least effective. When should a firm stop using debt to finance its operations or asset purchases?

Q4.3 **Calculating the Return on Shareholders' Equity.** When calculating a firm's return on shareholders' equity (ROE), some investment professionals modify the ROE ratio by subtracting any dividends paid by the firm to its preferred stock shareholders as follows:

$$\text{Return on shareholders' equity} = \frac{\text{(Net income} - \text{Preferred stock dividends)}}{\text{(Total shareholders' equity} - \text{Preferred stock equity)}}$$

This modified ROE ratio is often referred to as the "return on common equity," or ROCE. Discuss why and when ROCE might be a superior assessment of a firm's return on equity.

Q4.4 **Unlevering the Return on Assets.** When calculating a firm's return on total assets (ROA) ratio, some investment professionals modify the ROA ratio by adding back the interest expense paid by a firm to its creditors, on a net-of-taxes basis, as follows:

$$\text{Return on assets} = \frac{[\text{Net income} + i(1 - \text{Tax rate})]}{\text{Total assets}}$$

where i is the actual interest expense paid by a firm and the tax rate is a firm's "effective tax rate" (income tax expense divided by pre-tax net income). Adjusting net income for the interest expense paid by a firm is called "unlevering net income" because the adjustment yields a measure of net income as if the firm were all equity financed (with no debt financing). Discuss when and why unlevering ROA might produce a more useful measure of the return on assets of a firm.

Q4.5 **Evaluating a Firm's Liquidity and Solvency.** The Manhattan Company has $265 million in assets, $90 million in current liabilities, $135 million in noncurrent liabilities, and $40 million in shareholders' equity. Of the company's $85 million in current assets, the company's cash and cash equivalents total $23 million, accounts receivable total $24.5 million, inventory totals $26.4 million, and other current assets total $11.1 million. Is the Manhattan Company solvent? Why or why not? Is the company liquid? Why or why not?

Q4.6 **Evaluating a Firm's Liquidity and Solvency.** The Fremont Company has $465 million in assets, $70 million in current liabilities, $125 million in noncurrent liabilities, and $270 million in shareholders' equity. Of the company's $185 million in current assets, the company's cash and cash equivalents total $63 million, accounts receivable total $64.5 million, inventory totals $36.4 million, and other current assets total $21.1 million. Is the Fremont Company solvent? Why or why not? Is the company liquid? Why or why not?

Q4.7 **Evaluating Capital Intensity.** Presented below are selected financial data (in millions) for Bristol-Myers Squibb, The Coca-Cola Company, and the General Electric Company. Calculate the capital intensity ratio for each of the three firms and discuss the relative capital intensity of the firms. Why is it important or useful to know the relative capital intensity of a company?

	Total Assets	Net Sales
Bristol-Myers Squibb	$ 31,748	$ 16,560
The Coca-Cola Company.	90,093	44,294
General Electric Company	492,692	117,386

Q4.8 **Identifying the Unknown Companies.** Presented below are common-sized income statement data for three well-known companies representing three different industries (pharmaceutical, beverage, and diversified):

- Bristol-Myers Squibb
- The Coca-Cola Company
- General Electric Company

Identify which of the three companies goes with each of the common-size data profiles. Discuss the rationale for your choice.

	Company 1	Company 2	Company 3
Common-size income statement			
Net sales.	100.0%	100.0%	100.0%
Cost of goods sold.	30.9	44.3	59.8
Marketing, selling & admin.	22.6	13.0	32.6
Research & development	18.3	6.0	—
Other expenses	12.6	26.0	4.9
Net income.	15.6%	10.7%	2.7%

Q4.9 **Evaluating the Return on Assets.** Presented below are selected financial data for two competitors. Discuss why the return on assets increased for Company A but decreased for Company B.

	Return on Assets		Return on Sales		Asset Turnover	
	Year 1	Year 2	Year 1	Year 2	Year 1	Year 2
Company A.	7.9%	10.7%	12.3%	15.6%	.637	.683
Company B	9.2	6.9	21.6	15.7	.427	.436

Q4.10 **Evaluating the Return on Equity.** Presented below are selected financial data for two competitors. Discuss why the return on equity decreased for each firm.

	Return on Equity		Return on Sales		Asset Turnover		Financial Leverage	
	Year 1	Year 2	Year 1	Year 2	Year 1	Year 2	Year 1	Year 2
Company X.	8.5%	6.3%	12.0%	8.0%	1.0	1.1	7.1	7.2
Company Y.	24.9%	19.1%	9.9%	10.1%	1.2	0.9	2.1	2.1

Q4.11 **(Ethics Perspective) Ethics and Financial Analysts.** Explain why a sell-side analyst might be less objective than a buy-side analyst in his/her research reports. If an analyst is working for Merrill Lynch, where should the analyst's loyalties lie—with Merrill Lynch, with the companies that the analyst reviews and evaluates, or with the clients who purchase the analyst's research?

Assignments with the (MBC) logo in the margin are available in BusinessCourse.
See the Preface of the book for details.
CHECK FIGURE indicates that check figures are available on the book's Website.

EXERCISES

E4.12 **Analyzing Financial Statement Data.** Presented below are summary financial data from the Bristol-Myers Squibb 2015 annual report. Using the ratio definitions from Exhibit 4.6, calculate the following ratios: return on equity, return on assets (levered), return on sales (levered), asset turnover, and financial leverage. Does the company appear to be a good investment? Why or why not?

TA 1

MBC

(amounts in millions)	2015	2014
Balance sheet		
Total assets	$31,748	$33,749
Shareholders' equity	14,424	14,983
Income statement		
Net sales	$16,560	$15,879
Net income.	1,631	2,029

E4.13 **Analyzing Financial Statement Data.** Presented below are summary financial data from the Pfizer, Inc., 2015 annual report. Using the ratio definitions from Exhibit 4.6, calculate the following ratios: return on equity, return on assets (levered), return on sales (levered), asset turnover, and financial leverage. Does the company appear to be a good investment? Why or why not?

TA 1
CHECK
FIGURE
MBC

(amounts in millions)	2015	2014
Balance sheet		
Total assets	$167,460	$167,566
Shareholders' equity	64,998	71,622
Income statement		
Net sales	$ 48,851	$ 49,605
Net income.	6,986	9,168

TA 1   **E4.14**   **Analyzing Financial Statement Data.**   Presented below are summary financial data from the Johnson & Johnson 2015 annual report. Using the ratio definitions from Exhibit 4.6, calculate the following ratios: return on equity, return on assets (levered), return on sales (levered), asset turnover, and financial leverage. Does the company appear to be a good investment? Why or why not?

(amounts in millions)	2015	2014
Balance sheet		
Total assets	$133,411	$130,358
Shareholders' equity	71,150	69,752
Income statement		
Net sales	$70,074	$74,331
Net income.	15,409	16,323

TA 1   **E4.15**   **Analyzing Financial Risk.**   Presented below are summary financial data from the Bristol-Myers Squibb 2015 annual report. Using the ratio definitions from Exhibit 4.6, calculate the following liquidity and solvency ratios: cash and marketable securities to total assets, quick ratio, current ratio, long-term debt to total assets, long-term debt to shareholders' equity, and the interest coverage ratio. Evaluate Bristol-Myers' liquidity and solvency.

(amounts in millions)	2015	2014
Balance sheet		
Cash and cash equivalents	$ 2,385	$ 5,571
Marketable securities.	1,885	1,864
Accounts receivable (net).	4,299	3,390
Total current assets	10,415	14,608
Total assets	31,748	33,749
Current liabilities	8,017	8,461
Current portion of long-term debt	0	0
Long-term debt	6,550	7,242
Shareholders' equity	14,424	14,983
Income statement		
Interest expense	$ 184	$ 203
Net income before taxes	2,077	2,381

TA 1   **E4.16**   **Analyzing Financial Statement Data.**   Presented below are summary financial data from The Boeing Company 2015 annual report. Using the ratio definitions from Exhibit 4.6, calculate the following ratios: return on equity, return on assets (levered), return on sales (levered), asset turnover, and financial leverage. Does the company appear to be a good investment? Why or why not?

(amounts in millions)	2015	2014
Balance sheet		
Total assets	$94,408	$92,921
Shareholders' equity	6,397	8,790
Income statement		
Net sales	$96,114	$90,762
Net income.	5,176	5,446

TA 1   **E4.17**   **Analyzing Financial Risk.**   Presented below are summary financial data from the General Electric Company
CHECK   2015 annual report. Using the ratio definitions from Exhibit 4.6, calculate the following liquidity and solvency
FIGURE   ratios: cash and marketable securities to total assets, quick ratio, current ratio, long-term debt to total assets, long-term debt to shareholders' equity, and the interest coverage ratio. Evaluate General Electric's liquidity and solvency.

(amounts in millions)	2015	2014
Balance sheet		
Cash and cash equivalents	$ 70,483	$ 70,025
Marketable securities.	31,973	35,505
Accounts receivable (net).	27,022	23,237
Total current assets	151,993	146,456
Total assets	492,692	654,954
Current liabilities	105,112	111,669
Current portion of long-term debt	42,773	38,988
Long-term debt	145,301	186,596
Shareholders' equity	98,274	128,159
Income statement		
Interest expense	$ 3,463	$ 2,723
Net income before taxes	8,186	10,263

E4.18 **Analyzing Financial Risk.** Presented below are summary financial data from the The Coca-Cola Company TA 1
2015 annual report. Using the ratio definitions from Exhibit 4.6, calculate the following liquidity and solvency
ratios: cash and marketable securities to total assets, quick ratio, current ratio, long-term debt to total assets, long-
term debt to shareholders' equity, and the interest coverage ratio. Evaluate the company's liquidity and solvency.

(amounts in millions)	2015	2014
Balance sheet		
Cash and cash equivalents	$15,631	$18,010
Marketable securities.	4,269	3,665
Accounts receivable (net).	3,941	4,466
Total current assets	33,395	32,986
Total assets	90,093	92,023
Current liabilities	26,930	32,374
Current portion of long-term debt	2,677	3,552
Long-term debt	28,407	19,063
Shareholders' equity	25,764	30,561
Income statement		
Interest expense	$ 856	$ 483
Net income before taxes	9,605	9,325

E4.19 **Analyzing Financial Risk.** Presented below are summary financial data from The Boeing Company 2015 TA 1
annual report. Using the ratio definitions from Exhibit 4.6, calculate the following liquidity and solvency ratios:
cash and marketable securities to total assets, quick ratio, current ratio, long-term debt to total assets, long-term debt
to shareholders' equity, and the interest coverage ratio. Evaluate The Boeing Company's liquidity and solvency.

(amounts in millions)	2015	2014
Balance sheet		
Cash and cash equivalents	$11,302	$11,733
Marketable securities.	750	1,359
Accounts receivable, net	8,713	7,729
Total current assets	68,234	67,767
Total assets	94,408	92,921
Current liabilities	50,412	48,233
Current portion of long-term debt	1,234	929
Long-term debt	8,730	8,141
Shareholders' equity	6,397	8,790
Income statement		
Interest expense	$ 275	$ 333
Net income before taxes	7,155	7,137

TA 1   **E4.20**   **Analyzing Asset Management Effectiveness.**   Presented below are selected financial data from the Bristol-Myers Squibb 2015 annual report. Using the ratio definitions from Exhibit 4.6, calculate the following ratios: receivable turnover, receivable collection period, inventory turnover, and the inventory-on-hand period. Evaluate Bristol-Myers' receivable and inventory asset management effectiveness.

(amounts in millions)	2015	2014
Balance sheet		
Accounts receivable (net)..	$ 4,299	$ 3,390
Inventory	1,221	1,560
Income statement		
Net sales	$16,560	$15,879
Cost of goods sold	3,909	3,932

TA 1
CHECK
FIGURE

E4.21   **Analyzing Asset Management Effectiveness.**   Presented below are selected financial data from the The Coca-Cola Company 2015 annual report. Using the ratio definitions from Exhibit 4.6, calculate the following ratios: receivable turnover, receivable collection period, inventory turnover, and the inventory-on-hand period. Evaluate Coca-Cola's receivable and inventory asset management effectiveness.

(amounts in millions)	2015	2014
Balance sheet		
Accounts receivable (net)..	$ 3,941	$ 4,466
Inventory	2,902	3,100
Income statement		
Net sales	$44,294	$45,998
Cost of goods sold	17,482	17,889

TA 1   **E4.22**   **Analyzing Asset Management Effectiveness.**   Presented below are selected financial data from The Boeing Company 2015 annual report. Using the ratio definitions from Exhibit 4.6, calculate the following ratios: receivable turnover, receivable collection period, inventory turnover, and the inventory-on-hand period. Evaluate the company's receivable and inventory asset management effectiveness.

(amounts in millions)	2015	2014
Balance sheet		
Accounts receivable (net)..	$ 8,713	$ 7,729
Inventory	47,257	46,756
Income statement		
Net sales	$96,114	$90,762
Cost of goods sold	82,024	76,783

TA 1   **E4.23**   **Debt Covenants and Financial Analysis.**   During 2015, The Mann Corporation borrowed $500,000 from The Biltmore National Bank. The loan agreement included a debt covenant restricting the company's level of debt relative to shareholders' equity. The covenant specified that Mann's long-term debt to shareholders' equity ratio could not exceed 1-to-1 at any time during the loan period. The Mann Corporation's 2015 year-end balance sheet appeared as follows:

	2015
Total assets...	$2,001,600
Current liabilities...	$ 542,100
Long-term debt	625,500
Shareholders' equity	834,000
	$2,001,600

Calculate The Mann Corporation's long-term debt to shareholders' equity ratio at year-end 2015. What is the company's maximum borrowing capability at year-end 2015 without violating the long-term debt to shareholders' equity covenant of the existing loan agreement? What is the maximum dividend that the company can pay at year-end without violating the debt covenant? If the company pays a cash dividend of $100,000 at year-end 2015, what is the company's maximum borrowing capability without violating the debt covenant?

E4.24   **Estimating Sustainable Growth.**   The following information is taken from Procter & Gamble's 2015 annual   TA 2
report:

(in millions)	2015	2014	2013
Income statement			
Net sales	$76,279	$80,510	$80,116
Net earnings	7,036	11,643	11,312
Balance sheet			
Shareholders' equity	63,050	69,976	68,709
Statement of cash flows			
Dividends to shareholders	7,287	6,911	6,519

Calculate the company's actual and sustainable rate of growth in sales for 2015 and 2014. How do the two
growth rates compare? What advice would you give to P&G's management on the basis of these two rates of
growth?

E4.25   **Estimating Sustainable Growth.**   The following information is taken from the Fossil, Inc. 2015 annual   TA 2
report:

(in thousands)	2015	2014	2013
Income statement			
Net sales	$3,228,836	$3,509,691	$3,259,971
Net earnings	220,637	376,707	378,152
Balance sheet			
Shareholders' equity	932,543	983,801	1,075,367
Statement of cash flow			
Dividends to shareholders	0	0	0

Calculate Fossil's actual and sustainable rate of growth in sales. How do the two rates of growth compare?
What advice would you give to Fossil's management on the basis of these rates of growth?

PROBLEMS

P4.26   **Analyzing Financial Statements.**   Presented below are selected financial data from the 2015 annual report of   TA 1
the Bristol-Myers Squibb Company:

(amounts in millions)	2015	2014
Balance sheet		
Cash and cash equivalents	$ 2,385	$ 5,571
Marketable securities	1,885	1,864
Accounts receivable (net)	4,299	3,390
Inventory	1,221	1,560
Other current assets	625	2,223
Total current assets	10,415	14,608
Total assets	31,748	33,749
Current liabilities	8,017	8,461
Noncurrent liabilities	9,307	10,305
Shareholders' equity	14,424	14,983
Income statement		
Net sales	16,560	15,879
Cost of goods sold	3,909	3,932
Interest expense	184	203
Net income before taxes	2,077	2,381
Net income	1,631	2,029

Required

Using the ratio definitions from Exhibit 4.6, calculate the financial ratios for Bristol-Myers Squibb and determine whether the company is a good investment. Assume an effective tax rate of 30 percent.

TA 1   **P4.27**   **Analyzing Financial Statements.** Presented below are selected financial data from the 2015 annual report of **The Boeing Company**:

(amounts in millions)	2015	2014
Balance sheet		
Cash and cash equivalents	$11,302	$11,733
Marketable securities.	750	1,359
Accounts receivable (net).	8,713	7,729
Inventory	47,257	46,756
Total current assets	68,234	67,767
Total assets	94,408	92,921
Current liabilities	50,412	48,233
Noncurrent liabilities	37,599	35,898
Shareholders' equity	6,397	8,790
Income statement		
Net sales	$96,114	$90,762
Cost of goods sold	82,024	76,683
Interest expense	275	333
Net income before taxes	7,155	7,137
Net income.	5,176	5,446

Required

Using the ratio definitions from Exhibit 4.6, calculate the financial ratios for The Boeing Company and determine whether the company is a good investment. Assume an effective tax rate of 30 percent.

TA 1   **P4.28**   **Analyzing Financial Data: Trend Analysis.** Presented below is selected financial data for **Apple Inc.**, for the five-year period 2010 to 2014.

(in millions)	2014	2013	2012	2011	2010
Net sales.	$182,795	$170,910	$156,508	$108,249	$65,225
Net income.	39,510	37,037	41,733	25,922	14,013
Dividends per share	1.82	1.64	0.38	0	0
Total assets.	231,839	207,000	176,064	116,370	75,183
Noncurrent liabilities.	56,844	39,793	19,312	10,100	5,531
Total shareholders' equity	111,547	123,549	118,210	76,615	47,791
Cash, cash equivalents, and					
marketable securities	155,239	146,761	121,251	81,570	51,011

Required

1. Comment on the relationship between the growth in net sales and the growth in net income over the period 2010 to 2014 and what that implies regarding cost expenses.
2. Comment on the company's financial leverage over this period.
3. Comment on the company's asset turnover.
4. The company declared its first dividend in 2012. Do you agree with this decision? Why?

TA 1   **P4.29**   **Financial Statement Analysis and Debt Covenants.** Wilmot Real Estate Co. had the following balance
CHECK   sheet at year-end 2015:
FIGURE

WILMOT REAL ESTATE CO.		
Balance Sheet		
Year-end 2015		
Assets		**Liabilities and Shareholders' Equity**
Current assets . . . . $ 60,000		Current liabilities. $ 45,000
Real estate investments. 250,000		Long-term liabilities 150,000
Other noncurrent assets. 25,000		Shareholders' equity 140,000
Total assets. $335,000		Total liabilities & shareholders' equity $335,000

In early 2016, the company took out a $200,000 two-year bank loan to finance new real estate investments. The loan specified that Wilmot must maintain a current ratio of at least 2-to-1 at all times during the loan period. Failure to satisfy this debt covenant would represent a "technical default" of the loan agreement, enabling the bank to demand immediate repayment of the outstanding loan balance and any accrued interest.

During 2016, Wilmot experienced the following events:

1. Generated $750,000 in revenues, of which $700,000 was collected by year-end 2016.
2. Incurred $650,000 in expenses, of which $575,000 was paid in cash.

Required

1. Prepare a balance sheet at year-end 2016 assuming that Wilmot invested the maximum allowable amount of the bank loan in new real estate investments in early 2016.
2. Evaluate Wilmot's compliance with the current ratio debt covenant assuming (a) the bank loan is included in current liabilities and (b) the bank loan is included in long-term liabilities.
3. Calculate the maximum dividend that Wilmot can distribute to its shareholders in 2016 assuming the bank loan is included in long-term liabilities.

P4.30   Financial Statement Analysis and Ratios: International.   Presented below are the consolidated balance sheets and income statements for Tesco, PLC, the world's third largest retailer, for the years 2016 and 2015. Tesco is based in the United Kingdom.

TA 1

TESCO, PLC **Group Income Statement** **For the years ended February 2016 and 2015**		
(£ millions)	**2016**	**2015**
Continuing operations:		
Revenue	£54,433	£56,925
Cost of sales.	(51,579)	(59,128)
Gross profit (loss)	2,854	(2,203)
Administrative expenses	(1,852)	(2,574)
Profit on property-related items	44	(973)
Operating profit (loss).	1,046	(5,750)
Share of post-tax profits of joint ventures and associates.	(21)	(13)
Finance income	29	80
Finance costs	(892)	(651)
Profit (loss) before tax.	162	(6,334)
Taxation	54	670
Profit (loss) for the year from continuing operations	216	(5,664)
Discontinued operations:		
Loss for the year from discontinued operations.	(87)	(102)
Profit (loss) for the year	**129**	**(5,766)**
Attributed to:		
Owners of the parent	138	(5,741)
Non-controlling interests	(9)	(25)
	£ 129	**£ (5,766)**

TESCO, PLC
Group Balance Sheet
As of February 27, 2016 and February 28, 2015

(£ millions)	2016	2015
Non-current assets		
Goodwill and other intangible assets	£ 2,874	£ 3,771
Property, plant, and equipment	17,900	20,440
Investment property	78	164
Investment in joint ventures and associates	785	940
Other investments	1,135	975
Loans and advances to customers	4,723	3,906
Derivative financial instruments	1,532	1,546
Deferred tax assets	49	514
	£29,076	**£32,256**
Current assets		
Inventories	£ 2,430	£ 2,957
Trade and other receivables	1,607	2,121
Loans and advances to customers	3,819	3,814
Derivative financial instruments	176	153
Current tax assets	15	16
Short-term investments	3,463	593
Cash and cash equivalents	3,082	2,165
	14,592	11,819
Assets of the disposal groups and non-current assets classified as held for sale	236	139
	£14,828	**£11,958**
Current liabilities		
Trade and other payables	£ (8,568)	£ (9,922)
Borrowings	(2,826)	(2,008)
Derivative financial instruments and other liabilities	(62)	(89)
Customer deposits and deposits by banks	(7,479)	(7,020)
Current tax liabilities	(419)	(95)
Provisions	(360)	(671)
	(19,714)	**(19,805)**
Liabilities of the disposal groups classified as held for sale	—	(5)
Net current liabilities	**(4,886)**	**(7,852)**
Non-current liabilities		
Borrowings	(10,711)	(10,651)
Derivative financial instruments and other liabilities	(889)	(946)
Post-employment benefit obligations	(3,175)	(4,842)
Deferred tax liabilities	(135)	(199)
Provisions	(664)	(695)
	(15,574)	**(17,333)**
Net assets	**£ 8,616**	**£ 7,071**
Equity		
Share capital	£ 407	£ 406
Share premium	5,095	5,094
Other reserves	(141)	(414)
Retained earnings	3,265	1,985
Equity attributable to owners of the parent	**8,626**	**7,071**
Non-controlling interests	(10)	—
Total equity	**£ 8,616**	**£ 7,071**

Required

1. Calculate the following ratios for Tesco:

a.	Return on equity	*i.*	Interest coverage ratio
b.	Return on assets	*j.*	Accounts payable turnover
c.	Return on sales	*k.*	Receivable turnover
d.	Financial leverage	*l.*	Inventory turnover
e.	Total debt to shareholders' equity ratio	*m.*	Fixed asset turnover
f.	Long-term debt to shareholders' equity ratio	*n.*	Asset turnover
g.	Current ratio	*o.*	Common-size income statements
h.	Quick ratio	*p.*	Common-size balance sheets

   (*Hint:* Assume no current portion of long-term debt is due.)

2. Comment on the company's performance in 2016 relative to 2015.

P4.31   **(Appendix 4B) Pro Forma Financial Statements.**   Handy Dan, Inc., operates warehouse-style stores, sell- TA 5
ing a variety of home building products and lawn and garden supplies. Presented below are Handy Dan's
historical financial statements for 2014 and 2015:

HANDY DAN, INC.
Statement of Income

(amounts in millions)	2015
Sales.	$980
Cost of goods sold.	727
Gross profit.	253
Depreciation expense.	8
Other operating expenses	217
Operating income.	28
Interest expense.	21
Income before taxes.	7
Income tax expense.	2
Net income.	$ 5

HANDY DAN, INC.
Balance Sheets

(amounts in millions)	2014	2015		2014	2015
Assets			**Equities**		
Cash.	$ 10	$ 14	Accounts payable	$ 74	$104
Accounts receivable (net).	27	38	Short-term loans payable	10	29
Inventory	153	214	Long-term debt	207	289
Total current assets	190	266	Total liabilities.	291	422
Property & equipment (cost) . . .	199	279	Contributed capital	50	62
Accumulated depreciation.	(9)	(17)	Retained earnings	39	44
	190	262	Total shareholders' equity	89	106
Total assets.	$380	$528	Total liabilities & shareholders' equity . . .	$380	$528

HANDY DAN, INC.
Statement of Retained Earnings

(amounts in millions)	2015
Retained earnings (2014)	$39
Add: Net income	5
Less: Dividends	0
Retained earnings (2015)	$44

HANDY DAN, INC. Statement of Cash Flow	
(amounts in millions)	**2015**
Operations	
Net income.	$ 5
Depreciation expense	8
Accounts receivable (net).	(11)
Inventory	(61)
Accounts payable	30
Cash flow from operations.	(29)
Investing activities	
Purchase of property & equipment	(80)
Cash flow from investing	(80)
Financing activities	
Short-term borrowing	19
Long-term borrowing.	82
Stock sales	12
Dividend payment	0
Cash flow from financing.	113
Change in cash.	4
Beg. cash	10
End. cash	$ 14

Required

Using the following set of assumptions, prepare pro forma financial statements for Handy Dan, Inc. for 2016:

- Sales are projected to grow by 40 percent.
- Cash is expected to increase at the same rate as sales.
- Assume the following ratios to forecast the identified accounts:

Account	Financial Ratio	
Accounts receivable.	Receivable turnover	= 25.9x
Inventory.	Inventory turnover	= 3.39x
Property & equipment	Fixed asset turnover	= 3.52x
Cost of goods sold.	Gross profit margin ratio	= 25.9%
Operating expenses.	Operating expenses ÷ sales	= 22.1%
Accounts payable.	Payable turnover	= 7.55x

- Depreciation expense is based on a 30-year expected life with no salvage value; any property and equipment acquired during the year is depreciated for only one-half year.
- Interest expense is based on a six percent short-term cost of debt and eight percent cost of debt; only one-half year of interest is charged on loans taken out during the year.
- Effective income tax rate is 33.33 percent.
- Assume no dividends will be paid in 2016.
- The mix of short-term loans payable, long-term debt and contributed capital is set to satisfy an existing debt covenant that requires the company to maintain a current ratio of 2.0 (or greater) and a total debt-to-total assets ratio of 80 percent (or less).

Discuss the expected profitability and operating cash flow of Handy Dan in 2016.

TA 1 **P4.32** **Benchmarking Firm Performance.** Presented below are profitability ratios for three competitors: Bristol-Myers Squibb (BMY), Pfizer, Inc. (PFE), and Johnson & Johnson (JNJ):

2015	BMY	PFE	JNJ
Return on equity (ROE).	11.3%	10.7%	21.7%
Return on assets (ROA)	5.1%	4.2%	11.6%
Return on sales (ROS)	9.8%	14.3%	22.0%
Asset turnover	0.52	0.29	0.53

Required

Compare the relative profitability of the three firms. Which one appears most profitable? Which one would you prefer to add to a portfolio of securities? Why?

P4.33 **Evaluating Financial Performance.** Presented below are selected financial statement data for three global energy firms: TA 1

(amounts in millions)	Chevron Corporation	Conocophillips Corporation	Marathon Oil Corporation
Balance sheet			
Total assets	$266,103	$97,484	$32,311
Short-term debt	4,928	1,427	1,729
Long-term debt	33,584	23,453	7,276
Total debt	112,217	57,402	13,758
Shareholders' equity	153,886	40,082	18,553
Income statement			
Revenues	$129,925	$29,564	$ 4,951
Net income	4,710	(4,371)	(2,204)
Cash flow from operations	19,456	7,572	1,565
Ratios			
Receivable collection period	36.1 days	55.7 days	67.2 days
Inventory-on-hand period	33.1 days	33.0 days	67.4 days
Long-term debt to total assets	12.6%	24.1%	22.5%
Return on assets	1.8%	(4.5)%	(6.8)%
Return on equity	3.1%	(10.9)%	(11.9)%

Required

1. Compare the three firms in terms of their size and their financing strategy.
2. Evaluate the performance of the three firms. Was performance linked to firm size?

P4.34 **(Appendix 4A) Calculating ROE Using Unlevered Financial Ratios.** Presented below are summary financial data from the 2017 annual report of Natalie Company. Using the ratio definitions from Appendix 4A, calculate the following financial ratios: unlevered return on sales, asset turnover, financial leverage, and common equity share of operating earnings. Evaluate the trend in the company's return on equity. Assume an effective income tax rate of 30 percent. TA 4

(amounts in thousands)	2017	2016
Balance sheet		
Total assets	$28,138	$30,435
Shareholders' equity	11,208	10,202
Income statement		
Net sales	26,000	28,000
Interest expense	349	310
Net income after taxes	4,516	4,418

P4.35 **(Appendix 4C) Calculating the Cost of Equity.** The following information is available for The Philippi Winery Company, Inc. TA 6

	2015	2014	2013
Beta	1.20	1.15	1.18
Risk-free rate of return	2.50%	2.30%	2.10%
Equity risk premium	7.40%	7.50%	7.30%

Calculate the company's cost of equity capital for 2015, 2014, and 2013 using the Capital Asset Pricing Model discussed in Appendix 4C.

CORPORATE ANALYSIS

TA 1   **CA4.36**   **The Procter & Gamble Company.**   The 2015 annual report of The Procter & Gamble Company (P&G) is available at www.pginvestor.com. After reviewing P&G's annual report, respond to the following questions:

a.   Prepare common-size income statements for the period 2013 through 2015. What major trends can you identify from this data?

b.   Prepare common-size balance sheets for 2014 and 2015. What major trends can you identify from this data?

c.   Calculate the following ratios for P&G for 2014 and 2015:
   - Return on shareholders' equity
   - Return on assets (levered)
   - Return on sales (levered)
   - Gross profit margin ratio
   - Receivable turnover
   - Receivable collection period
   - Inventory turnover
   - Inventory-on-hand period
   - Asset turnover
   - Quick ratio
   - Current ratio
   - Long-term debt to total assets
   - Interest coverage ratio
   - Financial leverage

   What major trends can you identify from this data?

d.   Develop an overall assessment of the financial performance of P&G for the period 2013 through 2015.

TA 1   **CA4.37**   **Internet-based Analysis.**   Consider a publicly held company whose products you are familiar with. Some examples might include:

Company	Product	Corporate Website
• Johnson & Johnson............	• Band-Aids	• www.jnj.com
• Microsoft Corporation..........	• Windows software	• www.microsoft.com
• Apple, Inc.	• Cellular phones	• www.apple.com
• Intel Corporation	• Pentium processors	• www.intel.com
• Kimberly-Clark Corporation.......	• Kleenex	• www.kimberly-clark.com

Access the company's public website and search for its most recent annual report. (Note: Some companies will provide access to their financial data through an "investor relations" link, while others will provide a direct link to their "annual reports.") After locating your company's most recent annual report, open the file and review its contents. After reviewing the annual report for your selected company, prepare answers to the following questions:

a.   Prepare common-size income statements and common-size balance sheets for the past two years. What significant trends can you identify from these common-size statements?

b.   Calculate the following ratios for the past two years. (Note: Use the ratio definitions in Exhibit 4.6.)

Gross profit margin ratio	Cash and marketable securities to total assets
Return on sales	Quick ratio
Return on assets	Current ratio
Return on shareholders' equity	Accounts payable turnover
Receivable turnover	Days' payable period
Receivable collection period	Long-term debt to total assets
Inventory turnover	Long-term debt to shareholders' equity
Inventory-on-hand period	Interest coverage ratio
Asset turnover	

What significant trends in the company's profitability, asset management, liquidity, or solvency can you identify from your calculations?

  c. Identify several key competitors of your selected company. Go to Yahoo.Finance.com and benchmark your company against its key competitors on the following metrics:

Market capitalization	Return on assets
Return on sales	Return on equity

  d. Review the company's long-term debt footnotes. Is the company subject to any debt covenants? If so, what are the covenants and is the company currently in compliance with the covenant(s)?

CASE

THE CHUBB CORPORATION: AN ANALYSIS OF 2004–2012 RETURN ON EQUITY

Who insures you doesn't matter. Until it does.

(Chubb Corporation annual review, 2009)

Paula Kelly was a buy-side analyst with SunnyDale Advisors, a midsize (more than $5 billion in managed assets) investment management firm based in Stamford, Connecticut. She was asked by Richard Haines, one of SunnyDale's portfolio managers, to help him evaluate the Chubb Corporation (Chubb) as a potential investment candidate. It was March 2012, and Haines was looking to diversify his portfolio to include a property casualty insurer. He only had interest in those companies that had steady records of delivering returns, and Chubb certainly fit that mold. The company's stock performance was inspiring, tripling in value since 2004 and outperforming its peers (**Exhibits 1** and **2**). But Haines's own initial screening indicated weakness on some key financial statement metrics: low top-line premium growth, rising costs, low investment returns, and, most important of all, a flat-to-falling return on equity (ROE). Haines asked Kelly to complete a summary of Chubb's key drivers of financial performance that would explain the company's strong stock performance. (Chubb's financial statements are displayed in **Exhibits 3**, **4**, and **5**.)

Company Background

In 1882, Thomas Chubb and his son Percy founded Chubb & Son as a marine underwriting business that insured ships and their cargoes. Located in the seaport district of New York City, the company was initially capitalized by raising $100,000 from 100 prominent merchants in the area. The risk-sharing model was an immediate success, and it did not take long for the company to grow in both reputation and size. By the 1920s, the company had expanded into other insurance lines, including fidelity, surety bonds, and general casualty insurance.[6] Regardless of the product offered, a hallmark of the company from its early days was to treat all customers with fairness and integrity, from the point of contract sale to the payment of a claim. Thomas, Percy, and, later, Percy's brother Hendon all managed the company, keeping this simple but important tenet in mind. The company was consistently rated among the best in the industry by both its customers and its employees.

The Chubb Corporation in its holding-company form was established in 1967. The company's evolution had been anything but dull. In fact, its existence as a stand-alone entity was almost short-lived when, in January 1969, First National City (later Citicorp) tried to acquire Chubb, but the proposed merger was abandoned after the Department of Justice publicly announced it would attempt to bar the acquisition on antitrust grounds. In the ensuing years, Chubb found its footing, purchasing additional subsidiaries, undertaking forays into specialty products such as rain and drought insurance, underwriting entertainment and multimedia industry risks, and issuing credit default swaps. The company made international headlines in the early 1990s for issuing a personal liability umbrella policy to President Bill Clinton and assuming legal costs in lawsuits brought against him.

Given its emphasis on property and casualty insurance, catastrophic events frequently hit the company hard. In 2001, Chubb paid out close to $900 million in claims related to the September 11 terrorist attacks and the Enron collapse. In 2002, the company took a $700 million charge for asbestos and toxic waste claims. Environmental issues initiated by the Clinton administration and state legislatures put considerable pressure on profitability due to policies issued decades earlier. Hurricanes Ike (2008) and Sandy (2012) both struck areas heavily insured by the company, and losses from these events totaled more than $1 billion.

Chubb became a publicly traded company listed on the New York Stock Exchange in 1984. By 2012, Chubb's employee base numbered more than 10,000, and the company had 120 offices in 26 countries. Revenues and assets exceeded $13 billion and $52 billion, respectively. Also by 2012, Chubb operated three main businesses (**Exhibit 6**):

- Chubb Personal Insurance (CPI) provided customers with insurance for their homes, cars, yachts, jewelry, fine art, and antiques, as well as personal excess liability coverage (to protect wealth from lawsuits) and group accident and health products.

---

[6] Fidelity insurance was a type of insurance that protected companies from frauds and other acts by its employees. Surety bonds were agreements to pay one party in the event that another party defaults on a performance obligation. Casualty insurance was coverage against damage, losses, or other liabilities.

- Chubb Commercial Insurance (CCI) provided property, liability, auto, workers' compensation, marine, and multiple peril insurance while specializing in serving niche markets for midsize businesses.
- Chubb Specialty Insurance (CSI) provided highly specialized insurance for directors' and officers' liability, errors and omissions, employment practices liability, fidelity, crime, kidnap and ransom, and surety.

In 2003, John Finnegan, former chairman and president of General Motors Acceptance Corporation, took over as Chubb's chairman, president, and CEO. A first critical strategic move was the company's exit from the credit derivatives business, which was housed in the Chubb Financial Solutions segment. Finnegan reduced credit default swap notional exposure from $43 billion to $9 billion during 2004 and then to $1 billion by the end of 2005.

Finnegan's overall corporate strategy had targeted three areas: underwriting discipline, expense management, and returning value to shareholders. In his March 2005 letter to shareholders in the company's 2004 annual report, he stated that "underwriting discipline is paramount and premium growth desirable only if it leads to underwriting profit." His message had stayed consistent over the years. In early 2009, he commented on the company's 2008 performance:

> Chubb has always believed in the need to earn an underwriting profit rather than rely on returns on our investment portfolio to cover underwriting losses. Accordingly, we insure niche segments that we know, and if we cannot get the right price for the risk we have been asked to assume, we will not write the business.[7]

An indicator of Chubb's success at underwriting discipline and expense management was the combined ratio. This ratio conveyed the percentage of each premium dollar spent on claims-related expenses. It was calculated as the sum of the ratio of losses and loss expenses to premiums, and the ratio of statutory underwriting expenses to premiums.[8] **Exhibit 7** provides Chubb's combined ratio from 2004 to 2012.

Just as Finnegan was emphasizing disciplined expense management to bolster Chubb's ability to be profitable in a changing market environment, the financial crisis was taking its toll on other insurers. Chubb had entered and exited that period of time relatively unscathed, but certain macro events had still affected the company. For example, Hurricane Ike hit the entire property and casualty insurance industry hard in 2008. Chubb's total incurred net catastrophe losses were $607 million in 2008, 5.1 percentage points of the company's loss ratio; approximately half of those losses were related to this one event. In 2012, 9.6 points of catastrophe losses were recorded; Hurricane Sandy was the major signature event.[9] In early 2010, Finnegan stated his goals regarding shareholder value:

> We believe Chubb is in the enviable position of having excess capital. In the current environment, we are unable to deploy that excess capital at an acceptable rate of return. The prevailing market conditions of the property and casualty industry and the soft market preclude our ability to use it to support growth in our core businesses. In addition, there are fewer attractive investment opportunities for our conservative portfolio given the current capital market environment. Finally, our stock is trading at a ratio of price to book value that is lower than our historical valuation.[10]

And in early 2013, Finnegan discussed the company's 2012 results:

> From the time our share repurchases began in December 2005 through the end of 2012, we have bought back 47% of the shares that were outstanding when the buybacks began. During that period, we have returned a total of $13.9 billion to shareholders through $10.6 billion of share repurchases and $3.3 billion of dividends.[11]

Paula Kelly's Analysis

Kelly began to pull together Chubb's financial data, starting with 2004. Her objective was to understand how the company had navigated the financial crisis of 2008–2009 and to capture its overall financial performance under John Finnegan's leadership. Her analysis culminated with a decomposition of Chubb's ROE through time (**Exhibit 8**). After

---

[7] Chubb Corporation, "CEO Report," annual review, 2008.

[8] The standard insurance industry calculation reduced the denominator, premiums, by dividends paid to policyholders. Analysts external to the firm frequently estimated the combined ratio as total operating expenses divided by total premiums.

[9] Chubb Corporation, "CEO Report," annual review, 2012.

[10] Chubb Corporation, "CEO Report," annual review, 2009.

[11] Chubb Corporation, "CEO Report," annual review, 2012.

her review, she was satisfied she could provide Haines with the explanation of Chubb's strong financial performance that he desired.

Required

An evaluation of the past performance of Chubb is provided in the case. You do not need to perform a comprehensive review of each exhibit. Rather, read the case, review the exhibits, and focus your attention on the following:

i.   The Chairman of Chubb has identified a number of "levers" the company has used to enhance profitability. What specific actions has the company taken to grow its ROE? Where in the financial statements would you observe the success or failure of those levers?

ii. Exhibit 7 summarizes numerous financial ratios that drive return on equity (ROE) and return on assets (ROA). It specifically outlines how each can be broken down to component parts. In your review of Exhibit 7, what does the data tell you led to the drop in ROE experienced by Chubb in recent years? Does your identification of key ROE drivers link back to Finnegan's strategy and statements? Why or why not? (*Hint:* Review Exhibit 7 and look for trends in the data that may support or refute the factors that have led to changes in ROE and ROA).

This public-sourced case was prepared by Richard F. Green, Research Assistant, and Paul J. Simko, Associate Professor of Business Administration. It was written as a basis for class discussion rather than to illustrate effective or ineffective handling of an administrative situation. Copyright © 2015 by the University of Virginia Darden School Foundation, Charlottesville, VA. All rights reserved. *To order copies, send an e-mail to* sales@dardenbusinesspublishing.com. *No part of this publication may be reproduced, stored in a retrieval system, used in a spreadsheet, or transmitted in any form or by any means—electronic, mechanical, photocopying, recording, or otherwise—without the permission of the Darden School Foundation.*

EXHIBIT 1	The Chubb Corporation: An Analysis of 2004–2012 Return on Equity Stock Price Performance

Data source: Yahoo! Finance.

EXHIBIT 2	The Chubb Corporation: An Analysis of 2004–2012 Return on Equity Key Competitor Financial Metrics		
		Chubb	**Progressive**	**CNA Finl**

	Chubb	Progressive	CNA Finl
Earnings per share	$ 5.73	$ 1.15	$ 2.17
Premium growth	1.67%	7.49%	4.23%
Investment yield	3.57%	3.10%	5.00%
Losses to premiums earned	63.4%	74.6%	70.8%
Expenses to premiums written	34.6%	21.1%	34.0%
Combined ratio	98.0%	95.7%	104.8%
Return on assets	2.7%	3.1%	0.8%
Return on equity	9.7%	13.5%	4.2%
Profit margin (net income/revenue)	10.4%	4.1%	5.0%
Asset turnover (revenue/total average assets)	0.26	0.75	0.17
Financial leverage (average assets/average equity)	3.58	4.35	5.01
Beta	0.80	0.85	1.20
Stock price (12-31-12)	$ 75.32	$ 21.10	$ 28.01
Price-to-earnings (PE)	13.1	18.3	12.9
Price-to-book (PB)	1.2	2.1	0.6
Price-to-sales (PS)	1.5	0.8	1.3
Shares outstanding (millions)	261.8	604.0	269.4
Market capitalization ($ millions)	$19,716	$12,744	$ 7,546

Data source: Company 10-Ks, 2004–12.

EXHIBIT 3	The Chubb Corporation: An Analysis of 2004–2012 Return on Equity Balance Sheets								

As of Dec. 31 (in $ millions):	2012	2011	2010	2009	2008	2007	2006	2005	2004
Assets									
Invested assets:									
Short-term investments	$ 2,528	$ 1,893	$ 1,905	$ 1,918	$ 2,478	$ 1,839	$ 2,254	$ 1,898	$ 1,308
Fixed maturities	38,076	37,184	36,519	36,578	32,755	33,871	31,966	30,523	28,009
Equity securities	1,663	1,512	1,550	1,433	1,479	2,320	1,957	2,212	1,841
Other invested assets	1,954	2,180	2,239	2,075	2,026	2,051	1,516	0	0
Total invested assets	$44,221	$42,769	$42,213	$42,004	$38,738	$40,081	$37,693	$34,633	$31,158
Cash	50	58	70	51	56	49	38	36	42
Premiums receivable	2,185	2,161	2,098	2,101	2,201	2,227	2,314	2,319	2,336
Reinsurance recoverable	1,941	1,739	1,817	2,053	2,212	2,307	2,594	3,769	3,483
Deferred policy acquisition costs	1,206	1,630	1,562	1,533	1,532	1,556	1,480	1,445	1,435
Other assets	2,581	2,508	2,489	2,707	3,690	3,107	3,538	3,782	3,952
Total assets	$52,184	$50,865	$50,249	$50,449	$48,429	$49,327	$47,657	$45,984	$42,406
Liabilities									
Unpaid losses and loss expense	$23,963	$23,068	$22,718	$22,839	$22,367	$22,623	$22,293	$22,482	$20,292
Unearned premiums	6,361	6,322	6,189	6,153	6,367	6,599	6,546	6,361	6,356
Long-term debt	3,575	3,575	3,975	3,975	3,975	3,460	2,466	2,467	2,814
Other liabilities	2,458	2,326	1,837	1,848	2,388	2,200	2,489	2,267	2,818
Total liabilities	$36,357	$35,291	$34,719	$34,815	$35,097	$34,882	$33,794	$33,577	$32,280
Shareholders' Equity									
Common stock and paid-in-capital	550	562	580	596	525	721	1,950	2,575	1,515
Retained earnings	20,009	19,176	17,943	16,235	14,509	13,280	11,711	9,600	8,119
Other comprehensive income	1,431	1,195	790	720	(735)	444	202	367	703
Treasury stock	(6,163)	(5,359)	(3,783)	(1,917)	(967)	0	0	(135)	(211)
Total shareholders' equity	$15,827	$15,574	$15,530	$15,634	$13,332	$14,445	$13,863	$12,407	$10,126
Total liabilities and equity	$52,184	$50,865	$50,249	$50,449	$48,429	$49,327	$47,657	$45,984	$42,406

Data source: Company 10-Ks, 2004–12.

EXHIBIT 4	The Chubb Corporation: An Analysis of 2004–2012 Return on Equity Income Statements

Year Ended Dec. 31 (in $ millions):	2012	2011	2010	2009	2008	2007	2006	2005	2004
Revenues									
Premiums earned	$11,838	$11,644	$11,215	$11,331	$11,828	$11,946	$11,958	$12,176	$11,636
Investment income	1,556	1,644	1,665	1,649	1,732	1,738	1,580	1,408	1,256
Realized investment gains (losses), net	193	288	426	23	(371)	374	245	384	218
Other revenues	8	9	13	13	32	49	220	115	67
Total revenues	$13,595	$13,585	$13,319	$13,016	$13,221	$14,107	$14,003	$14,083	$13,177
Expenses									
Losses and loss expense*	7,507	7,407	6,499	6,268	6,898	6,299	6,574	7,813	7,321
Amortization of deferred policy acquisition costs	2,411	2,330	2,183	3,021	3,123	3,092	2,919	2,931	2,843
Other insurance operating costs	1,362	1,312	1,309	416	441	444	550	512	630
All other expenses	319	337	340	349	352	335	435	380	315
Total expenses	11,599	11,386	10,331	10,054	10,814	10,170	10,478	11,636	11,109
Income before income tax	1,996	2,199	2,988	2,962	2,407	3,937	3,525	2,447	2,068
Federal and foreign income tax	451	521	814	779	603	1,130	997	621	520
Net income	$ 1,545	$ 1,678	$ 2,174	$ 2,183	$ 1,804	$ 2,807	$ 2,528	$ 1,826	$ 1,548
Per Share Data									
Weighted ave. shares outstanding—basic	269,500	289,300	319,200	350,100	361,100	393,600	412,500	396,400	379,800
Weighted ave. shares outstanding—diluted	271,400	291,400	321,600	353,000	366,800	400,300	422,400	408,400	386,400
Net income per share—basic	$5.73	$5.80	$6.81	$6.24	$5.00	$7.13	$6.13	$4.61	$4.08
Net income per share—diluted	$5.69	$5.76	$6.76	$6.18	$4.92	$7.01	$5.98	$4.47	$4.01
Dividends per share	1.64	1.56	1.48	1.4	1.32	1.16	1	0.86	0.78
*Includes $ effect of catastrophic (CAT) losses	$1,136	$1,036	$1,043	$91	$607	$363	$167	$682	$349

Data source: Company 10-Ks, 2004–12.

EXHIBIT 5	The Chubb Corporation: An Analysis of 2004–2012 Return on Equity Statements of Cash Flow

Year Ended Dec. 31 (in $ millions):	2012	2011	2010	2009	2008	2007	2006	2005	2004
Net income	$ 1,545	$ 1,678	$ 2,174	$ 2,183	$ 1,804	$ 2,807	$ 2,528	$ 1,826	$ 1,548
Increase in unpaid losses and loss expense	691	361	145	262	389	350	986	1,904	2,288
Realized investment losses (gains)	(193)	(288)	(426)	(23)	371	(374)	(245)	(384)	(218)
Other operating activities	256	127	438	13	(20)	408	73	410	471
Cash flow from operating activities	$ 2,299	$ 1,878	$ 2,331	$ 2,435	$ 2,544	$ 3,191	$ 3,342	$ 3,756	$ 4,089
Net sales (purchases) of fixed maturities	(686)	256	(33)	(1,783)	(807)	(1,503)	(1,556)	(3,042)	(5,497)
Decrease (increase) in short term investments	(629)	11	38	563	(654)	455	(355)	(591)	1,388
Other investing activities	343	313	62	346	135	(601)	(458)	(218)	(19)
Cash flow from investing activities	$ (972)	$ 580	$ 67	$ (874)	$(1,326)	$(1,649)	$(2,369)	$(3,851)	$(4,128)
Repayment of long-term debt	—	(400)	—	—	515	1,000	—	(301)	—
Repurchase of shares	(959)	(1,707)	(2,003)	(1,060)	(1,336)	(2,185)	(1,228)	(135)	—
Dividends paid to shareholders	(438)	(450)	(472)	(487)	(471)	(451)	(403)	(330)	(291)
Other financing activities	62	87	96	(19)	81	105	660	855	320
Cash flow from financing activities	$(1,335)	$(2,470)	$(2,379)	$(1,566)	$(1,211)	$(1,531)	$ (971)	$ 89	$ 29
Net increase (decrease) in cash	(8)	(12)	19	(5)	7	11	2	(6)	(10)
Cash at beginning of year	58	70	51	56	49	38	36	42	52
Cash at end of year	$ 50	$ 58	$ 70	$ 51	$ 56	$ 49	$ 38	$ 36	$ 42

Data source: Company 10-Ks, 2004–12.

EXHIBIT 6	The Chubb Corporation: An Analysis of 2010–2012 Return on Equity Segment Performance		
Year Ended Dec. 31 (in $ millions):	**2012**	**2011**	**2010**
Personal Insurance (CPI)			
Premiums written			
Automobile	$ 691	$ 682	$ 638
Homeowners	2,554	2,477	2,382
Other.	880	818	805
Total personal	4,125	3,977	3,825
Other adjustments	(101)	(60)	(57)
Earned premiums	4,024	3,917	3,768
Expenses			
Insurance losses.	2,417	2,508	2,210
Amortization of deferred acquisition costs.	942	900	836
Other insurance operating costs	458	436	397
Other expenses	15	26	22
Total expenses	3,832	3,870	3,465
Net income—CPI	$ 192	$ 47	$ 303
Commercial Insurance (CCI)			
Premiums written			
Multiple peril	$1,119	$1,136	$1,094
Casualty	1,641	1,639	1,532
Workers' Compensation.	1,014	860	756
Property and marine	1,400	1,416	1,294
Total commercial	5,174	5,051	4,676
Other adjustments	(30)	(106)	(29)
Earned premiums	5,144	4,945	4,647
Expenses			
Insurance losses.	3,512	3,366	2,807
Amortization of deferred acquisition costs.	970	929	866
Other insurance operating costs	620	617	621
Other expenses	(2)	32	6
Total expenses	5,100	4,944	4,300
Net income—CCI	$ 44	$ 1	$ 347
Specialty insurance (CSI)			
Premiums written			
Professional liability	$2,273	$2,388	$2,398
Surety	295	332	329
Total specialty.	2,568	2,720	2,727
Other adjustments	98	49	60
Earned premiums	2,666	2,769	2,787
Expenses			
Insurance losses.	1,622	1,558	1,503
Amortization of deferred acquisition costs.	499	501	481
Other insurance operating costs	293	278	289
Other expenses	(10)	5	2
Total expenses	2,404	2,342	2,275
Net Income—CSI	$ 262	$ 427	$ 512

Data source: Company 10-Ks, 2010–12.

EXHIBIT 7	The Chubb Corporation: An Analysis of 2004–2012 Return on Equity Combined Ratio Summary								

Year Ended Dec. 31:	2012	2011	2010	2009	2008	2007	2006	2005	2004
Premiums earned ($ millions)	$11,838	$11,644	$11,215	$11,331	$11,828	$11,946	$11,958	$12,176	$11,636
Loss ratio	63.4%	63.6%	57.9%	55.3%	58.3%	52.7%	55.0%	64.2%	62.9%
Other expenses	34.6%	34.2%	34.2%	33.4%	33.1%	32.4%	32.6%	31.4%	32.6%
Total combined ratio.	98.0%	97.8%	92.1%	88.7%	91.4%	85.1%	87.6%	95.6%	95.5%
By Segment:									
Personal insurance (CPI)	94.4%	98.3%	91.5%	84.1%	87.1%	84.8%	81.7%	86.6%	92.5%
Commercial insurance (CCI).	99.0%	99.3%	92.3%	89.9%	93.9%	85.8%	83.1%	92.4%	82.5%
Specialty insurance CSI	91.3%	85.1%	82.2%	84.1%	83.3%	77.4%	87.5%	97.3%	100.3%

Data source: Company 10-Ks, 2004–12.

EXHIBIT 8	The Chubb Corporation: An Analysis of 2005–2012 Return on Equity DuPont Analysis—ROE and ROA							

		2012	2011	2010	2009	2008	2007	2006	2005
	Return on Equity Analysis								
Level 1	Return on average equity: ROE	9.70%	10.02%	12.57%	14.95%	14.84%	18.37%	18.31%	14.35%
Level 2	Net profit margin: profitability	10.41%	10.97%	14.46%	16.67%	15.32%	18.50%	17.10%	11.24%
	Total assets turnover: utilization	0.260	0.263	0.256	0.263	0.278	0.283	0.294	0.310
	Average assets/average equity (leverage) . . .	3.58	3.47	3.40	3.41	3.48	3.51	3.64	4.12
Level 3	See Level 3 ROA analysis.	See below	—	—	—	—	—	—	—
	Return on Assets Analysis								
Level 1	Return on average assets: ROA	2.71%	2.88%	3.70%	4.38%	4.26%	5.24%	5.02%	3.48%
Level 2	Net profit margin: profitability	10.41%	10.97%	14.46%	16.67%	15.32%	18.50%	17.10%	11.24%
	Total assets turnover: utilization	0.260	0.263	0.256	0.263	0.278	0.283	0.294	0.310
Level 3	**Profitability Drivers (common size costs)**								
	Losses and loss expense to sales	56.0%	55.7%	50.4%	48.2%	50.8%	45.9%	47.8%	57.0%
	Amortization of DAC to sales	18.0%	17.5%	16.9%	23.3%	23.0%	22.5%	21.2%	21.4%
	Other insurance operating costs to sales. . . .	10.2%	9.9%	10.2%	3.2%	3.2%	3.2%	4.0%	3.7%
	All other expense to sales	2.4%	2.5%	2.6%	2.7%	2.6%	2.4%	3.2%	2.8%
	Total expenses to sales	86.5%	85.6%	80.1%	77.4%	79.6%	74.1%	76.2%	84.9%
	Income taxes to sales.	3.4%	3.9%	6.3%	6.0%	4.4%	8.2%	7.2%	4.5%
	Efficiency Drivers (individual asset performance)								
	Net investment yield	3.57%	3.86%	3.95%	4.08%	4.39%	4.46%	4.36%	4.28%
	Premium receivable to sales.	6.13	6.15	6.15	6.18	6.18	6.17	5.95	5.91
	Reinsurance recoverable to sales.	6.90	7.65	7.10	6.33	6.14	5.95	5.30	3.63
	DAC to sales.	11.11	8.16	8.25	8.48	8.87	8.83	9.30	9.48
	Other assets turnover.	5.19	5.30	5.18	4.80	3.68	4.42	3.89	3.62

Data source: Company 10-Ks, 2005–12.

SOLUTIONS TO REVIEW PROBLEMS

Solution 4.1

THE DANA POINT COMPANY
Balance Sheets

Assets	Percentage Change 2016	Common Size 2016	Liabilities & Shareholders' Equity	Percentage Change 2016	Common Size 2016
Cash	(76.7)%	2.2%	Accounts payable...........	4.0%	20.7%
Accounts receivable....	12.5%	21.3%	Wages payable.............	(22.1)%	11.7%
Inventory.............	117.8%	15.5%	Total current liabilities........	(7.2)%	32.3%
Prepaid insurance......	33.3%	1.9%	Bank loan payable	(2.4)%	26.2%
Total current assets	10.7%	40.9%	Capital stock	0.0%	23.7%
Building (net).........	(1.3)%	59.1%	Retained earnings	54.8%	17.8%
Total	3.3%	100.0%	Total	3.3%	100.0%

Note: Columns may not total exactly due to rounding.

THE DANA POINT COMPANY
Income Statements

	Percentage Change 2016	Common Size 2016
Revenues	11.6%	100.0%
Less: Cost of goods sold	4.2%	52.1%
Gross margin	21.1%	47.9%
Less: Depreciation expense....................	0.0%	4.6%
Wage expense	4.7%	18.8%
Insurance expense........................	0.0%	3.3%
Interest expense..........................	(2.9)%	1.4%
Net income before taxes	61.1%	19.9%
Less: Tax expense	60.7%	6.0%
Net income..................................	61.4%	13.9%

Note: Columns may not total exactly due to rounding.

Solution 4.2

1. Ratio Analysis

	2016	2015
Return on equity	50.8%	37.1%
Return on sales	13.9%	9.6%
Asset turnover	1.51	1.40
Financial leverage	2.41	2.75
Receivable collection period	51.3 days	50.9 days
Inventory-on-hand period	71.5 days	34.2 days
Days' payable period	95.6 days	95.8 days
Long-term debt to total assets	26.2%	27.7%
Long-term debt to shareholders' equity	63.1%	76.2%
Interest coverage ratio	15.5	9.7
Quick ratio	0.7	0.8
Current ratio	1.3	1.1
Gross profit margin ratio	47.9%	44.2%

2. The profitability of The Dana Point Company is up dramatically from 2015 to 2016, as revealed by the trend in the return on equity and return on sales ratios. The gross profit margin ratio increase suggests that the company was able to realize some economies of scale over this same period. Overall, the company's asset management was up from 2015 to 2016, as revealed by the trend in the total asset turnover ratio, despite a small increase in the receivable collection period and a larger increase in the inventory-on-hand period. The cash collection cycle grew dramatically, however, from minus 10.7 days in 2015 to over 27 days in 2016 (a swing of over 37 days). The financial riskiness of the company improved from 2015 to 2016, as indicated by a decline in the use of financial leverage (see the financial leverage and the long-term debt to shareholders' equity ratios). This improvement is also reflected in an improving interest coverage ratio and current ratio.

Solution 4.3

1.

	2016	2015	2014	2013
ROS (NI/Revenue)	6.6%	6.3%	6.7%	5.8%
AT (Revenue/Total assets)	1.33	1.33	1.37	1.32
LEV (Total assets/SE)	1.54	1.55	1.52	1.62
ROE	13.5%	13.1%	13.9%	12.4%

2.

	2016	2015	2014	2013
Sales growth	5.0%	5.2%	6.7%	3.4%
ROE	13.5%	13.1%	13.9%	12.4%
DRR	40.0%	40.0%	40.0%	40.0%
SGR	5.4%	5.2%	5.6%	5.0%

Overall, the Ventura Company's sustainable growth rate equaled or exceeded its growth in revenues in all years except 2014, indicating that it is doing a solid job of managing its growth.

When you complete this chapter you should be able to:

1. Illustrate the operating cycle of a retail organization. (page 176)
2. Explain how retail, service, and manufacturing companies recognize their operating revenue. (page 177)
3. Describe how revenue is recognized under the completed contract and percentage of completion methods. (page 181)
4. Explain how accounts receivable are valued and how the allowance for uncollectible accounts and bad debt expense are estimated. (page 186)
5. Describe why the effective management of accounts receivable is important for a business. (page 194)
6. Identify the processes for monetizing a company's accounts receivable—factoring, pledging, and securitization. (page 196)
7. Understand basic analysis techniques for revenue recognition and receivables policies. (page 198)
8. Summarize the general guidance on revenue recognition. (page 201)

Operating Cycle, Revenue Recognition, and Receivable Valuation

The big 5 is the chapter number image.

EMBRAER S.A.

Embraer, S.A. otherwise known by its parent holding company name, Empresa Brasileira de Aeronáutica S.A., was created in 1969 as a Brazilian state-owned enterprise. In its initial years the company produced a variety of small aircraft for the Brazilian air force and small commercial airlines. By the mid-1980s it had shifted to larger aircraft and the Brazilian government sought to fully privatize the company. Embraer was soon acquired by a Brazilian bank holding company and two private pension funds who listed the company on the Sao Paulo and NYSE stock exchanges (tickers EMBR3 and ERJ). Embraer has been a solidly performing international aircraft manufacturer ever since. The company competes with Bombardier, Boeing, and Airbus.

Embraer manufactures and sells a variety of regional and business jets, including its popular ERJ-190 and 195 models, and two small-cabin jets introduced in 2009—the Phenom 100 and 300. Total sales for fiscal year 2014 topped $6.2 billion across both the commercial and military segments, and even more impressive was an order backlog of almost $23 billion. But what constitutes a "sale" at Embraer? Is it as simple as just making and selling a plane? An analysis of Embraer accounting policies reveals that it sells its aircraft under a number of different arrangements, and each has its own unique impact on Embraer's revenue account. For straightforward commercial or executive aircraft sales, revenue is recognized when delivery is made and all benefits and risk of ownership are transferred to the buyer. In contrast, in cases where all of the company's contractual obligations have not been met, the value of pending obligations is recorded in unearned income. Military aircraft sales are typically arranged through long-term development contracts with Brazilian and foreign governments. Revenue on these contracts is realized under the percentage of completion method. Embraer also delivered aircraft under leasing arrangements, typically meaning that rental income was recorded under the straight line method over the lease period (i.e., and operating lease contract). Finally, many sales contained multiple-element arrangements, wherein training, technical assistance, spare parts and other concessions were included in the aircraft purchase price.

A review of the company's balance sheet also provides interesting insights into Embraer's sales activities. The following select accounts are particularly relevant:

December 31: (in millions)	2014	2013
Assets		
Trade accounts receivables, net	$703.8	$ 578.7
Customer and commercial financing	68.6	73.7
Collateralized accounts receivable	425.6	425.9
Liabilities		
Advances from customers	828.6	1,007.0
Unearned income	328.9	274.7

Each of these balance sheet accounts relates directly to the revenue recognition policies being applied by the management at Embraer. In this chapter, we explore the important accounting concept of revenue recognition and its influence on such balance sheet accounts.

EXECUTIVE OUTLINE

Operating Cycle, Revenue Recognition and Receivable Valuation

Operating Cycle of a Business
- Operating Cycle of a Retail Company

Valuing and Reporting Accounts Receivable
- Percentage of Credit Sales Method
- Aging Method

Monetizing Accounts Receivables
- Factoring
- Pledging
- Securitization

Fundamentals of Revenue Recognition
- For Retail and Service Companies
- For Manufacturing Companies

Managing Accounts Receivable
- Sales Discounts
- Sales Returns

Analyzing Revenue and Receivables
- Revenue Recognition
- Receivables Valuation

eLectures
MBC

Takeaway 1
Illustrate the operating cycle of a retail organization.

OPERATING CYCLE OF A BUSINESS

Almost all companies have an identifiable cycle of activities that reflect the ongoing operations of the business. This repetitive cycle of events is commonly referred to as the **operating cycle**. Exhibit 5.1 presents, for example, the operating cycle of a typical retail operation. It reveals that retail companies buy inventory ready for sale, then sell the inventory, and ultimately, receive payment from their customers.

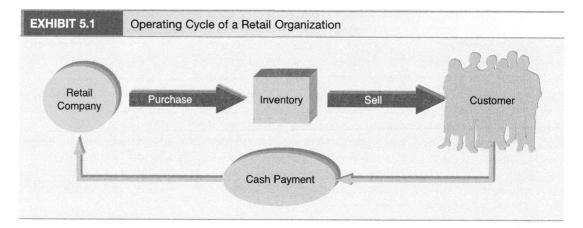

| **EXHIBIT 5.1** | Operating Cycle of a Retail Organization |

Illustrative of these events are the operating cycles of Wal-Mart and Ford, both international retail businesses.[1] Wal-Mart, for example, uses its operating resources to buy inventory for sale to its customers; but, because the products it sells are relatively inexpensive, and because its business strategy is to be a low-cost, low-profit margin, but high-volume business, almost all of Wal-Mart's sales transactions are in cash or using a debit/credit card. In short, Wal-Mart does not generally extend credit to its customers.[2] Ford, on the other hand, operates in the highly competitive automotive industry and sells an expensive product to its customers, most of whom could not afford to buy that product for cash. Thus, Ford, through its financing subsidiary, arranges for most of its customers to purchase on credit. As these

---

[1] Ford Corporation is, technically, a manufacturing company; however, the company maintains a network of dealers that specialize in the sale and maintenance of Ford products. We are referring here to that retail network of dealers.
[2] Wal-Mart does carry some receivables on its balance sheet. These primarily relate to amounts due from (i) insurance companies from pharmacy sales, (ii) suppliers for marketing and incentive programs, and (iii) certain real estate transactions.

examples reveal, depending upon the relative cost of a product, the financial capability of the customer, and the competitiveness of a given business environment, a company may (or may not) sell its products or services to its customers on credit.

In this chapter we explore the various ways that companies recognize their operating revenues, and if they extend credit to their customers, we review the accounting rules, the risks, and the attendant costs associated with this important business practice.

FUNDAMENTALS OF REVENUE RECOGNITION

Revenue refers to the inflow of assets (such as cash, accounts receivable, or bartered assets) to a company that occurs as a direct consequence of providing goods or services to customers. In Chapter 2, the topic of revenue recognition was introduced. At that time, we said that revenue could be **recognized**— that is, revenue could be reported on the income statement as having been earned—at the point in time at which a company provides goods or services to its customers, and when collectibility of any unpaid cash from the customer is reasonably assured.

Recognizing revenue is a significant economic event. It signifies that the company has successfully performed its primary activity of selling a product or providing a service. In the view of most investment professionals, recognizing revenue is the most important event affecting a business since it indicates the market's acceptance of the firm's product or service. Since revenue recognition increases shareholders' wealth, it is also considered to be a primary driver of firm share price, and thus, a key driver of firm value.

When revenue is recognized and then matched with the expenses incurred to produce that revenue, net income (loss) results. In Chapter 2, the financial data of the Russian River Valley Winery was used to illustrate how financial statements could be produced from a series of economic events and transactions. In that illustration, the winery recognized revenue from the sale of its wine at the time that it was sold to the company's customers (when legal ownership of the wine passed from the winery to the customer). But there were other points in time where it could reasonably be argued that the winery might have recognized its revenue, for example, when the wine was delivered if delivery occurred after the sale, or at the point of cash collection if customers were allowed to purchase the wine on credit. The question then is: What criteria should be used to determine the timing and amount of revenue recognition? The answer can have a significant impact on a firm's reported results.

In essence, the key business conditions that must be satisfied before a firm may recognize revenue include: (1) the revenue must be earned; and (2) the revenue must be **realized** or **realizable**. The first condition refers to the fact that the company must satisfy its obligations to a customer under the terms of the sales agreement. If the revenue relates to a service, then this typically means that the service has been performed. If the revenue relates to a product, then this typically means that ownership right (e.g., title) of the product has passed to the customer. The second condition refers to the fact that the company has been paid or can reasonably expect to be paid. In other words, there must be the expectation that the sale will ultimately result in the customer fulfilling his or her responsibility. While these conditions may seem relatively clear cut, inaccurate revenue recognition is by far the leading cause for U.S. Securities and Exchange Commission (SEC) enforcement actions against U.S. exchange-listed companies. The revenue recognition inaccuracies range from differences of opinion regarding the application of revenue recognition rules to outright fraud. We will have more to say about this problem later in this chapter.

The large number of inaccurate, usually aggressive or premature, revenue recognition practices adopted by firms led the SEC to issue, in 1999, explicit guidance regarding the recognition of revenue in Staff Accounting Bulletin (SAB) 101 (see Appendix 5A). In May 2014, the revenue recognition standards again were significantly revised, further testament to both the importance of these amounts reported by companies, and to the complexities in determining the proper timing in their recording. Importantly, the most recent changes reflect a joint effort between the IASB and the FASB, and are the result of more than a decade of collaboration on the topic.

The new standard is ASC 606, *Revenue from Contracts with Customers*, and it will replace current IFRS and GAAP revenue recognition requirements. The effective date for ASC 606 is for fiscal periods beginning after December 15, 2017, if the entity is publicly traded, and for all other companies after December 15, 2018. During this transition period, however, preparers and users of financial statements should be aware of revenue recognition criteria under both the new standard as well as the old. Accordingly, within this chapter we provide detailed explanations of the revenue recognition rules currently applicable to published financial statements. We follow this with a brief illustration highlighting how, in

Takeaway 2
Explain how retail, service, and manufacturing companies recognize their operating revenue.

general, grey areas in interpretation of revenue recognition rules have led to the numerous controversies surrounding the recording of revenue. In Appendix 5B we describe greater details pertaining to ASC 606.

According to SAB 101, the following must be satisfied before revenue can be recognized by a company following GAAP:

- Persuasive evidence of a sales arrangement must exist;
- Delivery of the product or service must occur;
- The seller's price to the buyer is fixed or determinable; and
- Collectibility of any unpaid cash is reasonably assured.

Notice that Embraer's revenue recognition criteria described in the vignette at the start of this chapter closely mirrors the criteria required by SAB 101.[3]

Under ASC 606, the primary principle of revenue recognition is more basically identified: that revenue is to depict the transfer of promised goods or services to customers in an amount that reflects the consideration expected in return for those goods or services. Rather than specify criteria, ASC 606 provides a five-step model that can be applied regardless of the type of transaction or industry. It also can be used for the recognition of gains and losses on the sale of assets that are not part of a company's ordinary activities, such as sales of property, plant and equipment. The five steps under the new standard are:

1. Identify the contract with a customer.
2. Identify the separate performance obligations in the contract.
3. Determine the transaction price.
4. Allocate the transaction price to the separate performance obligations in the contract.
5. Recognize revenue when the company satisfies a performance obligation.

Unfortunately, under current revenue recognition standards (SAB 101) many grey areas arise within the interpretation of exactly when to recognize revenue. A partial list of some controversial issues over the years include: (1) what constitutes persuasive evidence of a sales arrangement; (2) how to treat certain consignment sales; (3) at what stage does a right-of-product-return policy influence revenue recognition; (4) what if the product is complete and paid for but not yet delivered; (5) what if the seller acts as a middleman between the retailer and the customer; and, (6) what if the sale involves a barter transaction. Appendix 5A to this chapter provides an analysis of some of these controversial issues through a set of hypothetical scenarios. ASC 606 is designed to provide more structure around these decisions, although the jury is still out as to whether it will succeed when it is ultimately put into practice. Appendix 5B to this chapter provides more detail regarding the five-step model under the new standard.

To provide more context behind why revenue recognition, in general, can be so complex, Exhibit 5.2 depicts various points in time when some managers might justify the recording of revenue. Moving from right to left, these points represent a continuum of increasing risk that the amount of revenue recognized will not become true increase in wealth for the firm.

For instance, if revenue is recognized before production of a product even begins (see the far left end of the continuum), there is a much higher probability that the amount of recorded revenue will not actually be earned or realized. Many events may occur before the product is ultimately produced, sold, and delivered to the final consumer that could change its final selling price, and thus, the appropriate amount of revenue to be recognized.

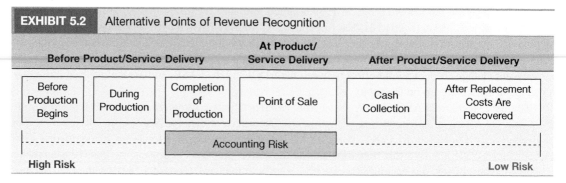

EXHIBIT 5.2   Alternative Points of Revenue Recognition

---

[3] Embraer uses a variety of revenue recognition policies owing to the variety of different customer needs it must satisfy.

To help you see the intuition behind the revenue recognition principles, let's use the spectrum in Exhibit 5.2 for the case of a jewelry manufacturer, such as Tiffany & Company, that uses diamonds and gold in its finished products. If the jeweler were to recognize revenue for a ring that has not even been produced, the jeweler would have to be very certain that the price of diamonds and gold would not change, that the cost of labor would remain stable, and that the ring would be sufficiently attractive so that there would be no trouble finding a buyer at the planned selling price. But one or all of these assumptions is likely to be false, and hence, revenue (and net income) would be potentially overstated, and very likely incorrectly reported. Thus, the left-most point on the risk spectrum—before production begins—is too early to recognize revenue even if the company has a guaranteed purchase commitment from a customer at a specified purchase price (such as a signed purchase contract). The company has yet to *earn* the revenue and, therefore, cannot recognize the revenue.

The second point, when the company is actively producing inventory for sale, indicates that the risk of being able to produce the product has been at least partially resolved. The risks that remain, however, include finding a buyer for the product at the anticipated selling price and collecting the full purchase price in cash, among others. Revenue still cannot be recognized.

At the third point production of the product is complete, and thus, the risk of production has been eliminated; but, the risk that remains is that a buyer will need to be found who is willing to pay the specified selling price. If a purchase order from a customer is received, and that is all, this would indicate that the customer is convinced of the product's value, and thus, it may seem that revenue recognition could be justified. This is not the case, however, since the earnings process has not been completed. The act of taking possession conveys that the risks of ownership transfer to the buyer. Until then, revenue cannot be recognized.

At the fourth point, the point of sale, all of the risks of successful production have been resolved and a final consumer has been identified. At this point, the principal remaining risks are that of cash collection, assuming that the jewelry store allows its customers to buy its goods on credit, and the risk of customer dissatisfaction, assuming that it offers its customers the opportunity to return unwanted or defective goods. For all businesses, there is the risk that some customers will be unable or unwilling to pay for previously purchased goods and services, as well as the risk that some products will be returned. While the point of delivery is the customary point at which revenue is properly recognized, questions may still remain as to whether the revenue has been earned and whether collection is reasonably assured. If a right-of-return policy exists or if collection of cash is not assured, it is premature to recognize the entire revenue amount. In such cases, companies must establish certain allowances or reserves to provide for the contingency that the product will be returned or will not be paid for. We illustrate such reserves later in the chapter. In sum, in the case of a jewelry store, revenue recognized at this point would appear to be appropriate.

At the fifth point, the point of cash collection, all revenue realization risks have been eliminated except for product-return risk. The product has been successfully produced; a final customer has been identified; and, the expected cash has been received. The remaining risks at this stage involve customer dissatisfaction and inflation. In the case of customer dissatisfaction, if a business maintains a policy of allowing customers to return unwanted and/or defective products, the risk of product return will persist until any product-return-guarantee period has expired. With respect to inflation, a business must be able to generate sufficient cash flow from its sales to replace its sold inventory; otherwise, it will be unable to survive in the long-term. In most situations, this business risk is unavoidable and is simply a matter of degree; however, a carefully constructed product pricing policy, which links retail prices to expected rates of inflation, can successfully manage inflation risk.

At the right-most final point, recognizing revenue after product replacement costs have been recovered, there are no revenue realization risks remaining unless the company's product-return-guarantee period has not yet expired. Also, at this point, all business risks have been successfully encountered. But, is it necessary for a business to wait until this point in time is reached before recognizing its revenue? Definitely not. Generally accepted accounting practice around the world provides considerable flexibility to companies to select the point of revenue recognition that makes the most economic sense for a given business model. This flexibility is possible because the accrual accounting system has built-in mechanisms that allow the measurement and reporting of any remaining revenue realization risks (such as bad debts, sales returns, etc.). Thus, it is possible to recognize revenue at a point in time with some remaining revenue risk so long as these risks are estimable and reported in the financial statements.

Revenue Recognition by Retail and Service Companies

Most retail companies buy goods completely manufactured and ready for sale to the final consumer, whereas service companies provide a service to the final customer. For these companies, the selection of a revenue recognition method is usually limited to the following two options:

- Point of sale or completion of service
- Point of cash collection

Global retail companies like Wal-Mart typically recognize revenue at the point of sale (which coincides with product delivery) because they rarely grant credit to their customers. Wal-Mart customers pay with cash, debit card, credit card, or by writing a check. For those retail or service companies, such as the consulting firm Accenture, that do grant credit to their customers, point of sale is still the most common method of revenue recognition *unless* there is significant doubt regarding the debt-paying ability of a customer. When account payment is not assured, companies instead must recognize revenue at the point of cash collection, or what is commonly called the **installment method**.

Under the installment method of revenue recognition, revenue is recognized only to the extent of any cash received. This de facto satisfies the "collectibility is assured" criterion. For instance, if a used car dealer sells an automobile to a customer with poor credit (who is unable to obtain bank financing for the purchase), the dealer may choose to recognize the revenue from the transaction on an installment basis given ultimate cash collection is somewhat at risk. To illustrate, assume that the dealer sold a car for $15,000 that had a

> **Accounts receivable** refer to short-term (usually 30, 60, or 90 days in duration) credit arrangements that are typically interest-free. **Notes receivable**, on the other hand, refer to credit that is longer term (perhaps as long as three to five years) for large amounts, and consequently, is likely to involve interest charges.

cost basis to the dealer of $12,000. Under the terms of the purchase agreement, the customer made an initial down payment of $1,500 (ten percent of the purchase price) and signed a promissory **note receivable** requiring nine additional monthly payments of $1,500.

Under the installment method, the car dealer will recognize only the initial down payment of $1,500 as revenue and record cost of goods sold of $1,200 (ten percent of $12,000). As each monthly payment is received, the dealer will recognize $1,500 in revenue and $1,200 in cost of goods sold, yielding a profit of $3,000 ($15,000 − $12,000) after all cash payments have been received. Since receipt of the entire $15,000 is in doubt because of the customer's poor credit history, the dealer appropriately only recognizes revenues and costs to the extent of the cash received. Note however, because the dealer effectively helped finance the customer's purchase over a nine-month period, there is a hidden **opportunity cost** to the dealer because of the time value of money. (If you are unclear about the time value of money, please read Appendix A at the end of this textbook.) If the dealer has a cost of borrowing of, say, one percent per month, the opportunity cost to the dealer implicit in the transaction would be $651, calculated as follows:

Deferred payments made by customer	$13,500
Less: Present value of 9 payments of $1,500 @ 1%: $1,500 × 8.56602	(12,849)
Opportunity cost	$ 651

Thus, the dealer's real economic profit in current dollars is only $2,349 ($3,000 − $651). To recover such opportunity costs, companies that sell their product on credit over extended periods (such as greater than 90 days) often charge their customers interest on any unpaid balances. We will have more to say about the concept of opportunity costs in Chapter 9.

REVIEW PROBLEM 5.1

The Hilton Company sells inexpensive furniture on installment plans to customers that have poor credit. Many of the company's customers are sometimes not able to make the required payments, forcing The Hilton Company to repossess the furniture. Assume The Hilton Company sells a bedroom set with a sales price of $3,000 that requires 10% down at time of purchase and the remaining balance due in 12 monthly payments. The cost of the bedroom set to The Hilton Company is $2,000.

continued

Required

Compute the required revenue and cost of goods sold to be recognized, by month, assuming accounting under either (1) point-of-sale, or (2) an installment basis.

The solution is on page 216.

Revenue Recognition by Manufacturing Companies

Manufacturing companies take one or more raw materials and produce a product themselves. To allow these companies to focus on the task of producing a product, most manufacturers do not sell directly to the final consumer of their products but rather sell to retailers who specialize in product distribution. For example, General Motors manufactures cars and trucks but does not sell these products directly to the final consumer. Instead, GM sells its cars and trucks to a network of dealers who specialize in retailing to consumers.

For most manufacturers, revenue recognition will occur at the point of product delivery or the point of cash collection if collection is uncertain. In some industries, manufacturers produce goods under contract when production may span several fiscal periods. In these situations, special rules apply that allow revenue recognition either during production or after production when the product is complete. Companies that manufacture a product under contract include such firms as Boeing, one of the world's leading manufacturers of commercial aircraft, and General Dynamics Corporation, one of the world's leading manufacturers of aerospace and defense systems. Because the cost of the products sold by these companies is quite large, they begin the manufacture of a product only after a purchase contract has been signed by the customer and a deposit customarily paid, principally to help minimize their business risk.

To illustrate the timing effects on the financial statements of alternative revenue recognition approaches for long-term manufacturing contracts, we will consider a contract signed by ProFlight Inc., a manufacturer of private corporate jets. For simplicity we will assume that immediately before the contract signing, the balance sheet of ProFlight consisted of only $4 million in cash and common stock. In 2015, the company signed a contract to build five jets over a two-year period for TransGlobal Airlines. Under the contract, ProFlight will receive total revenues of $10 million and anticipates that its cost to build the planes will equal $8 million, yielding a gross profit of $2 million. Data regarding the contract is presented in Exhibit 5.3.

EXHIBIT 5.3	Revenue Recognition by a Company Manufacturing Under Contract			
Percentage of Work Completed	**2015** **20%**	**2016** **80%**	**2017**	**Total**
Costs incurred by ProFlight	$2,000,000	$6,000,000	—	$ 8,000,000
Progress billings to TransGlobal.	1,000,000	9,000,000	—	10,000,000
Cash collected by ProFlight from TransGlobal.	500,000	4,500,000	$5,000,000	10,000,000

Exhibit 5.3 reveals that in 2015, ProFlight completed 20 percent of the work required under the contract, sent an invoice for $1 million to TransGlobal, and received a payment of $500,000. In 2016, ProFlight completed the remaining 80 percent of the project on budget at $8 million in total costs, delivered the five planes, sent an invoice for the remaining $9 million to TransGlobal, and received a $4.5 million payment. In early 2017, after completing flight testing of the aircraft, TransGlobal remitted the final $5 million in cash to ProFlight.

Revenue Recognition During Production. If ProFlight recognizes revenue as production of the planes proceeds, it will recognize revenue on the basis of the percentage of work actually completed each period. According to Exhibit 5.3, ProFlight completed 20 percent of the work in 2015 and the remaining 80 percent in 2016. This would suggest that ProFlight should recognize $2 million as revenue (20 percent of $10 million) in 2015 and $8 million as revenue (80 percent of $10 million) in 2016. This method of revenue recognition is commonly referred to as the **percentage of completion method**—that is, revenue is recognized in proportion to the amount of work actually completed each fiscal period.[4]

Takeaway 3
Describe how revenue is recognized under the completed contract and percentage of completion methods.

---

[4] Note that it is most common for companies to recognize revenue in proportion to the work completed, but the actual allocation can be based on any reasonable method. These might include costs incurred, certain milestones (fuselage completed, wings attached, etc.) or even units of production. There is an underlying requirement though that the recognition of both revenue and profits be related to the work performed.

The spreadsheet below summarizes the transactions for 2015 and the ending balance sheet for that year. ProFlight records revenues of $2 million (20% of $10 million) and costs of production of $1.6 million (20 percent of $8 million). Of the $2 million in revenue, only $1 million is actually billed to the customer; the remaining $1 million is accounted for as an **unbilled account receivable**. An unbilled account receivable is an internal billing for revenue which, for contractual reasons, is not yet sent to a customer for payment, but for all practical purposes is an amount owed by the customer. During 2015, ProFlight collected $500,000 on account and acquired $2 million in production materials which it paid for at year-end. The remaining $400,000 in production material is not recognized as a cost of production on the income statement and is therefore carried on ProFlight's balance sheet as an asset, called **production-in-progress**.

ProFlight Inc. Transaction Summary—Year 2015
Percentage of Completion Method

(in $ thousands)	2015 Beginning Balance Sheet	Contract Signing (no entry)	Acquire Production Items on Credit	Bill Customer	Collect Cash	Record Production Costs	Pay Suppliers	2015 Ending Balance Sheet
Assets								
Cash.	4,000				500		(2,000)	2,500
Accounts receivable.				1,000	(500)			500
Production-in-progress			2,000			(1,600)		400
Unbilled accounts receivable.				1,000				1,000
Total assets.	**4,000**							**4,400**
Liabilities and Shareholders' Equity								
Accounts payable.			2,000				(2,000)	0
Total liabilities	**0**							**0**
Common stock.	4,000							4,000
Retained earnings								400
Revenue					2,000			
Cost of production						(1,600)		
Total liabilities and shareholders' equity . . .	**4,000**							**4,400**

To complete the illustration, in 2016, ProFlight records the remaining $8 million in revenue, collects $4.5 million in cash, and records $6.4 million in production costs (80 percent of $8 million). In 2017, ProFlight collects the remaining $5 million in cash. The transaction summary for 2016 and 2017 is provided below. Note that at the end of the contract, total earnings of $2 million has been recorded, allocated in total as $400,000 in 2015 and $1.6 million in 2016, consistent with the percentage of work completed in those years.

One of the challenges to effectively implementing the percentage of completion method is estimating the amount of work actually completed in a given fiscal period. A frequently utilized approach is to compare the actual costs incurred to the total budgeted costs. This method can be effective when project costs can be forecasted with relative certainty. When there exists uncertainty regarding the costs to complete a project, alternative estimation techniques may be required, for example using work completion estimates provided by engineering consultants. Of course, utilizing work completion estimates based on uncertain cost estimates may cause the forecasted level of revenues in a given period to be too high or too low, and consequently, overstate or understate firm performance.

ProFlight Inc. Transaction Summary—Years 2016 and 2017
Percentage of Completion Method

(in $ thousands)	2015 Ending Balances	Acquire Production Items on Credit	Bill Customer	Collect Cash	Record Production Costs	Pay Suppliers	2016 Ending Balances	Collect Cash	2017 Ending Balances
Assets									
Cash.	2,500			4,500		(6,000)	1,000	5,000	6,000
Accounts receivable.	500		9,000	(4,500)			5,000	(5,000)	0
Production-in-progress	400	6,000			(6,400)		0		0
Unbilled accounts receivable.	1,000		(1,000)				0		0
Total assets.	**4,400**						**6,000**		**6,000**

continued

(in $ thousands)	2015 Ending Balances	Acquire Production Items on Credit	Bill Customer	Collect Cash	Record Production Costs	Pay Suppliers	2016 Ending Balances	Collect Cash	2017 Ending Balances
Liabilities and Shareholders' Equity									
Accounts payable.............	0	6,000				(6,000)	0		0
Total liabilities..................	**0**						**0**		**0**
Common stock.................	4,000						4,000		4,000
Retained earnings	400						2,000		2,000
Revenue			8,000						
Cost of production					(6,400)				
Total liabilities and shareholders' equity..........	**4,400**						**6,000**		**6,000**

Revenue Recognition at the Completion of Production.

If ProFlight recognizes its revenue, costs of production, and hence gross profit when the project is complete, no revenues or expenses will be reported on the income statement until 2016. (ProFlight will consider the contract to be satisfied upon delivery of the planes at the end of 2016; TransGlobal Airlines, however, might consider the contract to be complete after successful flight testing of the aircraft in 2017.)

Since no revenue is recognized in 2015, the $1 million billed to TransGlobal in 2015 will be accounted for as **deferred revenue**, a liability account on ProFlight's balance sheet. The deferred revenue account has a meaning just as it sounds, revenue whose recognition on the income statement has been deferred to the future until other criteria have been met. In this case the relevant criterion is the completion of the project. When the project is complete at the end of 2016, the deferred revenue will then be considered earned, and the balance in the deferred revenue account will be transferred to the revenue account on the income statement (and retained earnings on the balance sheet). Similarly, the $2

> **In Practice 5.1** *Revenue Recognition Method: A Glimpse of a Sample of Fortune 1000 Companies*   The following table identifies the method used by a sample of 83 Fortune 1000 companies to account for revenue under long-term contracts. Over 51 percent of the firms surveyed used the percentage of completion method:
>
> | Accounting Method | Number | Percentage |
> |---|---|---|
> | Percentage of completion .... | 43 | 51.8 |
> | Units of delivery .... | 32 | 38.6 |
> | Completed contract .... | 8 | 9.6 |
> | Total .... | 83 | 100.0 |
>
> Source: Accounting Trends & Techniques

million spent on production costs in 2015 will be accounted for as production-in-progress, an asset account on ProFlight's balance sheet until the project is complete, at which time the balance in the production-in-progress account is transferred to the cost-of-production account on the income statement. As a consequence, no profit is recognized in 2015 and instead is deferred until 2016 when all work is completed. This method of revenue recognition is called the **completed contract method**, and the events using this revenue recognition approach are presented in ProFlight's transaction summary that follows. For consistency with the above example we again separate the transactions into those for 2015 and those for 2016–17. For 2015:

ProFlight Inc. Transaction Summary—Year 2015 **Completed Contract Method**							
(in $ thousands)	2015 Beginning Balance Sheet	Contract Signing (no entry)	Acquire Production Items on Credit	Bill Customer	Collect Cash	Pay Suppliers	2015 Ending Balance Sheet
Assets							
Cash..	4,000				500	(2,000)	2,500
Accounts receivable.........................				1,000	(500)		500
Production-in-progress			2,000				2,000
Total assets..............................	**4,000**						**5,000**

continued

continued from previous page

(in $ thousands)	2015 Beginning Balance Sheet	Contract Signing (no entry)	Acquire Production Items on Credit	Bill Customer	Collect Cash	Pay Suppliers	2015 Ending Balance Sheet
Liabilities and Shareholders' Equity							
Accounts payable.........................			2,000			(2,000)	0
Deferred revenue				1,000			1,000
Total liabilities......................	0						1,000
Common stock........................	4,000						4,000
Total liabilities and shareholders' equity	4,000						5,000

And the summary transactions for 2016 and 2017:

ProFlight Inc. Transaction Summary—Years 2016 and 2017
Completed Contract Method

(in $ thousands)	2015 Ending Balances	Acquire Production Items on Credit	Bill Customer	Collect Cash	Pay Suppliers	Recognize Revenue	Record Cost of Production	2016 Ending Balances	Collect Cash	2017 Ending Balances
Assets										
Cash..................	2,500			4,500	(6,000)			1,000	5,000	6,000
Accounts receivable......	500		9,000	(4,500)				5,000	(5,000)	0
Production-in-progress ...	2,000	6,000					(8,000)	0		0
Total assets............	5,000							6,000		6,000
Liabilities and Shareholders' Equity										
Accounts payable........	0	6,000			(6,000)			0		0
Deferred revenue	1,000		9,000			(10,000)		0		0
Total liabilities..........	1,000							0		0
Common stock..........	4,000							4,000		4,000
Retained earnings								2,000		2,000
Revenue						10,000				
Cost of production							(8,000)			
Total liabilities and shareholders' equity ...	5,000							6,000		6,000

A Comparison of Performance: Percentage of Completion and Completed Contract.

Exhibit 5.4 presents a comparison of gross profit for ProFlight under the two alternative revenue recognition methods. The results are equal, in total, however the percentage of completion method spreads the gross profit between 2015 and 2016, whereas the completed contract method recognizes all the gross profit in the year of completion.

EXHIBIT 5.4	Comparison of Gross Profit under Percentage of Completion and Completed Contract Revenue Recognition

(in $ thousands)	2015	2016	2017
Percentage of completion	$400	$1,600	$0
Completed contract	0	2,000	0

BUSINESS PERSPECTIVE

Microsoft Corporation is the world's largest software maker measured by revenues and is one of the world's most valuable companies by market capitalization. The company was founded in 1975 and operates worldwide in more than 100 countries. It develops, licenses, and supports a wide range of software products, services, and devices including Xbox gaming systems. According to Microsoft's 2015 annual report, revenue jumped from $86.8 billion in 2014 to over $93.5 billion in 2015. According to Microsoft's 2015 10-K:

> Unearned revenue at June 30, 2015 was comprised mainly of unearned revenue from volume licensing programs. Unearned revenue from volume licensing programs represents customer billings for multi-year licensing arrangements paid for either at inception of the agreement or annually at the beginning of each coverage period and accounted for as subscriptions with revenue recognized ratably over the coverage period. Unearned revenue at June 30, 2015 also included payments for: post-delivery support and consulting services to be performed in the future; Xbox Live subscriptions and prepaid points; Microsoft Dynamics business solutions products; Office 365 subscriptions; Skype prepaid credits and subscriptions; Bundled Offerings; and other offerings for which we have been paid in advance and earn the revenue when we provide the service or software, or otherwise meet the revenue recognition criteria.

Although unearned revenues are consistent with generally accepted accounting principles and sound accounting practice, many investment professionals view Microsoft's practice of deferring the recognition of a portion of the revenue from its retail products and OEM-licensed products as a form of **rear-end loading** of revenues. Rear-end loading of revenues—that is, the deferral of the income statement recognition of certain revenues until a later fiscal period—reduces the total level of revenues currently recognized, and thus, reduces currently reported operating income.

Analysts critical of Microsoft's revenue reporting argue that the practice creates an **earnings reserve** on the company's balance sheet, enabling the firm to manage its reported earnings and consistently meet or exceed Wall Street's earnings' expectations. Microsoft has met or exceeded the Street's annual earnings' expectations for 27 consecutive years. Wall Street pundits also note that the practice of revenue deferral enables Microsoft to appear less profitable, and hence, less monopolistic—an important feature as the company appeals the anti-competitiveness ruling brought against it in 2004 and again in 2006 by the European Union Committee on Competition.

Microsoft has been proactive in its disclosures of detail pertaining to the impact of revenue deferrals on future profits. The following table outlines the expected future recognition of unearned revenue as of June 30, 2015 as disclosed by the company:

Three Months Ending (in millions)	2015
September 30, 2015	$ 8,889
December 31, 2015	7,172
March 31, 2016	4,848
June 30, 2016	2,314
Thereafter	2,095
Total	$25,318

Thus, over $25 billion has been received in cash and recorded as an obligation to deliver by the company. As these obligations are fulfilled in the future, revenue will be recognized in those periods.

GLOBAL PERSPECTIVE

Until the full adoption of ASC 606 in 2018, as referenced earlier in this chapter, there are many notable differences between U.S. GAAP and IFRS in regards to revenue recognition. For example, U.S. GAAP requires that a product or service be delivered before revenue may be recognized, whereas IFRS allows a business to recognize revenue if a firm commitment to provide goods or services in the future at a fixed price exists, the revenue and costs can be reliably measured, and significant risks and rewards of ownership are transferred to the customer. In essence, IFRS allows future commitments to be recognized (under certain conditions) that would not be permitted under U.S. GAAP. Another important difference is that IFRS does not permit the use of the completed contract method, whereas under U.S. GAAP a company may elect to use either the completed contract or percentage-of-completion method if reasonable estimates of completion cannot be made.

REVIEW PROBLEM 5.2

The Arcadia Company bid on a multiyear contract to construct the new hockey arena for the Phoenix Coyotes. The contract required that construction begin not later than January 1, 2015, and be completed not later than December 31, 2017. Arcadia won the contract with a bid of $720 million. During the three-year period 2015 to 2017, the company incurred the following construction costs:

	Construction Costs	Percentage of Project Completed
2015	$144 million	30%
2016	144 million	30
2017	192 million	40
Total	$480 million	100%

Under the terms of the contract, The Arcadia Company was entitled to bill the city of Glendale, Arizona, for 25 percent ($180 million) of the total bid upon completion of 30 percent of the planned project. Thus, at the end of 2015, and again at the end of 2016, Arcadia sent progress billings to, and was paid by, the City of Glendale in the amount of $180 million each year. At the end of 2017, after receiving all necessary occupancy approvals, The Arcadia Company billed the City of Glendale for the remaining $360 million.

Required

Prepare income statements for The Arcadia Company for 2015, 2016, and 2017 assuming that the company recognizes revenue from the Coyote arena contract (*a*) on the cash basis, (*b*) on the completed contract basis, and (*c*) on the percentage-of-completion basis.

The solution is on pages 216-217.

VALUING AND REPORTING ACCOUNTS RECEIVABLE

Takeaway 4

Explain how accounts receivable are valued and how the allowance for uncollectible accounts and bad debt expense are estimated.

Companies extend credit to current and potential customers as a means to attract an additional source of profit. This decision is not made lightly by management, and granting credit to customers makes sense only when the expected profit from these incremental sales exceeds the costs associated with extending the credit—specifically, when the incremental profit from the sale is enough to offset both the opportunity cost of delaying the receipt of cash (the time value of money) and the risk that some customer accounts will not be collected.[5] Credit sales are commonly short-term and, therefore, do not carry an interest charge. The accounting process, therefore, does not reflect the opportunity cost related

[5] Most companies extend interest-free trade credit to their customers who are also businesses (i.e., a B2B transaction) while rarely extending trade credit to their customers who are not businesses (i.e., a B2C transaction).

to the time value of money for receivables. The accounting for uncollectible accounts, however, is not ignored and, in fact, is a necessity if the financial statements are to be a useful representation of company performance.

To help you understand why accounting for uncollectible receivables operates as it does, recall the following basics of how receivables are established in the first place. When a sale is made on credit and meets the criteria for revenue recognition, the revenue recorded on the income statement (and likewise the retained earnings on the balance sheet) will be balanced with an increase to the accounts receivable account. The account therefore reflects the expectation of receiving cash at a later date for a sale made at an earlier date. A problem arises though: when the credit sale is initially recorded there may be an overstatement of the actual receivables balance that will be received by the company if some accounts ultimately are not paid by the customer. The accounting process, therefore, requires that we record receivables at **net realizable value**, an amount that reflects the expected net collectibility of the total accounts receivable balance.

Company management knows that some customers will not pay for sales made on credit but they just don't know which ones. If they did, they certainly would have avoided extending credit to these customers in the first place! Companies can reduce, but not eliminate, this risk by acquiring information about their customers from credit information intermediaries such as Dun and Bradstreet. For a fee, Dun and Bradstreet will supply information about a customer's past credit history and will use credit scoring techniques to predict the likelihood that a customer will pay for goods and services on a timely basis. Easy to access FICO scores are also commonly used.

Given the fact that a company might not know by the end of a fiscal period with certainty how much of its receivables balance will be paid, and what its credit losses associated with its current period's revenue will be, the *matching principle* requires that an estimate of these losses be made to facilitate a full matching of revenue and expenses on the income statement. Likewise, the *conservatism principle* requires that accounts receivable on the balance sheet not be overstated relative to what will ultimately be collected in cash. There are a variety of methods available to help businesses estimate their expected credit losses. The two most widely used methods to accomplish these objectives are the **percentage-of-credit-sales method** and the **aging method**.[6] We discuss each in turn.

Percentage-of-Credit-Sales Method

Under the percentage-of-credit-sales method, a company estimates its expected future credit losses as a function of the relationship between its historical credit losses and its historical credit sales. The percentage of historical credit losses divided by historical credit sales is multiplied with current period credit sales to estimate a business's expected future credit losses. The principal limitations of this approach are that it fails to capture the changing payment patterns of customers in a timely manner and it lacks the estimation precision provided by the aging method.

To demonstrate the percentage-of-credit-sales method, assume that the Savanna Company recognized $600,000 of credit sales during the current fiscal period. Further, assume that Savanna's management has determined from prior experience that approximately three percent of all credit sales eventually must be written off due to collection failure. Since bad debts resulting from collection failure are a cost of doing business, it is necessary to match this expense with current period revenue. Consequently, Savanna will recognize a bad debt expense in the amount of $18,000 (3 percent of $600,000) on its income statement in the current period. Savanna will also establish a contra-account—the **allowance for uncollectible accounts**—on its balance sheet to reflect the amount of the outstanding receivables that are not expected to be collected. We will discuss this contra-account more fully shortly; but, what is important to note is that Savanna's management recorded their estimate of the expected bad debt expense in the current period rather than waiting until a future period at which time they will know with certainty which receivables are uncollectible and should be written off. Stated simply, the $18,000 is just an estimate.

---

[6] A third approach is the **direct write-off method**, in which no estimate of credit losses is matched with current revenue. Instead, the actual accounts receivable write-off is reported on the income statement as a bad debt expense in the period in which non-collectibility is confirmed. Assuming materiality, the direct write-off method is not allowable under GAAP because it fails to match the cost of extending credit to customers in the same period in which the corresponding revenue is recognized.

BUSINESS PERSPECTIVE

Airline Ticket Revenue Recognition at Delta Air Lines

Delta Air Lines is the largest airline in the world when measured by almost any metric: total revenue, fleet size, passenger miles flown, and number of passengers. The company is based in Atlanta, Georgia, the location of its primary hub, and it has helped make Atlanta's Hartsfield-Jackson International Airport the busiest in the world.

The sale of an airline ticket may seem straightforward from the consumer-perspective: buy a ticket, sometimes months in advance, then take the flight. But from Delta's perspective the sale involves other factors to consider regarding how much and when to record revenue. According to the company's footnotes to its financial statements, when tickets are sold a portion is initially recorded as a component of "air traffic liability," a current liability on the balance sheet (equivalent to deferred revenue or unearned revenue); and, if the passenger has a frequent flyer account, a portion is allocated to "frequent flyer deferred revenue." Delta's 2014 annual 10-K report filing with the U.S. Securities and Exchange Commission reports the amount of recognized revenue and deferred revenue for 2014 and 2013 was as follows:

(in millions)	December 31	
	2014	2013
Income Statement		
Revenues	$40,462	$37,773
Balance Sheet (liabilities)		
Air traffic liability	$4,296	$ 4,122
Frequent flyer deferred revenue—current.......................................	1,580	1,861
Frequent flyer deferred revenue—noncurrent....................................	2,602	2,559

These deferred revenue liability accounts are quite significant to Delta, approximating 21% and 23% of total revenues for 2014 and 2013, respectively.

The accounting for airline tickets in this way follows straight from the economics of what has been sold, and more specifically from the expectation of when Delta will meet its obligation to fly the passenger on the plane. Revenue recognition guidelines under SAB No. 101 require that any revenue must be earned before it can be recognized. Since Delta does not earn its revenue until it has provided air transportation to its customers, it appropriately defers the recognition of its revenue until the time of flight service. The air traffic liability account reflects this obligation.

The allocation of a portion of the ticket to deferred revenue for frequent flyer miles, however, recognizes that there is an additional obligation attached to each ticket sold. Delta must award a passenger ticket when the miles are used, thus in effect the passenger is purchasing a portion of a future flight. Delta must, therefore, estimate the value of each frequent flyer mile sold. The language used to describe this process in Delta's 2014 10-K was:

Mileage credits are a separate unit of accounting as they can be redeemed by customers in future periods for air travel on Delta and participating airlines, membership in our Sky Club and other program awards.... We defer revenue for the mileage credits related to passenger ticket sales and recognize it as passenger revenue when miles are redeemed and services are provided. We record the air transportation portion of the passenger ticket sales in air traffic liability and recognize these amounts in passenger revenue when we provide transportation or when the ticket expires unused. . . . We value each deliverable on a standalone basis. Our estimate of the selling price of a mileage credit is based on an analysis of our sales of mileage credits to other airlines and customers, which is re-evaluated at least annually. We use established ticket prices to determine the estimated selling price of air transportation. We allocate the total amount collected from passenger ticket sales between the deliverables based on their relative selling prices.

Savanna Company Transaction Summary Percentage-of-Credit-Sales Method			
	Sell Goods on Credit	Estimate 3% of Credit Sales Uncollectible	Subtotals
Assets			
::			
Accounts receivable......................................	600,000		600,000
Less: Allowance for uncollectible accounts..................		(18,000)	(18,000)
Accounts receivable, net			582,000
Shareholders' Equity			
::			
Retained earnings			582,000
Revenue	600,000		
Bad debt expense.....................................		(18,000)	

Aging Method

A more refined approach to credit loss estimation, and consequently, the most widely used approach, is the aging method. Here the focus is on the balance sheet, and specifically how much is owed to the company as of the balance sheet date. Under the aging method, a company first categorizes its outstanding accounts receivable according to how much time has elapsed since the credit sale took place. Then, using historical customer payment data to estimate the probability of nonpayment, the estimates are multiplied by the outstanding receivable age category balance to arrive at the expected credit loss. You should readily see that an aging approach has the distinct advantage of evaluating an entire receivables balance based on an objective measure—the time elapsed since payment. In this way the reported net realizable value of the accounts receivables account will reflect the increasing uncertainty of collectibility that comes with older accounts.

To illustrate this method, consider the following scenario. Pan American Enterprises Inc. sells its internationally recognized stained glass products on credit to construction companies throughout the United States. The company's credit terms require customers to pay their bills within 30 days of a transaction. The chief financial officer (CFO) of Pan American is concerned about the possibility of bad debts arising when customers fail to pay for previously purchased inventory. The CFO realizes that bad debts may occur, but offering the company's customers credit has generated much higher sales and profit levels.

Exhibit 5.5 shows that credit sales for Pan American Enterprises were $3.2 million in 2016, of which Pan American collected $2.85 million in cash. In Pan American's accounting, this information is reported as an increase in retained earnings (via revenue) and an increase in accounts receivable in the amount of $3.2 million, and an increase in cash and a decrease in accounts receivable in the amount of $2.85 million.

EXHIBIT 5.5	Pan American Enterprises, Inc.—Credit Sales and Write-offs		
Year	Credit Sales	Accounts Receivable (year-end)	Write-Off
2016..	$3,200,000	$350,000	—
2017..	5,300,000	800,000	$11,500

Even if Pan American Enterprises screens its customers carefully, it is unlikely that the entire $350,000 of outstanding accounts receivable at year-end 2016 will be collected. Further, prior to the preparation of an income statement for 2016, the matching concept requires that the cost of extending credit to its customers—that is, the **bad debt expense**—be estimated and matched with the sales revenue for 2016.

> Many companies consider receivables over 120 days old to be worthless, and consequently, remove these receivables from the balance sheet to avoid overstating the realizable value of accounts receivable. Worthless receivables are usually turned over to a collection agency to pursue collection.

To estimate Pan American's bad debt expense using the aging method, an aging schedule of Pan American's accounts receivable is prepared and is presented in Exhibit 5.6. For convenience, we show the aging schedules for both the years 2016 and 2017. This exhibit shows that, at year-end 2016, $145,000 in receivables have been outstanding for less than 30 days, $100,000 outstanding for 31 to 60 days, $70,000 for 61 to 90 days, $20,000 for 91 to 120 days, and $15,000 for over 120 days.

An analysis of Pan American's past customer payment experience is then used to estimate the amount that will be uncollected from each category. As shown in Exhibit 5.6, the CFO's analysis of prior credit customer payment behavior found that 0.5 percent of accounts 30 days or less fail to pay, one percent of accounts that are 31 to 60 days old fail to pay, and that as much as 20 percent of accounts outstanding for more than 120 days end up in default. The total amount that is not expected to be collected is the sum of the amounts in each category times the percentage estimated to be uncollectible. For example, $725 (0.5 percent times $145,000) of the less than 30-days accounts is expected to be uncollectible. For the total outstanding receivable balance of $350,000 as of year-end 2016, $10,925 is expected to be uncollectible.

EXHIBIT 5.6	Aging of Accounts Receivable—Pan American Enterprises					
			December 31, 2016		December 31, 2017	
Period Outstanding	**Estimated Uncollectible Percentage**		**Outstanding Receivable Balance**	**Estimated Bad Debt**	**Outstanding Receivable Balance**	**Estimated Bad Debt**
30 days or less..............	0.5%		$145,000	$ 725	$400,000	$ 2,000
31–60 days.................	1.0%		100,000	1,000	200,000	2,000
61–90 days.................	6.0%		70,000	4,200	100,000	6,000
91–120 days...............	10.0%		20,000	2,000	75,000	7,500
More than 120 days..........	20.0%		15,000	3,000	25,000	5,000
Total			$350,000	$10,925	$800,000	$22,500

To record the results of the aging analysis, Pan American will establish a contra-account—the **allowance for uncollectible accounts**—on its balance sheet to reflect the amount of the outstanding receivables that are not expected to be collected. The allowance for uncollectible accounts is a reserve for future expected losses resulting from uncollectible credit sales. Despite the fact that the future losses cannot be known with certainty at year-end, the matching concept nonetheless requires that an attempt be made to estimate those losses, recognizing that the estimate may prove incorrect as additional information is obtained. Thus, $10,925 will be the balance in the allowance for uncollectible accounts and this contra-account is subtracted from the total outstanding receivable balance on Pan American's balance sheet to arrive at the **net realizable value** ($350,000 − $10,925 = $339,075) of the outstanding accounts receivable. It is the net realizable value of Pan American's accounts receivable that will be included in the firm's total assets.

Because 2016 was Pan American Enterprises' first year of operations, the beginning balance in the allowance account is $0. Thus, $10,925 is the amount necessary to bring the allowance account to the required amount of $10,925, and hence, it is also the amount of the bad debt expense reported on Pan American's income statement for the period. In the following transaction summary, the bad debt expense reduces retained earnings by $10,925 and the allowance for uncollectible accounts decreases assets by the same amount. Since the allowance account is an offset to the accounts receivable account, this transaction effectively reduces the net balance of accounts receivable. Under this approach, total "gross" accounts receivable are not reduced directly because the allowance account is just an estimate of Pan American's expected future credit losses. Reporting the accounts in this way thus tells the user of Pan American's balance sheet two important pieces of information: (i) how much is owed to the company in total ($350,000), and (ii) how much is the estimate of what won't be collected ($10,925).

Pan American Enterprises Transaction Summary—2016 Aging Method				
	Sell Goods on Credit	Collect Cash from Customers	Recognize Bad Debt Expense	Subtotals
Assets				
Cash.		2,850,000		2,850,000
Accounts receivable.	3,200,000	(2,850,000)		350,000
Less: Allowance for uncollectible accounts.			(10,925)	(10,925)
Total assets.				**3,189,075**
Shareholders' Equity				
: :				
Retained earnings				3,189,075
Revenue	3,200,000			
Bad debt expense.			(10,925)	
Total shareholders' equity				**3,189,075**

Pan American's abbreviated income statement for 2016 discloses sales revenue, less the bad debt expense, of $3,189,075 (see Exhibit 5.7, Panel A), and Pan American's balance sheet at December 31, 2016, reflects an accounts receivable balance, net of the allowance for uncollectible accounts, of $339,075, representing the net cash that Pan American expects to collect from its credit customers (see Exhibit 5.7, Panel B).

EXHIBIT 5.7	Selected Financial Data—2016

Panel A

PAN AMERICAN ENTERPRISES INC. Income Statement (abbreviated)	2016
Sales revenue.	$3,200,000
Less: Bad debt expense.	10,925
Net income	$3,189,075

Panel B

PAN AMERICAN ENTERPRISES INC. Balance Sheet (accounts receivable accounts)	2016
Accounts receivable.	$ 350,000
Less: Allowance for uncollectible accounts.	10,925
Accounts receivable, net	$ 339,075

In early 2017, Pan American Enterprises received information from a number of its credit customers that they would be unable to pay their outstanding unpaid bills. As a consequence, Pan American's CFO immediately wrote off the identified uncollectible accounts receivable, which totaled $11,500. In the accounting transaction summary provided below, the **write-off of uncollectible accounts** is executed by reducing accounts receivable by $11,500 and adjusting the allowance for uncollectible accounts for an equivalent amount. To see why the transaction takes this form consider the following. Recall that the allowance account represents a reserve for expected future losses from uncollectible

In Practice 5.2 *Balance Sheet Caption: A Glimpse of a Sample of Fortune 1000 Companies* The following table identifies the caption used by a sample of 600 Fortune 1000 companies on their balance sheets to describe the allowance for uncollectible accounts:

Doubtful Account Captions	Number	Percentage
Allowance for doubtful accounts	325	54.2
Allowance.	141	23.5
Allowance for uncollectible accounts.	25	4.2
Allowance for losses.	13	2.1
Reserve for doubtful accounts.	17	2.8
Other.	4	0.7
Receivables shown net	23	3.8
No reference to doubtful accounts.	52	8.7
Total	600	100.0

Source: Accounting Trends & Techniques

Takeaway 5

Describe why the effective management of accounts receivable is important for a business.

MANAGING A COMPANY'S INVESTMENT IN RECEIVABLES

When a company extends credit to its customers by permitting them to buy goods and services on credit, the company is, in effect, making an investment in accounts receivable. Like any investment, an investment in accounts receivable should generate returns to the company that are sufficiently large to justify the risks associated with the investment—that is, the gross profit resulting from the incremental credit sales must exceed the cost of extending credit. The principal costs of extending credit to customers include the cost of the goods or services if a customer fails to pay for their credit purchases and/or the time value of money (the opportunity cost) when a customer takes a long time to pay.

Sales Discounts

By extending credit to customers, a company is effectively lending to its customers on an interest-free basis for the period of time that the account receivable is outstanding. To maximize the return on a company's investment in accounts receivable, and thus, the firm's overall profitability, it is important to keep the duration of these interest-free loans as short as possible. One way that companies attempt to manage account receivable **duration** is by giving customers an incentive to pay quickly. That incentive usually takes the form of a price discount. For instance, some companies offer their customers **credit terms** or **trade terms** of 2/10, n/30. The term "2/10" indicates that if customers pay their bill within ten days of purchase, they will be given a two percent reduction in the gross purchase price of the purchased items. The term "n/30"—pronounced "net 30"—indicates that if the customer fails to take advantage of the quick-payment incentive, the full purchase price is expected within 30 days of the sales transaction. The specific credit terms used by a company are usually dictated by the competitive conditions that characterize a given industry. Thus, in less competitive industries, terms of 2/10, n/30 are common, whereas in highly competitive industries, more generous trade terms of 3/10, n/90 may be required.

When a customer takes advantage of a quick-pay incentive, this price reduction is called a **sales discount** and is reported on the income statement as a deduction from gross revenue. The resulting amount is called **net revenue** or net sales. In accounting terminology, the sales discount account is a contra-revenue account.

To illustrate, consider a credit sale of $1,000 with trade terms of 2/10, n/30. For a customer who pays her bill in full within the ten-day period, the final purchase price will be reduced to $980 ($1,000 less two percent of $1,000). This is shown in the summary below. In contrast, a customer who pays after the ten-day "quick pay" window has expired will be expected to pay the full $1,000, and payment is expected not later than 30 days after the original sale transaction.

	Sell Goods on Credit	Cash Collections	Subtotals
Assets			
Cash...		980	980
Accounts receivable...	1,000	(1,000)	0
Shareholders' Equity			
Retained earnings...			980
Revenue...	1,000		
Less: Sales discounts...		(20)	

When customers fail to take advantage of existing quick-pay incentives, the seller is faced with another dilemma: The longer a receivable remains unpaid, the lower the real profit on the sale because of the time value of money. Thus, well-managed companies usually pay considerable attention to their **receivable collection period** to help monitor this potential problem area. As discussed in Chapter 4, the receivable collection period is calculated as follows:

$$\text{Receivable collection period} = \frac{365 \text{ days}}{\text{Net sales/Account receivable}}$$

To illustrate the use of this financial ratio, consider the following data for the Flow International Corp., a U.S. technology company that provides water jet cutting and surface preparation solutions:

(in $ thousands)	2012	2011
Net sales.	$253,768	$216,524
Accounts receivable (net).	$ 46,830	$ 47,082
Receivable collection period	$\dfrac{365}{(\$253,768/\$46,830)} = 67.4$ days	$\dfrac{365}{(\$216,524/\$47,082)} = 79.4$ days

The data suggest that the average credit customer for Flow International took from 79.4 days to 67.4 days to pay for their credit purchases in 2011 and 2012, respectively. Even with this improvement, if Flow International's credit terms are 2/10, n/60, then some of its customers have greatly exceeded the company's payment terms. How would Flow International benefit if the average payment period were reduced to 50 days? With an average payment period of 50 days and the same level of revenue, Flow International would have reported outstanding receivables of only $29.661 million and $34.763 million at year-end 2011 and 2012, respectively:

(in $ thousands)	2012	2011
Revised receivable balance	$\dfrac{50 \times \$253,768}{365} = \$34,763$	$\dfrac{50 \times \$216,524}{365} = \$29,661$
Increase in cash	$46,830 - $34,763 = **$12,067**	$47,082 - $29,661 = **$17,421**

The reduction in Flow International's outstanding accounts receivable balance and the associated reduction in the receivable collection period would have resulted in an increase in the company's operating cash balance by $17.421 million in 2011 or $12.067 million in 2012. What could Flow International do with the extra cash? Some possibilities would be to pay down interest-bearing debt, increase dividends, or invest in new operating assets.

TAX PERSPECTIVE

Revenue Recognition and Accounts Receivable

Throughout this chapter we have discussed how managers of firms should determine the proper period in which to recognize revenues under GAAP, and when those revenues are made by granting credit how GAAP requires the recording of reserves for expected uncollectible accounts. The treatment of these issues from the perspective of U.S. tax authorities can differ substantially. With respect to revenue, while GAAP requires that SAB 101 (prior to 2018) or ASC 606 criteria be applied in the determination of revenue recognition, the IRS follows a modified framework labeled the "all events" test when determining how much and when to record these amounts. Under the assumption that the contractual amount from the sale of a service or product can be determined with reasonable accuracy, the all-events test is met on the earliest of one of three dates: (1) when the company completes the task required to earn the income, (2) when the payment of the task is due from the customer, or (3) when the business receives payment for the task. Note that with respect to this latter date, GAAP would require the recording of a liability (deferred revenue) until SAB 101 or ASC 606 criteria are met. Tax authorities also allow for such deferral, but only under special elections made by the company when its tax return is filed. Executives and managers are encouraged to investigate and review these special circumstances carefully, as accelerating revenue recognition could materially affect the timing of tax cash outflows.

Receivables accounting is another area wherein there are stark differences between the tax and GAAP treatment of expense measurement. As we have seen GAAP is rooted in the concept of allowing for estimates of uncollectibles within a period, without specific knowledge of which customer account may in fact be the one that is ultimately not collected. The IRS gives no such leeway. Only when a specific account is deemed uncollectible can it be written off and charged against income. Thus, it is the write-off transaction that becomes expensed under tax law, not the bad debt expense estimate illustrated throughout this chapter. Here would be an example of IRS tax accounting rules biasing against potentially understating income, and putting in place less room for judgment and more certainty to deductions included on a tax return.

Sales Returns

Many companies allow their customers to return unwanted and/or defective products for a cash or credit refund or for store credit. Like uncollectibles, the amount of customer returns may not be known with certainty until well after the completion of a fiscal period. To ensure that a business's revenue is not overstated, managers must estimate the expected future customer returns at the end of each fiscal period before an income statement can be prepared. Customer returns are typically estimated on the basis of recent historical business experience.

The amount of any expected sales returns is reported in a contra-revenue account, the **sales returns** account, on the income statement as well as in a contra-asset account on the balance sheet, called the **allowance for sales returns**, if the original sale was on credit. Like the allowance for uncollectible accounts, the allowance for sales returns is a reserve for future losses associated with product returns and is subtracted from the balance in accounts receivable to arrive at the net realizable value of accounts receivable.

Sales returns can be a serious problem in some companies. The most effective way to manage this problem is through a program of continuous quality control of manufacturing processes to ensure the production of high-quality goods, as well as a diligent assessment of customer needs and preferences to ensure that a company's products are meeting or exceeding customer needs and expectations.

REVIEW PROBLEM 5.4

1. In an effort to increase collections, Bishop Company offers a 1/10, n/30 discount for early payment. Assume a sale of $150,000 made on August 1st. Determine the total sales, the sales discount, and the net sales when the customer makes a payment either on (a) August 7th, or (b) August 27th.

2. Bishop Company offers a generous return policy of 60 days, no questions asked, in order to increase its total sales. Unfortunately this policy has the drawback that many people return their purchases during the 60-day period. Bishop Company management has estimated at year-end that approximately six percent of $1,200,000 of eligible purchases will be returned. Of this $1,200,000 of total sales, determine the sales returns, net sales, and the allowance for sales returns.

The solution is on page 217.

MONETIZING ACCOUNTS RECEIVABLE TO MANAGE OPERATING CASH FLOW

Takeaway 6
Identify the processes for monetizing a company's accounts receivable— factoring, pledging, and securitization.

In addition to collecting accounts receivable as a means to generate operating cash, a company can also sell its receivables to an outside buyer, use the receivables as collateral in a borrowing arrangement, or securitize its receivables. Collectively, these actions are referred to as "monetizing" a company's accounts receivable. Each of these cash-management options is considered below.

Factoring

The process of selling accounts and notes receivable is called **factoring**. Many financial institutions have divisions devoted exclusively to buying accounts and notes receivable from companies that need cash quickly and are unable to wait for customer payment on outstanding credit transactions. Factors convert a company's receivables into cash at their face value less a service charge and a charge for the time value of money. Because factoring represents a form of an asset sale, accounts receivable are removed from the books, the cash received is recorded, and the difference charged against income as fees on the transaction.

> **Monetizing** is the process of converting a noncash asset into cash. In the case of accounts and notes receivable, these assets may be converted into cash by selling or factoring, by borrowing against the value of the asset (pledging), or by securitization through the creation of an SPE or SPV.

The service charge for factoring varies considerably depending upon the degree of collection risk assumed by the factor. Receivables that are sold **with recourse** means that if a factor is unable to collect on a particular account or note receivable, the factor has the right to return the uncollectible receivable to the seller and recover its money directly from the seller. In this case, the factor assumes no collection risk, and thus, the factor's service fee is likely to be low, ranging, for example, from five to ten percent of the face value of the sold receivables.[7]

When receivables are sold **without recourse**, the factor assumes all risk of collection and thus will charge a considerably higher fee (such as 12 to 15 percent or more) to compensate for the potential loss associated with any uncollectible receivables. When accounts and notes receivable are sold without recourse, the factor is unable to recover any uncollected amounts from the seller. To help estimate the extent of the assumed collection risk, factors frequently ask companies that sell their receivables to provide them with a copy of their aging schedule.

Because factoring is an expensive financing option for most companies, it is only used when less expensive options are unavailable (such as pledging, described below). For instance, a business with a 15 percent gross profit margin that sells its receivables to a factor charging a 10 percent service fee (sold with recourse) would see its profit margin on these credit sales decline by 67 percent!

Pledging

Another way that companies can use their accounts and notes receivable to expedite operating cash inflows is to use the receivables as collateral to obtain bank financing, usually in the form of working capital financing. Although the company typically retains ownership of its pledged receivables, as well as the responsibility and risk of collecting the receivables, the cash flow from account and note collection is usually "pledged" to pay the principal and debt service charges associated with such a loan. **Pledging** receivables is a common form of financing for most companies because it is a lower-cost option than factoring.

Securitization

A third approach to monetize accounts and notes receivable is to sell the receivables to a private legal entity created by a company for the exclusive purpose of buying its receivables. Entities established for this purpose are called **special purpose entities (SPEs)** or **special purpose vehicles (SPVs)**.

For example, General Motors (GM) Company disclosed in its 2014 annual report the following:

> GM Financial uses special purpose entities (SPEs) that are considered VIEs to issue variable funding notes to third-party bank-sponsored warehouse facilities or asset-backed securities to investors in securitization transactions. The debt issued by these VIEs is backed by the cash flows related to finance receivables and leasing related assets transferred by GM Financial to the VIEs (Securitized Assets). GM Financial holds variable interests in the VIEs that could potentially be significant to the VIEs. GM Financial determined that they are the primary beneficiary of the SPEs because: (1) the servicing responsibilities for the Securitized Assets give GM Financial the power to direct the activities that most significantly impact the performance of the VIEs; and (2) the variable interests in the VIEs give GM Financial the obligation to absorb losses and the right to receive residual returns that could potentially be significant. The assets and liabilities of the VIEs are included in GM Financial's consolidated balance sheets.

In essence, an SPE or SPV acts like a company-owned factor. The SPE borrows money from investors or from a financial services company and then uses the borrowed funds to buy accounts and notes receivable from its parent company. The advantage of **securitization** over pledging is that the parent company does not increase its leverage. Because of complex accounting rules, the borrowings of an SPE or SPV also sometimes remain off-balance-sheet to its parent company. This is not the case for GM, however, as the VIEs are fully consolidated by the company. The advantage of securitization over external factoring is that the cost of factoring to a company-sponsored SPE is less than would normally be incurred when selling receivables to an independent, unaffiliated factor. We will have more to say about SPEs and SPVs, as well as **variable interest entities (VIEs)**, in Chapter 8.

---

[7] The company selling a receivable with recourse also must record a "recourse liability" account for the expected amount that will not be collected, adding to the net cost of the factoring transaction.

Takeaway 7
Understand
basic analysis
techniques
for revenue
recognition and
receivables
policies.

ANALYZING OPERATING REVENUE AND RECEIVABLES

Because security prices are sensitive to earnings' news, some managers resort to the use of questionable accounting practices as a means to favorably impact their firm's share price. Two common approaches used by some managers to manage their company's reported earnings involve overestimating the amount of earned revenue and underestimating the amount of expected credit losses on accounts and notes receivable.

Revenue Recognition Policy

In the case of revenue, it is not uncommon to find that some companies have recognized revenue on the income statement before it is appropriate—that is, before goods or services have been delivered to the customer and/or when cash collection is doubtful. Recognizing revenue prematurely is often referred to as front-end loading. Consider, for example, the case of MicroStrategy, Inc. MicroStategy is a publicly-traded provider of business intelligence software ("data-mining" software) that enables firms to analyze their proprietary data to reveal trends about their business, and consequently, manage themselves more effectively. In early 2000, the shares of MicroStrategy traded at $333 per share, but fell to $140 per share in mid-March 2000 after announcing that the company would restate its operating results for 1999 and 2000 to comply with new SEC accounting guidelines on revenue reporting (see Appendix 5A to this chapter). MicroStrategy had reported its revenue for software service contracts at the time the contracts were signed, even though the contracts provided for services to be delivered over many future fiscal periods. In essence, the company front-loaded revenue that should have been deferred until the future services were actually delivered to the customer. The company originally reported 1999 earnings of $0.16 per share, but the firm's EPS were subsequently restated to a loss of $0.44 per share. By April 2000, MicroStrategy's share price had fallen to $33 per share, a decline of 90 percent.

While it is far more common to observe aggressive or premature revenue recognition, some firms actually attempt to delay the recognition of some of their company's revenue flows (see the "Microsoft Corporation" Business Perspective earlier in this chapter). Investment professionals frequently assume that a company that delays the recognition of some of its revenue, or what is often referred to as "rear-end loading" of revenue, is attempting to create a revenue reserve on the balance sheet (i.e., the deferred revenue account) to enable the firm to more readily meet or exceed future Wall Street earnings' expectations. To help evaluate whether a firm is engaging in either front-end loading or the rear-end loading of revenues, some investment professionals calculate a financial ratio called the *cash conversion ratio*, defined as cash sales divided by accrual sales (see Chapter 3). When the cash conversion ratio gets significantly below (above) one, it may indicate the presence of front-end (rear-end) loading of revenue.

Receivable Valuation Policy

In the case of receivable valuation, some managers intentionally understate the cash collection risk associated with their accounts and notes receivable as a means to minimize the bad debt expense and, in so doing, boost the level of currently reported earnings. Consider, for example, the case of Fairfield Communities, Inc., a U.S.-based developer of time-share resorts. Fairfield sells the annual right to vacation at any of the company's resorts for the duration of a buyer's lifetime. The purchase price is typically financed with a down payment of 15 percent and a seven-year, non-recourse note receivable for the balance. An analysis of Fairfield's allowance for uncollectible accounts revealed that Fairfield's expected credit losses amounted to only 4.7 percent of time-share revenue, as contrasted with the industry average of seven to nine percent. Some investment professionals alleged that Fairfield understated its expected credit losses on its notes receivable as a means to "pump up" its earnings by understating the allowance for uncollectible accounts, and hence, understating its bad debt expense on the income statement.

In a recent similar situation, following the 2008 financial crisis the large Wall Street banks have been accused of using available discretion in determining their balances in the allowance for uncollectible accounts to help significantly bolster quarterly earnings. In the third quarter of 2012 alone, Citigroup, Inc. cut $1.7 billion from its $27.6 billion allowance for uncollectibles account, and Bank of America cut $1.9 billion from its $30 billion allowance. At Citigroup, Inc. this change led to all of the company's third quarter profit. While management of these banks might justify the changes in the allowance for uncollectible accounts on the basis of an improving economy, and thus less of a need for large reserves, critics argued that during that same quarter economic indicators were pointing to rising delinquencies in most consumer credit categories, most notably home mortgages in which Citigroup, Inc. and Bank of America were significantly exposed.

To help evaluate whether a company is managing its bad debt expense as a means to positively impact its current net earnings, some investment professionals calculate the average percentage of total receivables the company estimates will not be collected. This calculation takes the form of the ratio of the allowance for uncollectible accounts divided by gross accounts receivable. Below is a summary of the calculation of this ratio for Citigroup over the 20 quarters ending with the 2015 third quarter:

Citigroup, Inc.: Percentage Expected Uncollectible Loans			
	(1)	(2)	(2)/(1)
Quarter (in billions)	Total Gross Loans Outstanding	Allowance for Uncollectible Loans	% Estimated Uncollectible
4th Qtr 2010	$648.79	$40.66	6.27%
1st Qtr. 2011	637.14	36.57	5.74%
2nd Qtr 2011	647.50	34.36	5.31%
3rd Qtr. 2011	637.24	32.05	5.03%
4th Qtr 2011	647.24	30.12	4.65%
1st Qtr. 2012	648.02	29.02	4.48%
2nd Qtr 2012	654.97	27.61	4.22%
3rd Qtr. 2012	658.42	25.92	3.94%
4th Qtr 2012	655.46	25.46	3.88%
1st Qtr. 2013	646.36	23.73	3.67%
2nd Qtr 2013	643.74	21.58	3.35%
3rd Qtr. 2013	657.55	20.61	3.13%
4th Qtr 2013	665.47	19.65	2.95%
1st Qtr. 2014	664.22	18.92	2.85%
2nd Qtr 2014	667.50	17.89	2.68%
3rd Qtr. 2014	653.83	16.92	2.59%
4th Qtr 2014	644.64	15.99	2.48%
1st Qtr. 2015	621.05	14.60	2.35%
2nd Qtr 2015	632.12	14.08	2.23%
3rd Qtr. 2015	622.44	13.63	2.19%

In the case of Citigroup, the ratio of uncollectible accounts to gross loans outstanding had dramatically improved steadily to 2.19 percent in the 2015 third quarter from 6.27 percent five years earlier. While these may seem like small percentage changes, note that a 1% shift downward in this ratio on Citigroup's approximately $650 billion loan portfolio, translates into $6.5 billion of pretax profit in the form of lower bad debt expense. Because of the magnitude of these changes, most investment professionals viewed Citigroup's decline in its allowance for uncollectible accounts, and the corresponding decline in bad debt expense and increase in pretax net income, with a skeptical eye.

ETHICS PERSPECTIVE

Financial Statement Account Presentation at Groupon

Groupon was founded in 2008 and less than two years later was valued at over $1 billion. The business concept that bolstered this fast growth is simple but innovative. The company offers to consumers goods and services from select merchants at deep discounts. Consumers are contacted about the offers via email after becoming subscribers and providing Groupon with a personal profile, thus the offers can be tailored to specific geographic locations and personal preferences. Once each day for each market served (e.g., Richmond metropolitan), a Groupon offer is made to each subscriber. As an example, the subscriber might be offered a discounted entrance ticket and meal to the Colonial Downs Racetrack in Richmond for only $15. Typically this might cost around $30, but by offering the discount the racetrack hopes to pick up customers it would not otherwise get and help build a more permanent customer base.

continued

continued from previous page

If a minimum number of pre-determined entrance tickets are sold then the deal becomes "live." This reduces both the risk to the retailer and enhances overall profits. Groupon and the retailer typically split the amount paid by the consumer, so in this example Groupon would net $7.50 for each offer sold, with the remainder going to Colonial Downs.

Groupon became a publicly traded company in October 2011 but the transition has not been without significant controversy. During the IPO process Groupon was forced to abandon a controversial metric it had been reporting, Adjusted Consolidated Segment Operating Income (ACSOI), wherein the company was treating marketing costs as assets. This treatment alone made Groupon appear to be reporting a profit, when in fact GAAP earnings were just below break-even when marketing costs were properly characterized as an expense. There was more, however, particularly as it related to revenue recognition. The company was applying a "gross" presentation for earned revenue rather than a "net" presentation. This means in the above example for Colonial Downs, for each purchase by the consumer Groupon would record $15 of revenue and a corresponding $7.50 cost (i.e., the amount received by the end retailer), rather than just a single value of $7.50 net. This alone did not inflate net income per se, but it did have the effect of making the company appear stronger, larger, and more successful than it may have otherwise appeared. Revenue appeared twice as high. Because Groupon never took title to the goods sold, bore no risk of loss, and was simply acting as a middle-man to help move a retailer's product, the treatment of all amounts sold as revenue to Groupon was clearly an aggressive stance. In late 2011, Groupon was forced to restate its prior financial statements for this accounting treatment. The impact on many important metrics was significant:

- The average revenue per subscriber and customer was cut in half,
- Marketing expense as a percent of revenue shot up, exceeding 90% for 2010,
- Net profit margins (net income divided by sales) was dramatically worse, and
- Year-to-year revenue growth appeared much slower.

Since its IPO, Groupon's company value has been on a steady decline, from about $12 billion at the IPO date to just over $3 billion as of early 2013. Many experts question its ongoing viability because its business model has not been the boon to the retailers originally sought. Repeat business has been lower than expected. The questionable accounting practices employed by management have certainly not helped. Like many companies before, it seems Groupon management had chosen to take the aggressive approach when faced with accounting judgments, but unfortunately causing reputational damage that will be difficult for many investors to forget.

EXECUTIVE SUMMARY

This chapter investigated the important concepts of revenue recognition and receivable valuation. We saw that depending upon the particular business circumstances encountered, a company could recognize its operating revenue at the point of sale and delivery, during the production process, at the end of the production process, or at the point of cash collection if collection was in doubt. We also saw that when businesses allow their customers to buy their products on credit, certain additional costs are likely to be encountered, specifically the opportunity cost of not immediately collecting the promised cash and the potential losses when an account is uncollectible. Approaches to manage these costs were discussed; in addition, approaches to monetize a firm's accounts and notes receivable were considered.

As a validation of your understanding of the content of this chapter, you should now be able to:

- Illustrate the operating cycle of a retail organization.
- Explain how service, retail, and manufacturing companies recognize their operating revenue.
- Explain how revenue is recognized under the completed contract and percentage of completion methods.
- Explain how accounts receivables are valued and how the allowance for uncollectible accounts and bad debt expense are estimated.
- Explain why the effective management of accounts receivable is important for a business.
- Identify the processes for monetizing a company's accounts receivable—factoring, pledging, and securitization.
- Understand basic analysis techniques for revenue recognition and receivables policies.
- Summarize the general guidance on revenue recognition.

In Chapter 6, we examine various inventory valuation approaches used by companies to measure the cost of their products sold and the inventory remaining on hand.

KEY CONCEPTS AND TERMS

Accounts receivable, 180
Aging method, 187
Allowance for sales returns, 196
Allowance for uncollectible
   accounts, 187, 190
Bad debt expense, 189
Completed contract method, 183
Credit terms, 194
Deferred revenue, 183
Direct write-off method, 187
Duration, 194
Earnings reserve, 185
Factoring, 196
Installment method, 180
Monetizing, 196

Net realizable value, 187, 190
Net revenue, 194
Notes receivable, 180
Operating cycle, 176
Opportunity cost, 180
Percentage of completion
   method, 181
Percentage-of-credit-sales
   method, 187
Pledging, 197
Production-in-progress, 182
Realizable, 177
Realized, 177
Rear-end loading, 185
Receivable collection period, 194

Recognized, 177
Revenue, 177
Sales discount, 194
Sales returns, 196
Securitization, 197
Special purpose entities (SPEs), 197
Special purpose vehicles (SPVs), 197
Trade terms, 194
Unbilled account receivable, 182
Variable interest entities (VIEs), 197
Without recourse, 197
With recourse, 196
Write-off of uncollectible
   accounts, 191

APPENDIX 5A: Revenue Recognition: SAB No. 101

Takeaway 8
Summarize
the general
guidance
on revenue
recognition.

Although the general criteria regarding revenue recognition is quite straightforward—the revenue must be earned and the collection of cash realized or realizable—revenue recognition issues dominate SEC enforcement actions involving exchange-traded companies. SEC Staff Accounting Bulletin (SAB) No. 101 on revenue recognition in financial statements was written in 1999 to provide guidance for those situations in which a straightforward interpretation was not obvious. It is applicable U.S. GAAP for all fiscal years beginning before December 16, 2016, at which time ASC 606 will be the governing standard (see Appendix 5B). Below are illustrative questions and answers extracted from SAB No. 101.[8]

General Guidance on Revenue Recognition

Under SAB 101, revenue should not be recognized until it is realized or realizable and earned. Revenue is generally realized or realizable and earned when all of the following criteria are met:

- Persuasive evidence of a sales arrangement exists.
- Delivery has occurred or services have been rendered.
- The seller's price to the buyer is fixed or determinable; and,
- Cash collectibility is reasonably assured.

Persuasive Evidence of a Sales Arrangement

Facts: Company A has product available to ship to Company B prior to the end of the period. It is customary for Company A to enter into a written sales agreement that requires the signature of the buyer company. Company B places a verbal order stating that it is highly likely that the contract will be approved one week after the end of the fiscal period. Company A ships the goods and Company B received the goods prior to the end of the period.

Question and Response: May Company A recognize revenue in the current period? It would not be appropriate to recognize revenue until the signed sales agreement is received since this is the general business practice of Company A. The signed agreement represents persuasive evidence of an agreement.

Facts: Company A enters into an arrangement with Customer B to deliver products to Customer B on a consignment basis. Title does not pass from Company A to Customer B until Customer B consumes the product. Company A delivers the product to Customer B under the terms of the arrangement.

Question and Response: May Company A recognize revenue upon delivery of its product to Customer B? No, consignment arrangements do not qualify for revenue recognition until a sale occurs. Revenue recognition is not appropriate since Company A retains the risks and rewards of ownership and title did not pass to Customer B.

   Another characteristic in a transaction that will likely preclude revenue recognition, even if title has passed, is if the buyer has a right of product return. In general, under this set of circumstances, revenue recognition will be precluded until the right-of-return period has expired, unless it can be established that a return is unlikely.

---

[8] For further discussion on revenue recognition and SAB No. 101 see "The Right Way to Recognize Revenue" by Phillips, Luehlfing and Daily published in the June 2001 issue of the Journal of Accountancy. This article can be found online at www.journalofaccountancy.com/Issues/2001/Jun/TheRightWayToRecognizeRevenue

Delivery and Performance

Facts: Company A receives a purchase order for products it has in stock; however, the customer is unable to take delivery at this time.

Question and Response: Can Company A recognize revenue if it either segregates the inventory in its own warehouse or ships to a third-party warehouse if Company A retains title to the product? Generally, no; delivery is not considered to have taken place until the customer has taken title and assumed the risks and rewards of ownership. This interpretation includes layaway sales where a seller takes a nonrefundable deposit and holds the merchandise for later pickup by the customer. Further, revenue should not be recognized, even after delivery, if uncertainty exists regarding customer acceptance. Uncertainty exists, for example, if the customer has the right to test the product or require additional services subsequent to delivery.

Facts: Companies often require up-front, nonrefundable fees from their customers. Examples include a lifetime membership fee in a health club or an activation fee by a wireless telephone provider.

Question and Response: When should the revenue related to nonrefundable, up-front fees be recognized? Deferral of revenue recognition is appropriate unless the up-front fee is in exchange for delivered products or the performance of services that represent the culmination of a separate earnings process. Health club membership fees or activation fees by wireless telephone providers generally do not qualify for immediate revenue recognition.

Fixed or Determinable Sales Price

Facts: Company B is a discount retailer that generates revenue from annual membership fees it charges customers to shop at its stores and from the sale of products at a discount price to those customers. The membership arrangements with retail customers require the customer to pay the entire membership fee at the start of the arrangement. The customer has the unilateral right to cancel the arrangement at any time during its term and receive a full refund of the initial fee.

Question and Response: May Company B recognize revenue for the membership at the beginning of the membership period? No; the earnings process is not complete, and the ability of the member to receive a refund raises an uncertainty as to whether the fee is fixed or determinable. A company's contracts may include provisions for the customer to cancel or terminate early. In addition, side agreements may be present providing additional rights for the customer. Provisions of this type raise questions as to whether the sales price is fixed or determinable. The sales price is neither fixed nor determinable until cancellation privileges expire. If the cancellation privilege expires ratably over a stated time period, the sales price is considered to become determinable ratably over the stated period.

Other Issues

Facts: Company A operates an internet site from which it sells the products of other companies. Company A receives orders, processes credit card payments, and passes the order to Company B which possesses the product. Company B then ships the product to the ultimate customer. The product is sold for $175, of which Company A retains a $25 commission.

Question and Response: Should Company A report revenue on a gross basis as $175 with a corresponding $150 cost of sales or report revenue on a net basis of $25? Company A should report revenue on a net basis unless it takes title to the product and assumes the risks and rewards of ownership.

APPENDIX 5B: New Revenue Recognition Standards: Revenue from Contracts with Customers

In May 2014, the Financial Accounting Standards Board (FASB) and the International Accounting Standards Board (IASB) issued joint standards on revenue recognition, the culmination of over a decade of work between the two boards to develop a common framework for this critical financial statement line item. The FASB issued Accounting Standards Update 2014-09 and the IASB issued IFRS 15, both titled *Revenue from Contracts with Customers*. The FASB has also created a new Accounting Standard Codification (#606) for this topic, or ASC 606 for short. ASC 606 and ASU 2014-09 supersede almost all of the prior existing U.S. GAAP related to revenue recognition. They will be effective for years beginning in 2018 (for public companies) and 2019 (for most all others). Along with these new guidelines there will be significant amendments to existing standards. The new standards are being hailed as a milestone advancement in financial reporting:

"The revenue recognition standard represents a milestone in our efforts to improve and converge one of the most important areas of financial reporting. It will eliminate a major source of inconsistency in GAAP, which currently consists of numerous disparate, industry-specific pieces of revenue recognition guidance." (FASB Chairman Russell Golden)

Existing rules under both U.S. and international standards before this were very different. In the U.S., relevant GAAP (primarily under SAB 101) had developed a uniqueness by industry and by transaction, and depending on the preparer and context frequently could result in very different accounting treatments for the same transactions. Under IFRS there was less guidance offered, and preparers would find requisite guidance lacking for the many complex transactions facing the firm. The disclosures required under both systems also lacked uniformity and an appropriate level of detail.

ASC 606 now unifies under a single umbrella the myriad of different revenue recognition rules that presently exist. The new standard applies a principles-based revenue recognition framework, asking management to provide more individual judgment in determining when to record revenue for their companies. Ideally this will help create more informative income measurements and a standard that is adaptable to many different business contexts. With more judgment comes the need to understand those decisions, so ASC 606 also expands required disclosures. Provided below is a broad overview of the new framework under the standard.

A Five-Step Process

Revenue is defined under ASC 606 as

> "Inflows or other enhancements of assets of an entity or settlements of its liabilities (or a combination of both) from delivering or producing goods, rendering services, or other activities that constitute the entity's ongoing major or central operations." (ASC-606-10-20)

While this definition sets the objective—what needs to be reported, it still requires significant judgment on a contract by contract basis to determine when an item has reached the threshold of meeting this revenue definition. With ASC 606, a five-step recognition model is offered that can ideally be applied to any type of transaction and for any industry. Because it is a sequence of steps, it is structurally sound enough that it also can be used for the recognition of gains and losses on the sale of assets that are not part of a company's ordinary activities, such as sales of property, plant and equipment. The specific five steps under the new standard are:

1. Identify the contract with a customer.
2. Identify the separate performance obligations in the contract.
3. Determine the transaction price.
4. Allocate the transaction price to the separate performance obligations in the contract.
5. Recognize revenue when the company satisfies a performance obligation.

Describing each of these steps in great detail is beyond the needed scope of our discussion herein. We do, however, provide an overview of some of the key considerations with each step in Exhibit 5.9. Beyond these highlights, interested readers are encouraged to review the details of the standards and descriptions of each step. Suffice to say that, similar to prior revenue recognition, under the new standard certain criteria still must be met for a contract to be accounted for using the five-step model. Preparers still must determine that it is probable that company will be paid by the customer. There still must be a performance obligation on the part of the company that has been satisfied. And a price still must be determined for each piece of the contract that can be separately identified. For this latter item, determining the transaction price for contracts that contain multiple elements still may be the most challenging of all. ASC 606 offers several methods that can be used to estimate the standalone selling price when one is not directly observable.

Disclosure Modifications

Because the new revenue recognition rules tend to be more principles-based, requiring more judgment by managers in their application, many more disclosures will become necessary. These expanded disclosures make good sense as users of financial statements will now require greater detail in order to understand the basis behind the enhanced management discretion, should it exist.

There are numerous areas under ASC 606 where revenue recognition disclosures have been expanded. First, companies must disclose the nature of any separate sources of revenue, disaggregated by amounts, timing, uncertainty, and reportable segment. The information must be sufficient for users to understand the relationship with revenue generation with each of these key sources. Second, any material performance obligations under the contracts must be referenced. These include such items as obligations for returns and allowances, warranties, and significant payment terms. Third, contract balances must be disclosed. These items relate to opening and closing balances of outstanding liabilities (e.g., deferred revenue), receivables, and impairment losses. Finally, disclosures must include details related to any and all significant judgments used to determine such items as transaction prices, amounts capitalized, and amortization policies.

EXHIBIT 5.9	Summary of Steps and Key Considerations under Revenue Recognition Topic ASC 606

Step	Key Considerations
1. Identify the contract with a customer.	• A contract can be written, oral or implied. • There exists identifiable and enforceable rights. • Payment terms are identifiable. • Collectability of payment is probable.
2. Identify the performance obligations in the contract.	• Transfer of distinct goods or services, that are either unique or as a series with substantially the same pattern of transfer. • Normally specified in the contract but can include implied promises.
3. Determine the transaction price.	• The amount of consideration that the company is entitled to receive. • Includes estimates of any variable consideration under the contract. • Includes estimates of fair value of non-cash consideration. • Can elect to exclude sales taxes collected on behalf of governmental authorities.
4. Allocate the transaction price to the performance obligations.	• Allocate to each separate component based on "stand-alone selling price." • Any excess of sum of stand-alone prices to be treated as a discount allocated to separate performance obligations.
5. Recognize revenue.	• Recognition upon the "transfer" of a good or service, defined as when a customer obtains control. • Control might be transferred over time, under either an input or an output method of allocation.

Implementation and Expected Implications

While the new revenue recognition guidelines will not be a panacea, by making managers address critical sequential questions in step-wise fashion much structure has been brought to the measurement issues for the critical account. The benefits to conformity across international and U.S. accounting regimes also cannot be understated. The mandatory effective date for ASC 606 is for fiscal periods beginning after December 15, 2017, if the entity is publicly traded, and for all other companies after December 15, 2018. If there is an impact on reported dollar values in the financial statements (i.e., more or less revenue to be recognized), companies will have one of two methods to report these effects on prior period financial statements.[9] The first option would be to apply ASC 606 to all prior years, retrospectively restating the financial statements. The second option would be to apply a single, cumulative adjustment to the opening balance of retained earnings, then apply the new standard to individual line items going forward.

Companies across many different industries are expected to see a material change in the dollar amount of revenue reported on the income statement. In the healthcare industry, for instance, executives are expecting significant changes in the way they record revenues for third party payer settlements, uninsured patients, and non-refundable entrance fees. Likewise software companies will see significant changes in the ways they must account for products with bundled elements and those with sales or usage based royalties.[10] But even if there are no dollar value changes, the more extensive footnote disclosure requirements will mean that all companies will be impacted to some extent by ASC 606. Anticipating the many hurdles companies might face in implementation, a joint FASB/IASB transition resource group was formed to identify implementation issues and advise the FASB and the IASB. The AICPA has also created task forces unique to 16 industries that are studying specific implementation issues.

A joint effort between the FASB and IASB culminated in May 2014 with a new standard on revenue recognition. The new standard is Accounting Standards Update 2014-09, *Revenue from Contracts with Customers*, and creates a new topic in the FASB's Accounting Standard Codification (#606), or ASC 606 for short. ASC 606 supersedes almost all of the existing U.S GAAP related to revenue recognition. This appendix provides an overview of its key elements. As of the writing of this textbook the new rules have not yet been implemented and their impact is thus not determinable in company financial reports.

---

[9] Note that companies are required by the SEC to report three years of income statements in their annual reporting.
[10] See "New Revenue Recognition Standard Hits Health Care Entities," (Trent Fast, March 1, 2016),
http://www.claconnect.com/resources/articles/new-revenue-recognition-standard-hits-health-care-entities
and "New Revenue Recognition Standard Means Big Changes for Software Companies," (Maria Murphy, March 22, 2016),
http://www.claconnect.com/resources/articles/new-revenue-recognition-standard-means-big-changes-for-software-companies.

QUESTIONS

Q5.1 **Revenue Recognition Criteria.** MicroStrategy, Inc., is a software company that sells its services to other companies under multiyear contracts (on average for three years). The contracts call for a minimum fee, paid monthly, and additional fees when the services provided exceed certain levels. The chief operating officer (COO) of MicroStrategy is uncertain when the most appropriate time is to recognize the revenue from such contracts: (*a*) at the time of contract signing; (*b*) monthly, when billings are sent to customers; or (*c*), when the contract is complete and all services have been rendered. Discuss the criteria that should be considered in reaching this accounting policy decision. What would you recommend to MicroStrategy's COO?

Q5.2 **The Materiality Concept.** The materiality concept is a financial statement disclosure guideline used by most businesses to help determine when a particular account balance or economic event should be separately disclosed in a firm's financial statements. Unfortunately, there are no generally accepted guidelines for determining when an amount is material. Assume that you are the chief operating officer of a company generating $100 million in revenue, $10 million in net income, and $150 million in total assets. Discuss the materiality standard that you believe would be appropriate for such a business. Be prepared to justify your decision.

Q5.3 **Accrual Accounting, Accounts Receivable, and Cash Flow.** A well-known poem about accounting was written by H.S. Bailey, Jr. and published in 1975 in Publishers Weekly:

> *Though my bottom line is black, I am flat upon my back.*
> *My cash flows out and customers pay slow.*
> *The growth of my receivables is almost unbelievable.*
> *The result is certain—unremitting woe!*
> *And I hear the banker utter an ominous low mutter—"Watch cash flow."*

Discuss the message that Mr. Bailey was trying to convey through this poem.

Q5.4 **Revenue Recognition, the Matching Principle, and the Bad Debt Expense.** Urcarco, Inc., was a publicly held used-car dealer that had defined its market niche as customers with a low or no credit rating. In some years, Urcarco's repossession rate had run as high as 40 percent of all vehicles sold. Discuss how Urcarco should recognize revenue from vehicle sales and how it should estimate its bad debt expense.

Q5.5 **Revenue Recognition in the Air Transportation Industry.** U.S. Airways recognizes revenue from airline ticket sales when a customer takes a flight or not later than one year from the date of sale (flight coupons have a useful life of one year from the date of purchase). Discuss the alternative revenue recognition policy options available to U.S. Airways.

Q5.6 **Managing Earnings and the Bad Debt Expense.** Total Networks, Inc., reported gross accounts receivable of $1.2 billion in 2008 and an allowance for doubtful accounts of $300 million. In 2009, the company's gross accounts receivable declined slightly to $1.1 billion and its allowance for doubtful accounts likewise declined to $150 million. Calculate the ratio of the allowance for doubtful accounts divided by gross accounts receivable for 2008 and 2009. Discuss how Total Networks, Inc., might be managing its earnings.

Q5.7 **Sales Channel Stuffing.** On April 14, 2006, *The Wall Street Journal* carried an article headlined "Research in Motion Skeptics Pipe Up." The article concerned Research in Motion Ltd. (RIM), the manufacturer of the BlackBerry. One week earlier, RIM had disappointed investors with a weaker-than-expected revenue forecast for the current quarter. In the one-week period following the revenue announcement, RIM's share price declined 9.5 percent.

The Wall Street Journal article expressed new concerns about RIM's financial performance. RIM generates revenue two ways:

1. 70 percent of its revenue comes from sales of the BlackBerry device; and,
2. 30 percent of its revenue comes from the sale of subscriptions to the wireless network that supports the BlackBerry.

Of concern to Wall Street analysts was the fact that a widening gap was beginning to build between the number of new BlackBerry network subscribers and the number of BlackBerry devices shipped to retailers. In the latest reporting period, RIM reportedly shipped 1.12 million BlackBerries, while new network subscribers totaled only 625,000, a difference of about 495,000. According to the company, the "gap" between units shipped and new network subscribers for the prior three quarters, respectively, was 475,000, 335,000, and 248,000.

Discuss whether RIM is engaging in "channel stuffing." (Note: Channel stuffing refers to the practice of shipping unwanted and unsolicited goods to retailers, usually with a guarantee to allow the return of any unsold goods.) Why is channel stuffing of concern to analysts and investors?

Q5.8   **Sales Forecasts and Share Prices.**   In early 2006, the Bausch & Lomb Company halted shipments of its ReNu contact lens product and recalled from retailers any unsold containers of its contact lens solution. The contact lens cleaning solution had been linked to an increasing number of serious eye infections caused by a fungus. ReNu products generated about $45 million in 2005 sales for Bausch & Lomb, but analysts predicted a wider decline in sales in related products as well. For 2006, equity analysts predicted that the company might lose $75 million to $100 million in lens-solution sales, or about 4.6 percent of the firm's total projected sales for 2006. Shares of Bausch & Lomb declined over $8 per share, or 15 percent, in response to the product recall.

Discuss the relationship between revenue forecasts and security prices. Did the capital market overreact to the Bausch & Lomb news about ReNu?

Q5.9   **Revenue Recognition by Software Companies.**   Microsoft, Inc., recognizes revenue from its licensed software products at the "time of sale" or "time of installation." Despite receiving such revenue in cash, Microsoft defers the recognition of a portion of its software revenue. The deferred portion represents the value of any future software upgrades that might be distributed free of charge, as well as the value of any technical support services provided free of charge during the software warranty period. Discuss Microsoft's revenue recognition policy. Do you agree with Microsoft's policy choice? Discuss the company's possible motivation for adopting this revenue recognition approach.

Q5.10   **Revenue Recognition by Aircraft Manufacturers.**   In September 2015, Boeing agreed to terms to sell 300 planes to China in one of the largest long-term airline contracts ever signed. With contracts to sell a plane, a company such as Boeing would typically require a deposit of as much as $100 million per aircraft prior to the start of construction, which may take as long as nine months to complete. Boeing also would likely receive periodic progress payments from China as certain aircraft construction milestones are met. Typically, ten percent of each airplane's purchase price is withheld by the buyer until flight testing is complete and title of the aircraft is transferred. The average cost of a commercial aircraft is approximately $350–$500 million. Discuss the possible approaches to revenue recognition that Boeing might adopt. Which approach do you prefer? Why?

Q5.11   **Ethics and the Tone at the Top.**   Discuss what is meant by the "tone at the top" and why it is important. Further, discuss whether you feel it is ethical to be a whistle-blower.

Assignments with the ⓜ logo in the margin are available in BusinessCourse.
See the Preface of the book for details.
CHECK FIGURE indicates that check figures are available on the book's Website.

EXERCISES

TA 2, 3   **E5.12**   **Revenue Recognition Policy Decisions.**   Consider the following independent situations:

1. An international health club sells lifetime memberships costing $1,500 which allow the purchaser unlimited use of any of the club's 300 facilities around the world. The initiation fee may be paid in 36 monthly installments, with a two percent interest charge on any unpaid balance.

2. Global Motors, Inc., has always offered a limited, 36-month warranty on its cars and trucks, but to counter the significant competition in the industry, the company has come to the conclusion that it must do something more. With that in mind, the company developed a new warranty program: For a $1,500 payment at the time of purchase, a customer can buy a seven-year warranty that will cover replacement of almost all parts and labor. The purchased warranty expires at the end of seven years or when the customer sells the vehicle, whichever occurs first.

3. Arcadia Promotions Inc. sells coupon books that give the holder a ten percent discount at any of 50 participating merchants. The buyer of the coupon book pays $25 for the book but can realize up to $500 in savings. Arcadia convinces merchants to participate in the program at no cost, arguing that participation will build customer traffic and will create the opportunity for repeat business from the coupon book-holders.

4. Luxury Furniture Inc. sells household furniture under installment purchase contracts. The contracts usually carry interest rates of 16 percent or more a year. When the company accumulates $500,000 of contracts with at least a year or more to go, it sells the contracts to a finance company on a nonrecourse basis. Luxury Furniture continues to service the contracts and is paid a service fee. If a contract is uncollectible, Luxury Furniture turns it over to a collection agency and has no further responsibility for it. In January, Luxury sold contracts with a face value of $1 million and received $1.06 million in cash from the finance company.

5. Community News, Inc., prints and distributes a weekly newspaper throughout the city. Local stores order a certain number of the papers each week and pay for them on delivery. Community News always takes back any unsold papers and gives the merchant a credit toward future purchases.

For each of these situations, describe the revenue recognition policy that you believe that the company should follow, explaining the basis for your recommendation.

E5.13   **Revenue Recognition.**   The Longo Corporation contracted with The Davis Company to manufacture various metal component parts that would be assembled by Longo before resale to Longo's customers. Longo placed its most recent order with Davis for 10,000 parts in December 2016. Because of existing work commitments, however, Davis indicated that work on the Longo order could not commence until January 2017, with an expected delivery date of February 2017. Davis provides its customers with trade credit terms of 2/10, n/30, and thus, didn't expect to be paid the contract price of $100,000 by Longo until March 2017.

In which month should Davis Company recognize the $100,000 in revenue from the Longo order? Why?

TA 2, 3, 5

E5.14   **Analyzing Accounts Receivable.**   The following information is taken from the annual report of The Lincoln Electric Company.

TA 4
CHECK
FIGURE

Balance Sheet	2014	2015
Accounts receivable, net of the allowance for uncollectible accounts of $2,460 and $2,700, respectively..........................	$79,500	$75,390

Calculate the ratio of the allowance for uncollectible accounts divided by gross accounts receivable for 2014 and 2015. Did this ratio increase from 2014 to 2015? If so, what does that indicate? The bad debt expense on Lincoln Electric's income statement did not equal $2,700. What might explain this?

E5.15   **Analyzing Accounts Receivable.**   The following information is taken from the annual report of the Couche Corporation.

TA 4

Balance Sheet	2014	2015
Accounts receivable, net of the allowance for uncollectible accounts of $4,500 and $4,100, respectively..........................	$125,650	$132,500

Calculate the ratio of the allowance for uncollectible accounts divided by gross accounts receivable. Did this ratio decrease from 2014 to 2015? If so, what does that indicate? The bad debt expense on the Couche Corporation's earnings statement did not equal $4,100. What might explain this?

E5.16   **Accounting for Quick-Pay Incentives.**   Charles Smith, Inc., is a manufacturer of small office equipment. Smith transacts most of its business on credit and offers its customers credit terms of 2/10, n/30. On July 1, Smith shipped an order valued at $120,000 to a customer and shipped a second order valued at $80,000 to another customer on July 10. Payment was received on the July 1st order on July 6, but payment on the July 10th order was not received until August 15. Calculate total sales, the sales discount, and net sales for Charles Smith, Inc., for July. Why do companies like Smith, Inc., offer sales discounts to their customers? Why are sales discounts valuable to the customers of Smith, Inc.?

TA 5

E5.17   **Preparing an Aging Schedule.**   M. Beall Inc. uses the aging method to estimate the company's bad debt expense. Mike Beall, the president of the company, collected information about the company's outstanding accounts receivable and their probability of collection:

TA 4

Account Age	Amount	Probability of Non-Collection
0–30 days...	$725,000	0.5%
31–60 days..	275,000	1.5
61–90 days..	170,000	2.5
91–120 days...	100,000	4.0
Over 120 days	40,000	20.0

Calculate the allowance for uncollectible accounts for M. Beall, Inc., the total balance in accounts receivable, and the net realizable value of the company's accounts receivable. Assume that M. Beall Inc. adopts a policy of writing off as worthless all unpaid accounts receivable over 120 days old. How will implementation of this policy impact the net realizable value of the company's accounts receivable? Why?

E5.18   **Analyzing Accounts Receivable.**   The following information is taken from the annual report of The Coca-Cola Company:

(amounts in millions)	2014	2015
Net sales.	$45,998	$44,294
Accounts receivable (net).	4,466	3,941

Calculate the receivable turnover ratio and the receivable collection period for 2014 and 2015. How much additional cash flow from operations could Coca-Cola generate in 2015 if it could reduce its receivable collection period to just 30 days?

E5.19   **Analyzing Accounts Receivable.**   The following information is taken from the annual report of The Mann Corporation:

(all amounts in millions)	2014	2015
Net sales.	$26,258	$25,649
Accounts receivable (net).	4,684	4,883

Calculate the receivable turnover ratio and the receivable collection period for 2014 and 2015. How much additional cash flow from operations could The Mann Corporation generate in 2015 if it could reduce its receivable collection period to 60 days?

E5.20   **Revenue Policy Change: Software Service Contracts.**   CA Technologies is a software company that designs, develops, installs, and services business software for manufacturing companies. Typically, CA Technologies provides its services over a multiyear period. Following the release of SAB 101, the company changed its method of recognizing revenue under its multiyear service contracts. Originally, CA Technologies recognized all contract revenue at the time that a contract was signed; however, consistent with SAB 101, the company decided to recognize contract revenue on a prorata basis over the life of each multiyear contract.

1. How will the change in revenue recognition policy affect the following items on the financial statements of CA Technologies?
    a. Revenue   *c.* Cash flow from operations
    b. Total assets   *d.* Total liabilities
2. Do you agree with the policy change implemented by CA Technologies? Why?

PROBLEMS

P5.21   **Installment Basis versus Point-of-Sale Revenue Recognition.**   The Apollo Company is a catalogue-based retailer. The following describes Apollo's operations in its first two years of business:

	2015	2014
Sales (all on account).	$400,000	$600,000
Cash collections from customers		
On 2015 sales.	180,000	220,000
On 2014 sales.	—	240,000
Cash purchases of merchandise inventory	360,000	480,000
Merchandise inventory-on-hand (year-end).	120,000	228,000
Operating expenses (other than inventory)	64,000	88,000

Required

1. Prepare an income statement for each year assuming that Apollo recognizes revenue using the point-of-sale method and assuming that all operating expenses are paid in cash.
2. Prepare an income statement for each year assuming that Apollo recognizes revenue using the installment method and assuming that all operating expenses are paid in cash.

P5.22   **Revenue Recognition.**   At the beginning of 2016, John Cornell decided to quit his job as a construction company supervisor and formed his own residential housing construction company. When he resigned, he had a contract to build a custom home at a price of $400,000. The full price was payable in cash when the house was completed.

By year-end 2016, Cornell's new company Luxury Homes, Inc. had spent $50,000 for labor, $107,740 for materials, and $3,800 in miscellaneous expenses in connection with the construction of the new home. Cornell estimated that the project was 70 percent complete at year-end. In addition, construction materials on hand at year-end 2016 had cost $2,600.

During the year, Luxury Homes, Inc., had also purchased a small house for $95,000, spent $32,000 fixing it up, and then sold it on November 1, 2016, for $175,000. The buyer paid $25,000 down and signed a note for the remainder of the balance due. The note called for interest at a rate of 12 percent per year, with a lump-sum payment for the outstanding balance payable at the end of 2018. John's wife, Karen, kept the accounting records for Luxury Homes, Inc., and on December 31, she prepared the following statement:

LUXURY HOMES, INC.
Where We Stand at Year-End

Assets		Debts and Owners' Capital	
Cash.	$ 21,000	Accounts payable.	$ 44,600
Materials.	2,600	Owners' investment	242,540
Renovation contract receivable	150,000	Sale of renovated house.	175,000
Construction in progress	161,540		
Cost of renovated house	127,000		
Total assets.	$462,140	Total debts & owners' capital.	$462,140

After reviewing the statement, John and Karen got into a discussion concerning the level of revenue the company had earned during the year. John argued that all of the revenue from the sale of the renovated home, along with 70 percent of the expected revenue from the new construction contract, had been earned. Karen, on the other hand, maintained that the revenue on the renovation project should be recognized only to the extent of the cash actually collected and that no revenue should be recognized on the new home construction until it was completed and available for occupancy. John and Karen agreed that there were four possible alternative approaches to measuring the company's revenue:

1. Report the entire amount of renovation revenue and a proportionate amount of the new construction contract revenue.
2. Report the entire amount of renovation revenue but none of the new construction contract revenue.
3. Report the renovation revenue in proportion to the amount of cash received and the new construction contract revenue in proportion to the amount of work completed.
4. Report the renovation revenue in proportion to the amount of cash received but none of the new construction contract revenue.

Required

Prepare the balance sheets and income statements that would result under each of the four approaches. Which set of statements do you believe best reflects the results of Luxury Homes, Inc. for 2016? Why?

P5.23 **Completed Contract Method versus Percentage-of-Completion Method.** The Miller Company won a contract to build a shopping center at a price of $240 million. The following schedule details the estimated and actual costs of construction and the actual cash collections under the contract:

TA 3, 4
CHECK
FIGURE

	Estimated (Actual) Costs of Construction	Cash Collections from Customer
Year 1.	$ 40,000,000	$ 48,000,000
Year 2.	60,000,000	60,000,000
Year 3.	70,000,000	60,000,000
Year 4.	30,000,000	72,000,000
	$200,000,000	$240,000,000

Required

1. Prepare an income statement for the Miller Company for each year assuming that the company recognizes revenue under the completed contract method.
2. Prepare an income statement for the Miller Company for each year assuming that the company recognizes revenue under the percentage-of-completion method.
3. Which set of income statements best reflects the actual performance of the Miller Company? Why?

TA 3, 4   **P5.24**   **Revenue Recognition Under Long-Term Construction Contracts.**   In June 2014, Biltmore Construction Company (BCC) was hired by the City of Phoenix, Arizona, to assist in constructing its new Trade Center complex. The construction agreement called for work to begin no later than August 2014 and required Biltmore to construct the concrete frame for the complex. Under the terms of the three-year contract, BCC was to receive a total of $10 million in cash payments from the City of Phoenix, to be paid as follows: 25 percent when the project was 30 percent complete, 25 percent when the project was 60 percent complete, and the remaining 50 percent, when the project was fully complete. The contract required that BCC's completion estimates be certified by an independent engineering consultant *before* any cash progress payments would be made.

In preparing its bid, Biltmore estimated that the total cost to complete the project would be $8.3 million, assuming no cost overruns. During the first year of the contract, BCC incurred actual costs of $2.49 million, and on June 30, 2015, the engineering firm of J. Graham & Associates determined that the project had attained a 30 percent completion level. (BCC's fiscal year ran from July 1 to June 30.) In the following year, BCC incurred actual costs of $3.1 million, and on June 30, 2016, the firm of J. Graham & Associates determined that the project had attained at least a 60 percent completion level. By May 2017, BCC had completed the remainder of the project. Actual costs incurred during the year to June 30, 2017, amounted to $3.11 million. The firm received a certification for the fully completed work.

Required

1.   Assuming that BCC had no other sources of revenue or expenses, determine the level of profits to be reported for the years ended June 30, 2015, 2016, and 2017, using the following revenue recognition methods:
     a.   Percentage of completion
     b.   Completed contract
     c.   Cash basis
2.   Which set of results best reflects the economic performance of the company over the period 2015–2017? Why?

TA 2   **P5.25**   **Revenue Recognition: R & D Company.**   Wind Technology, Inc., is an independent research laboratory that undertakes contractual research for a variety of corporate and governmental clients. In January 2014, scientists at Wind Technology began work on a number of projects involving wind-power generation. During 2014, costs incurred in these efforts amounted to $363,000. In May 2015, promising results emerged and were reported to the U.S. Department of Energy. Development costs incurred in 2015 through the end of May totaled $204,000.

At this point, Wind Technology tried to secure a government contract to support the remainder of the research effort. The Department of Energy (DOE) was reluctant to commit substantial sums until further tests had been completed. Nonetheless, to ensure that it retained access to the new technology, the DOE gave Wind Technology a seed grant of $50,000 to help support continuation of the studies. This grant carried a stipulation that the DOE would retain the right to acquire the results, patents, and copyrights from the research any time on or before December 31, 2016, for $2.4 million.

Further testing proved favorable, although additional development costs incurred in 2015 amounted to $325,000 and to $210,000 in 2016. On December 28, 2016, the DOE exercised its right and agreed to purchase the results, patents, and copyrights from the lab. As previously agreed, the DOE paid Wind Technology $300,000 immediately, with the remainder of the contract price payable in seven equal annual installments beginning on December 31, 2017, through December 31, 2023. On March 1, 2017, Wind Technology delivered all scientific and legal documents, test results, and samples to the DOE offices in Washington, D.C.

Required

Evaluate the facts and determine when Wind Technology, Inc., should recognize the various revenue streams associated with its work on this project: (*a*) the $2.4 million contract proceeds; (*b*) the $50,000 seed grant; and (*c*) the interest implicit in the seven-year deferred payment (assume a discount rate of ten percent).

TA 4   **P5.26**   **Aging of Accounts Receivable.**   The Miller Company's accounts receivable reveal the following balances
CHECK   by age category:
FIGURE

Age of Account	Receivable Balance
0–30 days.	$ 800,000
31–60 days.	180,000
61–90 days.	80,000
91–120 days.	40,000
	$1,100,000

The allowance for uncollectible accounts has an existing positive balance of $34,200. The company's internal auditors suggest that the following percentages be used to estimate the amount of outstanding receivables that will eventually prove to be uncollectible.

0–30 days..	0.5%
31–60 days...	1.0
61–90 days...	10.0
91–120 days...	70.0

Required

1. Calculate the projected new balance for (*a*) the allowance for uncollectible accounts and (*b*) the bad debt expense.
2. Why is there an existing balance of $34,200 in the allowance for uncollectible accounts? What could be inferred if the existing balance in the allowance for uncollectible accounts was a negative balance of $34,200?

P5.27   **Accounts Receivable Analysis.**   Kate Miller owns a dance studio in Los Angeles, California. Students can buy access to the dance classes by paying a monthly fee. Unfortunately, many of Kate's students are struggling actors and actresses who lack the ability to pay their bills in a timely manner. And, although the students were expected to pay for classes in advance, Kate began offering credit to many of her students to grow her business. This, however, has put Kate in a serious liquidity problem as revealed by the growing balance in the studio's outstanding accounts receivable:

TA 4, 5

Age Classification	Accounts Receivable Outstanding Balance	Historical Estimate of Non-Collection
0–30 days.......................................	$44,000	4%
31–60 days.....................................	31,000	8
61–90 days.....................................	22,000	12
91–120 days...................................	13,000	14
121–150 days.................................	9,000	20
> 150 days	5,000	50

Kate's accountant, Matt Thomas, tried to help her get a handle on the studio's accounts receivable problem, but to little avail. One trick he successfully used in the past to make Kate realize the seriousness of the problem was to overestimate the extent of Kate's bad debt problem; consequently, there currently exists a balance in the allowance for uncollectible accounts totaling $2,700.

Required

1. The first step to help get Kate's business back on track is to write off all receivables having a very low probability of collection (those accounts over 150 days). What balance sheet accounts will be affected, and in what amount, when Matt executes this action?
2. Prepare an aging of Kate's remaining accounts receivable. What balance should be in the allowance for uncollectible accounts account?
3. Kate is in need of an immediate cash infusion and Matt has advised her to sell some of her receivables. A local bank has offered her two alternatives:
   a. Factor $40,000 of "current" receivables (0–30 days old) on a nonrecourse basis at a flat fee of eleven percent of the value of the receivables sold.
   b. Factor $40,000 of "current" receivables on a recourse basis at a flat fee of six percent of the value of the receivables sold.
   Which option should Kate choose? Why?

P5.28   **Factoring versus Pledging of Accounts Receivable.**   Global Markets, Inc. was experiencing a shortage of cash. Consequently, the President was considering two options to provide an immediate inflow of cash. The first option was to sell $2 million of the company's accounts receivable on a nonrecourse basis. The factoring cost would amount to 15.5 percent of the value of the factored receivables. The second option was to obtain a

TA 5, 6

60-day loan from a local bank using its outstanding receivables as collateral. Under the loan agreement, Global Markets would be charged 13 percent annual interest on the outstanding loan and would pledge receivables equal to 122 percent of the loan amount (a loan-to-value ratio of 82 percent).

Required

Compare the cost under each financing option. Which option is better for the company? Why?

TA 5, 6   **P5.29**   **Improving Cash Flow Through Receivable Management.** Star Communications designs, manufactures, and sells telecommunication equipment, and provides services associated with their installation, operation, and maintenance in China, India, Korea, and Vietnam. During 2016, the company's share price traded as high as $23 per share; but, in January, 2016, the company disclosed that it would file its Form 10-K with the U.S. Securities and Exchange Commission late due to material internal control problems identified by its independent auditor. One of the identified concerns related to the company's recording of revenue and the related accounts receivable. In response, the company's share price sank to $6 per share. Following are selected financial data from Star Communications 2015 annual report:

	2015	2014
Net sales.	$2.56 billion	$1.78 billion
Accounts receivable (net).	0.81 billion	0.37 billion

Required

1. Calculate UTStarcom's receivable collection period for 2014 and 2015. Is the company's receivable management decreasing in quality, improving, or about the same?
2. If the company could improve its receivable collection period to the industry average of 60 days, how much additional cash flow from accounts receivable would have been generated in 2014 and 2015?

CORPORATE ANALYSIS

TA 2, 4, 5   **CA5.30**   **The Procter & Gamble Company.** The 2015 annual report of the Procter & Gamble Company (P&G) is available at www.pginvestor.com. After reviewing P&G's annual report, respond to the following questions:

  a.   When does P&G recognize revenue from its product sales?
  b.   Has net sales for P&G been rising or falling? By how much? Assume the growth in net sales realized from 2014 to 2015 will continue. How much will net sales be in 2016?
  c.   When does P&G recognize its sales discounts and sales product returns?
  d.   Calculate P&G's receivable turnover ratio and receivable collection period for 2014 and 2015. Are these ratios improving?
  e.   Assume that P&G's allowance for uncollectible accounts was $180 million at year-end 2014 and $205 million at year-end 2015. Calculate the ratio of the allowance for uncollectible accounts to gross accounts receivable for 2014 and 2015. Did this ratio improve? If so, what does that indicate?
  f.   Using your forecast of net sales for 2016 from question (b), and your 2015 receivable turnover ratio from question (d), forecast the balance of accounts receivable for 2016 (assuming that receivable turnover remains the same from 2015 to 2016).

TA 2, 4, 5   **CA5.31**   **Internet-based Analysis.** Consider a publicly held company whose products you are familiar with. Some examples might include:

Company	Product	Corporate Website
• Johnson & Johnson.	• Band-Aids	• www.jnj.com
• Microsoft Corporation.	• Windows software	• www.microsoft.com
• Apple Corporation	• Cellular phones	• www.apple.com
• Intel Corporation	• Pentium processors	• www.intel.com
• Kimberly-Clark Corporation.	• Kleenex	• www.kimberly-clark.com

Access the company's public website and search for its most recent annual report. (Some companies will provide access to their financial data through an "investor relations" link, while others will provide a direct link to their "annual reports.") After locating your company's most recent annual report, open the file and review its contents. After reviewing the annual report for your selected company, prepare answers to the following questions:

    a.   Identify whether the company is a retailer, a manufacturer, or a service provider.

    b.   Review the company's "Summary of Significant Accounting Principles." When does the company recognize its operating revenue? Can you identify an alternative method to recognize its operating revenue? If so, describe the alternative approach.

    c.   Review the company's balance sheet and related footnotes. Identify the gross accounts receivable and the allowance for uncollectible accounts for each of the last two years. Calculate the ratio of the allowance for uncollectible accounts divided by the gross accounts receivable for each of the last two years. Is this ratio increasing or decreasing? Why?

    d.   Calculate the company's receivable turnover and receivable collection period for each of the last two years. Is the receivable collection period increasing or decreasing? What might explain this increase or decrease?

    e.   Calculate the company's cash collections from sales for each of the last two years. Using this calculation, compute the company's cash conversion ratio (cash from sales divided by net sales). Is the cash conversion ratio increasing or decreasing? Is the cash conversion ratio at an acceptable level? Note that cash from sales is calculated as net sales plus/minus the change in accounts receivable plus/minus the change in unearned (or deferred) revenue. See Chapter 3.

CA5.32 **IFRS Financial Statements.** The 2014 financial statements of LVMH Moet Hennessey-Louis Vuitton   TA 2 S.A. are presented in Appendix C of this book. LVMH is a Paris-based holding company and one of the world's largest and best-known luxury goods companies. As a member-nation of the European Union, French companies are required to prepare their consolidated (group) financial statements using International Financial Reporting Standards (IFRS). Under IFRS, as is the case under U.S. GAAP, companies are required to disclose their accounting policies. In LVMH's Notes to the Consolidated Financial Statements (not presented in Appendix C), the company discloses its revenue recognition policy:

> Revenue mainly comprises retail sales within the Group's store network and sales through distributors. Sales made in stores owned by third parties are treated as retail transactions if the risks and rewards of ownership of the inventories are retained by the Group.
>
> Direct sales to customers are made through retail stores . . . (and) are recognized at the time of purchase by retail customers.
>
> Wholesale sales through distributors . . . (are recognized) when title transfers to third-party customers, generally on shipment.

Consider the following questions:

    a.   Describe LVMH's revenue recognition policy.

    b.   Contrast LVMH's revenue recognition policy with the policy that you would expect a retailer to use under U.S. GAAP.

CASE

LONE STAR POWER

Ward Johnson stared out the window. In the three months since he had assumed the role of chief investment officer at Lone Star Power, Johnson thought the company's communications with the investing public had been superb, particularly with respect to its SEC filings. A single letter from an apparently upset analyst had changed that view.

Lone Star Power was a midsize power generation and power distribution company based in the Southwest. It provided electrical power to more than 750,000 homes, businesses, and government agencies. In addition to power generation and distribution, Lone Star sold and installed a wide-ranging array of products, from appliances to power-generation backup systems. It also offered service and repairs to customers throughout its territory. Total revenues for the quarter ended December 31, 2016, had topped $1 billion for the first time. With only one exception, the company had managed to grow both revenues and profits in each quarter since 2000. Put in place in early 2014, the company's formal investor-relations function was relatively new. Prior to that, Lone Star had a small support staff that would send annual reports and similar literature in response to phone requests and handle other routine investor inquiries. In addition to his other duties, Johnson was expected to develop the investor-relations department in a way that would enhance Lone Star's standing with the investing community.

Marianne Relzo was a senior, all-star equity analyst with Pitt Financial, a well-regarded U.S. investment bank. In a letter to Johnson, Relzo detailed her discontent with the company's external financial communications. She complained about items as specific as Lone Star's financial-statement footnote disclosures and as general as the company's composite accounting policies. Johnson knew he would have to meet with Lone Star's senior financial staff and receive input as to whether these issues had merit and how he should respond. With a red pen in hand, he read the letter once again.

Pitt Financial Corporation
1607 Lower 5th Avenue
New York, NY 15003

February 23, 2017

Mr. Ward Johnson
Chief Financial Officer
Lone Star Power, Inc.
230 Lone Star Way
McCullian, Texas 78324

Dear Mr. Johnson:

I write this letter with some trepidation as it is usually not my style to openly question a company's financial reporting practices. My job, as you well know, is to objectively analyze a company through its public communications and to then state my conclusion regarding the merits of an investing strategy. I have followed your company for nearly five years and am increasingly concerned that your reported financial results do not reflect the actual underlying performance of your firm. Much of my concern comes from what was communicated through your company's most recent 10-K filing and from what I know to be trends in your business. Unfortunately, there were numerous areas of unnecessary ambiguity in your latest report.

Below are six specific examples I bring to your attention. These examples are chosen because they capture each of six items I find important in firms' financial reporting policies: (1) revenue recognition across periods, (2) consistent application of accounting policies, (3) cost allocation across periods, (4) classification of reported line items, (5) supplemental interpretive guidance from management, and (6) interim voluntary disclosures. I think you can understand that my reports are more favorable toward companies that meet a high standard of reporting on these dimensions, if for no other reason than I do not have to discount for significant uncertainties.

1. In your most recent 10-K your company's revenue recognition policy is described as "revenue is recognized based upon services rendered to customers during each accounting period." This is quite generic, of course, and I believe there are trends in your business that warrant elaboration.

    a. From your own segment disclosure, your Business Sales Division represents a large share of operations. Past conversations I have had with your staff reveal that a large chunk of the contracts in this division represent equipment sales, with the remainder ongoing service revenue contracted at the time of sale. This most recent quarter, conveniently, you have met your projected revenue growth of 4% for this segment, but I also note that accounts receivable have risen 25% over this time. I was hoping the MD&A would have provided some elaboration, but it merely listed these percentage changes.

    b. I know from conversations with some of your customers that in December there were significant discounts given for their prompt signing of a contract. Was there indeed a push-through of January 2017 contracts to boost 2016 revenue?

    c. I believe that in some cases the equipment portion of a contract with both an ongoing service component and an equipment sale was just a mere "pass-through sale" of the equipment (i.e., the equipment was delivered and installed by the third-party vendor of that equipment). How does Lone Star recognize revenue for pass-through equipment sales?

2. Your MD&A states that $52 million of assets were impaired during 2015 due to a lower than expected utility rate increase during 2014. Since these losses had such a material impact on operations, why didn't the company issue a press release or 8-K disclosure describing this event in a more timely fashion? In addition, what circumstances might have led to the impairment a full year after the rate effects were known?

3. Your accounting policy for marketing and promotions indicates these costs are "expensed as incurred." Incurred costs for these items are further provided by year as $25 million, $45 million, and $20 million for 2016, 2015, and 2014, respectively. I find it odd that for the year 2015 there was the spike in both expenses and cash outlays without much of a noticeable change in your promotional policies. I can find no evidence of these items being treated as prepaid assets. Are these amounts related to the large impairments taken in 2015?

continued

4. Do managers at the unit level have the ability to choose their own accounting policies? In the telecommunications industry, for instance, AT&T uses a group method, where the depreciation rate for a specific asset group is based on the average useful life for all assets in that group. This would avoid the unintended consequence of department managers manipulating profits by extending useful lives and decelerating depreciation charges. From prior conversations, I believe that when Lone Star acquires other companies it does not convert the acquired assets to a method consistent with existing assets. You recently merged with Texas Light and Gas. In a review of their financial statements just prior to the merger, I noticed they used different depreciation methods and lives than did Lone Star for similar assets. Now what is happening?

5. In response to a direct question during Lone Star's conference call, your CEO indicated that as of 2016 your company is now classifying all contract acquisition costs as an operating expense, as opposed to a net against top-line revenue. The argument made was that this would be consistent with industry disclosure practice. Why was this fact not addressed in your 10-K when revenue growth comparisons were made from 2015 to 2016?

6. During 2016 "net regulatory assets" increased by $75 million, the largest annual increase in the company's history. Since your operations were unaffected by acts of nature during 2016, and I know of no efficiency programs put into place during the year, how does one know that this asset growth is not the mere deferral of costs to a future period?

I am scheduled to issue a report on your company by March 1. I hope by then you can find the time to address my questions.

Sincerely,
Marianne C. Relzo
PFC Senior Vice President

Relzo's letter raised a number of issues for Johnson to consider. In the margins of the letter, he jotted notes regarding each one. From his experience, Johnson knew it was an analyst's objective to gather as much information about a company as possible. Regulation FD, however, defined the landscape regarding how he and other Lone Star officers should release information, but he was unsure what this implied regarding how he should deal with financial-reporting questions.

Johnson was not an accountant, and was not at all confident that he could articulate Lone Star's position on when revenues and expenses were recorded. On the expense side, in particular, he was perplexed as to why it was even an issue if the company were to negotiate a discount that required promotional fees to be paid in advance, charging net income when paid. By recording in this fashion, he thought Lone Star was only being conservative by accelerating a loss.

The company was also being questioned on its overall financial-reporting "transparency." Lone Star followed Generally Accepted Accounting Principles (GAAP) to the letter and filed timely reports with the SEC. Its financial statements were audited, and each major topic required in the Management Discussion and Analysis (MD&A) was dutifully disclosed. It seemed unreasonable to Johnson that the company be expected to provide real-time details on such items as negotiations with specific customers and write-offs of assets.

Required
1. What are Johnson's options regarding how he might respond to the issues raised by Relzo?
2. Items 1 and 3 deal specifically with revenue and expense recognition in the income statement. What principles and guidelines govern when and how each of these items should be recorded?
3. Relzo raises issues with the consistent application of accounting methods (item 4) and the consistent classification of certain line items (item 5). Do you think it is within the rights of a company to vary accounting methods and reclassify certain line items?

SOLUTIONS TO REVIEW PROBLEMS

Solution 5.1

1. Point-of-Sale

Month	Revenue	COGS
1	$3,000.00	$2,000.00
2	0	0
3	0	0
4	0	0
5	0	0
6	0	0
7	0	0
8	0	0
9	0	0
10	0	0
11	0	0
12	0	0
13	0	0
Total Recognized	$3,000.00	$2,000.00

2. Installment

Month	Revenue	COGS
1	$ 300.00	$ 200.00
2	225.00	150.00
3	225.00	150.00
4	225.00	150.00
5	225.00	150.00
6	225.00	150.00
7	225.00	150.00
8	225.00	150.00
9	225.00	150.00
10	225.00	150.00
11	225.00	150.00
12	225.00	150.00
13	225.00	150.00
Total Recognized	$3,000.00	$2,000.00

Solution 5.2

a. Cash basis:

(in millions)	2015	2016	2017	Total
Revenue	$180	$180	$360	$720
Less: Construction costs	144	144	192	480
Net income	$ 36	$ 36	$168	$240

b. Completed contract basis:

(in millions)	2015	2016	2017	Total
Revenue	$ 0	$ 0	$720	$720
Less: Construction costs	0	0	480	480
Net income	$ 0	$ 0	$240	$240

c. Percentage-of-completion basis:

(in millions)	2015	2016	2017	Total
Revenue	$216[1]	$216[1]	$288[2]	$720
Less: Construction costs	144	144	192	480
Net income.	$ 72	$ 72	$ 96	$240

[1] $720 million × 30% = $216 million.
[2] $720 million × 40% = $288 million.

Solution 5.3

1. Percentage-of-credit-sales method:

Bad debt expense	$800,000 × 0.02 = $16,000
Allowance for uncollectible accounts	$(16,000) + $(2,000) = $(18,000)

2. Aging method:

Period outstanding	Estimated Uncollectible	Outstanding Balance	Estimated Uncollectible
Current	0.4%	$220,000	$ 880
31–60 days	1.0%	120,000	1,200
61–90 days	5.0%	80,000	4,000
91–120 days	10.0%	20,000	2,000
Over 120 days	25.0%	40,000	10,000
Total		$480,000	$18,080

Allowance for uncollectible accounts	$18,080
Bad debt expense $18,080 − $(2,000) =	$16,080

Solution 5.4

1. *a.* Payment made August 7th:

Total sales.		$150,000
Sales discount	0.01 × $150,000 =	$ 1,500
Net sales.		$148,500

b. Payment made August 27th:

Total sales.	$150,000
Sales discount	$ 0
Net sales.	$150,000

2.

Total sales.	$1,200,000
Sales returns	$ 72,000
Net sales.	$1,128,000
Allowance for sales returns	$ 72,000

When you complete this chapter, you should be able to:

1. Describe how the initial cost of inventory is determined. (page 220)

2. Explain how inventory is measured using FIFO, LIFO, and the weighted-average cost method and how the resulting cost of goods sold is matched with revenue. (page 221)

3. Understand the mechanical differences between the different inventory valuation methods. (page 225)

4. Describe the conditions under which the lower-of-cost-or-market method is used to value ending inventory and how this method affects reported net income. (page 230)

5. Explain the LIFO reserve and how a LIFO inventory liquidation can increase a company's gross profit and net income. (page 232)

6. Identify the methods a company could use to minimize the costs associated with inventory management. (page 237)

7. Describe how accounts payable are valued and how the payment of these payables can be managed to positively impact a firm's operating cash flow. (page 237)

8. Explain the drawbacks to using LIFO and the due diligence procedures a professional should undertake to avoid misstatements. (page 240)

Operating Expenses, Inventory Valuation, and Accounts Payable

Ford Motor Company is the world's fifth largest automaker by sales, and second in the U.S. Founded in 1903 by Henry Ford and based in Dearborn, Michigan, Ford manufactures its cars and trucks on six continents under the primary brands of Ford and Lincoln. The company owns a small stake in the Mazda brand, but recently streamlined its business by selling the Volvo brand in 2010, the Jaguar and Land Rover brands in 2008, and discontinuing the Mercury line in 2011.

FORD MOTOR COMPANY

Ford is considered to be a capital-intensive company with a capital intensity ratio of 0.175—that is, the company's investment in property, plant and equipment and intangible assets represents 17.5 percent of total assets. Besides its significant investment in property, plant and equipment, Ford maintains a sizeable investment in inventory to service its worldwide network of dealers. Ford's investment in inventory represented approximately 3.8 percent of total assets in 2014 and 2013. A major challenge for Ford's management team is to keep its investment in inventory as low as possible without damaging its ability to effectively service its worldwide dealer network.

According to the company's 2014 annual report, Ford's investments in inventory totaled $7.9 and $7.7 billion for 2014 and 2013, respectively. The company's inventory turnover for these same fiscal years was 15.7 and 16.2 times, representing a slight increase in the days inventory on hand from 22.5 days in 2013 to 23.2 days in 2014. By way of comparison, **Toyota**'s, the recognized leader in efficiency in the industry, 2014 inventory turnover was 10.5, representing an inventory-on-hand period of over 34 days. For the industry as a whole, 2014 was a strong year overall. And for its part Ford was able to move its inventory relatively more quickly than the average auto company, even more so than the efficiency experts like Toyota.

In this chapter, we investigate the important accounting principle of matching and examine the various ways that companies like Ford can match the cost of manufacturing their inventory with the revenue produced when the inventory is sold. In the case of Ford, the company used the last-in, first-out (LIFO) method to account for 28 percent of its worldwide inventory and the first-in, first-out (FIFO) method to account for the remaining 72 percent.

EXECUTIVE
OUTLINE

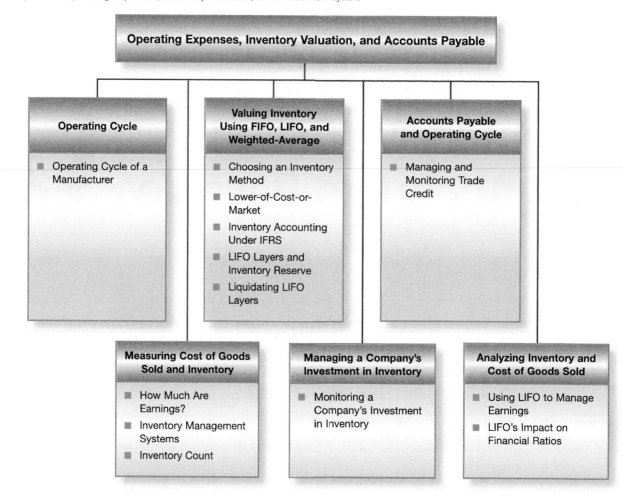

Operating Expenses, Inventory Valuation, and Accounts Payable

Operating Cycle

- Operating Cycle of a Manufacturer

Valuing Inventory Using FIFO, LIFO, and Weighted-Average

- Choosing an Inventory Method
- Lower-of-Cost-or-Market
- Inventory Accounting Under IFRS
- LIFO Layers and Inventory Reserve
- Liquidating LIFO Layers

Accounts Payable and Operating Cycle

- Managing and Monitoring Trade Credit

Measuring Cost of Goods Sold and Inventory

- How Much Are Earnings?
- Inventory Management Systems
- Inventory Count

Managing a Company's Investment in Inventory

- Monitoring a Company's Investment in Inventory

Analyzing Inventory and Cost of Goods Sold

- Using LIFO to Manage Earnings
- LIFO's Impact on Financial Ratios

OPERATING CYCLE OF A MANUFACTURER

eLectures

MBC

Takeaway 1
Describe how
the initial cost
of inventory is
determined.

Most businesses have an identifiable cycle of activities that reflect the day-to-day operations of the business. This cycle is known as its **operating cycle**. Exhibit 6.1, for instance, presents the operating cycle of a typical manufacturing company. In Chapter 5, we illustrated the operating cycle for a retail company (see Exhibit 5.1). In the case of a retailer, the company acquires inventory that is, for all practical purposes, ready for sale to its customers. Initially, the inventory is carried as an asset on the retailer's balance sheet, but upon its sale, the cost of the inventory is transferred from the balance sheet to cost of goods sold on the income statement, to be matched with the operating revenue produced by the sale. The inventory is subsequently replaced by cash, or an account receivable if sold on credit, on the balance sheet.

In the case of a manufacturing company, the operating cycle is more complex. A manufacturing company begins its operating cycle with the purchase of **raw material**, which then enters its production process. During the production process, the raw material is initially altered by the production-line workers and manufacturing equipment, yielding what is then known as **work-in-process inventory**. When the production process is finally complete, the ready-for-sale inventory is labeled **finished goods inventory**. As in the case of a retail company, the manufacturer's inventory (whether raw material, work-in-process, or finished goods inventory) is recognized as an asset on the balance sheet. When raw material enters the manufacturing process its value is transferred to the work-in-process inventory account. As work-in-process is completed, it is transferred to the finished goods account. Upon the sale of the finished goods inventory, the cost of the sold inventory is transferred to cost of goods sold on the income statement and replaced by cash or accounts receivable on the balance sheet.

Although retailers and manufacturers have clear differences in how they acquire inventory and get it ready for sale, an important commonality does exist in what amounts can be initially capitalized to the balance sheet as inventory. The fundamental rule-of-thumb is any cost necessary to get the inventory ready for sale should be capitalized. For retailers, this is the purchase price plus such other costs as taxes and shipping costs borne by the company. For manufacturers, the application of this concept is again much more complex. Consider the three stages of inventory represented above: raw materials, work-in-process, and finished goods. These themselves entail the acquisition of component parts (i.e., including raw materials) and the physical act of creating the final product (i.e., the work-in-process stage). Costs such as labor, depreciation on manufacturing equipment, and factory rent are all "necessary" to get the inventory ready for sale, and thus these costs become part of the inventory value recorded on the balance sheet. While the estimation of these amounts is a topic covered in depth with the study of *managerial* accounting, it is important to know how many different types of costs might be included in inventory when analyzing a company's financial reports.

In this chapter, we will focus on the operating cycle of two companies—Home Heating Oil Inc. and the Arizona Ice Cream Company Inc. We will see that one of the key **operating expenses** for each of these enterprises is cost of goods sold. In subsequent chapters, we will further consider some of the other typical operating expenses of such businesses—depreciation expense, employee compensation expense, interest expense, and income tax expense, among others.

EXHIBIT 6.1	Typical Business Operating Cycle of a Manufacturing Company

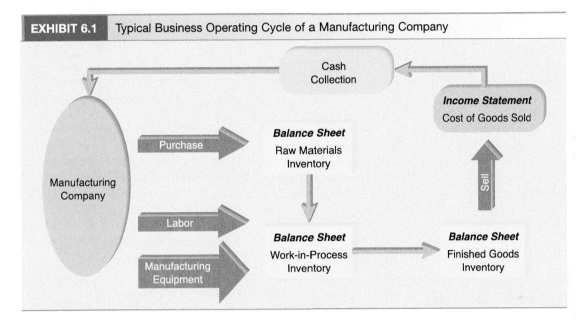

MEASURING COST OF GOODS SOLD AND ENDING INVENTORY

Inventory values on the balance sheet are charged to earnings in the period in which the inventory is sold. This is an example of the "matching" concept at work, wherein the effort (i.e., expense) is recorded in the same period during which any benefit is received by the company (i.e., revenue). We first introduced the matching concept in Chapter 1. When dealing with inventory, the charge matched against revenues is most commonly labeled "cost of goods sold"; and like its name suggests, what this account represents is the cost of the inventory that was sold to customers. The key to appreciating inventory accounting is that the "cost" in the term "cost of goods sold" is the amount that has been recorded on the balance sheet, nothing more and nothing less. This may sound simple enough on the surface, but in reality the measurement of cost of goods sold, and by default the value of inventory that remains on the balance sheet, is subject to numerous measurement issues. Consider the very frequent case when actual inventory items that a company owns for resale are physically identical, but the amounts that are recorded on the balance sheet vary greatly simply because of the timing of when they were purchased or manufactured. On the date one item is sold, how much is the value that needs to be recorded as the cost of that item? The revenue side is easy enough, the price paid by the consumer. But the cost of goods sold side must often be determined by assumption because the inventory records can contain many different cost values. And then how much is recorded as cost of goods sold on the income statement will determine how much remains as inventory on the balance sheet. Below we illustrate this point with a case illustration.

Takeaway 2
Explain how inventory is measured using FIFO, LIFO, and the weighted-average cost method and how the resulting cost of goods sold is matched with revenue.

Case Illustration: How Much are Earnings?

Home Heating Oil Inc. purchases heating oil from a major oil company and then resells and delivers the oil to its retail customers. The company began its first month of operations by acquiring one barrel of heating oil at a cost of $10 on January 1. It purchased another barrel of oil on January 12 for $16. On January 20, Home Heating sold one barrel for $25, by which time the wholesale price of heating oil had risen to $22 per barrel. This sequence of events is shown on the following timeline:

The chief executive officer (CEO) of Home Heating wondered exactly how much profit the company had made during the month of January and what value should be assigned to the barrel of oil that remained in inventory at the end of the month. After some review, the CEO concluded that there were four possible ways to think about the company's earnings and its remaining inventory. Applying the four possible approaches produced gross profit for the business that ranged from a high of $15 to a low of $3 and ending inventory valuations that ranged from $22 to $10 per barrel (see Exhibit 6.2). The CEO wondered if the company could choose any of the four methods. Method Four appeared to be the best choice for income tax purposes because taxable earnings would be only $3, whereas Method One would be more likely to impress the company's shareholders because earnings for the month would be $15.

EXHIBIT 6.2 Hypothetical Alternative Inventory Valuation Methods: Home Heating Oil Inc.				
	Method 1	**Method 2**	**Method 3**	**Method 4**
Income Statement				
Revenue	$25	$25	$25	$25
Cost of goods sold.	10	16	13	22
Gross profit.	$15	$ 9	$12	$ 3
Balance Sheet				
Inventory.	$16	$10	$13	$22
Summary of key inventory accounts:				
Cost of goods sold (on the income statement)	$10	$16	$13	$22
Inventory (on the balance sheet)	16	10	13	22
Total	$26	$26	$26	$44

To the CEO, the answer seemed clear: Use Method Four on the company's income tax return and Method One in the annual report to shareholders. That way Home Heating would pay low income taxes but report high earnings to its shareholders! The last idea sounded particularly appealing to the CEO whose year-end bonus was linked to reported earnings, and consequently, his personal income would be positively impacted.

Fortunately, Home Heating's chief financial officer (CFO) set the CEO straight about the constraints the company faced when selecting an inventory valuation method for the company's income tax return and when selecting a method for use in its audited financial reports to shareholders. Although Methods One, Two, and Three are acceptable under generally accepted accounting practice (GAAP) in the United States, Method

Four is not. Method Four—using the replacement cost to value inventory—could be used in some countries including Mexico, Australia, and the United Kingdom, but it was not allowable GAAP in the United States.[1]

The CFO informed Home Heating's CEO that Method One was known as **FIFO**—first-in, first-out—and as the name suggests, this approach assumes that the first units purchased are the first units sold, so Home Heating's cost of goods sold for January would be $10. The units remaining on hand are the units purchased more recently so the company's ending inventory would be $16, the cost of the last unit purchased on January 12. Method Two was known as **LIFO**—last-in, first-out. This method assumes that the units purchased most recently, the $16 unit purchased on January 12, are the first units sold. Hence, the unit in ending inventory would be the $10 unit purchased on January 1. Use of the LIFO method would result in reduced income taxes but there was a hitch—in the United States, the Internal Revenue Service requires businesses that use LIFO for income tax purposes to also use LIFO in the preparation of their audited financial reports to shareholders. This is known as the **LIFO conformity rule**. The CFO noted that this requirement would put a crimp in the CEO's desire to pay low taxes *and* report high earnings to shareholders. He would have to choose! LIFO also appeared to have the undesirable effect of reporting a low value for ending inventory ($10) on the balance sheet—a value that was considerably less than it would cost ($22) the business to buy a similar unit at the end of the month. Method Three, the **average cost method**, caused the unit sold and the unit in inventory to both be valued at $13, the average of the $10 and $16 purchase prices. Method Four, the **replacement cost method**, valued both the unit sold and the unit on hand at the inventory's replacement cost of $22.

> The **weighted-average cost method** differs from the average cost method in that each inventory price is weighted by the quantity of units purchased at a given price, whereas the average cost method calculates a simple average of the various inventory purchase prices without regard to the quantities purchased. The weighted-average cost method is widely regarded as being informationally superior to the average cost method, and consequently, is used by most firms not electing to adopt FIFO or LIFO. The weighted-average cost method is often simply referred to as the "average cost method" in many corporate financial reports.

Home Heating's CFO also informed the CEO that there was another option available to the company—the **specific identification method**. Under the specific identification method, if the CEO could identify exactly which barrel of heating oil was sold on January 20—the barrel purchased on January 1 or the barrel purchased on January 12—then the actual price of the identified barrel would be charged to cost of goods sold and the cost basis of the remaining barrel would also be known. Not surprisingly, the CEO could not clearly identify which barrel of oil was purchased on which date since the barrels were identical in appearance, content, and quality. Observing that the specific identification method was impractical for some companies, this option was discarded by both the CEO and CFO.

> The **specific identification method** tends to be used by manufacturers (such as Boeing) that produce a limited number of high-value products. For companies that produce in large volume, the additional record-keeping costs associated with this method are rarely justified.

After much debate, the CEO selected LIFO as the company's inventory valuation method. He decided that he would explain to shareholders that the operating cash flow saved by using LIFO for income tax purposes would enable the firm to pay more dividends, make additional investments in long-term assets, and reduce debt. That might keep the shareholders happy enough to pay him his bonus!

Inventory Management Systems

In addition to selecting an inventory valuation method, one of the decisions that must be made by a company like Home Heating Oil Inc. is the type of inventory management system that will be used to keep track of the inventory purchased, sold, and on hand. The choice involves two types of systems—periodic and perpetual.

As the name implies, a **periodic system** periodically updates such information as the cost and quantity of inventory on hand, but only when new goods are purchased and when a physical count of the on-hand inventory is undertaken. A periodic system presumes that management does not need minute-by-minute (or even daily) information regarding the quantity of inventory on hand or its cost. The deficiency of this system is that reliable information about a company's inventory available for sale is only periodically

---

[1] A key reporting convention followed under U.S. GAAP, and the GAAP of many other countries, is the **historical cost convention**, which stipulates that all assets be initially valued at their original or historical cost. Methods One, Two, and Three are consistent with this convention, whereas Method Four, which relies on the inventory's *future* replacement cost, is not. In addition, an inherent problem with Method Four, as can readily be seen, is that the total inventory purchases of $26 are not perfectly captured across the cost of goods sold and inventory accounts, and would necessitate recording a holding gain to increase the inventory balance to the replacement cost of $22.

available. For this reason, it is rarely used by well-run businesses because knowing how much inventory is available for sale is important for managers who try to provide the best possible service to their customers.

A **perpetual system**, on the other hand, updates a firm's inventory data after every purchase *and* every sale, providing a constant source of reliable information about the cost and quantity of goods available for sale. Perpetual systems are informationally superior to periodic inventory systems, but they are also more complex to implement. In today's competitive marketplace and with recent technological innovations, however, even small companies are now realizing the benefits of a perpetual system given the low cost of inventory management software.

A good way to understand the strengths and weaknesses of each inventory management system is by considering some illustrative inventory data. Assume that Home Heating Oil Inc. experienced the following events:

January 1	Purchased 100 barrels of oil at $10 per barrel, for a total expenditure of $1,000.
January 3	Sold 50 barrels at $15 per barrel, for a total sale of $750.
January 15	Purchased 100 barrels at $13 per barrel, for a total expenditure of $1,300.
January 20	Sold 125 barrels at $15 per barrel, for a total sale of $1,875.
January 30	Physically counted the available inventory, determining that 25 barrels were on hand.

Under a periodic system, the managers of Home Heating would not know exactly how many barrels of oil were on hand and available for sale until January 30, following a physical count of the inventory. Although a periodic system does capture information concerning units purchased, it does not record the cost of the sold units until a physical count of the inventory on hand verifies the quantity actually available. Thus, a periodic system records the quantities added to inventory on January 1 and January 15, but does not record the quantities removed from inventory on January 3 and January 20 until a physical count is executed on January 30. Hence, if an additional order for 30 barrels had been received on January 22 for delivery on January 25, Home Heating's managers would not have had the necessary information from the financial statement ledgers to know whether the company could satisfy the order because the inventory accounts had not been updated.

Under a perpetual system, however, the quantity of on-hand inventory is updated after every purchase and sale transaction. Thus, the system constantly provides current information about the quantity and cost of goods available for sale. Under a perpetual system, if an additional order for 30 barrels were received on January 22, Home Heating's manager could easily access the inventory management system to verify that the quantity on hand was insufficient to service the order. In this case, Home Heating's managers would find that there were only 25 barrels on hand, and thus, that five more barrels would first need to be ordered.

The Inventory Count

Even though a perpetual system provides up-to-the-minute information regarding inventory quantities, it is still important for a company to periodically physically count its inventory on hand. Almost all types of inventory are subject to damage, deterioration, and theft, and a physical count is the best way to identify the existence and magnitude of these problems.[2] In fact, GAAP requires that a physical inventory count by taken at least once a year so as to ensure the integrity of the inventory balances recorded on the financial statements. A physical inventory count serves as the basis to determine the quantity and value of ending inventory, along with the cost of goods sold for firms utilizing a periodic inventory system. In addition, the inventory count serves as a confirmation of the ending inventory balance for firms employing a perpetual inventory system. If the inventory value computed from the physical count differs from the inventory records maintained under the perpetual system, the company will adjust its records to match the physical count.

It should be noted that any amount needed to adjust ending inventory will affect not only inventory on the balance sheet but also cost of goods sold, and therefore net income on the income statement. Consider the case of the Watermark Company, a retail hardware store. Watermark Company maintains

[2] Retailers like Dillard's, Nordstrom's, and The Home Depot typically do a physical count of their merchandise inventory at least once a year, and more commonly, twice a year. To avoid interrupting normal daily sales activities, physical counts are usually executed at night, after store closing hours.

a perpetual inventory system and shows an ending inventory balance of $2,550 as of December 31. A physical count of the inventory on December 31, however, reveals that the actual inventory on hand is only $2,325, perhaps due to inventory breakage or theft. To recognize the inventory loss, it is necessary to enter a charge of $225 to cost of goods sold and a reduction of $225 to inventory (see the company's spreadsheet below). Note that this adjustment affects not only income in the current year—a reduction of $225—but will also affect earnings and inventory in the following year. This results because the ending inventory of $2,325 in the current year becomes the beginning inventory in the following year.

Watermark Company Spreadsheet			
	Balance Before Count	Inventory Count Adjustment	Ending Balance
Assets			—
Inventory	2,550	(225)	2,325
Shareholders' Equity			
Retained earnings:			
Cost of goods sold		(225)	(225)

The adjustments to cost of goods sold and inventory can be best understood by considering the following basic computation of cost of goods sold. This representation describing the relation between ending inventory, purchases, and cost of goods sold, is also useful when analyzing the balances in inventory accounts. The partition of inventory expenditures between the inventory account and the cost of goods sold is as follows:

Computation of Cost of Goods Sold
Beginning inventory
+ Purchases
= Goods available for sale
− Ending inventory
= Cost of goods sold

As can be seen from this basic formula, goods available for sale are partitioned into either ending inventory, an asset on the balance sheet, or cost of goods sold, an expense on the income statement. If the ending inventory balance is erroneously too high (low), then cost of goods sold will be erroneously too low (high). Further, ending inventory in one year becomes the beginning inventory for the next year. Since goods available for sale includes beginning inventory, any error in the previous year would be carried forward and would result in an error in cost of goods sold of equal magnitude, but opposite direction, the following year. For these reasons, periodic and accurate physical counts of inventory are an essential part of the financial accounting process.

VALUING INVENTORY USING FIFO, LIFO, AND WEIGHTED-AVERAGE—A CLOSER LOOK

The choice of inventory valuation method can yield vastly different amounts on the income statement and balance sheet, even though economically a company and its physical inventory are not any different regardless of the method chosen. From both a management and financial analysis perspective it is important to understand the mechanical differences that exist between these methods even though computers (or accountants) will keep track of the calculations. To illustrate these mechanics, we use a new set of facts.

Arizona Ice Cream Company (AICC) sells ice cream in large order sizes in Phoenix, Arizona. The current year is the company's first year of operations. The retail sales price of a ten-gallon bucket of ice cream is $20. The company has a sophisticated bar code scanner system that enables the company to operate a perpetual inventory system in each of its ten retail outlets. When ice cream is sold to a customer at one of its stores, the inventory system automatically updates the company's inventory records. It also sends a purchase order to a supplier when inventories fall to predetermined levels. The system records the cost of goods

Takeaway 3
Understand the mechanical differences between the different inventory valuation methods.

In Practice 6.1 *Income Statement Caption: A Glimpse of a Sample of Fortune 1000 Companies* The following table identifies the caption for cost of goods sold used on the income statement for a sample of 600 Fortune 1000 companies. The preferred label is "cost of sales:"

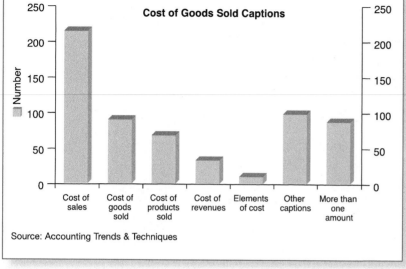

Cost of Goods Sold Captions

Source: Accounting Trends & Techniques

sold based on the specific inventory method the company uses, although AICC has not decided whether to use FIFO, LIFO, or the weighted-average cost method.

During the year, AICC made purchases of ice cream on September 5, October 22, November 15, and December 30 at prices that ranged from $10 to $15 per bucket. AICC purchased a total of 10,000 buckets of ice cream at an aggregate cost of $128,500. AICC also sold inventory on September 20, November 4, December 22, and December 31. Over these four dates total sales amounted to $160,000 (8,000 buckets at $20 per bucket). The two crucial financial accounting questions then become: How much profit did AICC make on its sales? And what was the value of its ending inventory? What you should first understand before these questions are answered is that the inventory balance on the balance sheet must be based on the 2,000 buckets remaining on hand and the cost of goods sold on

the income statement must be based on 8,000 buckets actually sold. The values that are assigned to these accounts reflect the decision that management must make when selecting an inventory accounting method. Under each possible method, there is a presumptive matching of cost of goods sold with revenue, but the profits determined under each approach are quite different.

If AICC uses FIFO to value its inventory, the results under a perpetual system would appear as presented in Exhibit 6.3. (We suggest that you work through the values in the columns labeled "FIFO Cost of Goods Sold" and "FIFO Ending Inventory" in Exhibit 6.3 to ensure that you understand how these values are calculated.) Using the FIFO perpetual method, AICC's cost of goods sold is $98,500, and gross profit is $61,500 ($160,000 − $98,500). Thus, the value of the 2,000 buckets of ice cream remaining in inventory for future sale is $30,000 ($128,500 − $98,500).

EXHIBIT 6.3	Valuing Inventory and Cost of Goods Sold using FIFO					
Date	Purchases (# buckets)	Purchase Price (per bucket)	Total Cost	Sales (# buckets)	FIFO Cost of Goods Sold	FIFO Ending Inventory
Sep 5	1,000	$10	$ 10,000			1,000 @ $10
Sep 20 ...				800	800 @ $10 $ 8,000	200 @ $10
Oct 22....	2,500	12	30,000			200 @ $10
						2,500 @ $12
Nov 4				2,600	200 @ $10 30,800	100 @ $12
					2,400 @ $12	
Nov 15 ...	4,500	13	58,500			100 @ $12
						4,500 @ $13
Dec 22 ...				3,400	100 @ $12 44,100	1,200 @ $13
					3,300 @ $13	
Dec 30 ...	2,000	15	30,000			1,200 @ $13
						2,000 @ $15
Dec 31 ...				1,200	1,200 @ $13 15,600	2,000 @ $15
Total	10,000		$128,500	8,000	$98,500	$30,000

If, on the other hand, AICC uses LIFO, the results under a perpetual system would appear as presented in Exhibit 6.4. Under the LIFO perpetual method, AICC's cost of goods sold is $101,200, and gross profit is $58,800 ($160,000 − $101,200). The value of the 2,000 buckets of ice cream remaining in inventory for future sale is $27,300 ($128,500 − $101,200).

The operating revenue that AICC would recognize from selling 8,000 buckets at $20 per bucket is $160,000 regardless of whether the company uses FIFO or LIFO. However, the cost of goods sold under FIFO and LIFO varies ($98,500 versus $101,200, respectively) as a consequence of the different inventory cost flow assumptions that characterize FIFO and LIFO. As a result, AICC's gross profit varies under the different inventory methods, as follows:

Income Statement Summary		FIFO	LIFO
Revenue.		$160,000	$160,000
Cost of goods sold.		(98,500)	(101,200)
Gross profit.		$ 61,500	$ 58,800

EXHIBIT 6.4	Valuing Inventory and Cost of Goods Sold using LIFO

Date	Purchases (# buckets)	Purchase Price (per bucket)	Total Cost	Sales (# buckets)	LIFO Cost of Goods Sold		LIFO Ending Inventory
Sep 5	1,000	$10	$ 10,000				1,000 @ $10
Sep 20 . . .				800	800 @ $10	$ 8,000	200 @ $10
Oct 22. . . .	2,500	12	30,000				2,500 @ $12
							200 @ $10
Nov 4				2,600	2,500 @ $12	31,000	100 @ $10
					100 @ $10		
Nov 15 . . .	4,500	13	58,500				4,500 @ $13
							100 @ $10
Dec 22 . . .				3,400	3,400 @ $13	44,200	1,100 @ $13
							100 @ $10
Dec 30 . . .	2,000	15	30,000				2,000 @ $15
							1,100 @ $13
							100 @ $10
Dec 31 . . .				1,200	1,200 @ $15	18,000	800 @ $15
							1,100 @ $13
							100 @ $10
Total	10,000		$128,500	8,000		$101,200	$27,300

Similarly, even though the quantity of inventory on hand for AICC is the same at the end of the year (2,000 buckets), the reported value of the ending inventory under FIFO versus LIFO varies ($30,000 and $27,300, respectively):

Balance Sheet Summary	Units	FIFO $	LIFO $	Difference
Beginning inventory	0	$ 0	$ 0	$ 0
Purchases.	10,000	128,500	128,500	0
Available for sale	10,000	128,500	128,500	0
Cost of goods sold.	(8,000)	(98,500)	(101,200)	(2,700)
Ending inventory.	2,000	$ 30,000	$ 27,300	$2,700

The gross profit for Arizona Ice Cream Company is highest under FIFO and lowest under LIFO. This outcome will occur when the cost of inventory is increasing. In this instance, the cost of AICC's inventory purchases increased from $10 to $12 to $13 per bucket, and finally to $15 per bucket. If, on the other hand, inventory costs are decreasing, LIFO will yield the highest gross profit and FIFO the lowest. If prices are perfectly stable, there will be no difference in the cost of goods sold or ending inventory under any of the methods.

But what if AICC decided to use the weighted-average cost method instead?[3] The results for the weighted-average cost method under a perpetual system are presented in Exhibit 6.5. Under this approach, AICC's cost of goods sold is $100,018, about midway between the cost of goods sold under FIFO and LIFO. The value of AICC's ending inventory is $28,482, again about midway between the value of ending inventory under FIFO and ending inventory under LIFO. Finally, gross profit is $59,982, about midway between FIFO gross profit of $61,500 and LIFO gross profit of $58,800. (Were you able to verify each of these figures by working through the two right-most columns of Exhibits 6.3, 6.4, and 6.5?) In essence, while FIFO and LIFO yield values representing the ends of a continuum, the weighted-average cost method yields results that fall somewhere within that continuum.[4]

EXHIBIT 6.5	Valuing Inventory and Cost of Goods Sold using Weighted-Average					
Date	Purchases (# buckets)	Purchase Price (per bucket)	Total Cost	Sales (# buckets)	Weighted-Average Cost of Goods Sold	Weighted-Average Ending Inventory
Sep 5	1,000	$10	$ 10,000			1,000 @ $10
Sep 20 . . .				800	800 @ $10 $ 8,000	200 @ $10
Oct 22. . . .	2,500	$12	30,000			2,700 @ $11.852[a]
Nov 4				2,600	2,600 @ $11.852 30,815	100 @ $11.852
Nov 15 . . .	4,500	$13	58,500			4,600 @ $12.975[b]
Dec 22 . . .				3,400	3,400 @ $12.975 44,115	1,200 @ $12.975
Dec 30 . . .	2,000	$15	30,000			3,200 @ $14.241[c]
Dec 31 . . .				1,200	1,200 @ $14.241 17,089	2,000 @ $14.241
Total.	10,000		$128,500	8,000	$100,018[d]	$28,482

a. [(200 × $10) + (2,500 × $12)]/2,700 = $11.852
b. [(100 × $11.852) + (4,500 × $13)]/4,600 = $12.975
c. [(1,200 × $12.975) + (2,000 × $15)]/3,200 = $14.241
d. rounding difference

Choosing an Inventory Method

With the diversity of cost of goods sold and ending inventory values provided under FIFO, LIFO, and the weighted-average cost method, how do managers decide which method is "best" for their company? In many cases, the inventory method decision is driven by the prevailing industry standard. For instance, the industry standard in the United States' automobile industry is LIFO; and thus, investment professionals expect to observe car and truck manufacturers using this inventory valuation method. If they observed otherwise, it might be a "red flag" raising concern about a company's reported financial results.

In some companies, the inventory method decision is linked to the physical flow of inventory through the business. Companies that supply perishable food products to hotels and restaurants, for example, frequently use FIFO. It is noteworthy, however, that it is not a requirement that the selected inventory method reflect the actual flow of goods through a business. A supermarket selling perishable food products can use LIFO or the weighted-average cost method even though store managers encourage customers to buy on a FIFO basis to minimize losses associated with food spoilage. The prevailing economic environment is also a contributing factor to the inventory method decision. In inflationary environments, LIFO is preferred over FIFO because it more effectively matches inflated selling prices with inflated inventory costs. Finally, for some firms, the inventory method selection is driven by a desire to report higher (or lower) earnings. For companies desiring to report the highest level of reported income, the FIFO method is often selected, at least when inventory costs are increasing. On the other hand, for firms desiring to

---

[3] The CEO and CFO decided that use of the specific identification method by Arizona Ice Cream Company, Inc., was not practical since the appearance, content, and quality of the buckets of ice cream were indistinguishable, and in any case, the additional record-keeping cost associated with the specific identification method did not appear justified.

[4] Worth noting is that as a company ages, weighted-average more closely approximates FIFO inventory balances rather than LIFO inventory balances. The reason for this is that LIFO inventory will always contain values from the first inventory units acquired, while FIFO by definition eliminates those units first. Thus, as long as a company acquires and sells its inventory at a reasonable pace, the weighted average methodology will place less weight on very old purchases, and more weight on more recent purchases, resulting in a closer approximation to FIFO relative to LIFO.

constrain the level of reported (or taxable) earnings, the LIFO method is often adopted.

Once a company has selected a particular inventory valuation method, does the company have to use that same method for all of its inventories? No. Companies that manufacture and/or sell multiple products may choose to use LIFO for one product, FIFO for another, and weighted-average for a third, although this is rarely done. Recall that at the beginning of this

> An important principle of accounting is the **consistency principle**, which stipulates that whenever possible, a business should utilize a consistent set of accounting policies from one fiscal period to the next. When companies change their accounting policies (such as a LIFO to FIFO switch), the analysis of financial statements is adversely impacted because a change in accounting policy is likely to induce variance in the reported accounting numbers unrelated to a firm's actual performance. For this reason, voluntary corporate accounting policy changes are widely regarded as a "red flag" by investment professionals.

chapter, Ford Motor Company disclosed that it used LIFO to account for 28 percent of its worldwide inventories, with the remainder accounted for using FIFO. Can a company change its method of inventory valuation? Under certain circumstances, yes, it can. GAAP provides companies with considerable flexibility. Not only can a company choose between different inventory valuation methods (FIFO, LIFO, specific identification, and weighted-average cost), but GAAP permits a LIFO company, for example, to switch to FIFO. Companies are encouraged, however, to be consistent from year to year in the accounting methods they apply in their financial reporting. Companies are allowed to switch methods if they can justify why a switch will provide a more meaningful financial statement presentation. Changing inventory valuation methods, however, is often viewed as a "red flag" by investment professionals who worry that such voluntary accounting policy changes may be motivated more by a desire to manage earnings than to use the most appropriate accounting method. In addition, the Internal Revenue Service, under Revenue procedure 92–20, requires taxpayers who have changed from LIFO to another method to wait five years before readopting LIFO unless extraordinary circumstances can be shown.

In Practice 6.2 *Inventory Method: A Glimpse of a Sample of Fortune 1000 Companies* The following table identifies the inventory methods used by a sample of 500 Fortune 1000 companies. Also shown for the LIFO firms is the extent of LIFO usage. The FIFO method was predominantly used by the sampled firms:

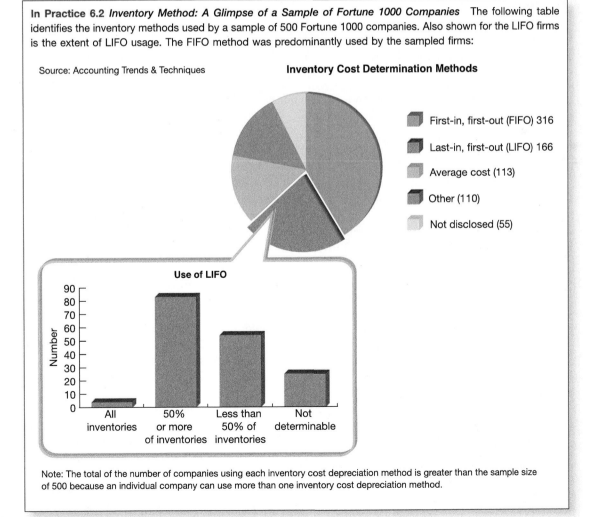

Source: Accounting Trends & Techniques

Inventory Cost Determination Methods

- First-in, first-out (FIFO) 316
- Last-in, first-out (LIFO) 166
- Average cost (113)
- Other (110)
- Not disclosed (55)

Use of LIFO

Note: The total of the number of companies using each inventory cost depreciation method is greater than the sample size of 500 because an individual company can use more than one inventory cost depreciation method.

REVIEW PROBLEM 6.1

The Arcadia Company is uncertain whether it should utilize the first-in, first-out (FIFO) method, the last-in, first-out (LIFO) method, or the weighted-average method to account for its inventory. The company's controller decided that she would compare the financial results under the three approaches as a way to reach a decision regarding which method to adopt. Data for the first two months of operations were as follows:

		Units	Unit Cost	Total
January				
Beginning inventory		6,000	$2.00	$ 12,000
Purchases:	Jan. 5	10,300	2.00	20,600
	Jan. 20	29,300	2.10	61,530
				$ 94,130
Sales:	Jan. 25	38,400		
February				
Beginning inventory		7,200		
Purchases:	Feb. 8	28,200	2.20	$ 62,040
	Feb. 23	15,300	2.60	39,780
				$101,820
Sales:	Feb. 27	40,700		
Ending inventory		10,000		

Required

a. Calculate the cost of goods sold for January and February for The Arcadia Company using FIFO, LIFO, and weighted-average methods.

b. Assume that revenue for the two-month period totaled $300,000. What inventory valuation method would you recommend that the company adopt? Why?

The solution is on pages 257–258.

Lower-of-Cost-or-Market (LCM)

Takeaway 4
Describe the conditions under which the lower-of-cost-or-market method is used to value ending inventory and how this method affects reported net income.

Under U.S. GAAP and IFRS, companies are required to ensure that the value of ending inventory carried on the balance sheet is recorded at an amount that does not exceed its current replacement cost. This reflects the desire to ensure that asset values are never overstated (although they are sometimes understated, for example as a consequence of the use of the historical cost convention). Under this practice, if the current replacement cost of inventory is less than its recorded book value, the company must write the value of its inventory down to its lower replacement cost. If, however, the replacement cost is higher than its recorded book value, the inventory is not written up to the higher value but remains valued at its cost. This convention is called the **lower-of-cost-or-market (LCM) method** and is an excellent illustration of the general conservative bias of financial accounting—losses on inventory are recognized immediately, even if the inventory is unsold, but gains are not. The practice of using the LCM method has a long history in the United States. In its 1921 annual report, General Motors announced that the company had written down its inventory by almost $17 million, to $109 million. Interestingly, by way of contrast, General Motors's December 31, 2014 inventory balance was valued at over $13.6 billion.

To illustrate the application of the LCM method, assume that AICC's CFO determined that the replacement cost of the company's ice cream was $14 per bucket at year-end. With 2,000 buckets in inventory, the replacement cost of AICC's inventory at December 31 would be $28,000 ($14 × 2,000).

> The LCM method reflects the **conservatism principle** of accounting, namely that losses should be recognized as soon as they are identified (even if unrealized), whereas gains should be recognized only after they are realized.

If AICC used FIFO, the LCM convention would require the company to write its ending inventory down by $2,000 ($30,000 less $28,000). No write-down would be required if AICC used

LIFO because its ending inventory would be stated at its LIFO cost of $27,300, which is lower than its replacement cost of $28,000. AICC's application of LCM under FIFO is demonstrated as follows:

Arizona Ice Cream Company Spreadsheet			
	Balance Before Count	**LCM Adjustment**	**End. Bal.**
Assets			
Inventory.	30,000	(2,000)	28,000
Shareholders' Equity			
Retained Earnings:			
Cost of Goods Sold		(2,000)	(2,000)

When an end-of-period write-down of inventory is necessary, as illustrated above, the adjustment is usually recorded as a component of cost of goods sold on the income statement; that is, both inventory and retained earnings are reduced by the amount of the LCM write-down, with the charge to retained earnings recorded as costs of goods sold on the income statement. If the amount of the write-down is material in amount, however, management often chooses to disclose the inventory write-down on the income statement as a separate line item (such as "loss on inventory write-down") so as to inform a user of the financial statements about all relevant detail pertaining to inventory-related charges.

One consequence of the LCM method is that while the immediate financial statement effect of an inventory write-down is to reduce current earnings by the amount of the inventory write-down, the effect in the future may be inflated earnings. For example, if AICC maintains its selling price of $20 per bucket, the LCM adjustment will lower current profit by $2,000, but raise future profit by the same amount when the inventory on hand is ultimately sold. In effect, the application of the LCM method may cause a shift in the profit on some sales from one period to the next.

TAX PERSPECTIVE

Inventory Accounting Under U.S. Tax Law

Inventory accounting rules specified by the U.S. Internal Revenue Service generally follow the same fundamental principles as U.S. GAAP but with two important exceptions. First, like U.S. GAAP, the amounts included in inventory for tax purposes must comprise all costs necessary to get the inventory ready for sale, and these costs generally may not be expensed until the inventory is sold. Uniform cost capitalization rules (UNICAP) under the Internal Revenue Code, however, provide for an expanded definition of which costs must be capitalized. Specifically, UNICAP requires that costs incurred that are not directly tied to production but that provide support for the production process, such as purchasing costs, technology, and general administrative costs, must be capitalized as inventory. As a consequence, the deferral of these additional costs to inventory delays the cash inflow from the tax deductibility of those costs.

Second, consistent with U.S. GAAP, a cost flow method must be determined and consistently applied for tax purposes. Valid methods include LIFO, FIFO, average cost and specific identification. The incentives with respect to the tax method choice, however, are almost always focused on minimizing current taxes due. Therefore, LIFO tends to be the preferred method for tax purposes as the expense deduction for cost of goods sold will typically be higher, and therefore, taxable income lower.

When inventory costs are rising, as is usually the case, management would obtain the optimal outcome by choosing FIFO for financial reporting (higher income) and LIFO for tax reporting (lower income). Referring back to Exhibits 6.3 and 6.4, notice the difference between the cost of goods sold reported by AICC under LIFO versus FIFO. LIFO was $2,700 higher, which would result in a lower tax bill. Recognizing the implicit motivation most managers would have to choose LIFO over FIFO, tax authorities require that companies use LIFO as a chosen tax method only if they also do so for financial reporting purposes. This requirement is called the **LIFO conformity rule**, and it has significantly limited the use of LIFO for tax purposes.

REVIEW PROBLEM 6.2

The Rock Creek Company has an ending inventory valuation using FIFO of $350,000. Had the company used LIFO the inventory would have been valued at $320,000. The company has determined the replacement cost of the inventory to be $325,000.

Required

Calculate the amount of any lower-of-cost-or-market adjustment that The Rock Creek Company will require.

The solution is on page 258.

Inventory Accounting Under International Financial Reporting Standards

The accounting for inventory under U.S. GAAP and IFRS differs in three significant ways. First and most important, IFRS does not permit the use of the LIFO method. The very old values of inventory resulting from LIFO accounting are perceived to reduce the relevance of the balance sheet to such a degree that under IFRS the method is deemed invalid. In Practice 6.2 reveals, however, that a significant percentage of companies in the United States use LIFO to account for at least a portion of their inventories. This means that analysts making comparisons of a U.S. company to one following IFRS would need to pay particularly close attention to the inventory method used. Further complicating the analysis is that the restriction of LIFO under IFRS puts companies desiring to switch to IFRS in a potentially unfavorable tax position. Given the LIFO conformity rule in the U.S., if a company were not to use LIFO for financial accounting purposes, the tax authorities would then require a switch to FIFO, potentially resulting in a significant tax increase.

A second critical inventory accounting difference between U.S. GAAP and IFRS relates to the method choice when there are various inventory product lines used by a company. Under U.S. GAAP a company may use multiple inventory methods to value inventory, regardless of the type of inventory under consideration. Under IFRS, however, a single inventory method must be used for inventory that is similar in nature or use. This does not preclude the use of multiple methods by an IFRS company, but only when the inventory is of a sufficiently different type. Finally, lower-of-cost-or-market (LCM) differs between the two systems. Under U.S. GAAP, "market" for purposes of applying LCM is generally defined as the inventory's net replacement value. Under IFRS, "market" is defined as the inventory's net realizable value which often approximates fair market value. Also, while U.S. GAAP only allows inventory to be written down under LCM when the inventory's replacement cost falls below its recorded cost, IFRS permits inventory to be written back up to the amount of the original write-down. Any write up in value above the book value of inventory is also added to a shareholders' equity account called the revaluation reserve. In essence, LCM under U.S. GAAP is a "one-way street," but under IFRS, it is a "two-way street" wherein both inventory value declines and (reversing) increases may be recognized.

Beyond the codified requirements under IFRS, in some countries the inventory method decision is further constrained by the allowable generally accepted business practices. For instance, the operating environment faced by a business frequently drives the inventory method decision. In Japan, for example, auto and truck manufacturers use FIFO because this industry has been able to implement just-in-time (JIT) inventory management techniques. For companies able to operate in a "lean manufacturing" environment, the inventory method decision has little impact on reported results because the required investment in inventory is kept to a minimum. In countries whose economies are characterized by high rates of inflation, several variants of LIFO may also be GAAP: **HIFO, highest-in, first-out**, and **NIFO, next-in, first-out**. Neither HIFO nor NIFO is acceptable under U.S. GAAP.

Takeaway 5
Explain the LIFO reserve and how a LIFO inventory liquidation can increase a company's gross profit and net income.

LIFO LAYERS AND THE LIFO INVENTORY RESERVE

As noted above, the value of AICC's ending inventory is highest under FIFO and lowest under LIFO because the cost of inventory purchases is increasing. Comparing the calculated cost basis of AICC's ending inventory on December 31 under the two methods reveals the following:

LIFO Ending Inventory	FIFO Ending Inventory
100 @ $10	
1,100 @ $13	
800 @ $15	2,000 @ $15
$27,300	$30,000

These figures illustrate that the entire FIFO ending inventory is valued at the most recent purchase price of $15 per bucket, whereas less than half of the LIFO inventory is valued at $15 per bucket. The LIFO ending inventory reflects a blend of purchase prices—100 buckets at $10, 1,100 buckets at $13, and 800 buckets at $15. These differing prices are referred to as **LIFO layers** and AICC has three such layers. Since the LIFO method assumes that the most recently purchased inventory is the first inventory to be sold, it is not unusual for a company like AICC to have multiple LIFO layers, often reflecting prices from several prior fiscal periods. As a consequence, when inflation is present, the value of ending inventory under LIFO may be much lower than its current replacement cost or its FIFO cost. For this reason many users of financial statements consider FIFO to yield more relevant inventory values on the balance sheet than LIFO.

Concerned that the LIFO method may produce misleading ending inventory values—that is, that the ending inventory (and hence, current assets) under LIFO may be materially undervalued relative to its current replacement value, and consequently, that comparability with non-LIFO firms may be impaired—accounting standard-setters require that companies using LIFO disclose the value of the **inventory reserve**, often called the **LIFO reserve**, in their footnotes. The inventory reserve is a measure of the difference ($2,700) between the FIFO cost of ending inventory ($30,000) and the LIFO cost of its ending inventory ($27,300). The disclosure of the inventory reserve in a company's footnotes is important because it enables financial statement users to use that value to determine a more current value of LIFO ending inventory by simply adding the value of the reserve ($2,700) to the value of the reported LIFO ending inventory. Notice that adding the inventory reserve to the value of LIFO ending inventory effectively restates the value of the ending inventory from the LIFO method to the FIFO method.

Disclosure of the inventory reserve is significant because it enables investment professionals to restate AICC's gross profit under LIFO ($58,800) to estimate what gross profit would have been had FIFO ($61,500) been used instead. The inventory reserve is a cumulative measure of the difference between the LIFO cost of ending inventory and the FIFO cost of ending inventory. This amount may accumulate over multiple periods as prices rise and as a company maintains certain minimum quantities of inventory on hand to service the needs of its customers. It is possible to disaggregate this accumulated amount on a period-by-period basis by calculating the change in the reserve from one period to the next. The change in the value of the inventory reserve from one fiscal period to the next is a good estimate of the difference between LIFO cost of goods sold and FIFO cost of goods sold on a period-by-period basis. Thus, adding the **change in the inventory reserve** to the LIFO gross profit yields an estimate of FIFO gross profit:[5]

Gross profit under LIFO	$58,800
Add: increase in inventory reserve ($2,700 − $0)	2,700
Gross profit under FIFO	**$61,500**

The restatement of the balance sheet and income statement amounts reported under LIFO to their as-if estimates under FIFO can be summarized with the following two formulas:

LIFO Inventory + LIFO Reserve = FIFO Inventory

LIFO Cost of Goods Sold − Change in LIFO Reserve = FIFO Cost of Goods Sold

Following is an excerpt of the inventory footnote disclosure for heavy equipment manufacturer **Caterpillar Inc.** that includes information about the company's LIFO reserve. Note in the first paragraph that

---

[5] If the inventory reserve decreases (increases) during the period, it is necessary to subtract (add) the decrease (increase) from the LIFO gross profit to compute FIFO gross profit.

the company indicates that for the year 2014 about 60 percent of its total inventory was valued using LIFO. This implies the remaining 40 percent was based on some other method (i.e., FIFO or average cost), a feature not unusual for companies with multiple types of inventory. The 2014 LIFO reserve for Caterpillar was $2.430 billion dollars, a decline from previous years' values of $2.504 billion and $2.750 billion.

> ***Summary of Significant Accounting Policies***: Caterpillar 2014 Annual Report
> Inventories are stated at the lower of cost or market. Cost is principally determined using the last-in, first-out (LIFO) method. The value of inventories on the LIFO basis represented about 60 percent of total inventories at December 31, 2014, 2013 and 2012.
>   If the FIFO (first-in, first-out) method had been in use, inventories would have been $2,430 million, $2,504 million and $2,750 million higher than reported at December 31, 2014, 2013 and 2012, respectively.

To illustrate the potential differences in magnitude of ending inventory values that can result under LIFO, In Practice 6.3 presents inventory data for the twenty U.S. companies having the largest LIFO inventory reserves. Consider again, for example, Caterpillar Inc. (see **bolded** area in In Practice 6.3). This company's ending inventory is valued at $12.205 billion under the combined use of LIFO and FIFO. Under FIFO exclusively, this same inventory would be valued at $14.635 billion ($12.205 + $2.430). Given Caterpillar's LIFO inventory reserve at the beginning of the period was $2.504 billion, the decline in the reserve for the period of $74 million suggests that the company's FIFO earnings before income taxes would have been $5.017 billion ($5.091 less $.074), as compared to the $5.091 reported. Additionally, since Caterpillar used LIFO for income tax purposes, we can infer that the company has deferred approximately $850.5 million in income taxes, assuming a 35 percent effective tax rate ($2.430 $\times$ 35% = $850.5 million). Although Caterpillar may ultimately pay these income taxes at some point in the future, in the interim, the U.S. government has effectively provided the company with $850.5 million in interest-free financing.

As a concluding point, it is worth noting that seven of the twenty companies in In Practice 6.3 come from the energy sector. While this clustering may seem surprising, what this simply indicates is that oil prices have been rising over time, along with increasing physical inventory volumes maintained by these companies to service the ever growing worldwide demand for energy products.

In Practice 6.3 *Twenty U.S. Companies with the Largest Inventory Reserves (in millions of dollars)*

	Ending Inventory	Cost of Goods Sold	Earnings Before Income Taxes	LIFO Reserve	LIFO Reserve/ Ending Inventory
Exxon Mobil Corp.	$16,678	$299,117	$51,630	$10,600	63.6%
Chevron Corp.	6,505	149,310	31,202	8,135	125.1%
Phillips 66	3,397	140,525	5,745	3,000	88.3%
Caterpillar Inc	**12,205**	**36,607**	**5,091**	**2,430**	**19.9%**
Walgreens Boots Alliance Inc.	6,076	53,495	3,557	2,300	37.9%
Deere & Co	4,210	24,457	4,790	1,528	36.3%
Kroger Co	5,688	85,512	2,649	1,245	21.9%
United States Steel Corp	2,496	15,455	170	1,000	40.1%
Rite Aid Corp	2,883	18,535	427	998	34.6%
Ford Motor Co	7,866	119,264	4,342	978	12.4%
Amerisourcebergen Corp	8,594	116,608	673	882	10.3%
Berkshire Hathaway	10,236	155,945	28,105	857	8.4%
Imperial Oil Ltd	1,121	28,141	5,021	857	76.4%
Valero Energy Corp.	6,623	123,018	5,552	857	12.9%
Mckesson Corp	14,296	166,833	2,657	768	5.4%
Alcoa Inc.	3,082	19,119	497	767	24.9%
Altria Group Inc	2,040	7,577	7,774	700	34.3%
Marathon Petroleum Corp	5,642	84,665	3,835	684	12.1%
Dow Chemical	8,101	45,134	5,265	569	7.0%
Nucor Corp.	2,745	18,474	1,205	567	20.7%

Source: Standard and Poor's Compustat. Based on data for fiscal years ending before June 30, 2015

BUSINESS PERSPECTIVE

Caterpillar Inc. (CAT) discloses the following information about inventories in its 2014 annual report:

7. Inventories

Inventories (principally using the LIFO method) are comprised of the following:

	December 31,		
(Millions of dollars)	2014	2013	2012
Raw materials.	$ 2,986	$ 2,966	$ 3,573
Work-in-process.	2,455	2,589	2,920
Finished goods.	6,504	6,785	8,767
Supplies	260	285	287
Total inventories	$12,205	$12,625	$15,547

We had long-term material purchase obligations of approximately $2,142 million at December 31, 2014.

During 2013 inventory quantities were reduced. This reduction resulted in a liquidation of LIFO inventory layers carried at lower costs prevailing in prior years as compared with current costs. In 2013, the effect of this reduction of inventory decreased Cost of goods sold by approximately $115 million and increased Profit by approximately $81 million or $0.12 per share. There were no significant LIFO liquidations during 2014 or 2012.

Footnote #7 for Caterpillar summarizes the components for the company's inventory by stage of production. Over half of total inventory is complete and ready for sale (i.e. "finished goods"), but notice there are significant portions of inventory in stages of production not yet ready for sale. The company notes that 2013 profits were aided by $81 million (after tax) from a reduction of inventory quantities and resulting LIFO liquidation. Recall from page 234 Caterpillar chose to disclose its LIFO reserve in its *Summary of Significant Accounting Policies*, and that in total the amount for 2013 was $2.5 billion. Thus, while the $0.12 per share boost to 2013 profits was material, the potential for even greater liquidations and boosts to future profits exists.

Liquidating LIFO Layers

Most companies have a number of operating objectives that they strive to meet. For example, a common corporate goal is to maximize shareholder wealth (maximize share price) while being a good member of the local community. Achieving these goals may involve trying to produce the highest-quality product or service at the lowest price, being attentive to customer needs, providing a healthy work environment for employees, being environmentally friendly, and trying to save on income taxes. Another goal may be to meet profit expectations as set by the board of directors, by Wall Street financial analysts, or by institutional investors.

Sometimes it is impossible to meet internal or external earnings expectations by increasing sales, and thus, managers may look for other ways to increase net income (such as cutting costs). One temporary profit-enhancing approach used by some managers of LIFO-accounted companies is the liquidation of LIFO layers. Liquidating a LIFO layer has the effect of lowering the reported cost of goods sold, and hence, raising gross profit because a lower cost of inventory is effectively matched with revenue.

To illustrate this phenomenon, consider again the case of the Arizona Ice Cream Company. AICC's LIFO layers consist of the following:

LIFO Layers

100 Buckets at $10 per Bucket

1,100 Buckets at $13 per Bucket

800 Buckets at $15 per Bucket

Companies grant credit to other businesses who are their customers, although they rarely grant credit to individuals who are the final consumer of their products or services. In this latter case, payment by cash, check, or debit/credit card is normally expected when the product or service is provided. When credit is extended to a business customer, **accounts payable** refers to relatively immaterial, short-term, non-interest-bearing credit balances. When the credit period exceeds 90 days or the amount involved is material, it is usually represented by an interest-bearing debt contract called a **note payable**.

equivalent to an opportunity cost of 36.5 percent (365/20 × 0.02). At that cost, a customer would be better off obtaining a bank loan to take advantage of such price discounts. But what happens if a customer's payment is not received within 30 days of the transaction date?

Failure to pay an outstanding accounts payable within the allotted period indicates that a buyer has violated the implied credit agreement with the seller and is in technical default. At this point most sellers start contacting their customers by mail, e-mail, or by telephone, suggesting that payment is required. And, in some cases, the seller may begin charging interest on the unpaid account payable balance.

Some customers intentionally violate the credit terms of their suppliers as a way to preserve their operating cash, particularly if there are no interest charges for doing so. In essence, these customers look to the credit provided by their suppliers as a source of interest-free financing for their own operations. One measure of the extent to which a firm utilizes this form of vendor financing is the **days' payable period**. This ratio indicates the average number of days that a company normally takes to pay its outstanding accounts payable:

$$\text{Days' payable period} = \frac{365}{\text{Cost of goods sold/Accounts payable}}$$

Some companies use the days' payable period as a component of their credit-granting review process. Customers that have historically taken a long time to pay for their credit purchases may be poor future credit risks. Comparing a customer's historical days' payable period with a seller's credit terms provides an easy approach to identify whether a customer is likely to pay for its credit purchases in a timely manner.

REVIEW PROBLEM 6.3

Walgreens Boots Alliance, Inc. ("Walgreens") is a global pharmacy, health and well-being company. It operates over 13,000 stores in 11 countries, generating net sales of $103.4 billion. The company's stated purpose is straightforward and direct—"to help people across the world lead healthier and happier lives." Walgreen's is one of the world's largest purchasers of prescription drugs and other health products, and has more than 370,000 employees worldwide.

According to Walgreen's 2015 annual report, the company values a portion of its inventory using the lower of last-in, first-out (LIFO) cost or market. It discloses the following in the footnotes to the financial statements:

> The Company values inventories on a lower of cost or market basis. Inventory includes product costs, inbound freight, direct labor, warehousing costs, overhead costs relating to the manufacture and distribution of products and vendor allowances not classified as a reduction of advertising expense. The Company's Retail Pharmacy USA segment inventory is accounted for using the last-in-first-out ("LIFO") method. At August 31, 2015 and August 31, 2014, Retail Pharmacy USA segment inventories would have been greater by $2.5 billion and $2.3 billion, respectively, if they had been valued on a lower of first-in-first-out ("FIFO") cost or market basis.

To interpret, Walgreen's inventory reserve as of year-end 2015 and 2014 was $2.5 billion and $2.3 billion, respectively, and therefore the change in the company's inventory reserve was $200 million ($2.5 less $2.3 billion). The income statements and balance sheets for Walgreen's follow:

Consolidated Statement of Earnings (in millions) For the years ended August 31:	2015	2014	2013
Net sales.	$103,444	$76,392	$72,217
Cost of sales.	76,520	54,823	51,098
Gross Profit	26,924	21,569	21,119
Selling, general and administrative expenses	22,571	17,992	17,543
Gain on sale of business	—	—	20
Equity earnings in Alliance Boots.	315	617	496
Operating Income.	4,668	4,194	4,092
Gain on previously held equity interest	563	—	—
Other income (expense)	685	(481)	120
Earnings Before Interest and Income Tax Provision.	5,916	3,713	4,212
Interest expense, net	605	156	165
Earnings Before Income Tax Provision.	5,311	3,557	4,047
Income tax provision	1,056	1,526	1,499
Post tax earnings from equity method investments.	24	—	—
Net Earnings.	4,279	2,031	2,548

Consolidated Balance Sheets (in $ millions) As of August 31:	2015
Assets	
Current Assets:	
Cash and cash equivalents.	$ 3,000
Accounts receivable, net	6,849
Inventories	8,678
Other current assets	1,130
Total Current Assets	19,657
Non-Current Assets:	
Property, plant and equipment, at cost, less accumulated depreciation and amortization	15,068
Equity investment in Alliance Boots.	—
Goodwill	16,372
Intangible assets.	12,351
Other non-current assets	5,334
Total non-current assets	49,125
Total assets.	$68,782
Liabilities and equity	
Current liabilities:	
Short-term borrowings	$ 1,068
Trade accounts payable	10,088
Accrued expenses and other liabilities.	5,225
Income taxes	176
Total current liabilities	16,557
Non-current liabilities:	
Long-term debt.	13,315
Deferred income taxes	3,538
Other non-current liabilities	4,072
Total non-current liabilities	20,925

continued

continued from previous page

Consolidated Balance Sheets (in $ millions) As of August 31:	2015
Commitments and contingencies (see Note 13)	
Equity:	
Preferred stock	—
Common stock	12
Paid-in capital	9,953
Employee stock loan receivable	(2)
Retained earnings	25,089
Accumulated other comprehensive (loss) income	(214)
Treasury stock	(3,977)
Total Walgreens Boots Alliance, Inc. shareholders' equity	30,861
Noncontrolling interests	439
Total equity	31,300
Total liabilities and equity	$68,782

Required

1. What would Walgreen's earnings before income tax provision have been (in millions) at year-end 2015 if the company had only used FIFO to value its inventory?
2. What would Walgreen disclose on its balance sheet at year-end 2015 as the value of its inventory (in millions) if the company had used FIFO instead of LIFO?
3. Approximately how much did the Walgreen Company save in income taxes (in millions) in 2015 by using LIFO to value its inventory?
4. What was Walgreen's inventory-on-hand period for 2015? 2014? (Inventory for 2014 was $6,076 million.)
5. Would Walgreen's inventory-on-hand period change if the company had used FIFO to value its inventory instead of LIFO? Compute that value for 2015.
6. What was Walgreen's days' payable period for 2015? 2014? (Accounts payable for 2014 were $4,315 million.)

The solution is on pages 258–259.

ANALYZING INVENTORY AND COST OF GOODS SOLD

Takeaway 8
Explain the drawbacks to using LIFO and the due diligence procedures a professional should undertake to avoid misstatements.

In this chapter, we examined the various ways that companies calculate their cost of goods sold and the value of their ending inventory. We learned that many U.S. public companies elect to use the LIFO method for this purpose. Since LIFO results in a lower taxable net income when input costs are rising, as compared to FIFO and weighted-average cost, we can speculate that the widespread usage of LIFO is linked to the income-tax sheltering afforded by the method, along with the U.S. Department of Treasury's LIFO conformity rule.

Despite LIFO's tax advantage, and the related positive impact on firm operating cash flow, some investment professionals charge that the method has a "dark side." For instance, some professionals allege that, as a consequence of LIFO's tax advantage, the method creates a "hidden earnings reserve" on the balance sheet in the form of undervalued ending inventory. The value of that earnings reserve on a pretax basis is, of course, the value of the LIFO inventory reserve that must be disclosed in the footnotes to the financial statements. Some investment professionals allege that LIFO-accounted firms can draw down on their LIFO reserve when additional income is needed to meet Wall Street earnings' expectations. While this is all true, it must be remembered that when a firm liquidates its LIFO earnings reserve—that is, when a firm liquidates its LIFO layers—the amount of the LIFO liquidation profits must be disclosed in the footnotes to the financial statements. So, it is a simple matter for a professional, as part of his or her due diligence review, to read the inventory footnote, determine the amount of LIFO liquidation profit, and restate a firm's net income as if the liquidation had not occurred.

LIFO liquidation profits are often derisively referred to as phantom profit because such profits do not result in a corresponding increase in a firm's cash flow from operations. In fact, a firm that liquidates its LIFO inventory reserve will reduce its operating cash flow as a consequence of the additional income taxes due on the LIFO liquidation profits.

Another LIFO-related concern expressed by some investment professionals is that the method causes distortions in many of the popular financial ratios used to evaluate firm performance. For example, the LIFO method causes cost of goods sold to be overstated and the value of ending inventory to be understated relative to a FIFO-accounted firm, assuming increasing inventory costs. And, as a consequence, a firm's inventory turnover ratio will be overstated and the inventory-on-hand period understated. Similarly, since net income under LIFO will be lower than net income under FIFO, some professionals worry that the return on sales, the return on assets, and the return on equity will be artificially misstated. Fortunately, using the techniques discussed in this chapter, it is possible to restate a firm's cost of goods sold and its pretax net income on the income statement and the ending inventory on the balance sheet to their approximate values as if FIFO had been used instead of LIFO. By making these financial statement restatements, it is possible to develop restated financial ratios that will facilitate interfirm comparisons of performance.

ETHICS PERSPECTIVE

One of the distinguishing characteristics of a profession is a code of ethics that its members are required to follow. The accounting profession is no exception. In order to be granted a certified public accounting (CPA) certificate, it is necessary to not only pass a competency exam but also an ethics exam. One reason for this requirement may be the public trust that is associated with membership in a profession and the fact that it is often difficult for a consumer to judge the quality of the service provided. This is certainly true regarding an audit, and is likely true regarding such services as tax planning and investing. Ultimately, the public's belief in how competently and ethically a profession performs will determine its ability to dictate how it does business. Prior to the Enron and WorldCom scandals, the accounting profession was largely self-policed by an internal organization, the American Institute of Certified Public Accountants (AICPA), which monitored the quality of the work of its members. Because of the profession's loss of credibility as a result of these corporate audit failures, the profession is now subject to oversight by the Public Company Accounting Oversight Board (PCAOB), a governmental organization.

EXECUTIVE SUMMARY

This chapter examined the important accounting issue of how to match operating revenue and operating expenses—specifically, how to match the cost of goods and services sold with the revenue produced by the sale of those goods and services. A number of inventory costing methods were considered—FIFO, LIFO, and the weighted-average cost method. Just which method a company adopts was shown to have a dramatic effect on reported gross profit and net income. Finally, the chapter illustrated that the choice of an inventory costing method was often linked to income tax and income reporting considerations.

As a validation of your understanding of the content of this chapter, you should now be able to:

- Describe how the initial cost of inventory is determined.
- Describe how inventory is measured using FIFO, LIFO, and the weighted-average cost method and how the resulting cost of goods sold is matched with revenue.
- Understand the mechanical differences between the different inventory valuation methods.
- Explain why the lower-of-cost-or-market method is sometimes used to value ending inventory and how this method affects reported net income.
- Explain the LIFO reserve and how a LIFO inventory liquidation can increase a company's gross and net profit.
- Identify the methods a company could use to minimize the costs associated with inventory management.
- Explain how accounts payable are valued and how the payment of these payables can be managed to positively impact a firm's operating cash flow.
- Explain the drawbacks to using LIFO and the due diligence procedures a professional should undertake to avoid misstatements.

In Chapter 7, our investigation of the matching concept continues; however, in the next chapter, the focus shifts to matching the cost of such long-lived assets as plant and equipment, intangible assets, and natural resources with the operating revenue produced by these assets.

KEY CONCEPTS AND TERMS

Accounts payable, 238
Average cost method, 223
Change in the inventory reserve, 233
Conservatism principle, 230
Consistency principle, 229
Days' payable period, 238
Finished goods inventory, 220
First-in, first-out (FIFO), 223
Highest-in, first-out (HIFO), 232
Historical cost convention, 223
Inventory-on-hand period, 237

Inventory reserve, 233
Last-in, first-out (LIFO), 223
LIFO conformity rule, 223, 231
LIFO layers, 233
LIFO reserve, 233
Lower-of-cost-or-market (LCM) method, 230
Next-in, first-out (NIFO), 232
Note payable, 238
Operating cycle, 220
Operating expenses, 221

Periodic system, 223
Perpetual system, 224
Phantom profit, 236
Raw material, 220
Replacement cost method, 223
Specific identification method, 223
Weighted-average cost method, 223
Work-in-process inventory, 220

QUESTIONS

Q6.1 **Consistency Principle.** The consistency principle stipulates that when a company begins using a given inventory valuation method (FIFO, LIFO, or the weighted-average cost method), the company should continue to use that method to prepare its financial statements until such time as its senior management, with concurrence from the firm's independent auditors, concludes that another method would more fairly present the company's financial condition and performance. Discuss why the consistency principle is important to investors and shareholders. If a company changes its method of accounting for its inventory, how will that change be disclosed in its financial statements?

Q6.2 **Physical Inventory Counts.** Although physically counting a business's inventory is integral to the periodic system of inventory recordkeeping, it is not an explicit component of the perpetual system. Nonetheless, most well-run businesses do annually (and sometimes, semiannually) conduct a physical count of their inventory. Discuss why physically counting a company's inventory is considered to be "best practice" regardless of which inventory recordkeeping system is utilized.

Q6.3 **Inventory Valuation Method Changes and Share Prices.** Voluntary accounting policy changes are said to be "unintended signals" about the financial health and future prospects of a firm from management to a firm's shareholders. Discuss how and why you would expect the capital markets to react to news that a company was voluntarily changing its inventory valuation policy from (a) LIFO to FIFO and from (b) FIFO to LIFO.

Q6.4 **Lower-of-Cost-or-Market Method.** The lower-of-cost-or-market method (LCM) is often referred to as a "one-way street" because under LCM, ending inventory values may be written down to a lower replacement value but are never written up when the expected replacement cost exceeds the inventory cost basis. What accounting principle is reflected in the application of LCM? What accounting principle is violated by the application of LCM? Discuss whether you think that LCM should be modified to become a "two-way street," allowing both inventory value write-ups and write-downs.

Q6.5 **Earnings Management and Inventory Valuation.** Investment professionals frequently develop concerns that earnings management may be present when they observe that a firm has voluntarily changed its inventory valuation policy from LIFO to FIFO. Similar concerns arise when the capital market discovers that a firm using LIFO is liquidating its inventory price layers. Discuss why these two financial statement disclosures might indicate the presence of earnings management. Discuss when these disclosures might *not* indicate the presence of earnings management.

Q6.6 **LIFO Inventory Reserve.** The LIFO inventory reserve is a measure disclosed in a company's footnotes and reveals the difference between the current value of a company's ending inventory and the LIFO value of its ending inventory. Discuss why and how this measure is useful to shareholders and investment professionals as they evaluate the financial condition and performance of a company that uses LIFO inventory valuation.

Q6.7 **LIFO and Earnings Management.** Some investment professionals refer to LIFO inventory valuation as an "earnings management" tool, suggesting that LIFO allows a company to create a hidden earnings reserve on a company's balance sheet, to be used in later periods to help meet Wall Street earnings expectations. Discuss why this assertion might be true and how to measure the size of a company's "hidden LIFO earnings reserve."

Q6.8 **Inventory Valuation Policy Change.** Riverwood International Corporation, a leading provider of paperboard, announced the following:

> During the fourth quarter, the Company changed its inventory valuation method from the last-in, first-out method to the first-in, first-out (FIFO) method as the Company determined that over time, FIFO more closely matches the Company's revenues with its costs.

Discuss why, and under what conditions, FIFO might enable Riverwood International to "more closely match" its costs with its revenue.

Q6.9 **LIFO Layer Liquidations.** Alleghany Technologies Incorporated disclosed in its annual report that:

> . . . inventory usage resulted in liquidations of LIFO inventory quantities. These inventories were carried at differing costs prevailing in prior years as compared with the cost of current manufacturing cost and purchases. The effect of these LIFO liquidations was to increase cost of sales by $1.5 million in 2012, increase cost of sales by $0.1 million in 2011 and decrease cost of sales by $1.8 million in 2010.

Discuss why a liquidation of LIFO inventory quantities would reduce a company's cost of goods sold. Does this event indicate that a firm is attempting to manage its earnings? Why or why not?

Q6.10 **Inventory Write-Down.** *The Financial Times* reported that Delphi, Inc., a manufacturer of automotive parts, would take a $100 million write-down of its inventory to reflect reduced demand for some of its products. The write-down was part of the company's efforts to restructure its money-losing operations. Discuss what accounting principle is being followed by Delphi when it implements the inventory write-down. Discuss how the write-down will affect the company's financial statements. Discuss how the write-down will affect the company's inventory turnover ratio and its inventory-on-hand period. Could an inventory write-down be used to manage earnings? If so, how?

Q6.11 **(Ethics Perspective) Code of Ethics.** It has been argued that to be classified as a professional one must offer services to the public rather than simply be an employee of an organization. As such, most employees of an organization, including accountants that are not CPAs, are not subject to their profession's ethical code of conduct. We have seen, however, that serious breaches of the public trust can result from the unethical conduct of some of these "professional" employees. Examples of such breaches include faulty construction in the city of Boston "Big Dig" and the scandal involving back-dated employee stock options. Do you feel that professionals working for an organization should be bound by the same code of ethical conduct as their colleagues that serve the public directly?

Assignments with the ⓜ logo in the margin are available in *BusinessCourse*.
See the Preface of the book for details.
CHECK FIGURE indicates that check figures are available on the book's Website.

EXERCISES

E6.12 **Compute the Missing Inventory Values.** The following information was disclosed in the 2015 annual report of The Arcadia Company.   TA 1

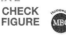

	2015	2014	2013
Beginning inventory	$?	$?	$11,560
Purchase of inventory	45,850	?	42,640
Inventory available for sale	?	?	54,200
Ending inventory	?	9,655	?
Cost of goods sold	13,600	42,480	43,715

Fill in the missing values.

E6.13 **Calculating FIFO Inventory Values.** The Mann Corporation began operations in 2015. Information relating to the company's purchases of inventory and sales of products for 2015 and 2016 is presented below.   TA 2
CHECK
FIGURE

2015			
January 1	Purchase	200 units @	$10 per unit
April 1	Sold	120 units @	$25 per unit
July 1	Purchase	100 units @	$14 per unit
September 1	Sold	130 units @	$25 per unit

2016			
January 1	Purchase	100 units @	$16 per unit
April 1	Sold	80 units @	$30 per unit
July 1	Purchase	100 units @	$18 per unit
September 1	Sold	100 units @	$35 per unit

Calculate the FIFO cost of goods sold and ending inventory for 2015 and 2016 assuming use of (*a*) the periodic method and (*b*) the perpetual method.

TA 2 **E6.14** **Calculating LIFO Inventory Values.** The Mann Corporation began operations in 2015. Information relating to the company's purchases of inventory and sales of products for 2015 and 2016 is presented below.

2015			
February 1	Purchase	200 units @	$10 per unit
May 1	Sold	120 units @	$25 per unit
August 1	Purchase	100 units @	$14 per unit
October 1	Sold	130 units @	$25 per unit

2016			
February 1	Purchase	100 units @	$16 per unit
May 1	Sold	80 units @	$30 per unit
August 1	Purchase	100 units @	$18 per unit
October 1	Sold	100 units @	$35 per unit

Calculate the LIFO cost of goods sold and ending inventory for 2015 and 2016 assuming use of (*a*) the periodic method and (*b*) the perpetual method.

TA 2 **E6.15** **Calculating Weighted-Average Cost Inventory Values.** The Mann Corporation began operations in 2015. Information relating to the company's purchases of inventory and sales of products for 2015 and 2016 is presented below.

2015			
March 1	Purchase	200 units @	$10 per unit
June 1	Sold	120 units @	$25 per unit
September 1	Purchase	100 units @	$14 per unit
November 1	Sold	130 units @	$25 per unit

2016			
March 1	Purchase	100 units @	$16 per unit
June 1	Sold	80 units @	$30 per unit
September 1	Purchase	100 units @	$18 per unit
November 1	Sold	100 units @	$35 per unit

Calculate the weighted-average cost of goods sold and ending inventory for 2015 and 2016 assuming use of (*a*) the periodic method and (*b*) the perpetual method.

TA 2 **E6.16** **FIFO versus LIFO: Ratio Analysis.** Presented below is financial data for two companies that are identical in every respect except that Company X uses the FIFO method to value its inventory and Company Z uses the LIFO method to value its inventory. Using this data, calculate the following ratios: return on sales, inventory turnover, inventory-on-hand period, and current ratio. Which of the two companies is the better investment opportunity? Why?

	Company X	Company Z
Sales.	$100,000	$100,000
Cost of goods sold.	47,500	56,400
Net income.	29,000	18,600
Inventory.	19,000	8,600
Current assets	64,000	53,600
Current liabilities.	21,000	21,000

E6.17   **Inventory Management.** The following financial information is taken from the annual report of Intel   TA 2
Corporation:

CHECK FIGURE · MBC

(amounts in millions)	2015	2014
Net revenues	$55,355	$55,870
Cost of goods sold.	20,676	20,261
Ending inventories	5,167	4,273

Using the above data, calculate the company's inventory turnover, inventory-on-hand period, and gross profit percentage for 2015 and 2014. Is the company's inventory management improving? Intel uses FIFO to value its inventory. Would these ratios look better if the company used LIFO instead? Why?

E6.18   **LIFO to FIFO Change.** At year end, Riverside Corporation announced that it would change its inventory   TA 2
valuation method from last-in, first-out (LIFO) to first-in, first-out (FIFO). The company also disclosed that the inventory valuation policy change would have a "positive impact on gross profit by $12.6 million." Presented below is Riverwood International's originally reported (using LIFO) financial results for the year.

(in thousands)	2015
Net sales.	$298,731
Gross profit.	49,766
Income from operations	10,201

Describe the financial effects of this policy change on the company's income statement, balance sheet, and statement of cash flow. Does the inventory method change materially impact the company's reported income from operations?

E6.19   **Ratio Analysis: Alternative Inventory Valuation Methods.** Exhibits 6.3, 6.4, and 6.5 in Chapter 6 present   TA 2
the financial results of the Arizona Ice Cream Company, Inc., using FIFO, LIFO, and the weighted-average cost method, respectively. Using this data, complete the following table for the company:

MBC

	FIFO	LIFO	Wt. Average
Inventory turnover	_____	_____	_____
Inventory-on-hand period.	_____	_____	_____
Gross margin percentage.	_____	_____	_____

Under which inventory valuation method does the company's performance appear most favorable? Using which inventory valuation method does the company's performance appear least favorable?

E6.20   **LIFO Reserve: Restating Financial Statements.** The following information is taken from the annual report   TA 5
of the Walgreens Boots Alliance, Inc.:

MBC

(in millions)	2015	2014
Cost of goods sold.	$76,520	$54,823
Net income before tax	5,311	3,557
Ending inventory.	8,678	6,076
Inventory reserve	2,500	2,300

Walgreens uses LIFO to value its inventory. Restate the company's financial results for 2015 assuming the use of the FIFO method. Assume an effective tax rate of 30 percent. Which method—FIFO or LIFO—should Walgreens use to report its financial results to its shareholders? Why?

TA 7   **E6.21   Calculating the Days' Payable Period.**   The following information is taken from the annual report of The Coca-Cola Company:

(amounts in millions)	2015	2014
Net revenue	$44,294	$45,998
Cost of goods sold	17,482	17,889
Inventories	2,902	3,100
Accounts payable	9,660	9,234

Using this information, calculate the accounts payable turnover ratio and the days' payable period for 2015 and 2014. Is Coca-Cola taking longer to pay its accounts payable to its suppliers? Do the ratios indicate that the company's credit risk is increasing? Why or why not?

TA 5   **E6.22   LIFO Layer Liquidations and Net Income.**   The following information is taken from the annual report of The Claremont Corporation:

(in millions)	2015	2014
Net income before tax	$360	$20

The company uses the LIFO method to value its inventory. In addition, the footnotes to the company's annual report revealed that, during 2015 and 2014, inventory usage resulted in liquidations of LIFO inventory quantities, and the effect of these liquidations was to reduce the cost of goods sold by $28 million and $6 million in 2015 and 2014, respectively. Calculate the company's net income before tax assuming that the LIFO inventory liquidations had not occurred. Discuss why the incremental profit from a LIFO-layer liquidation is often referred to as "phantom profit."

PROBLEMS

TA 2, 3, 4   **P6.23   Calculating the Value of Ending Inventory and Cost of Goods Sold: Periodic Method.**   Capstone Consolidated, Inc. is a leading manufacturer of steel products. The following inventory data relates to the firm's production during the first quarter of 2015:

Date of Purchase	Tons of Raw Steel Purchased	Purchase Price per Ton	Total Cost
Jan. 1	500	$40	$20,000
Jan. 15	700	35	24,500
Feb. 7	200	33	6,600
Feb. 21	450	30	13,500
March 15	350	42	14,700
	2,200		$79,300

At the end of the first quarter of 2015, Capstone's internal auditors determined that 1,700 tons of raw steel had been processed and sold.

Required

1. Calculate the cost of steel processed and sold during the quarter under each of the following methods, assuming use of a periodic inventory management system:
    a.   FIFO
    b.   LIFO
    c.   Weighted-average

2. Assume that the replacement cost per ton is $39 at the end of the quarter. What amount should Capstone's ending inventory be valued at on its March 31 balance sheet under each of the following methods?
    a. FIFO
    b. LIFO
    c. Weighted-average
3. Which method—FIFO, LIFO, or the weighted-average cost method—should Capstone use for reporting its financial results to its shareholders? Why? How does this decision constrain the company's method choice for income tax reporting?

P6.24   **Calculating the Value of Ending Inventory and Cost of Goods Sold: Perpetual Method.** Consider the following inventory data for the first two months of the year for CompX International:

TA 2, 3, 4
CHECK
FIGURE
MBC

	Total Units	Unit Cost	Total Cost
Beginning inventory on hand			
January 1	60,000	$2.00	$ 120,000
Purchases during month			
January 5	103,600	2.00	207,200
January 20	293,900	2.10	617,190
	457,500		$ 944,390
Sales of inventory			
January 25	383,900		
Beginning inventory at			
February 1	73,600		
Purchases during month			
February 8	282,200	2.20	$ 620,840
February 23	153,500	2.60	399,100
	509,300		$1,019,940
Sales of inventory			
February 27	407,600		
Ending Inventory	101,700		

Required
1. Calculate the cost of goods sold and ending inventory for January and February under each of the following methods, assuming use of a perpetual inventory management system:
    a. FIFO
    b. LIFO
    c. Weighted-average
2. Assume that the replacement cost of CompX International's ending inventory is $2.05 per unit on January 30 and $2.35 per unit on February 28. Calculate the value of the ending inventory for January and February under each of the following methods:
    a. FIFO
    b. LIFO
    c. Weighted-average
3. Which method—FIFO, LIFO, or the weighted-average cost method—should CompX International use when reporting its financial results to its shareholders? Why? How does this decision constrain the company's method selection for income tax reporting?

P6.25   **Calculating the Value of Ending Inventory and Cost of Goods Sold: Lower-of-Cost-or-Market Method.** The following inventory data is taken from the financial records of Fernandez, Inc., a personal computer software manufacturer.

TA 2, 3, 4
CHECK
FIGURE
MBC

	No. of Units	Unit Cost	Total Cost
Beginning inventory (Jan. 1)................................	160,000	$1.00	$160,000
Purchases: May 5	60,000	1.50	90,000
Sept. 3	60,000	2.00	120,000
Total available for sale	280,000		$370,000
Less: Sales*...	250,000		?
Ending inventory (Dec. 31)................................	30,000		?
Expected replacement cost per unit		1.40	

Sales for the year	No. of Units Sold
Feb 3...	120,000
Jun. 30	30,000
Oct. 5	100,000
	250,000

Required

1. Complete the following table.

	Periodic		Perpetual	
Method	Ending Inventory	Cost of Goods Sold	Ending Inventory	Cost of Goods Sold
FIFO				
LIFO				
Weighted-average				

2. Which inventory method would you recommend that Fernandez, Inc., use for income tax purposes? Why?
3. Which method would you recommend that Fernandez, Inc., use for accounting purposes if the company operates in a highly inflationary environment? Why?
4. Which method would you recommend that Fernandez, Inc., use for accounting purposes if the company operates in a deflationary environment? Why?

TA 5 **P6.26** **Restating Inventory Values Using the LIFO Inventory Reserve.** Presented below are the condensed financial statements of Global Enterprises, Inc. The company's inventory is valued using LIFO. The company's footnotes reveal that the LIFO reserve was as follows.

Year	LIFO Reserve (in thousands)
Year 1	$2,266
Year 2	2,152

Also, the footnotes indicate that net reductions in inventory levels resulted in a liquidation of LIFO layers amounting to $163,000 in Year 1 and $114,000 in Year 2.

GLOBAL ENTERPRISES, INC.
Condensed Balance Sheet

($ thousands)	Year 1	Year 2
Assets		
Quick assets	$ 7,327	$ 7,754
Inventory	3,029	3,158
Total current assets	10,356	10,912
Noncurrent assets	11,259	12,376
Total assets	$21,615	$23,288
Liabilities and Shareholders' equity		
Current liabilities	$ 8,153	$ 8,688
Long-term liabilities	3,099	3,162
Total liabilities	11,252	11,850
Shareholders' equity	10,363	11,438
Total liabilities and shareholders' equity	$21,615	$23,288

GLOBAL ENTERPRISES, INC.
Condensed Income Statement

($ thousands)	Year 1	Year 2
Sales of products	$26,500	$26,797
Cost of goods sold	(24,095)	(24,248)
Other income	312	450
Income taxes	(900)	(975)
Net earnings	$ 1,817	$ 2,024

Required

1. Restate the company's financial statements for Year 2 assuming the use of FIFO instead of LIFO.
2. Compare the tax consequences of using LIFO versus FIFO in Year 2, and for all prior years. (Assume an effective tax rate of 33 percent.)
3. Which method—FIFO or LIFO—should Global Enterprises use for reporting its financial results to shareholders? Why?

P6.27   Restating Inventory Values Using the LIFO Inventory Reserve.   Chemical Boost, Inc. is a manufacturer of chemical and derivative products. Presented below is select information from Chemical Boost's recent annual report.

TA 5
CHECK
FIGURE
MBC

CHEMICAL BOOST, INC.
Condensed Balance Sheet

($ millions)					
Assets	2015	2014	Liabilities & Shareholders' Equity	2015	2014
Inventory	$ 6,500	$ 6,200	Liabilities	$25,270	$24,520
Other current assets	13,560	13,900	Capital stock	7,460	7,180
Noncurrent assets	20,300	18,900	Retained earnings	7,630	7,300
Total	$40,360	$39,000	Total	$40,360	$39,000

CHEMICAL BOOST, INC. Condensed Statement of Earnings		
($ millions)	2015	2014
Revenues	$40,570	$41,900
Cost of goods sold.	27,650	28,240
Gross profit.	12,920	13,660
Other expenses	11,760	12,425
Income taxes	300	620
Net earnings.	$ 860	$ 615

The footnotes to the company's financial statements revealed that Chemical Boost, Inc. values most of its inventory using LIFO. The LIFO reserve was approximately $600 million and $300 million, respectively, at year-end 2015 and 2014. Assume an effective tax rate of 26%.

Required

1. If Chemical Boost, Inc. had used FIFO instead of LIFO to value its inventory, what value would have been reported for 2015 for the following accounts?
   - *a.* Ending inventory
   - *b.* Cost of goods sold
   - *c.* Net income before tax
   - *d.* Retained earnings
2. How much additional income tax would the company have paid if it had used FIFO instead of LIFO to value its inventory?

TA 2, 5   **P6.28   Inventory Valuation and Earnings.**   Dominick Portet Wines Inc. began operations to import fine wines from Australia to the United States. Sales and purchase information is provided below.

	Year 1	Year 2	Year 3
Sales.	170 units	220 units	300 units
Purchases.	250 units @ $10 each	200 units @ $8 each	? units @ $15 each
LIFO ending inventory	80 units @ $10	60 units @ $10	

Assume that Portet Wines uses the LIFO method of inventory valuation. The purchase amount for Year 3 has been left blank because Portet Wines has not yet decided the total number of units to purchase during the year. (Assume that all sales occur on the last day of the year, after all purchases for the year have been made. The company's year-end is December 31.)

Required

1. How many units should be purchased in Year 3 if the firm's objective is to maximize reported income for the year?
2. Compute the cost of goods sold for Year 3 assuming the number of units computed in (1) is purchased.
3. How many units should be purchased in Year 3 if the firm's objective is to minimize income taxes for the year?
4. Compute the cost of goods sold for Year 3 assuming the number of units computed in (3) is purchased.
5. Assume Portet Wines uses FIFO instead of LIFO and the company purchased just enough units to meet sales demand. What would the cost of goods sold be in Year 3? Assume that FIFO ending inventory is equal to 80 units at $10 in Year 1 and 60 units at $8 in Year 2.

TA 2, 5   **P6.29   Inventory Valuation and Earnings.**   Santiago, Inc., began operations as an importer of fine Chilean wine
CHECK FIGURE   to the United States. Sales and purchase information is provided below.

	Year 1	Year 2	Year 3
Sales.	250 units	140 units	300 units
Purchases.	300 units @ $10 each	200 units @ $15 each	? units @ $20 each
Ending Inventory	50 units @ $10 each	50 units @ $10 each	
		60 units @ $15 each	

Santiago, Inc., uses the LIFO method of inventory valuation. The purchase amount for Year 3 has been left blank because the company has not yet decided the total number of units to purchase during the year. (Assume that all sales occur on the last day of the year, after all purchases for the year have been made. The company's year-end is December 31.)

Required

1. How many units should be purchased in Year 3 if the firm's objective is to minimize income taxes for the year?
2. Compute the cost of goods sold for Year 3 assuming that the number of units computed in (1) is purchased.
3. How many units should be purchased in Year 3 if the firm's objective is to maximize reported income for the year?
4. Compute the cost of goods sold for Year 3 assuming that the number of units computed in (3) is purchased.

P6.30 **FIFO versus LIFO: Ratio Analysis.** Presented below are the financial statements of two companies that are identical in every respect except the method of valuing their inventories. The method of valuing inventory is LIFO for the LIFO Company and FIFO for the FIFO Company.

Comparative Income Statements	FIFO Company	LIFO Company
Sales.	$20,000,000	$20,000,000
Less: Cost of goods sold	9,200,000	11,280,000
Gross profit.	10,800,000	8,720,000
Less: Operating expenses	(5,000,000)	(5,000,000)
Net income before tax	$ 5,800,000	$ 3,720,000

Comparative Balance Sheets	FIFO Company	LIFO Company
Assets		
Cash.	$ 3,000,000	$ 3,000,000
Receivables	6,000,000	6,000,000
Inventory.	3,800,000	1,720,000
Total current assets	12,800,000	10,720,000
Total noncurrent (net)	20,000,000	20,000,000
Total	$32,800,000	$30,720,000
Liabilities and Equities		
Current liabilities.	$ 4,200,000	$ 4,200,000
Noncurrent liabilities.	9,000,000	9,000,000
Total liabilities.	13,200,000	13,200,000
Total shareholders' equity	19,600,000	17,520,000
Total	$32,800,000	$30,720,000

Required

Using the two sets of financial statements, calculate the ratios below for each firm. Ignore the effect of taxes (i.e., assume zero taxes for both firms).

1. Current ratio
2. Inventory turnover
3. Inventory-on-hand period
4. Return on assets
5. Total debt to total assets
6. Long-term debt to shareholders' equity
7. Gross profit margin ratio
8. Return on sales
9. Return on shareholders' equity
10. Earnings per share (assume 2 million shares outstanding)

Based on the above ratios, which company represents the better investment opportunity? The better acquisition opportunity? The better lending opportunity? Why?

P6.31 **Evaluating Firm Performance using FIFO and LIFO.** Costco Wholesale Corporation operates membership warehouses. As of August 30, 2015 Costco operated 686 warehouses, with 480 in the United States. In addition, the store sells merchandise through its website costco.com. Using selected parts of Costco's 2015 10-K report, answer the questions below. (The year 2015 refers to the year ending August 30, 2015. The effective tax rate is 33.2 percent.)

Required

1. Was 2015 a good year or a bad year for Costco Corporation? Why?
2. Costco Corporation accounts for its U.S. inventory and the related cost of goods sold using the last-in, first-out (LIFO) method. Inventory is stated at the lower of LIFO cost or market. The cumulative LIFO inventory reserve was $82 million and $109 million at year-end 2015 and 2014, respectively. Estimate the income before income taxes in 2015 assuming the company used FIFO to value its inventory.

COSTCO WHOLESALE CORPORATION
Consolidated Balance Sheets

(in millions)	August 30, 2015	August 31, 2014
Assets		
Current assets		
Cash and cash equivalents........................	$ 4,801	$ 5,738
Short-term investments	1,618	1,577
Receivables, net....................................	1,224	1,148
Inventory..	8,908	8,456
Deferred income taxes and other current assets	748	669
Total current assets..............................	17,299	17,588
Property, plant, and equipment, net..............	15,401	14,830
Other assets......................................	740	606
Total assets..................................	$33,440	$33,024
Liabilities		
Current liabilities		
Accounts payable.................................	$ 9,011	$ 8,491
Current portion of long-term debt	1,283	0
Other current liabilities	6,246	5,921
Total current liabilities	16,540	14,412
Long-term debt	4,864	5,093
Deferred income taxes and other liabilities	1,193	1,004
Total liabilities	22,597	20,509
Equity		
Preferred stock...................................	$ 0	$ 0
Common stock...................................	2	2
Additional paid-in capital	5,218	4,919
Accumulated other comprehensive income...............	(1,121)	(76)
Retained earnings	6,518	7,458
Noncontrolling interests...........................	226	212
Total equity	10,843	12,515
Total liabilities and equity......................	$33,440	$33,024

COSTCO WHOLESALE CORPORATION
Consolidated Statements of Income

(in millions)	August 30, 2015	August 31, 2014
Total revenue	$116,199	$112,640
Operating expenses		
Merchandise costs................................	101,065	98,458
Selling, general, and administrative	11,445	10,899
Preopening expenses.............................	65	63
Operating income	3,624	3,220
Other income (expense)		
Interest expense.................................	(124)	(113)
Interest income and other, net	104	90
Income before income taxes	3,604	3,197
Provision for income taxes........................	1,195	1,109
Net income including noncontrolling interests.............	2,409	2,088
Net income attributable to noncontrolling interests.........	(32)	(30)
Net income attributable to Costco.....................	$ 2,377	$ 2,058

CORPORATE ANALYSIS

CA6.32   The Procter & Gamble Company.   The 2015 annual report of the Procter & Gamble Company (P&G) is   TA 1, 2, 7
available at www.pginvestor.com. After reviewing P&G's annual report, respond to the following questions:

    a.   How does P&G value its inventory? What costs does P&G include in its cost of products sold? Do you agree with these policy decisions? How much of P&G's total assets are represented by its inventory?

    b.   Calculate P&G's inventory turnover ratio, inventory-on-hand period, accounts payable turnover ratio, and days' payable period for 2014 and 2015. What can you conclude from these ratios?

    c.   Assume that P&G needs to maintain an inventory of about $5.45 billion in 2016, the gross margin percentage remains the same as in 2015, and that in 2016, the company is able to raise its inventory turnover rate to 7.5 times. How much would its gross margin increase as a result of the improvement in the inventory turnover?

CA6.33   Internet-Based Analysis.   Consider a publicly held company whose products you are familiar with. Some   TA 1, 2, 7
examples might include:

Company	Product	Corporate Website
• Johnson & Johnson............	• Band-Aids	• www.jnj.com
• Microsoft Corporation..........	• Windows software	• www.microsoft.com
• Apple Inc......................	• Cellular phones	• www.apple.com
• Intel Corporation	• Pentium processors	• www.intel.com
• Kimberly-Clark Corporation......	• Kleenex	• www.kimberly-clark.com

Access the company's public website and search for its most recent annual report. (Some companies will provide access to their financial data through an "investor relations" link, while others will provide a direct link to their "annual reports.") After locating your company's most recent annual report, open the file and review its contents. After reviewing the annual report for your selected company, prepare answers to the following questions.

    a.   What method does the company use to account for its inventory? Do you agree with the company's selection of its inventory valuation method? Calculate the inventory as a percentage of total assets. Did the percentage increase or decrease over the last two years?

    b.   Calculate the inventory turnover ratio and the inventory-on-hand period for each of the last two years. Is the inventory-on-hand period increasing or decreasing? What might explain the change in the inventory-on-hand period?

    c.   Calculate the days' payable period for each of the last two years. Is the company paying its accounts payable faster or slower? What might explain this change?

CA6.34   IFRS Financial Statements.   The 2014 financial statements of LVMH Moet Hennessey-Louis Vuitton   TA 1, 2, 4
S.A. are presented in Appendix C of this book. LVMH is a Paris-based holding company and one of the world's largest and best-known luxury goods companies. As a member-nation of the European Union, French companies are required to prepare their consolidated (group) financial statements using International Financial Reporting Standards (IFRS). In LVMH's Notes to the Consolidated Financial Statements (not presented in Appendix C), the company discloses its inventory policy:

> Inventories are valued using the weighted average cost or FIFO methods. Inventories other than wine produced by the Group are recorded at the lower of cost (excluding interest expense) and net realizable value; cost comprises manufacturing cost (finished goods) or purchase price, plus incidental costs (raw materials, merchandise). Provisions for impairment of inventories are chiefly recognized . . . because of product obsolescence (end of season or collection, date of expiry, etc.) or lack of sales prospects.

Consider the following questions:

    a.   If LVMH followed U.S. GAAP, what inventory valuation method would you expect the company to use? Why?

    b.   Where would you expect to find the provision for inventory impairment in the company's financial statements?

CASE

TAO & WILLIS, INC.: INVENTORY ACCOUNTING METHODS

Tao & Willis, Inc. (TW), was a video gaming and entertainment company headquartered in Phoenix, Arizona. The company specialized in the manufacture and distribution of computer games and stand-alone gaming consoles. It sold its products all over the world, and experienced particularly strong demand in South America. High import tariffs in those countries, however, were cutting into profits. Under the leadership of John Gary Sommers, TW had become proactive. For years, Sommers had lobbied senior management to move manufacturing operations to Brazil, and his vision was finally a reality. The new subsidiary, TW-Brazil, would handle all manufacturing operations in the Western hemisphere south of the equator. TW had never before operated an entity in a foreign country, so this represented a true inflection point for the company. Sommers was put in charge and given full decision-making responsibility for all financial and operational aspects of TW-Brazil.

One of the early tasks Sommers assigned his CFO was to evaluate TW-Brazil's financial options related to inventory accounting. He specifically wanted comparisons of expected financial results for two different inventory cost flow methods: last in, first out (LIFO), and first in, first out (FIFO). Sommers knew that the inventory cost flow method that he ultimately chose would influence profits. TW was a publicly traded company and was thus always focused on maintaining margins and meeting EPS growth expectations. TW-Brazil was expected to help in this regard in 2016, but the longer-term benefits were not as obvious. Sommers fully understood that there was a company-wide expectation that 30% gross margins be maintained.

TW had established a healthy market share in the video game market over its 20-year history. Unlike the more well-known home-gaming systems (e.g., PlayStation and Xbox), TW was one of few remaining companies that built larger stand-alone gaming systems. These systems were used mainly in arcades, but also in restaurants and shopping malls. TW's primary customers were business owners desiring to either generate revenue per game played, or to simply attract customers to their stores. The company had only five years ago expanded its sales through multiple export distributors. It had begun selling its products in the South American market, specifically Paraguay, Uruguay, Argentina, Venezuela, and Brazil. These countries were all a part of the Mercosur customs union, and member nations maintained a common external tariff (CET). Brazil, however, was granted exceptions to the CET and maintained higher tariffs than its Mercosur partners on certain goods, including video games and consoles. These higher tariffs had forced TW to increase prices on its products and, not surprisingly, sales were negatively impacted relative to other South American markets (see Appendix 1 for a more detailed description of Mercosur).

TW-Brazil was opened in part to avoid the high import tariffs and keep prices competitive in the Brazilian market. Not only would opening TW-Brazil allow TW to better control costs within Brazil, but it would also allow for lower trade barriers between Brazil and the other members of Mercosur. With the 2016 budget due to TW's upper management in the coming few weeks, Sommers had to make a recommendation regarding which inventory cost flow method TW-Brazil would adopt. He also knew he would need to consider what varying production costs and the weakening of the Brazilian real would mean for South American profits. Exhibit 1 provides a summary of historical exchange rates and Sommers's forward expectations.

TW-Brazil manufacturing would begin by late 2015, and production and sales would commence in early 2016. Sommers's analysis included estimated production costs and sales prices for the next five years. He believed TW could sell its base model in Brazil for BRL2,250 in 2016, increasing this sales price incrementally over the next five years. Furthermore, Sommers estimated the total manufacturing costs for a single unit manufactured in Brazil would be BRL1,500 in 2016. Raw material and other manufacturing costs were also expected to increase each year for the next five years. The new plant's current manufacturing capacity was projected at 13,000 units per year. Longer term, Sommers expected robust demand for the product; he desired to slowly build unit inventory to about one-half of yearly demand. The remainder of his projections are summarized in Exhibit 2.

He passed this information to his CFO expecting a quick answer. Which method to use: LIFO or FIFO?

Required:

1. Compute the gross margins for 2016 through 2020 under both LIFO and FIFO [*Hint*: this requires computation of cost of goods sold under both methods]. Use R$ in all calculations. What do you conclude?
2. How much is the LIFO reserve, for each year, under the LIFO and FIFO accounting methods? What does this measure tell a user of financial statements?
3. Suppose in 2021 TW-Brazil produces no more units, and liquidates its remaining inventory at a sales price equivalent to its most recent production cost (R$ 2,150). What would be the gross margin realized in 2021?
4. For the operations in TW-Brazil, how do you think changing exchange rates would affect Tao & Willis' reported earnings?

EXHIBIT 1	Tao & Willis, Inc.: Inventory Accounting Methods

Brazilian Real/U.S. Dollar Historical and Sommers's Projected Exchange Rates

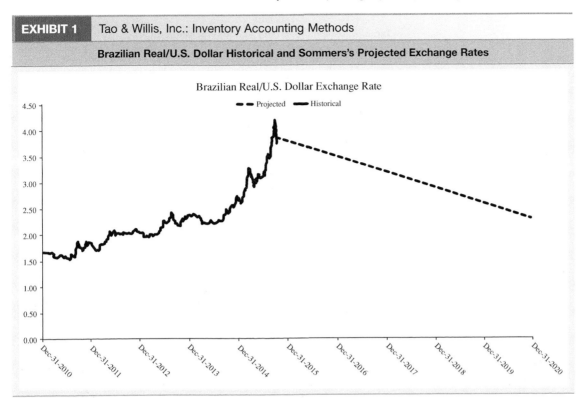

Source: All exhibits, unless otherwise noted, were created by author.

EXHIBIT 2	Tao & Willis, Inc.: Inventory Accounting Methods

Projected Production, Sales, and Exchange Rates

Year	Units Produced	Units Sold	Production Cost per Unit	Sales Price per Unit	Exchange Rate BRL/USD*
2016	13,000	10,000	BLR 1,500	BLR 2,250	3.50
2017	13,000	10,900	BLR 1,675	BLR 2,375	3.20
2018	13,000	11,280	BLR 1,800	BLR 2,550	2.90
2019	13,000	12,350	BLR 2,025	BLR 2,750	2.60
2020	13,000	13,700	BLR 2,150	BLR 2,995	2.30

*USD = U.S. dollars

Appendix 1
Tao & Willis, Inc.: Inventory Accounting Methods
Mercosur Overview[7]

A trading bloc in South America formed in 1991, Mercosur was often referred to as "the Common Market of the South." The goal of the bloc was to achieve fluid movement of goods, capital, services, and people among member states. The group acted as a customs union and a free-trade area, and membership depended on meeting certain political and economic criteria. For example, every country had to maintain a democratic system of governance. Member states included Argentina, Bolivia, Brazil, Paraguay, Uruguay, and Venezuela. In addition to member countries, Mercosur had several associate countries, including Chile, Columbia, Ecuador, Guyana, Peru, and Suriname. These countries were not members of the customs union and did not have voting power in terms of deterring Mercosur policies, but they had preferential access to the market.

A fundamental aspect of Mercosur was a common external tariff (CET), a schedule of taxes that applied to imports from nonmember countries. The CET varied, but averaged between 10% and 12%.[8] Any change to Mercosur economic policy required consensus from all members. But individual countries could ask that certain products be exempt from Mercosur policies in order to protect local industries. Brazil, for example, maintained higher tariffs on cell phones, telecommunications equipment, computers and computer printers, wind turbines, certain chemicals and pharmaceuticals, sardines, and mushrooms. For a listing of Brazil's largest importers in 2014, see the table below:

Company Name	Industry	Impact on Trade Balance (%)
Petrobras	Oil	16.43%
Samsung Electronica da Amazônia	Information technology, telecommunications, appliances	1.72%
Braskem SA	Chemical	1.18%
Cisa Trading	Automotive, aeronautic, cosmetic, pharma, tech	1.11%
Toyota do Brasil	Automotive	1.09%
Embraer SA	Aeronautic	1.02%
LG Electronics of Brazil	Electronics	1.00%
Ford Motor Company Brasil Ltda.	Automotive	0.87%
Flextronics International Tecnologia Ltda.	Electronics	0.85%
Yara Brasil Fertilizantes SA.	Chemical, fertilizer	0.67%
Volkswagen do Brasil	Automobile	0.62%
Syngenta Proteção de Cultivos Ltda..	Agribusiness	0.58%
GE Celma Ltda.	Aeronautic	0.57%
General Motors do Brasil Ltda.	Automotive	0.55%
BASF SA.	Chemical	0.53%
Bayer SA.	Chemical, pharma, agribusiness	0.47%
Renault do Brasil SA	Automotive	0.46%
Mercedes-Benz do Brasil Ltda.	Automotive	0.45%
Fertilizantes Heringer Ltda.	Agribusiness, chemicals	0.41%

Data source: Author adaptation of Marcelo Possato, "Top 20 Importing Companies in Brazil," *Brazil Business*, February 26, 2015.

In addition to the CET, member countries agreed to policies regarding currency exchange, investment, taxes, and educational exchanges in order to ease commerce between bloc members. In 2002, a free residence area was also established, permitting citizens of participating countries to obtain residence and the right to work in the participating countries without a visa. Furthermore, Mercosur had several free-trade agreements with other countries, including Chile, Columbia, Peru, Israel, and the Palestinian Authority.

---

[7] For a more detailed review, see Group Lamerica, L.L.C., "Mercosur Regional Trade Organization," 2015, http://grouplamerica.com/MERCOSUR; and Mark Keller, "Explainer: What is Mercosur?," Americas Society/Council of the Americas, August 2, 2012, http://www.as-coa.org/articles/explainer-what-mercosur-0 (both accessed July 7, 2016).
[8] Egil Fujikawa Nes, "Why are Taxes So High in Brazil?" *Brazil Business*, September 10, 2012.

SOLUTIONS TO REVIEW PROBLEMS

Solution 6.1

a. Cost of goods sold:

				Cost of Goods Sold
FIFO				
January	6,000 units	@	$2.00	$ 12,000
	10,300 units	@	2.00	20,600
	22,100 units	@	2.10	46,410
				$ 79,010
February	7,200 units	@	$2.10	15,120
	28,200 units	@	2.20	62,040
	5,300 units	@	2.60	13,780
Total				$169,950
LIFO				
January	29,300 units	@	$2.10	$ 61,530
	9,100 units	@	2.00	18,200
				79,730
February	15,300 units	@	$2.60	39,780
	25,400 units	@	2.20	55,880
Total				$175,390

Weighted average:

			Weighted-average	
January	6,000	units @	$2.00	$ 12,000
	10,300	units @	2.00	20,600
	29,300	units @	2.10	61,530
	45,600			94,130
Cost of goods sold	38,400	units @	2.06*	79,269
Ending inventory	7,200	units @	2.06*	14,863
February	7,200	units @	2.06*	14,863
	28,200	units @	2.20	62,040
	15,300	units @	2.60	39,780
	50,700			116,683
Cost of goods sold	40,700	units @	2.30**	93,667
Ending inventory	10,000	units @	2.30**	23,014
Total cost of goods sold				$172,936

* The unit cost is rounded for presentation purposes. The weighted-average calculation: $94,130/45,600 = $2.0643.
** The weighted-average calculation: $116,683/50,700 = $2.3014.

b. If the goal of the management of The Arcadia Company is to report the highest gross profit, the company should adopt the FIFO method:

	FIFO	LIFO
Revenues	$300,000	$300,000
Less: Cost of goods sold	(169,950)	(175,390)
Gross profit	$130,050	$124,610

If, however, the goal of the management of The Arcadia Company is to report the lowest gross profit, perhaps to minimize taxable net income, the company should adopt the LIFO method. The weighted-average method provides a result between the other two methods, thus not providing any compelling reason for its use.

Weighted-average	
Revenues	$300,000
Less: Cost of goods sold	172,936
Gross profit	$127,064

Solution 6.2

Because the company uses FIFO and has an ending inventory valuation before a LCM adjustment of $350,000, the LCM adjustment required will be $25,000 ($350,000 − $325,000). Had the company instead used LIFO, no LCM adjustment would have been needed.

Solution 6.3

1.

Net earnings before tax as reported.	$5,311
Add: Change in LIFO reserve	200
Net earnings before tax if the company had only used FIFO.	$5,511

2.

Inventory reported on balance sheet	$ 8,678
Add: LIFO reserve	2,500
Inventory if the company had only used FIFO	$11,178

3.

Average effective tax rate (1,056/5,311).	19.88%
Change in LIFO reserve	200
Estimated tax savings from use of LIFO (19.88% × 200)	$39.8 million

4.

$$\text{LIFO inventory-on-hand period} = \frac{365}{(\text{Cost of sales} / \text{Inventory})}$$

$$2015: \frac{365}{(76{,}520 / 8{,}678)} = 41.39 \text{ days}$$

$$2014: \frac{365}{(54{,}823 / 6{,}076)} = 40.45 \text{ days}$$

5.

$$\text{FIFO inventory-on-hand period for 2015} = \frac{365}{[(76{,}520 - 200) / (8{,}678 + 2{,}500)]} = 53.46 \text{ days}$$

6.

$$\text{Days payable period} = \frac{365}{(\text{Cost of sales} / \text{Accounts payable})}$$

$$2015: \frac{365}{(76{,}520 / 10{,}088)} = 48.12 \text{ days}$$

$$2014: \frac{365}{(54{,}823 / 4{,}315)} = 28.73 \text{ days}$$

When you complete this chapter you should be able to:

1. Describe how the acquisition cost of a long-lived asset is determined, and how the accounting treatment for ongoing costs related to these assets can differ. (page 262)

2. Understand why the matching of depreciation, depletion, and amortization expense with operating revenue is important. (page 264)

3. Explain how depreciation is calculated using straight-line, double-declining-balance, and the units-of-production methods. (page 264)

4. Define an asset impairment and how impairments are reflected in financial statements. (page 273)

5. Describe the accounting and reporting for intangible assets. (page 276)

6. Describe natural resources and how they are reported on the balance sheet. (page 278)

7. Compare the accounting for long-lived fixed assets between U.S. GAAP and IFRS. (page 280)

8. Understand a due diligence review of the financial statement disclosures associated with a firm's capital investments. (page 280)

Long-Lived Fixed Assets, Intangible Assets, and Natural Resources

7

Keurig Green Mountain, Inc. (GMCR) is a specialty coffee company based in Waterbury, Vermont. The company participates in a variety of beverage related businesses, including sourcing, producing, and selling over 200 varieties of coffee, cocoa, and teas. Many of its products come in single serving portion packs, although it also sells coffee in traditional packaging, whole bean and ground. GMCR sells its products primarily in North America through general retailers, restaurants, office coffee distributors, and directly to consumers through the internet. The company also manufactures gourmet single-cup brewing systems and brewing equipment. The company was founded in 1981 as a small café and by any measure has been a phenomenal success—by 2011 annual sales exceeded $2.6 billion.

KEURIG GREEN MOUNTAIN, INC.

But by early 2012 the luster had begun to wear off the GMCR story. On May 3, coincident with another solid quarter of earnings, the company forecast modestly slower growth and that day the stock shed almost 50 percent of its value. Compounding the problems caused by lofty growth expectations, some investors had become skeptical that the company was achieving past earnings targets by classifying some of its costs as capitalized assets, rather than immediately expensing them. One particularly vocal skeptic was David Einhorn, a hedge fund manager at Greenlight Capital.

In an October 2011 presentation at the Value Investing Conference in New York City, cynically titled "GAAP-uccino," Einhorn laid out what he thought were questionable capital expenditure forecasts for the company. His analysis showed that the historic change in K-cup unit sales did not correspond to the change in capital expenditures. He estimated that over half of the company's 2011 expenditures for long-term assets were unexplainable, arguing that as the company grew it should have achieved more scale with that growth. Capital expenditures for long-term fixed assets should have shown a company becoming more efficient, not less efficient. A New York Times article further questioned GMCR's announced capital expenditures of $175 million, versus analyst estimates of less than half that amount.

GMCR's responses to these inquiries, whether well-founded or not, were simply that the company adhered to required accounting standards and principles for its capital expenditures. The claims against the company, however, highlight the importance of accounting for long-term assets and the potential attention on these capital investments for many interested investors. In this chapter we explore these issues. We investigate the acquisition, use, and accounting for investments in long-lived fixed assets, intangible assets, and natural resources. We will see that the key issues surrounding these assets are (1) how to match their acquisition cost with the revenue generated by their use, and (2) the continuing asset value that should be reported on a company's balance sheet.

ACQUISITION COST OF A LONG-LIVED ASSET

Takeaway 1
Describe how the acquisition cost of a long-lived asset is determined, and how the accounting treatment for ongoing costs related to these assets can differ.

When an asset is initially acquired by a business, it is generally accepted accounting practice globally to **capitalize** the acquisition cost of the asset—that is, to place the value of the asset on the company's balance sheet at the asset's acquisition cost. This accepted practice reflects the historical cost principle discussed in Chapter 2. Frequently, the **acquisition cost** includes more than just its listed purchase price; it also includes any sales tax on the purchase price, transportation costs from the seller to the buyer's location, as well as a number of ancillary costs. As a general rule, all expenditures necessary to purchase an asset, transport the asset to the buyer's place of business, and place the asset into a revenue-producing state should be capitalized to the balance sheet as part of an asset's total acquisition cost. For example, if installation of an asset requires modification of the buyer's facilities (such as the installation of higher voltage electrical wiring or reinforced flooring), these costs should be capitalized to the balance sheet because without these expenditures the asset would not reach a revenue-producing state. While this accounting treatment might seem straightforward, many expenditures are less clear. For instance, if the use of a newly acquired asset requires special employee training, these costs may be capitalized to the balance sheet as part of the asset's acquisition cost because without them the asset would not be operational.

Some businesses self-construct the assets they utilize in their business. For example, automotive and truck manufacturers typically "retool" their production lines every three to five years. Retoolings often coincide with the introduction of a new model or the redesign of existing models. The cost of retooling is quite expensive, frequently involving billions of dollars. Rather than outsource these production-line changes, the automotive companies often undertake the retooling themselves. Consequently, the costs incurred during the retooling process are capitalized to the automotive company's balance sheet as a component of the plant and equipment account. Included in the amount capitalized would be any and all costs related to the retooling, such as wages paid to workers and depreciation on equipment and tools used in the retooling process.

Other, less obvious costs may also be capitalized under certain circumstances. The interest charges on any borrowed funds used to finance the retooling are appropriately capitalized to the balance sheet as part of the production-line cost during the period of retooling. However, once the retooling process is complete, the interest charges (and all other costs) may no longer be capitalized as part of the cost of the asset, and instead, must thereafter be expensed. When borrowing costs are capitalized, it is accepted practice to disclose the amount of the **capitalized interest** charges in the company's footnotes. Disclosure of these amounts serves an important purpose. Many investment professionals question the economic rationale behind the practice of capitalizing interest charges, preferring to see all financing costs expensed in the fiscal period in which they are incurred (recognizing the income statement deduction in the same fiscal period as the cost is incurred). Disclosure of the amount of capitalized interest costs in the footnotes to the financial statements enables these professionals to restate a company's financial statements as if the interest charges had been expensed, rather than capitalized.

Betterment Versus Maintenance Expenditures

After an asset has been placed in service, it is not uncommon to incur expenditures related to the asset's continued use. Just as with expenditures related to the initial acquisition of an asset, the financial reporting decision for expenditures made after the asset has been placed in service similarly relates to whether they are expensed immediately or capitalized to the balance sheet. Some post-acquisition expenditures involve routine maintenance of the asset (such as an oil change on a company truck) that is necessary to obtain the normal productive output from the asset. As a consequence, routine **maintenance expenditures** are expensed on the income statement in the fiscal period in which they are incurred. Other expenditures may be nonroutine, however, and consequently, may be more appropriately accounted for by capitalizing them to the balance sheet as part of the cost of an asset. For example, a factory with an expected useful life of 50 years may require a new roof every twenty years. The cost of replacing the factory roof is not a maintenance expense, but instead, is typically considered to be a **betterment** or improvement.

So how does one determine whether an expenditure is a betterment or maintenance? Betterment expenditures are frequently material in amount and must satisfy one of the following conditions:

1. extend the productive life of an asset,
2. improve the quality and/or quantity of an asset's output, or
3. reduce the operating expenses associated with the asset.

If one of these conditions is met, then the expenditures are capitalized to the balance sheet, to be depreciated over the asset's remaining expected useful life. Those expenditures that do not meet one of the above conditions are more appropriately classified and expensed as maintenance.

BUSINESS PERSPECTIVE

Capitalizing Versus Expensing at WorldCom

WorldCom Inc. was a discount long-distance telephone service provider founded in 1995 with the merger of Williams Telecommunications Group Inc. and LDDS Inc. By 2002, WorldCom had become the United States' second largest long-distance telephone company through more than 60 mergers and acquisitions. In 2003, a U.S. Securities and Exchange Commission complaint alleged that World-Com changed its accounting for the cost of landlines leased from such companies as AT&T and SBC, among others. Originally, the line costs—that is, the charges paid by WorldCom for access to other telephone company networks—were expensed to match the company's operating expenses with its operating revenue. However, beginning in 2000, WorldCom began inappropriately capitalizing these costs to its corporate balance sheet as an asset. An investigation by WorldCom's auditors KPMG revealed that as much as $7 billion in line costs may have been inappropriately capitalized to enable the struggling company to report positive earnings. The accounting change was masterminded to buoy WorldCom's sagging share price. In July 2002, WorldCom filed for bankruptcy, the largest in U.S. corporate history. In March 2005, former WorldCom CEO Bernard Ebbers was convicted of conspiracy to commit fraud by falsifying WorldCom's financial results, securities fraud by misleading investors and the public about WorldCom's true financial condition, and making false filings with the U.S. Securities and Exchange Commission that misrepresented WorldCom's financial position. In late 2005, Mr. Ebbers was sentenced to 25 years in prison; he began serving his prison sentence in September 2006.

Could an astute financial analyst have identified the pending WorldCom disaster? It is very likely that a rigorous financial analysis and review of WorldCom's financial statements would have provided analysts with "red flags" regarding the company's financial problems. For instance, WorldCom's **fixed asset turnover ratio**—that is, its net sales divided by net fixed assets—declined over the period 2000 to 2002 from 0.31 to a mere 0.19, a drop of nearly 40 percent, as the amount of capitalized landline costs increased. A decline of this magnitude should have raised concern among the investment professionals that followed the company.

The identification of just which expenditures are maintenance versus those that are betterments is often quite ambiguous. Since this accounting decision can have a significant impact on a business's current earnings, these decisions should be carefully reviewed by a firm's management in conjunction with its independent auditor. As with most financial reporting decisions, the earnings impact of the treatment of an expenditure as maintenance versus a betterment is a matter of timing. Betterment expenditures capitalized to the balance sheet do not immediately reduce current earnings but will reduce future earnings through increased depreciation expense. Maintenance expenditures that are expensed immediately, on the other hand, reduce current pretax profit. Managers who are compensated on the basis of reported earnings, or those otherwise pressured to meet short-term earnings expectations, often prefer to capitalize as many expenditures as can be justified to avoid the adverse effect on net income (and their compensation) caused by immediately expensing such outlays.

Takeaway 2
Understand why the matching of depreciation, depletion, and amortization expense with operating revenue is important.

MATCHING: THE ALLOCATION OF COSTS TO FUTURE PERIODS

Once the capitalized cost of a long-lived asset has been determined, the next accounting issue to be confronted is how best to allocate that cost over the asset's expected productive life. First, be aware that there are a variety of different terms used to describe the allocation of capitalized costs to future periods. The process of allocating the capitalized cost of a fixed asset over its expected useful life is most commonly referred to as **depreciation**, whereas the process of allocating the acquisition cost of an intangible asset over its productive life is called **amortization**. **Depletion**, on the other hand, refers to the allocation of the acquisition and development costs of a natural resource over its expected productive life. **Fixed assets** include such tangible assets as property, plant and equipment, whereas **intangible assets** include goodwill, the intellectual property represented by copyrights and patents, and other contract rights. **Natural resources** include such assets as standing timber, oil and gas reserves, iron ore, coal and gold mines.

The significance of the allocation process for long-lived assets arises as a consequence of the matching concept—that is, the desire within a given accounting period to match a company's operating revenues with **all** of the costs incurred to generate that revenue. Long-lived assets, by their nature, have the capacity to generate operating revenue over many years, and consequently, it is necessary to arrive at a logical and systematic way to distribute the capitalized value of these assets against the future revenue generated by their use.

For most long-lived fixed assets, it is difficult to know with certainty in what amount, or when, an asset's future revenue stream is going to occur since operating revenue is dependent on so many externalities such as product demand, competition, changing customer tastes, and innovation, among others. Consequently, given the ambiguity surrounding the revenue streams associated with such assets, the accounting community has developed a number of "logical and systematic" allocation schemes that have become accepted as GAAP. In the case of fixed assets, these generally accepted allocation approaches include:

- Straight-line method
- Accelerated methods
    - Double-declining balance
- Production-based methods
    - Units-of-production

In the case of intangible assets, amortization using the straight-line method is almost universally practiced worldwide. And, in the case of natural resources, the use of the units-of-production depletion approach is considered to be "best practice." Below we provide further detail on the application of each of these methods.

Takeaway 3
Explain how depreciation is calculated using straight-line, double-declining-balance, and the units-of-production methods.

Straight-Line Method

As its name implies, the **straight-line method** of depreciation (and amortization) allocates the capitalized cost of an asset equally over an asset's expected productive life. The amount of expense each period is determined using the following formula:

$$\text{Operating expense for the period} = \frac{1}{n}(\text{Acquisition cost} - \text{Residual value})$$

where n equals the asset's expected useful life in months or in years. The **useful life** of an asset is the length of time that the asset is expected to be productive (i.e., produce revenue) for the company. This length of time is generally shorter than the actual physical life of the asset. For example, a computer may have a ten-year physical life; however, the useful life for accounting purposes is sometimes much shorter, perhaps only four years or less, because of technological improvements in the area of information technology. Techno-logical advances, in fact, often render assets obsolete long before their productive years are complete. The estimated amount that an asset could be sold for at the end of its useful life is called the asset's **residual value**, scrap value, or **salvage value**. The residual value is important not only because of its inclusion in the straight-line expensing formula, but also because it represents a minimum balance sheet value for the asset at all times. That is, the asset value should not be depreciated or amortized below the residual value, as that amount represents the expected value that can be obtained by the company at the asset's ultimate disposition.

As an example, if the asset to be depreciated is a truck having an expected useful life of five years, costing $30,000, and with an expected residual value of $4,000 at the end of its five-year useful life, the annual straight-line depreciation charge would be $5,200 (1/5[$30,000 − $4,000]). Thus, in each of the asset's five years, a constant amount ($5,200) would be matched against the revenue produced by the truck. An implicit assumption underpinning the straight-line method is that an asset's productive capacity is approximately equal during each period of its useful life. Over the expected five-year useful life of the truck, the depreciation charges will aggregate to $26,000 (five years × $5,200 per year), representing the **depreciable cost** of the asset. The residual value of the asset ($4,000) should not be depreciated since this is the expected value that the asset can be sold for when retired from use.

How is depreciation calculated when an asset is acquired partway through a fiscal period? In recogni-tion of the reality that depreciation expense is just an estimate of the value of an asset that is consumed or used up in a given fiscal period, most companies employ a practice known as the **half-year convention**. Under this convention, no matter when an asset is acquired during a fiscal year, only one-half year of depreciation expense is taken in the first year of use. An alternative application of the half-year conven-tion used by some companies is that when an asset is acquired during the first six months of the year, the asset is assumed to have been acquired on the first day of the year and thus a full year of depreciation expense is taken. For assets acquired anytime during the second six months of the fiscal year, only one-half year of the first year's depreciation expense is taken.

When a company records its depreciation expense for the period, retained earnings is reduced by the amount of the expense and an equivalent amount is subtracted from the book value of the asset. However, in the case of long-term fixed assets, instead of reducing the original asset account directly, the current depreci-ation charge is placed in a contra-asset account called **accumulated depreciation**, which is then subtracted from the asset account. With the use of this account two important pieces of information are retained on the balance sheet: (1) the original cost of the asset and (2) the accumulated depreciation on the asset taken to date. The difference in these two amounts, the asset's remaining **net book value** ($24,800), is calculated as the acquisition cost ($30,000) minus the accumulated depreciation ($5,200) taken since the acquisition date. In the case of the truck, this information is illustrated below for the first year of depreciation.

	Acquire Truck	Depreciate Truck	End. Bal. (Summary)	
Assets				
Cash..........................	(30,000)		(30,000)	
::				
Property, plant and equipment.........	30,000		30,000	} Net book value = $24,800
Accumulated depreciation............		(5,200)	(5,200)	
Shareholders' Equity				
Retained earnings			(5,200)	} Retained earnings = ($5,200)
Depreciation expense.............		(5,200)		

As noted above the convention of using the accumulated depreciation account to record the deprecia-tion taken on an asset stems from a desire to preserve an asset's original acquisition cost while also dis-closing its current net book value. Comparing an asset's acquisition cost to its net book value reveals the relative age of an asset and, consequently, how soon the asset will need to be replaced. For example, the ratio of book value to acquisition cost for our $30,000 truck after one year of use yields a ratio of 83 percent ($24,800/$30,000). This suggests that only 17 percent of the asset has been consumed to date and, thus, that the asset will not need to be replaced for some years in the future. Knowing the relative age of a company's assets is useful as managers and investment professionals try to forecast future cash flow needs.

Accelerated Methods

Accelerated depreciation methods refer to those allocation methods that cause an asset to be expensed at a rate faster early in its useful life, then at a slower rate later in its life. The **double-declining-balance** method is the most commonly used accelerated method, yielding the fastest write-off of any generally accepted depreciation method. Under this approach, the annual depreciation expense is calculated as follows:

> The **double-declining-balance** (DDB) method is part of a family of declining-balance depreciation methods. The depreciation rate for DDB is 2/n, where n is the asset's expected useful life. But other rates are also permissible (such as 1.5/n, 1.25/n, etc.) so long as they do not exceed the DDB rate of 2/n.

$$\text{Operating expense for the period} = \frac{2}{n}(\text{Net book value})$$

where n equals the asset's expected useful life in months, quarters, or years.

In the case of the truck with a five-year life, costing $30,000, and with a residual value of $4,000, double-declining depreciation would be calculated each year as follows:

	Depreciation Expense	Double-Declining-Balance Calculations	Accumulated Depreciation	End of Period Book Value
Year 1 . . .	$12,000	2/5 × ($30,000)	$12,000	$18,000
Year 2 . . .	7,200	2/5 × ($30,000 − $12,000)	19,200	10,800
Year 3 . . .	4,320	2/5 × ($30,000 − $12,000 − $7,200)	23,520	6,480
Year 4 . . .	1,240*	1/2 × ($26,000 − $23,520)	24,760	5,240
Year 5 . . .	1,240*	1/2 × ($26,000 − $23,520)	26,000	4,000
	$26,000			

A close inspection of the truck's depreciation expense each year reveals that the double-declining-balance depreciation formula was not strictly applied in years 4 and 5 (indicated by the "*"). This departure is not unusual and was required because the DDB formula depreciates the truck so rapidly that by the end of Year 3, the remaining book value is only $6,480. Continuing to mechanically apply the DDB formula would cause the truck to be depreciated below its expected residual value of $4,000. Consequently, at this point, the convention typically applied is that the strict application of the DDB formula be abandoned, and thereafter, a straight-line approach utilized for the remaining costs to be depreciated. As of year 4, these amount to $2,480 ($6,480 − $4,000), and they are thus spread equally over the remaining two years of the truck's useful life ($2,480/2 years = $1,240).

Exhibit 7.1 provides a graphical comparison of the annual depreciation expense taken for the truck under the two distinct methods. From the graph you can readily see why one is labeled "straight-line" and the other "accelerated." Important to emphasize again is that the total depreciation taken under both methods across the five years is $26,000. *What differs is the timing of the allocation across periods.*[1]

---

[1] A second, but less widely used, accelerated depreciation method is the **sum-of-the-years' digits method**. The sum-of-the-years' digits (SYD) may be calculated as follows: SYD = n(n + 1)/2, where n is the asset's expected useful life. For an asset costing $30,000, with a useful life of five years (SYD = 15) and residual value of $4,000, the depreciation expense under this method would be calculated as follows:

	Depreciation Expense	Calculation
Year 1	$ 8,667	5/15 × ($30,000 − $4,000)
Year 2	6,933	4/15 × ($30,000 − $4,000)
Year 3	5,200	3/15 × ($30,000 − $4,000)
Year 4	3,467	2/15 × ($30,000 − $4,000)
Year 5	1,733	1/15 × ($30,000 − $4,000)
	$26,000	

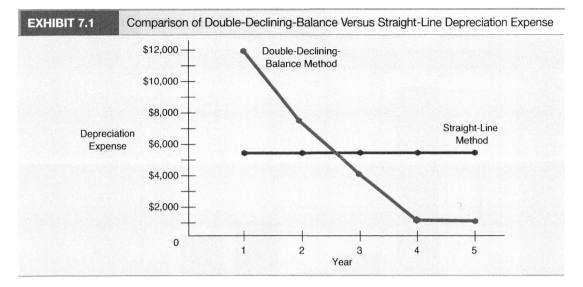

EXHIBIT 7.1 — Comparison of Double-Declining-Balance Versus Straight-Line Depreciation Expense

It is noteworthy that all generally accepted depreciation methods incorporate an asset's expected residual value in the calculation of the annual (or periodic) depreciation expense except the declining-balance methods. The declining-balance methods do not consider an asset's expected residual value except as a lower bound of total depreciation taken. In those situations when applying the method would cause the total depreciation expense taken on an asset to exceed its depreciable cost base, an adjustment to the depreciation formula will be necessary, typically to cap the depreciation expense taken so as not to allow the asset's net book value to drop below its residual value.

Exhibit 7.2 provides a graphical representation of balance sheet values related to the truck account under the straight-line and DDB methods, by year. Note once more that by the end of Year 5, the net book value under each method converges to $4,000.

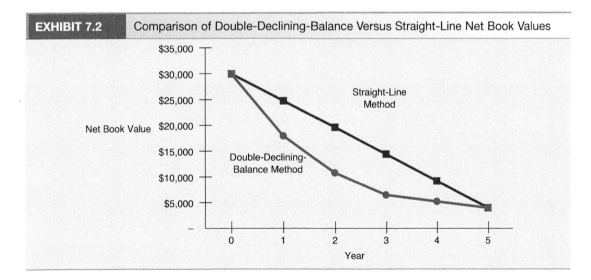

EXHIBIT 7.2 — Comparison of Double-Declining-Balance Versus Straight-Line Net Book Values

Units-of-Production Method

For some assets, calculating depreciation as a function of time (such as straight-line or declining balance) may not be relevant because the expected useful life of certain assets is more closely linked to their actual usage rather than the passage of time. For example, some equipment manufacturers have determined that their products have a reasonably well-defined useful life as measured by the number of machine-hours they are likely to run or the number of units they are likely to produce. For instance, the manufacturer of our truck costing $30,000 may believe that, based upon engineering statistics and actual utilization data, the truck's useful life is best defined in terms of expected miles to be driven (such as most truck leases are defined in terms of a maximum allowable mileage). Application of a straight-line or

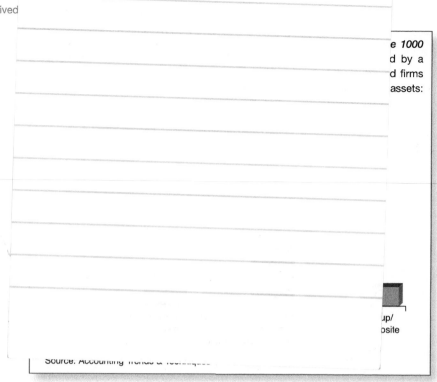

double-declining-balance method potentially would result in depreciation patterns unrelated to the earnings potential of the truck. Under these circumstances, the use of an output-based allocation method, such as the units-of-production method, may yield superior matching of revenue with expense.

Under the **units-of-production method**, the periodic depreciation charge is calculated as follows:

$$\text{Operating expense for the period} = \frac{\text{Output consumed this period}}{\text{Total estimated lifetime output}} \times (\text{Acquisition cost} - \text{Residual value})$$

As an illustration, if the truck is expected to be driven an aggregate 100,000 miles before replacement, and the actual mileage driven is 25,000 miles in Year 1, 25,000 miles in Year 2, 20,000 miles in Year 3, and 15,000, 12,000, and 12,000 miles in Years 4, 5, and 6 respectively, the units-of-production depreciation would be calculated as follows:

	Depreciation Expense	Units-of-Production Calculation
Year 1	$ 6,500	$\frac{25,000}{100,000} \times (\$30,000 - \$4,000)$
Year 2	6,500	$\frac{25,000}{100,000} \times (\$30,000 - \$4,000)$
Year 3	5,200	$\frac{20,000}{100,000} \times (\$30,000 - \$4,000)$
Year 4	3,900	$\frac{15,000}{100,000} \times (\$30,000 - \$4,000)$
Year 5	3,120	$\frac{12,000}{100,000} \times (\$30,000 - \$4,000)$
Year 6	780	$\frac{3,000}{100,000} \times (\$30,000 - \$4,000)$
	$26,000	

BUSINESS PERSPECTIVE

Units-of-Production

Exxon Mobil Corporation is one of the world's largest energy companies. It is involved in the exploration, production, and transportation of crude oil and natural gas products. As part of the systematic allocation of its balance sheet properties as charges against income, it depreciates proved oil reserves as they are extracted and ready for sale. How that is determined is not as easy as it sounds. Below are the disclosures made by Exxon Mobil in its 2014 annual report related to these activities. The first disclosure is from the company's Critical Accounting Policy (CAP) disclosure in Management's Discussion and Analysis (MD&A), and the second from the footnotes to the financial statements. Note how the company describes its ratio allocation, very similar to how a truck or car might be depreciated based on miles driven.

> The calculation of unit-of-production depreciation is a critical accounting estimate that measures the depreciation of upstream assets. It is the ratio of *actual volumes produced to total proved reserves* or proved developed reserves (those proved reserves recoverable through existing wells with existing equipment and operating methods), *applied to the asset cost* (emphasis added). The volumes produced and asset cost are known and, while proved reserves have a high probability of recoverability, they are based on estimates that are subject to some variability. While the revisions the Corporation has made in the past are an indicator of variability, they have had a very small impact on the unit-of-production rates because they have been small compared to the large reserves base.

> Acquisition costs of proved properties are amortized using a unit-of-production method, computed on the basis of total proved oil and gas reserves. Capitalized exploratory drilling and development costs associated with productive depletable extractive properties are amortized using unit-of-production rates based on the amount of proved developed reserves of oil, gas and other minerals that are estimated to be recoverable from existing facilities using current operating methods. Under the unit-of-production method, oil and gas volumes are considered produced once they have been measured through meters at custody transfer or sales transaction points at the outlet valve on the lease or field storage tank.

Like the straight-line method, units-of-production depreciation incorporates an asset's expected residual value, and consequently, the formula only allocates the truck's depreciable cost of $26,000 ($30,000 − $4,000) over its expected five-year life. The advantage of this method should be clear, however, in that the depreciation pattern is directly aligned to usage of the truck rather than its age.

Choosing a Depreciation Method

The process of allocating the cost of an asset over its useful life is done solely for the purpose of matching the acquisition cost of the asset with the revenue generated by the asset's use. The purpose is not to align the asset's balance sheet value—its net book value—with the actual market value of the asset. It will only be by coincidence that an asset's net book value will ever equal the market value of the asset at any time other than the point of initial purchase. It should also be noted that accumulated depreciation is nothing more than a running total offset to the acquisition cost of the asset. This account does not represent a fund of money that can be used for asset replacement as is sometimes thought by those who lack an understanding of accounting. In your review of each depreciation method illustrated above, be sure to observe that each method resulted in the same total depreciation taken over the asset's useful life—only the amount of the periodic depreciation charge, the timing, differed across the methods.

Given the variety of depreciation approaches that are considered acceptable under GAAP, how does the management of a company choose a method to depreciate its assets? Further complicating the answer to this question is that GAAP permits the use of a combination of depreciation methods—that is, some assets may be depreciated using the straight-line method while others may be depreciated using double-declining-balance or the units-of-production method—although most companies tend to use one approach for all of their depreciable assets, particularly for publicly disclosed financial statements.

In the United States, the depreciation method most commonly used in audited financial statements is the straight-line method. The popularity of the straight-line method in the United States appears linked to several considerations. First, for capital-intensive companies, depreciation expense is one of the largest operating expenses deducted against operating revenue. The straight-line method holds that expense stable, thereby enabling management to know with certainty a significant component of the operating expenses that they will need to cover each fiscal period. Some managers feel that this knowledge allows them to focus on other important issues when making operating decisions. Second, some investment professionals allege that companies attempt to "smooth" their reported earnings on the presumption that earnings stability is highly valued by the capital market (smooth earnings represent certainty, and hence, less risk). The straight-line method is thought to facilitate **income smoothing** because it provides a stable level of depreciation deductions over the life of an asset. Finally, relative to the accelerated methods, the straight-line method provides smaller depreciation deductions against operating revenues in the early years of an asset's life (see Exhibit 7.1). As companies grow and continue to add to their fixed asset bases, these differences will get increasingly exaggerated. For management concerned about reporting the highest possible earnings, the straight-line method tends to facilitate this financial reporting objective.

TAX PERSPECTIVE

Long-Term Assets Under U.S. Tax Law

Because long-term fixed assets are a significant part of nearly every business, managers and executives should be aware of certain important differences between the accounting required under U.S. GAAP and the rules that govern the tax treatment for those same assets. Here we provide a brief overview of some of the highlights.

Recall that a number of accounting issues were identified with regard to determining the amount of depreciation to be recorded on a company's income statement, and relatedly, the book value to be recorded on a company's balance sheet. These issues include the amount to be capitalized to the asset account and the choices surrounding the depreciation/amortization method for an asset (i.e., the asset's residual value and the asset's expected useful life). For U.S. income tax purposes, depreciation and amortization rules are generally more restrictive in choice. But the rate at which an item is allowed to be expensed is generally quite generous. This can be traced directly to economic stimulus considerations—the quicker a company can write-off a long-term fixed asset, the more likely the asset will be replaced with another.

Regarding the amount to be capitalized as an asset, U.S. tax authorities generally apply the same criteria as U.S. GAAP. All payments necessary to get an asset to its intended use, including its purchase price, sales tax, and shipping charges, are considered part of an asset's acquisition cost. Subsequent payments made for items other than routine maintenance that improve an asset's functionality, its profitability, or extend its useful life, would also be capitalized.

After the amount to be capitalized is determined, companies must follow a depreciation system called the **modified accelerated cost recovery system** (MACRS), a system that specifies the method and the rate at which various assets must be depreciated for tax purposes. The MACRS system provides for deductions that approximate the charges experienced under an accelerated method but with some qualifications. For tangible real property (i.e., buildings and real estate) and all intangibles, MACRS requires the use of the straight-line method. For all other tangible property, a manager can choose either an accelerated depreciation method (e.g., double declining balance) or straight-line.* Unlike U.S. GAAP where a manager is expected to consistently apply a depreciation method for assets of similar use, under tax law a company may elect either an accelerated or straight-line method for the tangible assets placed in service during a given year. Thus, the selected tax depreciation method may vary from year to year, forming the basis for effective tax planning.

The most significant difference between U.S. GAAP and tax accounting relates to the useful life restrictions placed on assets. Under GAAP, an asset's useful life is determined by management, whereas under tax accounting, it is predetermined by the IRS. Tables exist that categorize each asset type and give little room for deviation. Machinery and equipment, for instance, have a useful life for tax purposes of seven years. By way of contrast, under U.S. GAAP, managers may choose an expected life longer or even shorter than that used for tax purposes. As another example, under IRS rules, real property such as residential apartments or office buildings have lives ranging from 27.5 to 39 years, whereas for U.S. GAAP purposes, management may select a useful life longer or shorter than these periods.

* Because the former provides greater tax savings earlier, the accelerated method is virtually always selected. But, note that if expected tax rates for a company are lower in the earlier years of an asset's life, then a straight-line method may be preferred.

Related to the choice of depreciation method is the estimation of other assumptions embedded within the methods. Just as the choice of straight-line or accelerated methods can influence earnings, so too can estimates of an asset's useful life and residual (salvage) value. An accurate assessment of these two inputs at the date of acquisition is very difficult. But both must be made based on the best known facts and circumstances at the time the asset is placed in service. If managers were to assume a longer useful life, then the result would be a lower depreciation expense than otherwise would be reported. A higher residual value would result in a similar effect. GAAP provides no definitive guidelines for estimating the useful life and residual value of an asset, other than that these amounts should approximate the expected revenue generating life of the asset and its expected recoverable value at the end of that life, respectively. As with all accounting judgments made by management, these choices should be made consistently and conservatively, with appropriate levels of oversight and review.

REVIEW PROBLEM 7.1

The Arcadia Company is contemplating a large capital investment of $32 million in new production-line equipment, which is expected to have a useful life of six years, a residual value of $2 million at retirement, and be good for 800,000 units of production. The company's controller is uncertain whether the equipment should be depreciated using the straight-line method, the double-declining-balance method, or the units-of-production method. The CEO suggested that a decision be made only after comparing the financial effects of the three methods. The anticipated production in units for the new equipment is as follows:

Year 1	100,000
Year 2	120,000
Year 3	130,000
Year 4	150,000
Year 5	180,000
Year 6	120,000
Total	800,000

Required

Prepare a depreciation schedule for The Arcadia Company for the new equipment using each of the three methods of depreciation.

The solution is on page 294.

Accounting Policy Changes

Under the GAAP of most countries, companies are permitted to change the estimated useful life of a depreciable asset, its expected residual value, or the particular depreciation method in use. Frequent accounting policy changes, however, are normally not observed because it is well known that investment professionals regard any type of voluntary accounting policy change suspiciously, possibly indicating an attempt by management to "manage" reported earnings through the accounting policy change. Empirical evidence indicates that when a company's earnings increase as a consequence of an accounting policy change (such as a switch from double-declining-balance depreciation to straight-line depreciation), a firm's share price will tend to fall as the capital market speculates that such a change may forebode adverse future corporate news.[2] In essence, the capital market appears to "second-guess" the motivation behind voluntary corporate accounting policy changes. If the policy change results in an increase in accounting earnings, the market appears to infer that management is attempting to cover up poor expected future operating performance. If, on the other hand, an accounting policy change results in a decrease in accounting earnings, the market appears to infer that the firm's operating performance is expected to exceed management's projections, and consequently, the policy change is intended to "bank" some of the excess earnings for use in future periods (creating an earnings reserve to help meet future earnings' expectations).

There are three types of **accounting policy changes** permitted under GAAP: entity, estimate, and method. An **entity change** occurs when a company acquires, merges with, or divests itself of another company,

---

[2] D. Dharam and B. Lev, "The Valuation of Consequences of Accounting Changes: A Multi-Year Examination," *Journal of Accounting, Auditing and Finance* (1993).

BUSINESS PERSPECTIVE

Long-Lived Fixed Asset Disclosures

Financial statement disclosures of the H.J. Heinz Company for its fixed assets are presented below. The data reveals that Heinz uses the straight-line method to depreciate these assets (see footnote information). Since land is generally not depreciated, the depreciation expense of $295.718 million reported in Heinz's 2012 consolidated financial statements relates only to the company's buildings and equipment. Is it possible to estimate the average age of Heinz's buildings and equipment and their expected useful lives?

The aggregate cost of Heinz's depreciable assets in 2012 is $5.185 billion ($1.009 billion + $4.176 billion). Since the company uses the straight-line method, if we assume a zero residual value, the expected useful life of these assets can be estimated by dividing their aggregate cost by the depreciation for 2012 ($5.185 billion/$295.718 million), yielding an average expected useful life of approximately 17.5 years. With respect to the remaining useful life of the company's buildings and equipment, dividing the accumulated depreciation balance at year-end 2012 by the assets' aggregate capitalized cost ($2.782 billion/$5.185 billion) indicates that approximately 53.7 percent of the assets' expected useful lives have been used up, leaving 46.3 percent, or approximately 8.1 years (46.3 percent × 17.5 years), of remaining useful life. Thus, we can conclude that at the current rate of depreciation, Heinz will not need to replace these long-lived productive assets for about eight years.

H.J. HEINZ COMPANY		
Consolidated Balance Sheet		
(in thousands)	2012	2011
Property, plant and equipment		
Land	$ 81,185	$ 85,457
Buildings and leasehold improvements	1,009,379	1,019,311
Equipment, furniture and other.	4,175,997	4,119,947
	5,266,561	5,224,715
Less: Accumulated depreciation	2,782,423	2,719,632
Total property, plant and equipment, net	$2,484,138	$2,505,083

Consolidated Statement of Cash Flow		
(in thousands)		
Operating activities section:		
Depreciation	$295,718	$255,227
Investing activities section:		
Capital expenditures.	(418,734)	(335,646)
Proceeds from disposals of property, plant and equipment.	9,817	13,158

Footnote Disclosure (Note #1):

Land, buildings and equipment are recorded at cost. For financial reporting purposes, depreciation is provided on the straight-line method over the estimated useful lives of the assets, which generally have the following ranges: buildings—40 years or less, machinery and equipment—15 years or less, computer software—3 to 7 years, and leasehold improvements—over the life of the lease, not to exceed 15 years. Accelerated depreciation methods are generally used for income tax purposes. Expenditures for new facilities and improvements that substantially extend the capacity or useful life of an asset are capitalized. Ordinary repairs and maintenance are expensed as incurred. When property is retired or otherwise disposed, the cost and related accumulated depreciation are removed from the accounts and any related gains or losses are included in income. The Company reviews property, plant and equipment, whenever circumstances change such that the recorded value of an asset may not be recoverable. Factors that may affect recoverability include changes in planned use of the asset and the closing of facilities. The Company's impairment review is based on an undiscounted cash flow analysis at the lowest level for which identifiable cash flows exist and are largely independent. When the carrying value of the asset exceeds the future undiscounted cash flows, an impairment is indicated and the asset is written down to its fair value.

such as a subsidiary or division. In this case, the consolidated reporting entity is changed, and consequently, changes in the reported consolidated financial results are clearly imminent. To help financial statement users understand the effects of an entity change, companies are required to include pro forma financial data in their annual report—that is, data "as if" the entity change had not occurred—to enable statement users to evaluate the consolidated entity's performance independent of the entity change. The presentation of such pro forma information is normally required for only one year following an entity change.

An **estimate change**, on the other hand, is a change in an existing accounting estimate used by a firm in the preparation of its financial statements. Common financial statement estimates include the estimated bad debt expense, estimated sales returns, the estimate of an asset's residual value, and the estimated useful life of an asset. When a firm changes one of its estimates, the financial impact of the estimate change on the firm's net earnings must be disclosed in the company's footnotes. Consider, for example, the case of **Valley National Gas, Inc.** The company changed its estimate of the remaining expected useful life of its plant and equipment from 12 to 30 years. The change had the effect of reducing the company's annual depreciation expense by $2.3 million and increasing the company's net income after tax by $1.3 million. The change in accounting estimate raised Valley National's earnings per share by $0.14 per share, or approximately 80 percent.

Estimate changes like Valley National's expected useful life change are executed on a **prospective basis**; that is, no attempt is made to restate the historical financial statements of the company for the financial effects of the change. To illustrate, if after two years of depreciating a truck costing $30,000, with a residual value of $4,000 and expected useful life of five years using the straight-line method, it is determined that the truck will last eight years in total, no change would be required to the depreciation expense taken in years one and two. Those amounts would remain at $5,200 each year, or $10,400 for both years combined. But, the remaining depreciable cost of the truck of $15,600 ($26,000 − $10,400) will now be spread over the new remaining expected useful life of six years (8 years − 2 years). Consequently, the new depreciation expense will be $2,600 per year ($15,600/6 years), as compared to the original annual depreciation expense of $5,200. After 8 years, the total depreciation taken would amount to $26,000 as required.

Finally, a **method change** occurs when, for instance, a firm changes its revenue recognition policy from completed contract to percentage-of-completion or when a company switches its inventory valuation approach from LIFO to FIFO. Unlike estimate changes which are executed on a **prospective basis**, accounting method changes are generally reported on a **retrospective basis**. Under retrospective restatement, a firm recalculates each affected account balance under the new accounting policy for each affected fiscal

> Voluntary accounting policy changes are characterized by some investment professionals as an "unintended signal" from the management of a company to the capital market regarding the company's future operating prospects. This characterization of accounting policy changes reflects what has become known as **signaling theory**.

period. Since it is impractical and expensive to issue restated financial statements for all prior periods impacted by a method change, the restated results are reported only for those fiscal years included in the latest annual report. A lump-sum restatement to reflect the prior-period financial effect of the method change, called the **cumulative prior period effect of an accounting policy change**, is then made to beginning retained earnings in the statement of shareholders' equity. The retrospective approach is not required when it is impracticable, as is sometimes the case in accounting policy changes from FIFO to LIFO or when the policy change involves the depreciation, amortization, or depletion of long-lived, non-financial assets. In this latter case, the policy change is accounted for as "a change in accounting estimate due to a change in accounting principle" using the prospective approach.

As noted previously, accounting estimate and method changes are viewed skeptically by the capital market. Available empirical evidence, for example, suggests that a company's share price will tend to fall when a firm changes from an income-reducing method to an income-enhancing method (such as a switch from double-declining-balance depreciation to straight-line depreciation). Similarly, when a firm changes from an income-enhancing method to an income-reducing method (such as a FIFO to LIFO change), the company's share price will tend to increase.

REVALUING LONG-LIVED ASSETS

Takeaway 4
Define an asset impairment and how impairments are reflected in financial statements.

Two constructs that underpin the accounting frameworks of most developed countries are the **historical cost concept** and **conservatism**. The former stipulates that the assets of a business should initially be valued at their prior acquisition cost, and the latter that the expected losses of a business should be recorded as soon as they are identified, while expected gains should not be recorded until they are actually realized. As a consequence of these concepts, accepted accounting practice in the United States requires downward revaluations of all assets (such as the lower-of-cost-or-market rule for inventory) whereas upward asset revaluations are only selectively permitted. As will be seen in Chapter 8, marketable securities are often carried at their current market value, and thus, may be revalued upward or downward to reflect changes in their fair market value. But, this asset group is an exception to the general rule under U.S. GAAP.

In the U.S. long-lived assets may only be written down in value, and this may occur in two situations. First, as we saw earlier downward value adjustments are periodically recorded as depreciation expense to reflect the consumption of a long-lived asset associated with the ongoing operations of a business. Second, when the future earnings capacity of an asset declines unrelated to the depreciation process, the diminishment in value is recorded in the firm's income statement as an **impairment loss**. A depreciable long-lived asset is said to be "impaired" when the undiscounted sum of the future cash flow it is expected to help generate is less than its recorded balance sheet net book value. For assets subject to amortization, such as many intangibles, the relevant test for impairment is a comparison of the net book value to the asset's market value. In both cases, the write-down for impairment is made to the estimated market value of the asset, with a loss recorded on that period's income statement.

Often impairments occur when consumer demand for a product declines and the revenue-producing capacity of the long-lived assets used to produce the product, such as plant and equipment, cannot be utilized in the production of some alternative product. Consider the case of AMR Corporation, the parent company of American Airlines and American Eagle Airlines. Following the aircraft hijacking associated with the September 11, 2001, New York City terrorist attacks, AMR determined that the revenue-producing capacity of its fleet of aircraft had been impaired as consumer and business air travel declined significantly. Lacking an ability to convert its fleet of commercial aircraft to alternative revenue-producing activities, AMR took a $1.24 billion impairment charge at year-end 2001 and a second impairment charge of $0.46 billion at year-end 2002.

The use of annual asset revaluations in the U.K. and elsewhere reflects the commitment of standard-setters in these countries to the **market-value model of accounting**, in which all assets and liabilities are valued at their fair market value on the balance sheet.

In some countries, such as the United Kingdom, Australia, and New Zealand, when an asset appreciates in value, it is permissible to revalue the asset upward to reflect its appreciation in value. These upward revaluations may be executed annually and are reported in the financial statements by increasing the appreciated asset's balance sheet value and by increasing a shareholders' equity account called the **asset revaluation reserve** for the amount of the appreciation in asset value. The asset revaluation reserve is analogous to the "Unrealized gain/loss on available-for-sale securities" account found under U.S. GAAP that will be discussed in Chapter 8. These accounts represent unrealized wealth changes for a business and are reported as part of shareholders' equity on the balance sheet of the business because the wealth change has not yet been realized.

SALE OR RETIREMENT OF LONG-LIVED ASSETS

When long-lived assets are first acquired, they are recorded at their acquisition cost following the historical cost convention. These assets are then depreciated over their expected useful lives in order to properly match those past expenditures with the revenue that they contribute. When an asset is eventually sold or retired, it is necessary to remove the asset's remaining net book value from the company's books. Any difference between the proceeds from the sale of an asset and the remaining net book value of the asset is recorded as a gain if the proceeds exceed the net book value, or as a loss if the proceeds are less than the net book value. To illustrate, assume that Savanna Corporation sells a machine and receives $15,000. Further, assume that the machine was originally purchased for $60,000 and has accumulated depreciation to date of $50,000. Since the proceeds of $15,000 exceed the asset's remaining book value of $10,000 ($60,000 − $50,000), Savanna will record a $5,000 gain on the sale. This is shown in spreadsheet format below. Observe that not only is the original cost of the asset removed from the balance sheet at the time of sale but so too is any accumulated depreciation related to the asset sold. These amounts are replaced with the cash received, and the net difference reflected as a gain to income (and retained earnings).

	Acquire Machine	Depreciate Machine	Sell Machine	End. Bal. (summary)	
Assets					
Cash..............................	(60,000)		15,000	(45,000)	
::					
Property, plant and equipment......	60,000		(60,000)	—	
Accumulated depreciation........		(50,000)	50,000	—	
Shareholders' Equity					
Retained earnings				(45,000)	
Depreciation expense..........		(50,000)			Retained earnings = ($45,000)
Gain on sale			5,000		

There are a few other noteworthy points regarding the sale or retirement of a long-lived asset. First, in the case of an asset retirement, the accounting treatment is the same as if the asset were sold, but at a sales price of zero. Because nothing was received, the net book value becomes the amount of loss recorded on the transaction. Second, when an asset is sold, the depreciation and amortization up to the sales date must be recorded. This has the effect of properly categorizing the use of the asset for a portion of the period it was in use, and to also not understate the gain or overstate the loss on the sale itself. Finally, remember that any gains and losses are reported on the income statement on a net basis because this activity is usually peripheral to the company's primary business operations. In other words, the company does not report cash received from an asset sale as revenue and the net book value of the asset sold as an expense, but rather reports only a single number for income statement reporting purposes.

REVIEW PROBLEM 7.2

The McGee Company purchased a specialized machine five years ago for $250,000 and has taken $175,000 of depreciation to date. Suppose the company sells the machine for $50,000. Determine McGee's gain or loss on the sale.

The solution is on page 294.

Distortion Caused by Aging Assets

Since the book value of a long-lived asset declines as the asset ages, a reduction in book value can cause a distortion in some financial ratios when they are compared across time for a given company. For example, in cases when the productivity of an asset does not vary much during its early life, the return on assets (ROA) ratio will increase simply because the denominator of the ratio—total assets—decreases over time.

To illustrate, assume that Savanna Corporation purchases a single asset for $1,100,000 that is estimated to have a ten-year life and a salvage value of $100,000. Further assume that Savanna reports constant net income of $120,000 per year, including the annual $100,000 depreciation expense on its only asset. The return on assets ratio, defined as net income divided by ending total assets, will be 12 percent for the first year ($120,000/$1,000,000). After six years, however, the net book value of the asset will have declined to $500,000 and Savanna's ROA will have climbed to 24 percent, twice as high as the first year. Recall that net income has remained constant and Savanna is still operating with the same asset. The doubling of Savanna's ROA is simply a function of the reduction in net book value resulting from the annual depreciation charge on the asset. Results such as this can provide perverse incentives to managers, preventing them from making needed capital investments to replace their aging assets. The following table illustrates how the aging of long-lived assets can distort such important performance metrics as Savanna's ROA ratio:

	Acquisition Cost	Year 1	Year 2	Year 3	Year 4	Year 5	Year 6
Book value...........	$1,100,000	$1,000,000	$900,000	$800,000	$700,000	$600,000	$500,000
Depreciation.........		100,000	100,000	100,000	100,000	100,000	100,000
Net income..........		120,000	120,000	120,000	120,000	120,000	120,000
ROA		12%	13%	15%	17%	20%	24%
Asset age (in years)		1	2	3	4	5	6

down and a loss recorded if the new market value is less than the goodwill's book value. As a consequence of the two-step procedure followed to evaluate the current value of goodwill, goodwill impairment write-downs are rare and are likely to occur only in those cases in which an acquisition was materially overpriced or when an extraordinary externality impacts a business (such as AMR and the terrorist attack of 2001).

Marketing Costs

As a general rule, advertising and marketing costs are expensed when incurred under U.S. GAAP and IFRS. Similar to R&D accounting in the U.S., the conservative treatment of these operating expenditures stems from an inability to determine whether an advertising campaign has been successful, and if so, an inability to predict when the resulting increase in product sales associated with the advertising will occur. Thus, lacking reliable information about "when" and "how much," U.S. GAAP and the GAAP of most other countries recommend, but do not require, that advertising and marketing costs be expensed against operating revenue in the period in which the costs are incurred.

Occasionally, exceptions to this generally accepted practice will arise. Consider, for example, the case of Urban Outfitters, Inc. The company operates retail apparel stores under multiple brands, and relies heavily on catalog marketing to generate direct mail and internet sales. In its 2014 annual report the company notes the following.

The Company expenses the costs of advertising when the advertising occurs, except for direct-to-consumer advertising, which is capitalized and amortized over its expected period of future benefit. Advertising costs primarily relate to our Retail segment marketing expenses which are comprised of web marketing, catalog printing, paper, postage and other costs related to production of photographic images used in our catalogs and on our websites and mobile applications. **The catalog printing, paper, postage and other costs are amortized over the period in which the customer responds to the marketing material determined based on historical customer response trends to a similar season's advertisement.** Amortization rates are reviewed on a regular basis during the fiscal year and may be adjusted if the predicted customer response appears materially different from the historical response rate. The Company has the ability to measure the response rate to direct marketing early in the course of the advertisement based on its customers' reference to a specific catalog or by product placed and sold. The average amortization period for a catalog and related items is typically one to two months. **If there is no expected future benefit, the cost of advertising is expensed when incurred.** (Emphasis added by authors.)

NATURAL RESOURCES

eLectures

MBC

Takeaway 6
Describe natural resources and how they are reported on the balance sheet.

Natural resources include such assets as standing timber, oil and gas reserves, and iron ore, coal, gold, silver, and uranium mines. When these assets are purchased from other natural resource companies, they are reported on the balance sheet at their acquisition cost. Alternatively, when these assets are internally developed by a resource company the accounting treatment becomes much more complex. Two valuation approaches are available: the **full cost method** and the **successful efforts method**. Under the full cost method, all costs associated with the exploration for, and development of, natural resource assets are capitalized to the natural resource account on the balance sheet. Under this method, even the costs of unsuccessful exploration activities are capitalized to the balance sheet under the philosophy that the identification of new natural resource reserves is a speculative activity involving some inherent failure. In contrast, under the successful efforts method, only the costs associated with successful exploration and development activity are capitalized to the balance sheet. The cost of any unsuccessful activity is immediately expensed against net income.

Both the full cost and the successful efforts methods are generally accepted, and thus, both are available for use by managers of natural resource companies. In practice, however, only small resource companies tend to use the full cost method, whereas larger companies tend to utilize the successful efforts method. Can you think of a reason why small firms would prefer to use the full cost method?[3]

---

[3] If you thought about the adverse effect on net income associated with the successful efforts method, you are correct. Small firms have difficulty raising exploration and development capital, and this fund-raising is made more difficult when a firm reports little or no earnings. The full cost method capitalizes all exploration and development costs, making it more likely that a small firm will be able to report positive earnings, thus increasing its chances of raising future exploration capital.

To illustrate the difference between these two approaches, consider the case of an energy company involved in the exploration and development of oil and gas wells. Assume that the energy company owns the rights to explore for oil and gas on a given site and anticipates drilling four exploratory wells at a cost of $1 million each. The company's exploration program yielded three successful wells and one unsuccessful (or "dry") well. Under the full cost method, the entire $4 million spent on drilling the four exploratory wells would be capitalized to the company's balance sheet, whereas under the successful efforts method, only $3 million, representing the cost of the three successful wells, may be capitalized. The $1 million cost associated with the unsuccessful well would be expensed on the income statement.

For those amounts capitalized to the company's balance sheet, GAAP requires that those amounts be depleted over the resource's expected useful life. Unlike depreciation, there is only one generally accepted depletion approach, the units-of-production method. This method is procedurally equivalent to the units-of-production depreciation method utilized by some companies and illustrated earlier. Under this method, the first step is to estimate the number of units—barrels of oil, tons of ore, or board feet of timber—likely to be produced by a well, mine, or tract of land. Next, a depletion rate per unit is determined by dividing the capitalized resource cost by the asset's expected total output in barrels, tons, or board feet. For example, if the estimated number of tons of ore to be extracted from a mine is two million and the mine's original cost, less estimated residual value, is $10 million, the depletion rate per ton of extracted ore would be $5.00 ($10 million/2 million tons). If, during the first year of operations, 20,000 tons of ore are extracted, the depletion expense on the annual income statement would be $100,000 ($5 × 20,000 tons), and the book value of the mine on the balance sheet would be $9.9 million ($10 million − $100,000).

	Alternative Valuation Methods	
	Full Cost	**Successful Efforts**
Balance Sheet Account		
Long-term asset—wells	$4,000,000	$3,000,000
Retained earnings	0	(1,000,000)
Income Statement Account		
Exploration cost expense	0	1,000,000

4 wells drilled, $1 million each → 3 wells successful, 1 well "dry"

REVIEW PROBLEM 7.3

San Joaquin Company began exploration of oil in Texas by paying $600,000 for the drilling rights on a large tract of land. The company drilled 10 oil wells on the land. Seven of the wells were unsuccessful "dry" holes, but the other three wells struck oil. Assume the company paid $80,000 each for the wells. In addition, the company paid $75,000 in other infrastructure costs associated with the drilling project.

Required

Calculate the capitalized cost of San Joaquin Company's oil reserves under (a) the full cost method and (b) the successful efforts method.

The solution is on page 294.

LONG-TERM FIXED ASSET ACCOUNTING UNDER INTERNATIONAL FINANCIAL REPORTING STANDARDS

The accounting for property, plant and equipment (PP&E) under U.S. GAAP and International Financial Reporting Standards (IFRS) differs in two significant ways. First, under U.S. GAAP, while PP&E must be written down if an asset's value becomes impaired, the balance sheet value of these assets may not be written up if their value appreciates above recorded book value. The test for impairment requires

REVIEW PROBLEM 7.4

The Arcadia Company is contemplating a large capital investment of $32 million in new production-line equipment, which is expected to have a useful life of six years and a residual value of $2 million at retirement. The company's controller is uncertain whether the equipment should be depreciated using the straight-line method or the double-declining-balance method. The CEO suggested that a decision be made only after comparing the financial effects of the two methods.

Required

a. Prepare a depreciation schedule for The Arcadia Company for the new equipment assuming (1) use of the straight-line method and (2) use of the double-declining-balance method.

b. The Arcadia Company's net income exclusive of depreciation expense is expected to be $6 million each year for the next six years. Which depreciation method would you recommend to the CEO? Why?

The solution is on pages 294–295.

EXECUTIVE SUMMARY

This chapter investigated the accounting for long-lived fixed, intangible, and natural resource assets. Various depreciation methods used to match the cost of these long-lived assets with the operating revenue they produce were explored: straight-line, double-declining-balance, and units-of-production. In addition, the issues of amortization of intangible assets and depletion of natural resources were examined. Finally, the accounting for asset sales, asset impairments and asset revaluations was also investigated.

As a validation of your understanding of the content of this chapter, you should now be able to:

- Describe how the acquisition cost of a long-lived asset is determined and how the accounting treatment for ongoing costs related to these assets can differ.
- Understand why the matching of depreciation, depletion, and amortization expense with operating revenue is important.
- Explain how depreciation is calculated using the straight-line method, the units-of-production method, and the double-declining-balance method.
- Define asset impairment and how such impairments are reflected in financial statements.
- Describe the accounting and reporting for intangible assets.
- Describe natural resources and how they are reported on the balance sheet.
- Compare the accounting for long-lived fixed assets between U.S. GAAP and IFRS.
- Understand a due diligence review of the financial statement disclosures associated with a firm's capital investments.

In the next chapter, the accounting for intercorporate investments is considered, to include the equity method and consolidation accounting.

KEY CONCEPTS AND TERMS

Accelerated depreciation methods, 266
Accounting policy changes, 271
Accumulated depreciation, 265
Acquisition cost, 262
Amortization, 264
Asset revaluation reserve, 274
Betterment, 263
Capitalize, 262

Capitalized interest, 262
Conservatism, 273
Cumulative prior period effect of an accounting policy change, 273
Depletion, 264
Depreciable cost, 265
Depreciation, 264
Double-declining-balance, 266
Entity change, 271

Estimate change, 273
Fixed assets, 264
Fixed asset turnover ratio, 263
Full cost method, 278
Goodwill, 277
Half-year convention, 265
Historical cost concept, 273
Impairment loss, 274
Income smoothing, 270

Intangible assets, 264
Maintenance expenditures, 263
Market-value model of
    accounting, 274
Method change, 273
Modified accelerated cost recovery
    system, 270
Natural resources, 264

Negative goodwill, 277
Net book value, 265
Prospective basis, 273
Residual value, 265
Retrospective basis, 273
Salvage value, 265
Signaling theory, 273
Straight-line method, 264

Successful efforts method, 278
Sum-of-the-years' digits method, 266
Units-of-production method, 268
Useful life, 265
Voluntary accounting policy
    changes, 273

QUESTIONS

Q7.1 **Brand Names.** Williams-Sonoma, Inc., is a specialty retailer of products for the home. The retail segment of the company's business sells products through its retail concepts: Williams-Sonoma, Pottery Barn, Pottery Barn Kids, PBteen, West Elm, and Rejuvenation. The direct-to-customer segment sells similar products through its direct-mail catalogs and e-commerce websites. Williams-Sonoma stores offer a wide selection of culinary and serving equipment, including cookware, cookbooks, cutlery, informal dinnerware, glassware, and table linens. In addition, these stores carry a variety of quality foods, including a line of Williams-Sonoma food products, such as gourmet coffees and pasta sauces. The Williams-Sonoma brand name is well known in the United States. Discuss why the company doesn't report its brand name as an asset on its balance sheet. Is the company's brand name reflected anywhere in its financial statements?

Q7.2 **Depreciation, Depletion, and Amortization: The Matching Concept.** Depreciation, depletion, and amortization are allocation processes that distribute the acquisition cost of an asset to the many periods of the asset's expected useful life. Discuss how these processes reflect the matching principle and why they are important to the measurement of corporate profitability.

Q7.3 **Advertising Costs: Capitalize or Expense?** Johnson & Johnson discloses in its annual report that "costs associated with advertising are expensed in the year incurred and are included in selling, marketing and administrative expenses" on the income statement. Discuss why the expensing of advertising costs is considered to be "best practice." Can an argument be made that advertising costs should be capitalized?

Q7.4 **Revaluation of Long-lived Assets.** The Thunderbird Corporation was founded in 1947 on a decommissioned military installation that had been purchased from the U.S. government for a price of $1. Today, that same land carries a fair market value of $70 million. Consistent with the historical cost principle, The Thunderbird Corporation continues to value the land at its original purchase price of $1 plus the cost of any improvements (such as roadways, lights, and drainage). Discuss the financial statement problems created by the historical cost principle for entities like The Thunderbird Corporation that have significant investments in long-lived appreciating assets (such as land). Should these companies be allowed to revalue these assets? Why? How would a land revaluation be reflected in the financial statements?

Q7.5 **Capitalization of Interest Costs and Earnings Quality.** Under U.S. GAAP, a company may capitalize any interest costs associated with borrowings used in the self-construction of a business asset. Any capitalized interest is added to the cost basis of the asset and then depreciated over the expected useful life of the asset. Some investment professionals question the appropriateness of interest capitalization, observing that the interest costs associated with general corporate borrowings are expensed when paid and are not capitalized. These professionals allege that interest capitalization is a form of rear-end loading of expenses, and when material in amount, draws into question the quality of a firm's reported earnings. Discuss the validity of these arguments.

Q7.6 **Changing Depreciation Methods.** The Tomoegawa Paper Company Ltd. (TPC) is a well-known public company headquartered in Tokyo, Japan. In TPC's annual report, the company revealed that it had changed its method of depreciating its fixed assets from the straight-line method to the declining-balance method. Discuss the various financial effects of this accounting policy change on TPC's financial statements. Why do you think the company made this voluntary accounting policy change?

Q7.7 **Changing the Estimated Useful Life of a Long-lived Asset.** McCormick & Company revealed in its annual report that it had changed the estimated useful life of certain capitalized software costs from five to eight years. Discuss the effect of this accounting policy change on the company's financial statements. How would you expect the capital markets to react to this voluntary accounting policy change?

Q7.8 **Exploration and Development Costs in the Natural Resource Industry.** Under U.S. GAAP, research and development costs are expensed as incurred; however, in the natural resource industry, the cost of finding and developing natural resources may be capitalized to the balance sheet under the full cost and successful efforts methods. Are these methods inconsistent with the general treatment of research and development costs under U.S. GAAP? If so, why? What explanation can you offer for this inconsistency in accounting treatment of similar outlays under U.S. GAAP?

4. The company purchased a patent from another biotechnology company for $700,000. Unfortunately, this patent was also challenged in court and Intelligencia lost the case, incurring legal fees of $175,000.

Do you think the above costs should be capitalized to the balance sheet as an intangible asset or expensed on the income statement? Why or why not?

TA 3, 4
CHECK FIGURE

E7.24   **Changing the Estimated Life of a Depreciable Asset.**   At the beginning of the year, The Claremont Company purchased a 100-ton press for $750,000. The equipment had an estimated useful life of ten years and a salvage value of $30,000. The company decided to depreciate this equipment using the straight-line method. After eight years of trouble-free use, The Claremont Company concluded that it would be able to utilize the equipment for up to a total of 14 years; and consequently, at the end of year eight, changed its estimate of the equipment's expected life to 14 years, adding four more years to the asset's remaining useful life. Calculate the depreciation expense on the equipment in years eight and nine.

PROBLEMS

TA 2, 3   **P7.25**   **Calculating Depreciation.**   The Miller Company purchased a new headquarters building on January 1 at a cost of $40 million. The building is expected to last 20 years, at which time its residual value is expected to be $5 million.

Required
Calculate the depreciation expense for each of the first three years on the new headquarters building using each of the following methods:

1. Straight-line
2. Double-declining-balance

Does the selection of a depreciation method affect a company's cash flow from operations? In what ways?

TA 1, 2   **P7.26**   **Capitalize versus Expense.**   In 2015, Autoparts Company retooled its production line in order to accommodate the required changes to auto parts for new car models. The retooling costs were capitalized to Autoparts' balance sheet. Company observers suggested that the retooling costs should have been charged against income at the time of purchase rather than capitalized to the company's balance sheet.

Required
If Autoparts Company switched from capitalizing and amortizing the costs of retooling to immediately expensing them (for reporting to shareholders only), indicate how the following financial statement items would be affected:

1. Operating expenses
2. Assets
3. Cash flow from operations
4. Liabilities
5. Operating revenue

TA 4, 5   **P7.27**   **Intangible Assets.**   Global Music Enterprises, Inc., had a balance sheet loaded with intangible assets—copyrights on music, goodwill from various prior acquisitions, and internet customer lists purchased from other online music retailers. During the year, several accounting policy decisions were required regarding various intangible asset-related expenditures.

Required
What accounting policy should be adopted for the following expenditures?

1. Acquisition of new music rights from the estate of a deceased artist.
2. Advertising costs intended to create customer loyalty.
3. Purchase of online customer lists from Amazon.com.
4. Marketing costs to promote the new music library.
5. Computer programmer costs to fully convert the new music library to a digital format.

TA 1   **P7.28**   **Betterment versus Maintenance Expenditures.**   During the year, Graham International made the following expenditures relating to plant, machinery, and equipment:

•   Completed regularly scheduled repairs at a cost of $250,000.
•   Overhauled several stamping machines at a cost of $500,000 to improve production efficiency.
•   Replaced a broken cooling pump on a 100-ton press at a cost of $25,000.

Required
Identify which expenditures should be expensed as a maintenance expense or capitalized as a betterment outlay.

P7.29   **Depletion Expense.**   In 2015, Ottawa Oil Corporation paid $40 million for a partial interest in a Canadian oil   TA 2, 3, 6, 7
field with proven reserves. The company's share of the future production was capped at eight million barrels.

Required

1. Assuming that the oil field attains its expected future output, calculate Ottawa's depletion charge per barrel.
2. If in 2016, Ottawa's share of the field's total production amounts to two million barrels, what is the firm's depletion expense for 2016?
3. Go to the following Internet website www.irs.gov and locate Publication 535 "Business Expenses." Section 9 of this publication is entitled "Depletion." Read this section to determine how oil and gas companies in the United States calculate their depletion expense for U.S. income tax purposes. How does this tax practice compare to U.S. GAAP?

P7.30   **Estimating Depreciation Expense and Book Value.**   Equipment costing $29,000, with a scrap value of   TA 3
$5,000 was purchased on January 1, by Global Communications, Inc. The estimated useful life of the equipment was four years and it was expected to generate 80,000 finished units of production. Units actually produced were 14,000 in 2014 and 20,000 in 2015.

Required

Complete the following table. Can the selection of a depreciation method affect a company's asset replacement policy (i.e., the timing of its asset replacement)? If so, how?

| | Depreciation Expense | | Net Book Value | |
| | | | 2014 | 2015 |
Depreciation Method	**2014**	**2015**	**year-end**	**year-end**
Straight-line	___	___	___	___
Double-declining-balance	___	___	___	___
Units-of-production	___	___	___	___

P7.31   **Successful Efforts Versus Full Cost Method.**   On January 1, 2015, Drummond Oil and Gas Company was   TA 2, 6
about to embark on a 50-well exploration program in Texas and Louisiana. The CEO estimated that the average cost to drill a well would run $800,000 per well, with a resulting success ratio of 60 percent (30 wells were expected to yield commercially viable quantities of oil while 20 wells were expected to be commercially unproductive). In aggregate, the CEO estimated that the 30 successful wells would yield ten million barrels of oil, to be extracted at the following rates.

| | | Estimated Per Barrel | |
Year	**Production (in barrels)**	**Selling Price**	**Lifting Cost**
2015	1,000,000	$30	$5
2016	1,500,000	30	5
2017	1,500,000	35	6
2018	2,500,000	40	7
2019	3,500,000	45	8
	10,000,000		

The CEO of Drummond Oil and Gas Company was concerned about how the accounting for the exploration project would affect the firm's overall reported results. The exploration program would be financed with a $40 million bank loan acquired on January 1, 2015 with an interest rate of 10 percent per year on the balance of the loan outstanding as of the beginning of the year. The loan would be repaid in four installments of $10 million per year, with the first payment occurring on December 31, 2016.

Required

Assume that this is the company's only exploration project. Prepare the firm's income statements and balance sheets for 2015 through 2019 assuming the use of:

1. The full cost method
2. The successful efforts method

TA 4, 5   **P7.32   Impairment of Long-Lived Assets: Goodwill.**   Dean Foods Company, a food and beverage company headquartered in Dallas, Texas, is one of the nation's largest processors and direct-to-store distributors of fluid milk. Consistent with U.S. GAAP, Dean Foods annually performs an impairment test of its goodwill. In its 2011 annual report, Dean Foods reports the following information regarding its annual impairment test of goodwill. (At the time, Dean Foods had three reporting units: Fresh Dairy Direct, WhiteWave-Alpro, and Morningstar.)

> "Based on the results of analysis, we recorded a $2.1 billion, non-cash charge ($1.6 billion net of tax), during 2011. This impairment charge did not impact our operations, compliance with our debt covenants or our cash flows."

They concluded the implied fair value of our Fresh Dairy Direct goodwill was $87 million.

Required

1. What were the financial effects on Dean Food's 2011 financial statements (income statement, balance sheet, statement of cash flow) associated with its 2011 goodwill impairment write-off?
2. Assume that Dean Food had substantial borrowings secured by its U.S. assets and under these credit agreements, the company is subject to a number of debt covenants that required a certain level of debt to total assets. How would the 2011 goodwill impairment and related write-off have affected the company's ability to meet its debt covenants?

TA 4   **P7.33   Intangible Assets: Deferred Subscriber Acquisition Costs.**   The ADT Corporation provides monitored electronic security, interactive home and business automation, and related monitoring services in the United States and Canada. Clients typically lease the monitoring system and ADT retains ownership of the security system. The company reports:

> "For transactions in which the Company retains ownership of the security system non-refundable fees (referred to as deferred subscriber acquisition revenue) received in connection with the initiation of a monitoring contract are deferred and amortized over the estimated life of the customer relationship."

Selected information from ADT's 2015 annual report is presented below:

THE ADT CORPORATION Consolidated Balance Sheets		
(in millions)	Sept. 25, 2015	Sept. 26, 2014
Deferred subscriber acquisition costs, net.	$ 631	$ 571
Total assets.	10,726	10,549

THE ADT CORPORATION Consolidated Statements of Operations For the Years Ended		
(in millions)	Sept. 25, 2015	Sept. 26, 2014
Revenue	$3,574	$3,408
Cost of revenue	1,575	1,457
Selling, general, and administrative expenses	1,305	1,231
Other operating expenses	55	61
Operating income	639	659
Interest income	4	1
Interest expense	(209)	(193)
Other income (expense)	3	(35)
Income before taxes	437	432
Income tax expense	(141)	(128)
Net income	$ 296	$ 304

THE ADT CORPORATION
Consolidated Statements of Cash Flows
For the Years Ended

(in millions)	Sept. 25, 2015	Sept. 26, 2014
Cash flows from operating activities:		
Net income.	$ 296	$ 304
Amortization of deferred subscriber acquisition costs.	141	131
Deferred subscriber acquisition costs	(209)	(184)
Net cash provided by operating activities	1,605	1,519

Required

1. How much did ADT record as the expenditure of cash for deferred subscriber acquisition costs in 2015?
2. How much would the company's total assets be at September 25, 2015, if the company had always expensed its subscriber acquisition costs?
3. If ADT had always expensed its expenditures for subscriber acquisition costs in its financial statements to shareholders, would the cash flow from operations be higher, the same, or lower? Why?
4. What would the company's income before income taxes be in 2015 if ADT had always expensed its expenditures for subscriber acquisition costs?

P7.34   **Depreciation Choices and Outcomes.**   Mulligan Co. purchased a new machine on January 1. The following   TA 1, 3
information pertains to the purchase:

Life of asset	5 years
Salvage value	$ 3,000
Purchase price	18,000
Sales tax.	1,000
Freight cost	800
Electrical set-up	700
Custom programming	500
Estimated annual labor savings	3,500
Additional revenue generated	$ 8,000

Required

a.   Determine the capitalized cost of the new machine

b.   Compute annual depreciation, accumulated depreciation, and the machine's book value for the first three years assuming
     i.   Straight-line depreciation
     ii.   Double-declining-balance method

c.   Assume the machine is sold for $8,000 at the end of the third year after depreciation has been calculated. Determine the gain or loss assuming
     i.   Straight-line depreciation
     ii.   Double-declining-balance method

d.   Given your answer in part c, if Mulligan was able to perfectly predict the future that the machine would be sold for $8,000 at the end of the third year, which depreciation method should Mulligan choose? Ignore taxes.

CORPORATE ANALYSIS

CA7.35   **The Procter & Gamble Company.**   The 2015 annual report of The Procter & Gamble Company (P&G)   TA 2, 3, 4
is available at www.pginvestor.com. After reviewing P&G's annual report, respond to the following questions:

a.   What percentage of P&G's total assets is represented by its net property, plant and equipment? What percentage of P&G's total assets is represented by its net goodwill and other intangible assets? Which category of noncurrent assets is larger? Calculate the capital intensity ratio. (Recall that in Chapter 4, the capital intensity ratio was defined as the sum of fixed assets plus intangible assets divided by total assets.) Is P&G a capital-intensive company?

    b.   Calculate the fixed asset turnover ratio and the intangible asset turnover ratio. What do these ratios tell you about P&G's operations?

    c.   How much depreciation expense and amortization expense was taken in 2014 and 2015? What depreciation method does P&G use? What is the relative age of P&G's fixed assets (what percentage of the assets has been used up and what percentage remains available)?

TA 2, 3, 4, 5   **CA7.36** **Internet-based Analysis.** Consider a publicly-held company whose products you are familiar with. Some examples might include:

Company	Product	Corporate Website
• Johnson & Johnson.................	• Band-Aids	• www.jnj.com
• Microsoft Corporation..............	• Windows software	• www.microsoft.com
• Apple Inc..........................	• Cellular phones	• www.apple.com
• Intel Corporation	• Pentium processors	• www.intel.com
• Kimberly-Clark Corporation..........	• Kleenex	• www.kimberly-clark.com

Access the company's public website and search for its most recent annual report. (Note: Some companies provide access to their financial data through an "investor relations" link, while others provide a direct link to their "annual reports.") After locating your company's most recent annual report, open the file and review its contents. After reviewing the annual report for your selected company, prepare answers to the following questions:

    a.   How does the company depreciate its property, plant and equipment (PP&E)? Calculate the ratio of the accumulated depreciation divided by gross PP&E for the past two years. How old are the company's PP&E assets? What percentage of their useful life remains?

    b.   Does the company have any intangible assets? If so, what are they? What percentage of total assets do they represent?

    c.   Did the company invest in new PP&E or new intangible assets during the past two years? If so, in what amount?

    d.   Calculate the total asset turnover, the PP&E turnover, and the intangible asset turnover for each of the past two years. Are these turnover ratios increasing or decreasing? What might explain these trends?

TA 4, 7   **CA7.37** **IFRS Financial Statements.** The 2014 financial statements of **LVMH Moet Hennessey-Louis Vuitton S.A.** are presented in Appendix C of this book. LVMH is a Paris-based holding company and one of the world's largest and best-known luxury goods companies. As a member-nation, French companies are required to prepare their consolidated (group) financial statements using International Financial Reporting Standards (IFRS). In LVMH's Notes to the Consolidated Financial Statements (not presented in Appendix C), the company discloses its accounting policy regarding brand and trade names, an important asset for a luxury goods company:

> Only acquired brands and trade names that are well known and individually identifiable are recorded as assets based on their market values at their dates of acquisition.
>
> Costs incurred in creating a new brand or developing an existing brand are expensed. Brands, trade names and other intangible assets with finite useful lives are amortized over their estimated useful lives. The classification of a brand or trade name as an asset of definite or indefinite useful life is generally based on the following criteria:
>
> - the brand or trade name's positioning in its market expressed in terms of volume of activity, international presence and notoriety;
> - its expected long-term profitability;
> - its degree of exposure to changes in the economic environment;
> - any major event within its business segment liable to compromise its future development;
> - its age.
>
> Amortizable lives of brands and trade names with definite useful lives range from 15 to 40 years, depending on their estimated period of utilization.
>
> Any impairment expense of brands and trade names and, in some cases, amortization expense, are recognized within "Other operating income and expenses."

Consider the following questions:

    a.   Describe the key components of LVMH's accounting policy for brand names.

    b.   How might LVMH determine whether a brand name had a finite or infinite useful life?

CASE

LEWIS DRISCOLL AND DELTA CARGO

Lewis Driscoll was excited about the proposal that had just crossed his desk. As logistics manager for Delta Cargo, located near the mouth of the Mississippi River, Driscoll and his team were responsible for loading and unloading barges with a wide variety of goods shipped in standard shipping containers. Delta Cargo was an operating division of Delta Transportation, a company that provided a host of transportation services in the Gulf Coast region. With 10 forklifts to load and unload barges, Delta Cargo employees operated around the clock. A sales representative from the J. M. Crane Company had recently demonstrated a new crane that would allow Delta to replace its forklifts, improving both efficiency and speed. Although it sounded like a great idea, Driscoll began to wonder if corporate management would approve the expenditure. The crane would allow cargo to be processed much more efficiently. As the first company to utilize the technology, Delta would have an advantage over its numerous competitors in the Mississippi River freight market, which handled 175 million tons a year.

The crane investment would certainly affect Delta's profitability as the forklifts were nearly fully depreciated and the new crane would involve a substantial capital investment. Driscoll recalled the business-management class that Delta had sponsored after his last promotion. How much depreciation would Delta incur for this new investment? But did it really matter as depreciation affected profits but was not an actual cash outflow? Would his selection of a particular depreciation method—straight-line, double-declining-balance, sum-of-the-years' digits, or tax-based MACRS—affect Delta's bottom line and total profitability?

Driscoll also knew that retaining the forklifts would be unnecessary, as the crane's capacity was much larger than Delta needed. If the crane were indeed purchased, what disposal options would he have? And how would that affect profitability? Although the forklifts had been substantially depreciated, Driscoll expected that any disposal would result in a loss to Delta. New technologies on the market rendered the forklifts obsolete; thus, although the crane investment certainly made sense for the company under any valuation method, it would be very expensive and corporate management might hesitate both to bear the cost and to write off its previous forklift investment.

Capitalized Costs

Driscoll began to evaluate the proposal. The crane itself—a brand-new United Industries BH115—was a real beauty: a 115-ton hydraulic crawler crane with a 150-foot boom, a 70-foot tubular jib, and a quiet Cummins diesel engine. Priced at $2.1 million, it would have to be shipped in pieces from Savannah, Georgia, adding another $50,000 in shipping, assembling, and handling costs. Driscoll budgeted in his calculations that Delta could defray some of the assembly costs by having its own dockworkers assemble parts of the crane, at a savings of about $20,000, approximately what Delta would pay the dockworkers for their normal loading duties. As the dockworkers were occasionally idle, Driscoll viewed this as a real cost savings. Management would require a Delta Cargo stencil to be placed on the crane, which would cost $3,000, as well as a special paint job ($30,000) so that the crane would not rust from the intense moisture and salt at the Delta docks. Moreover, Delta would have to spend $40,000 on support beams for the dock so that it would be able to withstand the additional weight of the crane. Driscoll expected the beams would last approximately as long as the crane itself.

Other costs included mandatory training of the crane operators (estimated at $15,000) and severance pay of $25,000 for the forklift operators who could not be reassigned. Although severance costs were clearly one-time charges, OSHA regulations required all persons operating the crane to be periodically recertified, so that training costs would be an ongoing expenditure. Training activities included, but were not limited to, how to use correct hand signals, how to read load charts, proper rigging and inspections, and procedures for boom assembly and disassembly. The J. M. Crane Company would provide a consultant for one month (at $5,000) to assist in those operations while Delta workers were being trained.

Driscoll was having difficulty determining which costs should be capitalized and which costs would need to be expensed immediately (Exhibit 1).

Depreciation Methods and Financial Statement Implications

Driscoll realized that, after he had determined the total capitalized value of the crane, he would have to decide how to depreciate it. He knew of at least four depreciation methods: straight-line, double-declining-balance, sum-of-the-years' digits, or the tax-based modified accelerated cost-recovery system (MACRS). Each had its advantages and disadvantages, but he was unsure how to weight them. Straight line was simple and helped with earnings consistency. Double-declining-balance and sum-of-the-years' digits were accelerated methods so the company could write off more of the cost in the early years, thus benefiting later years. MACRS was the tax method prescribed by the IRS, but Driscoll was unsure if it could even be used for book purposes. Driscoll decided to compare the expenses that would be recorded using the straight-line method (the simplest of the four) and the double-declining-balance method to determine how much they would affect income (Exhibit 2). Driscoll estimated the crane's salvage value to be $100,000 at the end of 10 years, its expected useful life. The asset was to be purchased at the beginning of the company's fiscal year 2015, so that any half-year convention measures would be unnecessary.

Recalling a conversation he had had with Tom Spilbane, Delta Cargo's controller, Driscoll remembered that Spilbane had mentioned that Delta should not necessarily use the same method of depreciation for both book and tax purposes. The IRS allowed companies to use the straight-line method for book purposes and a modified form of double-declining-balance (i.e., MACRS) for tax purposes. Driscoll wondered if this would be advantageous for Delta and what other implications it might have for the firm's profitability. The two methods had different depreciation expenses each year and, therefore, different net book values at year-end. How would Delta manage those differences on its balance sheets and income statements?

Forklift Disposal

Driscoll could not ignore the issue of what to do with the 10 forklifts that Delta would no longer need. Each forklift had cost $60,000 four years earlier, and each had been depreciated to a net book value of $12,000 (for both book and tax purposes). Driscoll knew of only one immediate buyer, who was willing to pay just $8,000 per forklift. He also suspected that management would not be happy about a loss of $40,000, especially as that amount would factor negatively into bonus-pool calculations. Because the forklifts had been depreciated to their salvage value, Driscoll considered leaving them unused in a corner of the lot until the next fiscal year. That strategy might work as another buyer had previously approached Driscoll, but he required extensive refurbishing of the forklifts at Delta's expense. On the plus side, the refurbishing would take several months, and the buyer would reimburse Delta for the additional costs. Driscoll estimated those costs to be $6,000 per forklift. The buyer would then purchase each forklift for $14,000, possibly allowing the recognition of a small gain on each forklift.

Profit Impact

After calculating the depreciation for years one through five, Driscoll had a conversation with Spilbane regarding which method he should use to depreciate the crane purchase. Spilbane mentioned a possible complication that Driscoll had not considered. A large part of Driscoll's income—and the income of all the other managers—was derived from the company's bonus plan. Delta Cargo managers were allocated a portion of a bonus pool based on a percentage of Delta's earnings before interest and taxes. Driscoll thought that, although an accelerated method was required for tax purposes, his bonus would be lower because of the larger expense associated with that method if it were used for financial purposes. Driscoll reviewed his budgeted operating profit to see how this would affect the 2015 bonus calculations (**Exhibit 3**).

Required

1. Driscoll is faced with determining the current and future profit impacts of a number of costs. In general terms, what should guide the determination of whether an acquisition cost is capitalized or expensed? In the case of the crane, which costs should be capitalized and which should be expensed? Complete Exhibit 1.
2. Once it is determined how much should be capitalized, what other factors should guide Driscoll's final determination of depreciation expense?
3. Complete Exhibit 2.
4. Driscoll is considering two options for disposing of the old forklifts. Which of the two alternatives would you recommend?

EXHIBIT 1	Lewis Driscoll and Delta Cargo			
Crane Costs to Be Capitalized or Expensed				
Category		**Cost**	**Capitalize**	**Expense**
Crane		$2,100,000		
Shipping, handling, and assembling		50,000		
Additional in-house assembly cost		20,000		
Operator training		15,000		
Consultant operator		5,000		
Severance for forklift operators		25,000		
Support beams for dock		40,000		
Special paint work		30,000		
Delta Cargo stencil		3,000		
Cumulative maximum costs		$2,288,000	☐	☐
Salvage value			$100,000	
Depreciable cost			☐	

EXHIBIT 2	Lewis Driscoll and Delta Cargo

Depreciation-Method Comparisons

Depreciable cost = _____

	Straight Line (SL)		Double Declining (DDB)		
	Expense	Net Book Value	Expense	Net Book Value	Depr. Expense Difference
2005					
2006					
2007					
2008					
2009					
2010					
2011					
2012					
2013					
2014					
2015					
2016					
2017					
2018					
2019					
Totals					

EXHIBIT 3	Lewis Driscoll and Delta Cargo

Bonus-Plan Calculations[1]

Budgeted Income Statement	2015 (SL)	2015 (DDB)
Revenues	$2,238,500	$2,238,500
Selling, general, and administrative expenses	$ 552,250	$ 552,250
Earnings before interest, taxes, depreciation, and other income	$1,686,250	$1,686,250
Depreciation		
Earnings before interest, taxes, and other		
Loss on sale of assets		
Interest expense	$38,000	$38,000
Earnings before taxes		
Taxes (35%)		
Net income		
	SL	DDB
Earnings before interest and taxes		
20% allocated to bonus pool		

[1] Assumes efficiencies from crane acquisition. Bonus is calculated as 20% of earnings before taxes.

SOLUTIONS TO REVIEW PROBLEMS

Solution 7.1

	Straight-line Method	Double-Declining-Balance Method	Units-of-Production Method
Year 1	$ 5,000,000	$10,666,667	$ 3,750,000
Year 2	5,000,000	7,111,111	4,500,000
Year 3	5,000,000	4,740,741	4,875,000
Year 4	5,000,000	3,160,494	5,625,000
Year 5	5,000,000	2,160,494	6,750,000
Year 6	5,000,000	2,160,493	4,500,000
Total	$30,000,000	$30,000,000	$30,000,000
Book value	$ 2,000,000	$ 2,000,000	$ 2,000,000

Solution 7.2

Original cost	$250,000
Less: Accumulated depreciation	175,000
Book value	75,000
Less: Proceeds on sale	50,000
Loss on sale of machine.	$ 25,000

Solution 7.3

	Full Cost Method	Successful Efforts Method
Drilling rights.	$ 600,000	$600,000
Infrastructure	75,000	75,000
Wells.	800,000	240,000
	$1,475,000	$915,000

Solution 7.4

a. Depreciation schedule

	Straight-Line Method	Double-Declining-Balance Method
Year 1	$ 5,000,000	$10,666,667
Year 2	5,000,000	7,111,111
Year 3	5,000,000	4,740,741
Year 4	5,000,000	3,160,494
Year 5	5,000,000	2,160,494
Year 6	5,000,000	2,160,493
Total	$30,000,000	$30,000,000
Book value	$ 2,000,000	$ 2,000,000

b.   If The Arcadia Company earns net income, exclusive of depreciation expense, of $6 million per year, its net income after depreciation expense but before income taxes would be as follows:

	Straight-Line Method	Double-Declining-Balance Method
Year 1	$1,000,000	$(4,666,667)
Year 2	1,000,000	(1,111,111)
Year 3	1,000,000	1,259,259
Year 4	1,000,000	2,839,506
Year 5	1,000,000	3,839,506
Year 6	1,000,000	3,839,507
Total	$6,000,000	$ 6,000,000

The analysis reveals that The Arcadia Company will report substantial losses in Years 1 and 2 under the double-declining-balance method, turning profitable in Year 3 and thereafter, effectively rear-end loading the firm's profitability into Year 3 through Year 6. The straight-line method, however, enables the company to report a smooth earnings stream throughout the six-year period. Unless the CEO has some reason to rear-end load the company's earnings, perhaps to create an earnings reserve in anticipation of lower future operating results, the CEO is likely to prefer the stable earnings under the straight-line method for the company's financial reports to shareholders.

When you complete this chapter you should be able to:

1. Explain why companies acquire ownership interests in other entities. (page 298)

2. Describe how to account for investments in debt and equity securities, including the application of mark-to-market accounting, the equity method, and consolidation accounting. (page 299)

3. Explain and illustrate accounting for passive investments. (page 301)

4. Explain and illustrate accounting for equity investments. (page 307)

5. Explain the accounting for joint ventures and special purpose entities. (page 315)

6. Understand the foreign currency accounting issues that arise with investments in foreign entities. (page 318)

7. Discuss the considerations in analyzing intercorporate investments. (page 321)

Investing In
Other Entities

The acquisition of the corporate equity of one company by another is usually strategic in purpose and can be very complex. BHP Billiton's (BHP) proposed 2010 acquisition of Potash Corp. of Saskatchewan, Canada, is one example. BHP is the

BHP BILLITON

world's largest natural resources company, and its many diversified businesses produce aluminum, copper, coal, iron ore, gold, lead, silver, and diamonds. Its operations span the globe, with the heaviest concentration in Asia and Europe. The company has an employee and contractor base totaling about 80,000 individuals. For its fiscal year ending June 30, 2015, revenues exceeded $44 billion, and its market capitalization approximated $100 billion.

In late 2010, BHP launched a $40 billion hostile takeover bid for Potash, a premium of 20 percent over Potash's then market capitalization. Potash was the world's largest fertilizer company and the largest producer of potash, with an estimated 11 percent of global production and 20 percent of global capacity. The acquisition was squarely aimed at meeting BHP's strategy of becoming a leading miner of potash, a complement to its existing natural resource portfolio. The deal would involve a buyout of Potash shareholders, and to finance the acquisition, BHP planned to use cash plus debt. Analysts expected approximately $30 billion of new debt would need to be issued; they further expected goodwill on BHP's balance sheet to increase by over $20 billion on a post-acquisition basis. The deal was expected to be immediately accretive to BHP's earnings per share.

The BHP offer, however, was quickly rejected by the Potash board of directors as both too low and not in the best interest of the company's numerous stakeholders, especially its Canadian investors. Because so many Canadian citizens would be affected by the purchase, the Canadian government noted that any final approval of the deal must not result in any major economic shifts in the region. The line of those opposed to the deal did not stop there. Other stakeholders opposed to the acquisition included the Chinese government, whose concern centered around the acquisition's impact on the pricing and world-wide supply of fertilizers, a critical element of the agricultural growth of that country.

Rejection of the initial offer did not deter BHP's management. The company commenced a newspaper advertisement campaign targeting existing Potash shareholders and the community, and eventually raised its offer price. To assuage the fears of the Canadian people, BHP hailed the numerous benefits of the acquisition. The company publicly announced it was committed to being a strong corporate citizen in Saskatchewan. It would keep its President and management in the region, maintain current employment levels, and proposed a Canadian nominee to stand for election to the BHP board. Further, any planned capital programs of Potash would be maintained, and any spending commitments on community programs would be honored. In the end BHP was unsuccessful. The Canadian government ultimately blocked the deal, citing that it would not be a "net benefit" for Canada. Even though BHP was within its rights to fight this decision, it abandoned the deal.

In this chapter, the investment decisions of companies like BHP are examined in closer detail. Specifically, we will see that companies invest in other companies for a variety of reasons, and from those diverse reasons comes financial reporting that is diverse in its application. Further, we will see that the accounting for investments is driven largely by the size of the ownership interest acquired.

EXECUTIVE OUTLINE

Takeaway 1
Explain why companies acquire ownership interests in other entities.

INVESTMENTS IN OTHER ENTITIES

Transactions such as BHP's proposed acquisition of Potash, even though unsuccessful, are a regular part of corporate life as companies frequently buy and sell the shares of other businesses. The amount of equity shares acquired varies from relatively small amounts to 100 percent of the outstanding shares, as in the case of the proposed Potash takeover. When a company acquires a relatively small percentage of the outstanding shares of another entity (defined as less than 20 percent under U.S. GAAP guidelines), it usually indicates an expectation that the investment will provide an acceptable rate of return on idle corporate funds, and that the investor-company does not intend to take an active role in the management and operations of the investee.

When a company acquires a significant stake in another company—ownership interests of 20 percent or more—it is usually because the investor-company desires to take an active and influential role in the investee's business activities. Gaining control of the business affairs of another company may be of considerable economic value to an investor. It may enable an investor to generate incremental operating profit from cost savings and/or operating revenue enhancements. Operating cost/revenue synergies may be created by eliminating excess productive capacity, dropping unprofitable products, or generating incremental product sales. The investment might, for instance, be in a company that is vertically integrated within a product's manufacturing process, such as a supplier, thus enabling more control over the investor's value chain. An investor-company may also acquire a significant stake in an investee in order to oust an inefficient management team or because the investor believes that the investee's shares are temporarily undervalued and present an opportunity to profit from the capital market mispricing of the investee's shares. The combination of two companies may also be justified on financing grounds—one or both firms may have unused debt capacity capable of providing low-cost financing for growth of the combined entity. An investor-company may acquire shares in an investee to gain access to various skills, technology, or resources that would be more expensive to obtain in other ways. Finally, an investment might be made simply to diversify and put idle resources to work, as is the case with many diversified conglomerates such as Berkshire Hathaway and General Electric.

Overview of Accounting for Debt and Equity Securities

The accounting for corporate investments can be quite diverse as a variety of accounting methods are required. The selection of which method to use depends on (i) the degree of ownership control obtained in the target company, and, (ii) when an investment is for less than 20 percent voting control, the intent of the company making the investment. Exhibit 8.1 summarizes the general considerations that determine which accounting methods to apply across the spectrum of possible debt and equity investments. The last line of the exhibit illustrates there are potentially five different accounting methods that may come into play. It further identifies the factors that must be considered when selecting the appropriate accounting, such as whether the investment involves debt or equity, the percent of voting control acquired, and the investment "intent" of the investor-company. Taken together there is no doubt that these factors make investment accounting a complex topic.

Takeaway 2

Describe how to account for investments in debt and equity securities, including the application of mark-to-market accounting, the equity method, and consolidation accounting.

EXHIBIT 8.1	Determining Which Investment Accounting Method to Apply

Ownership Interest Less Than 20 Percent

Exhibit 8.2 summarizes the three broad categories of investments defined by the ownership level acquired in the investee-company and the amount of control assumed. The first category is for investments in which the ownership level is relatively small—less than 20 percent of the outstanding voting shares—and is referred to as **marketable securities**. These securities can take the form of debt securities (e.g., corporate bonds) or equity securities (e.g., preferred stock or common stock). Provided that a ready market exists for trading these securities—such as the New York Stock Exchange or the NASDAQ—there exists a special accounting treatment known as **mark-to-market accounting**. This is quite different from the accounting approach taken for most other assets on the balance sheet. For most assets, GAAP requires that a company carry their value at historical cost, with reductions for such issues as impairments and depreciation. The general argument in these cases is that while the resulting historical cost number may lack a degree of relevance, it is reliably and objectively measured. Mark-to-market accounting is an exception to this generally accepted practice and allows assets to be written up or down to their current fair value. This accounting is permitted because a ready resale market exists such that an investment's current value can be reliably ascertained.

The next critical step in the application of mark-to-market accounting is dependent on the investment intent of management. From that "intent" arises differences in how changes in fair values are treated on the financial statements. Marketable debt and equity securities that are held with the intent to be sold at any time to take advantage of short-term price changes are called **trading securities**. As summarized in Exhibit 8.2, these investments are valued at their fair value on the balance sheet, with any unrealized gain (loss) in a security's value included directly in the investor's net income. An **unrealized gain (loss)** is an increase (decrease) in the value of an asset that has not yet been sold. When the asset is sold, the gain (loss) is said to be "realized."

Alternatively, investments in debt and equity securities that management intends to hold for the longer term but which, under the right circumstances management might still liquidate quickly are referred to as **available-for-sale securities**. As described in Exhibit 8.2, these investments are also valued on the balance sheet at their fair value but any unrealized gain (loss) in value is reported in a separate shareholders' equity account on the balance sheet. For companies using U.S. GAAP, the unrealized gains (losses) on available-for-sale securities are considered to be part of **accumulated other comprehensive income**, often called "AOCI" for short, a category of yet-to-be-realized wealth increases or decreases disclosed in the shareholders' equity section of the balance sheet. We will have more to say about accumulated other comprehensive income in Chapter 11.

EXHIBIT 8.2	Overview of Accounting for Debt and Equity Securities	
Ownership Interest	**Equity Securities**	**Debt Securities**
Less than 20 percent	***Marketable Equity Securities*** **Trading securities** • Valued at fair value on balance sheet • Unrealized gain/loss included in income • Dividends included in income **Available-for-sale** • Valued at fair value on balance sheet • Unrealized gain/loss included as a component of shareholders' equity on balance sheet • Dividends included in income	***Marketable Debt Securities*** **Trading securities** • Valued at fair value on balance sheet • Unrealized gain/loss included in income • Interest revenue included in income **Available-for-sale** • Valued at fair value on balance sheet • Unrealized gain/loss included as a component of shareholders' equity on balance sheet • Interest revenue included in income
Between 20 and 50 percent	**Equity Method** • Investment in Equity Affiliate valued at cost plus share of earnings less share of dividends on balance sheet • Proportionate share of affiliate's earnings included in income of investor-company	

Greater than 50 percent	**Consolidation Accounting**
	• On parent-company books, investment is accounted for using the equity method.
	• Upon consolidation:
	  • Assets and liabilities of subsidiary are added to those of parent, with Investment in Equity Affiliate eliminated and noncontrolling interest shown on balance sheet
	  • Transactions between parent and subsidiary are netted out
	  • Revenue and expenses of subsidiary are combined with those of parent company, with noncontrolling interest in subsidiary's income deducted from consolidated earnings
		Held-to-maturity
		• Valued at amortized cost on balance sheet
		• Interest revenue included in income

Debt securities by definition carry ownership interests less than 20 percent so mark-to-market accounting under trading or available-for-sale may apply. However, because debt has a fixed term and over time the fair value of the debt security will converge to the face amount owed, a third investment category exists for debt. Debt securities that management intends to hold until maturity are referred to as **held-to-maturity debt securities**. These investments are valued at their **amortized cost**—that is, the original purchase price of the debt plus (minus) the amortization of any purchase discount (premium). We will have more to say about the amortization of purchase discounts (premiums) on debt instruments in Chapter 9.

Ownership Interest Between 20 and 50 Percent

The second investment category summarized in Exhibit 8.2 is for investments in equity securities wherein the investor-company can exercise significant influence over an investee-company's operating policies but that are not sufficiently large to represent voting control—between 20 and 50 percent of the outstanding voting shares. Investments in this category are by definition equity investments, as debt carries no voting control, and these investments are accounted for using the **equity method**. Under the equity method (see Exhibit 8.2), the Investment in Equity Affiliate account on the balance sheet is reported at its original cost plus a proportionate share of the affiliate's net earnings less a proportionate share of any dividends paid by the affiliate. The investor-company is also required to report the proportionate share of the affiliate's net earnings as part of its own income, and frequently you will see this separately classified on the income statement in an account called **equity in the earnings (loss) of an unconsolidated affiliate**.

> When preparing a statement of cash flow for an investor-company, it is necessary to (1) subtract (add) the "equity in the earnings (loss) of an unconsolidated affiliate" and (2) subtract (add) any unrealized gains (losses) on trading securities from net income when calculating the cash flow from operations. All cash flows related to non-consolidated investments are captured in the investing section of the statement of cash flow.

Ownership Interest Greater Than 50 Percent

Finally, investments in equity securities in which an investor-company establishes voting control over an affiliate—over 50 percent ownership—are accounted for using **consolidation accounting**. Under consolidation accounting, the operating results of the affiliated company are combined with those of the investor. Thus, shareholders in the investor-company receive a single set of combined financial statements representing both the investor and affiliate-company financial results. Affiliate companies in which an investor-company owns more than 50 percent of the outstanding voting shares are often referred to as "subsidiaries."

ACCOUNTING FOR MARKETABLE DEBT AND EQUITY SECURITIES—PASSIVE INVESTMENTS

To illustrate the accounting for, and the financial statement disclosures associated with, passive investments in marketable debt and equity securities, we refer to the investing activities of The New South Wales Trading Company, Inc. (NSWT). Assume that NSWT raised $50 million in cash in Year 1 from an initial public offering of its common shares. The company planned to use most of the cash to establish a chain of fast food restaurants specializing in Australian cuisine. Since the company's planned capital investments would take place over a three-year period, NSWT decided to temporarily invest some of its cash in debt and equity securities having a high degree of liquidity. The company settled on three investments:

Takeaway 3
Explain and illustrate accounting for passive investments.

Investment	Acquisition Date	Acquisition Cost	Classification	Fair Value at Year-End
(1) Qantas Inc. 10% Notes due in Year 6	September	$10.0 million	Held-to-maturity	$9.8 million
(2) 100,000 shares of JWS Inc. common stock	November	6.1 million	Trading	6.8 million
(3) 200,000 shares of Coles Inc. common stock . . .	December	8.4 million	Available-for-sale	8.2 million

In September Year 1, NSWT invested $10 million in Qantas Inc. 10 percent notes. The company planned to hold the notes until Year 6 when they matured and the principal of $10 million is repaid. The notes paid $1 million in interest income (10 percent of $10 million) on December 31 each year. The notes were classified by NSWT's chief financial officer (CFO) as **held-to-maturity debt securities**.

In November, NSWT invested $6.1 million in 100,000 shares of JWS Inc. common stock at $61 per share. Since JWS was a growth company, it paid no dividends to its shareholders. NSWT's CFO thought the shares were substantially undervalued, and consequently, placed an order to sell the JWS shares when they hit $80 per share. JWS's shares were classified by the CFO as **trading securities**.

In December, NSWT purchased 200,000 shares of Coles Inc. common stock at $42 per share for a total cost of $8.4 million. Like JWS, Coles had a policy of paying no dividends. The NSWT CFO thought the shares were fairly valued but that NSWT would sell them in the unlikely event that the Coles shares traded above $50 per share. The Coles shares were classified as **available-for-sale securities**.

The accounting for the IPO and the acquisition of the three securities in Year 1 is illustrated in the first four columns of Exhibit 8.3. The investment in Qantas Inc. notes reduces cash by $10 million and increases held-to-maturity debt securities by $10 million. The investments in JWS and Coles common shares reduce cash by $6.1 and $8.4 million, respectively, and increase trading equity securities and available-for-sale equity securities by $6.1 and $8.4 million, respectively.

| EXHIBIT 8.3 | Accounting for Marketable Debt and Equity Securities: The New South Wales Trading Company |

(in $ thousands)	Sept. IPO Common Shares	Sept. Qantas Debt Investment	Nov. JWS Stock Investment	Dec. Coles Stock Investment	Dec. 31 Qantas Interest Receipt	Dec. 31 Adjust JWS Value	Dec. 31 Adjust Coles Value	Year 1 End. Bal. (summary)
Assets								
Cash...........................	50,000	(10,000)	(6,100)	(8,400)	1,000			26,500
: :								
Held-to-maturity debt securities		10,000						10,000
Trading securities.........................			6,100			700		6,800
Available-for-sale securities				8,400			(200)	8,200
Total assets............................								**51,500**
Shareholders' Equity								
Common stock.........................	50,000							50,000
Retained earnings								1,700
Interest income........................					1,000			
Unrealized gain—trading................						700		
Accumulated other comprehensive inc........								(200)
Unrealized gain (loss)—available-for-sale....							(200)	
Total liabilities and shareholders' equity								**51,500**

Valuation Adjustments

At year-end, NSWT must consider several important events concerning its investments. These are shown as the last three transactions in Exhibit 8.3. First, NSWT received an interest payment of $1 million on the Qantas notes, increasing cash and retained earnings (interest income) by $1 million. Second, the fair values at year-end of NSWT's investments differed from their acquisition costs.

Since the Qantas notes are held-to-maturity securities, they are valued at their acquisition cost, requiring no downward adjustment to their fair value of $9.8 million. NSWT's trading securities (JWS shares), however, must be valued at their fair value with any unrealized gain (loss) in value taken into income. NSWT's trading securities have a fair value of $6.8 million versus an acquisition cost of $6.1 million. Thus, the trading equity securities account is increased by $700,000 to reflect its fair value of $6.8 million and retained earnings is increased by $700,000 to reflect the unrealized gain includable as current income.

The fair value of the Coles shares, however, is just $8.2 million versus an acquisition cost of $8.4 million; consequently, this investment must be written down to fair value with the unrealized loss reported as an AOCI component of shareholders' equity. Specifically, recording the unrealized loss reduces available-for-sale securities by $200,000 and reduces the shareholders' equity account unrealized gain (loss) on available-for-sale securities by $200,000. The shareholders' equity account unrealized gain (loss) on available-for-sale securities is classified as a component of accumulated other comprehensive income under U.S. GAAP.

Following these end-of-year adjustments, NSWT's balance sheet at year-end is presented in Exhibit 8.4. The balance sheet shows NSWT's investment in held-to-maturity debt securities at cost and its investments in trading and available-for-sale securities at their fair value. Shareholders' equity reflects the unrealized loss on available-for-sale securities and the unrealized gain on the trading securities, split across AOCI and retained earnings, respectively. NSWT's partial income statement for the year is also presented in Exhibit 8.4. It shows the interest income of $1 million and the $700,000 of unrealized gain on trading securities. These amounts you will note reconcile to the balance of retained earnings.

Recording the Sale of Investment Securities

The sale of investment securities, similar to other assets, requires recording the amount received from the sale and removing the balance sheet values of the securities sold. The gain or loss on the transaction

EXHIBIT 8.4	Financial Statement Summary, Year 1: Marketable Debt and Equity Securities

THE NEW SOUTH WALES TRADING COMPANY, INC.
Balance Sheet

($ thousands)	Dec. 31
Assets:	
Cash.	$26,500
Investments	
Held-to-maturity debt securities.	10,000
Trading equity securities.	6,800
Available-for-sale equity securities.	8,200
Total assets.	**$51,500**
Shareholders' Equity:	
Common stock.	$50,000
Retained earnings.	1,700
Accumulated other comprehensive income	
Unrealized loss on available-for-sale securities	(200)
Shareholders' equity	**$51,500**

THE NEW SOUTH WALES TRADING COMPANY, INC.
Partial Income Statement

($ thousands)	Dec. 31
Interest income.	$ 1,000
Unrealized gain on trading equity securities	700
Net income	**$ 1,700**

is, therefore, the difference between the amounts received and the book values of the items sold. This fundamental accounting treatment results in one further important distinction between securities classified as trading and those classified as available-for-sale. For trading securities, because the unrealized fair value changes have been recorded as income each period as they occur, when a security is sold only the *gain or loss attributable to the period of sale* is recorded for that period. For available-for-sale securities, however, when a security is sold the *entire gain or loss* since the year of acquisition is recorded as income. This difference is a direct result of deferring all prior period unrealized changes in fair values under available-for-sale accounting, and mechanically because these amounts have been previously reflected in the AOCI account on the balance sheet.

To illustrate, assume that during Year 2 NSWT liquidated both equity investments in its portfolio, selling the JWS shares for $64 per share and the Coles shares for $47 per share. To assess the gain (or loss) related to each sale, the sale proceeds received are differenced against the book value of the securities held. Because both investments are recorded at fair value at each balance sheet date, the book values are the last recorded fair value. But the amount of gain or loss recorded as current income can be tricky. For the JWS stock, the loss recorded as income amounts to $400,000, representing the decline of $4 per share from the prior year ($68 − $64) times the number of shares sold (100,000). For Coles Inc. it is not that simple. Because the security was classified as available-for-sale, the prior period change in fair value that was recorded in AOCI must also be removed from the balance sheet. This has the desired effect of recording that value in current income, as it was deferred from income in the prior year. To help you see the accounting a bit clearer, a summary of the total gain realized on each security from acquisition to sale, and how that gain was allocated to the income statement over the two periods, is provided below. Note that the total realized gain for the JWS stock is $300,000 (calculated as ($64 − $61) × 100,000 shares), recorded as a $700,000 gain in year 1 and a $400,000 loss in year 2. The Coles shares, on the other hand, were sold for a total realized gain of $1,000,000 (calculated as ($47 − $42) × 200,000 shares), and all of this amount was recorded in the income statement in the year of sale. Exhibit 8.5 summarizes the transaction effects and the final balance sheet for the two investment sales.

Summary Calculation of Gain (Loss) from Securities Sales		
($ thousands)	**JWS Inc.**	**Coles Inc.**
Total income statement gain from sale in Year 2:		
Proceeds received	$6,400	$9,400
less: Investment on balance sheet	6,800	8,200
plus: AOCI previously not recognized as income	n/a	(200)
Total year 2 income statement gain (loss)	$ (400)	$1,000
Total realized gain (loss) from acquisition to sale:		
Proceeds received	$6,400	$9,400
less: Acquisition cost	6,100	8,400
Total realized gain (loss)	$ 300	$1,000
Recorded as income by year:		
Year 1	$ 700	$ —
Year 2	(400)	1,000
Total	$ 300	$1,000

EXHIBIT 8.5	Accounting for Sales of JWS and Coles Securities: The New South Wales Trading Company

	Year 1 End. Bal.	Sale of JWS Shares	Sale of Coles Shares	Balance Sheet after Sales
Assets				
Cash	26,500	6,400	9,400	42,300
: :				
Held-to-maturity debt securities	10,000			10,000
Trading securities	6,800	(6,800)		—
Available-for-sale securities	8,200		(8,200)	—
Total assets	**51,500**			**52,300**
Shareholders' Equity				
Common stock	50,000			50,000
Retained earnings	1,700			2,300
Gain (loss) on sales of securities		(400)	1,000	
Accumulated other comprehensive income	(200)			—
Unrealized gain—available-for-sale			200	
Total liabilities and shareholders' equity	**51,500**			**52,300**

REVIEW PROBLEM 8.1

Sherwin Corporation invests its excess cash in equity securities when such funds are not needed to support operations. At the beginning of the year the company's portfolio consisted of the following stock securities:

Security	Cost Basis
Valentine	$ 80,000
Shadow	35,000
Twin Lakes	50,000
	$165,000

continued

At year-end the market values of the three securities were as follows:

Security	Market Value
Valentine.	$ 90,000
Shadow	30,000
Twin Lakes	55,000
	$175,000

Required

Calculate the amount of earnings reported by Sherwin Company for these investments under the following scenarios: (a) all securities are classified as trading; (b) all securities are classified as available-for-sale; (c) Valentine and Shadow are classified as available-for-sale and Twin Lakes is classified as trading.

The solution is on page 336.

Managerial Discretion

One might question why there is an inconsistent treatment of unrealized gains and losses between trading and available-for-sale securities. The difference in treatment coincides with the expected length of the holding period for the two investment categories—a relatively short holding period for trading securities and an uncertain holding period for available-for-sale securities. It could be argued that unrealized gains and losses should never be included in current income since the amount ultimately realized on a sale could be much different than the amount recognized in the current period. In fact, large swings in fair values, over which management has no control, may distort current period performance as measured by net income. This argument is the principal reason why unrealized gains and losses for available-for-sale securities are classified as accumulated other comprehensive income on the balance sheet rather than as current period income on the income statement. Trading securities, on the other hand, are expected to be sold within a relatively short time frame. Hence, large changes in fair value are much less likely to occur; and consequently, recognizing these unrealized gains and losses on the income statement in the current period is considered justifiable.

By classifying the shares of JWS Inc. as trading securities rather than as available-for-sale, the unrealized gain of $700,000 in the first year is included in NSWT's earnings rather than as a component of shareholders' equity on the balance sheet. Similarly during that year, classifying the shares in Coles Inc. as available-for-sale rather than as trading securities causes the unrealized loss of $200,000 to be included in shareholders' equity and not in NSWT's current earnings. Perhaps NSWT's CFO antici-pated this situation and strategically classified these securities to cause the most favorable impact on reported firm performance. Such a conclusion implies that the CFO has an ability to forecast future share prices, a talent that might lead him to resign his current position and become a professional stock picker. Yet, such strategic decision-making is more plausible in the CFO's decision to sell securities. If a boost in earnings is required for a given year, perhaps because operating profit has fallen short of expectations, a company's CFO could simply choose to sell the available-for-sale securities that are in winning positions, enabling an otherwise unrealized gain that would flow to shareholders' equity to manifest itself as a realized gain in current earnings. In some circles, such behavior is known as "cherry picking"—that is, selectively selling securities to include realized gains but not losses in a firm's current earnings. According to U.S. regulators, the Federal National Mortgage Association (also known as Fannie Mae), a publicly-held company chartered by the U.S. Congress to provide financ-ing for home mortgages, did just that. The Office of Federal Housing Enterprises Oversight charged in 2005 that Fannie Mae violated GAAP by pursuing an accounting policy that allowed it to keep the best mortgage-backed securities and to sell less attractive ones to investors, a practice that they labeled "keep the best, sell the rest."[1]

---

[1] *The Wall Street Journal*, "Fannie Mae Accused of Rule Breaking," April 7, 2005.

BUSINESS PERSPECTIVE

Fair Market Value Estimates

Companies reporting under U.S. GAAP are required to provide a set of comprehensive disclosures related to their estimates of fair market value. The objective is to help users of the financial statements understand both the composition of the investment portfolio and the degree of certainty regarding the measurement of fair value. Not all investments have readily available fair market values, so the FASB established a hierarchy of evidence that must be used when disclosing these estimates. Companies must classify their fair value estimates along three dimensions:

> Level 1—quoted market prices for identical items in active markets.
>
> Level 2—inputs to valuation that are directly or indirectly observable with reference to existing data.
>
> Level 3—unobservable inputs, requiring management judgment through estimates or assumptions.

These disclosure requirements were established in 2007, coinciding with the U.S. financial crisis that began around the same time. The timing of the new requirements was significant as many companies were invested in highly risky assets, for instance collaterized debt obligations (CDOs) and other mortgage-backed securities.

The fair value disclosures highlighted to a greater degree the extent to which measurement risk was embedded in a company's investment portfolio. Level 1 provides the greatest confidence as to the accurate measurement of fair value. As a company has more of its portfolio categorized as level 3, arguably there is greater uncertainty and greater risk related to those investments.

Below is an illustrative excerpt from the 2014 annual report of The Chubb Corporation. Chubb was a property and casualty insurance company based in Warren, New Jersey. Notice that the predominant amount of the company's $42.06 billion investment portfolio was comprised of level 2 assets ($39.76 billion); and, only a very small portion allocated to level 3, which would have provided investors some comfort. About five percent ($2.16 billion) of the Chubb portfolio involved traded securities in active markets, and then only stock equity investments.

The fair value hierarchy prioritizes the inputs to valuation techniques used to measure fair value into three broad levels as follows:

> Level 1—Unadjusted quoted prices in active markets for identical financial instruments.
>
> Level 2—Other inputs that are observable for the financial instrument, either directly or indirectly.
>
> Level 3—Significant unobservable inputs.

The fair value of financial instruments categorized based upon the lowest level of input that was significant to the fair value measurement was as follows:

	December 31, 2014			
Assets	**Level 1**	**Level 2**	**Level 3**	**Total**
	(in millions)			
Short term investments	$ 206	$ 1,112	$ —	$ 1,318
Fixed maturities				
Tax exempt...	—	19,769	3	19,772
Taxable				
U.S. government and government agency and authority obligations	—	2,007	—	2,007
Corporate bonds....................................	—	8,912	116	9,028
Foreign government and government agency obligations	—	6,663	9	6,672
Residential mortgage-backed securities.................	—	210	1	211
Commercial mortgage-backed securities...............	—	1,090	—	1,090
	—	18,882	126	19,008
Total fixed maturities................................	—	38,651	129	38,780
Equity securities.....................................	1,958	—	6	1,964
	$2,164	$39,763	$135	$42,062

EQUITY METHOD AND CONSOLIDATION ACCOUNTING

When an investor-company acquires enough shares such that it can exert significant influence over the investee, generally 20 percent or more, the accounting requirements for these investments change radically from the mark-to-market accounting described above. To illustrate the accounting for the acquisition of a significant shareholding—20 to 100 percent of a company's shares—we examine three scenarios involving the financial statement disclosures of Savanna Inc. and Waterloo Inc. Summary financial information for the two companies is provided in Exhibit 8.6. Savanna Inc. is the larger company in terms of assets—$150 million for Savanna versus $100 million for Waterloo—and has twice the revenue.

Takeaway 4
Explain and illustrate accounting for equity investments.

> The threshold of 20 percent voting power is presumed to be the tipping point of significant influence, although amounts less than 20 percent can qualify as well. For instance, even with less than 20 percent ownership when the board of directors of the investee is controlled by the investor, or there are key patents that the investor controls, these may be considered in the determination of whether significant influence exists.

EXHIBIT 8.6	Summary Financial Data for Savanna Inc. and Waterloo Inc.

Pre-Investment Balance Sheet
As of January 1

($ millions)	Savanna Inc.	Waterloo Inc.
Cash	$ 50	$ 20
Inventory	100	80
Total assets	**$150**	**$100**
Long-term debt	$ 50	$ 80
Common stock	100	20
Liabilities & shareholders' equity	**$150**	**$100**

Income Statement
Year Ending December 31

($ millions)	Savanna Inc.	Waterloo Inc.
Revenue	$200	$100
Expenses	170	90
Net income	**$ 30**	**$ 10**
Dividend	$ 0	$ 5

To simplify the illustration, we assume that (1) all revenue, expenses, and dividends are paid in cash; (2) there are no income taxes; (3) interest on long-term debt is ignored; (4) neither company initially holds debt or equity securities in the other; and, (5) Savanna pays no dividend during the year while Waterloo pays a $5 million cash dividend. Finally, we assume that there are no intercompany sales between the two companies.

> Consolidation accounting requires that prior to the combination of financial results, any profits on intercompany sales between related companies be eliminated. This requirement stems from the accounting principle that only profit from **arms-length transactions** be included in the income statement; that is, it is inappropriate to include the profit on a sale between two divisions of the same company in the consolidated results. In some circumstances, the profit on transactions between a parent company and an *unconsolidated* affiliate may be included in the consolidated income statement, but this situation (if material) must be disclosed in the footnotes to the consolidated financial statements as a **related-party transaction**.

Case 1. Savanna Inc. acquires 40 percent of the common shares of Waterloo Inc. for $8 million on January 2; the fair market value of Waterloo's net assets equals their book value of $20 million ($100 million in assets minus $80 million in liabilities).

Since Savanna's investment of $8 million is equal to 40 percent of the fair market value of Water-loo's net assets (40 percent of $20 million), there is no goodwill associated with the Waterloo investment. **Goodwill** is the excess of total consideration paid for an equity interest over the fair market value of the acquired net assets. The size of Savanna's investment in Waterloo's shares (40 percent) indicates that Savanna desires a significant but not controlling interest in Waterloo's operating decisions. As a consequence, Savanna should use the equity method to account for its investment in Waterloo. Savanna's accounting for its investment under the *equity method* is summarized below and is displayed in the spreadsheet in Exhibit 8.7:

There are many reasons why an acquiring company will pay an amount in excess of the fair value of an acquiree's identifiable assets, thus requiring an amount to be recorded as goodwill. The acquiring firm may believe that there are synergies that can be realized upon the acquisition, or alternatively, that certain "unidentified assets" such as technological know-how or managerial talent may be present in the acquired firm. Consequently, it should not be concluded that the existence of goodwill in an acquisition implies that the acquiring firm simply erroneously paid too much for an acquiree.

1. On January 2, Savanna decreases cash by $8 million for its investment in Waterloo and also increases the investment in equity affiliate account by $8 million.

2. During the year, Savanna reports its earnings as an increase in cash of $30 million and an increase in retained earnings of $30.

3. During the year, Savanna reports its 40 percent share of Waterloo's earnings, or $4 million (40 percent of $10 million), as an increase in the asset account investment in equity affiliate of $4 million and as an increase in retained earnings of $4 million (equity in the earnings of an unconsolidated affiliate). Under the equity method, Savanna reports a portion of Waterloo's earnings as both a source of earnings on its own income statement and as an increase in its investment in Waterloo on its balance sheet. If Waterloo had reported a loss instead of a profit, Savanna would report its ownership share of Waterloo's loss on its income statement and as a reduction in the investment account on its balance sheet.

4. During the year, Savanna reports its 40 percent share of Waterloo's cash dividend, or $2 million (40 percent of $5 million), by increasing cash by $2 million and decreasing the investment in equity affiliate by $2 million. Under the equity method, the payment of a dividend by an affiliate is treated as a reduction in (or liquidation of) the investment and not as a source of earnings. In effect, the affiliate's dividend is accounted for by the parent company (Savanna) as a return of investment, not a return on investment.

A dividend that is considered to be a return of capital, rather than a return on capital, is often called a **liquidating dividend**.

EXHIBIT 8.7	Accounting for Investments Using the Equity Method: Case 1						
($ millions)	Beginning Balance Sheet	Acquire Waterloo Shares	Savanna's Earnings for Year	40% of Waterloo Earnings	40% of Waterloo Dividends	Ending Balance Sheet
Assets						
Cash..........	50	(8)	30		2	74
Inventory.....	100					100
Investment in equity affiliate.....		8		4	(2)	10
Total assets.....	150					184
Liabilities						
Long-term debt	50					50
Shareholders' Equity						
Common stock.....	100					100
Retained earnings						34
Savanna's earnings for the year			30			
Equity in earnings of unconsolidated affiliate				4		
Total liabilities and shareholders' equity	150					184

The balance sheet for Savanna on January 2 after the initial investment in Waterloo's common shares and at the end of the year is shown in Exhibit 8.8. Savanna's investment in equity affiliate increases from $8 million at the time of the investment to $10 million at the end of the year. The income statement for Savanna is also shown in Exhibit 8.8 and reveals that Savanna's earnings include not only its own net earnings of $30 million, but also Savanna's 40 percent share of Waterloo's earnings ($4 million).

| EXHIBIT 8.8 | Financial Statements: Case 1 |

SAVANNA, INC.
Balance Sheet

($ millions)	January 2	December 31
Cash.	$ 42	$ 74
Inventory.	100	100
Investment in equity affiliate.	8	10
Total assets.	$150	$184
Long-term debt	$ 50	$ 50
Common stock.	100	100
Retained earnings	0	34
Liabilities & shareholders' equity	$150	$184

SAVANNA, INC.
Income Statement

($ millions)	December 31
Revenue	$200
Expenses	170
Operating income.	30
Equity in the earnings of unconsolidated affiliate.	4
Net income	$ 34

It may appear strange at first to see Savanna increasing its investment account for a portion of Waterloo's earnings, even if they are not received, and then decreasing the investment account for any dividends actually received. There is, however, logic behind this accounting treatment. Savanna's investment account represents its percentage ownership interest in Waterloo's shareholders' equity. Savanna initially paid an amount exactly equal to its percentage share of Waterloo's equity, so the investment account equaled 40 percent of $20 million or $8 million. During the year Waterloo reported net income of $10 million and paid dividends of $5 million. These amounts increase Waterloo's shareholders' equity (retained earnings) by $10 million and decrease its retained earnings by $5 million. Correspondingly, Savanna's investment account was increased by 40 percent of these amounts, $4 million minus $2 million, or $2 million. At year-end, Waterloo's shareholders' equity totals $25 million and Savanna's investment account is 40 percent of this amount, or $10 million. You may wish to try to replicate this reconciliation between Savanna's investment account and Waterloo's shareholders' equity for Case 2.

Finally, worth noting is that one important exception exists to the use of the equity method by U.S. companies. GAAP allows an investor to elect to use a fair value option rather than the equity method for minority ownership investments that exceed a 20% ownership interest. The fair value option, if elected, is irrevocable. Under this option, an investor reports its investments in a manner consistent with the treatment of trading securities, with any unrealized gains and losses resulting from changes in an investment's fair value reported on the income statement. Under the fair value option, the investor does not recognize its proportionate share of the investee's net income, but does report any dividends from the investee as dividend income. The fair value election is similar to the accounting provided under international accounting standards and reflects the continuing effort of the FASB to harmonize U.S. GAAP with IFRS.

Case 2. Savanna acquires 80 percent of Waterloo's common shares for $16 million; the fair market value of Waterloo Inc.'s net assets equals their book value of $20 million.

Since the total consideration paid of $16 million is equal to 80 percent of the fair market value of Waterloo's net assets (80 percent of $20 million),

Although it is generally true that when a company acquires a majority shareholding in another, the investor will report its financial results with those of the subsidiary on a consolidated basis, the presentation of consolidated financial statements is not required in every country (such as India). Consolidated financial statements are intended to help investors avoid the problem of **information overload** (giving investors too much financial information to comprehend).

In Practice 8.1 *Equity in the earnings of an unconsolidated affiliate* Care should be exercised when analyzing the income statements of investor-firms reporting affiliate earnings under the equity method since these earnings are often not received in cash. An analysis of public-company filings in 2015 found many companies reported earnings from affiliate-companies in excess of the cash dividends received from these affiliates. Moreover, in several cases, the affiliate-company earnings accounted for most of the investor-firms' reported net income:

Company	Unremitted portion of unconsolidated affiliate-company earnings as reported under equity method ($ millions)	Consolidated income before extraordinary items and discontinued operations ($ millions)
Alexander & Baldwin Inc	34.20	29.60
Alliancebernstein Holding Lp	212.50	188.18
Armstrong World Industries	66.10	52.60
Brookfield Property Prtrs Lp.	1,591.00	1,065.00
Chevron Corp.	4,684.00	4,587.00
Cosan Ltd.	197.90	116.13
Enbridge Inc.	475.00	251.00
Kinder Morgan Inc	333.00	253.00
Molson Coors Cda Inc	720.74	492.12
Nacco Industries-Cl A	50.47	21.98
Royal Dutch Shell Plc.	3,527.00	1,939.00
Surgery Partners Inc.	3.78	1.43
Teekay Corp.	102.87	82.15
Tejon Ranch Co	6.32	2.95
Valener Inc	58.26	47.15
Worthington Industries.	87.48	76.79

Source: Standard & Poor's Compustat

---

no goodwill is associated with the Waterloo investment. The size of Savanna's investment indicates that it has acquired a controlling interest in Waterloo's business, and therefore, Savanna should *consolidate* Waterloo's financial results. Savanna will initially account for its investment in Waterloo using the equity method on its unconsolidated financial statements and then prepare consolidated financial statements at the end of the fiscal period by making various consolidating adjustments. We follow that approach in this illustration. Savanna's initial accounting for its investment under the equity method is summarized below and in Exhibit 8.9:

EXHIBIT 8.9	Accounting for Investments Using the Equity Method: Case 2					
($ millions)	Beginning Balance Sheet	Acquire Waterloo Shares	Savanna's Earnings for Year	80% of Waterloo Earnings	80% of Waterloo Dividends	Ending Balance Sheet
Assets						
Cash.	50	(16)	30		4	68
Inventory.	100					100
Investment in equity affiliate.		16		8	(4)	20
Total assets	**150**					**188**
Liabilities						
Long-term debt	50					50
Shareholders' Equity						
Common stock.	100					100
Retained earnings						38
Savanna's earnings for the year			30			
Equity in earnings of unconsolidated affiliate				8		
Total liabilities and shareholders' equity	**150**					**188**

1. On January 2, Savanna decreases cash by $16 million for its cash investment in Waterloo and increases the investment in equity affiliate account by $16 million.

2. During the year, Savanna reports its earnings as an increase in cash of $30 million and an increase in retained earnings of $30 million.

3. During the year, Savanna reports its 80 percent share of Waterloo's earnings, or $8 million, as an increase in the investment in equity affiliate by $8 million and an increase in retained earnings by $8 million (equity in the earnings of unconsolidated affiliate).

4. During the year, Savanna reports its 80 percent share of Waterloo's cash dividend, or $4 million, by increasing cash by $4 million and decreasing the investment in equity affiliate by $4 million.

The financial statements for Savanna and Waterloo at December 31 are shown in Exhibit 8.10. Waterloo's assets of $105 million reflect its beginning assets of $100 million plus earnings for the year of $10 million less the dividends paid to its shareholders of $5 million. Since Savanna owns 80 percent of Waterloo's common shares, it must report its financial results and those of Waterloo on a consolidated basis. Thus, Waterloo's assets of $105 million are added to Savanna's assets. Similarly, Waterloo's $80 million of long-term debt is added to Savanna's liabilities. However, to avoid overstating the total consolidated assets and liabilities, certain adjusting (eliminating) entries are required. First, the investment in equity affiliate ($20 million) must be removed from the consolidated balance sheet to avoid double-counting some of Waterloo's assets. This amount is offset against Waterloo's common stock and retained earnings. Second, the 20 percent of Waterloo's common stock and retained earnings not legally owned by Savanna belong to

> The **noncontrolling interest** account was formerly called the "minority interest" account and is disclosed on the consolidated balance sheet as a component of shareholders' equity because it represents an ownership interest in the consolidated entity. For purposes of financial statement analysis, however, many financial analysts regard this account as a component of debt for purposes of calculating such ratios as the debt-to-equity ratio and the total debt-to-total assets ratio.

another group of shareholders whose claim on Waterloo's net assets, valued at $5 million (20 percent of $20 million plus 20 percent of $5 million), is known as the **noncontrolling interest** since Savanna is the controlling or majority shareholder. Noncontrolling interest refers to the portion of a subsidiary's net assets not owned, but still consolidated, by the parent company. Under consolidation accounting, 100 percent of an affiliate's assets and liabilities are consolidated with those of the parent company (Savanna) even though legal ownership may be less than 100 percent. The process of consolidating all of a subsidiary's assets and liabilities even though legal ownership is less than 100 percent is known as **full consolidation**.

EXHIBIT 8.10	Financial Statement Disclosures: Case 2			
Panel A: Balance Sheet ($ millions)	**Equity Method Savanna Inc. December 31**	**Waterloo Inc. December 31**	**Consolidating Adjustments**	**Consolidated Savanna Inc. December 31**
Cash.	$ 68	$ 25		$ 93
Inventory.	100	80		180
Investment in equity affiliate.	20	0	$(20)	0
Total assets.	**$188**	**$105**	**$(20)**	**$273**
Long-term debt	$ 50	$ 80		$130
Common stock.	100	20	$(20)	100
Noncontrolling interest in consolidated subsidiary			5	5
Retained earnings	38	5	(5)	38
Liabilities and shareholders' equity	**$188**	**$105**	**$(20)**	**$273**

Panel B: Income Statement ($ millions)	**Equity Method Savanna Inc. December 31**	**Waterloo Inc. December 31**	**Consolidating Adjustments**	**Consolidated Savanna Inc. December 31**
Revenue.	$200	$100		$300
Expenses	(170)	(90)		(260)
Operating income.	30	10		40
Equity in the earnings of unconsolidated affiliate.	8	—	$ (8)	
Noncontrolling interest in the earnings of consolidated subsidiary . . .	—	—	(2)	(2)
Net income	**$ 38**	**$ 10**	**$(10)**	**$ 38**

By adding across the left three columns, we arrive at Savanna's consolidated balance sheet in Exhibit 8.10, Panel A. The consolidated balance sheet shows that the net assets of $143 million ($273 million in assets less $130 million in long-term debt) are equal to the $138 million of Savanna's pre-consolidated equity claims ($188 of assets less $50 of long-term debt) plus the $5 million in claims by the minority shareholders. In essence, Savanna's $20 million Investment in Equity Affiliate account has been replaced with the assets and liabilities of Waterloo, less the 20% adjustment for noncontrolling interests.

Savanna's consolidated income statement is shown in Exhibit 8.10, Panel B. All of Waterloo's operating revenue and operating expenses are added to those of Savanna despite the fact that Savanna legally owns only 80 percent of Waterloo. To avoid double-counting Waterloo's earnings, it is necessary to eliminate the $8 million of equity in the earnings of unconsolidated affiliate and to subtract the 20 percent share of Waterloo's earnings, or $2 million (20 percent of $10 million), attributable to the claims of the minority or noncontrolling shareholders. Savanna's consolidated financial statements in Exhibit 8.10 reflect what is commonly referred to as the **acquisition method**.

Notice in Panel B of Exhibit 8.10 that the $38 million of net income reported by Savanna under the equity method is the same as the consolidated net income reported under consolidated accounting. This illustrates that consolidation accounting and the equity method produce similar income statement bottom-line results. Both revenue and expenses, however, are inflated under consolidation to reflect the aspect of control. The same is not true for the balance sheet: Total assets and long-term debt are higher under consolidation accounting than under the equity method.

The equity method enables a parent company to engage in what is commonly referred to as **off-balance-sheet financing**—that is, avoiding the disclosure of a subsidiary's debt on the parent-company balance sheet. To see this, note that Savanna would report a long-term debt-to-equity ratio of 0.94 ($130 million divided by $138 million) under the acquisition method of consolidation accounting but a ratio of only 0.36 ($50 million divided by $138 million) under the equity method. By maintaining an equity holding of 50 percent or less, a company is permitted to use the equity method to account for its intercorporate investments. Under U.S. GAAP, and that of many countries, parent-companies are required to disclose the aggregate assets, liabilities, revenue, and expenses of equity affiliates in the parent-company footnotes. Does it matter if a subsidiary's debt is disclosed in the footnotes rather than reported on the parent's balance sheet? If investors are reasonably astute they should be able to make the necessary adjustments to the parent's unconsolidated balance sheet to derive "as if" consolidated financial statements that reflect the debt of the subsidiary. Nevertheless, some managers go to great lengths to keep debt off the consolidated balance sheet, presumably under the belief that financial statement users don't make full and complete adjustments for off-balance-sheet debt. By keeping such debt off the balance sheet, these managers hope to make their companies appear less risky, and thus, positively impact the company's credit rating and the share price of the company's stock.

Case 3. Savanna acquires 100 percent of Waterloo's common shares for $25 million; the book value of Waterloo's assets and liabilities equals their fair market value except inventory, which has a current value of $82 million versus a book value of $80 million. Thus, the fair market value of Waterloo's net assets is $22 million ($20 million plus $2 million representing the understatement of inventory).

Savanna's acquisition of 100 percent of Waterloo's shares indicates that Savanna should prepare consolidated financial statements. Further, since Savanna paid a total consideration of $25 million for net assets having a fair market value of $22 million, *goodwill* in the amount of $3 million is present in the Waterloo acquisition. Finally, since Waterloo's inventory has a fair value of $82 million but a book value of only $80 million, Savanna must increase, or "step-up," the value of Waterloo's inventory by $2 million before the consolidated balance sheet is prepared. Under the acquisition method of consolidation accounting, all of the assets and liabilities of the acquiree are written up (or down) to their fair market value prior to the preparation of the consolidated financial statements.

As in Case 2, Savanna will initially account for its investment in Waterloo using the equity method, and at the end of the fiscal period, prepare consolidated financial statements. Savanna's equity method accounting for its investment in Waterloo is summarized below and in the Exhibit 8.11 transaction summary:

1. On January 2, Savanna increases the Investment in Equity Affiliate account by $25 million and decreases Cash for an equivalent amount.

2. During the year, Savanna reports its earnings for the year as an increase in Cash of $30 million and an increase in Retained Earnings of $30 million.

3. During the year, Savanna reports its 100 percent share of Waterloo's earnings, or $10 million, as an increase in the Investment in Equity Affiliate account and as an increase in Retained Earnings of $10 million (equity in the earnings of unconsolidated affiliate).

4. During the year, Savanna reports its 100 percent share of Waterloo's cash dividend, or $5 million, by increasing Cash by $5 million and decreasing the Investment in Equity Affiliate by $5 million.

EXHIBIT 8.11	Accounting for Investments Using the Equity Method: Case 3					
($ millions)	**Beginning Balance Sheet**	**Acquire Waterloo Shares**	**Savanna's Earnings for Year**	**100% of Waterloo Earnings**	**100% of Waterloo Dividends**	**Ending Balance Sheet**
Assets						
Cash......................................	50	(25)	30		5	60
Inventory.................................	100					100
Investment in equity affiliate..........		25		10	(5)	30
Total assets.........................	**150**					**190**
Liabilities						
Long-term debt	50					50
Shareholders' Equity						
Common stock..........................	100					100
Retained earnings						40
Savanna's earnings for the year			30			
Equity in earnings of unconsolidated affiliate				10		
Total liabilities and shareholders' equity	**150**					**190**

The balance sheets for Savanna and Waterloo at December 31 are shown in Exhibit 8.12, Panel A. The purchase price of $25 million exceeds the fair value of Waterloo's net assets of $20 million, with the excess of $5 million represented by a $2 million step-up in the value of Waterloo's inventory and goodwill in the amount of $3 million. As before, the investment in equity affiliate of $30 million is eliminated against Waterloo's common stock of $20 million, retained earnings of $5 million, the creation of goodwill for $3 million and the inventory write-up of $2 million. Consolidated financial statements are presented in Exhibit 8.12.

EXHIBIT 8.12	Financial Statement Disclosures: Case 3			
Panel A: Balance Sheet				
($ millions)	**Equity Method Savanna, Inc. December 31**	**Waterloo Inc. December 31**	**Consolidating Adjustments**	**Consolidated Savanna, Inc. December 31**
Cash.......................................	$ 60	$ 25		$ 85
Inventory..................................	100	80	$ 2	182
Investment in equity affiliate..........	30	0	(30)	0
Goodwill	—	—	3	3
Total assets.........................	**$190**	**$105**	**$(25)**	**$270**
Long-term debt	$ 50	$ 80	—	$130
Common stock...........................	100	20	$(20)	100
Retained earnings	40	5	(5)	40
Liabilities & shareholders' equity	**$190**	**$105**	**$(25)**	**$270**
Panel B: Income Statement				
($ millions)	**Equity Method Savanna, Inc. December 31**	**Waterloo Inc. December 31**	**Consolidating Adjustments**	**Consolidated Savanna, Inc. December 31**
Revenue	$200	$100		$300
Expenses	170	90		260
Operating income........................	30	10		40
Equity in earnings of unconsolidated affiliate..................	10	—	$(10)	—
Net income	**$ 40**	**$ 10**	**$(10)**	**$ 40**

REVIEW PROBLEM 8.2

The Arcadia Company made an offer to purchase all of the outstanding shares of The Claremont Company at a price of $10 per share, or an aggregate of $22 million. Immediately prior to the purchase offer, the balance sheets of the two companies appeared as follows:

	The Arcadia Company	The Claremont Company
Assets		
Cash.	$ 26,000,000	$ 2,000,000
Inventory.	12,000,000	7,000,000
Fixed assets, net	50,000,000	15,000,000
Intangible assets	30,000,000	18,000,000
Total Assets	$118,000,000	$42,000,000
Liabilities		
Accounts payable.	$ 7,000,000	$ 4,000,000
Bonds payable	25,000,000	19,000,000
Total	32,000,000	23,000,000
Shareholders' Equity		
Capital stock	56,000,000	14,000,000
Retained earnings	30,000,000	5,000,000
Total	86,000,000	19,000,000
Total liabilities and shareholders' equity.	$118,000,000	$42,000,000

During its due diligence review, Arcadia determined that while the liabilities of The Claremont Company were fairly valued, the reported value of Claremont's inventory was understated by $1,000,000 as a consequence of using the LIFO method, and the intangible assets of The Claremont Company were overstated by $4,000,000 because an impairment in the value of certain intangible assets had not yet been recorded in the company's financial statements.

Required

a. Calculate the value of the goodwill implicit in the offer price of $22 million.

b. Prepare the unconsolidated balance sheet of The Arcadia Company immediately following a successful acquisition of 100 percent of the outstanding shares of The Claremont Company.

c. Prepare the consolidated balance sheet for The Arcadia-Claremont Company assuming a successful acquisition offer.

The solution is on page 337.

Deconsolidation

Just as firms consolidate the financial statements of their majority-owned subsidiaries, they must reverse this process when their ownership interest falls below 50 percent. The **deconsolidation** process most commonly occurs when a parent company sells a business division or distributes its ownership shares to its existing shareholders. The distribution of ownership of a business division from a company to its shareholders is called a **spin-off** and is usually executed as a tax-free distribution.

Consider, for example, the July 20, 2015 spin-off of PayPal Holdings by eBay, Inc. eBay separated PayPal by distributing 100 percent ownership to its existing shareholders, one share of PayPal for each share of eBay. The spin-off reduced eBay's net worth by two-thirds (the book value of the net assets transferred to PayPal), and eBay's share price declined from $66.29 per share prior to the spin-off to $28.57 post-spin-off. The decline in eBay's share price approximated the opening fair market value of the PayPal (about $40 per share). Following the spin-off, PayPal became a separate exchange-traded entity and thus independent of eBay. Following the announcement of the spin-off, about 9 months earlier, eBay's share price rose 8 percent, suggesting that the equity market perceived the transaction to be a value-enhancing decision for eBay's shareholders. Spin-offs are a mechanism by which companies can unlock value for their shareholders when the consolidated entity is undervalued by the capital market. Other examples of recent high-profile spin-offs are General Electric's of Synchrony Financial in 2015, Sears Holdings' of Lands' End in 2014, Time Warner's of AOL in 2009, Verizon's of Frontier Communications in 2010, and ADT by Tyco International in 2012. Conglomerates like these, which are made up of a variety of businesses, often trade at a discount from the sum of their stand-alone fair market values. This discount is known as the **conglomerate discount**.

The accounting for a spin-off is executed like a reverse consolidation—that is, the book value of the division's assets and liabilities is removed from the consolidated balance sheet and placed on a new, separate unconsolidated balance sheet representing the new corporate entity. Parent-company shareholders receive shares in the spun-off entity in proportion to their ownership interest in the parent, and subsequently, can trade the shares of the newly created corporate entity separately from the parent company.

BUSINESS PERSPECTIVE

The first footnote to the financial statements typically is a summary of significant accounting policies adopted by a company. Certainly for any company engaged in large investments, understanding the accounting policies for those investments would be critical. As an example below, MGM Resorts International disclosed the following information in "Note 2—Basis of Presentation and Significant Accounting Policies," in its 2014 annual report:

Principles of consolidation The consolidated financial statements include the accounts of the Company and its subsidiaries. The Company's investments in unconsolidated affiliates which are 50% or less owned are accounted for under the equity method. The Company does not have significant variable interests in variable interest entities. All intercompany balances and transactions have been eliminated in consolidation. In September 2014, the Company resumed accounting for the investment in Borgata under the equity method and has adjusted prior period financial statements retroactively. **Investments in and advances to unconsolidated affiliates.** The Company has investments in unconsolidated affiliates accounted for under the equity method. Under the equity method, carrying value is adjusted for the Company's share of the investees' earnings and losses, amortization of certain basis differences, as well as capital contributions to and distributions from these companies. Distributions in excess of equity method earnings are recognized as a return of investment and recorded as investing cash inflows in the accompanying consolidated statements of cash flows. The Company classifies operating income and losses as well as gains and impairments related to its investments in unconsolidated affiliates as a component of operating income or loss, as the Company's investments in such unconsolidated affiliates are an extension of the Company's core business operations.

The Company evaluates its investments in unconsolidated affiliates for impairment whenever events or changes in circumstances indicate that the carrying value of its investment may have experienced an "other-than-temporary" decline in value. If such conditions exist, the Company compares the estimated fair value of the investment to its carrying value to determine if an impairment is indicated and determines whether the impairment is "other-than-temporary" based on its assessment of all relevant factors, including consideration of the Company's intent and ability to retain its investment. The Company estimates fair value using a discounted cash flow analysis based on estimated future results of the investee and market indicators of terminal year capitalization rates, and a market approach that utilizes business enterprise value multiples based on a range of multiples from the Company's peer group. See Note 6 for results of the Company's review of its investment in certain of its unconsolidated affiliates.

Accounting for Joint Ventures

In some cases, a business may establish a **joint venture** with another company to produce a product or provide a service. These ventures are often quite effective because each company typically has some unique skill, knowledge, or resource that makes it more efficient to partner with another company than to attempt the undertaking alone. These partnering arrangements are often established as separate corporate entities in which each partner owns 50 percent of the venture's equity, although owning exactly 50 percent is not a necessary condition to establish a joint venture. When each partner owns half of the joint venture's equity, these ventures are accounted for using the equity method.

eLectures

MBC

Takeaway 5
Explain the accounting for joint ventures and special purpose entities.

For example, the Starbucks Coffee Company disclosed in its 2012 annual report that it had ongoing joint ventures to produce and distribute Starbucks-branded products across the globe. Two such ventures were The North American Coffee Partnership, a 50/50 joint venture with the Pepsi-Cola Company to produce and distribute bottled Frappuccino coffee, and another with Shanghai President Coffee Company, Ltd. wherein the two companies would jointly open retail operations in China. Starbucks accounts for these investments using the equity method. The asset section of Starbucks' balance sheet is presented in Exhibit 8.13, and shows the company's investment in its joint ventures, called Equity and Cost Investments, as a line item in the noncurrent assets section (see **bolded** area in Exhibit 8.13). The data reveal that the value of Starbucks' joint ventures, plus any other equity method investments, increased from 2011 to 2012 by $87.6 million ($459.9 million − $372.3 million). This account would capture Starbucks' original investment, its 50 percent ownership interests in the joint venture's net income, less its 50 percent interest in any dividends paid by the joint ventures to their parent companies.

EXHIBIT 8.13	Financial Statement Disclosures: Joint Ventures		
STARBUCKS CORPORATION **Consolidated Balance Sheet**			
Fiscal Year Ended (in millions)		**Sept. 30, 2012**	**Oct. 2, 2011**
Cash and cash equivalents		$1,188.6	$1,148.1
Short-term investments		848.4	902.6
Accounts receivable, net		485.9	386.5
Inventories		1,241.5	965.8
Prepaid expenses and other current assets		196.5	161.5
Deferred income taxes, net		238.7	230.4
Total current assets		4,199.6	3,794.9
Long-term investments—available-for-sale securities		116.0	107.0
Equity and cost investments		**459.9**	**372.3**
Property, plant and equipment, net		2,658.9	2,355.0
Other assets		385.7	409.6
Goodwill		399.1	321.6
Total assets		$8,219.2	$7,360.4

Accounting for Special Purpose Entities

Special purpose entities (SPEs) or **special purpose vehicles (SPVs)** refer to separate legal entities created by a parent company along with other independent investors for a legitimate business purpose. Under U.S. GAAP, an SPE or SPV need not be consolidated by a parent company if certain conditions are met. The reporting rules governing these entities have recently been revised, including a new label for this type of entity, **variable interest entity** or **VIE**.

Unfortunately, the accounting rules that permitted majority-owned SPEs to remain unconsolidated were integral to several high-profile corporate scandals, most notably the Enron Corporation case from the early 2000s. It is now known that Enron made extensive use of SPEs, largely as an off-balance-sheet financing tool. An examination of Enron's footnotes concerning its unconsolidated equity affiliates reveals that Enron had extensive off-balance-sheet debt (see Business Perspective on page 317). What was not revealed in Enron's footnotes, however, was the extent to which Enron was contingently liable for much of the debt of its unconsolidated SPEs. The alleged abuses of SPEs led the FASB to revisit the reporting rules governing these entities. The FASB had trouble defining an SPE and instead defined a broader category of entity called a variable interest entity, or VIE. Many former SPEs that previously escaped consolidation are now required to be consolidated under the new accounting rules. Specifically, a VIE must be consolidated with the sponsoring parent company if the VIE is not independent from the sponsoring company and does not have sufficient capital to operate separately from the sponsoring company. If there is more than one sponsoring company, the VIE should be consolidated with the sponsoring company that will absorb the majority of the VIE's expected losses or receive a majority of the VIE's expected residual returns.

BUSINESS PERSPECTIVE

SPE Disclosures

Enron's abbreviated balance sheet at December 31, 2000, is presented below. The balance sheet reveals that Enron disclosed $8.55 billion of long-term debt and $5.294 billion of Investments in and Advances to Unconsolidated Equity Affiliates at year-end 2000. The use of this latter account indicates that Enron used the equity method to account for its unconsolidated SPEs (see **bolded** area).

ENRON CORPORATION		
Abbreviated Balance Sheet		
December 31 ($ millions)	2000	1999
Assets		
Current assets		
Total current assets	$30,381	$ 7,255
Investments & other assets		
Investments in & advances to unconsolidated equity affiliates	**5,294**	**5,036**
Assets from price risk management activities	8,988	2,929
Goodwill	3,638	2,799
Other	5,459	4,681
Total investments & other assets	23,379	15,445
Property, plant & equipment (net)	11,743	10,681
Total assets	$65,503	$33,381
Liabilities & shareholders' equity		
Total current liabilities	$28,406	$ 6,759
Long-term debt	**8,550**	**7,151**
Total deferred credits & other liabilities	13,759	6,471
Minority interests*	2,414	2,430
Company-obligated preferred securities of subsidiaries	904	1,000
Total shareholders' equity	11,470	9,570
Total liabilities & shareholders' equity	$65,503	$33,381

* Enron used the label minority interests to refer to its noncontrolling interest. Minority interest was the correct label for noncontrolling interests at the time these statements were prepared.

Enron's footnotes provided summary balance sheet information about its unconsolidated SPEs and revealed that its SPEs held $9.717 billion of related long-term debt. In simple terms, consolidating Enron's SPEs would have added another $9.717 billion of assets and long-term debt to Enron's consolidated balance sheet and consequently, increased Enron's reported debt-to-equity ratio from 0.75 ($8,550/$11,470) to 1.59 ($8,550 + $9,717)/$11,470—an increase of more than 100 percent! As is now known, an important objective in Enron's use of the equity method to account for its many SPEs was to keep the massive debt held by its unconsolidated SPEs off its consolidated balance sheet so that investors and investment professionals would perceive Enron to be less risky than it really was. Even such knowledgeable risk-rating agencies as Moody's and Standard & Poor's failed to correctly identify the financial risk inherent in Enron's financial arrangements. Enron filed for its much publicized bankruptcy in late 2001.

Companies that sell goods or services on credit, for example, often create an SPE to buy outstanding accounts receivable from the parent company. In essence, the SPE acts like a financial services company, borrowing from the investment community to then buy accounts receivable from the parent company. The following are excerpts related to one such transaction from the 2012 annual report of Marriott International. These excerpts highlight how Marriott was required under new accounting rules to consolidate certain VIEs related to timeshare notes receivable that were in place during the year 2010.

Note 1: **Adoption of New Accounting Standards Resulting in Consolidation of Special Purpose Entities** On January 2, 2010, the first day of the 2010 fiscal year, we adopted the new Transfers of Financial Assets and Consolidation standards (which were originally known as Financial Accounting Standards Nos. 166 and 167). Prior to the spin-off date, our former Timeshare segment used certain special purpose entities to securitize Timeshare segment notes receivables, which prior to our adoption of these new standards we treated as off-balance sheet entities. Our former Timeshare segment retained the servicing rights and varying subordinated interests in the securitized notes. Pursuant to GAAP in effect prior to the 2010 fiscal year, we did not consolidate these special purpose entities in our financial statements because the securitization transactions qualified as sales of financial assets. As a result of adopting the new Transfers of Financial Assets and Consolidation standards on the first day of 2010, we consolidated 13 existing qualifying special purpose entities associated with past securitization transactions.

Note 20: **Variable Interest Entities** In accordance with the applicable accounting guidance for the consolidation of variable interest entities, we analyze our variable interests, including loans, guarantees, and equity investments, to determine if an entity in which we have a variable interest is a variable interest entity. Our analysis includes both quantitative and qualitative reviews. We base our quantitative analysis on the forecasted cash flows of the entity, and our qualitative analysis on our review of the design of the entity, its organizational structure including decision-making ability, and relevant financial agreements. We also use our qualitative analyses to determine if we must consolidate a variable interest entity as its primary beneficiary.

ETHICS PERSPECTIVE

The Enron scandal was arguably the most complex financial fraud ever uncovered in the United States. Somewhat surprisingly, it was not Enron's external auditors, Arthur Andersen, or U.S. regulators that are credited with exposing the company's accounting improprieties. Instead, it was an Enron employee, Sherron Watkins, who stepped forward to warn that Enron would "implode in a wave of accounting scandals." It is often whistle-blowers such as Sherron Watkins at Enron and Cynthia Cooper at WorldCom that have the necessary knowledge to expose these financial frauds. Inside knowledge, unfortunately, is not always enough to get whistle-blowers to come forward with the information to expose corporate wrongdoing. Some corporate managers have made exposing fraud very costly to the whistle-blower through threats, intimidation, and character attacks. The Sarbanes-Oxley Act, passed into law in 2002, recognized the value of having a system in place such that employees would be more likely to report corporate wrongdoing. Provisions under Section 307 of the legislation make it easier for an employee to report items in a confidential matter while Section 806 prohibits retaliation by a company against any employee reporting questionable activities.

eLectures
MBC

ACCOUNTING FOR INVESTMENTS IN FOREIGN ENTITIES

Takeaway 6
Understand the foreign currency accounting issues that arise with investments in foreign entities.

With increasing globalization, even small companies now consider manufacturing and/or selling their goods and services abroad. Many U.S. companies, for example, have located manufacturing plants as far away as Asia to take advantage of large pools of skilled but relatively inexpensive labor. But another reason that companies locate their operations in other countries is to take advantage of natural currency hedges that exist when receipts from product sales and outlays for production costs are denominated in the same currency. A **currency hedge** is an attempt by a company to avoid the potential losses that may accompany an exchange rate movement between two currencies.

Currency Exchange Rate Fluctuations

A company may locate a sales office in a foreign country or it may establish an entire subsidiary that operates relatively autonomously from the parent company. One of the issues that must be addressed when locating a production and/or sales organization in another country is the resulting exposure to currency exchange rate fluctuations. If, for instance, a manufacturing facility is built in Mexico by a U.S. company, the value of the Mexico-based business to the U.S. parent company will rise and fall as the exchange rate between the U.S. dollar and the Mexican peso rises and falls. Currency exchange rate problems do not exist between countries in which the currencies are pegged to one another, as for example between the United States and Guatemala or Panama. But they are very real risks to companies that operate in countries with no such agreements, including doing business in all countries of the Euro-zone.

Before any consolidated financial statements that include the results of foreign-based subsidiaries can be prepared, the financial results of any foreign subsidiary must first be converted from its local currency into the currency of the parent company. Under U.S. GAAP and the GAAP of most countries, the **current rate method** is used to translate the foreign-currency denominated financial statements of foreign subsidiaries that are self-contained business units.

> The financial results of foreign subsidiaries that are not self-contained are usually translated using the **temporal method**. Under the temporal method, monetary assets and liabilities are translated at the current or closing exchange rate, whereas nonmonetary assets and liabilities are translated at historical exchange rates.

Under the current rate method, a foreign subsidiary's assets and liabilities are translated at the current or closing exchange rate as of the balance sheet date while shareholders' equity is translated at the historical exchange rate when the subsidiary was established. Income statement items, on the other hand, are translated at the average exchange rate for the fiscal period. Any foreign currency translation gains/losses—that is, any changes in the translated value of the foreign subsidiary assets and liabilities over the fiscal period—are reported as a component of shareholders' equity and do not flow through to the income statement. Foreign currency translation gains (losses) represent unrealized wealth changes, much like the unrealized gains (losses) on available-for-sale securities. And, as a consequence, the accumulated balance of any foreign currency translation gains (losses) are reported on the balance sheet as a component of accumulated other comprehensive income under U.S. GAAP.[2]

Illustration of Current Rate Method

Jimbo Inc., is a U.S. manufacturer and distributor of food preparation equipment. To take advantage of growth opportunities outside the United States, the company established a self-contained operating subsidiary in Mexico. The Mexican subsidiary—Jimbo de Mexico SA de CV—was established on January 1 when the exchange rate was 10 pesos (P) to $1. At the inception of the Mexican subsidiary, its balance sheet appeared as follows:

JIMBO DE MEXICO **Balance Sheet** **January 1**			
(P millions)			
Cash.	P1,500	Long-term debt	P 900
Accounts receivable.	300	Common stock.	900
Total assets.	**P1,800**	**Liabilities & shareholders' equity**	**P1,800**

How would Jimbo de Mexico report its balance sheet in U.S. dollars on January 1? Exhibit 8.14, Panel A, shows Jimbo de Mexico's balance sheet in Mexican pesos and in U.S. dollars. The company's assets and liabilities are translated at the current exchange rate of 10 pesos per dollar while shareholders' equity is translated at the historical exchange rate, which in this instance is also 10 pesos per dollar.

Now assume that on January 2, the Mexican peso depreciated to an exchange rate of 15 pesos per U.S. dollar. How would Jimbo de Mexico report its balance sheet in U.S. dollars following the devaluation? Jimbo de Mexico's post-devaluation balance sheet in U.S. dollars is shown in Exhibit 8.14, Panel B. After the devaluation, the company's assets and liabilities are translated at the new current exchange rate of 15 pesos per U.S. dollar while shareholders' equity is translated at the historical rate of 10 pesos per U.S. dollar. The **cumulative foreign currency translation adjustment** (CTA) of negative $30 million is required to ensure that the translated balance sheet actually balances. The CTA represents the exposure that Jimbo's shareholders suffered from the currency devaluation on their investment in Jimbo de Mexico. The $30 million unrealized loss is equal to the equity investment in Jimbo de Mexico times the change in the exchange rate [900 million pesos $\times$ (1/10 − 1/15)].

---

[2] This is the same account that is used to reflect the unrealized holding gains or losses on available-for-sale securities discussed earlier in this chapter.

EXHIBIT 8.14 | Translating Balance Sheets: Current Rate Method

Panel A. Pre-devaluation

JIMBO DE MEXICO
Balance Sheet

(in millions)	January 1 (Mexican pesos)	Exchange Rate (pesos per $1)	January 1 (U.S. dollars)
Cash.	P1,500	10	$150
Accounts receivable.	300	10	30
Total assets.	P1,800		$180
Long-term debt	P 900	10	$ 90
Common stock	900	10	90
Cumulative foreign currency translation adjustment	0		0
Liabilities & shareholders' equity	P1,800		$180

Panel B. Post-devaluation

JIMBO DE MEXICO
Balance Sheet

(in millions)	January 2 (Mexican pesos)	Exchange Rate (pesos per $1)	January 2 (U.S. dollars)
Cash.	P1,500	15	$100
Accounts receivable.	300	15	20
Total assets.	P1,800		$120
Long-term debt	P 900	15	$ 60
Common stock.	900	10	90
Cumulative foreign currency translation adjustment	0		(30)
Liabilities & shareholders' equity	P1,800		$120

The foreign currency translation account may carry either a negative (net unrealized loss) or positive (net unrealized gain) balance. The account balance will increase or decrease each period in response to the changing exchange rate between the currency of the country of the parent and the currency of the country of the subsidiary. The balance at any point in time represents the gain (loss) that could be realized by the parent company if the foreign subsidiary were sold for a price equivalent to its current book value, with the net proceeds from the sale repatriated back to the parent's currency.

GLOBAL PERSPECTIVE

Investment Accounting under International Financial Reporting Standards

The accounting for investments across U.S. GAAP and IFRS are on the whole quite similar. Passive investments are accounted for at mark-to-market, and the equity method is required for non-consolidated investments with significant influence. The most stark difference relates to the requirement of when consolidation must take place. Consolidation accounting is required under U.S. GAAP only when a firm acquires more than a majority shareholding (greater than 50 percent) in another entity. Under IFRS, however, consolidation accounting may be required when a firm's ownership interest is less than 50 percent but where it effectively controls another entity. This situation may arise when a firm owns a substantial ownership interest, for example 40 percent or more, and the entity's remaining ownership shares are widely held. Evidence of de facto control may be provided by membership of an acquirer's CEO or other executives on the board of directors of an acquiree. In essence, IFRS requires that considerable judgment be used in determining whether consolidation accounting is warranted or not in situations where ownership is significant but less than a majority.

continued

Although investment accounting in U.S. GAAP and IFRS have few differences, across the globe the practicalities of financial markets influence the ways in which investments are reported. In lesser developed countries where there are not actively traded markets for debt and equity securities, and thus not readily available or reliable market prices, the valuation of marketable debt and equity securities is often at the original cost of the investment. In some developed countries, a variant of the fair value approach called **lower-of-cost-or-market** is used. Under the lower-of-cost-or-market method, a security is valued at the lower of two values—its current fair value or its original cost. When a security's fair value falls below its cost, the security is written down to the lower amount and the unrealized loss is reported in current income.

REVIEW PROBLEM 8.3

On January 1st Mammoth Company established Juno Inc., a wholly-owned, self-sustaining British subsidiary with assets valued at 50 million pounds. The pound is the functional currency for Juno. The exchange rate at the time the subsidiary was established was .80 pounds per $1. On January 2nd, after the subsidiary was established, the exchange rate changed to .82 pounds per $1.

Required

1. What is the amount of total assets that Juno Inc. will show on its balance sheet in U.S. dollars on January 1st (before the exchange rate change)?
2. What is the amount of the cumulative foreign currency translation adjustment that Mammoth Company will report on its balance sheet after the exchange rate change?

The solution is on page 337.

ANALYZING INTERCORPORATE INVESTMENTS

The analysis of intercorporate investments—that is, an investment by one corporate entity in the equity of a second corporate entity—presents analytical challenges for financial statement users at several different levels. First, the managerial discretion that is required in the designation of marketable securities as being either trading securities or available-for-sale securities presents a significant opportunity for earnings' management. If, for example, the manager of an investor-company anticipates that an investee-company is likely to sustain operating losses that might adversely affect its fair value, he or she might selectively classify the investment as available-for-sale to avoid the potential negative income statement effect associated with an unrealized loss if the investment were classified as a trading security. Similarly, if an upward share price movement in the value of an investee-company were anticipated by the investor-company manager, he or she might selectively designate the investment as a trading security to enable any unrealized gain to flow through to the investor-company's income statement and positively impact its reported earnings. The manager might also selectively use investment sales transactions merely to influence the timing of reported gains and losses. In each of these cases, financial statement users would be wise to recall the definition of sustainable earnings from Chapter 3—sustainable earnings exclude any one-time or nonoperating events such as an unrealized gain on a trading security.

Second, with respect to equity method intercorporate investments, which include an investment in an unconsolidated affiliate, joint venture, or special purpose entity, some investment professionals regard the equity method as a form of off-balance-sheet financing. Under the equity method, an investor-company adjusts its carrying value for an investee-company for its proportionate share of the investee's operating earnings, losses, and dividends paid; but, the investor-company is not required to account for its implicit ownership interest in any changes in the level of debt financing of the investee. As a consequence, an investee may significantly increase its use of leverage, often for the express purpose of transferring the borrowed funds to the investor-company, but the investor is not required to reflect the increased investee borrowing on its own financial statements. The favorable accounting

Takeaway 7
Discuss the considerations in analyzing intercorporate investments.

treatment associated with the debt of an equity method investee was at the root of Enron Corporation's extensive use of off-balance-sheet special purpose entities.

A final consideration in the analysis of intercorporate investments is the issue of related-party transactions—that is, the profit or loss generated by transactions between two entities that are related by virtue of existing cross-firm equity investments. Although the elimination of any intercompany transactions among consolidated entities is required under existing GAAP, the financial effects of any intercompany transactions between an investor-company and an unconsolidated affiliate company are permitted to be included in the consolidated financial statements. Where such intercompany transactions are material in amount, details of the transactions must be disclosed in the footnotes to the financial statements. With this information, financial statement users are empowered to decide whether (or not) to restate the consolidated financial statements to eliminate the financial effects of these related-party transactions prior to assessing the value of a firm.

TAX PERSPECTIVE

Investment Accounting Under U.S. Tax Law

The accounting for investments in other entities outlined in Chapter 8 highlights a diverse set of income measurement rules dependent on the level of ownership. In most respects the income measurement principles followed by the IRS are more straightforward than U.S. GAAP. Here we review some of the highlights.

Recall that under U.S. GAAP, some unrealized losses (gains) are included as income (i.e., trading securities); however, no such treatment is allowed for tax reporting. For investments, the IRS follows an "ability to pay" approach wherein gains or losses are not taxed as income until the asset is sold and the cash has been received by the selling company. Likewise equity income in affiliates is not taxable income as those earnings have been taxed once at the affiliate level and are not required to be taxed again at the investor level. Only at the point of sale is the gain or loss on the investment taxable, and then on an investment account value that has not been increased or decreased by the earnings of the affiliate.

Dividends received by a corporation are also treated differently for tax purposes relative to GAAP. Recall that the treatment of dividends varied under GAAP as follows: (i) if the investment was less than 20 percent ownership, dividends were treated as income, (ii) if the equity method applied, the dividends were not income but rather a return of capital that lowered the investment account value, and (iii) dividends were eliminated between companies if the two were consolidated. For tax purposes most, but not all, of the dividends received from other corporations are not subject to tax. The logic here is to avoid what would effectively be triple taxation once the dollars finally made their way to the individual shareholders of the receiving corporation. The amount of the dividend received that is excludable from taxable income depends on the level of ownership in the company, but ranges from 70 percent for the smallest ownership levels to 100 percent if the subsidiary is wholly-owned.

Finally, we observed that companies that own over 50 percent of another entity are required under U.S. GAAP to consolidate their financial statements. No such requirement exists under the IRC. Each individual entity is expected to file its own separate tax return but with one exception: an affiliated group of corporations may elect, but is not required, to file a single consolidated tax return. "Affiliation" for these purposes is met when one corporation owns at least 80 percent of the voting stock of another.

EXECUTIVE SUMMARY

This chapter examined the accounting for investments in other corporate entities. We considered why such investments are made and how they are accounted for. In general, small equity investments (0 to 20 percent) are accounted for at their current fair value using mark-to-market accounting. Investments representing 20 to 50 percent of the outstanding equity are accounted for using the equity method, as are most joint ventures and special purpose entities; and, investments involving a controlling equity interest (greater than 50 percent) are accounted for using consolidated accounting.

As a validation of your understanding of the content of this chapter, you should now be able to:

- Explain why companies acquire ownership interests in other entities.
- Understand how to account for investments in debt and equity securities, including the application of mark-to-market accounting, the equity method, and consolidation accounting.

- Explain and illustrate accounting for passive investments.
- Explain and illustrate accounting for equity investments.
- Explain the accounting for joint ventures and special purposes entities.
- Understand the foreign currency accounting issues that arise with investments in foreign entities.
- Discuss the considerations in analyzing intercorporate investments.

In Chapter 9, we begin an exploration of corporate financing decisions, specifically how companies finance their operations and capital investments using debt.

KEY CONCEPTS AND TERMS

Accumulated other comprehensive income, 300
Acquisition method, 312
Amortized cost, 300
Arms-length transactions, 307
Available-for-sale securities, 300, 301
Conglomerate discount, 315
Consolidation accounting, 301
Cumulative foreign currency translation adjustment, 319
Currency hedge, 318
Current rate method, 319

Deconsolidation, 314
Equity in the earnings (loss) of an unconsolidated affiliate, 301
Equity method, 300
Full consolidation, 311
Goodwill, 308
Held-to-maturity debt securities, 300, 301
Information overload, 309
Joint venture, 315
Liquidating dividend, 308
Lower-of-cost-or-market, 321
Marketable securities, 299

Mark-to-market accounting, 299
Noncontrolling interest, 311
Off-balance-sheet financing, 312
Related-party transaction, 307
Special purpose entities (SPEs), 316
Special purpose vehicles (SPVs), 316
Spin-off, 314
Temporal method, 319
Trading securities, 299, 301
Unrealized gain (loss), 299
Variable interest entity or VIE, 316

QUESTIONS

Q8.1   **Accounting for Marketable Securities.**   Marketable securities are classified under U.S. GAAP as either trading securities or available-for-sale securities. Regardless of their classification, marketable securities are accounted for at their current fair value using mark-to-market accounting. Discuss why mark-to-market accounting is superior to accounting for marketable securities at their historical cost. Should mark-to-market accounting be adopted to account for all assets on the balance sheet? Why or why not?

Q8.2   **Equity Method Versus Consolidated Reporting.**   The equity method is often described as a "one-line consolidation." Discuss the similarities of the equity method and consolidated reporting. Discuss how these methods differ in their financial statement presentation.

Q8.3   **Noncontrolling Interest.**   The noncontrolling interest account arises on the consolidated balance sheet and is reported as a component of shareholders' equity. Many financial analysts, however, regard the account as a component of a firm's debt for purposes of financial statement analysis. Discuss whether the noncontrolling interest account on the balance sheet constitutes a component of debt or shareholders' equity.

Q8.4   **Accumulated Other Comprehensive Income.**   Accumulated other comprehensive income (AOCI) appears as a subsection of shareholders' equity on the balance sheet. Discuss the components of AOCI. What information does the AOCI convey to financial statement users about the financial health of a business?

Q8.5   **Cumulative Foreign Currency Translation Adjustment.**   The cumulative foreign currency translation adjustment (CTA) account appears on the balance sheet as a component of accumulated other comprehensive income. The CTA account may have either a positive (credit) or negative (debit) balance. Discuss the financial implications when the CTA account balance is negative and when it is positive.

Q8.6   **Goodwill.**   In 1989, PepsiCo Inc. acquired three international franchise-food operations—Pizza Hut, Taco Bell, and Kentucky Fried Chicken. PepsiCo paid an aggregate of $3.4 billion for the three businesses, which had been valued by investment professionals to be worth, in aggregate, $400 million. As a consequence, PepsiCo recorded $3.0 billion of goodwill on its consolidated balance sheet associated with the acquisitions. Discuss why PepsiCo may have been willing to pay so much above the fair market value of the three businesses.

Q8.7   **Trading Versus Available-for-Sale.**   Both trading and available-for-sale accounting methods are considered mark-to-market accounting for investments. Describe their similarities and differences. Which of the two methods do you think would make earnings inherently more volatile?

Q8.8   **Accounting for Long-term Investments.**   In 2006, CKX, Inc., a New York sports entertainment company, paid $50 million for an 80 percent ownership interest in G.O.A.T. LLC. (G.O.A.T. stands for "Greatest of All

Time" and is a business that licenses the name and image of former boxing champion Muhammad Ali.) The remaining 20 percent of G.O.A.T. LLC is owned by the Ali Trust. At the time of acquisition, financial statements reveal that the gross revenue of G.O.A.T. averages $5 million annually, giving the LLC an estimated fair market value of $30 million. Discuss how CKX's investment in G.O.A.T. LLC should be accounted for. How should the Ali Trust account for its 20 percent ownership interest in G.O.A.T.?

Q8.9 **Mergers, Acquisitions, and Share Price.** In 2006, Danaher, Inc. announced its intent to acquire Sybron Dental Specialties, Inc., a manufacturer of dental products. Danaher indicated that it had agreed to pay $47 per share for all of Sybron's outstanding shares. The cash tender offer, which included the assumption of $200 million of Sybron debt, was valued at $2 billion. In response to the acquisition announcement, Danaher's shares increased by 1.3 percent. Discuss how the capital market responds to merger and acquisition announcements, and specifically, the message implied by the market's response to Danaher's announcement of its planned acquisition of Sybron. What was the equity value of Sybron implicit in the transaction?

Q8.10 **Acquisition Bidding and the Winner's Curse.** Aztar Corporation is an operator of casinos and hotels. The company's flagship properties are the Tropicana Hotel & Casino located in Las Vegas, Nevada, and in Atlantic City, New Jersey. In early 2006, Aztar's common shares were trading at $29 per share. On March 12, 2006, Pinnacle Entertainment Inc. made a tender offer to buy all of Aztar's outstanding common shares for $38 per share, a premium of 31 percent above Aztar's market price. Two weeks later, Ameristar Casinos, Inc. made a competing tender offer to buy Aztar's outstanding shares at a price of $43 per share. On April 15, 2006, Columbia Sussex Corporation made an unsolicited offer to buy Aztar at $47 per share, a premium of over 62 percent above Aztar's share price before the bidding competition began. Then, on April 28, 2006, Pinnacle raised its bid to $48 per share, followed immediately by a $50 per share bid by Columbia Sussex. Finally, on May 10, 2006, Pinnacle again raised its bid for Aztar to $51 per share, only to again be outbid by Columbia, which offered $53 per share. Some industry analysts described the bidding war for Aztar as an example of "The Winner's Curse," a situation in auction-like settings in which the winner is the entity that most overvalues the item being bid on, and thus, winning the final bid actually signals that the winner has lost as a consequence of overpaying for the item.

Discuss whether you think the Aztar bidding war is an example of The Winner's Curse. Does the significantly higher bid by Columbia Sussex of $53 per share indicate that the market for Aztar's common stock prior to the bidding war was inefficient? Why would Columbia Sussex be willing to pay such a significant premium ($24 per share) for Aztar's shares?

Q8.11 **Goodwill Impairment.** On November 9, 2011, Dean Foods a Dallas Texas-based food and beverage company, announced that it would write off $1.6 billion, net of tax, in goodwill associated with its Fresh Dairy Direct acquisition. Discuss how Dean Foods will account for the write-off and why the company decided to make this adjustment to its goodwill account. How do you think the capital market reacted to this news announcement, and why?

Q8.12 **Divesting Long-term Investments.** BAE Systems, Europe's largest defense company, announced that it was selling its 20 percent shareholding in Airbus, Europe's largest aircraft manufacturer, to EADS, the Franco-German aerospace company that already owned 80 percent of Airbus. The CEO of BAE Systems stated that Airbus had been an excellent investment but "we believe that now is the right time for us to divest our Airbus shareholding to allow us to concentrate on our core strategy." BAE's cost basis of its investment in Airbus was believed to be $4.3 billion, with a current market value of approximately $7.8 billion. Prior to 2001, at which time BAE and EADS purchased their shareholdings in Airbus, the passenger aircraft manufacturer had been structured as a "consortium" whose assets were held by national companies in the United Kingdom, France, Germany, and Spain. Discuss how Airbus might have been accounted for prior to 2001. Following the sale of Airbus to BAE and EADS in 2004, how would each firm's investment in Airbus have been accounted for? Estimate BAE's gain on the divestiture of its Airbus shareholding.

Q8.13 **De-Merger and Share Prices.** In early 2006, Henry Silverman, chairman and CEO of Cendant Corporation, announced that the company's board of directors had approved the de-merger of Cendant into four operating companies—Avis Budget (a vehicle rental company composed of Avis, Budget, and Budget Truck), Wyndham Worldwide (a lodging company composed of such hotels and resort chains as Wyndham Resorts, Ramada Inn, Howard Johnson, and others), Realogy (a real estate franchise company composed of Century 21, Coldwell Banker, and Sotheby's, among others), and Travel Distribution (a travel company composed of Orbitz.com, CheapTickets.com, and RatesToGo.com, among others). Under the split-up plan, Wyndham Worldwide and Realogy would be de-merged by a public offering of shares, whereas Avis Budget and Travel Distribution would be spun off to existing Cendant shareholders.

The reason for the de-merger, according to Silverman, was that Cendant's earnings were not being properly reflected in its share price. "We were among the 100 most profitable companies in America in 2004, yet we were somewhere in the 300s in terms of market value." Discuss the reasons why Cendant's share price in 2004 may not have reflected its earnings in 2004. If the de-merger is successful, what should happen to the share price of the four operating companies? Why?

Q8.14 **Poison-Pill Defense.** Following a series of hostile acquisitions in the global steel industry, Nippon Steel Corporation announced the implementation of a "poison-pill" plan designed to fend off any hostile takeover bids for the Japanese steel company. Under the plan, if a hostile buyer attempts to acquire a stake of 15 percent or more in the company, the steelmaker's shareholders would be allowed to double the number of shares they own for a nominal amount. Executives of Nippon Steel indicated that adoption of the plan was aimed at fending off potential acquirers who might damage the firm's corporate value. Market analysts expressed concern that the poison-pill defense would adversely affect the firm's share price. Discuss how Nippon's poison-pill defense could prevent an unwanted takeover bid and why the plan might actually hurt the company's share price.

Q8.15 **Goodwill Impairment and Debt Covenants.** The October 12, 2006, edition of *The Wall Street Journal* carried an article entitled "Expedia Might Trip Debt Covenant." The article revealed that the share price of Expedia Inc., an online travel company, had recently declined by 33 percent following the company's spin-off from its parent company IAC/InterActive Corporation. IAC/InterActive had acquired Expedia several years earlier in an acquisition that involved $5.9 billion in goodwill.

When Expedia was spun off by its parent, the $5.9 billion in goodwill associated with the acquisition was downloaded from the consolidated balance sheet to Expedia's balance sheet. Further, a provision in Expedia's $1 billion borrowing arrangement required that the company maintain a shareholders' equity of $5.4 billion. With the decline in its share price to $16 per share, the company's market capitalization had dropped to just $5.2 billion. The company's book value at the time was just $5.8 billion. Discuss what action the company should take with respect to its $5.9 billion in acquisition goodwill. What are the consequences of those actions?

Q8.16 **(Ethics Perspective) Whistle-Blowing.** Whistle-blowers often question themselves as to whether they are doing the "right thing." Terms such as "snitch" and "tattletale" are often associated with an individual who exposes wrongdoing. Do you believe that it is ethical to report questionable activity as an anonymous whistle-blower, especially if you do not completely understand the events you are reporting?

Assignments with the ⓐⓑⓒ logo in the margin are available in BusinessCourse.
See the Preface of the book for details.
CHECK FIGURE indicates that check figures are available on the book's Website.

EXERCISES

E8.17 **Accounting for Short-term Investments.** The Claremont Corporation invests its excess cash in low-risk, TA 2, 3 dividend-paying equity securities until such funds are needed to support operations. At the beginning of the year, the company's portfolio consisted of the following securities:

Company	Cost Basis
Bristol-Myers Squibb (BMS)	$ 75,000
Johnson & Johnson (JNJ)	55,000
Pfizer, Inc. (PFE)	110,000
Total	$240,000

At year-end, the fair values of the three securities were as follows: BMS $82,000; JNJ $53,000; and PFE $100,000. Calculate the income statement effect of the company's short-term investments assuming: (a) all securities are classified as trading; (b) all securities are classified as available-for-sale; and (c) BMS and JNJ are classified as trading, while PFE is classified as available-for-sale. Does the classification of a security as trading versus available-for-sale affect a company's reported earnings? Will it affect the value of a company's share price? Will it affect the amount of income taxes that a company pays to the Internal Revenue Service?

E8.18 **Other Comprehensive Income.** The following financial data is taken from the annual report of The Emma TA 2, 3, 4 Company:

(in thousands)	2013	2014	2015
Net income	$20,493	$21,450	$21,846
Other comprehensive income (loss)			
Net unrealized gain (loss) on available-for-sale securities	(138)	219	33
Cumulative foreign currency translation adjustment	630	(549)	(96)
Total other comprehensive income	$20,985	$21,120	$21,783

Explain (a) what "other comprehensive income" is and how it differs from net income, (b) what happened to the value of The Emma Company's available-for-sale securities each year, and (c) what caused the cumulative foreign currency translation adjustment to increase or decrease each year. Explain why The Emma Company will pay income taxes on its net income but not its other comprehensive income.

TA 2, 3
CHECK
FIGURE

E8.19 **Available-for-Sale Securities.** The 2015 annual report of Bristol-Myers Squibb (BMS) reveals that the company maintains a large investment in available-for-sale securities:

(in millions)	2015	2014
Available-for-sale securities:		
Fair value	$6,502	$6,203
Amortized cost.	$6,524	$6,156

Did the company's available-for-sale securities experience a gain or loss in value in 2015 and/or 2014, and if so, in what amount? How did the company account for these gains and/or losses? Were these gains (losses) taxable (tax deductible) in 2015 and/or 2014?

TA 2, 3

E8.20 **Available-for-Sale Securities.** The 2015 annual report of Pfizer, Inc. (PFE) reveals that the company maintains a significant investment in short-term investments:

(in millions)	2015	2014
Short-term investments	$19,649	$32,779

During 2015, the company sold short-term investments (net of sales of short-term investments) totaling $5,768 million. Did the company's portfolio of short-term investments experience a gain or a loss during 2015, and in what amount? Assuming all of Pfizer's short-term investments are classified as available-for-sale securities, how did the company account for the gain or loss in 2015? Was the gain (loss) taxable (tax deductible) in 2015?

TA 2, 3

E8.21 **Long-term Equity Investments.** The 2015 annual report of Bristol-Myers Squibb (BMS) discloses the following amounts included within "other (income)/expense" on its consolidated statement of earnings:

(in millions)	2015	2014	2013
Equity in net income of affiliates.	$83	$107	$166

Assume that on the company's statement of cash flow, the following amounts appear as a subtraction from net earnings under the cash flow from operating activities:

(in millions)	2015	2014	2013
Undistributed income of affiliates.	$66	$7	$50

Calculate the amount of cash dividends received by BMS from its affiliates in 2015, 2014, and 2013. Assume that BMS neither sold nor purchased any equity interest in its affiliates in 2015, 2014, and 2013. What happened to the balance sheet value of the "investment in equity affiliates" account in 2015, 2014, and 2013?

TA 2, 3
CHECK
FIGURE

E8.22 **Long-term Equity Investments.** The annual report of The Arcadia Company discloses the following amounts on its consolidated statement of income:

	2013	2014	2015
Equity in earnings of unconsolidated affiliates.	$350	$415	$520

Further, on Arcadia's consolidated balance sheet, it reports the following amounts for its investment in its unconsolidated affiliates:

	2013	2014	2015
Investment in unconsolidated affiliates	$10,500	$10,715	$10,950

Calculate the amount of cash dividends received by The Arcadia Company from its unconsolidated affiliates in 2014 and 2015. Calculate the adjustment to net income that appears on Arcadia's statement of cash flow in 2014 and 2015 for "undistributed earnings of unconsolidated affiliates."

E8.23 **Equity Method.** The balance sheet of The Miller Corporation disclosed a long-term investment in the common shares of The Mann Corporation valued at $350,000 as of December 31, 2015. The investment had been purchased by The Miller Corporation in January, 2012. Further, the following financial information from The Mann Corporation is available: TA 2, 4

Year	Net Income (Loss)	Dividends Paid
2012	$ (30,000)	$ 0
2013	120,000	50,000
2014	150,000	60,000
2015	200,000	80,000

Determine how much The Miller Corporation paid for its investment in Mann common shares in January 2012 assuming that the investment represents a 25 percent ownership interest.

E8.24 **Equity Method.** On January 1, 2014, The Miller Corporation purchased 300,000 shares of The Mayfair Corporation for $5.7 million. The investment represented 25 percent of The Mayfair Corporation's outstanding common shares. During 2014, Mayfair reported net earnings of $2.25 million and paid a cash dividend of $0.15 per share. During 2015, Mayfair reported a net loss of $180,000 and again paid a dividend of $0.15 per share. Calculate the book value of Miller's investment in Mayfair as of December 31, 2014, and December 31, 2015.   TA 2, 4 CHECK FIGURE

E8.25 **Equity Method.** On January 2, 2015, Winstead & Company purchased 1,000,000 shares of the Secrest Company for $32 million. The investment represented 40 percent of the outstanding common shares of The Secrest Company. During 2015, Secrest reported net earnings of $1.05 per share and paid a cash dividend of $0.35 per share. During 2016, Secrest reported net earnings of $1.50 per share and paid a cash dividend of $0.40 per share. Calculate the book value of Winstead's investment in Secrest as of December 31, 2015, and December 31, 2016.   TA 2, 4

E8.26 **Accounting for Joint Ventures.** Starbucks Corporation and PepsiCo formed a joint venture to produce and distribute Starbucks' bottled Frappuccino coffee drink throughout North America. Assume that the 50/50 joint venture had a book value on the consolidated balance sheet of Starbucks Corporation of $90 million and $70 million at year-end 2012 and 2011, respectively. Further, assume that on Starbucks' 2012 statement of cash flow, the company disclosed an adjustment to net income for the PepsiCo joint venture as follows: TA 5

	2012
Equity in income of joint venture	$(22,000,000)

Calculate the joint venture's total earnings and total cash dividends for 2012.

PROBLEMS

P8.27 **Accounting for Marketable Equity Securities.** Tim Propp, CFO of Thunderbird, Inc., invested some of the firm's excess cash in the common shares of what he thought were three undervalued securities. At year-end, he reviewed how the portfolio of securities had done.   TA 2, 4

Security Name	Cost Basis	Fair Value at Year-End	Classification
Microsoft Corporation	$100,000	$122,000	Trading security
Pfizer, Inc.	75,000	73,000	Trading security
Boeing, Inc.	50,000	48,000	Available-for-sale security
	$225,000	$243,000	

Required

1. Calculate the value that would be assigned to the portfolio of securities on Thunderbird's balance sheet at year-end.

2. Calculate the income statement effect of the portfolio of securities at year-end.
3. Calculate the income statement effect of the portfolio of securities at year-end assuming all securities are classified as available-for-sale.
4. Are the company's reported earnings impacted by whether the portfolio of securities are classified as trading versus available-for-sale? Will the company's share price be impacted by the particular classification adopted? Will the company's income taxes be impacted?

TA 2, 4   P8.28

Accounting for Marketable Equity Securities.   Among the various responsibilities of the Chief Financial Officer (CFO) of the Amphlett Corporation was the management and oversight of the firm's cash reserves. During the year, the CFO had invested some of the firm's excess cash in what she thought were three undervalued stocks. All of the securities were classified as available-for-sale. At year-end, she reviewed how the portfolio of investments had done.

Investment	Cost Basis	Fair Value at Year-End
Bristol-Myers Squibb, Inc.	$ 50,000	$ 42,000
Titanium Metals, Corp.	50,000	55,000
Zila, Inc.	50,000	80,000
	$150,000	$177,000

Required
1. Calculate the value that would be assigned to the portfolio of marketable equity securities on the balance sheet of the Amphlett Corporation at year-end under each of the following approaches:
   a. Cost
   b. Lower-of-cost-or-market
   c. Fair value
2. How will the disclosure on the year-end balance sheet change if the entire portfolio is classified as "trading securities" versus "available-for-sale securities"?

TA 2, 4   P8.29
CHECK
FIGURE

Equity Method.   At midyear, National Steel Fabricators, Inc. purchased a 35 percent ownership interest in Keystone Consolidated, Inc. for $40 million. At year-end, Keystone reported an operating loss of $6 million, of which only $2 million related to the second half of the year. Despite the operating loss, Keystone paid its regular quarterly dividend of $1 million in both the third and fourth quarters.

Required
1. Calculate the income statement effect for National Steel at year-end associated with its investment in Keystone.
2. Calculate the book value that National Steel should record on its balance sheet for its investment in Keystone at year-end.

TA 2, 3   P8.30

Consolidation Accounting.   ABC Inc. purchased all of the outstanding common shares of XYZ Inc. for $100 million cash. At the time of the acquisition, the fair value of XYZ was $80 million. Presented below are the condensed balance sheets for ABC and XYZ immediately prior to the acquisition:

(in millions)	ABC Inc.	XYZ Inc.
Assets	$150	$100
Liabilities	$ 30	$ 20
Shareholders' equity	120	80
Total	$150	$100

Required
Prepare ABC's (a) unconsolidated balance sheet immediately after making the equity investment in XYZ and (b) the consolidated balance sheet immediately following the acquisition.

TA 2, 3   P8.31
CHECK
FIGURE

Consolidation Accounting.   Barranco, Inc., acquired all of the outstanding shares of Bemiller, Inc., by means of a share exchange valued at $50 million. At the time of the acquisition, the fair market value of Bemiller was $40 million. Presented below are the condensed balance sheets for Barranco, Inc. and Bemiller, Inc. immediately prior to the acquisition:

Balance Sheet	Bemiller, Inc.	Barranco, Inc.
Assets..	$50 million	$70 million
Liabilities......................................	$10 million	$20 million
Shareholders' equity	40 million	50 million
Total	$50 million	$70 million

Required

1. Prepare the unconsolidated balance sheet for Barranco immediately after making the investment in Bemiller.
2. Prepare the Barranco-Bemiller consolidated balance sheet following the acquisition.

P8.32   **Consolidation Accounting.** Graham Inc. acquired all of the outstanding shares of Mahoney Inc. through an exchange of common shares. The aggregate fair value of the Graham shares distributed to the Mahoney shareholders was $400,000. Further, at the time of the exchange, the fair value of Mahoney's net assets was equal to their book value, except for Mahoney's property and equipment, which was appraised at $540,000. Presented below are the pre-acquisition balance sheets of the two companies: TA 2, 3

Pre-acquisition Balance Sheets	Graham Inc.	Mahoney Inc.
Cash...	$ 60,000	$ 10,000
Accounts receivable (net).................................	140,000	80,000
Inventory (FIFO)	220,000	120,000
Property and equipment (net).............................	800,000	500,000
Other assets...	40,000	20,000
	$1,260,000	$730,000
Accounts payable...	$ 100,000	$ 25,000
Other current liabilities	100,000	15,000
Bonds payable	240,000	350,000
Common stock (no par value)	500,000	250,000
Retained earnings	320,000	90,000
	$1,260,000	$730,000

Required

Prepare the consolidated balance sheet for the new company immediately following the transaction.

P8.33   **Consolidation Accounting.** After an intense period of negotiation, Global Enterprises Corporation agreed to purchase all of the outstanding common shares of The Carlton Corporation. The agreed-upon price was $294 million, payable in Global Enterprise shares. According to the agreement, Global Enterprises would issue one share of its common stock in exchange for each share of The Carlton Corporation. Following the exchange, The Carlton Corporation would become a wholly-owned subsidiary of Global Enterprises. At the time of the negotiations, the market price of Global Enterprises' shares was $24.50 per share. Presented below are the pre-acquisition balance sheets of Global Enterprises and The Carlton Corporation: TA 2, 3

Pre-acquisition Balance Sheets	Global Enterprises Corporation	The Carlton Corporation
Assets		
Cash	$ 80,000,000	$ 25,000,000
Short-term investments	50,000,000	35,000,000
Accounts receivable (net)	75,000,000	50,000,000
Inventory (LIFO)	190,000,000	95,000,000
Property & equipment (net)	380,000,000	230,000,000
Other assets	45,000,000	15,000,000
Total assets	$820,000,000	$450,000,000
Liabilities & Shareholders' Equity		
Accounts payable	$ 95,000,000	$ 75,000,000
Other current liabilities	40,000,000	30,000,000
Bonds payable	110,000,000	—
Other long-term debt	75,000,000	125,000,000
Common stock ($10 par)	120,000,000	—
Common stock ($5 par)	—	60,000,000
Capital in excess of par value	70,000,000	20,000,000
Retained earnings	310,000,000	140,000,000
Total liabilities & shareholders' equity	$820,000,000	$450,000,000

As part of Global Enterprises' due diligence, the company determined that while the liabilities of The Carlton Corporation were fairly valued, some of the company's assets were not fairly valued. The fair value of Carlton's assets were as follows:

Asset	Fair Market Value	Under/(Over) Statement
Cash	$ 25,000,000	$ 0
Short-term investments	45,000,000	10,000,000
Accounts receivable (net)	35,000,000	(15,000,000)
Inventory (LIFO)	130,000,000	35,000,000
Property & equipment (net)	280,000,000	50,000,000
Other assets	0	(15,000,000)
Total	$515,000,000	$65,000,000

Required

Prepare the consolidated balance sheet immediately following the acquisition using consolidation accounting.

TA 2, 4, 6 **P8.34**   **Equity Investments: International.** Aussie Steaks Inc. operates a chain of steak restaurants in the United States. On January 1, 2015, the company had $500 million in assets.

MBC

On January 1, 2015, the company acquired 25 percent of the shares of Sun Devil Burgers, a hamburger chain of 200 outlets, for $10 million in cash. At the time of the acquisition, Sun Devil had total assets of $100 million and total liabilities of $60 million. In 2015, Sun Devil reported net income of $12 million and paid cash dividends of $4 million.

On March 6, 2016, Aussie Steaks established Zaijian Burgers, a wholly-owned self-sustaining Chinese subsidiary, with cash of RMB24 million. The Chinese RMB (renmimbi) is the functional currency for Zaijian Burgers. The exchange rate at the time the subsidiary was established was RMB8 per $1. Immediately after the subsidiary was established the exchange rate changed to RMB12 per $1. Aussie Steaks and its affiliates have a December 31 year-end.

Required

1. What amount will Aussie Steaks Inc. report on its January 1, 2015, balance sheet with regard to its investment in Sun Devil Burgers following the acquisition?
2. What amount will Aussie Steaks Inc. report on its December 31, 2015, balance sheet with regard to its investment in Sun Devil Burgers?

3. What is the amount of total assets that Zaijian Burgers will show on its balance sheet in U.S. dollars on March 6, 2016?

4. What is the amount of the cumulative foreign currency translation adjustment that Aussie Steaks will report on its consolidated balance sheet on March 6, 2016, following the exchange rate change?

P8.35 **Equity Investments: International.**   On January 1, 2015, Tradiciones, Inc., established Tradiciones de Mexico, a wholly-owned, self-sustaining Mexican subsidiary with assets valued at 48 million pesos. The peso (P) is the functional currency for Tradiciones de Mexico. The exchange rate at the time that the subsidiary was established was Ps8 per $1. On January 2, 2015, after the subsidiary was established, the exchange rate changed to Ps6 per $1.

TA 2, 4, 6
CHECK
FIGURE

Required

1. What is the amount of total assets that Tradiciones de Mexico will show on its balance sheet in U.S. dollars on January 1, 2015 (before the exchange rate change)?

2. What is the amount of the cumulative foreign currency translation adjustment that Tradiciones, Inc. will report on its balance sheet on January 2, 2015, after the exchange rate change?

3. At December 31, 2015, Tradiciones de Mexico reported the information below. Did the Mexican peso appreciate, remain unchanged, or depreciate against the U.S. dollar?

In millions of dollars	Common Stock	Accumulated Other Comprehensive Income	Retained Earnings	Total
Net income....................................			100	100
Accumulated other comprehensive income—foreign currency translation adjustment................		(5)		(5)

P8.36 **Consolidated Versus Unconsolidated Reporting.**   Global Enterprises Corporation (GE) is a manufacturing company whose principal products are microwave ovens, refrigerators, and conventional ovens. The company had a long history of selling high-quality, high-priced home appliances; however, recent reductions in the price of competitor products forced GE to consider ways to provide assistance to its customers to help them buy its products. As a consequence, GE started its own finance subsidiary, the GE Acceptance Corporation (GEAC), to assist customers in financing their purchases.

TA 1, 2, 5

GE Corporation is also associated with three other companies. It holds an 80 percent interest in Scrub-All, a company that makes automatic dishwashers. GE purchased the interest in Scrub-All because the company's product line complemented its own items and the products were a quality that GE would have had difficulty duplicating. Further, to ensure a steady supply of chrome parts for its appliances, GE obtained a 10 percent interest in the common stock of Acme Chrome Company. Well over 50 percent of Acme's sales were attributed to purchases by GE and Scrub-All. Further, to compete in the low-end market for various appliances, GE formed a joint venture (Spotless Appliance) with Whirlwind Products Co. to produce low-cost appliances. The following is a summary of GE's subsidiaries, affiliates, and equity investments:

> **GE Acceptance Corporation.** GEAC is a wholly-owned subsidiary that purchases consumer notes from its parent, GE Corporation. GEAC borrows funds from several banking institutions on a medium- and long-term basis and uses the margins between the short-term interest rates on the consumer notes and the rates on its medium- and long-term liabilities to cover its overhead costs. The parent company (GE) guarantees all of the borrowings of GEAC.
>
> **Scrub-All Company.** With an ownership interest of 80 percent of the common stock of Scrub-All, GE controls the strategic policies of Scrub-All Company through an interlocking board of directors. Scrub-All, like GE, sells its consumer notes to GEAC.
>
> **Acme Chrome Company.** To guarantee a steady supply of chrome parts, GE purchased a 10 percent interest in Acme Chrome Company. Over the years, a strong relationship had developed between GE and Acme. For example, Acme schedules the production run of its other customers around the production needs of GE and Scrub-All.
>
> **Spotless Appliance Company.** Both GE Corporation and Whirlwind Products Company (an otherwise unrelated company) contributed half of the funds necessary to start Spotless Appliance Company. Spotless Appliance Company makes low-end appliance models that are sold under the Spotless trade name or are labeled with various department store names.

GE CORPORATION
Consolidated Statement of Financial Position
December 31

Assets

Current assets	$ 37,500,000
Notes receivable	58,000,000
Investment in Spotless Appliance at equity (50%)	1,750,000
Investment in Acme Chrome Company (10%) at market	5,600,000
Other assets	101,500,000
Goodwill	3,200,000
Total assets	$207,550,000

Liabilities and Shareholders' Equity

Current liabilities	$ 31,500,000
Long-term liabilities	102,100,000
Common stock	15,000,000
Retained earnings	51,450,000
Noncontrolling interest	7,500,000
Total liabilities and shareholders' equity	$207,550,000

SCRUB-ALL COMPANY
Statement of Financial Position
December 31

Assets

Current assets	$16,400,000
Other assets	52,600,000
Total assets	$69,000,000

Liabilities and Shareholders' Equity

Current liabilities	$13,350,000
Long-term liabilities	18,150,000
Common stock	12,000,000
Retained earnings	25,500,000
Total liabilities and shareholders' equity	$69,000,000

ACME CHROME COMPANY
Statement of Financial Position
December 31

Assets

Current assets	$14,750,000
Other assets	36,250,000
Total assets	$51,000,000

Liabilities and Shareholders' Equity

Current liabilities	$ 5,000,000
Long-term liabilities	15,000,000
Common stock	18,750,000
Retained earnings	12,250,000
Total liabilities and shareholders' equity	$51,000,000

GE ACCEPTANCE CORPORATION Statement of Financial Position December 31	
Assets	
Current assets	$ 8,000,000
Notes receivable	58,000,000
Other assets	6,500,000
Total assets	$72,500,000
Liabilities and Shareholders' Equity	
Current liabilities	$ 5,000,000*
Long-term debt	47,100,000
Common stock ($1 par)	10,000,000
Retained earnings	10,400,000
Total liabilities and shareholders' equity	$72,500,000

*$3,000,000 of the current liabilities is a promissory note to GE Corporation. GE Corporation accounts for this as a long-term receivable in other assets.

SPOTLESS APPLIANCE COMPANY Statement of Financial Position December 31	
Assets	
Current assets	$ 8,500,000
Other assets	16,000,000
Total assets	$24,500,000
Liabilities and Shareholders' Equity	
Current liabilities	$ 3,000,000
Long-term debt	18,000,000
Common stock ($1 par)	6,000,000
Retained earnings	(2,500,000)
Total liabilities and shareholders' equity	$24,500,000

Required

1. Why are the investments in Acme Chrome and Spotless Appliance Companies shown on the GE Corporation consolidated balance sheet while the investments in Scrub-All and GEAC are omitted?
2. What is meant by the carrying value "at equity" for the investment in Spotless Appliance Company on GE's consolidated balance sheet?
3. Why is the investment in Acme Chrome Company shown "at market"?
4. Explain the Goodwill account on GE's consolidated balance sheet. To what company is this account related?
5. What is meant by "noncontrolling interest" on GE's consolidated balance sheet? To which company is this account related? Is this a liability or a shareholders' equity account?
6. What are GE Corporation's current ratio, total debt to equity ratio, and total debt to total asset ratio? Are these ratios correct?

CORPORATE ANALYSIS

CA8.37 The Procter & Gamble Company. The 2015 annual report of The Procter & Gamble Company (P&G)   TA 2, 4
is available at www.pginvestor.com. After reviewing P&G's annual report, respond to the following questions:

P&G's consolidated balance sheet reveals that the company has $47.316 ($53.704) billion in goodwill as of June 30, 2015 (2014). What percentage of total assets does goodwill represent in 2015 and 2014? Does P&G amortize its goodwill? If so, over what period? If not, why not? Did P&G recognize an impairment in its goodwill in either 2015 or 2014?

CA8.38 General Electric Company. The consolidated financial statements of General Electric Company (GE)   TA 2
combine the industrial manufacturing and services businesses of GE with the financial services businesses of

General Electric Capital Corporation (GECC). GE is the parent company of GECC. Because of the diverse nature of the businesses reflected in the operations of GE and GECC, GE presents its financial statements in two formats—a fully consolidated format (including the results of GE, GECC, and all other majority-owned entities) and a partially consolidated format (excluding the results of GECC). In GE's partially-consolidated financial statements, the investment in GECC is accounted for using the equity method.

a. Presented below are the partially consolidated income statements and balance sheets for GE and GECC for 2015. Do you think the 2015 fully consolidated statements for GE would include all of the amounts provided in each account presented?

b. Go to www.ge.com and review the company's 2015 consolidated statements. What significant differences do you notice about GE's financial statements on a partially consolidated basis versus a fully consolidated basis?

Statement of Earnings For the years ended December 31		
($ millions)	GE 2015	GECC 2015
Revenues		
Sales of goods	$ 74,565	$ 79
Sales of services	31,641	0
Other income	2,165	0
GECC earnings from continuing operations	(7,672)	0
GECC revenues from services	0	10,722
Total revenues.	100,700	10,801
Costs and Expenses		
Costs of goods sold.	59,970	69
Cost of services sold	20,858	2,273
Selling, general and administrative expenses	14,914	3,512
Interest and other financial charges.	1,706	2,301
Investment contracts, insurance losses and insurance annuity benefits.	0	2,737
Other costs and expenses	0	2,647
Total costs and expenses.	97,447	13,539
Earnings from continuing operations before income taxes	3,252	(2,739)
Benefit (provision) for income taxes.	(1,506)	(4,979)
Earnings from continuing operations before accounting changes.	1,746	(7,718)
Earning (loss) from discontinued operations, net of taxes.	(7,807)	(7,485)
Net earnings (loss)	$ (6,061)	$(15,202)

Statement of Financial Position At December 31		
($ millions)	GE 2015	GECC 2015
Assets		
Cash and equivalents	$ 10,372	$ 60,111
Investment securities	151	31,827
Current receivables	14,707	0
Inventories	22,449	66
Financing receivables—net	0	25,003
Other GECC receivables	0	15,865
Property, plant and equipment—net	20,145	34,781
Receivables from GECC	85,114	0
Investment in GECC	46,227	0
Goodwill	63,157	2,370
Other intangible assets—net	16,312	435
Contract assets	21,156	0
All other assets	13,281	25,287
Deferred income taxes	7,666	(4,561)
Assets of businesses held for sale	2,818	0
Assets of discontinued operations	9	120,942
Total assets	$323,562	$312,125
Liabilities and Shareholders' Equity		
Short-term borrowings	$ 19,799	$ 48,650
Accounts payable, principally trade accounts	19,250	1,745
Progress collections and price adjustment accrued	15,776	0
Dividends payable	2,167	0
Other GE current liabilities	23,595	0
Non-recourse borrowings of consolidated securitization entities	0	3,083
Long-term borrowings	83,770	129,062
Investment contracts, insurance liabilities and insurance annuity benefits	0	26,155
Non-current compensation and benefits	39,472	1,006
All other liabilities	15,573	9,351
Liabilities of businesses held for sale	1,409	0
Liabilities of discontinued operations	128	46,359
Total liabilities	220,938	265,411
Redeemable noncontrolling interests	2,972	0
Preferred stock (5,944,250 shares outstanding at year-end 2015)	6	6
GECC preferred shares (no shares outstanding at year-end 2015)	0	0
Common stock (9,379,288,000 shares outstanding at year-end 2015)	702	0
Accumulated other comprehensive income (loss)—net attributable to GE:		
Investment securities	460	456
Currency translation adjustments	(5,499)	(898)
Cash flow hedges	(80)	(112)
Benefit plans	(11,410)	(540)
Other capital	37,613	12,326
Retained earnings	140,020	34,988
Less common stock held in treasury	(63,539)	0
Total GE shareholders' equity	98,274	46,227
Noncontrolling interests	1,378	486
Total equity	99,651	46,713
Total liabilities and shareholders' equity	$323,562	$312,125

TA 2, 4, 5   **CA8.39**   **Internet-based Analysis.**   Consider a publicly held company whose products you are familiar with. Some examples might include:

Company	Product	Corporate Website
• Johnson & Johnson..............	• Band-Aids	• www.jnj.com
• Microsoft Corporation...........	• Windows software	• www.microsoft.com
• Apple, Inc......................	• Cellular phones	• www.apple.com
• Intel Corporation	• Pentium processors	• www.intel.com
• Kimberly-Clark Corporation......	• Kleenex	• www.kimberly-clark.com

Access the company's public website and search for its most recent annual report. (Note: Some companies provide access to their financial data through an "investor relations" link, while others provide a direct link to their "annual reports.") After locating your company's most recent annual report, open the file and review its contents. After reviewing the annual report for your selected company, prepare answers to the following questions:

    a.   Does the company have any short-term investments or marketable securities? If so, are they trading securities or available-for-sale securities? Over the past year, did the company experience any unrealized gains or losses on its marketable securities? If so, in what amount?

    b.   Does the company have any unconsolidated affiliates or joint ventures? If so, how are they accounted for? Did the unconsolidated affiliates or joint ventures produce a profit or loss last year?

    c.   Does the company have any consolidated subsidiaries? If so, how many? Does the company own 100 percent of all of its consolidated subsidiaries? How were you able to determine this?

    d.   Does the company have any goodwill from prior acquisitions? How does the company account for its goodwill? Has the goodwill been impaired in either of the last two years? If so, what amount was the impairment?

TA 2, 4   **CA8.40**   **IFRS Financial Statements.**   The 2014 financial statements of **LVMH Moet Hennessey-Louis Vuitton S.A.** are presented in Appendix C of this book. LVMH is a Paris-based holding company and one of the world's largest and best-known luxury goods companies. As a member-nation of the European Union, French companies are required to prepare their consolidated (group) financial statements using International Financial Reporting Standards (IFRS). In LVMH's Notes to the Consolidated Financial Statements (not presented in Appendix C), the company discloses its method of consolidation:

> The subsidiaries in which the Group holds a direct or indirect *de facto* or *de jure* controlling interest are fully consolidated. Jointly controlled companies are accounted for using the equity method. The assets, liabilities, income, and expenses of the Wines and Spirits distribution subsidiaries held jointly with the Diageo group are consolidated only in proportion to the LVMH group's share of operations. Companies where the Group has significant influence but no controlling interest are accounted for using the equity method.

How does LVMH's consolidation policy differ from U.S. GAAP?

SOLUTIONS TO REVIEW PROBLEMS

Solution 8.1

    a. $10,000 gain

    b.   no effect

    c. $5,000 gain

Solution 8.2

a. Goodwill

Purchase price		$22,000,000
Less: Fair market value		
Book value	$19,000,000	
Add: Inventory understatement	1,000,000	
Less: Intangible asset impairment	(4,000,000)	
		(16,000,000)
Goodwill		$ 6,000,000

b. Unconsolidated balance sheet

THE ARCADIA COMPANY
Unconsolidated Balance Sheet

Assets		Liabilities & Shareholders' Equity	
Cash	$ 4,000,000*	Accounts payable	$ 7,000,000
Inventory	12,000,000	Bonds payable	25,000,000
Investment in Claremont Co. . . .	22,000,000	Total	32,000,000
Fixed assets, net	50,000,000	Shareholders' equity	
Intangible assets	30,000,000	Capital stock	56,000,000
		Retained earnings	30,000,000
Total	$118,000,000	Total liabilities & equity	$118,000,000

* Cash: $26,000,000 − $22,000,000 = $4,000,000

c. Consolidated balance sheet

THE ARCADIA COMPANY
Consolidated Balance Sheet

Assets		Liabilities & Shareholders' Equity	
Cash	$ 6,000,000	Accounts payable	$ 11,000,000
Inventory	20,000,000	Bonds payable	44,000,000
Investment in Claremont Co. . . .	0	Total	55,000,000
Fixed assets, net	65,000,000	Shareholders' equity	
Intangible assets	44,000,000	Capital stock	56,000,000
Goodwill	6,000,000	Retained earnings	30,000,000
		Total	86,000,000
Total	$141,000,000	Total liabilities & equity	$141,000,000

Solution 8.3

1. 50,000,000/0.80 = $62,500,000
2. 50,000,000/0.82 = $60,975,610
   $62,500,000 − $60,975,610 = $1,524,390 loss

When you complete this chapter you should be able to:

1. Describe the characteristics of bonds and notes and explain how credit ratings are determined. (page 340)

2. Explain how bonds and notes are valued and reported in financial statements. (page 342)

3. Describe how companies account for debt when it is retired before its maturity. (page 346)

4. Explain the difference between a capital lease and an operating lease and how each is reported in the financial statements. (page 350)

5. Calculate the weighted-average cost of debt. (page 356)

6. Discuss how and why companies manage the amount of debt reported on their balance sheets. (page 357)

7. Determine whether a company's balance sheet adequately portrays the extent of a firm's use of leverage. (page 358)

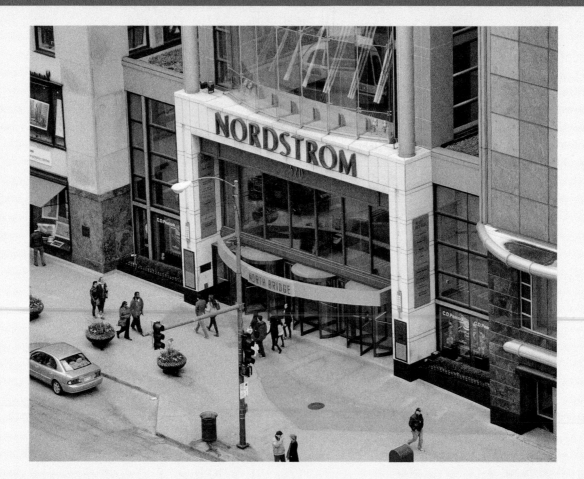

Debt Financing: Bonds, Notes, and Leases

John W. Nordstrom used his stake from the Alaska gold rush to open a small shoe store in Seattle, Washington, in 1901. This small store has since grown into an upscale U.S. apparel and shoe retail chain with 116 Nordstrom department stores and 167 outlet stores (Nordstrom Rack) across 38 states. It also serves customers online in 96 countries through Nordstrom.com The company is perhaps best known for its legendary reputation for top-rate customer service. In addition to its reputation for pleasing the customer, the company has also garnered attention for its treatment of its employees. Nordstrom is a Hall of Fame member of *Fortune* magazine's "100 Best Companies to Work For."

NORDSTROM

An examination of Nordstrom's balance sheet reveals that the company's largest single asset is its investment in land, buildings and equipment, valued at nearly $3.3 billion, 36 percent of total assets, as of fiscal year-end January 2015. Nordstrom financed these assets, along with other major assets such as over $1.7 billion of inventory, with a combination of debt and equity. The company's balance sheet reports long-term debt totaling over $4.0 billion and shareholders' equity of over $2.4 billion, representing a total debt-to-equity ratio of approximately 1.64.

Does the Nordstrom balance sheet portray a complete picture of the company's use of financing? Many investment professionals would say "no," and that to better understand how Nordstrom finances its assets, financial statement users need to dig into the footnotes to the financial statements. In particular, it is important to understand Nordstrom's use of off-balance-sheet financing. Nordstrom entered into various operating leases for the land and buildings for many of its stores. Generally accepted accounting principles allow Nordstrom to omit this form of financing, along with the corresponding leased assets, from its corporate balance sheet. The company's footnotes reveal that it is committed to approximately $2.3 billion in future lease payments associated with these leases as of January 2015. Failing to include these leased assets and lease liabilities in an analysis of the company's financial statements, however, can cause serious distortion to such important financial indicators as the debt-to-equity ratio and return-on-assets.

In this chapter, we consider various debt financing strategies and products, including the use of lease financing, available to companies like Nordstrom. In addition, we discuss a methodology that can aid in the analysis of corporate financial statements that rely on off-balance-sheet debt financing.

EXECUTIVE OUTLINE

FINANCING OPERATIONS AND ASSETS WITH DEBT: BONDS AND NOTES

Takeaway 1
Describe the characteristics of bonds and notes and explain how credit ratings are determined.

Most companies finance at least a part of their operations with debt. One of the reasons for this is that debt financing is almost always a less expensive form of financing than equity. Since creditors assume less risk than equity investors, it is appropriate that the expected rate of return to be earned by creditors should be less than that expected by shareholders. Remember that shareholders are likely to lose all of their invested capital if a business fails, whereas creditors are likely to lose only part, if any, because they have first claim on any remaining assets of the company. Debt also carries the advantage that it is anti-dilutive to the shareholder. That is, if a firm raises needed funds through debt financing, the existing ownership percentage in the company is unchanged. If those funds are raised through a stock issue to new shareholders, then the percentage ownership in the company to shareholders will fall.

The specific source of debt financing available to a borrower will depend on the desired length of the borrowing period, the amount of the borrowing, and the riskiness of the borrower. Small firms as borrowers, for example, are considered to be riskier than larger, established firms. A sustained history of operating performance makes lenders more comfortable with a firm's ability to repay debt, and small firms tend to lack a history of operating experience. Further, small firms tend to borrow smaller amounts, and since investment bankers are unlikely to engage in public debt offerings of less than $100 million, small borrowings are typically sourced from a single, private lender. Thus, most small firms have access to only a limited set of lenders—local financial institutions, business development companies, the Small Business Administration, friends and family, and in some cases, private equity and venture capital firms.

Larger, established firms, on the other hand, have many borrowing options, including financial institutions, insurance companies, pension funds, as well as the public debt market. Which lending segment is likely to be accessed is a function of the desired length of the borrowing period, called the loan **duration**. Banks and similar financial institutions prefer to limit their risk exposure to loans involving durations of one day to five years, whereas the public debt market is typically the source for borrowings of 5 to 20 years. Finally, borrowings involving durations greater than 20 years tend to be sourced from insurance companies and pension funds, which have the capacity and desire to place funds with borrowers for longer, extended periods of time.

The public debt market is most commonly composed of two similar lending products—bonds and notes. **Bonds** are publicly issued financial instruments that promise to pay the bondholder periodic payments over the life of the investment, usually 10 to 20 years, and then make a lump-sum principal repayment at maturity. **Notes** are similar instruments but have shorter maturities, usually one to ten years, and are frequently privately placed with large institutional investors or financial institutions. As long-term liabilities of the company bonds and notes have the same basic structure; the company receives cash up front and then agrees to repay that cash with an interest return to the lender. Bonds and notes also often have the following notable common features:

■ No voting rights at the annual shareholders' meeting.

■ An **indenture agreement** that specifies covenants, often based on accounting ratios, which may restrict the borrower's ability to pay dividends, issue additional debt, undertake mergers and acquisitions, or sell assets.

■ A **trustee**, such as a bank or trust company, which administers the provisions of the indenture agreement and acts as an independent party to protect the interests of the lenders.

■ Priority in receiving interest and principal repayments over any payments to common and preferred shareholders, such as dividends or payments in liquidation.

A number of additional features may be included with bonds and notes. For instance, bonds and notes may be **secured**—that is, the lender has a priority claim on specific assets of the borrower in the event of default—or **unsecured** (having no claim on specific assets in the event of a default). Unsecured debt, also known as **debentures**, may be **subordinated**—that is, the claim of the unsecured debtholder has a lower priority, or is "junior" to, the claims of secured creditors. **Unsubordinated** or senior debt has a priority claim equivalent to that of suppliers who hold the accounts payable of a firm, and thus, typically hold a claim against specific operating assets (such as inventory) of a business.

Bonds and notes may also be **convertible** into the common shares of the borrower. Convertible bonds and notes carry a share conversion ratio indicating the number of common shares to be received in the event of conversion, and are convertible at the option of the debtholder (usually, however, only after some portion of the debt duration has expired). Some bonds and notes are **callable** at the option of the borrower. A callable bond or note is one that may be mandatorily redeemed or retired prior to maturity. Callable bonds or notes are also often convertible to provide debtholders with an option to either (i) accept cash if the bond or note is called, or (ii) convert the bond or note into the common shares of the borrower. Finally, some bonds are commodity-based in which the interest or principal repayment is indexed to the price of a commodity like gold, silver, or oil, often with an option to receive the commodity instead of cash at maturity. As you might expect, commodity-based bonds are used by companies that have reason to protect against (i.e., hedge) the risk of commodity movements (e.g., gold miners).

Evident from this discussion is that the potential features of bonds and notes are many. They exist though for the simple reason that lenders require some compensation for the risk they will bear relative to their expected return on a company loan. While these features may affect the appeal of the bond or note to the lender, and ultimately its value, the accounting for these debt instruments remains generally unaffected by these features. As we will see the liability on the borrowing company's books is valued at its present value, and interest expense is charged on that liability each period.

Credit Ratings and the Cost of Debt

The interest on debt that is earned by the lender and paid by the company, often labeled the **cost of debt**, is dependent on many factors. These include the inherent riskiness of the lending company, the current economic and political environments, the set of alternative investments available to the lender, and the many features that may attach to the bonds or notes, as described above. One important additional item that affects the cost of debt for publicly issued bonds and notes is the **credit-risk rating**. This rating is a "score" that indicates the likelihood that the borrower will make all interest and principal payments on a timely basis. (Nonpublic debt is often unrated.) Credit rating agencies such as *Moody's* and *Standard & Poor's* make a grading assessment of the probability of default of a bond or note using a letter rating system as follows:

Credit Risk	Moody's	Standard & Poor's
Investment Grade..............	Aaa	AAA
	Aa1, Aa2, Aa3	AA+, AA, AA−
	A1, A2, A3	A+, A, A−
	Baa1, Baa2, Baa3	BBB+, BBB, BBB−
Junk	Ba1, Ba2, Ba3	BB+, BB, BB−
	B1, B2, B3	B+, B, B−
	Caa1, Caa2, Caa3	CCC+, CCC, CCC−
	Ca	CC
	C	C
		D

Recall that there is a positive relationship between risk and reward—that is, the higher the credit risk associated with a debt contract (i.e., the risk of nonpayment or default), the higher the expected return demanded by the lender. Thus, bonds and notes rated AAA will carry a low interest rate because available evidence indicates that there is a very low probability of default by these investment-grade borrowers. Junk bonds and notes (especially ones rated D, which are in default), on the other hand, should be avoided by investors who have a low tolerance for risk. **Junk bonds**, also known as high-yield bonds, have a significantly higher probability of default, and thus, carry higher rates of interest. Nordstrom has provided information on its credit ratings and debt covenants in its January 2015 annual report. The company reports that the interest rate paid on the debt will change if the credit rating on the debt changes, and that it expects to be in compliance with its primary debt covenant during 2015.

Credit rating agencies are not without fault and have recently been subject to much criticism related to their roles in the 2007-2009 financial crisis. The U.S. **Securities and Exchange Commission (SEC)** cited 10 rating agencies with "apparent failures" during the crisis ranging from not following prescribed methodologies to not managing potential conflicts of interest. The biggest cost to the financial markets arose when many agencies assigned 'AAA' ratings to structured mortgage backed credit instruments (e.g., CDOs) that subsequently defaulted.

Credit rating agencies perform a valuable service to the debt investor community by serving as independent analysts of a company's credit worthiness. Their ratings have significant influence directly on the company's cash flows, as a lower credit rating or a downgrade virtually guarantees higher borrowing costs, and therefore lower cash flows. How do *Moody's* and *Standard & Poor's* arrive at a borrower's credit rating? The process is lengthy but the financial statement analysis skills discussed in Chapter 4 are an integral part of the process. Additionally, these organizations use proprietary bankruptcy prediction models, such as the Z-score and Zeta Analysis, to help identify a borrower's probability of default.[1]

Takeaway 2
Explain how bonds and notes are valued and reported in financial statements.

VALUING BONDS AND NOTES

Under U.S. GAAP, and the GAAP of most other developed countries, liabilities are generally valued at their **present value**. (See Appendix A at the end of this book for a review of present value concepts.) Exceptions to this rule include such current liabilities as accounts payable, accrued expenses and dividends payable, and such long-term liabilities as deferred income tax liabilities, which will be discussed in Chapter 10. Since the present value of an account payable due in 30, 60, or 90 days is extremely close to its maturity value, discounting of these short-term obligations is not required on practical grounds—that is, there is very little difference between the present value and the future value of a liability payable in just a few months. For long-term obligations, however, there can be a substantial difference between the present value of the debt—that is, how much cash would be required to pay the obligation off today—and its future settlement value. Consider, for instance, Jacob De Haven's $450,000 loan to the revolutionary army of General George Washington in 1777 (see Appendix A at the end of this book). At five percent interest, the settlement or **maturity value** of the De Haven loan would cost the U.S. government over $52 billion today!

To calculate the present value of a bond or note, it is necessary to know the following facts:

- The maturity value and maturity date of the debt
- The coupon, or stated, rate of interest on the debt
- The number of interest payment, or compounding, periods
- The yield, or effective, rate of interest on the debt

The **coupon rate** is the cash rate of interest on a debt instrument whereas the **yield rate** is the effective, or market, rate of interest. The coupon rate is used only to determine the periodic cash flow paid as interest to the bondholder or noteholder. The yield rate, on the other hand, is used to discount both the periodic cash interest payments and the lump-sum repayment of principal at maturity. These two rates are rarely the same, and it is important to understand their different uses to understand bond and note accounting. Think of the coupon rate as a pre-specified, agreed upon numerical value, between the lender and borrower, that defines how much cash will be paid each period over the life of the loan. This value technically can be anything, including zero. The coupon rate though is normally fixed over the maturity period of the bond or note. Once

[1] E. Altman, "Financial Ratios, Discriminant Analysis and the Prediction of Corporate Bankruptcy," *Journal of Finance*, September 1968; E. Altman, R. Haldeman, and P. Narayanan, "Zeta Analysis: A New Model to Identify Bankruptcy Risk of Corporations," *Journal of Banking and Finance, 1977.*

the cash payment structure has been defined by the coupon rate, then the value of those cash payments is determined by how much those receiving that cash desire to earn as their investment return. This rate of return is the yield, or effective rate. It can fluctuate markedly over time, as general economic conditions change, or as the financial condition of the company making the cash payments changes.

To illustrate the valuation of, and accounting for, bonds and notes, consider the following scenario:

> On January 1, 2016, Midwestern Airlines Inc. issued $100 million face value (maturity value) of mortgage notes with an annual coupon rate of eight percent and a maturity of ten years. The notes pay interest on June 30 and December 31 of each year. The company was considered a high risk investment at the time the notes were issued, and the market yield rate of interest demanded by investors on equivalent risk-rated notes was ten percent. Five years later, on December 31, 2020, the market yield rate of interest on equivalent-risk-rated notes increased to twelve percent.

Ignoring any transaction costs associated with selling the notes to the investing public, the Midwestern Airlines notes would generate proceeds of $87.538 million when issued to the investing public. But how was this value calculated? There are two cash flow streams associated with a bond or note—a lump-sum payment of principal at maturity and the periodic payment of interest. In the case of the Midwestern Airlines' notes, the payment of $100 million in principal will occur in ten years, or 20 compounding periods, on December 31, 2025. Further, with an annual coupon rate of eight percent and interest paid semiannually on June 30 and December 31, noteholders will receive an annuity of 20 payments of $4 million each [($100 million × 8 percent)/2].

> Transaction costs associated with selling bonds or notes to the investing public can be quite significant, averaging one to three percent of the value of the issued debt.

Thus, the present value of the Midwestern notes on the date of issuance is the sum of (1) the present value of $100 million to be paid in ten years, compounded semiannually, discounted at five percent per period (½ of ten percent) and (2) the present value of a 20-period annuity of $4 million per period, also discounted at five percent. Hence:

Present value of $100 million in 20 periods @ 5%: $100 million × 0.37689	=	$37.689 million
+ Present value of $4 million per period for 20 periods @ 5%: $4 million × 12.46221	=	49.849 million
Present value of notes		$87.538 million

The (rounded) present value factors of 0.37689 and 12.46221 were obtained from Tables 1 and 2 in the appendix at the end of this book (n = 20; i = 0.05).

Since the Midwestern Airlines notes carried a coupon rate of only four percent per period (one-half of eight percent) while investors were expecting five percent (one-half of ten percent), perhaps to compensate investors for the higher credit risk associated with the airline company, the notes would, of necessity, be sold at a discount from their face value of $100 million. If the selling price of the notes were not discounted (or lowered), investors would be unwilling to buy the notes and would instead seek out other higher yielding investments. The **discount** of $12.462 million ($100 million − $87.538 million) equals the amount of additional income demanded by investors to earn an effective rate of return of five percent per period over the twenty periods. If investors hold the notes until maturity, they will receive the $12.462 million as part of the lump-sum payment of the $100 million maturity value. Thus, over the life of the notes, investors will receive a total of $180 million—that is, $87.538 million as a return *of* investment and $92.462 million in interest income ($80.0 million + $12.462 million) as a return *on* their investment. From Midwestern's perspective the same holds true, although they will be charged $92.462 in *interest expense* over the life of the loan. The following time-line representation of these cash flows should make this more clear:

	1/1/16	6/30/16	12/31/16	6/30/17		12/31/24	6/30/25	12/31/25
Lump-sum payment....								(100)
Coupon payments		(4)	(4)	(4)		(4)	(4)	(4)

Total payments = (180)

Summary of cash payments over the life of the notes (in millions):

	Total Cash Paid by Midwestern	Cash Received at Issue
Lump-sum	$100.000	$87.538
Coupon payments	80.000	*plus*
	$180.000	
		Total Interest Expense on Note
		$92.462

On January 1, 2016, when the $100 million face value of notes are sold, Midwestern Airlines will show an increase in cash of $87.538 million, an increase in notes payable for the future value of the debt of $100 million, and an increase in the **note discount** account in the amount of $12.462 million (see the first column of Midwestern's transaction analysis in Exhibit 9.2; we will have more to say about the other transactions later in the chapter). The note discount account is a **contra-liability** account; it is subtracted from the notes payable account to arrive at the book value of the debt. It is rare to see the note discount account on the face of a corporate balance sheet because these amounts are typically netted out against the maturity value of the debt.

Since bond investors demanded an annual rate of return of ten percent but the Midwestern Airlines' notes were offering only eight percent, why didn't Midwestern just change the coupon rate to enable the notes to be sold at their full face value of $100 million? Before any debt or equity securities can be sold in the U.S. capital market, the issuing company must register the securities with the U.S. Securities and Exchange Commission. This requirement is intended to protect investors by ensuring that all publicly issued securities meet certain disclosure standards. As part of the registration statement for the debt securities, called a **prospectus**, the issuing company must contractually establish certain characteristics of the security—the amount to be borrowed, the length of the borrowing period, the purpose of the borrowing, the method of repayment, and the coupon rate, among other things.[2] Thus, once registered, an issuing company is unable to change its coupon rate, or any other security features reported in the filing, even if the goal is to meet or satisfy investor expectations. As the registration statement becomes the equivalent of a binding contract, the only characteristic of the debt instrument that can be altered to meet changing investor expectations is the security's actual selling price, which is not part of the firm's registration statement.

In the case of the Midwestern Airlines' notes, the selling price of the notes was lowered—that is, the notes were sold at a **discount** from their face value—to enable investors to earn the higher expected rate of return. If, on the other hand, investors had demanded only a six percent annual rate of return (or three percent per compounding period), the Midwestern Airlines' notes would have been sold at a price above their face value—that is, the notes would have been sold at a **premium**.[3] Finally, in that rare instance in which the rate of return demanded by investors is exactly equal to the coupon rate provided by a bond or note, the debt instruments will sell at a price exactly equal to their **par** or **face value**.

> As a general rule, companies issuing debt set the offered coupon rate slightly below the expected market yield rate so that the bonds or notes will sell at a small discount from their face value. This practice is undertaken principally for marketing purposes.

Interest Expense

On June 30, 2016, Midwestern Airlines will make its first cash payment of $4 million to its noteholders. But how much interest expense did Midwestern incur during this first six-month period? **Interest expense**, or the cost of debt financing, is a reflection of the lenders' charge for the use of their cash during a given period. Thus, very similar to how interest on a home mortgage or credit card would be computed, as the loan amount outstanding times the interest rate charged, the same holds true with GAAP financial statements. For Midwestern Airlines, interest expense for the first half of 2016 is calculated by simply multiplying the yield rate on the debt (five percent in this case) times the book value of the debt as of the beginning of the fiscal period; hence,

$$\text{Interest expense} = 5\% \times \$87.538 \text{ million} = \$4.3769 \text{ million}$$

Midwestern's interest expense of $4.3769 million exceeds its actual cash payment of $4.0 million by $0.3769 million. The excess of $0.3769 million represents the portion of the $12.462 million note

---

[2] A prospectus is also required for any new issue of stock equity securities.

[3] With a coupon rate of eight percent, a yield rate of six percent, and semiannual compounding, the Midwestern Airlines' notes would sell for $114.878 million, a premium of $14.878 million. Can you verify this calculation using Tables 1 and 2 in the appendix to this book?

discount that is allocated to the period January 1, 2016, to June 30, 2016. The $12.462 million to be paid to noteholders on December 31, 2025, represents the additional interest necessary to enable the investors to earn a ten percent rate of return on the Midwestern notes and must be allocated over the twenty interest payment periods. It would be inappropriate and distortive to the financial statements to consider the entire $12.462 million portion of the payment as all interest expense in the year paid (2025).

The process of allocating a bond discount (or bond premium) over the various interest compounding periods is called **amortization**. Amortizing a discount (or premium) using the present value tables from Appendix A of this book is called the **effective interest method**. Discounts and premiums may also be amortized in a straight-line fashion, but only if this method does not differ materially from the effective interest method. The straight-line method is not widely used among public companies; and, in any case, straight-line amortization of discounts (premiums) is not recognized as economically meaningful in modern financial theory.

Exhibit 9.1 presents an **amortization schedule** for the Midwestern Airlines' notes. It details the periodic cash interest payments of $4 million (Column 1), Midwestern's interest expense on a period-by-period basis (Column 2), the amortization of the note discount on a period-by-period basis (Column 3), the remaining balance of the note discount (Column 4), the face value of the notes (Column 5), and the book value of the notes (Column 6). Observe that Column 6 is equal to Column 5, the face value of the notes, minus Column 4, the unamortized note discount.

EXHIBIT 9.1	Note Amortization Schedule (in millions)*						
(Principal = $100; Coupon rate = 8%; Yield rate = 10%)							
Date	Period	Cash Payments (1)	Interest Expense[1] (2)	Amortized Note Discount[2] (3)	Note Discount Balance[3] (4)	Face Value of Notes (5)	Book Value of Notes (6)	Market Value of Notes
01/01/16	0				$12.45	$100.00	$ 87.55	
06/30/16	1	4.00	$4.38	0.38	12.08	100.00	87.93	
12/31/16	2	4.00	4.40	0.40	11.68	100.00	88.32	
06/30/17	3	4.00	4.42	0.42	11.26	100.00	88.74	
12/31/17	4	4.00	4.44	0.44	10.82	100.00	89.18	
06/30/18	5	4.00	4.46	0.46	10.38	100.00	89.62	
12/31/18	6	4.00	4.48	0.48	9.90	100.00	90.10	
06/30/19	7	4.00	4.51	0.51	9.39	100.00	90.61	
12/31/19	8	4.00	4.53	0.53	8.86	100.00	91.14	
06/30/20	9	4.00	4.56	0.56	8.31	100.00	91.69	
12/31/20	10	4.00	4.58	0.58	7.72	100.00	92.28	$ 85.28
06/30/21	11	4.00	4.61	0.61	7.11	100.00	92.89	
12/31/21	12	4.00	4.64	0.64	6.46	100.00	93.54	
06/30/22	13	4.00	4.68	0.68	5.79	100.00	94.21	
12/31/22	14	4.00	4.71	0.71	5.08	100.00	94.92	
06/30/23	15	4.00	4.75	0.75	4.33	100.00	95.67	
12/31/23	16	4.00	4.78	0.78	3.55	100.00	96.45	
06/30/24	17	4.00	4.82	0.82	2.72	100.00	97.28	
12/31/24	18	4.00	4.86	0.86	1.86	100.00	98.14	
06/30/25	19	4.00	4.91	0.91	0.95	100.00	99.05	
12/31/25	20	4.00	4.95	0.95	0.00	100.00	100.00	100.00
12/31/25	20	100.00						

Figures are rounded to two decimal places. Your calculations may differ slightly due to rounding differences.

[1] Column 2 = Column 6_{t-1} × 5 percent
[2] Column 3 = Column 2 − Column 1
[3] Column 4 = Column 4_{t-1} − Column 3_t

On December 31, 2016, Midwestern Airlines must make its second cash payment of $4 million to its noteholders. But how much interest expense did Midwestern incur from June 30 to December 31, 2016? Using the formula to calculate the periodic interest expense (Interest expense = Yield rate × Book value of debt as of the beginning of the period), Midwestern's interest expense for the second compounding period is calculated as follows:

$$\text{Interest expense} = 5\% \times \$87.9149 \text{ million} = \$4.3958 \text{ million}$$

Be sure to observe that on June 30, the book value of the notes is now $87.9149 million ($100 − $12.462 + $0.3769), and thus, the interest expense for the second interest payment period is $4.3958 million. The cash interest payment of $4 million is unchanged, and thus, the discount amortization for the second period is $0.3958 million. After considering the discount amortization, the book value of the Midwestern notes at December 31, 2016, is $88.3107 million (see **bolded** area in Exhibit 9.1), or $87.9149 million plus $0.3958 million.

While the amortization schedule in Exhibit 9.1 is highly mechanical and very descriptive of the entire note liability, there is one very important simplifying feature worth re-emphasizing that is important to understanding the financial statements themselves. Recall we stated that at any balance sheet date long-term liabilities are generally valued at present value. Column (6) of the table identifies the book value of the Midwestern Airlines notes, measurable as the face value less the unamortized note discount account. It is this book value that will be reported on Midwestern's balance sheet at each date specified in the amortization table. For any period referenced in the table, however, net book value is computable directly by calculating the present value of the remaining cash flows to be paid on the note as of a given date. For instance, the net book value on December 31, 2020, of $92.28 million, is the present value of a $4 million annuity paid for the remaining *10 periods*, plus the present value of the lump-sum paid in 10 periods, both at 5 percent (try this on your own to verify). Once this number is computed, the current period discount is known ($100 − $92.28) and the next period's interest can be computed ($92.28 × 5% = $4.61). The importance of recognizing this feature is that you need not perform a complete amortization table to understand how to measure and understand the amounts reported as long-term liabilities at any balance sheet date.

Market Rates of Interest and the Book Value of Debt

Implicit in the Midwestern Airlines illustration is the assumption that the book value of the notes equals their present value and that the yield rate of interest on the Midwestern notes remains constant over time. In reality, market yield rates are constantly changing in the public debt market to reflect changing investors' expectations regarding the economic and political conditions of the local, national, and global economy. For financial statement purposes, however, the changing market perceptions and related changing market yield rates are generally ignored. On the financial statements of Midwestern, the $100 million notes are reported as if the yield rate on the notes remains a constant ten percent.

What will happen to the actual market value of the Midwestern notes if the market rate of interest demanded by investors increases to, say, twelve percent on December 31, 2015 (with ten interest payment periods remaining)? Using the formula to calculate the present value of a debt instrument, the market value of the Midwestern notes would be $85.28 million, calculated as follows:

Present value of $100 million in 10 periods @ 6%: $100 million × 0.55839 . . . . =	$55.84 million
+ Present value of $4 million per period for 10 periods @ 6%: $4 million × 7.36009 . . . . =	29.44 million
Market value of notes	$85.28 million

The book value of the notes on Midwestern's balance sheet, however, remains at $92.28 million, reflecting the assumption that the company's cost of debt is unchanged at ten percent (see **bolded** area in Exhibit 9.1).

The new market value of the Midwestern notes ($85.28 million) demonstrates an important relationship between the market value of fixed interest rate debt instruments and market rates of interest: As market rates of interest increase (decrease), the fair value of debt instruments with a fixed rate of return will decline (increase) to compensate investors for the changing time value of money. Since the coupon rate of interest on the Midwestern notes must remain fixed at four percent per period, but investors are now demanding a yield rate of six percent per period (one-half of twelve percent), the market price of the notes must decline to enable investors to earn the higher expected market rate of return. If the market price of the Midwestern notes did not adjust downward to enable investors to earn their expected rate of return, other investors would be unwilling to buy the notes.

eLectures
MBC

Takeaway 3
Describe how companies account for debt when it is retired before its maturity.

Early Debt Retirement

Companies sometimes find that they no longer need their existing debt financing, perhaps because the business has been successful at generating operating cash flow or because their current debt is at a higher rate than current market rates and refinancing can lower the firm's cost of debt financing. When this situation arises, firms will sometimes repurchase, or retire, their outstanding interest-bearing debt. When this

Fair Values of Liabilities on the Balance Sheet

There is one important exception to the requirement of using the interest rate in place when long-term debt is first issued for all of the future accounting associated with that long-term debt. Beginning in 2007, GAAP now allows firms to elect to use the fair values of liabilities as of the balance sheet date in lieu of its amortized value. This still can be viewed as recording long-term liabilities at their present value, however the current market yield, rather than the yield when issued, is used to value the debt. Very few companies have adopted the fair value option due to the increased financial statement volatility that might occur. But some have adopted, including many of the major Wall Street banks.

Under the original GAAP rules, if the fair value option for liabilities was adopted by a company any changes in the market value of liabilities from period to period due to fluctuating market interest rates were reportable as income. In the first quarter of 2012, falling interest rates caused a spike in the value of Morgan Stanley's long-term debt on the balance sheet. A quarterly loss of $78 million was reported by the company, rather than what would have been income of $1.4 billion. Volatility of earnings became the norm, as Morgan Stanley's valuation adjustments swung from $216 million in the fourth quarter of 2011 to a $1.5 billion loss the next quarter. Further whipsawing earnings, while most major banks reported approximately $4 billion total valuation gains during 2011 from liability fair value adjustments, in 2012 that total was expected to reverse as interest rates fell. Bank of America and Citigroup were expected to record losses in excess of $2 billion alone.

Reacting to this important accounting issue, in late 2012 the FASB tentatively agreed to remove the requirement that companies adopting a fair value accounting approach for liabilities report any changes in value as income. Any valuation adjustments would bypass net income and be reportable as a component of "Accumulated Other Comprehensive Income" (see Chapter 11 for a discussion of this shareholder's equity account).

occurs, because the book value removed from the balance sheet rarely equals the cash paid to retire the debt, a gain or loss will result:

Book value of debt − Cash paid to repurchase or retire debt = Gain (loss) on debt retirement

Returning to the Midwestern Airlines illustration, assume that the company decides to retire all of its outstanding eight percent notes on December 31, 2020. As indicated above, the market value of the notes is $85.28 million assuming a prevailing market yield rate of twelve percent, whereas the book value is $92.28 million (see **bolded** area in Exhibit 9.1). Ignoring transaction costs that may be necessary to facilitate the note repurchase, Midwestern will pay $85.28 million to retire the debt early. Thus, the company's cash will decline by $85.28 million, notes payable will decline by $100 million, the note discount account will decrease by $7.72 million ($100 million − $92.28 million), and retained earnings will increase by $7 million ($92.28 million − $85.28 million). By retiring the notes early, Midwestern will record a gain on early debt retirement of $7 million (see the Midwestern transaction summary in Exhibit 9.2), largely as a consequence of the increase in the market rate of interest from ten to twelve percent.

EXHIBIT 9.2	Accounting for Bonds and Notes: Midwestern Airlines, Inc.				
($ millions)	Jan.1, 2016 Issue Notes	June 30, 2016 Pay Coupon	Dec. 31, 2016 Pay Coupon	... ...	Dec. 31, 2020 Retire Notes
Assets					
Cash......................	87.538	(4.000)	(4.000)		(85.280)
Liabilities					
Notes payable	100.000				(100.000)
Note discount..............	(12.462)	0.377	0.396		7.720
Shareholders' Equity					
Retained earnings:					
Interest expense		(4.377)	(4.396)		
Gain on early retirement					7.000

Gains and losses on financing transactions like the early retirement of bonds or notes require special consideration when analyzing a company's income statement. These one-time gains or losses should not be considered as part of a firm's recurring or sustainable earnings. If material in amount, the gains or losses should be separately disclosed on the income statement; however, if immaterial, the gains or losses will need to be identified by financial statement users through a review of the footnotes and then removed from any estimate of sustainable earnings. During the preparation of a statement of cash flow, it is necessary to remove any gains or losses from financing transactions (such as the early retirement of debt) from cash flow from operations, and report the cash outflow to retire the debt as part of cash flow from financing.

Zero-Coupon Bonds and Notes

The public market for bonds and notes is made up of many investors and institutions with diverse risk preferences. Some investors prefer debt instruments that pay regular and routine payments, whereas others are willing to forego the regular receipt of cash in exchange for a higher rate of return. Zero-coupon bonds and notes are designed with this latter group of investors in mind.

As the name implies, **zero-coupon bonds** and notes have no coupon rate, and thus, pay no periodic cash interest payment. Instead, the regular but unpaid interest is added to the principal value of the bond (or note)

> Zero-coupon bonds and notes pay no regular interest payments to investors, and thus, are considered to be riskier investments than interest-bearing bonds and notes. As a consequence, zero-coupon debt may carry returns as much as 200 basis points (i.e., 2 percent) higher than interest-bearing debt. The higher returns reflect the opportunity cost that must be borne by investors who purchase zero-coupon debt.

and is paid as a lump sum at maturity. Zero-coupon bonds are important financing tools for companies with limited current cash flow since the issuing company is not required to pay the regular debt servicing associated with traditional interest-bearing bonds or notes.

To illustrate the valuation of, and accounting for, zero-coupon bonds and notes, consider the following scenario:

> On January 1, 2016, Midwestern Airlines, Inc. issued $100 million face value of zero-coupon mortgage notes with a maturity of ten years (in 2025), with semiannual compounding. At the time of issuance, the market yield rate on equivalent risk-rated debt instruments was twelve percent.

Assuming no transaction costs, how much would Midwestern Airlines receive from the sale of the notes? Unlike interest-bearing notes, the Midwestern zero-coupon notes have only one cash flow stream to discount, namely the lump-sum payment of principal in 2025. Using the present value formula, the proceeds from the sale of the notes would be $31.18 million, calculated as follows:

Present value of $100 million in 20 periods @ 6%: $100 million × 0.31180 = $31.18 million

Thus, the Midwestern zero-coupon notes would be sold at a discount of $68.82 million ($100 million − $31.18 million). The discount of $68.82 million represents the total periodic cash interest payment to be paid to an investor at maturity, assuming a six percent return per period compounded over 20 periods.

Jan.1, 2016:	Issue Zero-coupon Notes	
Assets		
Cash......................	31.18	
Liabilities		
Notes payable	100.00	Book value of Notes = $31.18
Note discount..............	(68.82)	

Although Midwestern will not make any payment until 2025, the company will still accrue interest expense on its mortgage notes on its income statement. On June 30, 2016, for example, the company's effective cost of borrowing is $1.87 million, or six percent times $31.18 million. Although the interest is unpaid, it is added to the book value of the notes. Thus, the zero-coupon notes are said to be valued at their **accreted value**—that is, the original issue price plus any accrued, but unpaid, interest. On June 30, 2016, for example, the accreted value of the zero-coupon notes is $33.05 million ($31.18 million + $1.87 million).

For the next six-month period ended December 31, 2016, Midwestern's cost of borrowing on the notes is $1.98 million ($33.05 million × 6 percent), and this amount would also be reported as interest expense on Midwestern's income statement. Therefore, total interest expense on the notes for the year 2016 would be $3.85 million ($1.87 + $1.98). Further, the accreted value of the notes at year-end 2016 will be reported as $35.03 million ($33.05 million + $1.98 million) on the airline's balance sheet. Exhibit 9.3 summarizes the amortization of these zero-coupon bonds.

EXHIBIT 9.3	Zero-Coupon Note Amortization Schedule (in millions)					
Date		Cash Payments (1)	Interest Expense (2)	Amortized Note Discount (3)	Note Discount Balance (4)	Face Value of Notes (5)	Book Value of Notes (6)
01/01/16	0				$68.82	$100.00	$ 31.18
06/30/16	1		1.87	1.87	66.95	100.00	33.05
12/31/16	2		1.98	1.98	64.97	100.00	35.03
06/30/17	3		2.10	2.10	62.86	100.00	37.14
12/31/17	4		2.23	2.23	60.64	100.00	39.36
06/30/18	5		2.36	2.36	58.27	100.00	41.73
12/31/18	6		2.50	2.50	55.77	100.00	44.23
06/30/19	7		2.65	2.65	53.12	100.00	46.88
12/31/19	8		2.81	2.81	50.30	100.00	49.70
06/30/20	9		2.98	2.98	47.32	100.00	52.68
12/31/20	10		3.16	3.16	44.16	100.00	55.84
06/30/21	11		3.35	3.35	40.81	100.00	59.19
12/31/21	12		3.55	3.55	37.26	100.00	62.74
06/30/22	13		3.76	3.76	33.49	100.00	66.51
12/31/22	14		3.99	3.99	29.50	100.00	70.50
06/30/23	15		4.23	4.23	25.27	100.00	74.73
12/31/23	16		4.48	4.48	20.79	100.00	79.21
06/30/24	17		4.75	4.75	16.04	100.00	83.96
12/31/24	18		5.04	5.04	11.00	100.00	89.00
06/30/25	19		5.34	5.34	5.66	100.00	94.34
12/31/25	20		5.66	5.66	$ 0.00	$100.00	$100.00
12/31/25	20	$100.00					

Your calculations may differ slightly due to rounding differences.

BUSINESS PERSPECTIVE

Century Bonds

In 1996, International Business Machines Corporation (IBM) made financing history in the U.S. debt market by launching the largest ever issue of 100-year debentures, or what are now known as **century bonds**. Prior to the IBM debt placement, 21 companies had issued century bonds in the U.S. capital market but none were as large as the $850 million IBM offering. The development of the century bond was patterned after the 1894 sale of $87.3 million (U.S. dollar equivalent) of gold bonds by the Imperial Government of Russia. A unique feature of the Russian gold bonds was that redemption was only by lottery drawing, conducted at the pleasure of the Russian government, causing some pundits to refer to the bonds as "perpetuity bonds" or "permanent debt."

IBM's century bond placement was possible because of the low, stable interest rate environment that characterized the U.S. debt market, as well as the significant demand for very long-term investment products by pension funds and insurance companies. The yield on the IBM century bonds was only 10 to 20 basis points higher than the yields on comparable 30-year bonds. (Note: One hundred basis points equal one percentage point of interest.) One adverse aspect of the IBM bonds was that the U.S. Treasury Department had threatened to rule that the bonds were a form of "permanent capital," and consequently, disallow the tax-deductibility of interest charges on grounds that the interest payments were equivalent to dividend payments, which are not tax deductible under U.S. tax statutes. In 1997, the U.S. Treasury Department enacted tax regulations that eliminated the tax-deductibility of any interest payments on debt instruments after 40 years (such as during the last 60 years of the IBM century bonds).

Zero-coupon Bonds and Taxes

In general, the tax treatment of zero-coupon bonds and notes follows the GAAP accounting treatment—that is, the accrued interest on the debt is tax-deductible in the period incurred, not when paid at maturity. Thus, zero-coupon bonds have two cash flow advantages: (1) the periodic interest cost remains unpaid until maturity, and (2) the unpaid periodic interest cost is currently tax-deductible, providing an immediate interest tax shield to the issuing company.

From the perspective of the IRS, the tax effect of zero-coupon bonds is essentially tax-neutral. The unpaid interest expense is tax-deductible to the issuing firm but is taxable income to the buyer of the bonds in the period in which the interest is effectively earned, not the period when it is received.

REVIEW PROBLEM 9.1

The Arcadia Company issued $50 million of five-year bonds on January 2. The bonds carried an annual coupon rate of six percent, with interest paid semiannually, and were issued at a time when similar risk-rated securities were yielding eight percent. Within twelve months of the debt issuance, however, market yield rates had risen to ten percent.

Required

a. Calculate the proceeds from the five-year debt offering on January 2.
b. Calculate the interest expense for the Arcadia Company on June 30 and on December 31.
c. Calculate the market value of the five-year bonds on December 31.
d. If the Arcadia Company elects to retire the bonds on December 31, how much gain (loss) would the company recognize?
e. Is the decision to retire the bonds on December 31 a good decision?

The solution is on pages 376-377.

LEASE FINANCING

Takeaway 4
Explain the difference between a capital lease and an operating lease and how each is reported in the financial statements.

A lease is a contract that conveys usage rights from an owner of property, the **lessor**, to a user of that property, the **lessee**. Leasing has become one of the most frequently utilized financing strategies for acquiring access to business assets. Office buildings, equipment, airplanes, trucks—almost any business asset—can be leased.

Companies lease assets for a variety of reasons. Some firms lease because they lack sufficient cash to purchase an asset outright—bank financing, for example, often requires a substantial down payment. Other firms lease because they have a poor credit rating and are too risky to secure bank financing. Financially healthy companies, on the other hand, often lease because they have better alternatives for investing their cash. And, some companies lease to avoid the risks that come with full ownership, such as with technology that may soon become outdated. Finally, some firms lease to take advantage of the special accounting treatment accorded certain types of leases. Leasing, however, is not without certain disadvantages. For instance, the interest rates implicit in some leases may be higher than typical long-term borrowing rates, and because ownership has not transferred there are often restrictions on asset use. The bottom line, however, is that the decision to lease an asset is a strategic financing decision with both pros and cons.

Accounting for Leases

Leasing is a vehicle for financing the short- or long-term use of an operating asset. The financial reporting issue faced by companies engaged in lease contracts is whether sufficient property rights have been transferred from the lessor to the lessee such that the recording of those rights is warranted. In most countries, this determination is made by reference to the terms of the contract and then, depending on those terms, leases are classified into one of two categories—capital leases and operating leases. A **capital lease** is treated as an asset purchase agreement involving a deferred payment plan; and, as such, the operating asset acquired under a capital lease and the related obligation to make lease payments are capitalized to the lessee's balance sheet. (The lessor accounts for the leased asset as if it has been sold to the lessee.) An **operating lease**, on the other hand, represents a straightforward contractual relationship wherein the lessor is deemed to provide only temporary access to the leased asset to the lessee. Because access to the leased asset under an operating lease is conditional (it is contingent on its future availability), current accounting standards do not require that the leased asset or the related obligation to make lease payments be capitalized to the lessee's balance sheet. Critics of the accounting for operating leases contend that this accounting treatment effectively provides a form of **off-balance-sheet financing** in that the lessee gains access to the productive capacity of the leased asset but is not required to report the future payments needed to finance that access on its balance sheet. Critics also observe that the accounting for operating leases effectively understates a lessee's true debt position, possibly leading to inefficiencies in the public and private debt markets. A recent U.S. Securities and Exchange Commission study found that of 200 publicly held companies analyzed, 77 percent had off-balance-sheet operating leases, valued at approximately $1.25 billion.

The limitations of lease accounting that allow for off-balance-sheet accounting were heard by accounting regulators. In response to the concerns expressed by users of financial statements, in February 2016 the FASB issued new guidance on lease accounting. These rules will be effective for fiscal years beginning after December 15, 2018, although early adoption is allowed. Because current lease rules will remain in effect until calendar years beginning in 2019, within this chapter we describe the *current* state of rules governing lease accounting. After this discussion, we review the lease accounting changes you can expect to see under the new guidelines.

The criteria used to identify when a lease is a capital lease vary from country to country. Under current lease accounting rules in the United States, a lease must be reported as a capital lease if *any* of the following conditions apply to the lease:

■ The lease agreement transfers legal ownership of the leased asset to the lessee by the end of the lease term.

■ The lease agreement contains a "bargain purchase" option—that is, the lessee has the right to buy the leased asset at a price less than its fair market value.

■ The lease term is 75 percent or more of the leased asset's remaining economic life.

■ The present value of the minimum contractual lease payments is equal to or greater than 90 percent of the leased asset's fair market value.[4]

The evaluation as to whether a lease is a capital or operating lease is made at the inception of a lease. If a lease is determined to be a purchase contract (i.e., a capital lease), capitalization of both the leased asset and a lease liability is required. Otherwise, the lease is accounted for as a **contingent liability**, and the existence, key terms, and characteristics of the operating lease agreement are disclosed in the footnotes to the financial statements but not on the face of the balance sheet. We will have more to say about contingent liabilities in Chapter 10.

On the lessee's income statement, the cost of an operating lease is reported as lease expense (or rent expense), whereas for a capital lease, the income statement effect is reported as depreciation on the capitalized leased asset and interest expense on the capitalized lease liability. It is rare that the lease expense under an operating lease will equal the sum of the depreciation expense plus the interest expense under a capital lease in any given year largely as a consequence of the allocation assumption inherent in most depreciation methods. Over the duration of the entire lease period, however, the total expense will be the same regardless of which lease accounting treatment is applied. On the statement of cash flow, the total cash flow of the two lease categories is the same each year because the cash paid, the lease payment, is equivalent under both lease forms.[5]

To illustrate the similarities and differences between an operating lease and a capital lease, consider the case of Midwestern Airlines Inc., which entered into a ten-year lease agreement for flight equipment. The equipment has a fair market value of $100 million and an implicit interest rate of ten percent per year.

---

[4] Many leases contain "escalation clauses" linking the actual lease payment to the level of revenues generated by the leased asset. Thus, while the minimum contractual lease payment is known at the time of lease signing, the actual lease payment cannot be known until the level of future revenue is determined.

[5] There are differences between operating and capital leases in the classification of cash flows across operating, investing and financing activities. Cash payments under capital leases are split between interest (operating) and principal (financing). Cash payments under operating leases are classified entirely as operating cash flows.

The annual lease payments are $16.27 million and are paid annually at the end of each year.[6] The leased equipment had an expected remaining useful life of 13 years.

In Practice 9.1 *Long-Term Leases: A Glimpse of a Sample of Fortune 1000 Companies*   The following table identifies the types of leases disclosed by a sample of 600 *Fortune 1000* companies. The data reveal that 53 percent of the surveyed firms use operating leases exclusively:

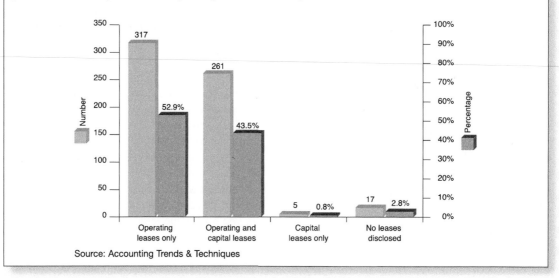

Source: Accounting Trends & Techniques

Capital Lease.   Although the Midwestern Airlines' lease agreement does not provide for a transfer of ownership at any time during the life of the lease or provide the lessee with a bargain purchase option, there are two reasons why this lease should be accounted for as a capital lease. First, the length of the lease period (ten years) exceeds 75 percent of the leased asset's remaining economic life of 13 years (75 percent × 13 years = 9.75 years). Second, the present value of the minimum contractual lease payments is greater than 90 percent of the equipment's fair market value. In fact, the present value of the lease payments is $100 million, which is exactly 100 percent of the equipment's fair market value. (Can you verify that the present value of ten payments of $16.27 million at ten percent interest is $100 million?)

When discounting the future minimum lease payments under a capital lease, the appropriate discount rate is the interest rate implicit in the lease agreement. The rate implicit in a lease is not always known, however, and thus, it is accepted practice to use a firm's incremental cost of borrowing (the rate at which the firm could borrow an equivalent amount of money given its existing debt structure) to discount the lease payments. When the incremental cost of debt is unknown, a firm's weighted-average cost of debt or an inferred rate based upon a firm's credit rating (if known) can be used.

Assuming treatment as a capital lease, the value of the leased flight equipment will be capitalized to Midwestern's balance sheet as a long-term asset at its present value of $100 million, with a lease liability for the same amount also reflected on the balance sheet. This information is illustrated in Midwestern Airlines' transaction summary in Exhibit 9.4. At the end of the first year of the lease, a cash payment for $16.27 million is made, reducing cash by $16.27 million, the lease liability by $6.27 million, and retained earnings by $10 million. The retained earnings effect represents interest expense on the outstanding lease liability ($100 million × 10 percent). In addition, depreciation expense on the capitalized asset must be recorded, again reflected in retained earnings. Assuming the use of the straight-line method, a useful life of ten years (the life of the lease agreement), and a zero residual value since the leased asset reverts to the lessor at the end of the lease period, the depreciation expense would amount to $10 million per year ($100 million/10 years).

A lease **amortization schedule** for Midwestern Airlines is presented in Exhibit 9.6. Consider, for example, Year 2 of the Midwestern equipment lease (see **bolded** area in Exhibit 9.6). According to the amortization schedule, Midwestern's lease payment of $16.27 million in Year 2 will reduce the lease liability by $6.9 million, with the remainder of the payment ($9.37 million) applied as interest expense ($93.73 million × 10 percent). This information is recorded in Midwestern's transaction summary in Exhibit 9.4. You will note that the interest expense recorded each year will fall as the lease liability balance is reduced by payments.

---

[6] A constant set of payments made at the end of each period is referred to as an **ordinary annuity** or an **annuity-in-arrears**.

EXHIBIT 9.4	Capital Lease Accounting Transaction Summary: Midwestern Airlines							

| | | Year 1 | | | | Year 2 | | |
| | | | | | | | | |
(in $ millions)	Lease Signing	Lease Payment	Recognize Depreciation Expense	Balance Sheet Year 1	Lease Payment	Recognize Depreciation Expense	Balance Sheet Year 2
Assets							
Cash....................................		(16.27)		(16.27)	(16.27)		(32.54)
::							
Equipment	100.00			100.00			100.00
Accumulated depreciation...................			(10.00)	(10.00)		(10.00)	(20.00)
Total assets.......................				**73.73**			**47.46**
Liabilities							
Lease liability	100.00	(6.27)		93.73	(6.90)		86.83
Shareholders' Equity							
Retained earnings				(20.00)			(39.37)
Depreciation expense....................			(10.00)			(10.00)	
Interest expense		(10.00)			(9.37)		
Total liabilities and shareholders' equity				**73.73**			**47.46**

Operating Lease.

Operating lease accounting is much more straight-forward. If the Midwestern Airlines' equipment lease is accounted for as an operating lease, no asset or liability is capitalized to the company's balance sheet. The annual lease payment of $16.27 million is recorded on the income statement as a lease expense and as a reduction in cash on the balance sheet. This is shown in Midwestern's transaction summary in Exhibit 9.5.[7]

EXHIBIT 9.5	Operating Lease Accounting Transaction Summary: Midwestern Airlines				

(in $ millions)	Lease Payment	Balance Sheet Year 1	Lease Payment	Balance Sheet Year 2
Assets				
Cash..	(16.27)	(16.27)	(16.27)	(32.54)
::				
Total assets........................		**(16.27)**		**(32.54)**
Liabilities				
Lease liability		—		—
Shareholders' Equity				
Retained earnings		(16.27)		(32.54)
Lease expense	(16.27)		(16.27)	
Total liabilities and shareholders' equity		**(16.27)**		**(32.54)**

As Exhibit 9.6 highlights, the total cash outflow for the Midwestern Airlines' lease is $162.75 million over the ten-year life of the lease, regardless of whether the lease is accounted for as an operating lease or as a capital lease. The total expenses deducted against revenues over the life of the lease are also equivalent ($162.75 million) under either lease accounting treatment. The key financial statement difference between the two types of leases involves the balance sheet disclosure—capital leases are reported on Midwestern's balance sheet as an asset and as a form of debt, whereas operating leases are not.

---

[7] Important to note—this summary for operating lease accounting is provided for illustration purposes only. Midwestern would not be able to use this accounting treatment for this specific contract as the criteria for capital lease accounting have been met.

EXHIBIT 9.6	Lease Amortization Schedule

Ten-year lease with implicit interest rate of 10 percent per year; straight-line depreciation of leased asset

Year	Lease Liability Balance[1] (1)	Interest Expense[2] (2)	Principal Reduction[3] (3)	Lease Payment (4)	Asset Depreciation (5)	Total Expenses Under Operating Lease	Total Expenses Under Capital Lease
0	$100.00						
1	93.73	$10.00	$ 6.27	$ 16.27	$ 10.00	$ 16.27	$ 20.00
2	86.82	9.37	6.90	16.27	10.00	16.27	19.37
3	79.23	8.68	7.59	16.27	10.00	16.27	18.68
4	70.88	7.92	8.35	16.27	10.00	16.27	17.92
5	61.69	7.09	9.19	16.27	10.00	16.27	17.09
6	51.59	6.17	10.10	16.27	10.00	16.27	16.17
7	40.48	5.16	11.11	16.27	10.00	16.27	15.16
8	28.25	4.05	12.23	16.27	10.00	16.27	14.05
9	14.80	2.82	13.45	16.27	10.00	16.27	12.82
10	0.00	1.48	14.80	16.27	10.00	16.27	11.48
Total		$62.75	$100.00[4]	$162.75	$100.00	$162.75	$162.75

Your calculation of these numbers may differ slightly due to rounding differences.
[1] Column 1 = Column 1_{t-1} − Column 3
[2] Column 2_t = Column 1_{t-1} × 10%
[3] Column 3_t = Column 4 − Column 2

> Both methods yield the same total expenses.

TAX PERSPECTIVE

Lease Accounting Under U.S. Tax Law

Throughout this text we have highlighted critical differences between the accounting rules required under GAAP and those required under U.S. tax law. Although the primary focus of this book is on the former, in any successful organization the financially astute executive must be aware of both perspectives when those differences are material. While understanding the financial statement implications for external reporting under GAAP is important to meet the needs of stakeholders such as creditors and investors, the tax regulation perspective is critical as it can have substantial impact on cash flow in a current period (i.e., taxes paid or saved). Lease accounting is one such area that requires special attention.

Under U.S. GAAP we have described how leases are characterized as operating leases or capital leases, depending on whether any of the four criteria for meeting a capital lease have been satisfied. The characterization has far reaching effects on what is reported on corporate balance sheets as assets and liabilities, and on income statements as expense line items. This important reporting issue exists solely because under lease contracts there is often no clear line drawn as to whether "ownership" has actually transferred to the lessee from the lessor.

A similar reporting issue faces the tax authorities as they enforce the rules that govern the taxation of leases. Has ownership transferred? If so, the payments made under the lease contract would be deemed repayments of a loan (i.e., interest and principal), and depreciation would be allowable based on the value of the leased asset. If not, then rent expense would be charged as each lease payment is made. The difference with GAAP, however, lies in the criteria the IRS uses to determine lease classification. The IRS classifies each lease as either a "True Tax Lease," wherein the lessor has retained ownership, or a "Non-Tax Lease," wherein ownership has deemed to have transferred. A lease is not considered a True Tax Lease by the IRS if any of the following are satisfied:

- A part of the lease payment is applied to an equity position in the asset,
- The lessee will acquire ownership (title) of the asset based upon the payment terms,
- The total amount paid is an exceedingly large proportion of the amount required to outright buy the asset,
- The lease payments exceed the current fair rental value,
- The title to the asset may be acquired for an exceedingly small purchase option price in relation to its actual value, or

continued

- Any portion of the lease payments is specifically designated as interest.

You may note with these criteria that they sound very similar to those under GAAP, but the IRS is focused more on the substance, rather than the form, of the lease contract. GAAP rules are more restrictive and definitive, and most tax professionals will note that a leased asset classified as an operating lease under GAAP will virtually always be classified as a True Tax Lease by the IRS. The reverse is not true, however, as many True Tax Leases are not classified as operating for financial reporting purposes. Unlike under GAAP where there typically exist strong incentives to keep a leased asset "off the books" (i.e., an operating lease), for tax purposes a company generally will benefit from treatment as a "Non-Tax Lease" by the IRS. This is because many purchased assets qualify for accelerated depreciation and sometimes even full expensing in the year acquired, and thus there can be huge early tax savings if a leased asset is classifiable as owned rather than rented.

Lease Accounting, Disclosures and Security Prices

Although the annual cash outflow of $16.27 million for Midwestern Airlines is the same under each lease treatment, the periodic balance sheet and income statement effects differ. Under the operating lease, Midwestern's lease expense totals $16.27 million each year, whereas under a capital lease the lease-related expenses total $20 million in Year 1 and $19.37 million in Year 2, respectively. On the balance sheet, a capital lease requires the creation of an asset and liability, whereas the operating lease does not. Do the financial statement differences associated with the accounting for operating leases and capital leases affect the perceived riskiness of a firm? And, do the financial statement differences between the two lease forms affect security prices? Available empirical research suggests that investors *do* include the financial risk associated with off-balance-sheet operating leases in their assessment of share prices, indicating that investors are not misled by the differing accounting treatment of the two lease forms.[8] Stated alternatively, investors see the two lease forms as economically equivalent forms of asset financing.

One reason that investors are not misled by the difference in accounting treatment for leases relates to the required footnote disclosure for these items. Accounting standards setters recognized that balance sheets can look drastically different under operating lease accounting, so companies are required to disclose the schedule of expected minimum lease payments that exist under the contracts for both types. Exhibit 9.7 provides an illustrative disclosure extracted from Nordstrom's 2015 annual report. The

EXHIBIT 9.7 Excerpts from Nordstrom, Inc. Lease Footnote—2015

Note 10: Leases
We lease the land or the land and buildings at many of our stores. Additionally, we lease office facilities, warehouses and equipment. Most of these leases are classified as operating leases and they expire at various dates through 2080. The majority of our fixed, noncancelable lease terms are 15 to 30 years for Nordstrom full-line stores and 10 to 15 years for Nordstrom Rack stores. Many of our leases include options that allow us to extend the lease term beyond the initial commitment period, subject to terms agreed to at lease inception. Most of our leases also provide for payment of operating expenses, such as common area charges, real estate taxes and other executory costs, and some leases require additional payments based on sales, referred to as "percentage rent." Future minimum lease payments as of January 31, 2015 are as follows (in millions):

Fiscal year	Capital Leases	Operating Leases
2015	$2	$ 210
2016	2	231
2017	1	229
2018	1	227
2019	—	219
Thereafter	—	1,202
Total minimum lease payments	6	$2,318
Less: amount representing interest	(1)	
Present value of net minimum lease payments	$5	

[8] K. Ely, "Operating Lease Accounting and the Market's Assessment of Equity Risk," *Journal of Accounting Research* (1995).

the various ways that a company can gain access to productive operating assets while not disclosing the obligation to pay for that access on its balance sheet. Examples of off-balance-sheet financing discussed thus far include the use of operating leases to finance operating assets and the use of the equity method to account for unconsolidated affiliates, joint ventures, and special purpose entities. We will have more to say about other forms of off-balance-sheet financing in Chapter 10.

BUSINESS PERSPECTIVE

Is Debt Bad?

All of us have likely heard at one time or another that we should avoid debt if at all possible. We are told by our parents that we should save our money and only buy things when we have enough money to afford them. We have also heard numerous examples of how debt can destroy not only individuals but also companies, or even countries, such as Greece. The story we often hear concerning a company's debt goes something like this:

As debt increases so does the risk of non-payment to creditors. This increase in risk leads to a decrease in credit ratings issued by firms like Moody's or Standard and Poor's. Lower credit ratings means higher cost of borrowing through increased interest rates. Higher cost of borrowing means fewer new growth opportunities, and fewer positive net present value projects, since higher returns are needed to overcome the higher cost of financing. With decreased growth opportunities the company's stock price will likely suffer since future growth is often a key consideration in determining a stock's value.

So is debt really bad? The answer is not nearly as clear as the above would imply. The above argument is only true up to the point the debt becomes too high. Most firms have plenty of debt capacity and can take on additional debt without suffering a decline in their credit rating. In addition, if the firm can earn a higher return on borrowed funds than the cost of those funds, the result is positive leverage leading to an increase in the company's return on stockholders' equity. This concept is demonstrated with the following stylized example.

Assume a world with neither taxes nor transaction fees on any real estate transaction. Further assume you purchase a condo for $500,000 cash and sell it exactly one year later for $600,000. Since there are no taxes or transaction fees you clear $100,000, leading to a return of 20 percent. Since there were no borrowed funds both return on assets and return of equity are both the same at 20 percent.

Now assume that instead of paying entirely with your own cash, you only put down 10 percent ($50,000), taking a loan of $450,000 at 7 percent annual interest. Under this scenario you would pay interest of $31,500 and therefore clear only $68,500. But what about your return? The ROA on the investment remains at 20 percent ($68,500 + $31,500)/$500,000 = 20 percent, but the ROE is now 137% since your equity is only $50,000 ($68,500/$50,000) = 137 percent. This can be seen as follows:

20 percent ROA + (20 percent return on borrowed funds less 7 percent cost of borrowed funds) × $450,000/$50,000 percentage of borrowed funds to equity or 0.20 + (0.20 − 0.07) × 450,000/50,000 = 137 percent

The 13 percent (20 percent − 7 percent) excess earnings on the borrowed funds flows straight to the equity holders resulting in an increase in ROE over ROA. This happens whenever the project earns a return in excess of the cost of the funds. Beware, however, that leverage is a double edged sword, and the opposite will occur if the project earns less than the cost of the borrowed funds.

---

eLectures
MBC

Takeaway 7
Determine whether a company's balance sheet adequately portrays the extent of a firm's use of leverage.

ANALYZING A COMPANY'S USE OF LEVERAGE

The first point that a financial statement user should consider when analyzing a firm's debt financing is whether the reported financial statement numbers accurately reflect the use of leverage. As discussed in this chapter, GAAP provides business managers with the opportunity to finance the acquisition of a firm's operating assets with leases and avoid any balance sheet recognition of the lease liability, provided that the lease qualifies as an operating lease. As a consequence, current applicable GAAP provides managers with a perverse incentive to structure their company's lease financing to satisfy the criteria for operating-lease accounting. This does not preclude the financial statement user, however, from undertaking various financial statement adjustments to place these obligations on the balance sheet, especially where it is determined that the amount of debt involved is material. U.S. GAAP requires that a company financing its assets with operating leases disclose sufficient information in the footnotes to permit a financial statement user to value the off-balance-sheet debt and to capitalize any lease obligations, along with the corresponding leased assets, on a firm's balance sheet.

Operating lease obligations, however, are only one of several off-balance-sheet financing arrangements that should be considered as part of any financial statement due diligence. In Chapter 8, for example, we examined how the use of the equity method enables parent-companies to report only the net assets of an affiliate company, rather than fully reporting the affiliate's assets and liabilities. We also learned that the equity method was principally used to account for joint ventures and variable interest entities (VIEs), enabling the parent-company of such entities to keep any debt off the parent's balance sheet. In Chapter 10, additional off-balance-sheet liabilities, such as commitments and contingencies, are examined. We will see that, like operating lease obligations, the key elements of these potential obligations are disclosed in the footnotes to the financial statements; and consequently, it is possible for financial statement users to determine whether to include this risk-related information in any assessment of a firm's use of leverage.

BUSINESS PERSPECTIVE

AMR Lease Disclosures Under Bankruptcy

AMR Corporation is the parent company of American Airlines and the regional carrier American Eagle. On November 29, 2011, AMR filed Chapter 11 bankruptcy, an event that required the company to begin operations as a "debtor-in-possession" under the jurisdiction of the bankruptcy courts. As a debtor-in-possession the company is allowed to continue to operate as an ongoing business but may not engage in transactions outside the ordinary course of business without the prior approval of the bankruptcy court. The following is the lease disclosure made by AMR in their fiscal year 2011 annual report. It highlights an important facet of the significant debt-load that was carried by the company.

AMR's subsidiaries lease various types of equipment and property, primarily aircraft and airport facilities. As allowed under Section 365 and other relevant sections of the Bankruptcy Code, the Debtors may assume, assume and assign, or reject certain executory contracts and unexpired leases. Consequently, the company anticipates that its liabilities pertaining to leases will change significantly in the future.

The future minimum lease payments required under capital leases, together with the present value of such payments, and future minimum lease payments required under operating leases that have initial or remaining noncancelable lease terms in excess of one year as of December 31, 2011, were (in millions):

	Capital Leases Subject to Compromise	Operating Leases
Year ended December 31:		
2012	$ 167	$ 1,176
2013	149	1,091
2014	129	942
2015	118	779
2016	78	685
2017 and thereafter	477	5,940
	$1,118	$10,613
Less amount representing interest	439	
Present value of net minimum lease payments	$ 679	

AMR's abbreviated balance sheet is presented below and reveals that the company has $11.434 billion ($11.041 billion + $0.393 billion) invested in equipment and property as of year-end 2011, of which

continued

continued from previous page

$0.393 billion was financed using capital leases. This total fails to include, however, the $10.613 billion that AMR expects to pay in the future for equipment and property financed using operating leases. AMR's lease disclosures reveal that the company relies extensively on operating leases as a form of financing. Interestingly, look what happens to the liability accounts during 2011, the year in which AMR entered Chapter 11 bankruptcy. In 2010 there was only $0.604 billion ($0.497 billion + $0.107 billion) reported by AMR as lease-related debt, a small amount relative to its total lease commitments and total long-term debt, but by 2011 these amounts had dropped to zero. The "Liabilities subject to compromise" explains this change, as under the bankruptcy many of the company's debt obligations ($4,843 million to be exact), including those under capital leases, are subject to being restructured as the company attempts to exit bankruptcy.

AMR CORPORATION Debtors and Debtors-in-Possession Consolidated Balance Sheets		
(in millions)	2011	2010
Current assets	$ 6,757	$ 6,838
Equipment and property, net	11,041	12,264
Equipment and property under capital leases	841	824
Less accumulated depreciation	(448)	(580)
	393	244
Other assets	5,657	5,742
Total assets	$23,848	$25,088
Current liabilities	$ 8,630	$ 8,780
Long-term debt, less current maturities	6,702	8,756
Obligations under capital leases, less current obligations ($0 and $107 in 2011 and 2010, respectively)	—	497
Other liabilities and credits	10,784	11,000
Liabilities subject to compromise	4,843	—
Shareholders' equity	(7,111)	(3,945)
Total liabilities and shareholders' equity	$23,848	$25,088

As lawyers and judges work through the terms of AMR's bankruptcy, one question certainly being addressed is how to deal with the company's $10.613 billion of commitments under operating leases. Financial analysts and investors often ask these questions as well, but rather as "What would be the financial impact on the financial statements if the company's operating leases were accounted for as capital leases (the leased assets and lease liabilities were capitalized to the balance sheet)?" To see this type of computation we will apply the analysis to AMR's lease disclosures as reported above. If we assume that the interest rate implicit in AMR's operating leases is ten percent, the present value of the company's minimum lease payments under its operating leases is $6.027 billion, calculated as follows:

Year	Future Minimum Lease Payments Under Operating Leases (billions)	Present Value Factor (10%)	Present Value of Minimum Lease Payments (billions)
2012 . . .	$ 1.176	0.90909	$1.069
2013 . . .	1.091	0.82645	0.902
2014 . . .	0.942	0.75131	0.708
2015 . . .	0.779	0.68301	0.532
2016 . . .	0.685	0.62092	0.425
2017 . . .	0.685	0.56447	0.387
2018 . . .	0.685	0.51316	0.352
2019 . . .	0.685	0.46651	0.320
2020 . . .	0.685	0.42410	0.291
2021 . . .	0.685	0.38554	0.264
2022 . . .	0.685	0.35049	0.240
2023 . . .	0.685	0.31863	0.218
2024 . . .	0.685	0.28966	0.198
2025 . . .	0.460	0.26333	0.121
Total . . .	$10.613		$6.027

continued

The footnote information reports the first five years of minimum lease payments (through 2016) along with a summation of the minimum lease payments for all years following the fifth year. In order to compute the present value of the future lease payments, we assume that the minimum lease payment after 2016 remains constant (years 2017 through 2024 in this example) with any remainder to be paid in the final year.

Excluding AMR's operating leases, the company's total liabilities at year-end 2011 totaled $30.959 billion ($23.848 billion plus $7.111 billion). Including the present value of AMR's operating leases on the company's balance sheet brings the company's total liability position to $36.986 billion ($30.959 billion + $6.027 billion). These figures reveal the extent to which AMR relies on the use of operating leases as a form of debt financing, but also the extent to which the company uses off-balance-sheet financing to gain access to its operating assets. Over 19 percent ($6.027 billion ÷ $30.959) of AMR's liabilities are carried off-balance-sheet! As a consequence, failure to consider AMR's operating leases as a form of debt financing materially understates the firm's total use of leverage.

In Chapter 4, we examined several financial ratios that can prove useful when evaluating a firm's use of leverage, including the long-term debt to total assets ratio and the long-term debt to shareholders' equity ratio. Both of these ratios provide information regarding a firm's use of debt financing relative to its use of equity financing. As a general rule, debt financing can be used to enhance shareholder returns so long as the firm is able to earn a return on its borrowed funds that exceeds its cost of borrowing the funds; thus, for most firms, the use of debt financing provides a good approach to build shareholder value. For some firms, however, increasing levels of debt financing will destroy shareholder value, especially when excessive debt levels impair management's operational flexibility. A final ratio that can help assess whether a firm has excessive levels of debt is the interest coverage ratio. By comparing a firm's current level of debt service charges with its operating earnings, the financial statement user can develop an informed opinion regarding a firm's liquidity and its solvency.

ETHICS PERSPECTIVE

Numerous reasons were cited in this chapter as to why some firms use leasing as a financing approach for acquiring capital assets. One reason is the managerial desire to avoid disclosing the operating lease liability on a company's balance sheet. It can be argued that there should not be any difference to financial statement users whether a lease obligation appears on the face of the balance sheet or is disclosed in the footnotes to the financial statements. As demonstrated in this chapter, it is a simple procedure for financial statement users to adjust the balance sheet for this type of off-balance-sheet debt. Nonetheless, many managers behave as if they believe that financial statement users will not undertake the necessary financial statement adjustments to develop a complete assessment of a firm's debt exposure. Available evidence, however, indicates that financial markets are not fooled by off-balance-sheet financing, and instead, market participants appear to incorporate this information in their assessments of the risk premium associated with public companies utilizing off-balance-sheet financing. Even so, the FASB has now taken steps to close this form of off-balance-sheet financing with proposed new lease accounting standards.

REVIEW PROBLEM 9.2

The following data was obtained from the financial records of the Costa Mesa Company for 2016:

Total liabilities	$15,000
Total assets.	22,000

Long-term Borrowings	Interest Rate
$4,000	4.5%
6,500	7.0%
3,000	5.5%

continued

continued from previous page

Minimum lease payments on operating leases

2017	$ 975
2018	890
2019	750
2020	670
2021	630
Thereafter	1,920
Total	$5,835

The Costa Mesa Company's operating leases carry an implicit interest rate of six percent.

Required

1. Estimate the present value of the company's operating lease payments.
2. Estimate the company's total liabilities to total assets ratio treating the leases as (i) operating leases, and (ii) capital leases.
3. Compute the company's weighted-average cost of debt treating the leases as (i) operating leases, and (ii) capital leases.

The solution is on page 377.

EXECUTIVE SUMMARY

This chapter investigated the strategic financing decision of companies, specifically how companies finance their operations and asset purchases with bonds, leases, and notes. We saw that most liabilities were valued at their present value. We also examined how and why some firms lease their long-term revenue-producing assets. Finally, we illustrated how to calculate the weighted-average cost of debt of a company. In Chapter 10, our investigation of debt financing continues with a consideration of commitments and contingent liabilities, retirement obligations, deferred income tax liabilities, and financial instruments and derivatives.

As a validation of your understanding of the content of this chapter, you should now be able to:

■ Describe the characteristics of bonds and notes and explain how credit ratings are determined.
■ Explain how bonds and notes are valued and reported in corporate financial statements.
■ Explain how a company accounts for debt when it is retired before its maturity.
■ Explain the difference between a capital lease and an operating lease and how each is reported in the financial statements.
■ Calculate the weighted-average cost of debt.
■ Explain how and why companies manage the amount of debt reported on their corporate balance sheets.
■ Determine whether a company's balance sheet adequately portrays the extent of a firm's use of leverage.

KEY CONCEPTS AND TERMS

Accreted value, 348
Amortization, 345
Amortization schedule, 345, 352
Annuity-in-arrears, 352
Bonds, 340
Callable, 341
Capital lease, 350
Century bonds, 349
Contingent liability, 351
Contra-liability, 344
Convertible, 341
Cost of debt, 341
Coupon rate, 342
Credit-risk rating, 341
Debentures, 341

Discount, 343, 344
Duration, 340
Effective interest method, 345
Face value, 344
Indenture agreement, 341
Interest expense, 344
Junk bonds, 342
Lessee, 350
Lessor, 350
Maturity value, 342
Net debt, 357
Note discount, 344
Notes, 340
Off-balance-sheet financing, 351, 357

Operating lease, 351
Ordinary annuity, 352
Par value, 344
Premium, 344
Present value, 342
Prospectus, 344
Secured, 341
Subordinated, 341
Trustee, 341
Unsecured, 341
Unsubordinated, 341
Weighted-average cost of debt, 357
Yield rate, 342
Zero-coupon bonds, 348

QUESTIONS

Q9.1   **Financing with Debt Versus Equity.**   It is commonly understood that the cost of financing a business's asset purchases with debt is cheaper than financing those purchases with equity. Discuss why debt financing is cheaper than equity financing. Is there a set of circumstances when the cost of debt financing would exceed the cost of equity financing? If so, when?

Q9.2   **Credit Ratings.**   In 2005, The General Motors Corporation (GM) reported a net loss of $10.6 billion. Moreover, the automobile manufacturer had been losing U.S. market share to increasing competition from Japanese automakers. In response, Standard & Poor's rating service indicated that it was reviewing whether to lower GM's debt rating from its current B rating (five levels below investment grade status). Standard & Poor's also reported that it was "putting GM's debt on its CreditWatch list with negative implications" because the automaker disclosed that as much as $3 billion in lease obligations could be subject to possible covenant violations that might cause an acceleration of debt repayment. The credit-rating agency also expressed concern that the company's recent disappointing performance might affect the firm's access to its $5.6 billion standby credit facility. Discuss why credit ratings are important to a company like GM. Discuss the consequences to a company when it violates its existing debt covenants. (GM filed for Chapter 11 bankruptcy in 2009.)

Q9.3   **Credit Ratings.**   In early 2006, The General Motors Corporation (GM) took significant steps to improve its deteriorating financial condition. Besides downsizing its workforce and closing certain inefficient plants, the company also sold its ownership interest in several of its subsidiaries. For instance, GM sold its equity stake in Japan's Isusu Motors for $300 million and sold a majority shareholding in its financing subsidiary, General Motors Acceptance Corporation (GMAC), for $14 billion. In response to these GM actions, U.S. credit-rating agencies took the following actions:

- Fitch, Inc. revised its outlook on GMAC's bonds to "positive."
- Standard & Poor's reported that it might raise the ratings on GMAC's bonds from BB to BB+.
- Moody's indicated that it might downgrade the GMAC bonds.

Discuss why a favorable credit rating is important to a company like GM. Do you agree with Moody's response (a possible credit-rating downgrade) to the GM actions? Why?

Q9.4   **Long-Term Debt Disclosures.**   Johnson & Johnson reported the following borrowings in note 7 of its 2014 annual report:

7. Borrowings

The components of long-term debt are as follows:

(Dollars in Millions)	2014	Effective Rate %
2.15% Notes due 2016	898	2.22
3 month LIBOR + 0.07% FRN due 2016	800	0.31
0.70% Notes due 2016	398	0.74
5.55% Debentures due 2017	1,000	5.55
1.13% Notes due 2017	697	1.15
5.15% Debentures due 2018	898	5.15
1.65% Notes due 2018	597	1.70
4.75% Notes due 2019 (1B Euro 1.2199)/(1B Euro 1.3683)	1,216	5.83
1.88% Notes due 2019	497	1.93
3.00% Zero Coupon Convertible	158	3.00
2.95% Debentures due 2020	543	3.15
3.55% Notes due 2021	446	3.67
2.45% Notes due 2021	349	2.48
6.73% Debentures due 2023	250	6.73
3.38% Notes due 2023	812	3.17
5.50% Notes due 2024 (500MM GBP 1.5542)/(500MM GBP 1.6414)	772	6.75
6.95% Notes due 2029	297	7.14
4.95% Debentures due 2033	500	4.95
4.38% Notes due 2033	865	4.23
5.95% Notes due 2037	995	5.99
5.85% Debentures due 2038	700	5.86
4.50% Debentures due 2040	539	4.63
4.85% Notes due 2041	298	4.89
4.50% Notes due 2043	499	4.52
Other	105	—
Subtotal	15,129	4.08%
Less current portion	7	
Total long-term debt	$15,122	

Discuss the difference between a "note" and a "debenture." Of Johnson & Johnson's (J&J) total long-term borrowings of $15,129, what amount will appear as a current liability and what amount will appear as a non-current liability? Were the 2.95% debentures, due 2020, originally sold at a discount, at their par value, or at a premium? Why? Were the 3.38% notes, due 2023, originally sold at a discount, at their par value, or at a premium? Why? Which of J&J's borrowings were sold at their par value? How do you know this?

Q9.5   **Selling Bonds at a Discount, at Par, and at a Premium.**   It is widely accepted that bonds may sell at a discount from their par value, at their par value, or at a premium above their par value. Discuss why, and under what circumstances, a bond would sell at a discount, at its par value, and at a premium.

Q9.6   **Accounting for Bonds at a Constant Yield Rate.**   When bonds are sold by a company, they are recorded on the issuing firm's financial statements at their selling price. This price reflects the yield rate on the date of sale for equivalent risk-rated debt instruments. Although the market yield rate for a given bond may fluctuate widely in the debt market, the changing market rate is ignored for accounting purposes; and instead, the debt instrument remains on the financial statements of the issuing company at the yield rate prevailing at the time of sale. Discuss the implications of this accounting treatment. Do you believe that bond values should be periodically revised to reflect a changing interest-rate environment? Why or why not?

Q9.7   **Credit Ratings.**   In 2015 Moody's Investors Service (Moody's) lowered Advanced Micro Devices, Inc.'s (AMD) corporate family rating to B3 from B2, and the ratings on the senior unsecured notes to Caa1 from B2. Moody's stated "The downgrade of the corporate family rating to B3 reflects AMD's prospects for operating losses over the next year and negative free cash flow, in contrast to our previous expectations of modest profitability and positive free cash flow." Discuss why credit ratings are important to a company like AMD.

Q9.8   **Operating Leases and Market Efficiency.**   Many businesses use operating leases as a method to finance their operating assets. One of the frequently stated reasons for the popularity of operating leases (as opposed to capital leases) is that operating leases are carried off-balance-sheet—that is, operating leases are a form of off-balance-sheet financing. Discuss whether you think the capital market is "efficient" with respect to operating leases. Stated alternatively, discuss whether you believe that the capital market treats operating leases as off-balance-sheet debt or as on-balance-sheet debt. Be prepared to justify your answer.

Q9.9   **Zero-Coupon Convertible Debentures.**   In 2000, ALZA Corporation, a wholly owned subsidiary of the Johnson & Johnson (J&J) Company, sold zero-coupon convertible debentures at a price of $551.26 per $1,000 principal amount at maturity. The twenty-year debentures were also convertible into J&J shares. Discuss the reasons why ALZA might issue zero-coupon convertible debentures. Estimate the yield to maturity on the debentures.

Q9.10   **Converting Notes Payable into Common Stock.**   In 2006, US Airways Group announced that more than 99 percent of its convertible senior notes had been converted into the airline's common stock. The $112 million of 7.5 percent notes, due 2009, had been called for redemption and noteholders had been given six weeks to either convert the notes into common stock or redeem the notes for approximately $1,050 in cash per $1,000 of notes. The notes were convertible into 34.376 shares of US Airways stock, which had recently been trading at $36 per share. Why did the US Airways noteholders convert their notes into the airline's common stock? Why hadn't they converted their notes earlier? Explain how a conversion of debt into common stock might benefit US Airways Group.

Q9.11   **Collateralized Debt Obligations.**   Collateralized debt obligations (CDOs) are bonds issued by a bank, real estate investment trust, or financial institution, which are backed by loans collateralized by commercial real estate (such as shopping malls, hotels, office buildings). In short, CDOs represent an interest in a pool of real estate loans and mortgages. Discuss why a bank, real estate investment trust, or financial institution would sell CDOs instead of issuing debentures backed by the firm's credit rating.

Q9.12   **Debt-for-Equity Exchange.**   The May 9, 2006, edition of the *Wall Street Journal* carried the following headline:

Accounting Gain Masks UAL Loss of $306 Million

The related article explained that UAL Corporation, parent company of United Airlines, reported first quarter net income of almost $23 billion thanks to a $24 billion gain from "discharging its obligations to unsecured creditors in exchange for giving them 115 million UAL common shares." Without the noncash gain, UAL would have reported a net loss of $306 million. UAL emerged from bankruptcy in February 2006. UAL common shares traded at $39 per share prior to the May 9, 2006, announcement. Discuss the financial effects of UAL's exchange of its stock for its unsecured debt. What was the market value of the UAL stock given to creditors? What was the book value of the UAL debt?

Q9.13   **(Ethics Perspective) Avoiding the Recording of Leases on Balance Sheet.**   Why do you suppose that managers desire to keep debt off the balance sheet even when they know that the obligation will be fully disclosed in the footnotes? Do you feel that it is ethical to choose to lease an asset rather than to purchase the asset if the only reason for the accounting policy choice is to avoid the balance sheet recognition of the lease obligation?

Assignments with the logo in the margin are available in BusinessCourse.
See the Preface of the book for details.
CHECK FIGURE indicates that check figures are available on the book's Website.

EXERCISES

E9.14   **Coupon Rates, Yield Rates, and Bond Issuance Prices.**   The relation between a bond's coupon rate and   TA 2
yield rate is known to influence a bond's issuance price. Presented below are coupon rates and yield rates
for a selection of corporate bonds. Identify whether each bond was sold at a discount, at its par value, or at a
premium, and explain why.

Bond	Coupon Rate	Yield Rate
A........................	7.35%	7.55%
B........................	8.9	8.0
C........................	5.0	5.0
D........................	3.5	3.4
E........................	8.8	9.2

E9.15   **Calculating Bond Issuance Prices.**   Presented below are annual coupon rates, yield rates, and expected   TA 2
duration for a series of debentures. Calculate the issuance price for each debenture assuming that the face value   CHECK
of each bond is $1,000 and that interest is paid semiannually.   FIGURE

Bond	Coupon Rate	Yield Rate	Duration
A........................	4.0%	6.0%	5 years
B........................	12.0	10.0	6 years
C........................	6.0	8.0	10 years
D........................	0.0	6.0	15 years
E........................	8.0	8.0	10 years

E9.16   **Bond Discounts and Effective Interest Rates.**   On January 1, 2015, the Mayfield Corporation issued $500   TA 2
million of zero-coupon debentures, due December 31, 2025. The proceeds of the bond sale totaled approximately
$192.772 million. Assuming semi-annual compounding, estimate the effective interest rate on the zero-coupon
debentures. Calculate the interest expense incurred by the Mayfield Corporation during the first year that the debt
was outstanding.

E9.17   **Calculating the Fair Value of Debt.**   The Longo Corporation issued $60 million maturity value in notes,   TA 2
carrying a coupon rate of six percent, with interest paid semiannually. At the time of the note issue, equivalent   CHECK
risk-rated debt instruments carried yield rates of eight percent. The notes matured in five years.   FIGURE
    Calculate the proceeds that Longo Corporation will receive from the sale of the notes. How will the notes
be disclosed on Longo's balance sheet immediately following the sale? Calculate the interest expense for
Longo Corporation for the first year that the notes are outstanding. Calculate the balance sheet value of the
notes at the end of the first year.

E9.18   **Building a Note Amortization Table.**   Balsoom, Inc. issued $100 million maturity value of three-year   TA 2
notes, which carried a coupon rate of four percent and which paid interest semiannually. At the time of the
note sale, equivalent risk-rated debt instruments carried a yield rate of six percent. Develop a note amortization
table for Balsoom's four percent, three-year notes.

E9.19   **Accounting for Bonds Sold at a Discount.**   The Biltmore National Bank raised capital through the sale of   TA 2
$150 million face value of eight percent coupon rate, ten-year bonds. The bonds paid interest semiannually
and were sold at a time when equivalent risk-rated bonds carried a yield rate of ten percent.
    Calculate the proceeds that The Biltmore National Bank received from the sale of the eight percent bonds.
How will the bonds be disclosed on Biltmore's balance sheet immediately following the sale? Calculate the
interest expense on the bonds for the first year that the bonds are outstanding. Calculate the book value of the
bonds at the end of the first year.

E9.20   **Market Yield Rates and Bond Values.**   Smith & Company issued $100 million maturity value of ten-year   TA 2
bonds, which carried a coupon rate of six percent, with interest paid semiannually. At the time of the debt
offering, equivalent risk-rated bonds were yielding eight percent. One year after the six-year bond offering,

yield rates had fallen to four percent; but, by the second anniversary of the bond sale, the yield rate on similarly risk-rated debt instruments had risen to ten percent.

Calculate the proceeds from the sale of the six percent, six-year bonds. Calculate the book value of the bonds after one year and after two years. Calculate the market value of the bonds after one year and after two years. What is the relationship between market yield rates and bond values?

TA 2

CHECK FIGURE

E9.21　Accounting for Notes Issued at a Premium. The Longo Corporation issued $50 million maturity value of six percent coupon rate notes, with interest paid semiannually. At the time of the note issuance, equivalent risk-rated debt instruments carried a yield rate of four percent. The notes matured in five years.

Calculate the proceeds that the Longo Corporation would receive from the sale of the notes. How will the notes be reported on Longo's balance sheet immediately following the sale? Calculate the interest expense on the notes for the first year. Calculate the book value of the notes at the end of the first year.

TA 3　**E9.22　Issuing Zero-Coupon Bonds.** On July 28, 2016, Shannon Corporation, a biotechnology firm located in Virginia, completed a private placement of zero-coupon convertible subordinated debentures. The zero-coupon debentures were issued at a price of $551.26 per $1,000 principal amount at maturity. Although the zero-coupon bonds paid no periodic interest payments, interest was assumed to be compounded semiannually. The bonds mature in 2036.

Estimate the yield rate on the zero-coupon bonds at the time of issuance. Why would Shannon Corporation issue non-interest-bearing bonds? Why would Shannon attach a conversion feature to the zero-coupon bonds? Calculate Shannon's implicit interest expense for the first year.

TA 3　**E9.23　Retiring Debt Early.** Smith & Company issued $100 million maturity value of six-year bonds, which carried a coupon rate of six percent and paid interest semiannually. At the time of the offering, the yield rate for equivalent risk-rated securities was eight percent. Two years later, market yield rates had risen to ten percent, and since the company no longer needed the debt financing, executives at Smith & Company decided to retire the debt.

Calculate the gain or loss that Smith & Company will incur as a consequence of retiring the debt early. Is the early retirement of the debt a good decision? What factors should be considered in making this decision?

TA 4　**E9.24　Operating Leases.** Johnson & Johnson disclosed in its annual report that it leases various vehicles and machinery using operating lease agreements. According to its footnotes the minimum payments required under the noncancelable operating lease agreements were as follows:

Year Ending ($ millions)	Operating Leases
2015	$200
2016	157
2017	111
2018	80
2019	66
After 2019	77
Total	$691

If the interest rate implicit in each of the lease agreements is four percent, what is the present value of the company's noncancelable lease payments? Johnson & Johnson's long-term debt-to-equity ratio at year-end was 26.9 percent ($18,760/$69,752). If the company's operating leases were accounted for as capital leases instead of operating leases, how would the firm's long-term debt-to-equity ratio change?

TA 4　**E9.25　Capitalizing Operating Leases.** The following information is taken from the 2014 annual report of Delta Air Lines, Inc. (in millions):

Total assets	$54,121
Total liabilities	$45,308
Stockholders' equity	$ 8,813

Operating Leases

Years Ending December 31, (in millions)	Delta Lease Payments	Contract Carrier Aircraft Lease Payments	Total
2015	$ 1,363	$ 344	$ 1,707
2016	1,187	306	1,493
2017	1,056	267	1,323
2018	881	239	1,120
2019	747	182	929
Thereafter	5,873	296	6,169
Total minimum lease payments	$11,107	$1,634	$12,741

Assume that the cost of debt implicit in the company's operating leases is five percent. Calculate the present value of Delta's operating leases at year-end. Calculate the company's total liabilities to total assets ratio for the year (a) with and (b) without considering the company's operating leases. Does the presence of operating leases impact a firm's financial risk?

PROBLEMS

P9.26   **Debt Valuation: Interest-Bearing Debentures.**   At the beginning of the year, Global Minds Inc. issued   TA 2, 3
$100 million (maturity value) of 20-year debentures. The debentures carried a two percent per period coupon   MBC
rate (i.e., 4% annually), were subject to semiannual compounding, and had been issued at a time when the yield
rate was three percent per period (i.e., 6% annually).

Required
1. Calculate the proceeds received by Global Minds when the bonds were sold.
2. Explain why the Global Minds bonds were sold at a discount.
3. Calculate the market value of the bonds if, after ten years, the market yield rate is five percent per period (i.e., 10% annually).
4. Calculate the cost of retiring the Global Minds bonds after 15 years assuming that the market yield rate is five percent per period at the time of retirement. Does the retirement result in a gain or loss? If so, where will the gain/loss be reported on the company's statement of cash flows?

P9.27   **Debt Valuation: Zero-Coupon Debentures.**   At the beginning of the year, KMF Inc. issued $200 million   TA 3
(maturity value) of 15-year, zero-coupon debentures, at a time when the yield rate was four percent per period.   MBC
The KMF, Inc. bonds would be subject to semiannual compounding.

Required
1. Calculate the proceeds to be received by KMF Inc. when the bonds are sold.
2. Calculate the cost to repurchase and retire the bonds after five years assuming that the market yield rate at that time is five percent per period. Is the early retirement of debt a good decision in this set of circumstances? What factors did you consider in reaching your decision?
3. Under what circumstances would a company consider issuing zero-coupon debentures instead of regular interest-bearing debentures?

P9.28   **Debt Retirement.**   MTF Inc. is a manufacturer of electronic components for facsimile equipment. The compa-   TA 3
ny financed the expansion of its production facilities by issuing $100 million of ten-year bonds carrying a coupon   MBC
rate of eight percent with interest payable annually on December 31. The bonds had been issued on January 1.
At the time of the issuance, the market rate of interest on similar risk-rated instruments was six percent.

Two years later, the market rate of interest on comparable debt instruments had climbed to twelve percent.
The CEO of MTF realized that this might be an opportune time to repurchase the bonds, particularly because
an unexpected surplus of cash made the outstanding debt no longer necessary.

Required
1. Calculate the proceeds received by the company when the debt was initially sold.
2. Calculate the interest expense for each of the two years that the bonds were outstanding.
3. Calculate the amount of cash needed to retire the debt after two years assuming a market yield rate of twelve percent. Does the retirement result in a gain or loss? If so, where will the gain/loss be reported on the company's statement of cash flow?

TA 2, 3
CHECK
FIGURE

P9.29 **Note Valuation.** Microsoft Corporation reported the following information on its long-term debt in its 2015 annual report (in millions):

Due Date	Face Value June 30, 2015	Face Value June 30, 2014	Stated Interest Rate	Effective Interest Rate
Notes				
September 25, 2015...........	$ 1,750	$ 1,750	1.63%	1.80%
February 8, 2016	750	750	2.50%	2.64%
November 15, 2017...........	600	600	0.88%	1.08%
May 1, 2018	450	450	1.00%	1.11%
December 6, 2018	1,250	1,250	1.63%	1.82%
June 1, 2019...............	1,000	1,000	4.20%	4.38%
February 12, 2020	1,500	0	1.85%	1.94%
October 1, 2020	1,000	1,000	3.00%	3.14%
February 8, 2021	500	500	4.00%	4.08%
December 6, 2021	1,950	2,396	2.13%	2.23%
February 12, 2022	1,500	0	2.38%	2.47%
November 15, 2022	750	750	2.13%	2.24%
May 1, 2023	1,000	1,000	2.38%	2.47%
December 15, 2023	1,500	1,500	3.63%	3.73%
February 12, 2025	2,250	0	2.70%	2.77%
December 6, 2028	1,950	2,396	3.13%	3.22%
May 2, 2033	613	753	2.63%	2.69%
February 12, 2035	1,500	0	3.50%	3.60%
June 1, 2039...............	750	750	5.20%	5.24%
October 1, 2040	1,000	1,000	4.50%	4.57%
February 8, 2041	1,000	1,000	5.30%	5.36%
November 15, 2042	900	900	3.50%	3.57%
May 1, 2043	500	500	3.75%	3.83%
December 15, 2043	500	500	4.88%	4.92%
February 12, 2045	1,750	0	3.75%	3.80%
February 12, 2055	2,250	0	4.00%	4.06%
Total	$30,463	$20,745		

Required

1. Are the June 1, 2019 notes recorded at a discount or a premium? Why?
2. How much would the June 1, 2019 notes have been sold for if the market rate of interest at the time of sale had instead been six percent per year? Assume the notes originally had a 10-year (20 interest payment) term.
3. Assume Moody's reports that the October 1, 2020 notes were rated as Aaa.
   a. If the rating had been Aa1 instead, would the yield rate on the notes have been lower, higher, or the same?
   b. If the notes had been secured, would the yield rate have been lower, higher, or the same?
4. Assume the company reported that the fair market value of the company's October 1, 2040 notes was $1,100 million on June 30, 2015. Assume further that the recorded value of the notes was just slightly less than the $1,000 face value. If the company repurchased all of the notes on June 30, 2015, would a gain or loss have been recorded?

TA 4   **P9.30** **Note Valuation.** The Jefferson Company is a multinational manufacturer of electrical equipment and components. Selected financial information is as follows:

Consolidated Statements of Income			
For Period Ended (In millions)	2016	2015	2014
Net sales..	$9,682.00	$9,597.60	$7,819.00
Operating income...................................	$ 523.20	$1,089.40	$1,079.70
Interest expense.................................	(253.00)	(255.30)	(183.50)
Other income (expense), net.....................	(6.80)	35.80	3.10
Noncontrolling interests	(20.10)	(39.30)	(29.10)
Earnings before income taxes	243.30	830.60	870.20
(Benefit) provision for income taxes	(2.90)	284.40	307.10
Earnings from continuing operations..................	246.20	546.20	563.10
Discontinued operations (net of tax)	—	123.20	28.00
Net earnings..	$ 246.20	$ 669.40	$ 591.10

Abbreviated Consolidated Balance Sheet		
(in millions)	2016	2015
Total assets.......................................	$11,063.70	$11,052.60
Long-term debt	$ 2,900.70	$ 1,540.40
Shareholders' equity	$ 3,916.60	$ 3,481.20
Total liabilities and stockholders' equity.............	$11,063.70	$11,052.60

Note 8–Long-Term Debt and Credit Facilities		
(in millions)	2016	2015
5.75% Notes Due 2018.............................	$ 700.00	$ 0
Total long-term debt...............................	$2,900.70	$1,540.40

Required

1. The company reported that on February 1, 2016, the company issued $700 million of 5.75 percent secured notes due February 1, 2018.
   a. Were the notes sold at a discount, a premium, or at par value?
   b. How much interest expense did the company record on August 1, 2016, assuming semiannual compounding?
   c. How much would the company have raised through the sale of the notes if the market rate of interest had been six percent per year?
2. Moody's reports that the notes were rated **A3**.
   a. If the rating had been A1 instead, would the yield rate have been higher, lower, or the same?
   b. If the notes had been unsecured, would the yield rate have been higher, lower, or the same?
   c. The company reports that the fair market value of the company's long-term debt at December 31, 2016, was $2,996.70 million. If the company repurchased all of the outstanding long-term debt on December 31, 2016, how much gain (loss) would be recognized?
   d. Assume Moody's only used the long-term debt to equity ratio and the interest coverage ratio in making its rating decision. Would the rating on the 5.75 percent notes have been higher, the same, or lower if the notes had been issued in 2015 instead of 2016?

TA 4   **P9.31**   **Valuing a Lease.**   On January 1, the president of KMF Inc. signed an eight-year lease agreement for retail space at a lease rate of $50,000 per year. During the negotiations, the president had learned that the lessor had built an implicit borrowing cost of ten percent per year into the lease contract. The agreement called for the lease payments to be made annually at the beginning of each year. Hence, the first payment of $50,000 was made immediately after the lease agreement was signed on January 1.

Required
1.   Assume that the lease agreement is to be accounted for as a capital lease by KMF. How will the lease commitment be reflected on the company's financial statements? At what value?
2.   At the beginning of the second year of the lease, what financial effects will be recorded in the financial statements of KMF? At the beginning of the third year?
3.   Which lease accounting treatment—operating lease versus capital lease—provides the most preferred income tax treatment (i.e., provides the greatest income tax benefits) to the company?
4.   How would your answers to the above questions differ under the new lease accounting rules required beginning in 2019?

TA 4   **P9.32**   **Lease Accounting.**   On January 1, Durant Inc. entered into a noncancelable ten-year lease for cooking equip-
CHECK   ment with a fair value of $100 million and requiring annual year-end lease payments. The company's year-end
FIGURE   is December 31.

Required
1.   If the implicit interest rate on the lease is six percent, what is the annual lease payment?
2.   Assuming that the lease is accounted for as a capital lease, what financial effects will be recorded in the financial statements with regard to the lease on January 1?
3.   Assuming that the lease is accounted for as a capital lease, what financial effects will be recorded with regard to the lease on December 31 (at the end of the first year)?
4.   What are the total expenses associated with the lease in the second year if it is accounted for as an operating lease? As a capital lease?
5.   How would your answers to the above questions differ under the new lease accounting rules required beginning in 2019?

TA 4   **P9.33**   **Lease Accounting.**   On January 1, Longo Inc. entered into a noncancelable 15-year lease for cooking equipment with a fair value of $150 million and requiring annual year-end lease payments. The company's year-end is December 31.

Required
1.   If the implicit interest rate on the lease is seven percent, what is the annual lease payment?
2.   Assuming that the lease is accounted for as a capital lease, what financial effects will be recorded in the financial statements with regard to the lease on January 1?
3.   Assuming that the lease is accounted for as a capital lease, what financial effects will be recorded with regard to the lease on December 31 (at the end of the first year)?
4.   What are the total expenses associated with the lease in the second year if it is accounted for as an operating lease? As a capital lease?
5.   How would your answers to the above questions differ under the new lease accounting rules required beginning in 2019?

TA 4   **P9.34**   **Capitalizing Operating Leases.**   McDonald's Corp. was the lessee at 14,139 restaurant locations through ground leases at December 31, 2011. The lease terms are generally for 20 years. The company is also the lessee under noncancelable leases covering certain offices and vehicles. The company's footnotes also revealed that at year-end 2011, the minimum lease commitments under noncancelable operating leases were:

(In millions)	Restaurant	Other	Total
2012	$ 1,172.6	$ 74.4	$ 1,247.0
2013	1,104.8	62.8	1,167.6
2014	1,019.5	55.4	1,074.9
2015	921.9	43.1	965.0
2016	813.9	37.9	851.8
Thereafter	6,039.1	208.8	6,247.9
Total minimum payments	$11,071.8	$482.4	$11,554.2

The following represents a condensed balance sheet for McDonald's for 2011:

MCDONALD'S CORPORATION Consolidated Balance Sheet	
($ millions)	**2011**
Assets	
Current assets	$ 4,403.0
Noncurrent assets	28,586.9
Total assets.	$32,989.9
Liabilities and Shareholders' equity	
Current liabilities.	$ 3,509.2
Long-term debt	12,133.8
Other noncurrent liabilities	2,956.7
Shareholders' equity	14,390.2
Total liabilities and shareholders' equity.	$32,989.9

Required

1. Calculate the present value of the company's operating leases assuming an interest rate of 6 percent.
2. Restate the company's balance sheet assuming that all operating leases are capitalized.
3. Calculate the:
    a. Long-term debt to shareholders' equity ratio, both with and without capitalization of operating leases.
    b. Total debt to total assets ratio, both with and without the capitalization of the operating leases.

   How would the company's debt rating be affected if all leases (both capital and operating) were capitalized to the balance sheet?

CORPORATE ANALYSIS

CA9.35 The Procter & Gamble Company. The 2015 annual report of the Procter & Gamble Company (P&G) is available at www.pginvestor.com. After reviewing P&G's annual report, respond to the following questions.   TA 2, 4, 5

   a. Calculate P&G's total debt to total assets ratio for 2014 and 2015. Is the company principally debt or equity financed? What is the trend in P&G's use of debt financing? What was P&G's short-term and long-term weighted-average cost of debt? What is the trend in P&G's cost of borrowing?
   b. Calculate P&G's return on assets for 2014 and 2015. Is the company's financing strategy sound? What is P&G's short-term and long-term credit rating? Does P&G have an "investment grade" rating or a "junk grade" rating?
   c. P&G's "total debt" in 2015 was $30.350 billion. What is the composition of P&G's "total debt"? Why would P&G issue notes denominated in British pounds, EU euros, Japanese yen, as well as in U.S. dollars? Is P&G subject to any debt covenants under its various borrowings? If so, what are the covenants and is the company satisfying the covenants?
   d. Does P&G use operating leases to finance any of its operating assets? If so, what are the future minimum operating lease payments for future years? Calculate the present value of P&G's operating leases assuming an implicit cost of borrowing of four percent. Is P&G's use of operating leases material?

CA9.36 Internet-based Analysis. Consider a publicly held company whose products you are familiar with. Some examples might include: TA 2, 4, 5

Company	Product	Corporate Website
• Johnson & Johnson.	• Band-Aids	• www.jnj.com
• Microsoft Corporation.	• Windows software	• www.microsoft.com
• Apple, Inc.	• Cellular phones	• www.apple.com
• Intel Corporation	• Pentium processors	• www.intel.com
• Kimberly-Clark Corporation.	• Kleenex	• www.kimberly-clark.com

Access the company's public website and search for its most recent annual report. (Some companies provide access to their financial data through an "investor relations" link, while others provide a direct link to their "annual reports.") After locating your company's most recent annual report, open the file and review its contents. After reviewing the annual report for your selected company, prepare answers to the following questions:

a. Calculate the total debt to total assets ratio for the past two years. Is the company principally debt-financed or equity-financed? Do you agree with this strategic decision?

b. Review the company's long-term debt footnote. What kinds of debt—bonds, notes, zero-coupon bonds—does the company have outstanding? Are the debt instruments denominated in U.S. dollars? If not, why not?

c. What is the company's weighted-average cost of debt? What is the company's return on assets? Can the company use leverage effectively?

d. Does the company use leases to finance any of its assets? If so, what kind of leases—operating or capital—does the company use?

e. Calculate the company's interest coverage ratio for the past two years. What is the trend in this ratio? Why? What is your assessment of the company's liquidity and solvency? What did you base your opinion on?

TA 2, 6   **CA9.37 IFRS Financial Statements.**   The 2014 financial statements of LVMH Moet Hennessey-Louis Vuitton S.A. are presented in Appendix C of this book. LVMH is a Paris-based holding company and one of the world's largest and best-known luxury goods companies. As a member-nation of the European Union, French companies are required to prepare their consolidated (group) financial statements using International Financial Reporting Standards (IFRS).

Review the company's IFRS financial statements. Is the company principally debt or equity financed? Calculate the company's long-term borrowings to total equity ratio for 2013 and 2014. Is the company's use of debt financing increasing or decreasing over the two-year period?

CASE

BHP BILLITON GROUP: LONG-TERM DEBT (A)

The historically low interest rate environment characterizing the years 2008–2010 led many international companies to tap the world's corporate bond markets. Companies large and small, investment grade and junk, were rushing to strengthen their balance sheets and lock in attractive rates. Worldwide corporate bond sales in 2009 totaled a record $3 trillion. Yields on 10-year U.S. Treasuries had fallen below 3.5%, approximately half the yields of a decade earlier, and were trending lower (**Exhibit 1**). The BHP Billiton Group (BHP), headquartered in Melbourne, Australia, was one of the many companies to issue new debt in 2009 under these favorable debtmarket conditions.

BHP Billiton Group

BHP was the world's largest natural-resources company, and its many diversified businesses produced aluminum, copper, coal, iron ore, gold, lead, silver, and diamonds. Its operations spanned the globe, with the heaviest concentration in Asia and Europe (**Exhibit 2**). The company had an employee and contractor base spread across more than 25 countries totaling almost 100,000. Revenues exceeded $50 billion, and its market capitalization approximated $144 billion.

BHP was organized as a dual-listed company (DLC) between BHP Billiton PLC and BHP Billiton Limited. The DLC structure meant that each entity retained its own corporate identity, but the entities were operated and managed together as a single unified economic entity. Their boards and senior management teams comprised the same individuals. As a DLC, it was also allowed a primary listing on the Australian Securities Exchange (ASX) and the London Stock Exchange (LSE), with American Depository Receipts (ADRs) traded on the New York Stock Exchange.

BHP's business model depended on the prices it received for the various commodities that it produced. The company's policy was to sell its products at prevailing market prices, relying on a diverse mix of products as insulation from the normal fluctuations in prices that occurred. With the global slowdown spawned from the U.S. financial crisis, however, commodity prices fell precipitously during 2009. **Table 1** summarizes average price quotes for select commodities during the years 2007–2009:

Table 1. Average price quotes as of June 30, 2007–2009.	2009	2008	2007
Crude oil ($/bbl)	70.49	96.98	63.00
Aluminum ($/t)	1,920	2,718	2,699
Copper ($/lb)	2.23	3.53	3.21
Nickel ($/lb).	6.03	12.93	17.15
Iron ore ($/dmtu).	0.9700	1.4466	0.0842
Energy coal ($/t)	94.49	94.60	51.52
Gold ($/oz)	931	930	650
Silver ($/oz).	13.98	17.58	12.51

Data sources: BHP Billiton 2009 annual report and Kitco Metals, Inc. (http://www.kitco.com).
Note: The abbreviation for barrel is (bbl), for ton (t), for pound (lb), for dry metric ton unit (dmtu), and for ounce (oz).

The $3.25 Billion Bond Issue

The global economic slowdown coupled with falling commodity prices put unexpected pressure on BHP's cash flow. So on March 18, 2009, BHP Billiton Finance, the wholly owned finance subsidiary of BHP, filed a prospectus with the U.S. Securities and Exchange Commission to sell $3.25 billion of senior notes. Even though the company was well capitalized (**Exhibit 3**), because its credit ratings were so strong and its borrowing rates so low, a prime opportunity to capitalize on these favorable lending conditions existed. The notes would be issued in two tranches with five- and ten-year maturities. A summary of the offering terms is provided in **Exhibit 4**.

The new debt was unsecured, carried no restrictive covenants, and would rank equally with the company's other indebtedness. Rating agencies provided upper-medium grade ratings: A+ by S&P, A1 by Moody's, and A by Fitch. The bond issue would only have a modest effect on the company's leverage. Total proceeds from the issue were $3.226 billion, not quite reaching the full stated principal. The company used 18 different underwriters in connection with the offering, with underwriter discounts approximating 0.35% and 0.45% for the 5.5% and 6.5% issues, respectively (see **Exhibit 5** for a list of underwriters). The net issue prices after underwriter discounts were expected to be $99.316 and $99.229. Other total expenses amounted to approximately $410,000.

Going Forward

Although the March 2009 bond issue seemed to be well timed, by the summer of 2010, interest rates and corporate bond yields continued to fall. On August 24, 2010, the two 2009 debt issues were quoted as shown in **Table 2**:

Table 2. Quotes of two debt issues trading on August 24, 2010.		
	5.50% Senior Notes	**6.50% Senior Notes**
Due date	**April 1, 2014**	**April 1, 2019**
Price (8/24/10)	114.84	124.83
Yield to maturity (YTM) (%).	1.253	3.173
Current yield (%).	4.789	5.207

But what appeared to be unfavorable conditions for BHP's existing debt would be a potential windfall for future debt. The management of BHP was again considering the company's debt and equity financing needs, although this time in connection with a mid-August $39 billion hostile bid for leading fertilizer producer Potash Corporation Inc. of Saskatchewan. The sustained low rate environment made debt financing this deal particularly attractive.

Required:

BHP Billiton Group issued $3.25 billion of debt during March of 2009 in two tranches, 2014 and 2019. Answer the following questions as they relate to the 2014 notes. For simplicity assume the bonds were issued on 4/1/2009:

a. Prepare an amortization schedule for the 2014 notes referenced in the case.

b. Approximately what will be the long-term debt liability related to these 2014 notes at the end of 2009? 2010? 2011?

c. Approximately how much interest expense will be recorded as a charge to income in 2010 for the 2014 notes? How much interest will be paid in cash?

d. On 8/24/10 the notes were trading at a premium relative to the time issued. Approximately how much was that premium on that date? How should BHP account for this difference?

e. In practice, how would the company deal with the 6-day lag between the quarter end date and the issue date of the debt (no calculations required)?

| EXHIBIT 1 | BHP Billiton Group: Long-Term Debt (A) |

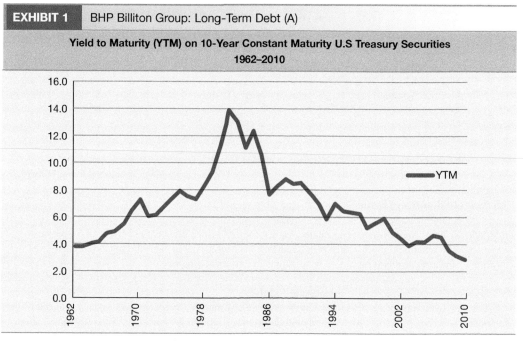

Data source: Federal Reserve, http://www.federalreserve.gov.

| EXHIBIT 2 | BHP Billiton Group: Long-Term Debt (A) |

Fiscal Year 2009 Geographical Segment Revenue, Assets, and Capital Expenditures

	Revenues	Assets	Capital Expenditures
Australia	$ 4,621	$31,902	$6,215
China	9,873	unallocated	unallocated
Europe	10,806	3,241	unallocated
Japan	7,138	unallocated	unallocated
North America	4,020	8,507	903
Other Asia	9,280	unallocated	unallocated
South America	1,652	11,977	1,210
Southern Africa	1,374	5,430	738
Rest of the world	1,447	1,323	270
Unallocated assets	—	16,390	—
Totals	$50,211	$78,770	$9,336

Data source: BHP Billiton 2009 annual report, 192.

EXHIBIT 3	BHP Billiton Group: Long-Term Debt (A)

Summary of Balance Sheet Capitalization and Indebtedness—December 31, 2008

Current interest bearing liabilities.	$ 2,156	
Non-current interest bearing liabilities		
Secured.	777	
Unsecured	8,430	
Total Interest Bearing Liabilities		$11,363
Equity		
Share capital		
BHP Billiton Limited	$ 1,227	
BHP Billiton PLC	1,116	
Treasury shares held	(522)	
Reserves	1,168	
Retained earnings	35,783	
Minority interests	877	
Total Equity		$39,649
Total Capitalization		$51,012

Data source: BHP Billiton Finance (USA) Prospectus, March 18, 2009.

EXHIBIT 4	BHP Billiton Group: Long-Term Debt (A)

The Bond Offering

Notes Being Offered	5.50% senior notes due 2014 (the "2014 notes") and 6.50% senior notes due 2019 (the "2019 notes" and, together with the 2014 notes, the "notes").
Issuer	BHP Billiton Finance (USA) Limited.
Guarantors	BHP Billiton Plc. and BHP Billiton Limited.
Principal Amount	2014 notes: US$1,500,000,000 aggregate principal amount.
	2019 notes: US$1,750,000,000 aggregate principal amount.
Issue Price	2014 notes: 99.666%.
	2019 notes: 99.679%.
Maturity Date	2014 notes: April 1, 2014.
	2019 notes: April 1, 2019.
Interest Rate	The 2014 notes will bear interest at the rate of 5.50% per year from March 25, 2009, based upon a 360-day year of 12 months with 30 days.
	The 2019 notes will bear interest at the rate of 6.50% per year from March 25, 2009, based upon a 360-day year of 12 months with 30 days.
Interest Payment Dates	Interest on each series of the notes will be payable semiannually in arrears on April 1 and October 1 of each year, commencing October 1, 2009 and ending on the respective maturity date.
Ranking	The notes will be unsecured obligations of BHP Billiton Finance (USA) and will rank equally in right of payment with all other unsecured and unsubordinated debt obligations of BHP Billiton Finance (USA). The guarantees will be unsecured obligations of BHP Billiton Plc. and BHP Billiton Limited and will rank equally in right of payment with all other unsecured and unsubordinated debt obligations of BHP Billiton Plc. and BHP Billiton Limited, except, in each case, indebtedness given preference by applicable law.
Use of Proceeds	We anticipate the net proceeds from the issue and sale of the notes, after deducting underwriting discounts and commissions, and our estimated expenses will be approximately US$3,225,837,500. We intend to use the net proceeds from the offering of the notes for general corporate purposes. See Use of Proceeds.

Data source: BHP Billiton Finance (USA) Prospectus, March 18, 2009.

EXHIBIT 5	BHP Billiton Group: Long-Term Debt (A)	
Bond Underwriters		
	2014 Notes	**2019 Notes**
Barclays Capital Inc.*	$ 300,000,000	$ 350,000,000
Citigroup Global Markets Inc.*	300,000,000	350,000,000
Goldman, Sachs & Co.*	300,000,000	350,000,000
BNP Paribas Securities Corp.	105,000,000	122,500,000
HSBC Securities (USA) Inc.	105,000,000	122,500,000
Santander Investment Securities Inc..	60,000,000	70,000,000
Banc of America Securities LLC	33,000,000	38,500,000
BBVA Securities	33,000,000	38,500,000
Commerzbank Capital Markets Corporation	33,000,000	38,500,000
Daiwa Securities SMBC Europe Ltd.	33,000,000	38,500,000
Lloyds TSB Bank plc.	33,000,000	38,500,000
Mizuho Securities USA Inc.	33,000,000	38,500,000
National Australia Bank Ltd	33,000,000	38,500,000
Scotia Capital (USA) Inc.	33,000,000	38,500,000
The Toronto-Dominion Bank	33,000,000	38,500,000
UBS Securities LLC	33,000,000	38,500,000
Total	$1,500,000,000	$1,750,000,000

*Barclays Capital Inc., Citigroup Global Markets Inc., and Goldman, Sachs & Co. were the joint book runners for the offering of the notes.
Data source: BHP Billiton Finance (USA) Prospectus, March 18, 2009.

SOLUTIONS TO REVIEW PROBLEMS

Solution 9.1

a. Proceeds of debt offering:

Present value of $50 million in 10 periods @ 4%: $50,000,000 × 0.67556	=	$33,778,000
+ Present value of $1,500,000 per period for 10 periods @ 4%: $1,500,000 × 8.11090	=	12,166,350
Proceeds		$45,944,350

b. Interest expense:

June 30: $45,944,350 × 0.04	=	$1,837,774
December 31: ($45,944,350 + $337,774) × 0.04	=	$1,851,285

c. Market value:

Present value of $50 million in 8 periods @ 5%: $50,000,000 × 0.67684	=	$33,842,000
+ Present value of $1,500,000 per period for 8 periods @ 5%: $1,500,000 × 6.46321	=	9,694,815
Market value		$43,536,815

d. Gain on retirement:

Book value of bonds	$45,944,350
Discount amortization (06/30)	337,774
Discount amortization (12/31)	351,285
Book value (12/31)	$46,633,409
Less: Market value.	(43,536,815)
Gain on early retirement.	$ 3,096,594

e. The Arcadia Company will recognize a gain of $3,096,594 on the debt retirement as a consequence of the decline in the market value of the bonds, associated with the market interest rate increase from eight to ten percent. Thus, if the debt is no longer needed to finance the operations of the company, the decision would be a good decision.

Solution 9.2

1.

Year	Minimum Lease Payment	PV of Minimum Lease Payment
2017	$ 975	$ 920
2018	890	792
2019	750	630
2020	670	531
2021	630	471
2022	630	444
2023	630	419
2024	630	395
2025	30	18
Total	$5,835	$4,620

2.

	(i) Without Capitalization	(ii) With Capitalization
Total liabilities to total assets	68.2%	73.7%*

*($15,000 + $4,620)/($22,000 + $4,620)

3. (i) as an operating lease

Amount of Borrowing	Interest Rate	Interest Expense
$ 4,000	4.5%	$180
6,500	7.0%	455
3,000	5.5%	165
$13,500		$800

Simple average of interest rates. 5.67%
Weighted-average (800/13,500). 5.93%

(ii) as a capital lease

Amount of Borrowing	Interest Rate	Interest Expense
$ 4,000	4.5%	$ 180
6,500	7.0%	455
3,000	5.5%	165
4,620	6.0%	277
$18,120		$1,077

Simple average of interest rates. 5.75%
Weighted-average (1,077/18,120) 5.94%

When you complete this chapter you should be able to:

1. Explain the difference between a commitment and a contingent liability. (page 380)

2. Describe deferred income tax and how this account increases and decreases. (page 382)

3. Explain how employee retirement obligations are reported and disclosed. (page 392)

4. Understand the importance of judgment in analyzing the balance sheet presentation of contingent liabilities. (page 397)

5. Describe how financial instruments and derivatives are valued and reported in corporate financial statements. (page 399)

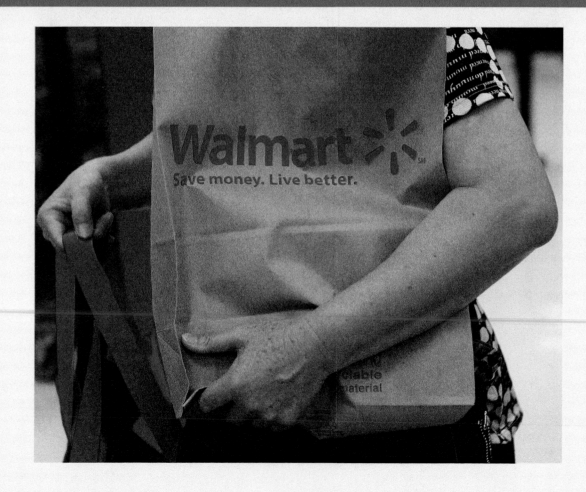

Commitments and Contingent Liabilities, Deferred Tax Liabilities, and Retirement Obligations

Wal-Mart Stores Inc., with its motto of "Low prices, always," has used its low-price strategy to fuel tremendous growth. Sam Walton, the company founder, opened the first Wal-Mart store in 1962 (called Walmart Discount City) and incorporated the business as *Wal-Mart Stores Inc.* in 1969, by which time it had expanded to 38 stores. As of January 2016, Wal-Mart was the world's largest retailer with over 11,500 retail units in 28 countries.

WAL-MART STORES INC.

The company refers to its 2.2 million employees as "associates." In addition, Wal-Mart stores in the United States and Canada have designated "greeters," whose role is to welcome shoppers at the store entrance and play a role in inventory loss prevention. It has been reported that 80 percent of U.S. residents shop at Wal-Mart at least once a year. Each week, over 200 million customers visit a Wal-Mart store and sales for fiscal year 2012 topped $440 billion. The company sells its goods in retail outlets, online and through mobile phone apps. In 2015 Wal-Mart was experimenting with online grocery delivery in select markets.

While Wal-Mart may be cheered by consumers for its low prices, others are more critical of the company. Wal-Mart has been criticized and sued by community groups, trade unions, and environmental groups for, among other things, its extensive foreign product sourcing, treatment of employees and product suppliers, environmental policies, use of public subsidies, and store impacts on local communities and businesses. One such investigation relates to the practices of Wal-Mart's Mexico subsidiary. The following description appeared in the company's 2015 annual report:

FCPA Investigation and Related Matters: The Audit Committee (the "Audit Committee") of the Board of Directors of the Company, which is composed solely of independent directors, is conducting an internal investigation into, among other things, alleged violations of the U.S. Foreign Corrupt Practices Act ("FCPA") and other alleged crimes or misconduct in connection with foreign subsidiaries, including Wal-Mart de México, S.A.B. de C.V. ("Walmex"), and whether prior allegations of such violations and/or misconduct were appropriately handled by the Company. The Audit Committee and the Company have engaged outside counsel from a number of law firms and other advisors who are assisting in the on-going investigation of these matters.

The Company has been informed by the DOJ and the SEC that it is also the subject of their respective investigations into possible violations of the FCPA. The Company is cooperating with the investigations by the DOJ and the SEC. A number of federal and local government agencies in Mexico have also initiated investigations of these matters. Walmex is cooperating with the Mexican governmental agencies conducting these investigations. Furthermore, lawsuits relating to the matters under investigation have been filed by several of the Company's shareholders against it, certain of its current directors, certain of its former directors, certain of its current and former officers and certain of Walmex's current and former officers.

Presented below is the liabilities section of Wal-Mart's 2015 balance sheet. Where does Wal-Mart disclose the potentially massive legal liability associated with the DOJ and SEC investigations?

(continued on next page)

Current liabilities:	
Short-term borrowings...	$ 1,592
Accounts payable..	38,410
Accrued liabilities..	19,152
Accrued income taxes...	1,021
Long-term debt due within one year...	4,810
Obligations under capital leases due within one year...........................	287
Total current liabilities...	65,272
Long-term debt...	41,086
Long-term obligations under capital leases......................................	2,606
Deferred income taxes and other..	8,805
Commitments and contingencies	—

If you guessed that the investigation is disclosed under "commitments and contingencies" with a zero balance, you are correct. Under U.S. GAAP, a company is required to record its potential litigation exposure only if the company concludes that it is highly probable that it will lose the ruling and if the amount of any potential award can be reasonably estimated. Wal-Mart is either unable to reasonably estimate the possible loss that may result from this investigation, or it expects to be exonerated. Consequently, the company is not required to record a liability for its potential loss.

In this chapter, we examine the important category of potential liabilities called commitments and contingencies, along with two other corporate obligations, deferred income tax liabilities and employee retirement obligations. In Appendix 10B we examine another potential obligation—financial instruments and derivatives.

EXECUTIVE OUTLINE

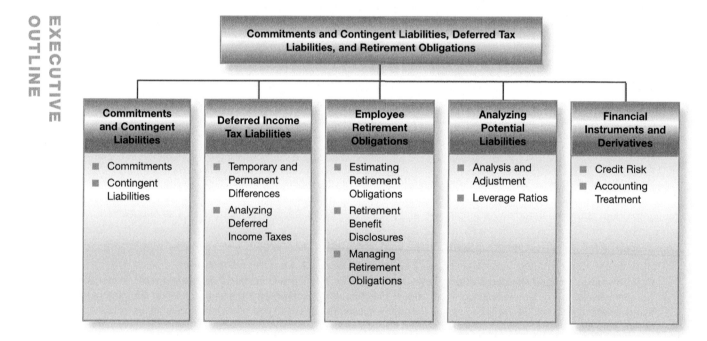

Commitments and Contingent Liabilities, Deferred Tax Liabilities, and Retirement Obligations

Commitments and Contingent Liabilities	Deferred Income Tax Liabilities	Employee Retirement Obligations	Analyzing Potential Liabilities	Financial Instruments and Derivatives
■ Commitments ■ Contingent Liabilities	■ Temporary and Permanent Differences ■ Analyzing Deferred Income Taxes	■ Estimating Retirement Obligations ■ Retirement Benefit Disclosures ■ Managing Retirement Obligations	■ Analysis and Adjustment ■ Leverage Ratios	■ Credit Risk ■ Accounting Treatment

COMMITMENTS AND CONTINGENT LIABILITIES

eLectures
MBC

Takeaway 1
Explain the difference between a commitment and a contingent liability.

In the day-to-day running of most businesses, it is common for the managers of a company to engage in **executory contracts** on behalf of the business. An executory contract is an agreement that calls for some form of future performance by both parties to the agreement, often involving an exchange of assets. For example, we reviewed a most basic type of executory contract in Chapter 9—a short-term rental agreement. A company signs a contract agreeing to pay a fixed rent, and in exchange the property owner explicitly agrees to provide the use of the property (i.e., an operating lease). As another example of an executory contract, management may sign a **purchase commitment** with one of a company's key suppliers, committing the firm to buy certain quantities of raw materials in the future. Since financial statements portray "what is" or "what has been" and not "what will be," executory contracts and the related future obligation to perform are not reported in the financial statements, although they are frequently described in the footnotes to the financial statements.

In accounting language, executory contracts are referred to as **commitments**—that is, an unexecuted contract in which the amount of the pending obligation is *relatively certain*. Examples include bank lines of credit, operating leases, purchase commitments, and take-or-pay contracts. In the case of a bank **line of credit**, when a borrower draws down on a credit line, the executory component of the contract is executed—the lender has provided cash and the borrower is now obligated to pay—and the amount of the borrowing must be reported on the borrower's balance sheet along with the amount of borrowed cash. Similarly, in the case of a purchase agreement, as

> A **line of credit** is a guaranteed loan, which may be used by a borrower in whole or in part. The borrower pays a fee to gain access to the line of credit and pays interest on any borrowed amounts.

soon as the promised product is delivered, a contractual obligation to pay the supplier is created and must be recorded on the face of the purchaser's balance sheet, along with the newly acquired inventory. Until those events occur, however, the obligation to buy the goods at some point in the future or the obligation to repay unborrowed funds under a line of credit need only be disclosed in the footnotes to the financial statements.

Closely related to commitments are **contingent liabilities**—that is, an obligation contingent upon the occurrence of some future event in which the amount of the pending obligation is *relatively uncertain*. Examples include the financial settlement of a pending lawsuit, environmental clean-up responsibilities, loan guarantees, and the potential reimbursement associated with accounts receivable sold with recourse. In the case of an **account receivable sold with recourse**, the seller of an account receivable is uncertain what its future reimbursement obligation to a **factor** will be until the factor tries, and fails, to collect on a specific account receivable. Similarly, in the case of a pending lawsuit, until a court verdict is rendered in which the defendant-firm is judged to have damaged the plaintiff and an award to the plaintiff is assessed, there is uncertainty as to whether an award will occur and how large the award will be.

> A **"factor"** is a third party that purchases accounts receivable from companies at a discount. The factor will then attempt to collect the receivables from the original customer. When receivables are factored without recourse, the transaction is treated as a sale of the receivables by the company. When sold with recourse, if the recourse provision cannot be valued at the transaction date, the transaction is treated as a loan to the company with the accounts receivable the collateral.

GLOBAL PERSPECTIVE

The accounting for some executory contracts under U.S. GAAP and IFRS differs significantly. For example, under U.S. GAAP, purchase commitments are not reported on the balance sheet but instead are disclosed in the footnotes to the financial statements. These executory contracts fail to meet the definition of an accounting liability under U.S. GAAP, although it is widely acknowledged that they represent economic liabilities to an entity. Under IFRS, however, purchase commitments are disclosed on the balance sheet when a company has a clear and demonstrable commitment to another entity. In effect, IFRS is more effective in restricting the incidence of off-balance-sheet debt than is U.S. GAAP.

How and where contingencies are disclosed in corporate financial statements is determined based on the probability of occurrence of the future event and whether an amount can be reliably estimated. **Gain contingencies**, such as the expectation of winning a financial settlement in a lawsuit, are almost never accrued on the financial statements and are rarely even disclosed in the footnotes. Instead, under the **conservatism principle** (see Chapter 6), gain contingencies are normally only recognized when they are realized (i.e., when the event occurs). Liabilities from **loss contingencies**, on the other hand, are commonly disclosed and sometimes must be accrued on the financial statements if certain conditions are met. Specifically, if a loss contingency is both *probable* and can be *reliably estimated*, then it must be accrued as a liability on the balance sheet, with the corresponding loss recorded on the income statement and as a reduction to retained earnings. If, however, a loss contingency is probable but the amount cannot be reliably estimated, or the probability of occurrence is only *reasonably possible*, the contingency must be disclosed via the footnotes but not accrued on the financial statements. The investigation of Wal-Mart described in the vignette at the beginning of this chapter falls under this category, and therefore, Wal-Mart elected to disclose but not accrue for this loss contingency. Finally, if the probability of occurrence of a loss is deemed to be only *remote*, then it can be ignored (i.e., not recorded on the balance sheet and not disclosed in the footnotes). It should be noted that existing accounting standards do not provide detailed definitions as to what level of probability is considered probable, reasonably possible, or remote. Therefore, a company's management team has considerable discretion as to which contingencies are accrued, which are disclosed, and which are simply ignored. Often legal considerations and risk management figure into the financial statement disclosure decision—management may feel it is safer to disclose a loss contingency in the footnotes even if they truly believe that the contingency is remote.

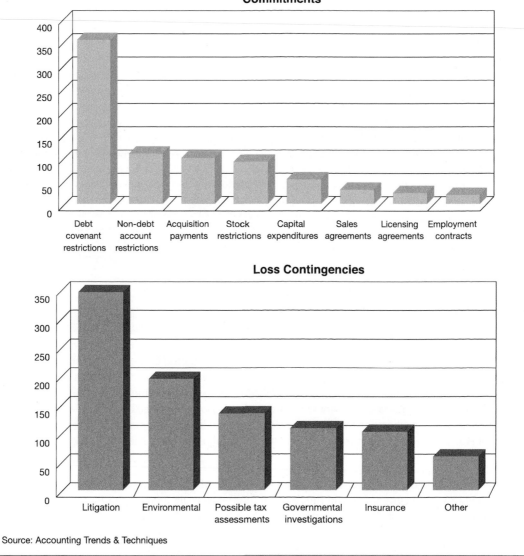

In Practice 10.1 *Commitments and Contingencies: A Glimpse of a Sample of Fortune 1000 Companies*   The following graphs summarize the types of commitments and loss contingencies disclosed by 500 sampled companies with fiscal years ending in 2010. As can be seen, debt covenant restrictions represent the most frequently disclosed commitment, while litigation is the most frequently disclosed source of loss contingency:

Source: Accounting Trends & Techniques

The commonality of commitments and contingent liabilities is that if and when a specific future event occurs, the firm will face an economic obligation, in most cases involving the payment of cash. Commitments and contingent liabilities are most commonly disclosed in the footnotes to the financial statements, especially if they are material in amount. They constitute an important source of information about a firm's future credit risk and cash flow obligations, and they should be carefully considered by investors and shareholders as they evaluate the future financial well-being of a company.

Takeaway 2
Describe deferred income tax and how this account increases and decreases.

DEFERRED INCOME TAX LIABILITIES

One frequently hears that firms "keep more than one set of books." This statement is often erroneously interpreted to indicate that a firm is doing something unethical, illegal, or at best, "shady." Quite the contrary, most firms are forced to maintain at least two sets of accounting records since the rules governing

BUSINESS PERSPECTIVE

Microsoft Corporation

Contingent liabilities are important disclosures, and they are very common. To inform investors of potential damaging litigation losses, Microsoft Corporation had disclosed for 12 consecutive years the details of a pending lawsuit with Novell in its annual reports. In November 2004, Novell, Inc. ("Novell") filed a complaint against Microsoft asserting antitrust and unfair competition claims related to Novell's ownership of WordPerfect and other applications. After the trial court dismissed or granted summary judgment on a number of Novell's claims, litigation of the one remaining claim took place in late 2011. The result was a mistrial. In July 2012, the trial court granted Microsoft's motion for judgment as a matter of law, and Novell later appealed this decision to the U.S. Court of Appeals for the Tenth Circuit. The appeals court affirmed the trial court's decision in September 2013, and the Supreme Court denied Novell's petition for review in April 2014. Over all of this time, no litigation loss had been disclosed by Microsoft, but status updates were included as supplements to the financial statements. Had a litigation loss (and liability) been reported by Microsoft, a reversal of this accounting would have been required in 2014.

financial accounting, as determined by GAAP, differ in many respects from the rules governing the calculation of **taxable income**, as determined in the United States by the Internal Revenue Code (IRC). It should not be surprising that there are significant differences between the measurement of net income under GAAP and the measurement of taxable income under IRC tax regulations. Throughout prior chapters, where appropriate, we have highlighted many of the more important key differences. The motivation for developing effective accounting standards differs from that associated with legislating tax policies. The goal of the FASB, for example, is to develop accounting practices that enable firms to measure and report their financial performance for investors and lenders in a "fair" manner. In essence, accounting standards are designed to help users adequately assess current and potential future investments. Tax regulations, on the other hand, are enacted by elected and appointed governmental officials. Their goal is to raise revenues to help achieve various public policy objectives, such as providing for social services, encouraging investment in R&D, or funding the military. In most cases, the differences in pretax net income created by differing financial accounting practices and income tax regulations are only temporary, and over time, the financial effects of any differences will be eliminated. To appreciate this, consider that over the life of a company the total amount of aggregate income taxes actually paid to the taxation authority should (and in most cases, does) equal the aggregate income tax expense reported on the income statements for financial statement purposes. But in any given year the amounts paid and the amounts expensed frequently differ.

The questions that arise then are: "What amount should be reported as the income tax expense on a firm's income statement?" Should it be the amount of tax appearing on the firm's income tax return based on taxable income? Or should it be the estimated tax expense based on net earnings calculated under GAAP? It is the latter. U.S. GAAP requires that a firm compute its accounting income tax expense based on its GAAP earnings so as to properly *match* its

U.S. corporate income tax rates vary as a function of the level of taxable income. For 2015, those rates were as follows:

Taxable Income	Tax Rate %
0 to $50,000	15
$50,001 to $75,000	25
$75,001 to $100,000	34
$100,001 to $335,000	39
$335,001 to $10,000,000	34
$10,000,001 to $15,000,000	35
$15,000,001 to $18,333,333	38
Over $18,333,333	35

reported income tax expense with its revenues from the same period. Unfortunately, this creates some confusion because the reported financial accounting tax expense for a given period is unlikely to equal the firm's income tax liability for that same period according to the Internal Revenue Service (IRS) and other tax authorities. But understanding why this inequality occurs is important. The focus of GAAP on the accrual concept requires recording a tax charge (or benefit) for those amounts included in GAAP net income for that period. The actual timing of when that expense is paid may be based on what is currently due, or may be based on what is *deferred* to a future period.

The discrepancy between GAAP net income and taxable net income can arise from two types of policy differences—permanent and temporary differences. **Permanent differences** are those that never reconcile because they will never be taxed or be a deduction in computing taxes. Examples of permanent differences include the interest from municipal bonds, which is included in GAAP net income but excluded from IRC taxable income. The payment of fines in contrast is another example, as these amounts are often not deductible for income tax purposes but are recorded as a business expense on a firm's corporate income statement. **Temporary differences** are timing differences between GAAP and taxable income that will reverse over time, and hence, eventually fully reconcile. An example of a temporary difference is the income difference created by using straight-line depreciation for accounting purposes and MACRS depreciation for income tax purposes (see Chapter 7).

The **deferred income tax** account is used to reconcile the temporary timing differences between a firm's tax expense based on its GAAP earnings and the taxes actually paid to the U.S. Department of Treasury and other tax authorities (i.e., state and international government tax authorities). It can take the form of either an asset (i.e., amounts to be recovered in the future from tax timing differences) or a liability (i.e., amounts to be paid in the future from tax timing differences). Whether the deferred income tax account is an asset or a liability depends on the nature of the timing differences, but in all cases those timing differences must be temporary. The deferred income tax account does not reconcile the permanent GAAP versus Internal Revenue Code differences that exist between a firm's accounting and taxable earnings because, as the name implies, "permanent differences" will persist indefinitely. Thus, the deferred tax asset or liability would never be received or paid. Recall also from Chapter 2 that one of the disciplines imposed on the balance sheet is that it must always balance, and the deferred income tax account helps satisfy this requirement. The Deferred Income Tax account is the cumulative, after-tax effect of the difference between a firm's income tax expense reported in its income statement and the income taxes actually paid that result from the accounting/tax policy differentials that arise in the measurement of net income. Examples of these accounting/tax policy differentials include the following:

Income Statement Item	Example Accounting and Tax Policy Differences	
	Common Accounting Policy	Required Tax Policy
• Revenue	• Percentage-of-completion	• Completed contract
• Bad debt expense	• Expense estimated using an aging schedule	• Estimates not permitted; tax deduction based on actual receivable write-offs.
• Depreciation expense	• Straight-line method	• Modified accelerated cost recovery system (MACRS)
• Warranty expense	• Expense estimated based on historical experience	• Estimates not permitted; tax deduction based on actual payments for warranty repairs.
• Gain (loss) in value of trading marketable securities	• Unrealized gain (loss) recognized under mark-to-market accounting	• Unrealized gains (losses) not recognized until gain (loss) is realized

To illustrate how *temporary* differences between a firm's accounting income tax expense and the income taxes actually paid may arise, consider the case of Arcadia Inc. Arcadia purchased a piece of equipment costing $100,000, having an expected useful life of eight years, but with an uncertain residual value at retirement. Under the **Modified Accelerated Cost Recovery System (MACRS)** used to depreciate all business assets for U.S. income tax purposes, depreciable assets are first classified into a "life category" (such as a three-year asset, a five-year asset, etc.). Each asset life category then specifies how much depreciation may be taken on the asset in any year. If we assume that Arcadia's equipment qualified for depreciation as a five-year asset,[1] it would be depreciated at the following established MACRS rates:

---

[1] Although the expected useful life of Arcadia's asset was eight years, for MACRS purposes it qualified as a five-year asset. This is not unusual as the rapid write-off of assets for income tax purposes has been found to be an effective economic stimulus technique used for promoting business investment in new capital assets.

	MACRS Depreciation	
Five-Year Asset		**Depreciation Percentage**
1st Year.		20.00%
2nd Year		32.00
3rd Year		19.20
4th Year		11.52
5th Year		11.52
Residual value		5.76
		100.00%

If Arcadia depreciates the asset using the straight-line method for financial statement purposes over its expected useful life of eight years, and assuming no salvage value at retirement, the depreciation expense for GAAP financial accounting and income tax purposes would be as follows:

	Depreciation Expense		Annual	
	GAAP Books: Straight-line	**Tax Books: MACRS**	**Temporary Difference**	**Cumulative Temporary Difference**
1st Year.	$ 12,500	$ 20,000	$ 7,500	$ 7,500
2nd Year	12,500	32,000	19,500	27,000
3rd Year	12,500	19,200	6,700	33,700
4th Year	12,500	11,520	(980)	32,720
5th Year	12,500	11,520	(980)	31,740
6th Year	12,500	5,760	(6,740)	25,000
7th Year	12,500	0	(12,500)	12,500
8th Year	12,500	0	(12,500)	0
	$100,000	$100,000	$ 0	

Notice that the depreciation expense taken under the MACRS system for income tax purposes exceeds the straight-line depreciation charge for accounting purposes in Years 1 through 3; but, beginning in Year 4, the depreciation expense for accounting purposes exceeds the MACRS depreciation deduction. Over the life of the asset, the total depreciation expense reported for accounting and tax purposes is the same ($100,000), but the amount reported in any given year differs—and hence, the notion of a temporary difference. Exhibit 10.1 presents a graphical comparison of Arcadia's depreciation expense for GAAP and income tax purposes. The shaded area in Exhibit 10.1 represents the temporary difference between the GAAP and tax depreciation expense that will arise over the life of the asset as a consequence of the differing depreciation treatments.

Assuming Arcadia's pretax income before depreciation expense is $60,000 each year, the company's pretax income after depreciation and its subsequent income tax expense, assuming a 25 percent tax rate, for GAAP and tax purposes is presented in Exhibit 10.2. At the end of Year 1, Arcadia Inc. will make a cash payment of $10,000 to the IRS for its current year income taxes and will report an income statement deduction for its current tax expense of $11,875. To bring the financial statements into balance, it is necessary to create a deferred income tax liability of $1,875 on the company's balance sheet. Thus, Arcadia's **deferred income tax liability** represents the future taxes *to be paid* on the incremental income ($47,500 − $40,000 = $7,500) that has been reported to the shareholders of the company *but not yet* reported to the taxation authorities.

At the end of Year 2, Arcadia will make a cash payment of $7,000 to the IRS for its current income taxes. On the other hand, Arcadia will report an income statement deduction for its current period income tax expense of $11,875. To bring Arcadia's financial statements into balance, it is necessary to increase the deferred income tax liability by $4,875, for a cumulative total of $6,750 (see **bolded** value in Exhibit 10.2). By the end of Year 2, Arcadia has disclosed $27,000 ($7,500 + $19,500) more of net income to its shareholders that has not yet been reported to the IRS.

At the end of Year 3, Arcadia will make a cash payment of $10,200 for its current income taxes, while reporting an income statement deduction for its income tax expense of $11,875. To bring its financial statements into balance, Arcadia will increase its Deferred Income Tax liability by $1,675, for a total cumulative deferred income tax liability at the end of Year 3 of $8,425. By the end of Year 3, Arcadia has reported $33,700 ($7,500 +$19,500 + $6,700) in additional net income to its shareholders that has not yet been reported to the IRS for which it will eventually pay future taxes of $8,425 ($33,700 × 25 percent).

| EXHIBIT 10.1 | A Comparison of Depreciation Expense: GAAP Straight-line vs. MACRS |

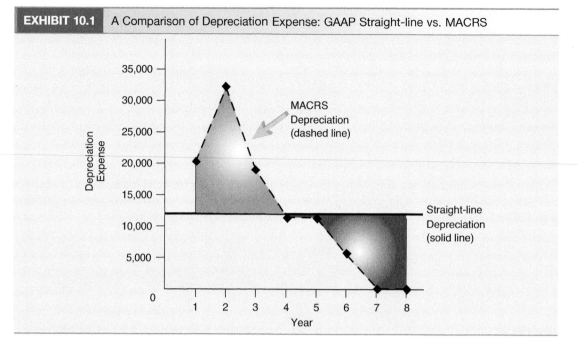

| EXHIBIT 10.2 | Calculating the Deferred Income Tax Liability |

	Pretax Income* After Depreciation		Tax Expense	Tax Due	Deferred Income Tax Expense	Cumulative Deferred Income Tax
	GAAP	**IRS**	**(GAAP × .25)**	**(IRS × .25)**	**(Benefit)**	**Liability**
1st Year.	$ 47,500	$ 40,000	$11,875	$10,000	$ 1,875	$1,875
2nd Year	47,500	28,000	11,875	7,000	4,875	**6,750**
3rd Year	47,500	40,800	11,875	10,200	1,675	8,425
4th Year	47,500	48,480	11,875	12,120	(245)	8,180
5th Year	47,500	48,480	11,875	12,120	(245)	7,935
6th Year	47,500	54,240	11,875	13,560	(1,685)	6,250
7th Year	47,500	60,000	11,875	15,000	(3,125)	3,125
8th Year	47,500	60,000	11,875	15,000	(3,125)	0
	$380,000	$380,000	$95,000	$95,000	$ 0	

*Pretax net income before depreciation is $60,000 annually. Assumed 25% tax rate.

At the end of Year 4, the temporary differences created in Years 1, 2 and 3 begin to reverse. (Observe in Exhibit 10.1, for example, that the MACRS line dips below the straight-line depreciation line.) Arcadia will make a cash payment of $12,120 to the IRS for its current period income taxes, but will show an income statement deduction for its income tax expense of only $11,875. As a consequence, the Deferred Income Tax liability account is reduced by $245, and thus, the cumulative deferred income tax liability at the end of Year 4 declines to $8,180. These financial effects are summarized in Arcadia's spreadsheet in Exhibit 10.3 (see **bolded** values). At the end of Year 4, the amount of income reported to Arcadia's shareholders but not yet reported to the IRS declines to $32,720 [$7,500 + $19,500 + $6,700 + ($980)].

The decline in the Deferred Income Tax liability account continues in Years 5, 6, 7, and 8 as the cash income taxes paid to the IRS grow relative to the income tax expense reported on Arcadia's income statement. This result occurs because the MACRS depreciation is heavily loaded into Years 1, 2, and 3 of the asset's life, and then dramatically declines to zero in Years 7 and 8, causing increasing amounts of Arcadia's net income to be exposed to income taxes in Years 4 through 8. In essence, MACRS provides a **depreciation tax shield** in the early years of the asset's life, and thereafter, increasingly exposes the company's income to taxation (see shaded areas in Exhibit 10.1).

By the end of Year 8, Arcadia's cumulative income reported to shareholders and to the IRS will total $380,000; and, the cumulative income taxes actually paid and the aggregate accounting tax expense will total $95,000 (see Exhibit 10.2). Thus, over the life of Arcadia's equipment, the differences in taxable income caused by using different depreciation approaches for income tax and accounting purposes are eliminated, reflecting their temporary nature.

In Practice 10.2 *Corporate Tax Rates Around the World*   The 35 percent statutory tax rate on income earned by U.S. corporations has been a political hot button for years. It is the highest corporate tax rate of any developed country, and opponents of such a high rate argue it puts U.S. companies at a competitive disadvantage. Others argue that many companies hardly ever pay the full 35 percent due to the numerous tax code loopholes. Two items cannot be disputed however. First, unlike most countries in the world, the U.S. has adopted a territorial taxation system whereby companies must pay U.S. taxes on their profits earned overseas that is repatriated to the U.S. This has caused many companies to "park" their earned profits in foreign countries to avoid the incremental tax that would be due. Second, many companies have chosen to relocate their corporate headquarters overseas (e.g., to Bermuda, where corporate income taxes are zero), by acquiring firms in lower tax countries to take advantage of lower rates. This technique is called a "tax inversion," and legislators have denounced such moves as unpatriotic. Recent examples of tax inversions include Medtronic (to Netherlands), Burger King (to Canada), and Actavis (to Ireland). Below is a 2015 listing of the statutory tax rates by select countries:

Country	Statutory Tax Rate
Argentina	35.0%
Australia	30.0%
Brazil	34.0%
Canada	15.0%
China	25.0%
France	33.3%
Germany	15.0%
India	30.0%
Ireland	12.5%
Italy	27.5%
Japan	23.9%
Mexico	30.0%
Portugal	21.0%
Russia	20.0%
Saudi Arabia	20.0%
Spain	28.0%
Switzerland	8.5%
Turkey	20.0%
United Kingdom	20.0%
United States	35.0%

Source: Deloitte Touche Tohmatsu Limited, 2015

EXHIBIT 10.3	Accounting for Deferred Income Taxes								
Year:	**1**	**2**	**3**	**4**	**5**	**6**	**7**	**8**	**Totals**
Assets									
Cash	(10,000)	(7,000)	(10,200)	**(12,120)**	(12,120)	(13,560)	(15,000)	(15,000)	(95,000)
Liabilities									
Deferred income tax	1,875	4,875	1,675	**(245)**	(245)	(1,685)	(3,125)	(3,125)	—
Shareholders' Equity									
Retained earnings:									(95,000)
Tax expense	(11,875)	(11,875)	(11,875)	**(11,875)**	(11,875)	(11,875)	(11,875)	(11,875)	

A = L + SE

Analyzing Deferred Income Taxes

The Arcadia Inc. illustration shows how one policy differential involving the depreciation of equipment affects not only a company's income statement but its balance sheet as well. These policy differences do not, however, affect the statement of cash flow as the amount of cash paid for income taxes is unchanged (it is based on the actual income taxes paid to the IRS).

Deferred income taxes can result from many accounting and tax policy differences, thus potentially creating both deferred income tax liabilities, as illustrated above, and **deferred income tax assets**. In general, the existence of a large deferred income tax liability is often viewed favorably by investment professionals who recognize that the balance of the deferred income tax liability effectively represents an interest-free loan from the tax authorities. Financing a business with interest-free debt creates considerable shareholder value.

Deferred income tax liabilities are common on the financial statements of many U.S. corporations. In fact, a recent study by the U.S. General Accounting Office of the income taxes actually paid by U.S. corporations for the period 1989 to 2000, revealed that 63 percent of the companies paid no income taxes at all![2] Thus, for the majority of U.S. firms, most (and sometimes all) of the income tax expense reported on corporate income statements is effectively deferred, creating a substantial future obligation, as well as considerable interest-free financing from the U.S. Department of Treasury.

TAX PERSPECTIVE

Net Operating Losses

When a company experiences a net operating loss (NOL) during a period, IRS regulations allow the company to carry such losses back up to two years to offset any previously taxed income and obtain a refund of any previously paid income taxes. In the event that the operating loss is large enough to more than offset taxable earnings of the previous two years, the excess operating loss may be carried forward up to 20 years to reduce future income taxes. **NOL carryforwards** and **NOL carrybacks** are found in the tax provisions of most countries; however, the length of the carryback/carryforward period varies dramatically between countries.

The potential future tax savings associated with NOL carryforwards are usually disclosed in the footnotes to the financial statements because of their importance in estimating future operating cash flows. Also recognize that NOL carryforwards will create a *deferred tax asset* for a company. This is because under the matching concept the GAAP net operating loss reported will require an accrued tax benefit on the income statement, but the realization of that benefit for IRS purposes will be deferred to a future year. The tax authorities therefore "owe" the company.

Unlike most long-term corporate debt, accounting rules require that deferred income tax liabilities are not discounted; instead, they are valued at their future expected settlement value and not their present value. It also would not be possible to use the present value approach to value these liabilities since the exact date of their payment is unknown (payment of a deferred income tax liability depends upon the future performance of the firm, which of course, is unknown).

GLOBAL PERSPECTIVE

The amount of deferred income tax reported on the balance sheets of multinational corporations varies dramatically from country to country. In the United States, the U.K., and Canada, where significant accounting/tax policy differentials exist, the deferred income tax obligation of large, mature companies can be substantial. However, in Germany and Japan, the amount of permitted accounting/tax policy differentials is constrained, and as a consequence, the deferred income tax obligation of companies from these countries is frequently immaterial in amount.

BUSINESS PERSPECTIVE

General Electric and Corporate Taxes

General Electric (GE) is not only one of the most successful U.S. companies of all time, it also happens to be very adept at minimizing the amount of corporate taxes it pays to the U.S. government. In early 2011 the financial press stoked a controversy when it was reported that GE earned worldwide profit of $14.2 billion—but paid no taxes. In fact, the company claimed a tax benefit of $3.2 billion! While this made for some bad press for the company, minimizing the tax bill was nothing new for GE. The company had long mixed a combination of skilled tax accountants, aggressive tax strategies, and rigorous

continued

---

[2] *Wall Street Journal,* April 7, 2004.

lobbying to gain a tax advantage and help boost bottom line profits. A historical analysis by one trade group concluded that GE paid an average tax rate of just 2.3 percent over the decade ending in 2011, a far cry from the required 35 percent tax rate expected for companies of GE's size and profitability.* So how does the company pull this off? The reasons are many and complex, but most have concluded that GE's heavy push for favorable changes in the tax law, credits for such things as "green energy" initiatives undertaken by the company, and its vast overseas operations that are minimally taxed as long as the profits remain overseas, have all led to a tax burden much smaller proportionally than for other U.S. companies.

In the years since the 2011 publicity over its lack of paying U.S. corporate taxes, GE has continued to keep its tax rate well below the 35 percent statutory rate. However , the company has been unable to get its effective rate to zero. GE's effective tax rate for 2012 through 2014 has averaged nearly 10 percent.

* *New York Times*, March 24, 2011

Some analysts use the information contained in a company's income tax footnote to gain insight into the degree of discretion that management has used in its financial reporting. One measure of the degree of how aggressive a company's accounting policy choices have been is the **conservatism ratio**, defined as:

$$\text{Conservatism ratio} = \text{Net income before taxes/Taxable income}$$

The theory behind this ratio is that firms will choose to delay paying their income taxes as long as it is legally possible and will, therefore, make accounting policy choices that accelerate expenses and defer revenues in reporting taxable income, the denominator of the ratio. Thus, the more the ratio exceeds one, the more aggressive a firm's financial reporting can be assumed to be.

Pretax net income, the numerator in the conservatism ratio, can be taken directly from a company's income statement. Taxable income, on the other hand, must be computed from information contained in the income tax footnote, as follows:

$$\text{Taxable income} = \text{Current year tax liability/Effective tax rate}$$

Utilizing data from Kohl's fiscal year 2014 footnote disclosures, (see upcoming Business Perspective) we see that the current year income tax liability is $436 million ($400 million + $36 million) and the effective tax rate is 35.7 percent. The estimate of taxable income is, consequently, $1,221 million ($436 million/35.7 percent). Since pretax net income on the income statement is reported to be $1,349 million, Kohl's conservatism ratio is 1.10 ($1,349 million/$1,221 million). Given that Kohl's conservatism ratio is only slightly above 1, we can infer that Kohl's financial versus tax reporting is fairly neutral, or at worst only mildly aggressive.

BUSINESS PERSPECTIVE

Deferred Income Tax Disclosures

Kohl's Corporation operates over 1,100 specialty department stores throughout the United States. The company's consolidated balance sheets for the fiscal years 2014 (year ended January 31, 2015) and 2013 (year ended February 1, 2014) are presented below. The balance sheets reveal that Kohl's reports deferred income taxes both as an asset and as a liability (see bolded areas). Combining the deferred income tax asset and the deferred income tax liability reveals that Kohl's had a net deferred income tax liability of $252 million ($368 million − $116 million) and $197 million ($339 million − $142 million), respectively, in 2014 and 2013. These amounts are clearly material in amount, representing approximately three percent and two percent, respectively, of Kohl's outstanding obligations.

continued

continued from previous page

KOHL'S CORPORATION
Consolidated Balance Sheets

($ millions)	Jan. 31, 2015	Feb. 1, 2014
Assets		
Current assets		
Cash and cash equivalents.	$ 1,407	$ 971
Merchandise inventories.	3,814	3,874
Deferred income taxes.	**116**	**142**
Other.	361	327
Total current assets.	5,698	5,314
Property and equipment, net	8,515	8,745
Other assets.	218	298
Total assets.	$14,431	$14,357
Liabilities and Shareholders' Equity		
Current liabilities		
Accounts payable.	$ 1,511	$ 1,365
Accrued liabilities	1,160	1,138
Income taxes payable.	78	116
Current portion of capital lease and financing obligations.	110	139
Total current liabilities	2,859	2,758
Long-term debt	2,793	2,792
Capital lease and financing obligations	1,858	1,930
Deferred income taxes.	**368**	**339**
Other long-term liabilities.	562	560
Shareholders' equity		
Common stock—367 and 364 million shares issued	4	4
Paid-in capital.	2,743	2,598
Treasury stock, at cost, 166 and 153 million shares.	**(8,744)**	**(8,052)**
Accumulated other comprehensive loss	**(20)**	**(34)**
Retained earnings.	12,008	11,462
Total shareholders' equity.	5,991	5,978
Total liabilities and shareholders' equity.	$14,431	$14,357

KOHL'S CORPORATION
Consolidated Income Statements

($ millions)	2014	2013	2012
Net sales.	$19,023	$19,031	$19,279
Cost of merchandise sold	12,098	12,087	12,289
Gross margin	6,925	6,944	6,990
Selling, general, and administrative expenses	4,350	4,313	4,267
Depreciation and amortization	886	889	833
Operating income.	1,689	1,742	1,890
Interest expense, net	340	338	329
Income before income taxes.	**1,349**	**1,404**	**1,561**
Provision for income taxes	**482**	**515**	**575**
Net income.	$ 867	$ 889	$ 986

continued

10-K Income Tax Note

Deferred income taxes consist of the following:

($ millions)	Jan. 31, 2015	Feb. 1, 2014
Deferred tax liabilities		
Property and equipment......................................	$1,385	$1,416
Deferred tax assets		
Merchandise inventories.......................................	24	24
Accrued and other liabilities, including stock options	182	223
Capital lease and financing obligations	773	813
Accrued step rent liability......................................	100	94
Unrealized loss on investments		7
Unrealized loss on interest rate swap.............................	13	15
Federal benefit on state tax reserves..............................	41	43
	1,133	1,219
Net deferred tax liability	$ 252	$ 197

The components of the provision for income taxes are as follows:

($ millions)	2014	2013	2012
Current federal	$400	$473	$592
Current state..	36	45	60
Deferred federal	48	6	(68)
Deferred state..	(2)	(9)	(9)
	$482	$515	$575

The provision for income taxes differs from the amount that would be provided by applying the statutory U.S. corporate tax rate due to the following items:

Fiscal Year	2014	2013	2012
Provision at statutory rate	35.0%	35.0%	35.0%
State income taxes, net of federal tax benefit	1.3	2.2	2.2
Tax-exempt interest income...	—	(0.2)	(0.1)
Other federal tax credits...	(0.6)	(0.3)	(0.3)
Provision for income taxes...	35.7%	36.7%	36.8%

The footnotes to Kohl's financial statements reveal the sources of the company's net deferred tax liability. The income tax footnote data reveals that Kohl's accounting/tax policy differential involving depreciation on its property and equipment resulted in a deferred income tax liability of $1,385 million as of fiscal year 2014; however, this is offset by its accounting/tax policy differentials involving such items as inventory, accrued expenses, and unrealized losses that resulted in a deferred income tax asset of $1,133 million as of fiscal year 2014. In essence, Kohl's tax treatment of inventory and accrued expenses was less tax-advantaged than was its tax treatment of depreciation.

Kohl's income statement reports a fiscal year 2014 provision for income taxes—income tax expense—of $482 million on pretax income of $1,349 million. The increase in the net deferred income tax liability of $55 million ($252 million − $197 million) from fiscal year 2013 to fiscal year 2014 represents the amount of Kohl's current period income tax expense that will be paid at a later date. Kohl's income tax expense of $482 million on pretax income of $1,349 million yields an effective income tax rate of 35.7 percent, which differs from the U.S. statutory income tax rate of 35 percent largely as a consequence of state income taxes.

pension footnote due diligence is required to evaluate a firm's pension liability exposure under the prior pension plan accounting rules. In addition, it is prudent for financial statement users to consider whether the pension assumptions reported in the footnotes, including the discount rate, the estimated rate of wage increase, and the expected return on plan assets, are reasonable.

Chapter 9 discussed three ratios that are helpful when analyzing a firm's use of leverage. Those ratios include the long-term debt to total assets ratio, the long-term debt to shareholders' equity ratio, and the interest coverage ratio. These ratios can be useful for assessing a firm's solvency, with the caveat that it may be necessary to modify the level of reported debt for any material off-balance-sheet obligations reported in the footnotes.

ETHICS PERSPECTIVE

Different Sets of Books

Many firms maintain multiple sets of financial data for income tax purposes and for financial reporting purposes because of different rules governing GAAP-based financial reporting and income tax reporting governed by the U.S. Internal Revenue Code. No one should question a firm's ethical standards for maintaining these multiple sets of books since the firms are simply complying with external reporting requirements. In addition to the record keeping required for GAAP financial reporting and tax reporting, firms sometimes keep a third set of books. This supplemental financial reporting is often used for internal decision-making and for incentive compensation contracts. Unlike GAAP reporting and income tax reporting, the assumptions used for internal reporting purposes are rarely, if ever, disclosed to individuals outside the firm to protect a firm's competitive market position.

EXECUTIVE SUMMARY

This chapter concludes our investigation of corporate liabilities. Specifically, we examined the valuation and financial statement disclosure of such potential obligations as commitments and contingent liabilities, deferred income tax liabilities, unfunded retirement obligations, and financial derivatives (see Appendix 10A). In Chapter 11, we consider the shareholders' equity section of the balance sheet and examine how companies raise capital through the sale of equity instruments.

As a validation of your understanding of the content of this chapter, you should now be able to:

- Explain the difference between a commitment and a contingent liability.
- Explain deferred income tax and how this account increases and decreases.
- Explain how employee retirement obligations are reported and disclosed.
- Understand the importance of judgment in analyzing the balance sheet presentation of contingent liabilities.
- Explain how financial instruments and derivatives are valued and reported in corporate financial statements (see Appendix 10A).

KEY CONCEPTS AND TERMS

Account receivable sold with
  recourse, 381
Benefit cost, 394
Commitments, 381
Conservatism ratio, 389
Contingent liabilities, 381
Contributory, 392
Counterparties, 399
Deferred income tax, 384
Deferred income tax assets, 388
Deferred income tax liability, 385
Defined benefit plans, 392
Defined contribution plans, 392
Depreciation tax shield, 386

Derivative financial instruments, 399
Executory contracts, 380
Factor, 381
Financial instruments, 399
Funding status, 393
Gain contingencies, 381
Interest cost, 393
Interest rate swap, 399
Investment return, 393
Line of credit, 381
Loss contingencies, 381
Modified Accelerated Cost Recovery
  System (MACRS), 384
Noncontributory, 392

Permanent differences, 383
Plan assets at fair value, 394
Projected benefit obligation
  (PBO), 394
Purchase commitment, 380
Repo agreement, 399
Service cost, 393
Taxable income, 383
Temporary differences, 384
Trustee, 392
Zero-sum game, 399

APPENDIX 10A: Financial Instruments and Derivatives

As businesses have come under increasing pressure from shareholders to maximize firm value, more and more firms have begun utilizing exotic financial contracts to minimize the risk of business losses and maximize the likelihood of business gains. Examples of such contracts include financial instruments and derivative securities.

Financial instruments are financial contracts that impose an obligation on a business that uses these instruments to exchange cash (or some other financial asset) under potentially unfavorable conditions. (Not all financial instruments are obligations; some are assets. We restrict our consideration to those financial instruments that impact a firm's credit risk.) Examples include repurchase or repo agreements, forward purchase agreements for securities or commodities, and various hybrids of these instruments. For example, a business with excess cash, desiring to maximize its return on its excess cash, might purchase a portfolio of bonds from a brokerage firm under a repurchase agreement. During the term of the **repo agreement**, often six months to one year, the business receives interest income from its investment in the portfolio of bonds. However, at the end of the agreement, the business is obligated to sell the portfolio of bonds back to the brokerage firm at their original purchase price; and, as a consequence, the buyer is protected from any loss due to a decline in the principal value of the bond investment. Both parties to the repo agreement, however, are exposed to market risk—that is, the risk that the market value of the portfolio of bonds could be greater than or less than the amount that the purchaser originally paid for them. If the bond portfolio declines in value because of an increase in market interest rates, the brokerage firm loses while the purchaser gains. On the other hand, if the portfolio gains in value, the brokerage firm gains and the purchaser loses. A repo agreement is, in effect, a **zero-sum game**—one party gains what the other party loses! Why would a company engage in a repo arrangement? In an attempt to maximize the return on its excess cash, and thus, maximize shareholder value.

Derivative financial instruments are financial contracts that derive their value from some other asset or index. Examples include options, forward contracts, futures contracts, and interest rate swaps. For example, to illustrate the mechanics of an **interest rate swap**, assume that Firm A has an outstanding note payable with a face value of $100,000 that bears interest at the rate of 7 percent, payable annually on December 31. Firm A has the option of repaying the note anytime prior to its maturity in five years; however, the amount of the repayment will be determined based on the market value of the note at the time of repayment. Firm A is worried that interest rates may fall and cause the value of the note to increase. Firm Z also has an outstanding note payable with a face value of $100,000 with payments due annually on December 31. In contrast to the Firm A note, Firm Z's note has a variable interest rate based on the prime lending rate. Firm Z is concerned that its cash flow will be harmed if interest rates increase, causing its interest payments to increase. To mitigate these risks, Firm Z may negotiate a contract to swap or exchange its interest payments with Firm A. This is typically accomplished through a swap dealer such as a bank that serves as an intermediary to bring together the two **counterparties** to the swap transaction. Under a swap arrangement, Firm A assumes responsibility for the payment of Firm Z's variable rate interest payment, whereas Firm Z assumes responsibility for the payment of Firm A's fixed rate interest payment. As a consequence of the swap, Firm Z locks in a fixed rate to protect its cash flow and Firm A will have a variable rate interest payment whose cash flow changes will be offset by the change in the fair value of its outstanding note. To illustrate the financial effects of an interest rate swap, assume that Companies A and Z agree to swap interest expense payments over a three-year period. Each firm has an outstanding loan obligation in the amount of $100,000, and while Company Z pays a variable rate equivalent to the London InterBank Offering Rate (LIBOR) as of the beginning of the year, Company A pays a fixed rate of 8 percent per year. At the beginning of the swap period, the LIBOR rate is also 8 percent, and hence, for the first year of the agreement, both firms pay interest charges of $8,000. At the beginning of the second year, however, the LIBOR rate rises to 10 percent; and, as a consequence, at year-end, Company A will make a variable payment of $10,000 while Company Z continues to pay $8,000 based on the fixed rate that it assumed in the swap. If, at the beginning of the third year, LIBOR resets to 12 percent, Company A's annual payment will amount to $12,000 while Company Z's payment remains fixed at $8,000. Over the three-year swap period, Company Z will have paid a total of $24,000 while Company A paid $30,000, $6,000 more than it would have paid had it not entered into the swap agreement. Company Z, on the other hand, saved $6,000 by entering into the swap agreement. Interest rate swaps are derivative instruments because they derive their value from movements in the general corporate borrowing rate. Like repo agreements, interest rate swaps are a zero-sum game in which one party gains while the other party loses.

Financial instruments such as repurchase agreements and derivative financial instruments such as interest rate swaps may constitute significant obligations for a company. Under U.S. GAAP, the accounting for these instruments depends upon a firm's intent in utilizing the instrument. Gains and losses on speculative hedge instruments that do not attempt to mitigate a business-related risk are reported in the income statement, whereas gains and losses on business-related hedges that qualify for hedge accounting treatment are matched with the corresponding gain or loss on the hedged item. If the gain (loss) on the hedged item is reported in current income, the loss (gain) on the related hedge instrument is likewise reported as part of current income. If, however, the gain (loss) on the hedged item is deferred to a later fiscal period, the loss (gain) from the related hedge instrument is reported in Other Comprehensive Income as a component of shareholders' equity. We will have more to say about unrealized gains and losses on derivative securities in Chapter 11. Under IASB GAAP, however, the unrealized gain (loss) on financial instruments is reported on the income statement rather than on the balance sheet as under U.S. GAAP. This divergence in practice between U.S. and IASB GAAP reflects the IASB's commitment to the use of market-value based accounting.

Takeaway 5
Describe how financial instruments and derivatives are valued and reported in corporate financial statements.

QUESTIONS

Q10.1 **Contingent Liability Accounting.** In September 2014, Home Depot stated that an estimated 56 million credit and debit cards were exposed during a five-month-long attack on its payment terminals. On September 19, 2014, the *New York Times* reported in "Ex-Employees Left Home Depot Data Vulnerable," that former employees of Home Depot, who asked to remain anonymous, alleged that the retailer's network was protected with outdated software, and that some cyber security team members left after managers allegedly dismissed their concerns. In the same article, the *New York Times* also stated that the breach may result in up to $3 billion in fraudulent charges. In the same month, a federal data breach class action lawsuit was filed against Home Depot on behalf of all customers nationwide whose personal information was compromised as a result of the data breach. The lawsuit alleged that Home Depot failed to take reasonable security measures to adequately protect its customers' personal data. It also asserted that Home Depot failed to disclose the data breach in a timely manner to its customers. Home Depot believed a loss from this litigation was reasonably possible, but that it was not able to estimate the costs, or a range of costs due to the uncertainty surrounding the entire matter. Discuss how Home Depot should have reported this litigation.

Q10.2 **Debt Covenants and Going-Concern Exceptions.** The May 2, 2006, edition of *The Financial Times* carried the following leading story headline:

Auditors to Warn over Sea Containers

The related article reported that Sea Containers Ltd., a Bermuda-based container leasing and passenger transport company, remained unable to file its 2005 financial statements with the U.S. Securities and Exchange Commission. The company reported that while it expected to receive an unqualified auditor's opinion on its 2005 financial report, it also "anticipated that there would be a paragraph (in the auditor's report) raising substantial doubt about (the company's) ability to continue as a going concern." When issuing an audit opinion, an audit firm may note one or more concerns that it has regarding a firm's reported results or its ability to continue to operate as a going concern. In March of 2006, Sea Containers disclosed to the public that it had violated some of its debt covenants when it wrote off $500 million of its leasing business, causing the firm's net worth to drop below required covenant minimums. Discuss why a violation of an existing debt covenant might cause an auditor to issue a going-concern exception about Sea Containers.

Q10.3 **Pension Accounting and Debt Covenants.** In 2006, the Financial Accounting Standards Board adopted new pension accounting guidance which required that, effective year-end 2007, pension and retirement-benefit plan surplus and deficit funding be disclosed on corporate balance sheets as an asset or liability, respectively. The new accounting, however, might adversely affect the ability of some businesses to satisfy their debt covenants on existing loan agreements. Consider, for example, Electronic Data Systems (EDS), which faced a debt covenant of a required minimum level of $6.42 billion in shareholders' equity. (EDS's shareholders' equity was $7.5 billion.) Under the new FASB pension accounting, EDS would be required to add $1.08 billion to its liabilities due to a pension plan funding deficit and also reduce its shareholders' equity to exactly the covenant minimum of $6.42 billion. Discuss how EDS should respond to the new pension accounting with respect to its creditors.

Q10.4 **Accounting for Pending Lawsuits.** On April 13, 2006, Bausch & Lomb Inc. pulled its ReNu contact lens solution from suppliers' shelves over mounting concerns that the product was linked to over 100 cases of a rare fungal eye infection (Fusarium Keratitis) that could lead to corneal damage and required corneal transplant. In a statement released on April 14, 2006, the Federal Food and Drug Administration indicated its support for the product recall/removal while the Center for Disease Control investigated Bausch & Lomb's production facilities for possible contamination. On May 9, 2006, the law firm of Weitz & Luxenberg filed a lawsuit against Bausch & Lomb on behalf of a Philadelphia client who was diagnosed with Fusarium Keratitis after using the ReNu product. Discuss how Bausch & Lomb should disclose the pending lawsuit in its 2006 annual report. Discuss the financial effects to Bausch & Lomb's financial statements associated with the ReNu product recall/removal.

Q10.5 **Interpreting Deferred Income Tax Assets.** The following information was taken from the 2014 annual report of Microsoft Inc.:

($ millions)	2014	2013
Current assets		
Deferred income taxes	$1,941	$1,632
Long-term liabilities		
Deferred income taxes	2,728	1,709

A review of the footnotes to Microsoft's annual report reveals that two major accounting policies affecting its deferred income taxes were (1) the accounting for unearned revenue and (2) the accounting for its portfolio of trading securities. When Microsoft sells a software product, it defers a portion of the revenue received to cover the cost of future technical service and free upgrades that may be provided during the warranty period. Discuss how Microsoft's accounting for unearned revenue and its accounting for its portfolio of trading securities could result in the creation of a deferred income tax asset. Discuss the difference between a current deferred income tax asset and a noncurrent deferred income tax asset.

Q10.6   **Interpreting Deferred Income Tax Liabilities.**   The following information is taken from the annual report of The Coca-Cola Company (KO):

($ millions)	2014	2013
Long-term deferred income tax liability	$5,636	$6,152

The footnotes to the company's annual report reveal that the primary contributor to its deferred income tax liability was its accounting for trademarks and other intangible assets. According to The Coca-Cola Company:

> Intangible assets are classified into one of three categories: (1) intangible assets with definite lives subject to amortization, (2) intangible assets with indefinite lives not subject to amortization and (3) goodwill. For intangible assets with definite lives, tests for impairment must be performed if conditions exist that indicate the carrying value may not be recoverable. For intangible assets with indefinite lives and goodwill, tests for impairment must be performed at least annually or more frequently if events or circumstances indicate that assets might be impaired.

Discuss why and how the company's accounting for intangible assets results in a deferred income tax liability. The long-term deferred income tax liability for trademarks and other intangible assets decreased by $172 million from 2013 to 2014; what does this decline suggest?

Q10.7   **Analyzing the Funding Status of a Pension Plan.**   The following information is taken from the annual report of The Coca-Cola Company:

Pension Plans ($ millions)	Year 1	Year 2
Benefit obligations (at end of year).	$2,576	$2,904
Fair value of plan assets.	1,810	2,221

Discuss whether Coca-Cola's pension plans are fully funded at year-end of Year 1 and Year 2. Did the company's funding improve from Year 1 to Year 2? The footnotes reveal that Coca-Cola changed the discount rate that it used to discount its benefit obligations from 5.8 percent in Year 1 to 5.4 percent in Year 2; how would this change likely impact the value of Coca-Cola's benefit obligation?

Q10.8   **Changing Pension Plan Assumptions.**   The annual report of Johnson & Johnson (J&J) disclosed the following information:

U.S. Retirement Plans	Year 1	Year 2	Year 3	Year 4
Discount rate	6.75%	6.00%	5.75%	5.75%
Expected long-term rate of return on plan assets	9.00	9.00	9.00	9.00
Rate of increase in compensation levels	4.50	4.50	4.50	4.50

Between Year 1 and Year 4, J&J lowered the discount rate used to calculate the present value of its projected benefit obligation from 6.75 percent to 5.75 percent, while it maintained the expected rate of return on plan assets at nine percent. Discuss how a lowering of the assumed discount rate while maintaining the expected rate of return on plan assets would impact J&J's pension obligations. Why would J&J lower the discount rate on its projected benefit obligation?

Q10.9   **Discounting Deferred Income Tax Liabilities.**   Deferred income tax liabilities arise because of differences in the policies used to account for revenue and expenses for financial reporting purposes versus the policies utilized to report revenue and expenses for income tax purposes. For instance, revenue might be recognized for financial reporting purposes at the point of sale, whereas for income tax purposes, revenue might be recognized at the point of cash collection using the installment method. It is generally accepted practice to discount liabilities to their present value for purposes of presentation on the balance sheet. Discuss why deferred income tax liabilities are not valued on corporate balance sheets at their present value.

Q10.10   **(Appendix 10A) Interest Rate Swaps.** The 2014 annual report of The Home Depot Inc. revealed the following information regarding its derivative securities:

> In November 2013, we entered into an interest rate swap that expires on September 10, 2018, with a notional amount of $500 million, accounted for as a fair value hedge, that swaps 2.25 percent fixed rate interest on the 2018 notes for variable interest equal to LIBOR plus 88 basis points. At February 1, 2015, the approximate fair value of this agreement was an asset of $8 million, which is the estimated amount we would have received to settle the agreement and is included in Other Assets in the accompanying Consolidated Balance Sheets.

Describe the financial effects of the swap for Home Depot. Why has Home Depot recorded the $8 million on its balance sheet? At what LIBOR rate does Home Depot lose from the swap? Discuss what is meant by a "zero-sum game."

Q10.11   **Underfunded Retirement Obligations and Firm Valuation.** In a prior annual report, Johnson & Johnson disclosed that its employee retirement obligations were underfunded by $2.063 billion at year-end. And, of this amount, only $475 million was reported on the company's balance sheet, leaving the remainder ($1.588 billion) as an off-balance-sheet liability. Discuss whether the off-balance-sheet portion of J&J's underfunded retirement obligation should be considered when calculating the value of Johnson & Johnson's capital stock.

Q10.12   **(Ethics Perspective) Multiple Sets of Books.** As noted in the ethics perspective at the end of this chapter, firms routinely maintain separate sets of books for their financial reporting and their tax reporting. Can you think of any reason why a firm would be justified in keeping a third, internal set of books? Do you feel that it is ethically acceptable to not fully disclose to shareholders how a company's internal books differ from those used for external reporting purposes?

Assignments with the 🌐 logo in the margin are available in BusinessCourse.
See the Preface of the book for details.
CHECK FIGURE indicates that check figures are available on the book's Website.

EXERCISES

TA 2   **E10.13**   **Calculating Deferred Income Taxes.** The Sample Corporation prepared the following income statements and income tax returns for Year 1 through Year 4.

Income Statement	Year 1	Year 2	Year 3	Year 4
Sales.	$1,000	$1,000	$1,000	$1,000
Operating expenses	650	650	650	650
Pretax net income	350	350	350	350
Provisions for income taxes	140	140	140	140
Net income	$ 210	$ 210	$ 210	$ 210

Income Tax Return	Year 1	Year 2	Year 3	Year 4
Sales.	$1,000	$1,000	$1,000	$1,000
Operating expenses	900	900	400	400
Taxable income	100	100	600	600
Income tax payable	40	40	240	240
After-tax net income.	$ 60	$ 60	$ 360	$ 360

Calculate the balance in the company's deferred income tax liability account at the end of each year. Explain what a growing balance in the deferred income tax liability is likely to indicate about a company's net income relative to its taxable income. Why might investment professionals view this situation positively? Negatively?

TA 2   **E10.14**   **Deferred Income Taxes and Changing Tax Rates.** The Waterloo Company uses straight-line depreciation
CHECK   accounting in its corporate financial reports but MACRS depreciation accounting for income tax purposes.
FIGURE   At the end of the year, Waterloo reported taxable income to the IRS totaling $100,000 and pretax net income

to its shareholders of $150,000. MACRS depreciation expense for the year totaled $70,000, while straight-line depreciation was only $40,000. Assume an effective tax rate of 35 percent; calculate Waterloo's deferred income taxes for the year. Is the company's deferred income tax effect an asset or a liability? If the income tax rate was lowered to 30 percent, how much will the company's deferred income taxes change? Explain the change in deferred income taxes.

E10.15   **Reporting the Provision for Income Taxes.**   Smith & Sons Company presented the following information   TA 2
in the income tax footnote in its annual report:

Note 13. Income Taxes   Provision for income taxes includes the following (in thousands)

	End-of-year
Current payable	
U.S.	$4,028
Foreign	438
Deferred	
U.S.	2,880
Foreign	(174)
Total	$7,172

How much tax expense did Smith & Sons report on its income statement for the year? How much of the reported income tax expense was paid currently and how much was deferred to a future period for payment? What is implied by the negative foreign deferred income taxes of $174?

E10.16   **Analyzing Retirement Fund Obligations.**   The following information is taken from the 2014 annual report   TA 3
of Johnson & Johnson (J&J):

($ millions)	2014	2013
Projected benefit obligation	$26,889	$21,488
Plan assets at fair value	22,575	20,901
Net amount recognized in the company's balance sheet (as a liability)	4,314	587

Calculate the amount that J&J's retirement fund obligations are underfunded as of each year-end. How much of the underfunding is reported on the company's balance sheet?

E10.17   **(Appendix 10A) Analyzing Foreign Currency Hedges.**   The Arizona Company, a U.S.-based manufacturer,   TA 5
ordered a piece of equipment from Sonora Inc., a Mexico-based supplier, agreeing to pay 300,000 Mexican pesos upon delivery of the equipment in three months time. At the time of the contract signing, the exchange rate between the U.S. dollar and the Mexican peso was 10P:$1. With concerns about a weakening U.S. dollar, The Arizona Company decided to hedge its currency exposure by purchasing a forward foreign exchange contract from a local bank. The forward contract committed The Arizona Company to pay $30,300 in three months in exchange for 300,000 pesos.

What was the forward foreign exchange rate implicit in the contract (assuming no transaction costs)? If the foreign exchange rate in three months was 9.8P:$1, how much did The Arizona Company save by purchasing the currency hedge? If the foreign exchange rate in 3 months was 9.0P:$1, how much did the company save by purchasing the currency hedge?

E10.18   **(Appendix 10A) Analyzing Interest Rate Swaps.**   The Phoenix Company purchases a piece of equipment   TA 5
from the Anthem Company by issuing a three-year note with a face value of $100,000. The two companies agree that the interest rate on the note will be pegged to LIBOR (London InterBank Offering Rate), which was currently six percent, and would be reset at the end of each year for the following year.

Because of concerns about rising interest rates, The Phoenix Company arranged an interest rate swap with its local bank. Under the swap agreement, The Phoenix Company agreed to pay the bank six percent annually for the three-year period, thus swapping its potentially variable-rate interest payment for a fixed-rate payment. Calculate the value of The Phoenix Company's loss over the three-year swap assuming that LIBOR drops to four percent at the end of the first year and remains there until the end of the swap agreement. Calculate the value of The Phoenix Company's gain over the three-year swap assuming that LIBOR goes to eight percent at the end of the first year and remains there until the end of the swap agreement.

TA 5   **E10.19**   **(Appendix 10A) Financial Instruments and Derivatives.**   The Portet Wine Company holds 20,000 gallons of wine in inventory at year-end. The company expects to age the wine for another six months before selling it as bulk wine. Given uncertainties surrounding the economic conditions in six months, Portet Wine Company decided to purchase a forward commodity contract in which it promised to sell the 10,000 gallons of wine in six months at a total fixed price of $1.2 million.

Ignoring transaction costs, what was the forward price per gallon of wine implicit in the commodity contract? If the purchase price per gallon of bulk wine in six months is $110 per gallon, was the decision to purchase a forward commodity contract a good decision? If so, why? If not, why not?

PROBLEMS

TA 1   **P10.20**   **Legal Proceedings: Patent Infringement.**   Bristol-Myers Squibb Company (BMS) engages in the discovery, development, license, manufacture, marketing, distribution, and sale of pharmaceutical and other health care products. Selected financial information for the company is as follows:

	Year 2	Year 1
Revenue	$19.4 billion	$20.9 billion
Net income	2.4 billion	3.1 billion
Total assets	30.4 billion	27.5 billion
Total liabilities	20.2 billion	17.7 billion

BMS's Year 2 annual report disclosed the following information in its footnote:

> **Legal Proceedings and Contingencies**   Various lawsuits, claims, proceedings, and investigations are pending against the Company and certain of its subsidiaries. In accordance with SFAS No. 5, *Accounting for Contingencies,* the Company records accruals for such contingencies when it is probable that a liability will be incurred and the amount of loss can be reasonably estimated. These matters involve antitrust, securities, patent infringements, the Employee Retirement Income Security Act of 1974, as amended (ERISA), pricing, sales and marketing practices, environmental, health and safety matters, product liability and insurance coverage. The most significant of these matters are described on the next page.
>
> **Plavix Litigation**   The Company's U.S. territory partnership under its alliance with Sanofi is a plaintiff in three pending patent infringement lawsuits instituted in the U.S. District Court for the Southern District of New York. Plaintiffs' infringement position is based on defendants' filing of their Abbreviated New Drug Application (ANDA) with the FDA, seeking approval to sell generic clopidogrel bisulfate prior to the expiration of the composition of matter patent in Year 9. Plavix is currently the Company's largest product ranked by net sales. Net sales of Plavix were approximately $3.3 billion and $2.5 billion for the years ended December 31, Year 2 and Year 1, respectively. Loss of market exclusivity of Plavix and the subsequent development of generic competition would be material to the Company's sales of Plavix and results of operations and cash flows and could be material to its financial condition and liquidity.

Required

1. Historically, the loss of patent protection on a brand name pharmaceutical product has resulted in a 70 percent decline in product sales. Assuming that (a) BMS's patent protection on Plavix is lost as of the beginning of Year 3, (b) revenue and earnings for Year 3 would, in the absence of the loss of patent protection, have equaled those of Year 2, and (c) the after-tax margin on Plavix is 60 percent, estimate BMS's revenue and earnings for Year 3. How material are these financial effects?
2. BMS's Plavix patent is carried on its balance as an intangible asset valued at $120 million. In the event of patent protection loss, how should the company reflect this in its financial statements?
3. How should the capital market react to (a) the disclosure that a patent infringement suit involving Plavix had been filed against BMS and (b) the disclosure that the suit had been lost (won)?

TA 1   **P10.21**   **Loss Contingency: Lawsuit Award.**   Microsoft Corporation is a leading designer and retailer of PC software applications. In its 2012 annual report, the company disclosed that the European Union Competition Commission had opened an investigation concerning a commitment to make browser choice selection easier in the company's Windows operating system:

> **Government Competition Law Matters**
>
> In December 2009, the European Commission adopted a decision that rendered legally binding commitments offered by Microsoft to address the Commission's concerns about the inclusion of Web browsing software in Windows. Among other things, Microsoft committed to display a "Browser Choice Screen" on Windows-based PCs in Europe where Internet Explorer is set as the default browser. Due to a technical error, we failed to deliver the requisite software to enable that display to PCs that came preinstalled with a version of Windows 7 called Windows 7 Service Pack 1. We did deliver the requisite software to PCs running the original version of Windows 7 and earlier editions of Windows. Following notification by the Commission of reports that some PCs were not receiving the update, we promptly fixed the error and advised the Commission of what we had discovered. PCs that come preinstalled with Windows 7 Service Pack are now receiving the Browser Choice Screen software, as intended. On July 17, 2012, the Commission announced that it had opened proceedings to investigate whether Microsoft had failed to comply with this commitment. The Commission stated that if a company is found to have breached a legally binding commitment, the company may be fined up to 10% of its worldwide annual revenue.

In March 2013 the European Union fined Microsoft $731 million for its failure to provide Windows PC users a Web browser choice screen.

Required

1. How should Microsoft account for the EU Competition Commission investigation in its 2012 annual report? Why?
2. How should Microsoft account for the potential fine of up to 10% of its worldwide annual revenue? Why?
3. How would the capital markets react to an announced investigation like that filed by the EU Competition Commission in 2012? How would the capital markets react to the announcement that a fine of $731 million was imposed?

P10.22 Deferred Income Taxes: Bad Debt Expense Policy. Claremont Enterprises, Inc. started operations in early 2015. During the first year of operations, Claremont generated sales of $2.5 million, and at year-end, had $250,000 in outstanding accounts receivable. Using collection estimates provided by its controller, the company estimated that its bad debt expense for 2015 would be $8,925.

TA 2
CHECK
FIGURE

During its second year of operations, Claremont generated sales of $4.2 million, and at year-end, had $750,000 in outstanding accounts receivable. Using an aging schedule, the controller estimated that Claremont's bad debt expense for 2016 would be $14,500. In June of 2016, Claremont received confirmation that one of its outstanding accounts receivable in the amount of $13,500 had gone into bankruptcy, and thus would not be collected.

In discussions with the firm's independent auditor, the CFO of Claremont Enterprises learned that while an estimate of expected uncollectible accounts was permitted for purposes of preparing its U.S. GAAP-based annual report, the U.S. Treasury Department only allowed firms to deduct actual, known uncollectible accounts for purposes of preparing their income tax returns.

Required

Prepare a schedule showing the company's income tax expense, its income tax payable, and its deferred income tax balance for 2015 and 2016. Assume an effective tax rate of 30 percent and that Claremont has no other expenses other than the bad debt expense. Do you agree with the tax policy of the U.S. Treasury Department regarding the treatment of bad debts? Why or why not?

P10.23 Deferred Income Taxes: Depreciation Accounting Policy. At the start of business, the Miller Company acquired a $100,000 piece of equipment that was to be depreciated on a straight-line method basis for financial statement purposes but on an accelerated depreciation basis for income tax purposes. The Miller Company employed a half-year convention under which only one-half of the first year's depreciation expense would be taken regardless of when an asset was purchased and placed in service. The company also followed the accounting practice that if the level of accelerated depreciation charges fell below the level of straight-line depreciation charges (such as in Year 4 in the schedule below), the company would switch from accelerated depreciation to a straight-line approach. The company's CFO prepared the following depreciation schedule for financial statement and income tax purposes.

TA 2

	Straight-Line Depreciation	Accelerated Depreciation
Year 1	$ 8,333	$ 16,667
Year 2	16,666	27,778
Year 3	16,667	18,519
Year 4	16,667	12,347
Year 5	16,667	8,230
Year 6	16,667	8,230
Year 7	8,333	8,229
	$100,000	$100,000

Required

Assuming a 30 percent effective tax rate, prepare a schedule illustrating the deferred income tax effects for Year 1 through Year 7 associated with this asset. Which are more likely to be favorably viewed by the capital markets—deferred income tax assets or deferred income tax liabilities?

TA 2 **P10.24** **Deferred Income Taxes: Natural Resource Accounting Policy.** The Herberger Oil & Gas Company explored for and developed oil and gas wells in Texas, Louisiana, and Oklahoma. Presented below are the company's income statements for a five-year period under the successful efforts method and the full cost method. Herberger Oil & Gas used the successful efforts method for purposes of preparing its income tax return but the full cost method for purposes of preparing its audited financial statements for its equity investors.

Income Statement Under the Successful Efforts Method						
($ millions)	Year 1	Year 2	Year 3	Year 4	Year 5	Total
Revenues	$40.0	$55.0	$62.5	$110.0	$167.5	$435.0
Less						
Lifting costs	5.0	7.5	9.0	17.5	28.0	67.0
Exploration costs	21.0	0.0	0.0	0.0	0.0	21.0
Interest expense	4.0	4.0	3.0	2.0	1.0	14.0
Depletion expense	2.4	3.6	3.6	6.0	8.4	24.0
Income before tax	$ 7.6	$39.9	$46.9	$ 84.5	$130.1	$309.0

Income Statement Under the Full Cost Method						
($ millions)	Year 1	Year 2	Year 3	Year 4	Year 5	Total
Revenues	$40.0	$55.0	$62.5	$110.0	$167.5	$435.0
Less						
Lifting costs	5.0	7.5	9.0	17.5	28.0	67.0
Exploration costs	0.0	0.0	0.0	0.0	0.0	0.0
Interest expense	4.0	4.0	3.0	2.0	1.0	14.0
Depletion expense	5.0	7.0	7.0	11.0	15.0	45.0
Income before tax	$26.0	$36.5	$43.5	$ 79.5	$123.5	$309.0

Required

Assuming an effective tax rate of 30 percent, calculate the deferred income tax effect for Herberger Oil & Gas Company for the five-year period Year 1 through Year 5.

TA 5 **P10.25** **(Appendix 10A) Interest Rate Swaps.** Global Enterprises (GE) acquired MNC Inc. As part of the acquisi-
CHECK tion, GE assumed responsibility for MNC's $250 million of six percent, senior notes. Global Enterprises sub-
FIGURE sequently guaranteed the senior notes to avoid having them called by the lender (the sale of MNC triggered an immediate redemption covenant in the note indenture). To hedge its interest rate risk associated with the senior note guarantee, Global Enterprises entered into the following three-year reverse swap arrangement:

The Company entered into a three-year reverse interest rate swap beginning June 1, 2015, and ending June 1, 2018. Under the terms of the swap, the Company receives a fixed interest payment of 2.9 percent and pays six-month LIBOR* for the prior six months on $250 million. The net effect of the swap is to convert the first three years of the six percent senior notes from a fixed rate obligation to a floating rate obligation (composed of a fixed payment of 3.1 percent plus a floating payment based on six-month LIBOR for the prior six months). The swap agreement increased the company's interest expense by $1.1 million in 2016 and reduced its interest expense by $1.3 million in 2015. *(LIBOR = London InterBank Offered Rate)

Required

1. Describe the financial effects of the reverse swap for Global Enterprises.
2. Under what LIBOR rate does Global Enterprises gain from the swap? Under what LIBOR rate does Global Enterprises lose?
3. How should GE account for this interest rate swap on its financial statements?

P10.26 **(Appendix 10A) Foreign Exchange Contracts.** The financial statements of MNE Corporation revealed the following: TA 5

The Company operates internationally and is exposed to fluctuations in currency values. The fluctuations can increase the costs of financing and operating the business.

The Company manages this risk to acceptable limits through the use of derivatives to create offsetting positions in foreign currency markets. The Company views derivative financial instruments as risk management tools and is not party to any leveraged derivatives.

The notional amounts of derivative contracts do not represent the amounts exchanged by the parties, and thus are not a measure of the exposure of the Company through its use of derivatives. The amounts exchanged by the parties are normally based on the notional amounts and other terms of the derivatives, which relate to exchange rates. The value of derivatives is derived from those underlying parameters and changes in the relevant rates.

At December 31, 2014, the Company had $154 million notional principal amount of outstanding currency swap contracts to hedge its foreign net assets, which were terminated in 2015.

Foreign currency commitment and transaction exposures are managed at the operating unit level as an integral part of the business and residual exposures that cannot be offset to an insignificant amount are hedged. Hedged items include foreign currency denominated receivables and payables on the balance sheet, firm purchase orders, and firm sales commitments.

At December 31, the Company had the following amounts related to foreign exchange contracts hedging foreign currency transaction and firm commitments:

($ millions)	2015	2014
Notional amount		
Buy contracts..	$1,685	$1,749
Sell contracts..	1,115	587
Gains and losses explicitly deferred as a result of hedging firm commitment		
Gains deferred..	$ 24	$ 34
Losses deferred...	(39)	(34)
	$ (15)	$ 0

Required

1. Why does MNE Corporation use foreign exchange derivatives? What is the likely form of these derivatives?
2. What is the "notional amount" of a derivative?
3. How are the gains/losses on MNE's foreign exchange derivatives accounted for?

P10.27 **(Appendix 10A) Interest Rate Swaps.** The Procter & Gamble Company is a U.S.-based multinational enterprise that manufactures and markets a range of consumer products worldwide. The company's 2015 annual report discloses the following: TA 5

Interest Rate Risk Management

Our policy is to manage interest cost using a mixture of fixed-rate and variable-rate debt. To manage this risk in a cost-efficient manner, we enter into interest rate swaps whereby we agree to exchange with the counterparty, at specified intervals, the difference between fixed and variable interest amounts calculated by reference to a notional amount.

Interest rate swaps that meet specific accounting criteria are accounted for as fair value or cash flow hedges. For fair value hedges, the changes in the fair value of both the hedging instruments and the underlying debt obligations are immediately recognized in Interest expense. For cash flow hedges, the effective portion of the changes in fair value of the hedging instrument is reported in OCI and reclassified into Interest expense over the life of the underlying debt obligation. The ineffective portion for both cash flow and fair value hedges, which was not material for any year presented, was immediately recognized in Interest expense.

Required

1. Describe Procter & Gamble's strategy involving its use of interest rate swaps.
2. What does P&G mean by the term "notional amount"?
3. What are the two types of hedges which the company states are used to account for interest rate swaps?
4. How did the company state that the change in fair value was accounted for under each type of hedge?
5. Was the company's use of interest rate swaps effective?

TA 3 **P10.28** **Retirement Obligations Funding Status.** McGonagall, Inc. is a worldwide manufacturer of plastic parts. The company's pension disclosures from its annual report were as follows:

Employee Benefit Plans The Company has defined benefit and defined contribution retirement plans for its employees. The defined benefit pension plans pay benefits to employees at retirement using formulas based on a participant's years of service and compensation. The funded status of the defined benefit plans is as follows:

($ thousands)	2015	2014
Assets available for benefits.	$287,482	$247,783
Projected benefit obligation		
Vested.	(244,050)	(182,005)
Nonvested.	(17,938)	(12,696)
Total accumulated benefit obligation	(261,988)	(194,701)
Effect of projected future compensation increases	(45,164)	(30,203)
Total actuarial projected benefit obligation	(307,152)	(224,904)
Assets (less than) in excess of projected obligation	$ (19,670)	$ 22,879
Consisting of amounts to be offset against (charged to) future pension costs		
Remaining assets in excess of obligation existing at adoption of SFAS 87 in 1986.	$ 5,598	$ 6,777
Unrecognized actuarial (loss) gain due to differences in assumptions and actual experience.	(15,977)	8,974
Unrecognized prior service cost.	6,262	7,199
Accrued pension costs.	(15,553)	(71)
	$ (19,670)	$ 22,879

The actuarial present value of the accumulated benefit obligation and the projected benefit obligation was calculated using a discount rate of 7.25 percent in 2015 and 8.0 percent in 2014, and the rate of increase in future compensation levels used was 5.5 percent each year. The expected long-term rate of return on assets was 10.0 percent in 2015 and 9.0 percent in 2014. The plan invests primarily in marketable securities and time deposits.

Required

1. Identify the following values of 2014 and 2015:
   a. Projected benefit obligation (PBO)
   b. Pension plan assets

   Is McGonagall's defined benefit plan over- or underfunded relative to its PBO? What financial statement adjustment would be required to fully reflect McGonagall's pension asset/debt position on its balance sheet?

2. What was the financial effect on McGonagall's PBO in 2015 when it lowered its discount rate from 8.00 percent in 2014 to 7.25 percent in 2015? What was the financial effect on McGonagall's plan assets in 2015 when it raised its expected long-term rate of return from 9 percent in 2014 to 10 percent in 2015? Do you agree with these changes?

CORPORATE ANALYSIS

CA10.29 The Procter & Gamble Company.   The 2015 annual report of The Procter & Gamble Company (P&G) is available at www.pginvestor.com. After reviewing P&G's annual report, respond to the following questions.   TA 1, 2, 3, 5

   a. Describe P&G's outstanding commitments and contingencies as of June 30, 2015. Does the company consider these commitments and contingencies to be material?
   b. What was the company's effective tax rate for 2015? How much of the 2015 tax expense was deferred? P&G discloses deferred income taxes as a current asset and deferred income taxes as a noncurrent liability on its balance sheet. What is the difference between these two accounts (what do they represent)?
   c. Describe some of P&G's financial instruments and derivatives that it uses to manage its various business risks.
   d. Describe P&G's postretirement benefit plans for its employees. Evaluate the funding status of the company's defined benefit pension plan in 2015. Is the plan fully funded relative to the benefit obligation (BO)? If not, how underfunded is this plan relative to the BO? Where is the underfunding reported on P&G's balance sheet?

CA10.30 Internet-based Analysis.   Consider a publicly held company whose products you are familiar with. Some examples might include: TA 1, 2, 3, 5

Company	Product	Corporate Website
• Johnson & Johnson...........	• Band-Aids	• www.jnj.com
• Microsoft Corporation..........	• Windows software	• www.microsoft.com
• Apple, Inc.	• Cellular phones	• www.apple.com
• Intel Corporation	• Pentium processors	• www.intel.com
• Kimberly-Clark Corporation......	• Kleenex	• www.kimberly-clark.com

Access the company's public website and search for its most recent annual report. (Some companies provide access to their financial data through an "investor relations" link, while others provide a direct link to their "annual reports.") After locating your company's most recent annual report, open the file and review its contents. After reviewing the annual report for your selected company, prepare answers to the following questions:

1. Review the company's commitments and contingent liabilities footnote. Describe the company's existing commitments. Is the company involved in any litigation? If so, what kind?
2. Does the company have any pension or retirement plans for its employees? If so, are they defined benefit plans or defined contribution plans? Are the plans underfunded or overfunded? If so, by what amount?
3. Does the company use derivatives to hedge its business risks? If so, what kinds of derivatives does it use and what kinds of business risks are being hedged?
4. Does the company have any deferred income taxes on its balance sheet? If so, are the deferred income taxes an asset or a liability? Is the amount of the deferred income tax asset or liability increasing or decreasing? What might explain this increase or decrease?

CA10.31 IFRS Financial Statements.   The 2014 financial statements of LVMH Moet Hennessey-Louis Vuitton   TA 1
S.A. are presented in Appendix C of this book. LVMH is a Paris-based holding company and one of the world's largest and best-known luxury goods companies. As a member-nation of the European Union, French companies are required to prepare their consolidated (group) financial statements using International Financial Reporting Standards (IFRS). In LVMH's Notes to the Consolidated Financial Statements (not presented

in Appendix C), the company discloses its off-balance-sheet commitments as purchase commitments (for grapes), operating leases (for retail space), pending litigation regarding brand rights and intellectual property rights, and various financial guarantees on outstanding loans. The undiscounted value of these off-balance-sheet commitments was approximately 10.2 million euros.

Consider the following:

1. Relative to LVMH's on-balance-sheet debt, is the aggregate value of the company's off-balance-sheet commitments material?
2. To evaluate the company's debt exposure, should the value of these commitments be considered as part of the company's outstanding debt? If so, describe how you might determine the current or present value of these commitments.

SOLUTIONS TO REVIEW PROBLEMS

Solution 10.1

Year	Net Income	Taxable Income	Tax Expense	Tax Due	Deferred Tax Expense (Benefit)	Cumulative Deferred Tax Liability
2012	$ 41,000	$ 36,000	$12,300	$10,800	$1,500	$1,500
2013	42,000	38,000	12,600	11,400	1,200	2,700
2014	47,000	48,000	14,100	14,400	(300)	2,400
2015	51,000	56,000	15,300	16,800	(1,500)	900
2016	60,000	63,000	18,000	18,900	(900)	—
	$241,000	$241,000				

Solution 10.2

Upland's retirement fund obligation is underfunded by $41,500 − $18,250 = $23,250
All of this amount was recognized as a liability on Upland's balance sheet.

When you complete this chapter you should be able to:

1. Compare the advantages and disadvantages of becoming a public company. (page 414)

2. Explain the accounting for share issuances and repurchases. (page 416)

3. Describe why companies issue dividends and the accounting for those dividends. (page 421)

4. Explain the motivation behind forward and reverse stock splits and their financial accounting treatments. (page 425)

5. Describe the components of other comprehensive income as reported on the balance sheet. (page 428)

6. Illustrate the accounting for stock options under the fair value method. (page 430)

7. Understand how to analyze reported shareholders' equity. (page 435)

Equity Financing and Shareholders' Equity

Microsoft Corporation was founded to develop and sell BASIC interpreters for the Altair 8800 computer. Under the guidance of its founder Bill Gates, the company grew to a position of dominance in the computer software industry. Microsoft is now a multinational company with global revenue of $93.6 billion and over 118,000 employees in over 100 countries. Although best known for its Windows operating system and Office productivity suite, Microsoft also sells a wide range of other software. In addition to software, the company markets such home entertainment products as the Xbox, hardware such as Lumia phones, and computer accessories such as the Microsoft mouse and keyboards. Microsoft is also involved in other endeavors, including a number of cloud-based services and mobile platforms with Nokia.

Microsoft went public in 1986 at a price of $21 per share. Since then, the stock has split nine times such that if you held one of the original IPO shares, you would now own 288 shares of the company. As of late 2015, Microsoft stock was trading at $54 per share, making an original $21 investment worth over $15,600, an annual share price appreciation rate in excess of 25 percent.

While Microsoft's share price has performed beyond the expectations of even the most optimistic investor, the company's share price performance has lagged since its peak in 1999. But despite the mediocre share price performance over the last 15 years or so, the same cannot be said of Microsoft's financial performance. Microsoft reported record net income of over $12 billion and cash flow from operations in excess of $29 billion for its fiscal year ending June 30, 2015. The company was also in the middle of a stock repurchase program announced in 2013. The following excerpt from Microsoft's 10-K provides the details:

Share Repurchases
On September 16, 2013, our Board of Directors approved a share repurchase program authorizing up to $40.0 billion in share repurchases. The share repurchase program became effective on October 1, 2013, has no expiration date, and may be suspended or discontinued at any time without notice. While the program has no expiration date, we intend to complete it by December 31, 2016. As of June 30, 2015, $21.9 billion remained of our $40.0 billion share repurchase program.

So by mid-2015 Microsoft had completed about 45 percent of the planned stock repurchase, using over $18 billion of its available cash. But why is the company buying back its shares? The following explanation appeared on Fool.com: "When a profitable company generates excess cash flow, one of the best ways to return that cash to shareholders is through a share buyback. If a company knows its shares are undervalued, and who else is in a better position to know whether a company's shares are undervalued, repurchasing shares is a surefire way for the company to create value. And even if a company thinks its shares are overvalued, a share buyback is almost always preferable to a cash dividend considering that dividends are taxed at the marginal individual income tax rate, which can be 30 percent or higher."

continued

(continued from previous page)

Many possible reasons exist for a company's share repurchases in addition to sending a signal to the market that management believes that the company's shares are undervalued. One reason, for example, is to acquire shares to be distributed to employees when they exercise their employee stock options. Buying back shares on the open market rather than issuing new shares to these employees prevents existing outstanding shares from being diluted.

In this chapter, we discuss the various types of corporate equity transactions, including share issuances and repurchases, dividends, stock splits, and employee stock options.

EQUITY FINANCING

Going Public

Takeaway 1
Compare the advantages and disadvantages of becoming a public company.

Small businesses start and grow for many years utilizing financing provided by its owners, family and friends, or from such external sources as the Small Business Administration, a business development company, or regional bank. After a history of operating performance has been established a small business might find equity funding available through an "angel" investor or possibly a venture capital firm. Only after a firm's business model has been vetted and refined, and a history of operating earnings and cash flow established, will the firm be ready to "go public" through an **initial public offering (IPO)** of its shares. Taking a company public provides the original founders and investors, and perhaps those angel and venture capital investors with an "exit strategy"—that is, a means to gain liquidity by converting some or all of their shareholdings in the business to cash.

Because most businesses do not have direct access to the many individual investors and mutual funds that comprise the capital market (see Chapter 1), companies desiring to go public typically hire an investment banker to assist with the public offering of their shares. Investment bankers have direct access to many potential investors who are their clients. Prior to an IPO, the executives of a firm, along with the lead investment banker for the IPO, will typically go on a "road show" visiting investment professionals, portfolio managers, and other investment bankers in key financial centers around the country. The purpose of the road show is to provide an opportunity for a company going public to explain and market its business plan and future prospects to financial advisors and investment professionals. The hope is that they, in turn, will recommend adding the firm's shares to their clients' investment portfolios.

For a fee, investment bankers advise companies about the appropriate IPO share price, the number of shares to offer for sale, and ultimately, help execute the sale of the firm's shares. Most commonly, IPOs are executed on a **best efforts basis** in which the investment bank attempts to place (sell) all of the shares available for sale but does not guarantee complete success. On some occasions, an IPO may be handled on a **firm commitment basis** in which the investment bank agrees to purchase any shares that remain unsold following an IPO. The investment banker's fees for a firm commitment IPO are naturally higher than the fees for a best efforts IPO, because the investment banker bears the market risk associated with any unsold shares.

BUSINESS PERSPECTIVE

Why Become a Public Company?

The increased need for capital or the desire of the original investors to gain liquidity often means the small, privately-held company will transform and become "public." By definition, a public company is one whose securities are traded on an open exchange and, therefore, subject to the reporting, disclosure, and other requirements of the federal securities laws. Thus, there are increased demands on the firm to provide financial information to those outside the organization. But why else would a private company ever choose to become public and thus open its records to intense scrutiny? The advantages and disadvantages are many. Some of those are summarized below:

Advantages of Becoming a Public Company	
Raise Growth Capital	At the IPO the company raises cash through a stock equity offering. Often the funds generated are larger but at lower costs than other financing sources.
Enhances Future Access to Capital	The company may return to the markets to raise additional cash in what are called "seasoned equity" offerings.
Established Market Value	Private companies are frequently valued significantly lower given illiquidity costs. The enhanced information flow associated with an established market value also often results in lower borrowing costs.
Stock as Currency	The ability to use stock as a "currency" facilitates mergers and acquisitions. In rapidly changing markets this can offer a substantial advantage over private competitors. Stock compensation plans are also measurable forms of compensation and benefits.
Liquidity	Liquidity results in the shareholders' ability to have relatively easy and unrestricted trading in the company's securities.
Perceived Stability and Stature	By being public the corporate image and perceived stability is frequently higher, helping to strengthen the competitive position. For instance, private companies sometimes encounter more questions from potential vendors about the firm's long-term stability. "Free" advertising from public markets also helps boost name recognition.

Disadvantages of Becoming a Public Company	
Management Distraction	Significant senior management time and attention are necessary for successful completion of a security offering.
Offering Expenses	The total aggregate costs of an equity offering may range from 10-15% of the gross offering proceeds.
Short-term Orientation	Because important strategic decisions will be subjected to public scrutiny, frequently management will face the choice between long-term goals and short-term financial results (e.g., quarter earnings releases and the pressure to "meet or beat" market expectations).
Voluminous Disclosures	Public companies are required to disclose volumes of information at both the IPO and on an ongoing basis.
Increased Litigation Risk	Given the requisite public disclosures, lawsuits against public companies claiming violations of securities laws have become commonplace.
Ongoing Expense and Effort	Taking a company public can be quite costly. In-house personnel additions often include a Chief Financial Officer (CFO), an investor relations department and related increases in staffing. External advisors and consultants are required. Routine decision making becomes more cumbersome and time consuming. There are also increased costs for such matters as premiums for directors and officers liability insurance, printing and distribution expenses associated with securities law compliance.

Adapted from: Aronson, Donald H., *Raising Capital for the Emerging Business: A Primer for Entrepreneurs*, Greenberg Traurig, LLP, Fourth Edition (2001).

Issuances and Repurchases of Equity

There are two basic forms of equity capital—common (or ordinary) shares and preferred (or preference) shares.

Common Shares.   **Common shares** are the purest form of equity capital and all corporations must have at least one common shareholder. But common shares are also the riskiest form of capital because in the event the firm liquidates, common shareholders are only paid if there is anything left after paying off all of the other investors in the firm. Thus, common shareholders are said to have a **residual interest** in the firm's net assets. With this high risk, however, comes the right to vote for the firm's board of directors and on other key corporate governance issues. In most companies, for instance, only the common shareholders may vote on such corporate governance matters as the selection of a firm's independent auditors, increasing or decreasing the firm's outstanding equity, whether to offer or amend an executive stock bonus plan, and whether to approve a proposed merger or acquisition. The total number of common shares that may be sold by a company is specified in the firm's **charter of incorporation**. These are referred to as the **authorized** shares of a firm. When shares are actually sold, they are said to be **issued**. The shares held at any date by investors are said to be those **outstanding**.

When shares are **repurchased** by a company with the intent of reissuing them for some future corporate purpose they are labeled **treasury shares**. While these shares are no longer outstanding they are still considered to be issued. Hence, the total number of shares issued is equal to the number of shares outstanding plus any shares held in treasury. Under International Financial Reporting Standards (IFRS) and U.S. GAAP, treasury shares are reported on the balance sheet as a contra-shareholders' equity account; that is, the repurchase cost of any treasury shares is reported as a negative value in total shareholders' equity. In addition, IFRS and U.S. GAAP precludes the recognition of any gain or loss by a company from share transactions involving its own equity. In contrast, some countries such as France and Japan allow treasury shares to be reported on the asset side of the balance sheet as an investment in marketable securities. Under IFRS and U.S. GAAP, treasury shares do not satisfy the definition of an asset, and therefore, cannot be reported as marketable securities. Instead, treasury shares are considered to be equivalent to authorized-but-unissued common shares, which have no value until sold to the investing public. A summary of the relation between authorized, issued, repurchased, and outstanding shares is provided below:

> Shares which are repurchased without any intent to reissue become canceled, reducing both the number of shares issued and outstanding.

Authorized shares ↓	Shares specified as available for issue in the company's charter of incorporation.
Issued shares ↓	Shares sold to investors, and not since retired, over the life of the company. These shares are accounted for in the "common (or preferred) stock" and "paid in capital" accounts.
Repurchased shares ↓	Shares that have been issued but then subsequently repurchased by the company. These shares are accounted for in the "treasury" stock account.
Outstanding shares	Shares currently held by investors in the firm. Outstanding shares can be computed as issued shares less repurchased shares.

There are several reasons why firms buy back their own shares. Companies that repurchase their own outstanding shares often do so as a means to take advantage of the stock market's undervaluation of its shares. (In some countries, share buybacks are illegal because they are viewed as a form of price manipulation.) This not only allows the company to benefit if and when the share price ultimately rises, but it also sends a positive signal to the financial markets about the company's prospects. The $40 billion Microsoft stock buyback program referenced at the introduction of this chapter is perhaps an example of such a corporate objective. Important to note is that any "gain" or "loss" from the repurchasing shares at one price and reselling at a different price is never reflected on the income statement as profit or loss. Rather the difference is captured in the additional paid-in capital accounts on the balance sheet. In this way the firm can show the economic benefits from the repurchase and resale transactions within stockholders' equity, but it does not report earnings from such transactions.

Other reasons for share repurchases relate to strategic benefits at both the shareholder and company levels. The profits on shares sold back to the company by investors are often taxed at lower capital gains

IPOs Around the World

Historically, the U.S. stock exchanges have attracted the vast majority of the world's initial public offerings (IPOs). Recently, however, as world economies and financial markets have grown, stock exchanges around the world have become attractive alternatives. The tables below from a recent Ernst & Young study confirm this fact; they summarize the top 12 worldwide IPOs for 2013 by the number of deals and by cumulative size. While the New York Stock Exchange (NYSE) still led the way in terms of total dollars of new capital, the NASDAQ and stock exchanges in Asia, Europe, Australia and South America were also very active. Hong Kong, in fact, raised the second highest total of IPO capital in 2013. The NYSE and NASDAQ combined had just over 25 percent of the world's 2013 IPOs.

2013 Global IPOs by Stock Exchange					
Top 12 Exchanges by Number of Deals			**Top 12 Exchanges by Capital Raised**		
Exchange	**No. of Deals**	**% of Global Total**	**Exchange**	**Capital Raised ($ mill.)**	**% of Global Total**
New York (NYSE)	114	13.2%	New York (NYSE)	$ 44,081	27.0%
NASDAQ.	108	12.5%	Hong Kong (HKEx)	16,548	10.2%
Hong Kong (HKEx)	68	7.9%	NASDAQ.	15,560	9.5%
Australia (ASX)	52	6.0%	London (LSE)	13,306	8.2%
London (AIM)	49	5.7%	Tokyo (TSE).	9,249	5.7%
KOSDAQ	37	4.3%	Sao Paulo (BM&F BOVESPA) . . .	8,479	5.2%
Bombay SME	30	3.5%	Australia (ASX)	5,854	3.6%
Indonesia (IDX)	29	3.4%	Thailand (SET)	5,195	3.2%
Tokyo MOTHERS	29	3.4%	Mexican (BMV)	4,805	2.9%
Hong Kong GEM	21	2.4%	Singapore (SGX)	4,647	2.9%
Thailand (SET)	21	2.4%	New Zealand (NZX).	3,893	2.4%
London (LSE)	20	2.3%	Deutsche Borse	3,288	2.0%
All other exchanges	285	33.0%	All other exchanges	28,110	17.2%
Total	863	100.00%	Global total.	$163,015	100.00%

Source: "EY Global IPO Trends Q4 2013," Ernst & Young

Even though the U.S. is still the world's leading capital market, IPOs in the United States have dropped precipitously over the last two decades. The accompanying graph from a recent finance study confirms this trend. The graph stratifies the IPOs by large firms (sales greater than $50 million, adjusted to 2009 dollars) and small firms (sales less than $50 million). One reason asserted to explain the declining popularity of the U.S. markets is the high regulatory costs imposed by the Sarbanes-Oxley Act (SOX). For example, in 2006 the largest IPO in history by the Commercial and Industrial Bank of China, scrapped plans to go public in New York citing the high costs of SOX, and instead raised $18.4 billion in Hong Kong. But researchers studying the systematic evidence more carefully generally conclude that SOX is not the only explanation. Other factors include the increasing quality of foreign stock exchanges as well as changes in the profiles of firms raising capital. The 2012 study by Gao, Ritter and Zhu, on which the graph below is based, concludes that many smaller firms have found that there are greater and quicker advantages to selling out to a larger firm, rather than take the company public.

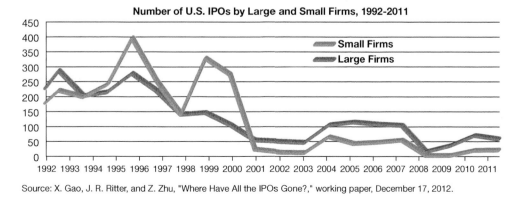

Source: X. Gao, J. R. Ritter, and Z. Zhu, "Where Have All the IPOs Gone?," working paper, December 17, 2012.

rates than the rate of taxation on ordinary income. At the corporate level, some companies repurchase their shares in order to have a sufficient number available to execute an acquisition through a share exchange, or to meet the demand for new shares when employees exercise their stock options. Alternatively, some companies repurchase as a takeover defense, for example, when the company's share price is below its intrinsic value per share and outsiders have been accumulating the shares. Finally, some companies repurchase their own shares as a means to build shareholder value—the firm has excess cash and a share repurchase is judged to create greater shareholder value than alternative discretionary managerial actions.

Depending upon the securities laws of the state or province of incorporation, a firm will issue either **no-par value** shares or **par value** shares. Par value, sometimes referred to as **stated value**, is an outdated legal concept that was developed when security markets were largely unregulated and there was a required protected value for a firm's common or preferred shares. It represented the amount of equity capital that cannot be impaired by management (such as paid out in the form of dividends to shareholders) unless a firm was legally restructuring or liquidating itself. In the United States, most shares are now issued without par, or because there are no statutes specifying the dollar amount of a firm's par value, it is not uncommon to see par values as low as $0.01 or $.001 per share. The assignment of a value to par often differs across countries, however. In Japan, for instance, all common shares carry a statutory par value of 50 yen.

In Practice 11.1 *Stock Repurchases versus Dividends*

Stock repurchases were relatively rare in the United States until the 1980s, but have mushroomed in recent years, from about $5 billion in 1980 to over $400 billion by 2011. In fact, share repurchases have become so popular that they now account for over half of all cash distributions to shareholders.

This means that on an annual basis, firms pay more to shareholders for stock repurchases than they do for dividends. The accompanying graph shows the total amount of operating income, dividends and stock repurchases for the S&P 500 by quarter from 2007 through 2011, a period of sharp peaks and troughs in the stock market. You will note how dividends remained relatively constant throughout the economic downturn spanning 2007 and 2008, and how repurchases follow the company's ability to fund those repurchases with income.

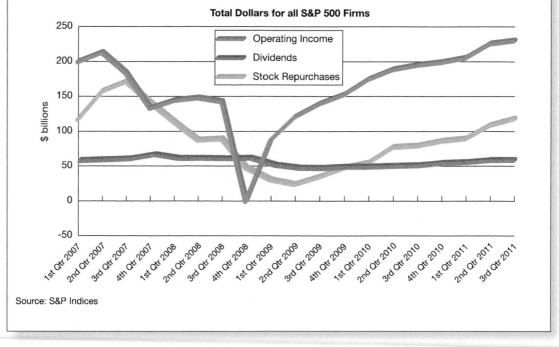

Total Dollars for all S&P 500 Firms

Source: S&P Indices

When common shares are issued, they are rarely sold at their par value, but instead for some greater amount reflecting the intrinsic value of the firm. **Intrinsic value** refers to the underlying economic value of a going concern—that is, the value that a business could be sold for in an efficient market. Investors acquiring a company's shares in the public stock markets will typically pay an amount that reflects this intrinsic value. Because intrinsic value is a market-based value, it almost always differs from a firm's **book value**, which is based on the accounting-based balance sheet value of shareholders' equity.

When shares are sold for an amount greater than their par value, any payment in excess of the par value is placed in a shareholders' equity account labeled **additional paid-in-capital**. The total **contributed capital** of a firm for shares issued, therefore, is the sum of the par value account and the additional paid-in-capital account. When common shares are issued without a par value, there is no additional paid-in-capital account, and hence, all proceeds from the sale of stock are placed in the common stock account.

In some companies, there may be multiple classes of common shares, often labeled Class A, Class B, Class C, etc. These categories refer either to the **voting rights** of the shares, or to the fact that one or more classes of shares represent **tracking shares**. Class A shares are often the shares issued to the original capital providers of a company (such as the founders of the business, angel investors, and venture capital investors) and may

> While additional paid-in-capital, or APIC for short, is the commonly used name for the excess above par, other labels used for this account are **capital in excess of par value**, **capital surplus**, or **share premium**.

> An extreme example of Class A voting power is the Adolph Coors Company. The founding Coors' family (and trusts) own 100 percent of the Class A shares of the Adolph Coors Company, whose value is just 3.5 percent of the firm's total market capitalization. Coors Company Class B shares, owned by the public and representing 96.5 percent of firm value, have no voting rights except in the case of a merger; all other issues are decided by the Class A shareholders.

carry voting rights greater than the voting rights of other share classes. In the case of tracking shares, market value of these shares is linked to the earnings of a particular operating division of the parent company—that is, the value of the shares is said to "track" the performance of a specific business unit or division. For example, during the 1990s, General Motors had three classes of common shares outstanding—GM, GM-E, and GM-H. The value of the GM common shares represented the overall value of the consolidated company, whereas GM-E and GM-H were tracking shares whose market values were tied directly to the earnings performance of the EDS and Hughes Aircraft divisions, respectively, of General Motors.

GLOBAL PERSPECTIVE

In some countries, when common shares carry a letter class designation, it is in reference to who may purchase the shares (a citizen of the country or a noncitizen). For instance, in China for many years, Class A shares could only be purchased by Chinese citizens whereas (until 2001) only noncitizens could purchase Class B shares. In 2003, as China began liberalizing its capital markets to facilitate increased foreign investment, its securities laws were relaxed to permit the sale of H shares in Hong Kong, L shares in London, N shares in New York, and S shares in Singapore.

To illustrate the accounting for share issuances and repurchases, consider the following equity transactions for the Ito Company. The Ito Company share transactions are displayed in the Exhibit 11.1 transaction summary below.

1. Ito Company issues 100 shares of $1 par value common stock at an initial market price of $10 per share.
2. The market value of the Ito common shares increases to $12 per share.
3. Ito repurchases 30 shares of its common stock at $12 per share.
4. The market value of the Ito common shares increases to $13 per share.
5. Ito reissues 10 shares of its treasury common shares at $13 per share.

EXHIBIT 11.1 Share Issue and Repurchase Transactions

THE ITO COMPANY						
	Transaction					Balance
	1	2	3	4	5	Sheet Totals
Assets						
Cash.	1,000		(360)		130	**770**
		No		No		
Shareholders' equity		Entry		Entry		
Common stock ($1 par)	100					100
Additional paid-in-capital	900				10	910
Treasury stock			(360)		120	(240)
Total shareholders' equity						**770**

Several items should be noted regarding the accounting for these equity transactions. As illustrated in the first transaction, the recognition of the initial issuance of the $1 par value common stock increases cash by the total proceeds of $1,000 ($10 × 100 shares), increases the common stock account by $100 ($1 par value × 100 shares), and increases the additional paid-in-capital on common stock account by $900, which equals the issuance price per share minus the par value per share times the number of shares issued [($10 − $1) × 100 shares]. Transactions two and four indicate that the Ito Company does not record the changes in the market value of its stock because these changes do not directly impact the firm (even though they do impact the firm's shareholders). Transaction three illustrates that treasury stock is recorded in a contra-shareholders' equity account that reduces shareholders' equity by $360 ($12 × 30 shares) and reduces cash by $360. GAAP allows two different methods to record treasury stock.[1]

Finally, transaction five reports that the reissuance of the treasury stock increases cash by the proceeds of $130, removes the 10 treasury shares from the treasury stock account at the price for which they were initially purchased ($12 × 10 shares), and increases additional paid-in-capital by $10, which equals the difference between the reissuance price per share minus the original purchase price per share times the number of shares reissued [($13 − $12) × 10 shares]. After the five transactions, the cumulative effect on the three shareholders' equity accounts totals $770, the amount of net cash proceeds received by the Ito Company.

What happens if the Ito Company eventually reissues the rest of its treasury stock and the reissuance price is below its cost of $12 per share? The company first reduces the additional paid-in-capital account for the difference between the reissuance price and the cost per share, and if the balance in the additional paid-in-capital account is insufficient to absorb the difference, Ito then reduces retained earnings for the remaining amount. For example, if Ito reissues the remaining 20 treasury shares for $9 per share, the transaction increases cash by $180 ($9 × 20 shares), eliminates the remaining balance of $240 ($12 × 20 shares) in the treasury stock account, and reduces additional paid-in-capital by the remaining $60 ($240 − $180). If the additional-paid-in-capital account were less than $60, the difference would reduce retained earnings.

Preferred Shares.   **Preferred shares**, or preference shares, take their name from the fact that this form of equity is legally entitled to receive dividends before any dividends are paid on the common stock. Unlike common stock, preferred stock receives a periodic fixed dividend, and in the event that the firm liquidates, is paid before the common shareholders. These "preferences" come at a cost, however, in that preferred shares rarely carry the right to vote at shareholder meetings. Further, since the market value of preferred shares is more closely linked to the amount of their fixed dividend payments than to the financial performance of the issuing company, preferred shares rarely experience the share price appreciation that characterizes common shares. For these reasons, investment professionals frequently treat preferred shares as a quasi-form of debt, often as part of a firm's **mezzanine financing**.

Preferred shares are frequently referred to as **mezzanine financing** along with the subordinated debt of a business. The concept of mezzanine financing takes its name from the fact that this type of financing is less risky than pure equity financing but is more risky than secured debt financing (bank debt)—that is, mezzanine financing falls somewhere in the middle of the risk continuum. Although accounted for as shareholders' equity on the balance sheet, many investment professionals consider preferred stock to be equivalent to debt for financial analysis purposes.

Preferred shares may also have a number of economically important investment features, most of which are designed to make the preferred shares more attractive to investors. For example, some preferred shares are **convertible** into common shares at a predetermined share conversion ratio. This enables the preferred shareholder to share in the success of the company, as reflected in any appreciation of the common shares. Preferred shares may also be **participating**, in which case if a company declares a special dividend for the common shareholders, the participating preferred shareholder will share in the special dividend. Some preferred shares are **cumulative**, in which case if a regular dividend is not paid, the com-

The share **conversion ratio** of convertible preferred shares (or convertible bonds and notes) into common shares is established at the time the securities are originally issued. The ratio, however, may be subsequently changed in the event that a firm undergoes a stock split. Changing the share conversion ratio following a forward stock split, for instance, protects the convertible preferred shareholder against the dilutive effect of the split.

pany will maintain a record of any unpaid dividends and the cumulative preferred shareholder must be paid the previously unpaid dividends before any new regular dividends can be distributed. An unpaid cumulative dividend is called a **dividend-in-arrears** and represents a contingent liability to the firm that

[1] The method presented here is called the "cost method," and its use is far more widespread than the alternate "stated value method." The stated value method, also known as the "par value method," is described in advanced courses.

is disclosed in the footnotes to the financial statements. Finally, some preferred shares are **callable**. A callable preferred share is one that can be mandatorily redeemed, or "called," by the issuing company. Companies that issue callable preferred shares often attach a conversion feature to the shares, creating callable convertible preferred stock, to enable preferred shareholders to convert their shares into a company's common shares in the event that the preferred shares are called by the issuing company.

REVIEW PROBLEM 11.1

The Arcadia Company began operations on January 1st, by issuing 500,000 shares of $1 par value common stock at a price of $10 per share. On July 1st of the same year the company repurchased 10,000 shares of its common stock for cash at a price of $15 per share.

Required

Using a spreadsheet approach, record these two transactions for the Arcadia Company.

The solution is on page 454.

DIVIDENDS

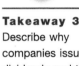

Cash Dividends

As a mechanism to provide an immediate cash return to a shareholder, as well as a means to attract investor interest in a company, some companies pay a **regular dividend** on their equity shares. In the case of preferred shares, regular dividends are paid at a fixed rate, much like interest on a bond. In the case of common shares, however, the dividend rate frequently changes over time as a company's performance and operating cash flows increase or decrease. Dividend-paying companies are evaluated by investors on the basis of their **dividend yield**—that is, the dividend paid per share divided by the market price per share. It is noteworthy that dividends on equity shares are never guaranteed; they must be formally approved and declared each fiscal period by the board of directors. In addition, dividends are not a liability of the firm until such time as they are declared by the board.

Once a dividend has been declared, a **record date** and a **distribution date** are established. To receive a dividend a shareholder must own the shares on the record date, typically four to six weeks after a dividend has been declared by the board of directors. Subsequent to the record date, a stock is said to be "ex-dividend;" that is, the stock is sold to a buyer who will not have the right to receive the latest declared dividend. The distribution date—that is, the date on which any dividend is actually paid—is approximately two weeks following the record date.

Since the payment of a cash dividend can affect the market price of a stock, dividend changes are approached cautiously by the board of directors. Dividend increases, for example, are rarely observed unless a firm's projected discretionary cash flow is sufficient to sustain the dividend increase for the foreseeable future. Dividend decreases, on the other hand, are received poorly by equity investors, often interpreted as a negative "signal" about a firm's future prospects. An announced reduction in a firm's dividend is typically accompanied by a dramatic drop in share price, and thus, dividend reductions are avoided by most firms.

Dividend increases, on the other hand, are

> As a general rule, companies that are considered to be "growth companies" rarely pay dividends on their common shares. Instead, these companies use their available operating cash flow to fund their growth. As the rate of revenue growth declines, companies will often begin to pay dividends as a means to retain their shareholders. Companies that pay large amounts of their earnings out as dividends are often referred to as "mature companies," having little or no revenue growth opportunities other than that caused by inflation or normal market expansion.

typically accompanied by only modest increases in share price. Since growth companies rarely pay dividends—that is, growth companies reinvest all available cash to fuel continued growth—an increase in a firm's dividend could be interpreted by the equity market as a negative signal about a firm's future prospects. For example, an increase in a firm's dividend may signal that a firm is no longer a growth company or that its industry is no longer a growth industry. To many investors, a dividend increase is a signal from management that they believe that shareholders have investment opportunities superior to those of the company (such as because of slowing industry or firm growth). Hence, under this scenario, a dividend increase is intended to maximize shareholder wealth by distributing cash directly to investors and enabling them to invest in their superior return-generating opportunities.

Takeaway 3
Describe why companies issue dividends and the accounting for those dividends.

In Practice 11.2 *Dividend Payout and Dividend Yield for the S&P 500* The **dividend payout ratio** is a measure of the amount of dividends paid by a firm relative to its current net income (dividend per share divided by earnings per share). As of early 2013 the average dividend payout for S&P 500 firms approximated 37%, well below its historical 50-year average of 53%. A related ratio is the dividend yield, calculated as follows: Dividend paid per share/Market price per share. A common misperception is that dividend-paying companies attempt to maintain a stable payout ratio. In reality, dividend-paying companies determine the dividend to be paid on the basis of their sustainable discretionary cash flow, and not net income. Below is a graph of the average dividend yield for S&P 500 firms since 1980, along with a list of the December 2015 dividend yields of the 30 stocks in the Dow Jones Industrial Average (data source: www.dividend.com).

S&P 500 Dividend Yield

Company	Ticker	Stock Price	Annual Dividend	Company	Ticker	Stock Price	Annual Dividend
Verizon	VZ	$ 45.39	$2.26	Microsoft	MSFT	54.19	1.44
Chevron Corp	CVX	89.01	4.28	United Technologies	UTX	98.22	2.56
Caterpillar Inc.	CAT	71.14	3.08	JP Morgan Chase	JPM	67.54	1.76
IBM Corp	IBM	138.50	5.20	3M	MMM	158.95	4.10
Exxon Mobil	XOM	79.79	2.92	Boeing Co.	BA	149.40	3.64
Procter & Gamble	PG	75.82	2.65	DuPont	DD	66.70	1.52
Pfizer	PFE	32.18	1.12	Travelers Co.	TRV	115.83	2.44
Merck	MRK	54.10	1.80	Home Depot	HD	130.21	2.36
Wal-Mart Stores	WMT	60.07	1.96	UnitedHealth Group	UNH	112.97	2.00
McDonald's	MCD	113.91	3.56	Apple Inc.	AAPL	119.30	2.08
Coca-Cola Co.	KO	42.43	1.32	American Express	AXP	72.42	1.16
Cisco Systems	CSCO	27.57	0.84	Goldman Sachs	GS	191.47	2.60
General Electric	GE	30.66	0.92	The Walt Disney Company	DIS	120.07	1.32
Johnson & Johnson	JNJ	102.48	3.00	Nike Inc.	NKE	132.65	1.28
Intel Corp	INTC	34.66	0.96	Visa	V	80.19	0.56

Occasionally, a firm facing a limited investment opportunity set, but with large amounts of available cash on hand, will pay its shareholders a **special dividend**. A special dividend is a one-time distribution of cash unrelated to a stock's regular dividend. A special dividend may be distributed to avoid an unwanted takeover bid or to maximize shareholder value when management believes that shareholders have superior investment opportunities. For example, by 1998 the Ford Motor Company had accumulated over $22 billion in cash on its balance sheet. With few acquisition opportunities available—Ford had already acquired Jaguar, Volvo, and Land Rover—and since any further automotive acquisitions would likely have encountered antitrust opposition from both the U.S. Federal Trade Commission and the EU Competition Commission, Ford distributed its excess cash to shareholders as a special dividend of $21.09 per share.

When a company pays a dividend, the share price of the dividend-paying company typically falls by an amount approximately equal to the value of the dividend. For example, in February 2015 Costco Wholesale Corp. paid its shareholders a special dividend of $5.00 per share. On the day prior to the ex-dividend date, the shares of Costco closed at $155.92 per share. On the ex-dividend date, the price of the shares dropped to a close of $149.09, a decline of $6.81 per share. Most of this decline, $5.00 to be exact, is attributable to the dividend now due to shareholders owning Costco shares on the prior date. The remainder of the decline can be attributed to other market movements. Notably though, the share price of a firm sometimes declines immediately following the announcement of a special dividend when the market perceives the payout as being so large as to impede the firm's future performance.

Regular or special cash dividends are a distribution of earned income that is accounted for by reducing both the cash account and retained earnings on the balance sheet. Although interest, the cost of debt financing, is considered to be an expense, dividends, or the cost of equity financing, are not. This differential treatment of the cost of debt and the cost of equity financing reflects the fact that the income statement is prepared from the perspective of a company's shareholders, before any distributions of earnings are made to shareholders.

BUSINESS PERSPECTIVE

Shareholders' Equity Disclosures

The shareholders' equity section of the balance sheet of Ford Motor Company is below:

December 31 ($ millions)	2011	2010
Shareholders' equity		
Capital stock (Note 24)		
Common stock, par value $0.01 per share		
(3,745 million shares issued of 6 billion authorized)	$ 37	$ 37
Class B stock, par value $0.01 per share		
(71 million shares issued of 530 million authorized)	1	1
Capital in excess of par value of stock	20,905	20,803
Retained earnings/(accumulated deficit)	12,985	(7,038)
Accumulated other comprehensive income/(loss)	(18,734)	(14,313)
Treasury stock (15 million common shares)	(166)	(163)
Total equity/(deficit) attributable to Ford Motor Company	15,028	(673)
Equity/(deficit) attributable to noncontrolling interests	43	31
Total equity/(deficit)	15,071	(642)
Total liabilities and equity	$178,348	$164,687

Ford's shareholders' equity section reveals that, at year end 2011, the company had 3.73 billion shares of Class A common stock outstanding (3,745 − 15 million) and 71 million shares of outstanding Class B common stock. Ford's total net contributed capital in 2011 amounted to $20.777 billion ($20,905 million + $37 million + $1 million − $166 million), whereas its earned capital (retained earnings + accumulated other comprehensive income) amounted to negative $5.389 billion. $43 million of shareholders' equity belongs to noncontrolling interests in consolidated affiliates. The company's book value, or shareholders' equity, of $15.071 billion, is well short of its end of year 2011 market value, or market capitalization, of $45 billion. The difference between these two amounts emphasizes the distinction between a company's book value and its market capitalization—the former reflects the company's past performance whereas the latter reflects the market's expectations regarding the firm's future performance. It is clear from the disparity of these two amounts that the market expects a bright future for Ford.

BUSINESS PERSPECTIVE

All in the Family

The equity ownership structure of U.S. and U.K. public companies is characterized by small diffuse investors, each of whom owns only a small fraction of the firm. But the ownership structure of public companies in most of the rest of the world is strikingly different, and is characterized by the presence of a large investor who holds a controlling interest in the company's stock. These large owners usually consist of families who are typically directly involved in managing the company's operations. The accompanying graph reports the percentage of public companies in seven East Asian countries that are controlled by families. It indicates that more than fifty percent of the public companies in each country are controlled by families and that South Korea has the highest with nearly 80 percent.

continued

continued from previous page

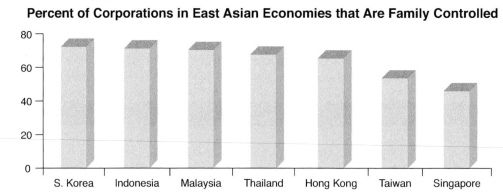

Percent of Corporations in East Asian Economies that Are Family Controlled

This difference in ownership structure means that public companies in the United States and U.K. have a somewhat different "agency" problem than companies in the rest of the world. While the agency problem for U.S. and U.K. firms involves conflicts of interest between the managers and outside owners, the agency problem in the rest of the world involves conflicts between the large insider-owners and the small minority shareholders.

Source: Fan, J., and Wong, T. J., 2002. Corporate ownership structure and the informativeness of accounting earnings in East Asia. *Journal of Accounting and Economics*.

Free Share Distributions

Investors in publicly held corporations may obtain their ownership interest by purchasing shares of stock through a firm's initial public offering, a secondary public offering, or by buying the shares from another investor on the open market. Sometimes a company will distribute additional shares of stock to its existing shareholders via a **free share distribution**. Free share distributions occur in two forms—a stock dividend or a stock split. Free share distributions take their name from the fact that investors receive the additional shares without having to pay for them.

BUSINESS PERSPECTIVE

Dividends, or the Lack Thereof, at Apple Inc.

Apple Inc. is unquestionably one of the most successful and innovative companies of the last quarter century. The company is a global corporate icon, best known today for its popular set of consumer electronics: the Apple Watch, the MacBook Air line of personal computers, and the iPod, iPad and iPhone handheld devices, among others. With the Apple platform, one of its original founders, Steve Jobs (deceased 2011), single-handedly is credited with revolutionizing the personal computer, the electronics, and the media distribution industries. Jobs' success at Apple has brought the company and its shareholders unprecedented financial success. It was the world's second largest corporation in terms of value as of late 2015 (market capitalization of approximately $665 billion), and during the fiscal year ending September 26, 2015 Apple earned over $53 billion in profits alone.

Despite Apple's innovative research focus, the company is surprisingly known to be overly conservative financially. The company carried little debt, and had accumulated a cash hoard (including marketable securities) of over $185 billion as of September 2015. In 2015, the company had committed to paying a $0.52 per share quarterly dividend, and with 5.6 billion shares outstanding this approximated a total dividend payment to shareholders of $11.6 billion annually ($0.52 × 4 quarters × 5.6 billion shares). While this may seem like a healthy payout, some of Apple's shareholders were not pleased given its under-utilized cash balance. One of Apple's largest shareholders, Greenlight Capital, had even threatened a lawsuit against the company for its poor "capital allocation strategy." With rates of return below 2 percent on most cash holdings, the arguments were sound—that this cash would be better served in the hands of shareholders, either through a new preferred stock issue that paid a dividend, a special cash dividend on the common stock, or a stock buyback. Apple management, as it always had before, said it was "considering all such options." Stay tuned.

Stock Dividends

Cash dividends—that is, a distribution of a firm's earned income—commonly occur as a regular or special dividend to shareholders. Occasionally, a business may distribute a **property dividend** to its shareholders by giving them the product (or a coupon for the product) that the firm produces. For example, McDonald's Holdings Company (Japan) Ltd. gives its shareholders a coupon book good for several free "Big Macs." Since customers at a McDonald's restaurant rarely eat just a sandwich, often also ordering french fries and a drink, it may be surmised that McDonald's property dividend is also intended to generate incremental food sales.

> The William Wrigley Company, the world's largest bubble gum manufacturer, sends its shareholders twenty free packs of gum around Christmas each year. Companies that distribute property dividends generally believe that this encourages their shareholders to retain their shares by becoming more informed about the company's products.

When a firm desires to reward its shareholders with a dividend but also desires to preserve its operating cash, it may resort to the distribution of a **stock dividend**—that is, the distribution of additional shares of common stock in proportion to the shares already owned by shareholders. For instance, if a firm declares a ten percent stock dividend, the number of new shares to be distributed to shareholders is equal to ten percent of the shares outstanding prior to the free share distribution.

It is important to observe that a firm is not transferring anything of value to the shareholders in a "free" share distribution. While the shareholders hold a larger number of shares after receiving a stock dividend, the value of the shareholders' investment is unchanged. There is some variation in the accounting for stock dividends, but the most common treatment is to reduce retained earnings by the market value of the distributed shares, increase the common stock account by the par value of the distributed shares, and increase the additional paid-in-capital account by the excess of market value above par value.

For example, consider the case of the Julius Company, with ten million shares outstanding, a par value of $1 per share, and a market value of $12 per share. If Julius declares a ten percent stock dividend it will issue an additional 1 million shares to its shareholders (10 percent times 10 million shares). To account for this stock dividend Julius decreases the retained earnings account by $12 million (1 million shares times $12 market value per share), increases the common stock account by $1 million (1 million shares times $1 par value), and increases the additional paid-in-capital account by $11 million, which equals the difference between the decrease in the retained earnings account and the increase in the par value account ($12 million minus $1 million). Thus, following a stock dividend, Julius's total shareholders' equity balance remains unchanged, while its retained earnings account declines by the fair value of the distributed shares and the paid-in-capital accounts (common stock at par value plus additional paid-in-capital) increase by the same amount. By transferring the market value of the distributed shares from retained earnings to paid-in capital, the accounting treatment for stock dividends permanently capitalizes a portion of Julius's retained earnings.

Because nothing of value is transferred to the shareholders, the stock's price per share following a stock dividend should fall exactly proportionately to the size of the stock dividend. Empirical evidence indicates, however, that the announcement of a stock dividend results in an increase in share price. One explanation for this increase in shareholder value is that by permanently capitalizing a portion of retained earnings, stock dividends signal to the market that managers expect greater future growth.[2]

An exception to the accounting described above for stock dividends does exist. When stock dividends are proportionally quite large—that is, when the quantity of the distributed shares is 25 percent or more of the existing number of outstanding shares—it is the standing policy of the New York Stock Exchange (and other stock exchanges) that the stock dividend be accounted for in the same way as a stock split, to which we now turn.

Stock Splits

Stock splits are used to both increase and decrease the number of outstanding shares, and hence, the market price per share. A **forward stock split**, for example, increases the number of outstanding shares, whereas a **reverse stock split** reduces the number of outstanding shares.

A forward stock split is used principally to lower the market value of a stock. For example, in January 2003, Microsoft Corporation announced a two-for-one split of its common stock. Prior to

Takeaway 4
Explain the motivation behind forward and reverse stock splits and their financial accounting treatments.

---

[2] G. Rankine and K. Stice, "Accounting Rules and the Signaling Properties of 20% Stock Dividends," *The Accounting Review*, 1997.

the split, the firm's shares traded at $48.30 per share. Immediately following the split, the stock traded at $24.96 per share, almost exactly one-half of its prior market value (see **red bold** area in Exhibit 11.2). Previously, Microsoft had split its stock on eight other occasions. Thus, an original IPO investor in Microsoft with one share of common stock would now own the equivalent of 288 post-split shares. These shares would have an aggregate market value in excess of $15,600 at the November 2015 approximate price of $54 per share. Microsoft originally went public in 1986 at $21.00 per share, with a par value of $.01.

EXHIBIT 11.2	Microsoft's History of Forward Stock Splits				
		Stock Split	Par Value	Share Price	
Date of Forward Stock Split		Ratio	After Split	Before Split	After Split
September, 1987		2:1	$0.005	$114.50	$53.50
April, 1990		2:1	0.0025	120.75	60.75
June, 1991		3:2	0.0016667	100.75	68.00
June, 1992		3:2	0.00111111	112.50	75.75
May, 1994.		2:1	0.0005556	97.75	50.63
December, 1996.		2:1	0.00025*	152.88	81.75
February, 1998		2:1	0.00025**	155.13	81.63
March, 1999.		2:1	0.000125	178.13	92.38
February, 2003		2:1	0.0000625	48.30	24.96

* Rounded from 0.000277
** Stock split effected as a stock dividend

At $15,600 per share (Microsoft's pre-split value per share), only institutional and wealthy investors could afford to buy Microsoft's stock. Thus, the purpose of a forward split is to lower a firm's share price to a price range affordable by most investors. Most stock exchanges charge the lowest transaction fees when shares are purchased or sold in "round lots"—that is, in lots of 100 shares. Thus, to receive the lowest transaction cost per share, a Microsoft investor would need to be able to invest $1,560,000 in the company's shares if they were trading at $15,600 per share, an amount beyond the means of most individual investors.

BUSINESS PERSPECTIVE

Berkshire Hathaway

A contrary example to those firms that use forward stock splits as a means to lower a firm's share price to a trading range affordable by most investors is Berkshire Hathaway. As of late 2015, the company's Class A common stock trades on the NYSE at approximately $204,000 per share and may be the most expensive price for a single share of stock worldwide. The company's CEO, Warren Buffett, does not believe in the notion of stock splits or stock dividends; however, to make the Berkshire Hathaway shares affordable to small investors, the company issued a Class B share, with unit values and fewer voting rights than the company's Class A common shares. The Class B shares trade at approximately $136 per share, this after a 2010, Class B stock split of 50-for-1 as part of Berkshire's takeover of Burlington Northern Santa Fe Corporation. After the split the relative value of Class B shares are 1/1,500 of Class A shares, but with only 1/10,000 of the voting rights.

The traditional accounting for a forward stock split is to proportionally lower the par value of the stock to compensate for the increase in the quantity of shares outstanding. Hence, if a company executes a two-for-one stock split when its par value is $.01, the number of shares outstanding will double and its par value will halve to $.005 per share. Following a stock split, the total par value of the firm is unchanged although the market value of the firm, and of a share of stock, may actually increase. Forward stock splits, like stock dividends, are frequently viewed by the market as a favorable signal about a

> Most stock exchanges maintain a minimum listing price. In the event that a firm's share price falls below the minimum listing price for a consecutive period of time, usually 30 days or more, the shares may be de-listed. Exchange de-listed shares may, and usually do, trade in the over-the-counter market.

firm's future operating prospects, and thus, the post-split share price tends to drift upward in anticipation of subsequent favorable corporate news.[3]

A reverse stock split, on the other hand, is used principally to raise the market value of a company's common stock. Consider, for example, the case of Titanium Metals Corporation. Titanium Metals Corporation was an integrated manufacturer of titanium sponge, the basic form of titanium metal used in processed titanium products. A major use of titanium metal is in the construction of aircraft. Prior to the terrorist attack on the New York City World Trade Center in September 2001, Titanium Metals' shares traded at approximately $15. In the days following September 11, 2001, Titanium Metals' share price fell to less than $3 per share, eventually falling to less than $1, as the demand for commercial aircraft, and hence titanium, declined. In early 2003, Titanium Metals announced a one-for-ten reverse split. Earlier the company had been informed by the New York Stock Exchange that since its share price had traded below $1 per share for more than 30 consecutive days, its shares were in danger of being de-listed. Hence, one reason why some firms attempt to raise their share price is to avoid stock exchange de-listing. When a company's shares are de-listed, shareholders face a liquidity crisis in that it is extremely difficult to find buyers for unlisted shares.

Another reason that some firms attempt to raise their share price through a reverse stock split involves the stock "screens" used by many institutional investors and mutual fund managers. There are over 19,000 publicly traded companies in the United States, and thus, portfolio managers need an approach to narrow the universe of companies that they consider for their portfolio selections. One way that mutual fund managers constrain the set of firms they evaluate is by the use of "screens," and one such screen is a minimum share price.

Many institutional investors and mutual fund managers do not consider companies as potential investments whose share price is consistently below $5 per share (unless, of course, the mutual fund specializes in "low-price" stocks). To be sure that mutual fund managers consider a firm's shares for possible purchase and inclusion in their portfolio, some companies execute a reverse split to get their share price above the $5 screen threshold. Stocks whose share price is below the price threshold don't attract institutional investors whose buying in large blocks often drives up share prices. A recent high profile example of a reverse stock split for these purposes is Citigroup, Inc. Following the financial crisis beginning 2008, Citigroup saw its stock price fall from a high of over $50 per share to at one point under $2 per share. After over a year lingering below the $5 level, Citigroup engaged in a reverse split of one-for-ten. From the day before the split to the day after the traded per share value of the stock was changed from approximately $4.50 per share to $45.00 per share.

In Practice 11.3 *Stock Splits: A Glimpse of a Sample of Fortune 1000 Companies*   The following chart identifies the stock split ratios disclosed by a sample of 600 *Fortune 1000* companies. The most commonly executed split is a 2-for-1 split:

Source: Accounting Trends & Techniques

---

[3] R.M. Conroy and R.S. Harris, "Stock Splits and Information: The Role of Share Price," *Financial Management*, 1999.

REVIEW PROBLEM 11.2

The Arcadia Company began operations on January 1st, by issuing 500,000 shares of $1 par value common stock at a price of $10 per share. On July 1st of the same year the company repurchased 10,000 shares of its common stock for cash at a price of $15 per share. During its second year of operations the company executed the following events in the sequence listed.

a. Declared a 2-for-1 forward stock split.

b. Declared and distributed a ten percent stock dividend on the outstanding shares at the time when the market price per common share was $18 per share.

c. Paid a cash dividend of $.10 per share on all outstanding common shares.

Required

Using a spreadsheet approach, record these second year transactions for the Arcadia Company.

The solution is on page 454.

Takeaway 5
Describe the
components
of other
comprehensive
income as
reported on the
balance sheet.

OTHER COMPREHENSIVE INCOME

Under U.S. GAAP, companies are required to report various increases and decreases in shareholder wealth that have not yet been realized, and thus, not yet reported on the income statement, as a component of shareholders' equity on the balance sheet called **other comprehensive income**. Examples of such wealth changes, which are not reportable as income include:

■ Foreign currency translation adjustments

■ Employee benefit adjustments

■ Unrealized gains (losses) on available-for-sale marketable securities

■ Unrealized gains (losses) on financial derivatives

Collectively these items represent changes in shareholders' equity, unrelated to amounts contributed by or distributed to shareholders, that are part of company performance but not recorded as income in the current period. Items of other comprehensive income taken together with reported net income will yield *total* "**comprehensive income**." The notion of comprehensive income is thus a more inclusive view of how well a company has performed. Note also that while retained earnings accumulates all recorded income statement earnings, less dividends paid, the account "**accumulated other comprehensive income**" (often labeled AOCI for short) serves as the repository for differences between net income and comprehensive income. Below we provide some background into some of the more common components of other comprehensive income.

As discussed in Chapter 8, when a firm maintains operations in a foreign country, the translated value of those foreign operations will fluctuate as the exchange rate between the currencies of the two countries fluctuates. These unrealized changes in value of the foreign operations are accumulated in a shareholders' equity account on the consolidated balance sheet called the **cumulative foreign currency translation adjustment** account, or more commonly, the CTA. To illustrate, consider the case of General Electric Company (GE), a U.S.-based manufacturing and financial services company with global operations. As of year-end 2013, the value of GE's overseas operations had decreased by $308 million as compared to the cost basis of its original investment due to currency fluctuations (see **red bold** area in Exhibit 11.3). By year-end 2014, the total unrealized loss in value had ballooned to $2.729 billion. Thus, from 2013 to 2014, as a consequence of the increase in the U.S. dollar relative to the foreign currencies of the countries in which GE maintained overseas operations, the value of GE's foreign operations decreased by $2.421 billion. If GE were to liquidate those foreign investments at exchange rates characteristic of year-end 2014 and repatriate those monies back to the United States, the firm could expect to realize a loss of as much as $2.421 billion. Until that unlikely event (until the loss is actually realized), GE is required to disclose the magnitude of the potential wealth decline on its balance sheet as part of its Other Comprehensive Income.

In Chapter 10, the accounting for retirement obligations was discussed. It was noted that, under U.S. GAAP, companies with underfunded pension plans—that is, a retirement plan in which the present value of the future employee retirement benefits exceeds the value of the pension plan assets—are required to record a liability for the amount of the underfunding. In some instances, the offsetting balance sheet effect

EXHIBIT 11.3	Other Comprehensive Income Disclosures			

GENERAL ELECTRIC COMPANY

December 31 ($ millions)	2014	2013	Change
Accumulated other comprehensive income, net			
Investment securities	$ 708	$ (374)	$ 1,082
Currency translation adjustments.	(2,729)	(308)	(2,421)
Cash flow hedges	234	467	(233)
Benefit plans	(7,279)	11,300	(18,579)
Total accumulated other comprehensive income, net	$(9,066)	$11,085	$(20,151)

to the pension liability is the creation of a contra-shareholders' equity account called the **pension liability adjustment**. (GE refers to this account as Benefit Plans in Exhibit 11.3.) In the case of GE, Exhibit 11.3 reveals that the company's pension liability adjustment amounted to $7.279 billion as of year-end 2014, having increased by $18.579 billion from 2013 to 2014. These amounts represent unrealized wealth declines for GE because the disclosed amount has not yet been paid into the GE pension fund nor expensed against the firm's earnings. In essence, the wealth decline remains unrealized until GE satisfies its pension obligation by actually contributing the cash to its pension fund.

GLOBAL PERSPECTIVE

There exist a number of significant differences between U.S. GAAP and IFRS with respect to the reporting of shareholders' equity. First, under U.S. GAAP, shareholders' equity includes the investment of both common and preferred shareholders, whereas under IFRS, equity includes only the investment of the common (or ordinary) shareholders. Under IFRS, preferred equity is considered to be a component of debt financing; however, this difference is under review by the joint FASB/IASB convergence project. Second, under U.S. GAAP, the financing component of the balance sheet is segmented into three categories—debt, mezzanine financing, and shareholders' equity. Under IFRS, this section of the balance is segmented into just two components—debt and equity. Under U.S. GAAP, the mezzanine financing section is the repository of those accounts which are neither debt nor equity. Finally, there exist a number of significant terminology differences under the two systems:

U.S. GAAP	IFRS
Common stock	Share capital
Additional paid-in-capital	Share premium
Retained earnings	Retained profits
Accumulated other comprehensive income	Other reserve accounts

In Chapter 8, the accounting for marketable securities was discussed. At that time it was noted that under U.S. GAAP, equity investments classified as "available-for-sale" are valued at their fair market value, with any increase (decrease) in value reflected as part of Other Comprehensive Income as long as the securities remain unsold, and hence, the wealth gain (loss) unrealized. Exhibit 11.3 reveals that GE investment securities classified as "available-for-sale" are in a $708 million net gain position, significantly better than the $374 million loss position in 2013.

Finally, in Appendix 10A, the accounting for financial instruments and derivatives was discussed. It was noted that such instruments should be valued at their fair market value and that any increase (decrease) in their market value above their original cost should be reported on the balance sheet as part of other comprehensive income. As long as the financial instruments remain outstanding, no gain or loss need be reported on the income statement until such time as the instrument expires or is eliminated. GE's accumulated other comprehensive income disclosure reveals that the company had cash flow derivative hedge positions with cumulative net gains of $234 million as of the end of 2014, a $233 million decline over the prior year.

In aggregate, Exhibit 11.3 reveals that GE's unrealized losses exceeded its unrealized gains by $20.151 billion during 2014. If all of GE's unrealized gains and losses disclosed as other comprehensive income in Exhibit 11.3 were realized, GE's 2014 pre-tax net income would decline by a massive $9.066 billion.

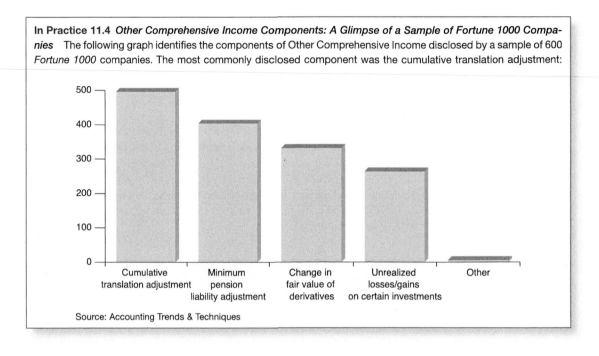

In Practice 11.4 *Other Comprehensive Income Components: A Glimpse of a Sample of Fortune 1000 Companies* The following graph identifies the components of Other Comprehensive Income disclosed by a sample of 600 *Fortune 1000* companies. The most commonly disclosed component was the cumulative translation adjustment:

Source: Accounting Trends & Techniques

Takeaway 6
Illustrate the accounting for stock options under the fair value method.

EMPLOYEE STOCK OPTIONS

An important component of the compensation of many corporate employees is the annual stock option grant.[4] **Stock options** grant employees the right to buy a company's common shares at a fixed price (the **strike price** or **exercise price**) within a specified period of time. A typical employee stock option does not vest—that is, it is not exercisable by the employee—for a number of years, often as long as five to ten years, cannot be sold or transferred, and is ultimately valuable only if the firm's common share price rises above the option strike price.

During the 1990s, stock options became an integral part of employee compensation packages in the United States as companies tried to more closely align the shareholder goal of share price maximization with the employee goal of increased compensation. And, since option exercise prices are typically set at the share's market price at the time of granting, an option is worthless to an employee unless their efforts are successful in raising the company's share price above its strike price. Because most employee stock options have no immediate or **intrinsic value** (they are issued "at the money"), and in any case, can't be exercised for years, the traditional accounting treatment was to ignore the options for financial statement purposes—that is, the options were described in the footnotes to the financial statements but were not actually reflected in the financial statements. This accounting approach, called the intrinsic value method, was quite controversial since it was believed by many investment professionals that stock options have a **fair value** at the time of granting since there is an expected value associated with the possibility that the options will be exercisable at a profit in the future when, and if, the share price increases. The FASB concluded that stock options represented a real employee compensation cost to the firm and proposed that the options be expensed in the period in which they were

---

[4] As one extreme example, in 2011 Apple Computer CEO Tim Cook received a salary of just $900 thousand, but on top of that he also received stock options valued at nearly $377 million.

granted. This proposal met with stiff opposition from the business community, and consequently, the proposal was defeated (recall the discussion from Chapter 1). The topic of expensing employee stock options resurfaced, however, following the accounting scandals at Enron and WorldCom, where some attributed the fraudulent activity of management at least in part to the earnings' management incentives provided by their stock options.

BUSINESS PERSPECTIVE

Controversy Over Employee Stock Options

The impact on the income statement of expensing stock options can be quite significant. To illustrate, consider the case of Cisco Systems, Inc., a worldwide leader in networking hardware and software for the internet. The following table presents Cisco's 2000 to 2003 earnings per share both with and without the cost associated with issuing employee stock options. The cost of employee stock options represents as much as $0.15 to $0.24 per share of the firm's total net income. For the year 2000, the options impact represented 42 percent of reported net income. For 2003 the impact was 36 percent. Thus, it is clear that Cisco's employee stock options had a material impact on the firm's reported performance. For the period 2000 to 2003, Cisco reported the financial impact of its employee stock options in its footnotes but not as an expense on its income statement.

Effect of Stock Options on Reported Net Income (Fiscal Year)	Net Income Per Share		
	As Reported	After Stock Option Expense	Difference
2000	$ 0.36	$ 0.21	(0.15)
2001	(0.14)	(0.38)	(0.24)
2002	0.25	0.05	(0.20)
2003	0.50	0.32	(0.18)

Source: U.S. Securities and Exchange filings

Stock options like those issued by Cisco must now be expensed, but controversy remains over how to measure an option's fair value. Two widely used approaches to estimate the value of employee stock options are the **Black-Scholes model** and the **binomial model**. Although easier to apply, the Black-Scholes model does not consider the likelihood that changes in a stock's market price will influence the timing of when employees exercise their options. As a consequence, the binomial model is becoming more widely used. Consider, for example, the American International Group, Inc. (AIG). AIG disclosed that in 2002, it changed the method it used to value its employee stock options from the Black-Scholes approach to the binomial approach. By switching methods, AIG was able to lower its option expense by $30 million in 2000 and by $18 million in 2001. In 2002, the company deducted $140 million as its cost of granting options under the binomial method, a savings of $30 million as compared to the Black-Scholes method. In 2007, the U.S. Securities and Exchange Commission approved a new approach to value employee stock options called ESOARS, or employee stock option appreciation rights securities. ESOARS use an auction process to assign value to employee stock options. Recently, Google Inc. announced that it would use an online auction process to enable its employees to trade, and hence value, their stock options granted by the company.

   In the response to the requirement that the cost of employee stock options be immediately expensed, a study by New Constructs research firm found that many firms affected by the new accounting requirement attempted to mitigate the adverse earnings effect of the new accounting by altering the projected volatility assumptions used in their option pricing models. The research study found that over 20 percent of the Russell 1,000 companies changed their model volatility assumptions to reduce the adverse earnings effect associated with recognizing the cost of employee stock options. The volatility assumption change refers to the degree to which the price of a company's shares fluctuate in the capital market. For some companies, the effect of the volatility assumption change reduced the negative earnings effect of expensing employee stock options by as much as 50 percent.

Statement of Shareholders' Equity

The fourth basic financial statement is the statement of shareholders' equity. This statement summarizes the changes during the year of each component of the shareholders' equity section of the balance sheet. Presented below is Ford Motor Company's 2011 statement of shareholders' equity, which reveals the 2011, 2010, and 2009 change in the balance of each of Ford's shareholders' equity components—capital stock, capital in excess of par value of stock, retained earnings, treasury stock, accumulated other comprehensive income, and equity attributable to noncontrolling interests. Ford's total shareholders' equity increased by $30.442 billion from a negative balance of $15.371 billion to start 2009 to a positive $15.071 billion to end 2011. Quite a turnaround! This $30.442 billion increase is shown in the statement of shareholders' equity to be related to a number of components, but principally to the net income reported in each of those three years (and recorded as part of retained earnings). In 2011 net income was $20.213 billion, accounting for the biggest contributor to the increase in equity. Note the purpose of the statement of shareholders' equity—to convey detail that is important to understanding Ford's shareholder equity accounts that might not be found elsewhere in the financial statements.

FORD MOTOR COMPANY and Subsidiaries
Consolidated Statement of Shareholders' Equity
For Years Ended December 31, 2011, 2010, and 2009

(in millions)	Capital Stock	Capital in Excess of Par Value	Retained Earnings (Accum. Deficit)	Accum. Other Compr. Income (Loss)	Treasury Stock	Total	Equity Attributable to Non-Controlling Interests	Total Equity (Deficit)
Year Ended December 31, 2009								
Balance at beginning of year	$24	$10,875	$(16,316)	$(10,123)	$(181)	$(15,721)	$350	$(15,371)
Comprehensive income/(loss)								
Net income/(loss)	—	—	2,717	—	—	2,717	—	2,717
Foreign curr. translation (net of $65 of tax)	—	—	—	2,235	—	2,235	—	2,235
Net gain/(loss) on derivative instruments (net of $0 of tax)	—	—	—	(127)	—	(127)	—	(127)
Employee benefit related (net of $302 of tax benefit & other)	—	—	—	(2,851)	—	(2,851)	—	(2,851)
Net holding gain/(loss) (net of $0 of tax)	—	—	—	2	—	2	—	2
Comprehensive income/(loss)						1,976	—	1,976
Common Stock issued	10	5,911	—	—	—	5,921	—	5,921
Impact of deconsolidation of AutoAlliance International, Inc.	—	—	—	—	—	—	(269)	(269)
Treasury stock/other	—	—	—	—	4	4	(40)	(36)
Cash dividends declared	—	—	—	—	—	—	(3)	(3)
Balance at end of year	$34	$16,786	$(13,599)	$(10,864)	$(177)	$ (7,820)	$ 38	$ (7,782)
Year Ended December 31, 2010								
Balance at beginning of year	$34	$16,786	$(13,599)	$(10,864)	$(177)	$(7,820)	$ 38	$ (7,782)
Comprehensive income/(loss)								
Net income/(loss)	—	—	6,561	—	—	6,561	(4)	6,557
Foreign curr. translation (net of $2 of tax benefit)	—	—	—	(2,233)	—	(2,233)	(1)	(2,234)
Net gain/(loss) on derivative instruments (net of $0 of tax)	—	—	—	(24)	—	(24)	—	(24)
Employee benefit related (net of $222 of tax benefit & other)	—	—	—	(1,190)	—	(1,190)	—	(1,190)
Net holding gain/(loss) (net of $0 of tax)	—	—	—	(2)	—	(2)	—	(2)
Comprehensive income/(loss)						3,112	(5)	3,107
Common Stock issued	4	4,017	—	—	—	4,021	—	4,021
Treasury stock/other	—	—	—	—	14	14	—	14
Cash dividends declared	—	—	—	—	—	—	(2)	(2)
Balance at end of year	$38	$20,803	$ (7,038)	$(14,313)	$(163)	$ (673)	$ 31	$ (642)
Year Ended December 31, 2011								
Balance at beginning of year	$38	$20,803	$ (7,038)	$(14,313)	$(163)	$ (673)	$ 31	$ (642)
Comprehensive income/(loss)								
Net income/(loss)	—	—	20,213	—	—	20,213	9	20,222
Foreign curr. translation (net of $2 of tax benefit)	—	—	—	(718)	—	(718)	(2)	(720)
Net gain/(loss) on derivative instruments (net of $67 of tax benefit)	—	—	—	(152)	—	(152)	—	(152)
Employee benefit related (net of $1,560 of tax benefit & other)	—	—	—	(3,553)	—	(3,553)	—	(3,553)
Net holding gain/(loss) (net of $0 tax)	—	—	—	2	—	2	—	2
Comprehensive income/(loss)						15,792	7	15,799
Common Stock issued	—	102	—	—	—	102	—	102
Treasury stock/other	—	—	—	—	(3)	(3)	5	2
Cash dividends declared	—	—	(190)	—	—	(190)	—	(190)
Balance at end of year	$38	$20,905	$12,985	$(18,734)	$(166)	$15,028	$ 43	$ 15,071

TAX PERSPECTIVE

Stock Options Under the U.S. Tax Law

Under U.S. GAAP a company must record compensation expense over the vesting period of stock options granted to all employees. However, the tax deductibility of those same options under U.S. tax law follows a different set of rules. First, some stock options, specifically *incentive* stock options (ISOs), are not deductible at all for tax purposes. This restriction exists because with ISOs the employee is able to avoid ordinary income tax when the option is exercised, as long as he or she meets certain holding period restrictions (e.g., the stock is held at least 1 year, among others). There are a number of other restrictive criteria and administrative burdens on companies that issue ISOs. These are too complex and many for our purposes here, but note that when these added costs are coupled with the inability of a company to reduce its taxes through a deduction against income, ISOs have become the less commonly granted type of options.

Any option that does not meet the requirements of being an ISO is by default classified as a *nonqualified* stock option. For IRS tax purposes, a nonqualified option is deductible under IRS rules in the year of exercise. And the measurement of "compensation expense" takes a different form. Whereas under U.S. GAAP the fair value estimate of option value at the date of grant determines total compensation (e.g., under a model such as Black-Scholes), under U.S. tax law the allowable deduction is the difference between (i) the fair market value of the company's stock on the exercise date, and (ii) the exercise price received by the company from the employee. In essence, in the eyes of the IRS the company has "given up" a difference in economic value as of the exercise date equivalent to the acquisition discount received by the employee. In the eyes of FASB, however, the grant date option fair value represents how much effort the employee has provided the company over the vesting period. Since these amounts are "earned" by the employee over the vesting period, they must be matched to revenues in the proper time periods consistent with accrual accounting. Noteworthy is that the IRS will typically tax as income to the employee who exercises nonqualified options the same amount that is allowed as a deduction by the corporation, and in the same year.

Because with nonqualified options the IRS allows a tax deduction if and when exercised, nonqualified options can yield temporary timing differences between book and tax income. These timing differences will create a deferred tax asset (see Chapter 10) on the company's balance sheet because the options are also expensed under GAAP, but sooner. The deferred tax asset must be eliminated on one of three dates: (i) the date the employee severs employment if before the options have vested, (ii) the vesting date if the options are out-of-the-money, or (iii) the exercise date because it is then that a deductible expense is finally recorded on the tax books.

As you can no doubt see, the accounting for options, both under GAAP and U.S. tax law, is complex and dependent on many different inputs. These complexities mean that managers and executives that grant or receive stock options need be aware of both the financial reporting and tax rules, as they can have large impacts on the company and its employees. This brief review only touched on some of the more general factors to consider, and thus it is important for those affected to research this topic more fully.

The FASB's proposal to expense stock options met with particularly strong opposition from companies in the high-tech industry. High-tech companies are some of the biggest stock option users and executives in this industry argued that expensing stock options would dramatically reduce their profitability. In response to claims that lower reported profits would hurt the competitiveness of U.S. businesses and cost jobs, the House of Representatives passed HR 3574 in 2004, a bill that outlawed the FASB from requiring companies to expense stock options. While the bill ultimately failed to become law, its existence demonstrates the political nature of accounting standard setting.

Internationally, the prevailing view has been that despite the fact that employee stock options are rarely granted "in the money," the options are valuable because they may assume significant future value for an employee if, and when, the share price rises. As a consequence, both the IASB and the FASB now require that companies granting employee stock options must estimate the fair market value of the options at the time of granting and deduct that value as employee compensation expense on a straight-line basis over the vesting period. The offset to the retained earnings from the compensation expense is an increase in the additional paid-in-capital account in shareholders' equity. This accounting method is known as the fair value method.

BUSINESS PERSPECTIVE

The Backdating Scandal

In 2004, finance Professor Erik Lie at the University of Iowa published research reporting that the option grant dates of many U.S. corporations happened to coincide with the day of the year in which the stock was at its annual low. This research was followed by a series of investigative articles in the *Wall Street Journal* in 2006 that alleged large numbers of U.S. companies were deceptively "backdating" their option grant dates. An example is UnitedHealthcare, a large managed health care company. UnitedHealthcare reported that it granted 250,000 options to its CEO in October 1998 when the stock was selling at $35 per share, and hence assigned a $35 exercise price to the options (see the accompanying graph). With a grant date and exercise price both equaling $35 per share, the options have an intrinsic value of zero, and the proper accounting is to make no adjustments to the books. In 2006, however, the SEC and the Internal Revenue Service launched investigations into allegations that the options were actually granted in December 1999, when the stock was trading at $85 per share. If true, the stock options actually had an intrinsic value of $12.5 million ($85 minus $35, times 250,000 options) and the proper accounting is to increase compensation expense by $12.5 million, an event that also has tax consequences. The SEC opened investigations of more than 130 companies suspected of backdating their executive stock options, including against such high profile companies as Apple and Dell. In October of 2006, UnitedHealthcare CEO William McGuire agreed to resign his position. In 2007, McGuire settled with the SEC, agreeing to repay $468 million, and under the Sarbanes-Oxley Act, was barred from serving as an officer or director of a public company for ten years.

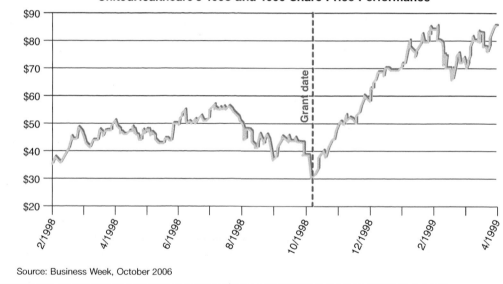

UnitedHealthcare's 1998 and 1999 Share Price Performance

Source: Business Week, October 2006

To illustrate the accounting for stock options under the fair value method, consider the following scenario for the Walsh Company. Assume that certain Walsh employees receive stock options on 200,000 shares of Walsh stock. At the time of grant the stock was trading for $40 per share, the options were issued at the money (i.e., the strike price is $40), and the options would vest in 5 years. The controller for Walsh estimated that the value of all the options on the date of grant equaled $10 million. Suppose further that five years after the options were granted the stock price of Walsh had risen to $75 per share, and during that fifth year all employees exercised their right to purchase shares at $40 per share. The 200,000 shares of stock were then issued, and they carried a par value of $1 per share. The yearly Walsh Company transactions related to their stock options are summarized in Exhibit 11.4 on the next page (for purposes of this illustration taxes are ignored).

Note from the summary transactions the systematic allocation (i.e., amortization) of the option fair value across each year prior to vesting. Stock compensation is recorded each year, but since no cash has changed hands, and since the company has no obligation to pay employees, the excess-paid-in-capital account must be increased by the amount of expense recorded each year. This treatment in effect records

| EXHIBIT 11.4 | Summary Transactions for Stock Option Grant and Exercise |

THE WALSH COMPANY
Summary Transactions for Stock Option Grant and Exercise

Transaction ($ thousands):	Year 1: Options Granted	Year 2	Year 3	Year 4: Options Vest	Year 5: Options Exercised	Balance Sheet Totals
Assets						
Cash.					$8,000	**$8,000**
Shareholders' Equity						
Common stock ($1 par)					200	200
Additional paid-in-capital.	2,500	2,500	2,500	2,500	7,800	17,800
Retained earnings						
Stock compensation expense.	(2,500)	(2,500)	(2,500)	(2,500)		(10,000)
Total shareholders' equity						**$ 8,000**

the compensation as-if the employee has contributed to the company as a shareowner. By the fourth year the entire $10 million of compensation has been recorded. When the option is exercised, Walsh Company simply treats the transaction as it would the issue of any new stock. Cash is received in the amount of $8 million, the common stock account is increased for the par value of $0.2 million (200,000 shares × $1 par), and additional-paid-in-capital balances the transaction ($7.8 million). Note if the stock price of Walsh Company never reached a value for which the options would be exercised, then this last transaction would not occur, but the prior expensing of the fair value would remain.

ANALYZING EQUITY FINANCING AND SHAREHOLDERS' EQUITY

The analysis of equity transactions requires a substantial amount of judgment on the part of financial statement users. As discussed in this chapter, there are multiple reasons why a firm may elect to engage in transactions such as issuing shares, share buybacks, or dividend payments. Companies issue shares usually because there exists a need for capital. The accounts that reflect a share issuance are recorded at historical cost as of the date of the stock issue, and thus financial statement users need to interpret those accounts with that in mind. Both share repurchases and dividend increases are often considered to be shareholder-value increasing events because they signal the market about management's optimistic beliefs regarding a firm's future prospects. For example, share repurchases often signal that management feels that the current share price undervalues a firm's intrinsic value, while increases in a firm's dividend payout signal that management believes that future operating cash flow will be more than adequate to support the larger dividend payments. Unfortunately, negative signals can also be associated with each of these events. Both share repurchases and dividend increases are sometimes interpreted by the capital market as indicating that a firm no longer has high revenue growth prospects.

Shareholder value creation can arise in two ways—share price appreciation and dividend payments. Two measures of the latter include the dividend payout ratio and the dividend yield. The dividend payout ratio compares the amount of dividends paid to shareholders relative to a firm's net income, while the dividend yield computes dividends paid relative to a firm's share price. According to financial theory, in the absence of income taxes, it should not matter to shareholders whether or not a firm chooses to pay dividends since any dividend paid would cause an equivalent decrease in share price. Still, many investment professionals pay close attention to the dividend policy adopted by a firm because many shareholders prefer a steady, dependable dividend to the uncertainty of share price appreciation.

As noted in prior chapters, it is the responsibility of the financial statement user to not only analyze the numbers that appear in a company's financial statements, but also to adjust the financial statements for any business risks (such as operating leases and pending lawsuits) that they feel are not adequately reflected in the financial data. Examples of the latter that are discussed in this chapter include dividends-in-arrears and employee stock option expense (for financial statements prior to 2007). Dividends-in-arrears result from the failure of a firm to pay dividends on its cumulative preferred stock.

Takeaway 7
Understand how to analyze reported shareholders' equity.

In Practice 11.5 *Title of the Shareholders' Equity Section on the Balance Sheet: A Glimpse of a Sample of Fortune 1000 Companies*   The following chart identifies the title used on the balance sheet for the shareholders' equity section by a sample of 600 *Fortune 1000* companies. Over 50 percent of the surveyed firms used the label "stockholders' equity:"

Stockholders' equity 50.3%

Shareholders' equity 38.0%

Shareowners' equity 3.1%

Shareholders' investment 1.3%

Common stockholders' equity 1.2%

Common shareholders' equity 0.7%

Term deficit or deficiency in title 4.2%

Other or no title 1.2%

Source: Accounting Trends & Techniques

Since dividends are not recorded as liabilities until they are actually declared by the board of directors, dividends-in-arrears represent a contingent liability and thus require only footnote disclosure. The presence of dividends-in-arrears, however, serves as a red flag to financial statement users that a firm is (or at least, was) in financial distress, and consequently, has been forced to conserve its operating cash flow by not paying its preferred stock dividends.

Prior to 2007 managers had considerable discretion as to how they reported the cost of employee stock options under U.S. GAAP. Most managers elected to simply disclose this cost in the financial statement footnotes rather than reporting the expense as a deduction against earnings on the income statement. Beginning in 2007, however, firms were required to expense employee stock option costs as an operating expense on the income statement. Nonetheless, if an analysis of a firm includes prior years (2006 and before), it is important to consider the earnings impact of the employee stock option expense that can be found in a firm's footnotes.

Finally, the financial statement user should pay careful attention to items that appear in the Accumulated Other Comprehensive Income section of shareholders' equity. The items reported in this section of the balance sheet represent unrealized wealth changes to a firm that bypass the income statement, at least temporarily. The financial statement user should, at a minimum, consider whether their inclusion is warranted in any analysis of a firm's future cash flow and sustainable earnings.

ETHICS PERSPECTIVE

One of the basic tenets of modern financial theory is that the primary goal of a public corporation is to maximize shareholder value. The rationale underlying this argument is that the shareholders are the owners of the corporation, and as the residual claimants, they bear all of the risks and rewards of ownership. Further, economic theory dating from the teachings of Adam Smith argues that capital will flow to those firms that provide the best returns and that this flow of capital will benefit society as a whole. The construct of shareholder value maximization, however, is not universally embraced. Some would call "stakeholder theory" a competing theory of the firm. Under stakeholder theory, shareholders are but one of the many stakeholders of the corporation, with other stakeholders being a company's employees, customers, suppliers, the government, the surrounding community, and the environment. Stakeholder theory proponents believe that it is the obligation of the corporation to balance the needs of each of its stakeholder groups, rather than to focus solely on shareholder maximization. Some have gone so far as to equate the doctrine of shareholder maximization with corporate greed.

REVIEW PROBLEM 11.3

The Arcadia Company began operations on January 1, by issuing 500,000 shares of $1 par value common stock at a price of $10.00 per share. During the first year of operations, the company generated revenue of $2 million and incurred expenses totaling $800,000. (Assume all transactions are in cash.) During its second year of operations, the company executed the following events in the sequence listed:

a. Declared a 2-for-1 forward stock split.

b. Repurchased 10,000 shares of its common stock for cash at a price of $15 per share.

c. Declared and distributed a ten percent stock dividend on the outstanding shares at a time when the market price per common share was $18 per share.

d. Paid a cash dividend of $.10 per share on all outstanding common shares.

e. Generated revenue of $3 million and incurred expenses of $1.2 million.

Required

Using a spreadsheet approach, record the transactions for Years 1 and 2 for The Arcadia Company. Using the account balances at the end of Year 2, prepare the shareholders' equity section of the balance sheet for The Arcadia Company.

The solution is on page 454.

EXECUTIVE SUMMARY

This chapter investigated the shareholders' equity section of the balance sheet. Specifically, we considered how companies raise equity capital through the sale of common and preferred shares, and how and why they sometimes execute free share distributions through stock dividends and stock splits. Finally, we examined the Other Comprehensive Income section of the shareholders' equity section of the balance sheet, and the accounting for, and disclosure of, employee stock options.

As a validation of your understanding of the content of this chapter, you should now be able to:

- Compare the advantages and disadvantages of becoming a public company.
- Explain the accounting for share issuances and repurchases.
- Describe why companies issue dividends and the accounting for those dividends.
- Explain the motivation behind forward and reverse stock splits and their financial accounting treatments.
- Describe the components of the other comprehensive income section of shareholders' equity on the balance sheet.
- Illustrate the accounting for stock options under the fair value method.
- Understand how to analyze reported shareholders' equity.

In the next and final chapter, we illustrate the discounted cash flow approach and the residual income approach to firm valuation.

KEY CONCEPTS AND TERMS

Additional paid-in-capital, 418
Authorized, 416
Best efforts basis, 414
Binomial model, 431
Black-Scholes model, 431
Book value, 418
Callable, 421
Capital in excess of par value, 419
Capital surplus, 419
Charter of incorporation, 416
Common shares, 416
Contributed capital, 418
Conversion ratio, 420
Convertible, 420
Cumulative, 420
Cumulative foreign currency
    translation adjustment, 428
Distribution date, 421

Dividend-in-arrears, 420
Dividend payout ratio, 422
Dividend yield, 421
Exercise price, 430
Fair value, 430
Firm commitment basis, 414
Forward stock split, 425
Free share distribution, 424
Initial public offering (IPO), 414
Intrinsic value, 418, 430
Issued, 416
Mezzanine financing, 420
No-par value, 418
Other comprehensive income, 428
Outstanding, 416
Participating, 420
Par value, 418
Pension liability adjustment, 429

Preferred shares, 420
Property dividend, 425
Record date, 421
Regular dividend, 421
Repurchased, 416
Residual interest, 416
Reverse stock split, 425
Share premium, 419
Special dividend, 422
Stated value, 418
Stock dividend, 425
Stock options, 430
Stock splits, 425
Strike price, 430
Tracking shares, 419
Treasury shares, 416
Voting rights, 419

QUESTIONS

Q11.1   **Book Value versus Market Capitalization.**   The Home Depot, Inc. reports a book value of approximately $9 billion in its February 1, 2015 annual report; however its market capitalization exceeds $100 billion (more than 11 times its book value). Discuss why Home Depot's book value is so much less than its market capitalization. Describe the circumstances in which a company's book value might exceed its market capitalization.

Q11.2   **Free Share Distributions.**   Stock dividends and stock splits are often referred to as "free share distributions." Discuss why the use of the label "free share distribution" is an appropriate description of these shareholders' equity transactions.

Q11.3   **Dividend-in-Arrears.**   When dividends are unpaid on a cumulative preferred stock, they are referred to as a dividend-in-arrears. Discuss why dividends-in-arrears are disclosed as a contingent liability in the footnotes to the financial statements and not as a liability on the balance sheet. What message do dividends-in-arrears convey about the financial health of a business?

Q11.4   **Multiple Classes of Voting Rights.**   During 2006 *The Wall Street Journal* carried the following headline and lead paragraph:

> **New York Times Faces Share Class Challenge**   The *New York Times Co.* became the latest newspaper company to come under fire from some of its restive investors, this time for its use of two classes of shares with unequal voting power. Morgan Stanley's money-management division, which holds more than 5% of the New York Times Class A shares, pressed the company to eliminate its Class B stock.

The Times' Class B shares, which are primarily owned by the family of Chairman Arthur Sulzberger, carry significantly more voting power than the newspaper company's Class A shares. Discuss why Morgan Stanley would want to see the two-class share structure eliminated. Why would the family of Chairman Sulzberger prefer to maintain a two-class share structure?

Q11.5   **Oversubscribed Initial Public Offering.**   In early 2006, India's Reliance Petroleum announced that it would hold an initial public offering (IPO) of its common shares. The announced IPO was for 1.8 million shares at an estimated price range of 57 to 62 rupees per share, or approximately $2.5 billion to $2.7 billion. Because of exceptionally strong investor interest worldwide for Reliance Petroleum company shares, and especially for oil and gas company shares, the Reliance Petroleum IPO was oversubscribed by 7.5 times (the total number of shares sought by investors was 13.5 million). Discuss what strategies Reliance Petroleum might adopt in response to this dramatic oversubscription of its initial public offering. If Reliance's outstanding shares total 7.2 million shares following the IPO, what is the implicit value of the entire company? (Reliance Petroleum's remaining outstanding shares were held by its parent company Reliance Industries.)

Q11.6   **Stock Splits and Share Prices.**   The Loews Corporation, a property and casualty insurance company, announced that its board of directors had approved a 3-for-1 forward stock split. At the time of the stock split announcement, Loews' common shares were trading at $99 per share but gained nearly $2 per share in after-hours trading following the announcement. In the year prior to the split announcement, the Loews shares had steadily increased in price from $70 per share to its current price of $99 per share, an increase of over 41 percent in just one year. Discuss why the board of directors might have approved the stock split. Is the announcement of a stock split "positive news" to the market? If so, why?

Q11.7   **Dividend Reduction.**   The Mills Corporation announced that it would cut its dividend payment to shareholders from $0.63 per share to just $0.25 per share. In response to the announcement, Mills' share price rose about $4 per share, or approximately 13 percent. Over the past year, Mills' share price had fallen about 53 percent, from $64 per share to $30 per share, after the real estate investment trust (REIT) company had revealed to its shareholders that it was incurring significant operating losses on a number of its real estate projects. Analysts had been predicting a dividend cut since Mills had been unable to cover its dividend payout through its ongoing operating cash flow. REITs are usually reluctant to cut their dividend because the dividend yield on such investments is one of the principal attractions for investors. Discuss how the equity market is likely to react to news of a dividend cut. Discuss how companies set their dividend policy and under what conditions they are likely to increase or decrease a dividend.

Q11.8   **Dividend Payout Ratio.**   The dividend payout ratio, or the percentage of net income paid out to shareholders in the form of a dividend (Dividends paid/Net income), is used by some investors to identify securities to add to their portfolio of investments. For example, in recent years, the dividend payout ratio for the Procter & Gamble Company averaged 37.6 percent, Johnson & Johnson averaged 36.4 percent, and for Pfizer, Inc.

averaged 68.7 percent. Discuss whether having a high payout ratio (such as Pfizer, Inc.) is a good strategy for a company. What type of investor would prefer a high payout ratio versus a low (or zero) payout ratio? What does a high payout ratio suggest about a company's future growth prospects?

Q11.9 **Cost of Employee Stock Options.** The April 19, 2006, edition of *The Wall Street Journal* carried the following headline: "Yahoo's Net Declines 22% After Accounting Change." The article explained that while the internet company's revenue had increased by 30 percent over the same period one year earlier, its profit had fallen 22 percent as a consequence of the mandatory adoption of a new accounting standard regarding the accounting for employee stock options. Without the adoption of the accounting change, Yahoo's first quarter earnings would have been $231 million, or $0.15 per share. Including the cost of employee stock options issued to Yahoo employees during the first quarter caused Yahoo's earnings to fall $71 million, or $0.04 per share, to just $160 million, or $0.11 per share. Yahoo's share price rose six percent in response to the news announcement while the S&P 500 index closed slightly down for the day. Discuss why the capital market may have responded positively to Yahoo's earnings announcement. Do you agree that the cost of employee stock options should be expensed in the period in which they are granted?

Q11.10 **Directors' Compensation.** In 2006, the Coca-Cola Company announced a major change in company policy regarding the compensation of its board of directors. Under the new director compensation plan, nonexecutive directors would be paid an annual director's fee of $175,000 only if the soft drink company met its target of eight percent compounded annual earnings growth over a three-year period. If the target was missed, directors would receive nothing. Coca-Cola director Warren Buffett hailed the program as "pioneering," noting that the new policy would align the interests of the board of directors and Coke's shareholders more closely than in any other large company. Discuss whether you think Coke's new director compensation scheme will achieve its intended goal.

Q11.11 **Repurchases of Stock versus Dividends.** On March 2, 2015, Best Buy Co. announced that it planned to repurchase up to $1 billion of its common shares, the first such repurchase since 2012. This was part of an existing $5 billion authorization. The company also announced on that day a $0.04 per share increase to its quarterly dividend, from $0.19 to $0.23, and a one-time special dividend of $0.51 per share. Over the past three fiscal years, the big electronics retailer had collected a windfall from a legal settlement related to the manufacture of liquid crystal displays it had sold. It decided to pass on this value to its shareholders in the form of the special dividend. Combined the company had committed to pay a total dividend of $0.74 per share to shareholders of record on March 19, 2015. On that date, March 19, Best Buy's share price closed at $41.60 per share. The following day the stock opened for trading day at $41.13. Describe the motivations of Best Buy management in their use of repurchases, regular dividends, and special dividends. Which method of returning capital to investors do you think they would view most favorably?

Q11.12 **(Ethics Perspective) Stakeholder Theory and Shareholder Wealth Maximization.** To whom do you feel corporate managers owe their responsibility? Do you feel that shareholder wealth maximization and stakeholder theory are necessarily competing theories? If you feel that managers owe a responsibility to more than just shareholders, how should they resolve the ethical dilemma of the competing needs of each group (such as profits for shareholders, quality and fair prices for customers, good wages for employees, etc.)?

Assignments with the ⓜ logo in the margin are available in BusinessCourse.
See the Preface of the book for details.
CHECK FIGURE indicates that check figures are available on the book's Website.

EXERCISES

E11.13 **Shareholders' Equity Transactions.** The following transactions occurred during the year for The Niagara Company:

TA 2, 3, 4

1. Generated net income of $2.5 million.
2. Sold common stock having a par value of $0.01 for $22 per share.
3. Paid a cash dividend of $2 per share to its preferred shareholders.
4. Issued a ten percent stock dividend on its outstanding common stock.
5. Repurchased 10,000 shares of common stock at $18 per share.
6. Declared a 2-for-1 forward stock split on its common stock.

Identify whether the above transactions increased, decreased, or had no effect on total shareholders' equity. Identify the specific shareholders' equity accounts affected by each transaction and indicate whether the accounts increased, decreased, or remained unchanged. How is the capital market likely to react to the ten percent stock dividend, the repurchase of 10,000 shares of common stock, and the 2-for-1 forward stock split? Why?

E11.14   **Accounting for Shareholders' Equity Transactions.**   The shareholders' equity section of the balance sheet of The Claremont Company appeared as follows at the end of the first year of operations:

Common stock, $0.10 par value	$ 600,000
Additional paid-in-capital...	89,400,000
Retained earnings	32,000,000
Treasury stock	(7,500,000)
Shareholders' equity	$114,500,000

During the second year of operations, the following transactions occurred:

1. Generated net income of $6 million.
2. Paid a cash dividend of $1.5 million.
3. Purchased 100,000 shares of common stock at $9.50 per share.
4. Executed a 1-for-2 reverse stock split.

Prepare the shareholders' equity section of the balance sheet of Claremont Company at the end of the second year of operations.

E11.15   **Accounting for Shareholders' Equity Transactions.**   The shareholders' equity section of the consolidated balance sheet of Perry Corporation appeared as follows at the beginning of the year.

Common stock, $1.00 par value	$ 100,000
Additional paid-in-capital...	1,200,000
Convertible preferred stock, no par value	800,000
Retained deficit	(600,000)
Treasury stock	(250,000)
Shareholders' equity	$1,250,000

The following transactions occurred during the year:

1. Generated net income of $80,000.
2. Paid cash dividends of $220,000.
3. Issued a ten percent common stock dividend; the fair value of the stock was $10 per share at this time.
4. Declared and issued a 2-for-1 forward stock split.
5. Converted 10,000 shares of convertible preferred stock with a book value of $300,000 into 30,000 shares of common stock.

Prepare the shareholders' equity section of the balance sheet of Perry Corporation at year-end. How is the capital market likely to react to the conversion of convertible preferred stock into common stock? Why?

E11.16   **Dividend Yield and Dividend Payout.**   The following information is available for West Texas Waste Management Inc. (WTWM).

	Year 1	Year 2	Year 3
Dividends per share	$ 0.04	$ 0.08	$ 0.16
Earnings per share	1.07	1.28	1.41
Market price per share	16.00	19.00	21.00

Calculate WTWM's dividend payout ratio and dividend yield for Year 1 through Year 3. Describe the trend in WTWM's dividend payout and dividend yield. Which factor—dividends or earnings—seems to be driving WTWM's share price movement?

E11.17   **Accounting for Stock Dividends and Stock Splits.**   The Irvine Corporation reported the following data at year-end:

Common stock, par value $1	$ 100,000
Additional paid-in-capital	300,000
Retained earnings	1,400,000
Treasury shares	(600,000)
Other comprehensive income	200,000
Total shareholders' equity	$1,400,000

The following transactions occurred during the year in the following sequence:

1. Declared and distributed a ten percent stock dividend on the outstanding common shares at a time when the common shares were selling for $15 per share.
2. Declared a 3-for-2 forward stock split on the outstanding common shares.
3. Declared and issued a 20 percent stock dividend on the outstanding common shares at a time when the shares were selling for $30 per share.
4. Declared a 2-for-1 forward stock split on the outstanding common shares.

Calculate the par value per share and number of shares outstanding at year-end. Prepare the shareholders' equity section of the balance sheet for the Irvine Corporation at year-end.

E11.18 Interpreting the Foreign Currency Translation Adjustment Account. The following information is taken from the annual report of The Home Depot, Inc.:   TA 5

Other Comprehensive Income (in millions)	January 31, 2016	February 1, 2015	February 2, 2014
Foreign currency translation adjustment account	$(412)	$(510)	$(329)

Discuss why the Foreign Currency Translation Adjustment account was negative for Home Depot in all three fiscal years. Are the changes in this account reported on the income statement or in the statement of cash flow for Home Depot? Why or why not? Why are changes in a company's "other comprehensive income" not subject to income taxation?

E11.19 Analyzing the Net Unrealized Gain on Available-for-Sale Securities. The following information is taken from the annual report of Smith & Sons Inc.:   TA 5

Other Comprehensive Income (in millions)	Year 1	Year 2	Year 3
Net unrealized gain (loss) on available-for-sale securities	$(9,324)	$47,230	$19,238

Explain why the net unrealized gain on available-for-sale securities was negative in Year 1. Explain why the account balance became positive in Year 2 but then declined in Year 3. Are the changes in this account reported on the company's income statement? Would this account appear on Smith & Sons' statement of cash flow? Why or why not?

E11.20 Adjusting Conversion Ratios for Stock Splits and Stock Dividends. R.J. Miller & Company has the following securities outstanding: TA 2, 4 CHECK FIGURE

- Common stock, $0.10 par value
- Convertible preferred stock
- Convertible debentures

The convertible preferred stock carried a conversion ratio of 3-to-1 (each share of preferred stock may be converted into three shares of common stock), whereas the convertible debentures carried a conversion ratio of 46-to-1 (each debenture may be converted into 46 shares of common stock). During the year, R.J. Miller & Company declared and issued a ten percent common stock dividend, followed by a 2-for-1 forward common stock split. Calculate the new conversion ratios for the convertible preferred stock and convertible debentures following the common stock dividend and common stock split. Why is it appropriate to adjust the conversion ratios of the convertible preferred stock and the convertible debentures following the stock dividend and stock split?

TA 2   **E11.21**   **Contrasting the Contributed Capital of a Firm with Treasury Stock.**   The following information is taken from the annual reports of Alpha Systems, Gamma Company, and Delta Industries:

Shareholders' Equity (amounts in millions)	Alpha Systems	Gamma Company	Delta Industries
Contributed capital..............................	$27,096	$ 7,698	$62,150
Retained earnings	22,957	38,994	(5,978)
Treasury stock	(27,153)	(10,637)	(8,057)
Other comprehensive income	274	127	0
	$23,174	$36,182	$48,115

For each company, calculate the ratio of treasury stock divided by contributed capital. What does this ratio tell you about each of the three companies?

TA 2, 3, 5   **E11.22**   **Analyzing Shareholders' Equity.**   Presented below is the consolidated statement of shareholders' equity for Johnson & Johnson (J&J) at year-end:

(in millions)	Total	Retained Earnings	Accumulated Other Comprehensive Income	Common Stock	Treasury Stock
Balance, December 28, 2014........................	$69,752	$97,245	$(10,722)	$3,120	$(19,891)
Net earnings.....................................	15,409	15,409			
Cash dividends paid..............................	(8,173)	(8,173)			
Employee stock compensation and stock option plans ...	1,920	(577)			2,497
Repurchase of common stock.....................	(5,290)				(5,290)
Other comprehensive income (loss), net of tax	(2,443)		(2,443)		
Other...	(25)	(25)			
Balance, January 3, 2016..........................	$71,150	$103,879	$(13,165)	$3,120	$(22,684)

The following information is provided in J&J's notes to the financial statements.

Accumulated Other Comprehensive Income
Components of other comprehensive income (loss) consist of the following:

(in millions)	Foreign Currency Translation	Gain/ (Loss) On Securities	Employee Benefit Plans	Gain/ (Loss) On Derivatives & Hedges	Total Accumulated Other Comp. Income (Loss)
December 28, 2014......	$(4,803)	$257	$(6,317)	$141	$(10,722)
Net 2015 changes	(3,632)	347	1,019	(177)	(2,443)
January 3, 2016.........	$(8,435)	$604	$(5,298)	$ (36)	$(13,165)

Based on your review of this data, consider the following questions:

1.   How much cash dividends did J&J pay during the year?
2.   What was the value of the common stock distributed to employees under J&J's stock compensation plan and stock option plan? Where did J&J get the shares to distribute to its employees?
3.   What was the value of the treasury stock repurchase during the year?
4.   What happened to J&J's currency translation adjustment account? Did the U.S. dollar appreciate, depreciate, or remain unchanged during the year?

E11.23 **Analyzing Shareholders' Equity.** Presented below is the Shareholders' Equity section of the consolidated   TA 2, 3, 4, 5
balance sheet of Pfizer Inc. The data is taken from the company's annual report:

(in millions)	2015	2014
Convertible preferred stock (no par)...............................	$ 26	$ 29
Common stock, $0.05 par value	459	455
Additional paid-in-capital...	81,016	78,977
Treasury stock, at cost..	(79,252)	(73,021)
Retained earnings	71,993	72,176
Accumulated and other comprehensive loss........................	(9,522)	(7,316)
Total shareholders' equity	$64,720	$71,301

Based on your review of this data, develop an explanation as to why each of the account balances changed from
2014 to 2015.

PROBLEMS

P11.24 **Accounting for Share Transactions.** At the beginning of the year, The Mann Corporation, a private entity,   TA 2, 3
decided to go public. A charter of incorporation was constructed which authorized the sale of ten million shares
of $1 par value common stock; 100,000 shares of $100 par value, eight percent preferred stock; and 200,000
shares of $5 no-par-value convertible preferred stock. The following shares were sold as part of the firm's
initial public offering:

- 1,000,000 shares of common stock at $10 per share.
- 100,000 shares of $100 par value, eight percent preferred stock at $105 per share.
- 100,000 shares of $5 convertible, no-par preferred stock at $55 per share.

At year-end, the full dividend was declared and paid on both preferred stock offerings.

Required
Using a spreadsheet, record the financial effects of the shareholders' equity transactions for The Mann Corporation for the year.

P11.25 **Accounting for Share Transactions.** The Mayfair Corporation went public on January 1, 2015, with an   TA 2, 3, 4
initial public offering of 10,000,000 common shares, $1 par value, at a market price of $3 per share. Since   CHECK
then, the following equity transactions had occurred: FIGURE

1. In 2016, a ten percent stock dividend was issued. At the time, the Mayfair common shares were trading
   at $6 per share.
2. In 2017, a three-for-one forward stock split was executed. At the time, the Mayfair common shares were
   trading at $12 per share.
3. In 2018, 500,000 common shares were repurchased on the open market at a price of $15 per share.
4. On December 31, 2018, the company declared and paid its first cash dividend of $0.10 per share on all
   outstanding common shares.

Required
1. Calculate the par value per share and the number of shares outstanding for the Mayfair Corporation on
   December 31, 2018.
2. Prepare a spreadsheet to illustrate the financial effects of each of the above share transactions.

P11.26 **Accounting for Share Transactions.** The shareholders' equity section of the consolidated balance sheet of   TA 2, 3, 4
Wilson Industries appeared as follows at the beginning of the year:

Shareholders' Equity	
Class A common stock, $.01 par value; 20,000,000 shares authorized;	
6,100,000 shares issued......................................	$ 61,000
Additional paid-in-capital...	118,127,000
Retained earnings	14,270,000
Currency translation adjustment	(2,412,000)
Total equity...	$130,046,000

The following events occurred sequentially during the year:

1. A 2-for-1 forward stock split was executed.
2. A ten percent stock dividend was distributed when the Wilson share price was $20 per share.
3. Treasury stock valued at $3,000,000 was repurchased when the Wilson share price was $15 per share.

Required

1. How many Class A common shares are outstanding following the above events?
2. What is the par value per share of the Class A common stock following the above events?
3. Identify the financial effects associated with the above three share transactions.
4. Calculate the total value of shareholders' equity following the above events.
5. How is the capital market likely to react to the forward stock split, the stock dividend, and the treasury stock purchase? Why?

TA 3 **P11.27** **Stock Dividends.** Mic Dundee, President of Aussie Steaks Inc., is contemplating issuing a stock dividend that would lower the company's share price to either the $24 or to the $25 per share range. Aussie Steaks' share price is currently trading at $30 per share. The shareholders' equity section of Aussie Steaks' balance sheet at year-end is as follows:

Common stock ($1 par)	$ 500,000
Additional paid-in-capital	2,000,000
Retained earnings	3,100,000
Total shareholders' equity	$5,600,000

For the past several years, Aussie Steaks has paid annual cash dividends of $0.08 per share. Mic would like to maintain this level of cash dividends after the stock dividend is issued. Mic expects net income for the next few years to average $300,000 per year. Some members of Aussie Steaks' board of directors want a 20 percent stock dividend; others want a 25 percent stock dividend.

Required

1. Identify the financial effects associated with a 25 percent stock dividend.
2. Identify the financial effects associated with a 20 percent stock dividend.
3. Is there any reason why the Aussie Steaks' shareholders would prefer a small stock dividend to a large stock dividend?
4. Should Aussie Steaks declare a 20 percent stock dividend or a 25 percent stock dividend? Why?
5. What event must have occurred if the shareholders' equity section of Aussie Steaks' balance sheet at January 1 of the following year was reported as shown below?

Common stock ($1 par)	$1,000,000
Additional paid-in-capital	1,500,000
Retained earnings	3,100,000
Total shareholders' equity	$5,600,000

TA 2 **P11.28** **Convertible Preferred Stock: A Redemption.** The *Financial Times* and the *Wall Street Journal* carried a legal notice entitled "The Thomas Regout Company has called for the redemption of all of its €3.50 Convertible Preferred Stock." According to the notice Thomas Regout, a Dutch company, had decided to exercise the redemption feature on its outstanding preferred stock and to redeem all of the outstanding shares at a price of €52.45 per share plus accrued dividends of €0.16 per share, for a total of €52.61, on August 31. The Thomas Regout preferred stock also carried a conversion feature that would permit the owner to convert the preferred stock into 1.9608 shares of common stock (par value of €1). The market price of the common stock on August 13 was €32.625 per share. The legal notice of redemption emphasized that the conversion feature of the preferred stock expired on August 27.

Required

1. Assume that Thomas Regout has 1 million shares of preferred stock outstanding and that its par value is €5. How would the company account for (1) the redemption of all of the preferred shares and (2) the conversion of all of the preferred shares?
2. If you held 100 shares of Thomas Regout preferred stock, which alternative (conversion or redemption) would you choose, and why?
3. If you were the CEO of Thomas Regout, which alternative (conversion or redemption) would you prefer, and why?

P11.29 **Analyzing Shareholders' Equity.** Microsoft Corporation is one of the world's leading developers and   TA 2, 3, 5
retailers of PC software. Presented below are excerpts from Microsoft's June 30, 2016 annual report regarding
its shareholders' equity:

Shareholders' Equity Statements			
Year Ended June 30 (In millions),	2016	2015	2014
Common stock and paid-in capital			
Balance, beginning of period	$68,465	$68,366	$67,306
Common stock issued	668	634	607
Common stock repurchased	(3,689)	(3,700)	(2,328)
Stock-based compensation expense	2,668	2,574	2,446
Stock-based compensation income tax deficiencies	0	588	272
Other, net	66	3	63
Balance, end of period	68,178	68,465	68,366
Retained earnings			
Balance, beginning of period	9,096	17,710	9,895
Net income.	16,798	12,193	22,074
Common stock cash dividends	(11,329)	(10,063)	(9,271)
Common stock repurchased	(12,283)	(10,744)	(4,988)
Balance, end of period	2,282	9,096	17,710
Accumulated other comprehensive income:			
Balance, beginning of period	2,522	3,708	1,743
Other comprehensive income (loss)*	(985)	(1,186)	1,965
Balance, end of period	1,537	2,522	3,708
Total stockholders' equity	$71,997	$80,083	$89,784

	2016	2015	2014
Other comprehensive income (loss):			
Net unrealized gains (losses) on derivatives	$(238)	$559	$(35)
Net unrealized gains (losses) on investments	(228)	(362)	1,737
Translation adjustments and other	(519)	(1,383)	263
Other comprehensive income (loss)	$(985)	$(1,186)	$1,965

Required

Prepare a list of the key events and their financial effects that impacted Microsoft's shareholders' equity in
2016. Where possible, explain why these transactions occurred. You may wish to access Microsoft's 2016
annual report at www.microsoft.com to assist you with your answer.

P11.30 **Other Comprehensive Income: Calculating the Cumulative Foreign Currency Translation Adjust-**   TA 5
ment. Graham International Ltd., an Australian Company, is a wholly owned but financially independent
operating subsidiary of its U.S.-parent company and reports its financial results in Australian dollars. As of
January 1, Graham International had a balance of $(10,780) U.S. in its cumulative foreign currency translation
adjustment account (see translated balance sheet). During the year, the exchange rates between the Australian
and U.S. dollars were as follows:

January 1:	0.75	($1A = $0.75 U.S.)
December 31:	0.78	($1A = $0.78 U.S.)
Average for year:	0.76	

Graham International Ltd.'s balance sheet as of January 1 was as follows:

January 1	$A	Exchange Rate	$US
Assets			
Cash......................................	$ 28,000	0.75	$ 21,000
Accounts receivable...........................	84,000	0.75	63,000
Inventory....................................	98,000	0.75	73,500
Property and equipment, net....................	476,700	0.75	357,525
Total....................................	$686,700		$515,025
Liabilities.................................	$434,700	0.75	$326,025
Common stock..............................	42,000	H *	25,830
Retained earnings..........................	210,000	H *	173,950
Translation adjustment.......................	—		(10,780)
Total....................................	$686,700		$515,025

*H = the historical exchange rate in effect at the time the account balance was created.

At the end of the year Graham International's income statement and balance sheet appeared as follows:

Income Statement (Australian Dollars)	
Sales...	$1,148,000
Less: Operating expenses......................................	(781,200)
Net income before taxes......................................	366,800
Income tax expense...	(186,200)
Net income...	$ 180,600

Balance Sheet: Year-End (Australian Dollars)	
Assets	
Cash...	$ 63,000
Accounts receivable...	103,600
Inventory...	140,000
Property and equipment, net....................................	462,000
Total...	$768,600
Liabilities..	$336,000
Common stock..	42,000
Retained earnings..	390,600
Total...	$768,600

Required

1. Translate Graham International's income statement using the average exchange rate for the year.
2. Translate Graham International's year-end balance sheet using the current rate method (all assets and liabilities are translated at the end-of-year exchange rate).
3. Explain the change in Graham's cumulative foreign currency translation adjustment from $(10,780) at the beginning of the year, to $392 at year-end. Why did the currency translation adjustment increase from an unrealized loss to an unrealized gain? When will this unrealized gain be realized?

TA 2, 4, 5   **P11.31**   **Analyzing Shareholders' Equity.**   Wal-Mart Stores, Inc. is the world's largest retailer as measured by total revenues. As of January 2016, the company operated 11,530 retail units under 63 banners in 28 countries and e-commerce websites in 11 countries. Wal-Mart Stores Inc. was founded in 1945 and is based in Bentonville, Arkansas. Presented below are selected parts of Wal-Mart's 2016 10-K report:

WAL-MART STORES, INC.
Consolidated Balance Sheet (selected)

(in millions)	Jan. 31, 2016	Jan. 31, 2015
Equity:		
Common stock.	$ 317	$ 323
Capital in excess of par value.	1,805	2,462
Retained earnings.	90,021	85,777
Accumulated other comprehensive income (loss)	(11,597)	(7,168)
Total Walmart shareholders' equity	80,546	81,394
Nonredeemable noncontrolling interest	3,065	4,543
Total equity.	83,611	85,937
Total liabilities and equity	$199,581	$203,490

WAL-MART STORES, INC.
Consolidated Statements of Stockholders' Equity

(Amounts in millions, except per share data)	Common Stock Shares	Common Stock Amount	Capital in Excess of Par Value	Retained Earnings	Accumulated Other Comprehensive Income (Loss)	Total Walmart Shareholders' Equity	Nonredeemable Noncontrolling Interest	Total Equity	Redeemable Noncontrolling Interest
Balances—February 1, 2013	3,314	$332	$3,620	$72,978	$ (587)	$76,343	$5,395	$81,738	$ 519
Consolidated net income	—	—	—	16,022	—	16,022	595	16,617	78
Other comprehensive income, net of income taxes.	—	—	—	—	(2,409)	(2,409)	(311)	(2,720)	(66)
Cash dividends declare ($1.88 per share)	—	—	—	(6,139)	—	(6,139)	—	(6,139)	—
Purchase of Company stock	(87)	(9)	(294)	(6,254)	—	(6,557)	—	(6,557)	—
Redemption value adjustment of redeemable noncontrolling interest	—	—	(1,019)	—	—	(1,019)	—	(1,019)	1,019
Other.	6	—	55	(41)	—	14	(595)	(581)	(59)
Balances—January 31, 2014	3,233	323	2,362	76,566	(2,996)	76,255	5,084	81,339	1,491
Consolidated net income	—	—	—	16,363	—	16,363	736	17,099	—
Other comprehensive loss, net of income taxes.	—	—	—	—	(4,172)	(4,172)	(546)	(4,718)	—
Cash dividends declared ($1.92 per share) . . .	—	—	—	(6,185)	—	(6,185)	—	(6,185)	—
Purchase of Company stock	(13)	(1)	(29)	(950)	—	(980)	—	(980)	—
Purchase of redeemable noncontrolling interest	—	—	—	—	—	—	—	—	(1,491)
Other.	8	1	129	(17)	—	113	(731)	(618)	—
Balances—January 31, 2015	3,228	323	2,462	85,777	(7,168)	81,394	4,543	85,937	—
Consolidated net income.	—	—	—	14,694	—	14,694	386	15,080	—
Other comprehensive income, net of income taxes.	—	—	—	—	(4,429)	(4,429)	(541)	(4,970)	—
Cash dividends declared ($1.96 per share) .	—	—	—	(6,294)	—	(6,294)	—	(6,294)	—
Purchase of Company stock.	(65)	(6)	(102)	(4,148)	—	(4,256)	—	(4,256)	—
Cash dividend declared to noncontrolling interest.	—	—	—	—	—	—	(691)	(691)	—
Other	(1)	—	(555)	(8)	—	(563)	(632)	(1,195)	—
Balances—January 31, 2016	3,162	$317	$1,805	$90,021	$(11,597)	$80,546	$3,065	$83,611	$ —

Required

1. During fiscal year ended January 31, 2016, Wal-Mart repurchased some of its outstanding shares. What was the average price paid for the repurchased treasury shares?

2. Wal-Mart reports a noncontrolling interest account on its consolidated balance sheet. What does the existence of this account reveal about Wal-Mart's investments in its subsidiaries?

3. Wal-Mart uses the current rate method to account for its foreign subsidiaries. During fiscal year ended January 31, 2016, did the U.S. dollar appreciate, remain unchanged, or depreciate relative to the currencies of the countries in which these subsidiaries operate? Assume other comprehensive income applies to foreign currency translation.

4. On March 4, 1999, the Company announced a two-for-one forward stock split in the form of a 100 percent stock dividend. Prior to the announcement, the company's stock price was $89 3/8 per share. What was the target share price that the company achieved with the March 1999 forward stock split?

5. On March 4, 1998, Wal-Mart's share price was $48 per share. Why did Wal-Mart split its stock in 1999?

6. How much would retained earnings change if Wal-Mart had declared a 20 percent stock dividend instead of a 100 percent stock dividend? The two-for-one stock split added 2,224 shares.

CORPORATE ANALYSIS

TA 2, 5   **CA11.32 The Procter & Gamble Company.**   The 2015 annual report of The Procter & Gamble Company (P&G) is available at www.pginvestor.com. After reviewing P&G's annual report, respond to the following questions.

    a.   What types of equity securities does P&G have outstanding? What is their par or stated value, how many shares are authorized, and how many shares are outstanding at year-end 2014 and 2015?

    b.   What percentage of P&G's assets are debt-financed versus equity-financed in 2014 and 2015? Why do you think the company has followed this strategic financing policy? What is P&G's cost of debt in 2015?

    c.   How many common shares did P&G repurchase in 2015 and at what aggregate price?

    d.   How many common shares were issued in 2015 to employees under P&G's employee stock option plan? If P&G had utilized the fair value method to account for its employee stock options, what would have been the effect on P&G's basic and diluted EPS for 2015?

TA 2, 3   **CA11.33 Internet-based Analysis.**   Consider a publicly held company whose products you are familiar with. Some examples might include:

Company	Product	Corporate Website
• Johnson & Johnson.............	• Band-Aids	• www.jnj.com
• Microsoft Corporation..........	• Windows XP software	• www.microsoft.com
• Apple Inc.	• Cellular phones	• www.apple.com
• Intel Corporation	• Pentium processors	• www.intel.com
• Kimberly-Clark Corporation......	• Kleenex	• www.kimberly-clark.com

Access the company's public website and search for its most recent annual report. (Some companies provide access to their financial data through an "investor relations" link, while others provide a direct link to their "annual reports.") After locating your company's most recent annual report, open the file and review its contents. After reviewing the annual report for your selected company, prepare answers to the following questions:

    a.   How many common shares are authorized, issued, and outstanding? What is the par (or stated) value of the common stock? What is the company's market capitalization?

    b.   Does the company have any preferred stock issued and outstanding? If so, what is its par (or stated) value and what is the amount of the annual dividend? Is the preferred stock callable, convertible, or participating?

    c.   Has the company repurchased any of its common shares in the last two years? If so, how much was spent on treasury stock in each of the last two years?

    d.   Does the company give stock options to its management team? If so, how many shares might be issued if all of the outstanding stock options are exercised? What would happen to the company's earnings per share if the options are exercised?

    e.   Does the company pay dividends on its common stock? If so, what is the company's dividend payout ratio? What is the company's dividend yield? Is the company a "growth" company?

TA 2   **CA11.34 IFRS Financial Statements.**   The 2014 financial statements of LVMH Moet Hennessey-Louis Vuitton S.A. are presented in Appendix C of this book. LVMH is a Paris-based holding company and one of the world's largest and best-known luxury goods companies. As a member-nation of the European Union, French companies are required to prepare their consolidated (group) financial statements using International Financial Reporting Standards (IFRS). After reviewing LVMH's consolidated statement of changes in equity in Appendix C, prepare answers to the following questions:

    a.   LVMH lists eight equity accounts—Share capital, Share premium account, Treasury shares and LVMH-share settled derivatives, Cumulative translation adjustments, Revaluation reserves, Net profit-group share, Other reserves, and Minority interests. Briefly describe each of these accounts using equivalent U.S. GAAP account titles.

    b.   At year-end 2014, LVMH reports that its Revaluation reserve totaled 1,019 million euros. If LVMH used a spreadsheet based on the balance sheet equation $(A = L + SE)$, what other account(s) would likely have been impacted by the recording of the Revaluation reserve?

CASE

PRUDENTIAL FINANCIAL, INC.:
STOCKHOLDERS' EQUITY AND BALANCE SHEET LEVERAGE

Prudential Financial was a financial-services company that operated in three divisions: Insurance, Investment, and International Insurance and Investments. The Insurance division offered life and disability insurance products, long-term care, and annuities to individuals and institutions. The Investment division encompassed asset management, financial advisory, and retirement-plan services. The International Insurance and Investments division offered individual life-insurance products and other financial services to affluent markets in Asia, Europe, and Latin America. The company was headquartered in Newark, New Jersey.

Prudential was founded in 1875 and went public on December 18, 2001. On that date, the company converted from a mutual life-insurance company to a stock life-insurance company (a demutualization from Prudential Insurance). After all membership interests in Prudential Insurance were abolished on the date of demutualization, eligible policyholders received shares of Prudential Financial common stock or the right to receive cash or policy credits, which were increases in policy values or increases in other policy benefits. At the time of demutualization, Prudential Financial issued two classes of common stock. The common stock was publicly traded and reflected the performance of the Financial Services Business. The Class B stock was privately held and reflected the performance of the Closed Block Business.[5]

Since the 2001 IPO, Prudential's stock value had seen a steady but remarkable rise, followed by a quick and very steep decline (**Exhibit 1**). The decline can be attributed to the financial crisis that took hold of the markets in 2008 and particularly to investor concerns regarding the financial leverage of financial-services companies during this time.

Required

Prudential's balance sheet, income statement, and statement of stockholders' equity are shown in **Exhibits 2**, **3**, and **4**, respectively. Each statement was presented by the company in its 2007 annual report to shareholders. Use the exhibits to answer the following questions:

1. Compare the stockholders' equity section of the balance sheet (**Exhibit 2**) with the statement of stockholders' equity (**Exhibit 4**). Describe in general terms how they relate.
2. How many shares of preferred and common stock (including Class B stock) were authorized, issued, and outstanding as of December 31, 2007? Why do companies issue different classes of stock?
3. Approximate Prudential's total market value of common stock equity as of December 31, 2007. You may use any public data source to help in your estimation of total market value of equity. Is this number larger or smaller than the amounts reported on the balance sheet? Why do you think they differ?
4. How many shares of treasury stock did Prudential repurchase or reissue during 2007? Estimate the cash paid or received from these transactions.
5. What was the amount of dividends declared by Prudential during 2007? Approximate the company's dividend payout and dividend yield.
6. What does the account "Accumulated other comprehensive income" likely represent for Prudential? What is the logic of including this account in the stockholders' equity section of the balance sheet?
7. Compute the balance sheet leverage of Prudential for the years 2007 and 2006. What do these values tell you about the company? Why do you think this specific ratio became so critical during the fall of 2008?

---

[5] The plan of reorganization at demutualization required Prudential to establish and operate a regulatory mechanism known as the Closed Block. The Closed Block provided for the expectations of holders of participating individual life-insurance policies and annuities included in the Closed Block for future policy dividends after demutualization by allocating assets that would be used for payment of benefits on these policies, including policyholder dividends. Prudential could, with the prior consent of regulators, enter into agreements to transfer to a third party all or any part of the risks under the Closed Block policies. As of year-end 2005, 90% of the Closed Block had been reinsured.

EXHIBIT 1	Prudential Financial, Inc.: Stockholders' Equity and Balance Sheet Leverage

Common Stock Price Performance: January 2002–November 2008

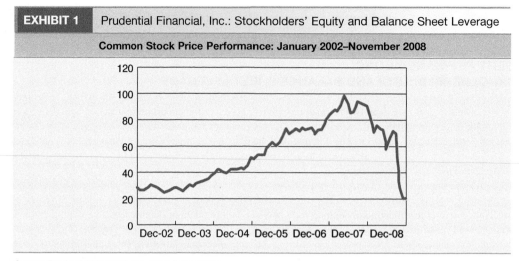

Source: Prudential Financial, Inc. 2007 Form 10-Ks.

EXHIBIT 2	Prudential Financial, Inc.: Stockholders' Equity and Balance Sheet Leverage

Balance Sheets: December 31, 2007 and 2006 (in millions, except share amounts)

	2007	2006
Assets		
Fixed maturities:		
Available for sale, at fair value (amortized cost: 2007—$160,137; 2006—$158,828)	$162,162	$162,816
Held to maturity, at amortized cost (fair value: 2007—$3,543; 2006—$3,441)	3,548	3,469
Trading account assets supporting insurance liabilities, at fair value	14,473	14,262
Other trading account assets, at fair value	3,163	2,209
Equity securities, available for sale, at fair value (cost: 2007—$7,895; 2006—$6,824).	8,580	8,103
Commercial loans.	30,047	25,739
Policy loans	9,337	8,887
Securities purchased under agreements to resell	129	153
Other long-term investments	6,431	4,745
Short-term investments	5,237	5,034
Total investments	243,107	235,417
Cash and cash equivalents	11,060	8,589
Accrued investment income.	2,174	2,142
Reinsurance recoverables	2,119	1,958
Deferred policy acquisition costs.	12,339	10,863
Other assets.	19,432	17,834
Separate account assets	195,583	177,463
Total assets	$485,814	$454,266
Liabilities and stockholders' equity		
Liabilities		
Future policy benefits.	$111,468	$106,951
Policyholders' account balances	84,154	80,652
Policyholders' dividends	3,661	3,982
Reinsurance payables	1,552	1,458
Securities sold under agreements to repurchase.	11,441	11,481
Cash collateral for loaned securities	6,312	7,365
Income taxes	3,553	3,108
Short-term debt	15,657	12,536
Long-term debt	14,101	11,423
Other liabilities	14,875	14,955
Separate account liabilities	195,583	177,463
Total liabilities.	$462,357	$431,374
Commitments and contingent liabilities (see Note 21)		
Stockholders' equity		
Preferred stock ($0.01 par; 10,000,000 shares authorized; none issued)	—	—
Common stock ($0.01 par; 1,500,000,000 shares authorized; 604,901,479 and		
604,900,423 shares issued at December 31, 2007 and 2006, respectively)	6	6
Class B stock ($0.01 par; 10,000,000 authorized; 2,000,000 issued and outstanding).	—	—
Additional paid-in capital	20,856	20,666
Common stock held in treasury, at cost (157,534,628 and 133,795,373 at		
year end 2007 and 2006)	(9,693)	(7,143)
Accumulated other comprehensive income.	447	519
Retained earnings	11,841	8,844
Total stockholders' equity	$ 23,457	$ 22,892
Total liabilities and stockholders' equity.	$485,814	$454,266

Source: Prudential Financial, Inc. 2007 Form 10-Ks.

EXHIBIT 3	Prudential Financial, Inc.: Stockholders' Equity and Balance Sheet Leverage		

Income Statements

Years Ended December 31, 2007, 2006 and 2005 (in millions, except per share amounts)	2007	2006	2005
Revenues			
Premiums	$14,351	$13,908	$13,756
Policy charges and fee income	3,131	2,653	2,520
Net investment income	12,017	11,320	10,595
Realized investment gains, net.	613	774	1,378
Asset management fees and other income	4,289	3,613	3,098
Total revenues	34,401	32,268	31,347
Benefits and expenses			
Policyholders' benefits.	14,749	14,283	13,883
Interest credited to policyholders' account balances	3,222	2,917	2,699
Dividends to policyholders.	2,903	2,622	2,850
General and administrative expenses	8,841	8,052	7,641
Total benefits and expenses.	29,715	27,874	27,073
Income from continuing operations before income taxes	4,686	4,394	4,274
Income taxes:			
Current	783	488	(59)
Deferred	462	757	862
Total income tax expense.	1,245	1,245	803
Income from continuing operations before equity earnings.	3,441	3,149	3,471
Equity in earnings of operating joint ventures, net of taxes.	246	208	142
Income from continuing operations	3,687	3,357	3,613
Income (loss) from discontinued operations, net of taxes	17	71	(73)
Net income.	$ 3,704	$ 3,428	$ 3,540
Earnings per share			
Financial services businesses			
Basic:			
Income from continuing operations per share of common stock	$ 7.72	$ 6.49	$ 6.59
Income (loss) from discontinued operations, net of taxes	0.03	0.14	(0.14)
Net income per share of common stock	$ 7.75	$ 6.63	$ 6.45
Diluted:			
Income from continuing operations per share of common stock	$ 7.58	$ 6.36	$ 6.48
Income (loss) from discontinued operations, net of taxes	0.03	0.14	(0.14)
Net income per share of common stock	$ 7.61	$ 6.50	$ 6.34
Dividends declared per share of common stock	$ 1.15	$ 0.95	$ 0.78

Source: Prudential Financial, Inc. 2007 Form 10-Ks.

EXHIBIT 4	Prudential Financial, Inc.: Stockholders' Equity and Balance Sheet Leverage

Statement of Stockholders' Equity

Years Ended December 31, 2007, 2006 and 2005 (in millions)	Common Stock	Class B Stock	Additional Paid-In Capital	Retained Earnings	Common Stock Held in Treasury	Accum. Other Compr. Income	Total Stockholders' Equity
Balance, December 31, 2004.	$ 6	$—	$20,348	$ 2,851	$(3,052)	$2,191	$22,344
Common Stock acquired	—	—	—	—	(2,090)	—	(2,090)
Stock-based compensation.	—	—	153	(32)	217	—	338
Dividends declared on Common	—	—	—	(393)	—	—	(393)
Dividends declared on Class B	—	—	—	(19)	—	—	(19)
Comprehensive income:							
Net income.	—	—	—	3,540	—	—	3,540
Other comprehensive loss	—	—	—	—	—	(957)	(957)
Total comprehensive income							2,583
Balance, December 31, 2005.	6	—	20,501	5,947	(4,925)	1,234	22,763
Common Stock acquired	—	—	—	—	(2,500)	—	(2,500)
Stock-based compensation.	—	—	165	(59)	282	—	388
Dividends declared on Common	—	—	—	(453)	—	—	(453)
Dividends declared on Class B	—	—	—	(19)	—	—	(19)
Adoption of SFAS No. 158	—	—	—	—	—	(556)	(556)
Comprehensive income:							
Net income.	—	—	—	3,428	—	—	3,428
Other comprehensive loss	—	—	—	—	—	(159)	(159)
Total comprehensive income	—	—	—	—	—	—	3,269
Balance, December 31, 2006.	6	—	20,666	8,844	(7,143)	519	22,892
Common Stock acquired	—	—	—	—	(3,000)	—	(3,000)
Stock-based compensation.	—	—	191	(34)	315	—	472
Conversion of Senior Notes	—	—	(1)	(90)	135	—	44
Dividends declared on Common	—	—	—	(521)	—	—	(521)
Dividends declared on Class B	—	—	—	(19)	—	—	(19)
Changes in accounting principles	—	—	—	(43)	—	—	(43)
Comprehensive income:							
Net income.	—	—	—	3,704	—	—	3,704
Other comprehensive loss	—	—	—	—	—	(72)	(72)
Total comprehensive income	—	—	—	—	—	—	3,632
Balance, December 31, 2007.	$ 6	$—	$20,856	$11,841	$(9,693)	$ 447	$23,457

Source: Prudential Financial, Inc. 2007 Form 10-Ks.

SOLUTIONS TO REVIEW PROBLEMS

Solution 11.1

	Issue Stock	Repurchase Shares
Assets		
Cash..	5,000,000	(150,000)
Shareholders' Equity		
Common stock.......................................	500,000	
Additional paid-in-capital......................	4,500,000	
Treasury stock		(150,000)

Solution 11.2

	THE ARCADIA COMPANY		
	a.	b.	c.
	2:1 Stock Split*	10% Stock Dividend **	Cash Dividend ***
Assets........................			
Cash.........................			(107,800)
Shareholders' Equity			
Common stock...................		49,000	
Additional paid-in-capital..........		1,715,000	
Retained earnings		(1,764,000)	(107,800)

*   No entry, but must reduce par value of common stock to $0.50 per share ($1.00/2)
**   980,000 outstanding shares × 10% × $0.50 par value = $49,000.
      980,000 outstanding shares × 10% × $18 per share = $1,764,000.
***   1,078,000 outstanding shares × $0.10 = $107,800.
Shares outstanding: 500,000 − 10,000 = 490,000 × 2 = 980,000 + (980,000 × 10%) = 1,078,000.

Solution 11.3

	THE ARCADIA COMPANY										
	Issue Stock	Generate Revenue	Incur Expenses	EOY 1 Balance Sheet	a. 2:1 Stock Split	b. Repurch. Shares	c. 10% Stock Dividend	d. Cash Dividend	e. Generate Revenue	e. Incur Expenses	EOY 2 Balance Sheet
Assets											
Cash	$5,000,000	$2,000,000	$(800,000)	$6,200,000		$(150,000)		$(108,900)	$3,000,000	$(1,200,000)	$7,741,100
Total assets				6,200,000	no entry						7,741,100
					::						
Shareholders' Equity					::						
Common stock ($1 par).....	500,000			500,000	reduce		$49,500¹				549,500
Additional paid-in-capital ...	$4,500,000			4,500,000	par		1,732,500				6,232,500
Retained earnings.........				1,200,000	to		$(1,782,000)¹	$(108,900)²			1,109,100
Revenues		$2,000,000			$0.50				$3,000,000		
Expenses			$(800,000)		::					$(1,200,000)	
Treasury stock............				—		$(150,000)					(150,000)
Total shareholders' equity ..				$6,200,000							$7,741,100

1.   990,000 outstanding shares × 10% × $0.50 par value = $49,500.   990,000 outstanding shares × 10% × $18 per share = $1,782,000.
2.   1,089,000 outstanding shares × $0.10 = $108,900.

THE ARCADIA COMPANY	
Partial Balance Sheet	
Shareholders' equity	
Common stock, $0.50 par value 1,099,000 shares issued; 1,089,000 shares outstanding	$ 549,500
Additional paid-in-capital	6,232,500
Retained earnings	1,109,100
Treasury stock	(150,000)
Total shareholders' equity	$7,741,100

When you complete this chapter you should be able to:

1. Construct pro forma financial statements and understand their purpose and use. (page 458)

2. Understand how accounting information is used in equity valuation. (page 463)

3. Understand how to develop cash flow data, useful in the valuation of a company, by using key accounting measurement concepts. (page 464)

4. Estimate the value of a company using the discounted cash flow model. (page 467)

5. Estimate the value of a company using the residual income model. (page 473)

6. Describe how price-earnings multiples are used in valuation. (page 475)

Using Accounting Information in Equity Valuation

12

John Mackey, along with two other Austin, Texas, investors, decided that the natural foods industry was ready for a super-market format. In 1980, they opened the first Whole Foods Market with a staff of only 19 people. The company is now the world's leading retailer of natural and organic foods, with 431 stores in the U.S., Canada, and the United Kingdom. For the fiscal year ended September 27, 2015, sales reached $15.4 billion, a nearly 24 percent compounded growth rate over the prior 24 years.

Whole Foods Market is a mission driven company with a strong belief in a "virtuous circle," including the food chain, people, and the planet. The company motto is "Whole Foods, Whole People, Whole Planet." It is consistently honored for its commitment to corporate social responsibility, ranking among "The Top 50 Best Corporate Citizens" by *Business Ethics* magazine and among "The Top 10 Companies To Work For" by *Fortune* magazine.

Whole Foods Market is also customer driven. The company strives to provide a high level of customer satisfaction and believes that by "offering the highest quality food available, we are helping to transform the diet of America, helping people live longer, healthier, more pleasurable lives while responding positively to the challenge of environmental sustainability." It has been recognized consistently for these efforts, and is ranked among the most socially responsible businesses by the U.S. Environmental Protection Agency.

Whole Foods Market understands that profits are an essential ingredient if it wishes to be a responsible corporate citizen and provide benefits to its many stakeholders. As the company states, profits are "the 'seed corn' for next year's crop. We are the stewards of our shareholders' investments and we are committed to increasing long-term shareholder value." The company utilizes Economic Value Added (EVA), a variation of the residual income method discussed in this chapter, to help evaluate the firm's progress in reaching this goal.

What does it mean to increase long-term shareholder value? Shareholder value is increased when the return on the shareholders' investment in a business enterprise is increased through a combination of dividend distributions and share price appreciation. To determine whether this goal is attained requires that a value be calculated as to what an enterprise is worth. In this chapter, we examine various methodologies that allow a financial statement user to estimate the value of a company like Whole Foods Market.

EXECUTIVE OUTLINE

Takeaway 1
Construct pro forma financial statements and understand their purpose and use.

PRO FORMA FINANCIAL STATEMENTS

We first considered pro forma financial statements in Appendix 4B. At that time, we observed that investment professionals, managers, and shareholders are often interested in knowing how a firm might perform in the future under various economic scenarios. Pro forma financial statements are a good source of information to address these kinds of questions, particularly with respect to equity valuation. Indeed, a complete set of forecasted financial statements yields most inputs needed in a variety of valuation models, such as those based on dividends, book values, earnings, or cash flows. An added advantage of pro forma financial statements is that they necessitate consideration of all possible financial aspects of the business. Examples include the required capital structure, the cash-generating ability of the company, solvency risk assessments, and sources of growth. In this chapter, we continue our exploration of pro forma financial statements as they relate to valuing the shareholders' equity of a company. As we will soon see, pro forma statements provide the raw data to develop an assessment of the fair value of a company.[1]

To facilitate the calculations necessary to develop pro forma financial statements, we recommend utilizing an electronic spreadsheet. To illustrate the process of setting up such a spreadsheet, we again turn to the financial data of the Russian River Valley Winery, Inc. developed in Chapter 2. In Chapter 2, we prepared a forecast of the firm's first year of operations in conjunction with the winery's request for bank financing. The winery's first-year results (here assumed to be 2015) were stronger than predicted as the firm was able to sell more wine than its owners initially forecasted (sales of $1.9 million were forecasted while actual sales of $2.2 million were achieved). In addition, cost of goods sold comprised only 15 percent of sales rather than the predicted 20 percent. This positive turn of events led to a higher than expected net income for the first year ($317,000 forecasted net income versus $521,000 actual net income). The second year of operations (2016) proved to be even better than the first, with an additional ten percent increase in sales (actual sales of $2.42 million). We now turn our attention to forecasting the next five years of performance for the winery to estimate the value of Matt's and Kate's investment in the business.

Exhibit 12.1 presents a spreadsheet summary for the winery, reflecting both its historical and forecasted financial performance. Columns two and three, for example, display the two years of actual performance data for the winery (2015 and 2016). This historical performance data, along with our knowledge of the operating environment of the winery, provides the necessary data for forecasting the winery's future financial performance. Our goal is to develop pro forma financial statements for the period 2017 through 2021.

---

[1] The term "pro forma" in Latin means "as a matter of form." In business this has come to mean financial statements prepared in advance of a planned transaction, investment, or period. The pro forma statements take the "form," therefore, of an anticipated set of results that summarize the future.

| EXHIBIT 12.1 | Pro Forma Financial Statements: Russian River Valley Winery, Inc. |

Panel A Income Statement

($ thousands)	Actual		Forecast					Terminal Year
	2015	2016	2017	2018	2019	2020	2021	
Sales (net)...............................	$2,200	$2,420	$2,662	$2,928	$3,221	$3,543	$3,897	$4,092
Cost of goods sold.......................	(330)	(363)	(399)	(439)	(483)	(531)	(585)	(614)
Gross profit...............................	1,870	2,057	2,263	2,489	2,738	3,012	3,312	3,478
SG&A expense............................	(506)	(557)	(612)	(673)	(741)	(815)	(896)	(941)
Depreciation and amortization...........	(275)	(275)	(275)	(275)	(275)	(275)	(275)	(289)
Interest expense..........................	(288)	(230)	(202)	(173)	(144)	(115)	(86)	(90)
Income before income taxes.............	801	995	1,174	1,368	1,578	1,807	2,055	2,158
Income taxes.............................	(280)	(348)	(411)	(479)	(552)	(632)	(719)	(755)
Net income...............................	$ 521	$ 647	$ 763	$ 889	$1,026	$1,174*	$1,336	$1,403

Panel B Balance Sheet

($ thousands)	Actual		Forecast					Terminal Year
	2015	2016	2017	2018	2019	2020	2021	
Cash.......................................	$ 860	$ 726	$ 799	$ 878	$ 966	$ 1,063	$ 1,169	$ 1,228*
Other current assets......................	1,180	968	1,065	1,171	1,288	1,417	1,559	1,637
Total current assets	2,040	1,694	1,864	2,050*	2,254	2,480	2,728	2,865
PP&E (net)	9,275	9,275	9,275	9,275	9,275	9,275	9,275	9,739
Intangibles	50	0	0	0	0	0	0	0
Total assets...............................	$11,365	$10,969	$11,139	$11,325	$11,529	$11,755	$12,003	$12,603*
Current debt..............................	$ 480	$ 480	$ 480	$ 480	$ 480	$ 480	$ 480	$ 504
Other current liabilities	384	605	666	732	805	886	974	1,023
Total current liabilities....................	864	1,085	1,146	1,212	1,285	1,366	1,454	1,527
Long-term debt	3,840	3,360	2,880	2,400	1,920	1,440	960	1,008
Total liabilities............................	4,704	4,445	4,026	3,612	3,205	2,806	2,414	2,535
Paid-in-capital	6,400	6,400	6,400	6,400	6,400	6,400	6,400	6,720
Retained earnings	261	124	713	1,313	1,924	2,549	3,189	3,348
Total shareholders' equity	6,661	6,524	7,113	7,713	8,324	8,949	9,589	10,068
Total liabilities and shareholders' equity..	$11,365	$10,969	$11,139	$11,325	$11,529	$11,755	$12,003	$12,603

Panel C Statement of Retained Earnings

($ thousands)	Actual		Forecast					Terminal Year
	2015	2016	2017	2018	2019	2020	2021	
Beg. retained earnings	$ 0	$261	$124	$ 713	$1,313	$1,924	$2,549	$3,189
+ Net income	521	647	763	889	1,026	1,174	1,336	1,403
− Dividends	(260)	(784)	(174)	(289)	(414)	(549)	(696)	(1,243)
= End. retained earnings	$261	$124	$713	$1,313	$1,924*	$2,549	$3,189	$3,348*

*minor rounding difference

continued next page

To begin, the single most important assumption when developing pro forma financial statements is the forecast of future sales revenue. The forecasting process begins with projected sales because, as you might expect, future assets and liabilities frequently arise directly from the revenue activities of a firm. A number of income statement costs then follow directly from the sales activity forecasted. Recurring costs—such as cost of goods sold and selling, general, and administrative expenses (SG&A)—are usually incurred to generate sales, and thus are typically some reasonable function of predicted sales. Because so many of the income statement and balance sheet accounts are dependent on a firm's future sales, a poor forecast with this line item is very likely to result in a poorly constructed set of pro forma financial statements, and hence, an incorrect estimate of firm value. Consequently, it is essential to utilize whatever data may be available, such as a firm's prior operating history, the expected demand for new products, demographic trends, and inflation to make the sales forecast as accurate as possible.

continued from previous page

EXHIBIT 12.1	Pro Forma Financial Statements: Russian River Valley Winery, Inc.

Panel D Statement of Cash Flow

($ thousands)	Actual		Forecast					Terminal
	2015	2016	2017	2018	2019	2020	2021	Year
Operating activities								
Net income..................................	$ 521	$ 647	$ 763	$ 889	$1,026	$1,174	$1,336	$1,403
+ Depreciation and amortization	275	275	275	275	275	275	275	289
− Increase in other current assets	(1,180)	212	(97)	(106)	(117)	(129)	(142)	(78)
+ Increase in other current liabilities....................	384	221	61	66	73	81	88	49
= Cash from operations	(0)	1,355	1,002	1,124	1,257	1,401	1,557	1,663
Investing activities								
− Capital expenditures............................	(9,550)	(225)	(275)	(275)	(275)	(275)	(275)	(753)
− Purchases of intangibles.........................	(50)	0	0	0	0	0	0	0
= Cash from investing	(9,600)	(225)	(275)	(275)	(275)	(275)	(275)	(753)
Financing activities								
+ Increase in debt...............................	4,320	(480)	(480)	(480)	(480)	(480)	(480)	72
− Dividends	(260)	(784)	(174)	(289)	(414)	(549)	(696)	(1,243)
Issuance of common stock	6,400	0	0	0	0	0	0	320
= Cash from financing	10,460	(1,264)	(654)	(769)	(894)	(1,029)	(1,176)	(851)
Change in cash...................................	$ 860	$ (134)	$ 73	$ 80	$ 88	$ 97	$ 106	$ 59
+ Beg. cash	0	860	726	799	878	966	1,063	1,169
Ending cash balance	$ 860	$ 726	$ 799	$ 878*	$ 966	$1,063	$1,169	$1,228

*minor rounding difference

The process of preparing pro forma financial statements typically progresses with the following set of steps:

1. Forecast sales revenue.

2. Forecast the cost of goods sold, gross profit, and other operating expenses on the income statement as a function of forecasted sales, using the historical common-size percentages for those accounts (as a percentage of sales) where a linear relationship with sales is evident.

3. Forecast the balance sheet working capital accounts such as cash, accounts receivable, inventory, and accounts payable needed to support the forecasted sales, using such historical relationships as revealed by the receivable, inventory, and payable turnover ratios.

4. Forecast the property, plant and equipment and intangible assets needed to support the forecasted level of sales, using such historical relationships as revealed by the fixed asset turnover and intangible asset turnover ratios.

5. Forecast depreciation and amortization expense as a function of forecasted property, plant, and equipment and intangible assets. (Investment professionals frequently adopt a half-year convention when forecasting the depreciation and amortization expense associated with these capital investments to compensate for the uncertainty regarding the timing of such investments.)

6. Forecast the level of debt financing based on such strategic factors as the desired capital structure and the forecasted growth in sales.

7. Forecast interest expense based on the level of forecasted debt.

8. Forecast any remaining items on the income statement (e.g., investment income and non-recurring items) and then forecast the income tax expense based on forecasted earnings before tax and the firm's effective tax rate.

9. Forecast the statement of retained earnings based on the forecasted income statement, including any expected dividend payments.

10. Prepare the pro forma statement of cash flow from the forecasted income statement and forecasted balance sheets using the indirect method (see Chapter 3).

11. Determine a **terminal year growth rate** for the pro forma terminal year. Practically speaking, it is unreasonable to continue to forecast indefinitely. The terminal year is the year following the final forecast period (2021 for the Russian River Valley Winery) wherein it is assumed that the firm has reached a steady state and constant growth will persist in perpetuity. More on the terminal year a bit later.

The above steps illustrate one approach to preparing pro forma financial statements. Other approaches also exist. For example, while accounts receivable, inventory, and accounts payable may be forecasted based on their respective turnover ratios, some investment professionals instead use the historical common-size balance sheet percentages to forecast these operating assets. And, some will use a combination of ratios and common-size percentages to develop their pro forma estimates. As a consequence of the alternative approaches that may be used to forecast the individual balance sheet accounts, it is typical for a pro forma balance sheet to be out-of-balance. When this occurs, a plug figure is required to achieve the necessary equality demanded by the balance sheet equation. Possible plug figures include cash and marketable securities when a plug figure is needed to balance the asset side of the balance sheet, and short-term debt or a line of credit when a plug figure is needed to balance the liability side of the balance sheet.[2] When determining what account should be the final plug, the most appropriate approach would be to determine first what the company would choose to do with any excess cash it might generate in the business. For instance, if the company would pay down debt, then long-term debt might be the final plug. If, alternatively, the company pays dividends with excess cash, then dividends (and retained earnings) might be the final plug account. For our illustration we will use dividends and retained earnings for this purpose.

Exhibit 12.2 presents the various representative assumptions that were used to construct the pro forma financial statements for the Russian River Valley Winery that appear in the forecast columns (2017 through 2021) of Exhibit 12.1. As detailed in Exhibit 12.2, the following assumptions were utilized:

- Sales are expected to grow by ten percent per year for five years and by five percent annually thereafter. As mentioned above, in practice a number of economic, industry and company specific factors would need to be evaluated to determine the appropriate level of expected sales.

- Cost of goods sold will remain a constant 15 percent of sales. This assumption equates to an expected 85 percent gross margin. As cost of sales relates directly to the purchase and distribution of wine products, any changes in expected margins should be considered and included in the forecast.

- Selling, general, and administrative (SG&A) expenses will remain a constant 23 percent of sales. Without any information to the contrary, the historical relation between these costs and sales is a reasonable approximation. The forecaster should be careful to incorporate any known fixed costs into the assumed relation if known. That is, if for example $0.5 million of Russian River Valley Winery's SG&A related to management salary and were known beforehand to be fixed, then the forecast should include a smaller percentage of SG&A that would be predicted to vary with the level of sales. The $0.5 million would be treated as a constant fixed cost.

- Since Russian River Valley Winery has sufficient capacity to produce enough wine to satisfy projected sales for the next five years without any new capital investment, PP&E is expected to remain constant for the next five years. As a consequence, depreciation will remain constant at the 2016 level. In practice, any known additional PP&E required to support a level of sales would be included in the forecast. The only capital outlay in the present case will be an amount equal to the annual depreciation expense.

- Interest expense will be six percent of the outstanding end-of-year balance of bank debt. This rate should be the assumed borrowing rate required for the level of bank debt carried by the company.

- Income taxes will be 35 percent of earnings before income taxes. This is typical of most tax rate assumptions, as 35 percent is the base U.S. corporate tax rate. To the extent the winery does business and earns profits in other tax jurisdictions (e.g., internationally, or within certain states), then these different tax rates should be what drive the tax rate assumption used in the forecast.

---

[2] Care must be taken, however, when choosing a plug figure account as there are many interdependencies in the financial statements. For example, if debt is used as a plug figure to balance the liability side of the balance sheet, then interest expense on the income statement will need to be recomputed each time that the level of debt changes. This will alter net income, and therefore retained earnings, forcing another change to debt. While such situations can be resolved with more advanced mathematical techniques, it is often easier to use an account that has fewer dependencies (such as cash). It is also possible to solve these "circular reference" situations with the iteration function within Excel.

■ Cash will be maintained at 30 percent of sales. Companies typically require a certain level of liquidity, and as the company grows, so often also does the cash balance.

■ Other current assets will be maintained at 40 percent of sales, and other current liabilities will remain a constant 25 percent of sales. As is often the case with cash, a required level of working capital is often needed to support ongoing sales.

■ The current debt will continue to be paid down at a constant rate ($480,000 per year) for five years. After 2021, debt will grow at a rate equal to sales growth. The forecast should always include any known reductions in debt, as well as new borrowings.

■ Dividend payments are forecasted as a plug figure to balance retained earnings on the balance sheet. Dividends here are considered a discretionary cash outlay after the other remaining needs of the business have been satisfied. This assumption also helps serve as the final balancing amount for the balance sheet.

The spreadsheet summary in Exhibit 12.1 reveals that based upon the above set of assumptions, the Russian River Valley Winery is projected to have both increasing profits and increasing cash flow from operations throughout the forecast period and beyond. Therefore, our assumptions regarding the need for debt and continuing dividend payments appear reasonable. One advantage of the electronic spreadsheet approach is that it is possible to conduct "what if" analyses—that is, to evaluate how the winery's financial performance would be affected if, for instance, sales growth is reduced to, say, five percent or if gross profit percentages are increased to reflect the realization of economies of scale that come with greater levels of output. In the next section, we will see how the pro forma financial statements can be used to help assess the equity value of a firm.

EXHIBIT 12.2	Summary Pro Forma Assumptions used for Russian River Valley Winery
Item	**Assumption**
Sales.	Grows annually at 10% until terminal year
Cost of goods sold.	15% of sales
SG&A expense	23% of sales
Depreciation.	Constant until terminal year
Interest expense.	6% of outstanding debt
Income taxes	35% of earnings before taxes
Cash.	30% of sales
Other current assets.	40% of sales
PP&E	Constant net PP&E until terminal year
Debt	Constant payments of $480 until terminal year
Other current liabilities	25% of sales
Dividends	Plug figure to balance the balance sheet
All items	Terminal 5% annual growth

REVIEW PROBLEM 12.1

Azusa Company reported the following financial results for 2016 and 2017:

AZUSA COMPANY Income Statements		
	2016	**2017**
Sales.	$3,000	$3,120
Cost of goods sold.	1,200	1,248
Gross profit.	1,800	1,872
SG&A expense	300	312
Depreciation.	1,200	1,200
Interest	250	150
Income before taxes.	50	210
Income taxes	15	63
Net income.	$ 35	$ 147

continued

Azusa Company Balance Sheets		
	2016	**2017**
Cash.	$ 700	$ 750
Other current assets.	1,050	1,125
Total current assets	1,750	1,875
PP&E(net)	12,000	10,800
Total assets.	$13,750	$12,675
Accounts payable.	$ 375	$ 450
Other current liabilities	1,625	328
Total current liabilities.	2,000	778
Long-term debt	5,000	5,000
Total liabilities.	7,000	5,778
Common Stock and Paid-in-capital.	5,500	5,500
Retained earnings	1,250	1,397
Total shareholders' equity	6,750	6,897
Total liabilities and shareholders' equity.	$13,750	$12,675

Azusa Company did not pay any dividends in 2016 or in 2017.

Required

Prepare pro forma income statements and balance sheets for Azusa Company for the years 2018–2020 using the following assumptions:

1. Sales are expected to grow annually by four percent.
2. Cost of sales will remain at a constant forty percent of sales.
3. Sales, general, and administrative (SG&A) expenses will remain at a constant ten percent of sales.
4. The company will not be purchasing any additional property, plant, and equipment for the next three years (i.e., net PP&E will only change by the annual depreciation expense).
5. Since there will not be any additional purchases of PP&E, nor any sales, depreciation expense will remain constant for the next three years.
6. The company does not foresee any need for additional debt or equity financing during the next three years. Long-term debt is interest only with the entire principal balance due in five years.
7. Interest expense is computed as five percent of the long-term debt balance.
8. Income taxes are computed at an effective tax rate of 30 percent.
9. There are no plans to pay dividends during the next three years.
10. Cash, other current assets, and accounts payable will remain constant during the next three years, at their 2017 level.
11. Other current liabilities are used as a plug figure to balance the balance sheet.

The solution is on pages 502–503.

Introduction to Equity Valuation

How much is the Russian River Valley Winery worth? Recall from Chapter 2 that Matt and Kate sold 200,000 shares of the winery's common stock to an outside investor for $2 per share. How could that outside investor determine if this was a reasonable price to pay for the Russian River Valley Winery shares? An important role for accounting information is its use in valuing a business. To answer the question of what a share of stock in the Russian River Valley Winery is worth, it is first necessary to select a valuation framework to estimate the company's value. There are several valuation models that are widely used. If done correctly and under a consistent set of forecasting assumptions, each model will yield the same estimate of firm value since they are based on the same fundamental theory of economic risk and reward. Which model is used is usually determined by individual investor preference, or practical considerations such as data availability.

Takeaway 2
Understand how accounting information is used in equity valuation.

The two models that we will illustrate are the discounted cash flow model, which is based on a firm's free cash flow, and the residual income model, which is based on a firm's accrual-based earnings. We also explore the popular price-earnings multiple model—a model whose popularity can be traced to its ease of use and ease in understanding.

Takeaway 3

Understand how to develop cash flow data, useful in the valuation of a company, by using key accounting measurement concepts.

USING CASH FLOW DATA TO VALUE A COMPANY

A fundamental tenet of modern financial theory is that the value of an asset or a bundle of assets (such as an entire company), is equal to the present value of the future cash flows that accrue from ownership. Thus, this tenet suggests that the primary source of firm value is a firm's operating cash flows that are not required to reinvest back into the company to keep it viable and growing. This excess cash flow is the lifeblood of the valuation process. Hence, the first task that investment professionals, equity investors, and managers face when trying to value a company is to forecast a firm's future cash flows freely available to distribute back to the owners, using pro forma financial statements, and to then value those projected future cash flows into today's dollar equivalent using an appropriate discount rate. This valuation framework is called the **discounted cash flow approach**.

Developing Cash Flow Data

Use of the discounted cash flow approach to firm valuation assumes an understanding of, and capability of, developing cash flow data. As indicated above, pro forma cash flow data is extracted from the pro forma income statements and balance sheets using the indirect method format. In Chapter 3, we illustrated a five-step process for preparing a statement of cash flow using the indirect method. That illustration was, of necessity, highly simplistic. We now return to that five-step process and consider a more sophisticated cash flow example that integrates some of the accounting measurement concepts and approaches discussed in Chapters 5 through 11. Specifically, we now consider how the accounting for zero-coupon bonds (Chapter 9); the use of the equity method to account for unconsolidated affiliates, joint ventures or special purpose entities (Chapter 8); and the accounting for a gain or loss on the sale or retirement of a long-lived asset (Chapter 7) affect the cash flow of a company.

Our illustration for this purpose involves the Arctic Sea Oil & Gas Company Ltd., a Canadian energy company. Financial information for the company for 2015 and 2016 is presented in Panels A and B of Exhibit 12.3. As discussed in Chapter 3, the five-step process to prepare a statement of cash flow using the indirect method format is as follows:

1. Measure the change in all balance sheet accounts by subtracting the beginning balance from the ending balance. Recall that the increase or decrease in the cash and cash equivalents account is the check figure for the cash flow statement.

2. Classify each of the balance sheet accounts into one of the three cash flow activity categories: Operating, Investing, or Financing.

3. Prepare a *preliminary* statement of cash flow using the values from Step 1 and the activity classifications from Step 2. Remember that the signs of the changes of the asset accounts are reversed, but the signs of the changes of the liability and shareholders' equity accounts are not.

4. Integrate the income statement data (such as depreciation and amortization expense) into the preliminary statement of cash flow, remembering that it is necessary to always balance to the change in cash.

5. Make any necessary refinements to the cash flow from operations (CFFO) to identify the sustainable operating cash flow of the business by removing any nonrecurring, nonoperating gains or losses.

Panel A of Exhibit 12.3 presents the results of Steps 1 and 2 of our five-step process; and, Panel C presents the results of Step 3—Arctic's preliminary statement of cash flow using only the company's balance sheet data. As required, Arctic's preliminary statement of cash flow balances to the change in cash on Arctic's balance sheet of negative $10.183 million. Can you replicate Arctic's preliminary statement of cash flow in Panel C using the data from Panel A of Exhibit 12.3?

Step 4 involves the introduction of Arctic's income statement data presented in Panel B of Exhibit 12.3. The adjustments (in thousands) to the preliminary statement of cash flow required at this step include the following:

1. Replace Arctic's change in retained earnings of $22,668 with net income of $46,168 in the operating activities section. The difference of $23,500 ($46,168 – $22,668) is also shown as a cash outflow for dividends paid to shareholders in the financing activities section.

2. Depreciation and depletion expense of $24,800, a noncash expense, is added back to accrual net income in the operating activities section and also subtracted from the change in the oil and gas properties (net) in the investing activities section.

3. Amortization expense of $750, a noncash expense, is added back to accrual net income in the operating activities section and subtracted from the change in intangible assets in the investing activities section.

4. Zero-coupon interest expense of $4,757, a noncash expense, is added back to accrual net income in the operating activities section and subtracted from the change in zero-coupon debenture issuance in the financing activities section.

5. The equity in the earnings of unconsolidated affiliates of $36,650, representing Arctic's ownership interest in the earnings of its affiliates that it does not control (and thus which remain unconsolidated), is subtracted from accrual net income in the operating activities section and added to the change in the investment in affiliated companies in the investing activities section.

6. The gain on the sale of property and equipment of $1,000, a nonrecurring and nonoperating event, is subtracted from net income in the operating activities section and added to the change in oil and gas properties (net) in the investing activities section.

EXHIBIT 12.3   Financial Statement Data: Arctic Sea Oil & Gas Company Ltd.

Panel A Consolidated Balance Sheet

(in thousands)	2016	2015	Change	Category
Assets				
Current assets				
Cash..	$100,067	$110,250	$ (10,183)	Check Fig.
Accounts receivable.............................	69,100	53,200	15,900	O
Inventory	58,950	46,800	12,150	O
Prepaid expenses	11,108	13,850	(2,742)	O
	239,225	224,100		
Investments				
In affiliated companies...........................	159,000	151,000	8,000	I
Marketable equity securities	2,500	0	2,500	I
Long-term assets				
Oil & gas properties, equipment (net)	237,850	246,900	(9,050)	I/O
Intangible assets	3,000	3,750	(750)	I/O
Total assets....................................	**$641,575**	**$625,750**	**$ 15,825**	
Liabilities and Shareholders' Equity				
Current liabilities				
Accounts payable	$ 1,650	$ 8,000	$ (6,350)	O
Income taxes payable	4,750	3,250	1,500	O
Long-term liabilities				
Zero-coupon debentures.........................	53,507	0	53,507	F
Deferred income taxes...........................	46,000	40,000	6,000	O
Employee retirement benefits	62,500	60,000	2,500	O
Total liabilities....................................	168,407	111,250		
Shareholders' equity				
Common shares at par	103,000	75,000	28,000	F
Capital in excess of par..........................	157,500	150,000	7,500	F
Preferred shares, no par	0	100,000	(100,000)	F
Retained earnings	212,168	189,500	22,668	O/F
Other comprehensive income				
Unrealized gain on available-for-sale securities	500	0	500	I
Total liabilities and shareholders' equity	**$641,575**	**$625,750**	**$ 15,825**	

continued

continued from previous page

EXHIBIT 12.3	Financial Statement Data: Arctic Sea Oil & Gas Company Ltd.

Panel B Consolidated Income Statements
(in thousands)

	2016
Revenue	$483,135
Costs and expenses	
Cost of goods sold	345,920
Depreciation and depletion expense.	24,800
Selling and general expenses	54,215
Amortization expense	750
Operating income.	57,450
Other (expense) income	
Interest expense	(4,757)
Equity in earnings of unconsolidated affiliates	36,650
Gain on sale of property and equipment.	1,000
Income before income taxes	90,343
Less: Income tax provision.	(44,175)
Net income	**$ 46,168**

Panel C Preliminary Statement of Cash Flow
(in thousands)

	2016
Operating activities	
Retained earnings	**$ 22,668**
Accounts receivable.	(15,900)
Inventory	(12,150)
Prepaid expenses	2,742
Accounts payable	(6,350)
Income tax payable	1,500
Deferred income taxes.	6,000
Employee retirement benefits	2,500
Cash flow from operations (preliminary).	1,010
Investing activities	
Investment in affiliated companies	(8,000)
Marketable equity securities	(2,500)
Unrealized gain on long-term marketable securities	500
Oil and gas properties, equipment (net).	9,050
Intangible assets	750
Cash flow for investing (preliminary)	(200)
Financing activities	
Zero-coupon debenture issuance	53,507
Common stock issuance.	35,500
Preferred share retirement	(100,000)
Cash flow for financing (preliminary)	(10,993)
Change in cash.	(10,183)
Beginning cash.	110,250
Ending cash	$100,067

Following the set of six adjustments, it is now possible to develop Arctic's final statement of cash flow using the indirect method format, and this final statement is presented in Exhibit 12.4. Arctic's statement of cash flow in Exhibit 12.4 reveals that the company's cash flow from operations is $17.167 million, its cash flow from investing is $11.9 million, and its cash flow for financing is negative $39.25 million, aggregating to a decrease in cash of $10.183 million. Now that you have a more complete understanding of how to construct a complex statement of cash flow, let's consider how this data can be used to value a company using the discounted cash flow approach.

EXHIBIT 12.4	Statement of Cash Flow: Arctic Sea Oil & Gas Company Ltd.

Consolidated Statement of Cash Flow

(in thousands)	2016
Operating activities	
Net income.	$ 46,168
Accounts receivable.	(15,900)
Inventory	(12,150)
Prepaid expenses	2,742
Accounts payable	(6,350)
Income tax payable	1,500
Deferred income taxes.	6,000
Employee retirement benefits	2,500
Depreciation and depletion expense.	24,800
Amortization expense	750
Zero-coupon interest expense.	4,757
Equity in earnings of unconsolidated affiliates	(36,650)
Gain on sale of property and equipment.	(1,000)
Cash flow from operations	**17,167**
Investing activities	
Investment in affiliated companies	28,650
Marketable equity securities	(2,000)
Oil and gas properties, equipment (net).	(14,750)
Cash flow for investing	**11,900**
Financing activities	
Zero-coupon debenture issuance	48,750
Common stock issuance.	35,500
Preferred share retirement.	(100,000)
Dividends paid.	(23,500)
Cash flow for financing	**(39,250)**
Change in cash.	(10,183)
Beginning cash.	110,250
Ending cash	**$100,067**

VALUATION USING THE DISCOUNTED CASH FLOW MODEL

Takeaway 4
Estimate the value of a company using the discounted cash flow model.

The Operating Value of a Firm

One of the well-documented limitations of humans is an inability to forecast the future. Meteorologists routinely forecast the temperature and weather conditions for days, and sometimes even weeks in advance with considerable accuracy; but, they rarely attempt to forecast weather conditions years in advance because they lack the skill to do so. This same difficulty confronts financial analysts and managers as they try to estimate the value of a business. Since firm value depends on events that will occur well into the future, it is necessary to forecast the unknown, or at least some part of the unknown.

In general, most financial analysts feel comfortable forecasting a firm's performance for the coming year, at least for most industries. But, that confidence quickly erodes as they attempt to forecast beyond one or two years. Fortunately, as a consequence of the discounting process, the value of near-term forecasts is far more important when assessing firm value than are longer-term forecasts (i.e., recall that the value of $1 in one year is considerably greater than the value of $1 in ten years).

Because of our inability to accurately forecast far into the future, we dichotomize a company's future into two time periods—a specific forecast period (the pro forma statement preparation period) and the period thereafter. The pro forma forecast period is that period of time for which financial analysts and managers feel confident in their ability to prepare specific pro forma financial statements, and thereafter is all periods in which they feel unable to do so. Using this dichotomy, we define the **operating value** of a business as follows:

$$\text{Operating Value of a Business} = \text{Present Value of Operating Cash Flows During the Specific Forecast Period} + \text{Present Value of Operating Cash Flows Thereafter}$$

The second component of operating value is commonly referred to as the **continuing value** of a business, or alternatively, as its **terminal value** (TV). It is the value of a business from the end of the specific forecast period (the pro forma statement preparation period) until the business is sold or otherwise terminated. Thus, we can refine the definition of firm operating value as follows:

$$\text{Operating Value of a Business} = \text{Present Value of Operating Cash Flows During the Specific Forecast Period} + \text{Present Value of a Firm's TV}$$

We will have more to say about computing terminal values shortly.

Free Cash Flow

As noted earlier, the primary source of a firm's value is its **operating cash flow**—that is, the cash generated from its sustainable, recurring operations. There are two approaches to discounting the operating cash flow to value a company. One approach is to utilize a measure of the cash flow to all capital providers, both creditors and equity investors. This approach leads to a value for the entire enterprise. To obtain a value for just the equity of a business—that is, the value of a business's common shares—it is necessary to obtain a separate value for the firm's debt (as discussed in Chapter 9). The value of a firm's debt is then subtracted from the enterprise's total value to yield its equity value.[3] In this chapter, we illustrate a second discounted cash flow approach that is used to directly value the equity of a firm.

To be a going concern, a business must constantly reinvest in itself, replacing those assets consumed by its operations each period. As discussed in Chapter 3, a firm's **free cash flow** (FCF) is defined as the cash flow from operations (CFFO) available to capital contributors (debtholders and shareholders) less the capital expenditures necessary to enable a firm to maintain itself as a going concern (to replace or replenish any assets consumed).[4] A variant of a firm's FCF is its **free cash flow to equity**, which is nothing more than the net cash distributions to common shareholders.[5] Free cash flow to equity can be measured in multiple ways; however, all definitions are equivalent and must yield the same result. Exhibit 12.5 illustrates the computation of free cash flow to equity for the Russian River Valley Winery utilizing the financial statement data from Exhibit 12.1.[6]

The first definition of free cash flow to equity in Panel A is perhaps the simplest and most straightforward. It merely looks to the financing section of the statement of cash flow and identifies the two items that are cash flow transactions involving the common shareholders. For the Russian River Valley Winery in 2017, projected dividend payments are $174,000, but there are no other forecasted cash flows to or from shareholders, such as no sales or repurchases of common shares. Therefore, the free cash flow to equity is $174,000.

The second definition of free cash flow to equity, illustrated in Panel B of Exhibit 12.5, uses the statement of cash flow and backs into the amount of cash flow to equity by removing all other cash flows. This definition starts with the CFFO and subtracts any increase in the cash account (if the cash account increased, this would suggest that the cash was not paid to shareholders). Next, any cash from investing is added if it is positive and subtracted if it is negative. Finally, any cash received from borrowings is added and any cash paid to a firm's creditors is subtracted. What remains is the free cash flow to equity since the cash retained by the firm, used to purchase assets, or used to retire debt has been removed. For the Russian River Valley Winery in 2017, projected cash flow from operations is $1,002,000; however, the company retained $73,000 of this amount. From this net cash of $929,000 ($1,002,000 − $73,000), $275,000 was invested in long-term assets and $480,000 was used to retire debt, yielding a cash flow to equity of $174,000 ($929,000 − $480,000 − $275,000).

The final definition of free cash flow to equity uses only the income statement and the balance sheet. As noted in Panel C, the free cash flow to equity is simply net income less any increase in common shareholders' equity. For the Russian River Valley Winery in 2017, projected net income is $763,000 and the only

---

[3] For an example of this first approach, see the News Corp. Business Perspective illustration on pages 471–472.
[4] Recall from Chapter 3 that we defined a firm's free cash flows (FCF) as: FCF = CFFO – Capital expenditures.
[5] We will refer to free cash flow to common equity as simply "free cash flow to equity" under the assumption that a firm does not have any preferred shareholders. Free cash flow to equity is also often labeled "levered free cash flow," and free cash flow to both debt and equity holders is often labeled "unlevered free cash flow."
[6] Valuation computations for the Russian River Valley Winery were done with the aid of the spreadsheet program eVal. See Russel Lundholm and Richard Sloan, *Equity Valuation and Analysis with eVal*. McGraw-Hill, 2004.

EXHIBIT 12.5	Free Cash Flow to Equity Computation: Russian River Valley Winery					
Year of Forecast (in 000's) Panel A	**2017**	**2018**	**2019**	**2020**	**2021**	**Terminal Year**
Financing flows						
Dividends paid........................	$ 174	$ 289	$ 414	$ 549	$ 696	$1,243
− Net issuance of common stock...........	0	0	0	0	0	(320)
Free cash flow to equity	$ 174	$ 289	$ 414	$ 549	$ 696	$ 923
Panel B						
Cash flow from operations................	$1,002	$1,124	$1,257	$1,401	$1,557	$1,663
− Increase in operating cash..............	(73)	(80)	(88)	(97)	(106)	(59)
+ Cash from investing....................	(275)	(275)	(275)	(275)	(275)	(753)
+ Increase in debt......................	(480)	(480)	(480)	(480)	(480)	72
Free cash flow to equity	$ 174	$ 289	$ 414	$ 549	$ 696	$ 923
Panel C						
Net income...........................	$ 763	$ 889	$1,026	$1,174	$1,336	$1,403
− Increase in common equity	(589)	(600)	(611)	(625)	(640)	(479)
Free cash flow to equity	$ 174	$ 289	$ 414*	$ 549	$ 696	$ 923*

* rounding error

change in common equity is an increase of $589,000 in retained earnings. Therefore, the free cash flow to equity is again computed to be $174,000 ($763,000 − $589,000).

Russian River Valley's free cash flows for years 2018 through 2021, along with the terminal year forecast, are calculated in a similar fashion and are presented in Exhibit 12.5. Having determined the free cash flow to equity for the winery, we now turn to the valuation of the firm's equity.

Valuing a Firm's Equity

The first step in valuing any asset, such as a piece of equipment or a whole company, is to realize that the payoffs received from ownership of the asset are worth less the longer it takes to receive the payoffs. This economic fact is referred to as the time value of money. (See Appendix A at the end of this book for a discussion of the time value of money.) In essence, $1 received in ten years is worth much less than $1 received immediately. In fact, $1 received in ten years would be worth only $0.39 if you could earn ten percent per year by putting your money in an investment elsewhere. Thus, if you were offered a deal in which you had to pay a sum of money today to receive $1 in ten years, the most you should be willing to pay is $0.39. The value today—$0.39—is called the present value of $1 to be received in ten years with a rate of return of ten percent per year. The ten percent per year is the opportunity cost or required rate of return on your investment. The opportunity cost is also known as the **discount rate** for the investment.

Financial theory postulates that the value of any financial asset is simply the sum of the future cash flows to be received from the asset, discounted at an appropriate risk-adjusted rate. In Chapter 9, we saw that the value of a bond could be calculated by discounting each of the future interest payments along with the final principal payment. While the same definition applies to the valuation of a firm's equity, several factors make the calculation more complex. The first complexity involves the degree of uncertainty associated with the future cash flows. We incorporate this uncertainty into our valuation analysis through the use of a discount rate based on the firm's cost of equity capital, an amount that is commonly several percentage points greater than a firm's cost of debt.

A widely accepted tenet of modern financial theory is that the appropriate rate to discount a stream of cash is that rate which best reflects the riskiness of the flows. In the case of a business's free cash flow to equity, since the cash flows are net of the interest expense paid to debtholders, the valuation model discounts these payoffs—that is, finds their present value—at the rate of return required by the firm's shareholders, or what is commonly referred to as the firm's **cost of common equity** (r_e). This topic is covered extensively in basic finance courses but the idea is simple. Finance professionals use the **capital asset pricing model** (CAPM) to establish the point that there is a linear relationship between a company's risk (β) and the expected return required by equity investors (r_e). The model says that if investors can earn the risk-free rate of return (r_f) by investing in government securities, the expected return on a risky investment should be the risk-free (r_f) rate *plus* a risk premium that is proportional to the company's risk. That is, $r_e = r_f + \beta*$risk premium, where β is the company's **beta**. (See Appendix 4C for additional information on CAPM.)

> Beta is a measure of the historical volatility of a company's share price relative to the capital market as a whole. Betas can be found in Standard & Poor's publications, Yahoo! Finance, or in ValueLine publications, among others.

To facilitate our illustration, assume that: (1) the beta for the Russian River Valley Winery is 0.8, compared to 1.0 for the U.S. stock market as a whole (such as the Standard & Poor's 500 index); (2) the yield rate on ten-year U.S. Treasury Bonds, a long-term risk-free rate of interest, is 2.8 percent; and (3) the historical risk premium of 9.0 percent is estimated as the average difference between the annual returns on U.S. Treasury Bonds and an index of common stocks over a long period of time. (The calculation of an appropriate risk premium is a hotly debated topic in financial circles; a full discussion of this issue is beyond the scope of this book.) Under these assumptions, the cost of equity (r_e) for the Russian River Valley Winery is 10.0 percent (2.8% + 0.8 × 9.0%).

The second complexity involves the timing and duration of the future cash flows associated with a business. When finding the value of a bond in Chapter 9, we knew when and for how long the various cash flows associated with the bond would be received. The same cannot be said for a firm's equity. In fact, we assume in most cases that a firm will continue indefinitely. Since the value of the equity requires us to discount to the present all future cash flows, we are presented with a dilemma. Fortunately, there is an accepted shortcut that allows us to forecast a relatively small number of years (such as five years for Russian River Valley Winery) and then create a terminal year forecast to reflect the cash flows for all years thereafter.

Because we assume that a business is a going concern, the terminal value is an aggregate measure of a business's free cash flows for all periods beyond the specific forecast period; it is a proxy measure for the future free cash flow of a business that an analyst is unable to forecast on a period-by-period basis using pro forma financial statements. As a practical matter, the longer the forecast period, the smaller will be the terminal value (TV). For short forecast periods (such as five years for the Russian River Valley Winery), the TV may constitute the majority of a business's total operating value.

A widely used approach to estimate a firm's TV is the **perpetuity growth formula**. Under the perpetuity growth formula, a business is assumed to grow at some constant annual rate, g, in perpetuity. Since g is likely to be unknown, it is common practice to set g equal to the expected rate of inflation. Under this formula, a firm's TV is estimated as follows:

$$TV = FCF/(r_e - g)$$

where FCF is the firm's free cash flow to equity in the terminal year and r_e is the firm's cost of equity capital, which can be calculated using the CAPM.

Valuing the Russian River Valley Winery Shares

Exhibit 12.6 presents a discounted cash flow analysis of the Russian River Valley Winery's operating cash flow assuming a five-year forecast horizon. The free cash flow to equity values were obtained from Exhibit 12.5. Each of these cash flows for the five-year forecast horizon is discounted to the present using the firm's ten percent cost of equity. The sum of these present values is shown to be $1.516 million.

EXHIBIT 12.6	Discounted Cash Flow Valuation of Russian River Valley Winery						
Year of Forecast (in 000's)		2017	2018	2019	2020	2021	Terminal Year
Free cash flow to common equity		$ 174	$289	$414	$549	$696	$923
Present value of FCF		158	239	311	375	432	
Present value of first 5 years		$ 1,515					
Present value beyond 5 years		$11,462					
Value attributable to common equity		$12,977					
÷ Common shares outstanding		6,200					
= Forecast price per share		$ 2.09					

The terminal year FCF of $923,000 produces a terminal value of $18.460 million ($923,000/0.05) using the perpetuity growth formula and assuming a growth rate of five percent and a cost of equity of ten percent. This value, discounted back to the present, equals $11.463 million.

$$PV(TV) = \frac{FCF}{(r_e - g)}/(1 + 0.10)^5$$

$$= \frac{\$923}{(0.10 - 0.05)}/(1 + 0.10)^5$$

$$= \$18,460/(1 + 010)^5$$

$$= \$11,462$$

The $12.977 million value of Russian River Valley equity is the sum of these two amounts ($1.515 million + $11.462 million), or $2.09 per share when divided by the 6.2 million shares outstanding. Obviously, this value is highly dependent on the reasonableness of the assumptions that were used to build the winery's pro forma financial statements in Exhibit 12.1. An error in any of the key assumptions, such as the growth rate of revenue, could result in a material error in the discounted cash flow estimate of firm value. Thus, considerable effort should be expended developing reasonable assumptions, and hence, generating reliable pro forma data.

In the next section, an accounting-based valuation model, the residual income (RI) model, is illustrated. This model uses accounting variables that are found in a company's basic financial statements to assess firm value. Following a discussion of RI valuation, valuation using price-earnings multiples is considered.

BUSINESS PERSPECTIVE

Needham and Company Valuation of News Corp. As we have described throughout this chapter, investors can use many different models in their valuation of a company. Analysts on Wall Street are no exception, and frequently in their research reports on a company's stock they will present more than one approach to support their buy, sell or hold recommendation. This is part of the analyst's due diligence, but it also serves to reassure potential investors that their quantitative analysis was not dependent on a single selected valuation approach. As an illustrative example of the application of discounted cash flow, Laura Martin prepared a report on June 27, 2012 recommending the purchase of News Corp. Martin is Managing Director and Senior Analyst at Needham and Company, an investment bank and asset management firm headquartered in New York City. News Corp. (ticker NWSA) is a diversified mass media company controlled by Rupert Murdoch. The company owns a number of popular U.S. media outlets such as Fox News, *The Wall Street Journal*, and Twentieth Century Fox. In 2011, Murdoch and his company received much unwanted press when staff at the *News of the World* (in Great Britain) were charged with hacking the phones and voicemails of private citizens. After the ensuing scandal News Corp. stock languished for about a year.

Laura Martin's June 2012 research report and recommendation were driven by new information that News Corp. would be spinning off its publishing net assets into a separate entity. Martin placed a "Buy" recommendation on the stock, citing (i) how the spinoff would create $5 per share of additional value, (ii) how the spinoff would simplify the company, and (iii) how projections for earnings were already just too low. Below are two excerpts from Martin's 20-page research report. The first is from the opening page, specifying the overall research conclusion and key quantitative facts. She provides her main conclusions, the "Buy" recommendation, and a $27.00 price target relative to a current value of only $21.76 per share.

News Corporation (NWSA) - Buy
NWSA: Upgrading to Buy with Target Price of $27

Rating Change

We are upgrading NWSA based on the following analytical building blocks:

➤ A potential spin-off would add more than $5/share of value to NWSA, in our view.
➤ We believe that NWSA earnings estimates are too low for FY13 owing to higher affiliate fees tied to recent negotiations. We are introducing a FY13E EPS estimate of $1.72, above consensus.
➤ Over the past year NWSA has been aggressively dealing with its non-consolidated assets, which simplifies valuations, raises EBITDA, and should drive multiple expansion.

We upgrade NWSA from Hold to BUY, with a 12-month target price of $27 per share.

Market Data	
Price (06/26/12)	$21.76
12-Month Price Target	$27.00
52-Week range	$21.76-13.62
Shares Out. (MM)	2,620.0
Market cap (MM)	$57,011.6
Avg. daily volume (000)	16,454.5

Financial Data	
Total Debt/Cap.	34.8%
Price/LTM Rev.	1.6x
Tangible BVPS	$2.08
Net Cash Per Share	($1.93)

continued

continued from previous page

The second excerpt below comes from Table 5 of the report. Here you see the conclusions of a DCF model as applied by Martin. The analysis has slightly more components than our summary valuation in Exhibit 12.6, not a surprise given News Corp. is a bit more complex than the Russian River Valley Winery, but the similarities should be apparent. First, note the forecast period spans 10 years (2013E-2022E, "E" means "estimate") and the conclusions for the "value of operations" are an almost even split between the present value of the FCF over the first 10 years ($35.174 billion) and the present value of the terminal value ($33.917 million). The DCF analysis performed then discounts the FCF values using a "WACC," an acronym for "**weighted average cost of capital**," which is a blend between the cost of borrowing and the cost of common equity. To this value Martin adds certain other "non-operating" items of value that are not reflected in her estimates of FCF. And because she uses a WACC approach rather than the cost of equity, long-term debt and interest bearing capital leases are later subtracted from the total enterprise value calculated, yielding a total common equity value of $67.803 billion. Dividing this amount by shares outstanding (2.509 billion) yields an estimated stock price of $27.02 per year, a 24% upside relative to the current stock price on June 27, 2012. Interestingly, to the right of the analysis is provided the analyst's view of the strengths and weaknesses of the general DCF model.

Table 5

News Corp: Target Price Calculation, 2013E-2022E
$ and shares in millions, except per share data

Valuation Conclusions		% of Total
Sum of PV of Free Cash Flow[1]	$35,174	40%
PV of Terminal Value Discounted at WACC[1]	$33,917	38%
Value of Operations (WACC Method)	**$69,090**	**78%**
Plus: Cash at 3/31/12	$10,686	
Plus: Non-Consolidated Assets (From PMV)	$10,886	
Less: Minority Interests (RSNs, Asian JVs, etc)	($500)	
Less: Unfunded Retirement Liabilities	($1,300)	
Enterprise Value	**$88,863**	**100%**
Less: LTDebt at 3/31/12	($15,460)	
Less: Lease Obligations	($4,600)	
Less: Preferred Stock Outstanding	$0	
Less: Value of Options & Restricted Sk, After-tax	($1,000)	
Common Equity Value	**$67,803**	**76%**
Fully Diluted Shares Out, 6/30/12E	2,509	
DCF Value/Share	**$27.02**	
Current Share Price @ 6/26/12	$21.76	
Upside Potential (DCF-Current Price/Current Price)	**24%**	

Traditional Discounted Cash Flow (DCF) Valuation
Why We Calculate: DCF is a rigorous bottoms-up valuation of the enterprise focusing on cash flows (not accounting)

Strengths
1 Focuses on operations. Removes financing
2 Focuses on FCF. Removes non-cash accounting
3 Explicitly forecasts capital needs (WC & CapX)
4 Uses a levered beta (widely available)
5 Ent value focus captures entire business model

Weaknesses
1 Many assumptions. Valuation can be manipulated
2 Terminal value big & based on low visibility projections
3 Model assumes constant debt/equity ratio
4 Complex to calculate
5 Calculates the enterprise value first, then equity value

Source: Martin, L. and D. Medina. "News Corporation (NWSA)—Buy—Upgrading to Buy with Target Price of $27," June 27, 2012. Needham and Company, LLC.

REVIEW PROBLEM 12.2

The following financial data was obtained from pro forma financial statements for Agnes Company.

Year	Cash Dividends	Change In Operating Cash	Net Income	Change In Debt	Net Issuance Of Common Stock	Change In Common Equity	Cash From Investing	Cash Flow From Operations
2018	$350	$195	$500	$20	$—	$150	$50	$475
2019	350	235	505	20	—	155	70	495
2020	350	290	525	20	—	175	80	540
2021	400	270	575	25	—	175	50	595
2022	400	260	600	25	—	200	55	580
Terminal Year . . .	$400	$295	$612	$25	$—	$212	$60	$610

Assume Agnes Company has a cost of equity of 8 percent and projects a terminal growth rate of 2 percent.

Required

1. Determine the free cash flow for Agnes Company for 2018–2022, and for the terminal year.
2. Use the free cash flow to equity computation to value the common equity of Agnes Company.

The solution is on page 503.

VALUATION USING THE RESIDUAL INCOME MODEL

Unlike the free cash flow model, the **residual income** model (RI) focuses on accounting variables rather than cash flows.[7] Residual income is derived from the basic financial tenet that a firm only adds value to its shareholders if it is able to earn a return greater than its cost of capital. As with the free cash flow to equity valuation model just discussed, the cost of capital is simply the firm's cost of equity (r_e). More formally, residual income, also known as **excess earnings**, is defined as the firm's net income, or **normal earnings**, less the opportunity cost associated with common shareholders' equity:

$$RI_t = NI_t - r_e CE_{t-1}$$

The opportunity cost associated with shareholders' equity, $r_e CE_{t-1}$, is defined as the firm's cost of equity times its beginning-of-period common shareholders' equity. In other words, residual income is the amount of net income the firm earns above the amount that could have been earned by the shareholders if they had invested their money elsewhere at their required rate of return. This is best illustrated by thinking of a savings account that pays five percent interest in which you deposit $1,000 at the beginning of the year. Your opportunity cost of withdrawing your savings and investing elsewhere is the foregone interest you would no longer earn—$50 in this case. If you took your savings and invested in a project that earned eight percent, the residual income would be the excess earnings of three percent (eight percent less five percent) times your investment of $1,000—$30 in this example ($80 − $50). Further, since this project can earn a rate of return in excess of the cost of capital, it will be popular with other investors. These other investors, in an effort to also earn the higher rate of return, will try to acquire ownership shares in the project, and in so doing, will bid up the price of the project so that your investment will be worth more than its original $1,000. In other words, by earning residual income, the project will be able to add value and this additional value is equal to the present value of all expected future residual income.

BUSINESS PERSPECTIVE

Whole Foods Market and EVA   As mentioned in the vignette at the beginning of this chapter, Whole Foods Market utilized a variation of the residual income method known as **Economic Value Added**. The company described its usage of this valuation approach in its 2014 annual report as follows:

> Most of our stores are located in high-traffic shopping areas on premier real estate sites and are either freestanding or in strip centers. We also have a number of urban stores located in high-density, mixed-use developments. In selecting store locations, we use an internally developed model to analyze potential sites based on various criteria such as education levels, population density and income levels within certain drive times. After we have selected a target site, our development group does a comprehensive site study and sales projection and works with our regional teams to develop construction and operating cost estimates. Each project must meet an internal Economic Value Added ("EVA") hurdle return, based on our internal weighted average cost of capital, which for new stores generally is expected to be cumulative positive EVA in five years or less. In its simplest definition, EVA is equivalent to net operating profits after taxes minus a charge on the cost of invested capital necessary to generate those profits. Our current internal weighted average cost of capital metric is 8%.

Under the RI approach, the value of a firm's equity (E_0)—that is, the value of its outstanding common shares—is equal to the book value of shareholders' equity (CE_0) from the balance sheet plus the sum of all future residual income (RI_t) over the life of the firm, all discounted at the cost of equity (r_e):

$$E_0 = CE_0 + \sum_{t=1}^{\infty} RI_t / (1 + r_e)^t$$

Stated alternatively, the residual income model assumes that a firm's equity value (E_0) is equal to the current book value of shareholders' equity (CE_{t-1}) plus the present value of the firm's expected future residual income (future earnings less normal earnings).

---

[7] For a complete discourse on the residual income valuation model, see S. Penman, *Financial Statement Analysis and Security Valuation,* 5th edition, McGraw-Hill International (2012).

eLectures

MBC

Takeaway 5
Estimate the value
of a company
using the residual
income model.

A natural question to ask is how a firm's equity can be valued as the present value of its future free cash flow to equity, a measure based on cash flows, and also as the present value of its future residual income, a measure based on earnings, and come to the same valuation result. You may even be wondering how it is even possible to perform a valuation using earnings given all the myriad of accounting policy choices and estimates present under the GAAP framework. How can a consistent valuation be achieved when so many different earnings numbers are possible depending upon which accounting policy choices and estimates are made? These are good questions and luckily there is a good answer for each.

First, it can be demonstrated mathematically that the present value of free cash flow and of residual income over the life of a firm are identical.[8] Likewise, with some algebra, it can also be demonstrated that operating cash flow and residual income valuation will lead to the exact same valuation result. Therefore, which method is used comes down to practical issues such as data availability and one's ability to forecast earnings versus cash flows.[9]

It can also be shown with some algebra that the types of accounting policy choices and estimates made by managers will not affect the ultimate equity valuation.[10] The reason behind this resides in the way that the balance sheet and the income statement work together, along with the way that the residual income computation is discounted. For example, if a firm's assets are depreciated using the double-declining-balance method, then net income will be lower in the early years. At the same time, the common equity account (through retained earnings) will also be lower, leading to a lower charge against net income to compute residual income. These offsetting amounts, when discounted at the cost of equity, exactly cancel each other out and lead to the same valuation result regardless of the accounting policy choices and estimates.

Valuing the Russian River Valley Winery Shares

Exhibit 12.7 illustrates the valuation of the Russian River Valley common equity using the residual income method. We first compute the residual income for the five-year forecast period, along with the terminal year. The computation begins with net income, which we obtain from Panel A of Exhibit 12.1. We then subtract the opportunity cost of the shareholders' investment, defined as beginning-of-year common equity (obtained from Panel B of Exhibit 12.1) multiplied by the firm's ten percent cost of equity capital (such as in 2017, 10 percent × $6.524 million = $652,400). For 2017, this yields residual income of $110,600 ($763,000 − $652,400). We next discount the future residual income values back to the present using the firm's ten percent cost of equity capital. The present values of the five years of forecasted residual income are then aggregated to $946,000. As we did with the free cash flow valuation, the terminal year residual income is first divided by the difference between the cost of equity capital (ten percent) and the assumed growth rate (five percent), and this amount is then discounted to the present at the cost of equity, yielding $5.515 million. These two amounts are combined with the initial common equity of $6.524 million to yield a $12.985 million valuation of common equity. When divided by the outstanding shares of 6.2 million, we get a value of $2.09 per share, exactly as with the free cash flow to equity valuation.

It is instructive to compare the results of the two valuation methods. While each yields the same valuation estimate for equity, the component parts of the valuation analysis are much different. The discounted cash flow approach attributes far more of the firm's value to the firm's terminal value—$11.462 million compared to $5.515 million—than does the residual income approach. In contrast, the residual income approach attributes far more of the firm's value to the first five years of forecasted operations—$7.470 million compared to $1.515 million. Why is this?

These differences are a consequence of how each approach considers value creation. The residual income approach considers the existing investment to have value—$6.524 million in this case—and then considers future excess earnings above the firm's cost of capital as incremental value. The discounted cash flow approach, in contrast, only considers future cash flows as value-relevant, and therefore, places a greater percentage of the equity's value on the firm's future cash flows.

[8] Note that the illustrated values for common equity computed under the free cash flow and residual income approaches (see Exhibits 12.6 and 12.7) differ only due to rounding errors.

[9] Ohlson, James A.,"Earnings, book value, and dividends in equity valuations," 1995. *Contemporary Accounting Research*, 11, pp. 661–687.

[10] R. Lundholm and R. Sloan, *Equity Valuation and Analysis with eVal*. 3rd ed. McGraw-Hill, 2013.

EXHIBIT 12.7	Residual Income Valuation of Russian River Valley Winery					
Year of Forecast (in 000's)	**2017**	**2018**	**2019**	**2020**	**2021**	**Terminal Year**
Net income.	$ 763	$ 889	$1,026	$1,174	$1,336	$1,403
Common equity at beginning of year. . . .	6,524	7,113	7,713	8,324	8,949	9,589
Residual income*	111	178	255	342	441	444
Present value of residual income*	101	147	191	233	274	
Present value of first 5 years	$ 946					
Present value beyond 5 years	$ 5,515					
Common equity as of 2017	$ 6,524					
Value attributable to common equity	$12,985					
÷ Common shares outstanding	6,200					
= Forecast price per share	$ 2.09					

*rounded

REVIEW PROBLEM 12.3

The following financial data was obtained from pro forma financial statements for Osprey Company:

Year	Beginning of Period Common Equity	Net Income
2018	$5,500	$590
2019	5,800	620
2020	5,920	635
2021	6,100	660
2022	6,125	680
Terminal Year	$6,200	$710

Assume Osprey Company has a cost of equity of 9 percent and projects a terminal growth rate of 4 percent.

Required

Use the residual income valuation method to value the common equity of Osprey Company.

The solution is on page 504.

VALUATION USING PRICE-EARNINGS MULTIPLES

Both the free cash flow to equity and the residual income valuation approaches are premised on the basic financial concept that the value of any asset is simply the present value of the future returns generated by the asset. Unfortunately, while these valuation methods are widely accepted as theoretically sound, they are not easy to apply. Each requires forecasted pro forma financial statements and each is subject to the various uncertainties inherent in forecasting the future. Academic research indicates that investment professionals often use a much simpler approach based on comparable firms to value a company, although they often later supplement this simple approach with one of the two approaches discussed.[11]

This simplified approach is based on the concept that equally risky financial assets that provide similar payouts should sell for prices that are similar. One of the most common forms of the comparable firms approach is **price-earnings (P/E)** multiples valuation. The P/E multiple—or the market price per share divided by the earnings per share—indicates the relative amount that investors are willing to pay for $1 of sustainable corporate earnings. Thus, a P/E multiple of 20 indicates that investors are willing to pay $20 for each dollar of future recurring income earned by a company.

Earnings multiples can be calculated for a variety of earnings-based metrics but are most often calculated for earnings after taxes (P/E), earnings before interest and taxes (P/EBIT), and earnings before interest, taxes, depreciation, and amortization (P/EBITDA). The two most popular earnings multiples are P/E and P/EBITDA, the latter largely because of its close proximity to a firm's cash flow from operations.

Takeaway 6
Describe how price-earnings multiples are used in valuation.

[11] Demirakos, N. Strong, and M Waller, "What Valuation Models Do Analysts Use," *Accounting Horizons*, December, 2004.

Earnings multiples can also be calculated for a variety of time periods. A **trailing multiple**, for example, is obtained by dividing a company's recent closing share price by its *historical* earnings per share (EPS) for the most recently completed fiscal period (quarter or year). (Most analysts use basic EPS but some use diluted EPS.) A **forward multiple**, on the other hand, is a company's current closing share price divided by *forecasted* earnings per share. Since a firm's share price is thought to be a function of future earnings, forward multiples are conceptually superior to historical multiples.

Most businesses routinely develop budgeted (or pro forma) financial statements for internal planning purposes; hence, forecasted EPS values are readily available to managers to assess a firm's value. These internal forecasts of profitability are rarely externally publicized, however; and thus, investment professionals and shareholders must develop their own forecasts of EPS, or alternatively subscribe to such data services as *Zacks Investment Research*, *Institutional Brokers' Estimate System*, or *First Call/Thomson Reuters* which provide consensus earnings forecasts for most publicly held companies. **Consensus earnings forecasts** are the average forecast of future earnings from a group of professional analysts that routinely follow a particular company's performance.

Perhaps the most difficult aspect of the comparable companies approach is to actually find the comparable companies. While most professionals simply look at similar-size firms in the same industry, care must be taken to consider such factors as firm risk, accounting policy differences, and growth options. Each of these factors should be value relevant and result in different P/E multiples. Once a group of comparable firms is determined, the P/E multiples approach is quite easy to implement. This process is best illustrated by way of an example.

To value the common equity of the Russian River Valley Winery, Kate and Matt found four wineries that appeared to be comparable. The earnings per share and share price, along with the computed P/E ratio of each winery, are presented in Exhibit 12.8.

EXHIBIT 12.8	Comparable Price-Earnings Ratios			
Winery		**EPS**	**Share Price**	**P/E Ratio**
A.		$0.50	$ 9.00	18
B.		$0.06	$ 1.32	22
C.		$1.25	$20.00	16
D.		$0.60	$14.40	24
Average				20

Russian River Valley's 2016 net income was $647,000. Since the outstanding number of shares was 6.2 million, the winery's EPS for 2016 is $0.104. Using an average P/E multiple of 20, based on the identified comparable firms (see Exhibit 12.8), yields a share price of $2.08 ($0.104 × 20) for the Russian River Valley Winery.

BUSINESS PERSPECTIVE

Johnson & Johnson To illustrate the use of P/E multiple valuation, consider the case of Johnson & Johnson (J&J), a leading pharmaceutical and consumer products' company. J&J reported EPS (adjusted for nonrecurring items) for the year ending December 28, 2014 of $5.70 per share and had a closing share price of $107.06 per share. Hence, the company's trailing P/E multiple was 18.8 times earnings:

$$\text{Trailing P/E Multiple} = \$107.06/\$5.70 = 18.8$$

The consensus EPS forecast of a survey of professional analysts that tracked the company was $6.86 for the following fiscal year, yielding a forward P/E multiple of:

$$\text{Forward P/E Multiple} = \$107.06/\$6.86 = 15.6$$

Presumably, J&J's year-end price of $107.06 reflects the consensus earnings estimate, and thus, conceptually, the forward multiple of 15.6 would more accurately reflect the market's consensus of the value of the firm.

continued

How can the forward multiple be used to value J&J? As new information is obtained, such as actual first quarter earnings for the following year, the multiple can be used to calculate whether the firm's current share price is undervalued (a buy), overvalued (a sell), or fairly valued (a hold). For instance, if J&J reports first quarter earnings of $1.50 per share, the annualized earnings would equal $6.00 per share (4 × $1.50). On the basis of its annualized earnings and a forward P/E multiple of 15.6, J&J's shares would be fairly priced at $93.60 per share. If J&J's share price is below (above) $93.60, it would be considered undervalued (overvalued) using the P/E multiple framework.

ETHICS PERSPECTIVE

Historically, there have been three approaches to developing and teaching ethics. Utilitarianism, which is closely associated with John Stuart Mill, teaches that ethical behavior leads to the best consequences. Deontology, associated with Immanuel Kant, teaches that ethics is a matter of finding the right rule. Finally, a virtue-based approach to ethics states that ethics is a matter of acquiring and putting into practice the relevant "virtue." Which of the three approaches do you feel most accurately describes your personal philosophy of ethics?

REVIEW PROBLEM 12.4

Muir & Sons is planning to go public with an initial public offering. The company would like to determine the potential price for its common stock based on comparable price-earnings multiples. Muir & Sons reported earnings of $2,300,000 and plans to issue 1 million shares of common stock.

The following data was obtained for three comparable companies:

Company	EPS	Share Price
Adams	$2.25	$31.50
Yosemite.	$1.10	$11.00
Sequoia	$1.50	$22.50

Required

Using the price-earnings multiples approach, determine the potential IPO price for Muir & Sons.

The solution is on page 504.

EXECUTIVE SUMMARY

Accounting information can be used to benchmark a firm's performance, to help managers make important operating decisions, and to help assess the value of a firm. The focus of this final chapter was firm valuation. Using the discounted cash flow framework, we saw that it was possible to value a firm by discounting the various operating cash flows expected to be generated by the firm. We also saw that it was possible to value a firm using its book value and its residual income. Finally, we saw that some professionals value a firm by reference to earnings multiples.

As a validation of your understanding of the content of this chapter, you should now be able to:

- Construct pro forma financial statements and understand their purpose and use.
- Understand how accounting information is used in equity valuation.
- Understand how to develop cash flow data, useful in the valuation of a company, by using key accounting measurement concepts.
- Estimate the value of a company using the discounted cash flow model.
- Estimate the value of a company using the residual income model.
- Describe how price-earnings multiples are used in valuation.

KEY CONCEPTS AND TERMS

Beta, 470
Capital asset pricing model, 469
Consensus earnings forecasts, 476
Continuing value, 468
Cost of common equity, 469
Discounted cash flow approach, 464
Discount rate, 469
Economic Value Added, 473

Excess earnings, 473
Forward multiple, 476
Free cash flow, 468
Free cash flow to equity, 468
Normal earnings, 473
Operating cash flow, 468
Operating value, 467
Perpetuity growth formula, 470

Price-earnings (P/E), 475
Residual income, 473
Terminal value, 468
Terminal year growth rate, 461
Trailing multiple, 476
Weighted average cost of capital, 472

QUESTIONS

Q12.1 **Discounted Cash Flow Versus Residual Income Valuation.** Describe the general steps followed to value the common equity of a business using (a) the discounted cash flow method and (b) the residual income method. Discuss what circumstances will yield equivalent valuation results under the two approaches.

Q12.2 **Pro Forma Financial Statements.** Describe the basic steps to be followed in developing pro forma financial statements. Discuss why it is unnecessary to make a separate set of pro forma assumptions for the statement of cash flow. Discuss why it is necessary to develop a terminal year projection.

Q12.3 **Free Cash Flow Versus Residual Income.** Discuss how (a) the free cash flow and (b) the residual income of a business are calculated. Describe how these two measures are related.

Q12.4 **Capital Asset Pricing Model and Beta.** Explain the Capital Asset Pricing Model. What does it mean if a company has a beta of 1.3? What does it mean if a company has a beta of 1.0?

Q12.5 **Analyzing and Reporting Operating Loss Carryforwards.** The following information is taken from the annual report of The Coca-Cola Company:

> We believe our remaining deferred tax assets will be realized because of the existence of sufficient taxable income within the carryforward period available under tax law. As of December 31, 2014, our net tax operating loss carryforwards totaled $167 million, of which $21 million expire between 2030 and 2034, and the remainder does not expire.

Discuss how the existence of operating-loss carryforwards affects firm value. Discuss how the financial effects of operating-loss carryforwards are reflected in the calculation of firm value using (a) the discounted cash flow model and (b) the residual income model.

Q12.6 **Forecasting the Cost of Goods Sold: Economies and Diseconomies of Scale.** Many investment professionals forecast the cost of goods sold on the pro forma income statement using recent historical common-size percentages. Common-size percentages, however, may be significantly impacted by economies of scale or diseconomies of scale. Discuss what an economy of scale is and how it can impact the historical relation of the cost of goods sold divided by sales. Discuss what a diseconomy of scale is; under what circumstances can diseconomies of scale arise?

Q12.7 **Unlevering Cash Flow from Operations.** Some investment professionals "unlever" the cash flow from operations by adding the following term $i(1-t_x)$ to the cash flow from operations (CFFO). Discuss why these professionals might modify the CFFO in this fashion. How does unlevering change the CFFO?

Q12.8 **Discounting Cash Flows and Earnings.** Under the residual income approach and the discounted cash flow approach to firm valuation, earnings and cash flows, respectively, are discounted using a firm's cost of equity. Discuss why the cost of equity is the appropriate discount rate to use to discount a firm's earnings and cash flows. Why is the cost of debt inappropriate to use to discount a firm's earnings or cash flows?

Q12.9 **(Ethics Perspective) Virtue-based Approach to Ethics.** The virtue-based approach to ethics asks the following questions—What role should an individual occupy in an organization? What good traits (or virtues) are needed to succeed at that role? And, how should someone with those virtues act when confronted with ethical dilemmas? Discuss the role that accountants are meant to occupy. Discuss the traits or virtues that an accountant should have to succeed in that role. Discuss how an accountant should act when faced with an ethical dilemma.

Assignments with the ⓜ logo in the margin are available in Business Course.
See the Preface of the book for details.
CHECK FIGURE indicates that check figures are available on the book's Website.

EXERCISES

E12.10 **Calculating the Cost of Equity.** Assume that the Coffman Company has a beta of 1.9 and that the risk-free rate of return is three percent. If the equity-risk premium is six percent, calculate the cost of equity for the Coffman Company using the capital asset pricing model.

TA 4

E12.11 **Calculating the Cost of Equity.** Assume that The Jackson Company has a beta of 0.8 and the risk-free rate of return is 4.5 percent. If the equity-risk premium is seven percent, calculate the cost of equity for The Jackson Company using the capital asset pricing model.

TA 4
CHECK
FIGURE

E12.12 **Valuation Using Price-Earnings Multiples.** The Claremont Company is planning an initial public offering (IPO) and management would like to have an idea of an appropriate price to charge for a share of its stock. The company plans to issue 100,000 shares. The Claremont Company's most recent earnings per share (EPS) are $1.25; however, the consensus forecast among analysts who follow the company is for EPS to be $1.50. The EPS and share price of four comparable firms are shown below:

TA 6

Firm	EPS	Share Price	P/E ratio
A...	$ 1.00	$ 18.00	18
B...	0.60	13.20	22
C...	10.00	140.00	14
D...	2.20	57.20	26

Compute the value of a share of Claremont Company stock using the price-earnings multiples method.

E12.13 **Valuation Using Price-Earnings Multiples.** The La Verne Company is planning an initial public offering (IPO) and management would like to have an idea of an appropriate price to charge for a share of its stock. The company plans to issue 250,000 shares. The La Verne Company's most recent earnings per share (EPS) are $3.00; however, the consensus forecast among analysts who follow the company is for EPS to be $3.25. The EPS and share price of four comparable firms are shown below:

TA 6

Firm	EPS	Share Price	P/E ratio
W	$ 1.50	$ 22.50	15
X	0.75	9.00	12
Y	12.00	108.00	9
Z	6.00	144.00	24

Compute the value of a share of La Verne Company stock using the price-earnings multiples method.

E12.14 **Calculating Terminal Values.** Scripps Inc. is projected to generate free cash flow (FCF) of $800,000 in its terminal year, at which point it is forecasted to have a four percent growth rate. The firm's cost of equity is estimated to be ten percent. Calculate the terminal value of Scripps Inc.

TA 4

E12.15 **Calculating Free Cash Flow.** Below are data from the financial statements of Sand and Glass Audio:

TA 3

Net income..	$ 900
Common stock issued (net)............................	200
Cash from operations (net)...........................	1,150
Cash from investing (net)............................	(400)
Change in debt (net).................................	(475)
Dividends paid......................................	300
Change in operating cash (net).......................	175
Change in common equity (net)........................	800

Compute the company's free cash flow to equity using three different methods. (Each method should yield the same answer.)

E12.16 Calculating Free Cash Flow. Below are data from the financial statements of Ann A. Logg Audio.

Net income.	$2,000
Common stock issued (net)	400
Cash from operations (net).	2,500
Cash from investing (net)	(800)
Change in debt (net).	(950)
Dividends paid	800
Change in operating cash (net)	350
Change in common equity (net)	1,600

Compute the company's free cash flow to equity using three different methods. (Each method should yield the same answer.)

E12.17 Residual Income Valuation. Presented below are data for Boso Audio:

	Forecast Year					
	1	2	3	4	5	Terminal
No. of outstanding shares	500	500	500	500	500	500
Terminal year growth rate						5%
Cost of common equity	10%	10%	10%	10%	10%	10%
Net income.	$ 79	$ 94	$111	$130	$150	$157
Beginning of year common equity	$649	$683	$720	$758	$797	$839
Free cash flow to common equity	$ 44	$ 58	$ 73	$ 90	$108	$115

Compute the value of a share of Boso common stock using the residual income method.

E12.18 Discounted Cash Flow Valuation. Presented below are data for Boso Audio:

	Forecast Year					
	1	2	3	4	5	Terminal
No. of outstanding shares	500	500	500	500	500	500
Terminal year growth rate						5%
Cost of common equity	10%	10%	10%	10%	10%	10%
Net income.	$ 79	$ 94	$111	$130	$150	$157
Beginning of year common equity	$649	$683	$720	$758	$797	$839
Free cash flow to common equity	$ 44	$ 58	$ 73	$ 90	$108	$115

Compute the value of a share of Boso common stock using the discounted cash flow method.

E12.19 Residual Income Valuation. Presented below are data for Hero Cable:

	Forecast Year					
	1	2	3	4	5	Terminal
No. of outstanding shares	1,000	1,000	1,000	1,000	1,000	1,000
Terminal year growth rate						4%
Cost of common equity	12%	12%	12%	12%	12%	12%
Net income.	$128	$148	$170	$194	$221	$230
Beginning of year common equity	$698	$738	$780	$824	$870	$919
Free cash flow to common equity	$ 88	$106	$126	$148	$172	$193

Compute the value of a share of Hero common stock using the residual income method.

E12.20   **Discounted Cash Flow Valuation.**   Presented below are data for Snap Imaging: TA 4

	Forecast Year					
	1	**2**	**3**	**4**	**5**	**Terminal**
No. of outstanding shares	800	800	800	800	800	800
Terminal year growth rate						3%
Cost of common equity	8%	8%	8%	8%	8%	8%
Net income.	87.86	118.28	136.47	162.07	180.27	185.68
Beginning of year common equity	169.81	242.68	300.95	382.42	454.49	539.79
Free cash flow to common equity	15.00	60.00	55.00	90.00	95.00	169.48

Compute the value of Snap Imaging stock using the discounted cash flow method.

E12.21   **Residual Income Valuation.**   Presented below are data for Snap Imaging: TA 5

	Forecast Year					
	1	**2**	**3**	**4**	**5**	**Terminal**
No. of outstanding shares	800	800	800	800	800	800
Terminal year growth rate						3%
Cost of common equity	8%	8%	8%	8%	8%	8%
Net income.	87.86	118.28	136.47	162.07	180.27	185.68
Beginning of year common equity	169.81	242.68	300.95	382.42	454.49	539.79
Free cash flow to common equity	15.00	60.00	55.00	90.00	95.00	169.48

Compute the value of Snap Imaging stock using the residual income method.

E12.22   **Price-Earnings Multiple Valuation.**   The Boeing Company (BA) is one of the world's leading aerospace   TA 6
and defense products and services companies. On May 3, 2015, the company's trailing (twelve months) earnings   CHECK
per share was $7.99, and with a market price per share of $144.67, indicated a trailing price-earnings multiple of   FIGURE   MBC
18.11.

Required
1. According to Thomson Reuters, the consensus forward price-earnings multiple is 15.56. What is the consensus forecasted earnings-per-share?
2. Using your consensus forecast of future earnings-per-share from part one, and the current trailing price-earnings multiple of 18.11, what should Boeing's target share price be? According to Thomson/First Call, the median of Boeing's one-year target price was $169 per share. How does this one-year target price compare to your target price?

E12.23   **Pro Forma Income Statements.**   Presented below is the consolidated statement of earnings for Mann &   TA 1
Miller, Inc.   MBC

MANN & MILLER, INC. Consolidated Statement of Earnings			
($ millions)	2015	2014	2013
Sales to customers.	$36,298	$32,317	$29,172
Cost of goods sold.	10,447	9,581	8,957
Gross profit.	25,851	22,736	20,215
Selling, marketing & administrative expense	12,216	11,260	10,495
Research expense	3,957	3,591	3,105
Purchased in-process research & development	189	105	66
Interest income.	(256)	(456)	(429)
Interest expense, net of portion capitalized.	160	153	204
Other (income) expense, net	294	185	(94)
	16,560	14,838	13,347

continued

continued from previous page

Earnings before provision for income taxes..................	9,291	7,898	6,868
Provision for income taxes............................	2,694	2,230	1,915
Net earnings......................................	$ 6,597	$ 5,668	$ 4,953
Basic net earnings per share	$2.20	$1.87	$1.65
Diluted net earnings per share........................	$2.16	$1.84	$1.61

Required

Using the Mann & Miller Inc. (M&M) consolidated statement of earnings as your base year, prepare pro forma income statements for M&M for 2016 and 2017 using an Excel spreadsheet. Relevant assumptions that you should use include:

- Sales growth is 10 percent per year.
- Gross profit margin is 65 percent.
- Effective income tax rate is 29 percent.
- Selling, marketing & administrative expenses, research expenses, and other income and expenses net all vary as a function of sales.
- Purchased in-process R&D, and interest income remain constant at the 2015 level.
- Interest expense is six percent of the beginning balance of long-term debt.
- Long-term debt at the end of 2015 is $2,750 and increases by five percent each year.

PROBLEMS

TA 3, 4   P12.24   Generating Cash Flow Information.   Presented below are recent financial statements for The Gamble Company.

THE GAMBLE COMPANY Consolidated Balance Sheet		
	2016	**2015**
Assets		
Cash & cash equivalents	$ 1,549	$ 2,350
Marketable securities..	857	760
Trade receivables..	2,781	2,738
Inventories	3,284	3,087
Prepaid expenses	1,511	1,190
Total current assets	9,982	10,125
Property, plant & equipment (net)	12,180	11,376
Intangible assets (net)	7,011	3,949
Deferred income taxes...	167	102
Other noncurrent assets	1,198	1,433
Total assets	$30,538	$26,985
Liabilities & Shareholders' Equity		
Accounts payable	$ 2,051	$ 2,203
Accrued expenses & other liabilities	3,942	3,802
Taxes payable	976	944
Debt due within one year.......................................	2,281	849
Current liabilities	9,250	7,798
Long-term debt	5,765	4,143
Other noncurrent liabilities	3,287	2,998
Shareholders' equity		
Capital stock (at par)	3,158	3,210
Additional paid-in-capital.......................................	907	559
Retained earnings	11,144	10,730
Cumulative translation adjustment account	(2,973)	(2,453)
Total liabilities & shareholders' equity	$30,538	$26,985

THE GAMBLE COMPANY Consolidated Statement of Earnings		
	2016	**2015**
Net sales.	$37,154	$35,764
Cost of goods sold*	(21,064)	(20,510)
Marketing research & administrative expenses**	(10,035)	(9,766)
Operating income.	6,055	5,488
Interest expense.	(548)	(457)
Other income (net)†	201	218
Earnings before income taxes	5,708	5,249
Income taxes	(1,928)	(1,834)
Net earnings.	$ 3,780	$ 3,415

* Includes depreciation on plant & equipment of $1,480 in 2016 and $1,387 in 2015.
** Includes amortization of intangible assets of $118 in 2016 and $1,000 in 2015.
† Includes one-time gains of $150 in 2016 and $125 in 2015 from the sale of equipment.

Required

Prepare a statement of cash flow using the indirect method. What does the company's statement of cash flow reveal about the company's financial health?

P12.25 Firm Valuation: Discounted Cash Flow. The Mann Corporation is a small manufacturer of office products. Until recently, the company was all equity-financed (shareholders' equity totaled $20 million), having a cost of equity of twelve percent. The company decided to expand its productive capacity by investing in new plant and equipment at a cost of $12 million. Executives at Mann decided to finance the capital investment with lower-costing debt financing that carried an interest rate of only eight percent. The CEO of The Mann Corporation wondered what the company was now worth following the plant expansion; consequently, the CEO instructed the company's CFO to prepare a forecast of the firm's free cash flows. The CFO's forecast was as follows:

(in thousands)	Year 1	Year 2	Year 3	Year 4
Free cash flow	$2,500	$4,675	$5,573	$ 5,930
Terminal value.				30,000

Required

1. Calculate the value of The Mann Corporation.
2. Is the company's decision to invest in new plant and equipment a good operating decision? Why?

P12.26 Generating Cash Flow Information. Presented below are recent financial data for The Coca-Cola Company.

THE COCA-COLA COMPANY Consolidated Balance Sheet		
	Year 9	**Year 8**
Assets		
Cash & cash equivalents	$ 1,611	$ 1,648
Marketable securities.	201	159
Trade accounts receivable (net)	1,798	1,666
Inventories	1,076	890
Prepaid expenses & other current	1,794	2,017
Total current assets	6,480	6,380
Equity investment in affiliated companies	6,792	6,686
Marketable securities.	2,124	1,863
Property, plant & equipment (net).	4,267	3,669
Goodwill & other intangibles (net).	1,960	547
Total assets.	$21,623	$19,145

continued

continued from previous page

THE COCA-COLA COMPANY Consolidated Balance Sheet		
	Year 9	Year 8
Liabilities & Shareholders' Equity		
Accounts payable & accrued expenses.	$ 3,714	$ 3,141
Loans & notes payable.	5,112	4,459
Current maturities of long-term debt	261	3
Accrued income taxes	769	1,037
Total current liabilities.	9,856	8,640
Long-term debt	854	687
Long-term pension liabilities	902	991
Deferred income taxes.	498	424
Shareholders' equity		
Common stock @ par.	867	865
Additional paid-in-capital.	2,584	2,195
Reinvested earnings.	20,773	19,922
Cumulated currency translation adjustment	(1,551)	(1,434)
Treasury stock	(13,160)	(13,145)
Total liabilities & shareholders' equity	$21,623	$19,145

THE COCA-COLA COMPANY Consolidated Statement of Income	
	Year 9
Net operating revenues	$19,805
Less: Cost of goods sold [1].	6,009
Gross profit.	13,796
Less: Selling and administrative expenses [2]	9,001
Other operating charges.	813
Operating income.	3,982
Interest expense (net of income)	(77)
Equity income (loss).	(184)
Other income (net)	68
Gains on issues of stock by equity investors.	30
Income before income taxes	3,819
Income taxes	1,388
Net income.	$ 2,431

[1] Includes depreciation on property & equipment of $528.
[2] Includes amortization of intangible assets of $264.

Required

Prepare a statement of cash flow for Year 9 using the indirect method format. What does the company's statement of cash flow reveal about the company's financial health?

TA 2   **P12.27**   **Generating Cash Flow Information: International.** China Yuchai International Ltd. is a Bermuda holding company that owns 76.4 percent of the outstanding common shares of Guangxi Yuchai Machinery Company Ltd. Guangxi Yuchai is one of the leading manufacturers of diesel engines in China. Presented below are recent financial statements for China Yuchai International:

CHINA YUCHAI INTERNATIONAL LTD. Consolidated Statement of Financial Position (in 000's of Chinese Yuan Renminbi ¥)	Year 3	Year 4
Assets		
Current assets		
Cash.	¥ 173,038	¥ 285,831
Inventories	301,366	292,192
Receivable from related company	98,270	60,263
Trade receivables (net)	548,128	475,254
Prepaid expenses	69,343	84,252
Investments	—	800
Total current assets	1,190,145	1,198,592
Noncurrent assets		
Property, plant, & equipment (net)	1,136,242	1,082,976
Investments	99,446	50,063
Goodwill (net)	263,211	246,353
Deferred income tax	21,703	22,322
Total assets	¥2,710,747	¥2,600,306
Liabilities & Shareholders' Equity		
Current liabilities		
Short-term bank loans	¥ 128,016	¥ 90,000
Current maturities of long-term loans	183,800	294,800
Trade accounts payable.	209,954	134,696
Income taxes payable	559	1,057
Accrued expenses payable	138,374	138,472
Total current liabilities	660,703	659,025
Long-term bank loans	208,800	60,000
Total liabilities.	869,503	719,025
Minority interest	358,589	354,926
Shareholders' equity		
Common stock	30,349	30,349
Contributed surplus	1,486,934	1,486,934
Statutory reserves	98,868	108,095
Accumulated deficit	(133,496)	(99,023)
Total liabilities & shareholders' equity	¥2,710,747	¥2,600,306

CHINA YUCHAI INTERNATIONAL LTD. Consolidated Statement of Operations (in 000's of Chinese Yuan Renminbi ¥)	Year 4
Net sales.	¥1,270,337
Cost of goods sold.	828,865[1]
Gross profit.	441,472
Selling, general & administrative expenses	309,995
Amortization of goodwill.	16,859
Impairment of plant & equipment.	4,449
Operating income.	110,169
Interest expense.	36,602
Income before income taxes & minority interest	73,567
Income tax expense.	11,217
Income before minority interest	62,350
Minority interest in income of consolidated subsidiaries	(18,650)
Net income.	¥ 43,700

[1] Includes depreciation expense of $127,892

Required

Prepare a statement of cash flow using the indirect method. What does the company's statement of cash flow reveal about the company's financial health?

TA 3   **P12.28**   **Statement of Cash Flow: International.**   Presented below are the financial statements of the Wacoal Corporation, a leading manufacturer of women's apparel in Japan. Wacoal's footnotes and other supplementary data revealed the following additional information:

1. Depreciation and amortization on property, plant, and equipment taken in Year 2 amounted to ¥3,265 million.

2. Effective April 1, Year 2, Wacoal changed its method of accounting for employee retirement benefits. As a result of this change in accounting principle, net income for Year 2 decreased by ¥1,429 million, **including** the cumulative effect of the change as of the beginning of the year of ¥1,286 million.

3. The consolidated statement of shareholders' equity revealed that cash dividends paid in Year 2 were ¥2,544 million, and that treasury stock in the amount of ¥2,803 million had been repurchased and had been deducted against retained earnings.

WACOAL CORPORATION Consolidated Balance Sheet		
(in millions of Yen)	Year 2	Year 1
Assets		
Cash.	¥ 7,634	¥ 9,403
Time deposits & certificates of deposit	33,562	40,486
Total cash & cash equivalents	41,196	49,889
Marketable securities.	34,499	24,178
Notes & accounts receivable		
Trade notes	2,651	2,902
Trade accounts	22,049	21,851
Allowance for returns & doubtful receivables	(2,869)	(2,633)
Inventories	25,601	25,515
Deferred income taxes.	4,647	4,142
Other current assets	1,734	1,890
Total current assets	129,508	127,734
Property, plant & equipment		
Land.	25,284	25,247
Buildings	55,197	54,784
Machinery & equipment.	11,530	11,148
Total	92,011	91,179
Accumulated depreciation.	(33,367)	(31,189)
Net property, plant, & equipment.	58,644	59,990
Other assets		
Investments in affiliates	8,670	7,305
Investments	28,877	37,327
Lease deposits & other	6,563	5,365
Total other assets.	44,110	49,997
Total	¥232,262	¥237,721
Liabilities and Shareholders' Equity		
Short-term bank loan.	¥ 8,088	¥ 8,125
Trade notes	8,513	7,391
Trade accounts	7,214	6,769
Accrued payroll & bonuses	7,743	8,053
Income taxes payable	3,093	3,033
Other current liabilities.	6,281	4,340
Current portion of long-term debt	517	779
Total current liabilities	41,449	38,490
Long-term liabilities		
Long-term debt	892	1,369
Liability for termination & retirement benefits	6,709	11,734
Deferred income taxes.	8,957	10,675
Total long-term liabilities	16,558	23,778
Minority interests	1,697	1,841

WACOAL CORPORATION
Consolidated Balance Sheet

(in millions of Yen)	Year 2	Year 1
Shareholders' equity		
Common stock par value of ¥50 per share-authorized, 237 million &		
240 million shares in Year 2 & Year 1; issued & outstanding 151,116,685		
and 154,116,685 shares in Year 2 & Year 1	13,260	13,260
Additional paid-in-capital	25,242	25,242
Retained earnings	132,322	126,780
Accumulated other comprehensive income (loss)		
Foreign currency translation adjustments	(2,418)	(3,231)
Unrealized gain on securities	4,152	11,561
Total	1,734	8,330
Total shareholders' equity	172,558	173,612
Total	¥232,262	¥237,721

WACOAL CORPORATION
Consolidated Statement of Income

(in millions of Yen)	Year 2
Net sales	¥162,023
Operating costs and expenses	
Cost of sales	87,493
Selling, general & administrative expense	64,906
Total operating costs and expenses	152,399
Operating income	9,624
Other income and expenses	
Interest income	395
Interest expense	(333)
Dividend income	268
Equity in net income of affiliated companies	1,271
Gain (loss) on sale, transfer or exchange of investments	11,025
Other (net)	(850)
Total other income and expenses	11,776
Income before income taxes, minority interests and cumulative effect of accounting change	21,400
Income taxes	
Current	5,181
Deferred	3,877
Total income taxes	9,058
Income before minority interests and cumulative effect of accounting change	12,342
Minority interests	(167)
Income before cumulative effect of accounting change	12,175
Cumulative effect of accounting change	(1,286)
Net income	¥ 10,889

Required

Prepare a statement of cash flow for Year 2 using the indirect method format. What does the company's statement of cash flow reveal about the company's financial health?

TA 3   **P12.29   Generating Cash Flow Information.**   Presented below are recent statements for the Chateau Company.

CHATEAU COMPANY Balance Sheet		
	2016	**2015**
Assets		
Cash	$ 150	$ 130
Marketable securities	225	250
Accounts receivable	365	325
Inventory	445	410
Other current assets	85	90
Total current assets	1,270	1,205
Property, plant, and equipment	925	850
Long-term investments	210	175
Total assets	$2,405	$2,230
Liabilities		
Accounts payable	$ 390	$ 410
Accrued expenses	180	175
Debt due within one year	165	155
Total current assets	735	740
Long-term debt	410	415
Total liabilities	1,145	1,155
Stockholders' equity		
Common stock	125	120
Additional paid-in-capital	925	875
Treasury stock	(520)	(270)
Retained earnings	730	350
Total stockholders' equity	1,260	1,075
Total liabilities and stockholders' equity	$2,405	$2,230

CHATEAU COMPANY Income Statement		
	2016	**2015**
Net sales	$2,100	$1,950
Cost of goods sold	1,240	1,239
Gross profit	860	711
Selling, general and administrative expense	215	155
Depreciation expense	95	80
Operating income	550	476
Other income	50	0
Income before income taxes	600	476
Income taxes	180	140
Net income	$ 420	$ 336

Other income on the income statement represents a gain on the sale of equipment. Cash dividends paid in 2016 were $40.

Required

Prepare a statement of cash flow for 2016 using the indirect method. What does the company's statement of cash flow reveal about the company's financial health?

P12.30 **Firm Valuation: Discounted Cash Flow**   The Canik Corporation is a small manufacturer of photography   TA 4
products. Until recently, the company was all equity-financed (shareholders' equity totaled $13 million), hav-
ing a cost of equity of ten percent. The company decided to expand its productive capacity by investing in new
plant and equipment at a cost of $15 million. Executives at Canik decided to finance the capital investment
with lower-costing debt financing that carried an interest rate of only eight percent. The CEO of The Canik
Corporation wondered what the company was now worth following the plant expansion; consequently, the
CEO instructed the company's CFO to prepare a forecast of the firm's free cash flows. The CFO's forecast
was as follows:

(in thousands)	Year 1	Year 2	Year 3	Year 4
Free cash flow	$4,000	$5,150	$6,100	$ 6,350
Terminal value				17,500

Required

1. Calculate the value of the Canik Corporation.
2. Is the company's decision to invest in new plant and equipment a good operating decision? Why?

P12.31 **Pro Forma Financial Statements.**   The venture capital division of a major U.S. financial institution has   TA 1
elected to fund an investment in an oil and gas exploration and production company that will operate both
onshore and offshore in Texas and Louisiana in the United States. The initial financing commitment from the
bank is for $40 million.

   The company's strategic plan calls for an aggressive drilling program to be carried out during 2012. Hofstedt Oil & Gas estimates that it will drill 50 wells at an average cost of $800,000 per well and that 30 of those
wells will yield aggregate crude oil reserves of approximately 10 million barrels. The remaining 20 wells are
expected to be dry or commercially unproductive. These forecasts were based on the expert opinion of geolo-
gists familiar with the properties and were confirmed by petroleum engineers employed directly by the bank.

   The company's production plan calls for a maximum exploration effort to earn the highest financial
return. Tom Hofstedt, president of the company, developed the following production scenario:

Year	Number of Barrels to Be Produced	Estimated Selling Price per Barrel	Estimated Lifting Cost per Barrel
2012	1,000,000	$30	$5
2013	1,500,000	30	5
2014	1,500,000	35	6
2015	2,500,000	40	7
2016	3,500,000	45	8

Hofstedt Oil & Gas is concerned about the impact of this operation on its financial statements and on the
company's stock price. Consequently, any available accounting policy choices loom as very important in the
overall evaluation of the investment. As a result, Hofstedt sent a terse memo to the company's controller, the
closing line of which stated, "Prepare pro forma statements showing the alternative accounting effects on cash
flow, income before tax, and financial position if we elect to use the successful efforts method or the full-cost
method." Under the full-cost method, the cost of all wells—successful and unsuccessful—are capitalized to
the balance sheet and then depleted over the expected productive life of the successful wells. Under the successful efforts method, only the cost of the successful wells are capitalized (the cost of any unsuccessful wells
are immediately expensed) to be depleted over their expected productive life.

Required
For purposes of pro forma statement preparation, assume that the $40 million loan agreement will be repaid as
follows: (1) $10 million principal repayment per year to be paid on December 31 beginning on December 31,
2013; and (2) interest payments of 10 percent per year on the balance of the loan outstanding as of the beginning of the year. Ignore income taxes and all other operations. Based on your pro forma cash flows, income
statements, and balance sheets for the period 2012 through 2016, what accounting method (successful efforts
or full cost) recommendation would you make to Hofstedt, and why?

TA 1 **P12.32** **Pro Forma Financial Statements.** Handy Dan, Inc., operates warehouse-style stores, selling a variety of home building products and lawn and garden supplies. Presented below are Handy Dan's historical financial statements for Year 1 and Year 2:

HANDY DAN, INC.
Statement of Income

($ millions)	Year 2
Sales	$980
Cost of goods sold	(727)
Gross profit	253
Depreciation expense	(8)
Other operating expenses	(217)
Operating income	28
Interest expense	(21)
Income before taxes	7
Income tax expense	(2)
Net income	$ 5

HANDY DAN, INC.
Balance Sheets

($ millions)	Year 1	Year 2	Equities	Year 1	Year 2
Assets			**Equities**		
Cash	$ 10	$ 14	Accounts payable	$ 74	$104
Accounts receivable (net)	27	38	Short-term loans payable	10	29
Inventory	153	214	Long-term debt	207	289
Total current assets	190	266	Total liabilities	291	422
Property & equipment (cost)	199	279	Contributed capital	50	62
Accumulated depreciation	(9)	(17)	Retained earnings	39	44
Net property & equipment	190	262	Total shareholders' equity	89	106
Total assets	$380	$528	Total equities	$380	$528

HANDY DAN, INC.
Statement of Retained Earnings

($ millions)	Year 2
Retained earnings (Year 1)	$39
Add: Net income	5
Less: Dividends	0
Retained earnings (Year 2)	$44

HANDY DAN, INC.
Statement of Cash Flow

($ millions)	Year 2
Operations	
Net income..	$ 5
Depreciation expense	8
Accounts receivable (net)..	(11)
Inventory	(61)
Accounts payable	30
Cash flow from operations.......................................	(29)
Investing	
Purchase of property & equipment	(80)
Cash flow from investing	(80)
Financing	
Short-term borrowing	19
Long-term borrowing...	82
Stock sales	12
Dividend payment	0
Cash flow from financing...	113
Change in cash...	4
Beginning cash...	10
Ending cash	$ 14

Required

Using the following set of assumptions, prepare pro forma financial statements for Handy Dan, Inc., for Year 3:

- Sales are projected to grow by 40 percent.
- Cash is expected to increase at the same rate as sales.
- Assume the following ratios to forecast the identified accounts:

Account	Financial Ratio		
Accounts receivable....................................	Receivable turnover	=	25.9x
Inventory..	Inventory turnover	=	3.39x
Property & equipment	Fixed asset turnover	=	3.52x
Cost of goods sold.....................................	Gross profit margin ratio	=	25.9%
Operating expenses....................................	Operating expenses/sales	=	22.1%
Accounts payable.......................................	Payable turnover	=	7.55x

- Depreciation expense is based on a 30-year expected life with no salvage value; any property and equipment acquired during the year is depreciated for only one-half year.
- Interest expense is based on a six percent short-term cost of debt and eight percent long-term cost of debt; only one-half year of interest is charged on loans taken out during the year.
- Assume no dividends were paid in Year 3.
- Effective income tax rate is 33.33 percent.
- The mix of short-term loans payable, long-term debt and contributed capital is set to satisfy an existing debt covenant that requires the company to maintain a current ratio of 2.0 (or greater) and a total debt-to-total assets ratio of 80 percent (or less).

P12.33 Residual Income Valuation. Lowe's Companies Inc. is the second largest retailer of home improve-   TA 5
ment products in the world, with a specific emphasis on retail do-it-yourself (DIY) and commercial business
customers. Lowe's specializes in offering products and services for home improvement, home decor, home
maintenance, home repair and remodeling, and maintenance of commercial buildings.

Required

Assume that on July 8, Year 6, Lowe's stock price closed at $45.30 per share. An analyst at a prominent Wall
Street bank set a price target of $52 per share based on an EPS forecast of $2.22 per share for fiscal Year 6.
Assume that the company's cost of equity is 14 percent. Use the Residual Income valuation model to calculate
the equity value of the Lowe's Companies. [As a base case, a company whose expected ROE is 25 percent per
year, whose cost of equity is 14 percent, and whose growth in book value is expected to be 20 percent per year
for the first ten years and five percent per year thereafter, would have an intrinsic value of 4.015 times current
book value.] Do you think Lowe's is worth $52 per share? Why?

LOWE'S COMPANIES INC.
Consolidated Balance Sheet

($ millions)	Year 5	Year 4
Assets		
Cash and cash equivalents	$ 853	$ 799
Short-term investments	273	54
Accounts receivable—net	172	166
Merchandise inventory	3,968	3,611
Deferred income taxes	58	93
Other current assets	244	197
Total current assets	5,568	4,920
Property, less accumulated depreciation	10,352	8,653
Long-term investments	29	22
Other assets	160	141
Total assets	$16,109	$13,736
Liabilities		
Short-term borrowings	$ 50	$ 100
Current maturities of long-term debt	29	59
Accounts payable	1,943	1,715
Employee retirement plans	88	126
Accrued salaries and wages	306	221
Other current liabilities	1,162	796
Total current liabilities	3,578	3,017
Long-term debt, excluding current maturities	3,736	3,734
Deferred income taxes	478	305
Other long-term liabilities	15	6
Total liabilities	7,807	7,062
Shareholders' Equity		
Preferred stock—$5 par value, none issued	—	—
Common stock—$.50 par value; shares issued and outstanding Year 5, 782; Year 4, 776	391	388
Capital in excess of par value	2,023	1,803
Retained earnings	5,887	4,482
Accumulated other comprehensive income	1	1
Total shareholders' equity	8,302	6,674
Total liabilities and shareholders' equity	$16,109	$13,736

LOWE'S COMPANIES INC.
Consolidated Statements of Income

($ millions except per share amounts for period ended)	Year 5	Year 4	Year 3
Net sales	$26,491	$22,111	$18,779
Cost of sales	18,465	15,743	13,488
Gross margin	8,026	6,368	5,291
Expenses:			
Selling, general and administrative	4,730	3,913	3,348
Store opening costs	129	140	132
Depreciation	626	517	409
Interest	182	174	121
Total expenses	5,667	4,744	4,010
Pretax earnings	2,359	1,624	1,281
Income tax provision	888	601	471
Net earnings	$ 1,471	$ 1,023	$ 810
Basic earnings per share	$ 1.89	$ 1.33	$ 1.06
Diluted earnings per share	1.85	1.30	1.05
Cash dividends per share	0.09	0.08	0.07

Selected Financial Data for Lowe's					
Lowe's Companies	Year 5	Year 4	Year 3	Year 2	Year 1
Net sales....	$26,491	$22,111	$18,779	$15,906	$13,331
Growth in net sales (%)	19.8%	17.7%	18.1%	19.3%	—
Net earnings...	1,471	1,023	810	673	500
Total assets....	16,109	13,736	11,358	9,007	7,087
Shareholders' equity	8,302	6,674	5,494	4,695	3,620
Growth in shareholders' equity (%)	24.4%	21.5%	17.0%	29.7%	—
ROE Analysis					
ROE (net earnings/beginning shareholder's equity)....	22.04%	18.62%	17.25%	18.59%	—
Return on sales (net earnings/net sales)	5.55%	4.63%	4.31%	4.23%	3.75%
Asset turnover (net sales/total assets)	1.64	1.61	1.65	1.77	1.88
Leverage (total assets/beginning shareholders' equity)....	2.41	2.50	2.42	2.49	—

P12.34 **Pro Forma Financial Statements and Firm Valuation.**   The Kat Company began operations in 2015. The   TA 1, 2, 4
year went very well with the company generating a positive net income, with strong demand for its products
providing management with a rosy forecast for the future. Management is contemplating possibly going public and would like a valuation of the company. Below are the balance sheet and the income statement for the
first year of operation, along with assumptions needed to calculate pro forma statements for the period 2016
through 2020, along with a terminal year projection.

KAT COMPANY Income Statement	
Sales....	$550.00
Cost of sales....	275.00
Gross profit....	275.00
SG&A	55.00
Depreciation....	60.00
Interest	14.47
Pretax income	145.53
Tax	43.66
Net income....	$101.87

KAT COMPANY Balance Sheet	
Cash....	$ 60.00
Accounts receivable....	5.00
Inventory....	8.00
Total current assets....	73.00
PP&E—gross	600.00
Accumulated depreciation	200.00
PP&E—net	400.00
Total assets	$473.00
Accounts payable....	$ 20.00
Other current liabilities	10.00
Total current liabilities	30.00
Notes payable	241.13
Total liabilities	271.13
Common stock....	100.00
Retained earnings	101.87
Total equity	201.87
Total liabilities and equity	$473.00

Assumptions:

- Sales will be $975 in 2016 then grow by 15 percent in 2017, ten percent in 2018, ten percent in 2019, and six percent in 2020. Terminal growth is assumed to be 5 percent.
- Gross profit is assumed to be 60 percent in each year.
- Sales, general, and administrative expenses are assumed to be 35 percent of sales in each year.
- Depreciation is assumed to be ten percent of end of year gross PP&E, and then grow at a 5 percent rate in the terminal year.
- Interest is assumed to be six percent of end of the year notes payable and then grow at a 5 percent rate in the terminal year.
- Taxes are assumed to be 30 percent of pretax income.
- The cash balance is projected to be 9.5 percent of sales.
- The accounts receivable turnover is assumed to be 8.
- The inventory turnover is assumed to be 5.
- Gross PP&E is assumed to be $850 in 2016 and 2017, $925 in 2018, and then growing by $25 in each year of 2019 and 2020, and finally growing by 5 percent in the terminal year.
- Accumulated depreciation is assumed to grow by the amount of yearly depreciation expense and then grow by 5 percent in the terminal year.
- Accounts payable turnover is assumed to be 9.
- Other current liabilities are assumed to be a constant $20 and then grow at a 5 percent rate in the terminal year.
- Notes payable are assumed to be as shown in the below table.

	2016	2017	2018	2019	2020	Terminal Year
Notes payable	$507.50	$399.95	$349.68	$240.38	$104.66	$109.88

- Common stock is assumed to be a constant $110 and then grow at a 5 percent rate in the terminal year.
- Retained earnings is assumed to grow at the rate of annual net income less dividends paid. Dividends are assumed to be as shown below.

	2016	2017	2018	2019	2020	Terminal Year
Dividends paid	$15.00	$60.00	$75.00	$90.00	$95.00	$165.33

- Assumed terminal year growth is 5 percent.
- Kat Company's cost of common equity is 10 percent.

Required
1. Prepare pro forma income statements, balance sheets, and statements of cash flow for the five-year period 2016 through 2020, along with the terminal year.
2. Determine the company's free cash flow for the five-year period 2016 through 2020, along with the terminal year.
3. Determine the equity value of Kat Company using the residual income method.
4. Determine the equity value of Kat Company using the discounted cash flow method.

TA 4, 5, 6   P12.35   Integrative Case Analysis.   CSK Auto Corp. is the largest retailer of automotive parts and accessories in the Western United States and one of the largest retailers of such products in the United States based on the number of stores. As of February 4, 2001, the company operated 1,152 stores as one fully integrated company under three brand names: Checker Auto Parts, Schuck's Auto Supply, and Kragen Auto Parts. Presented below is selected information from CSK Auto Corp.'s 2001 10-K report. Assume an effective tax rate of 40 percent.

Required
1. On March 17, 1998, the Company completed an initial public offering (IPO). What was the average price (net of underwriting fees) that CSK sold its shares for?
2. In 1999, CSK Auto spent $260.221 million on investing activities. How did the company finance this investment?
3. On February 4, 2001, the company's share price was $6.10 per share. The Board of Directors believes that the company's share price is too low and has recommended a share buyback program. What would be the financial effect of a share buyback, and what accounts would be affected if the company repurchased ten percent of its outstanding shares?

4. On March 1, 2000, the company participated in the formation of a new joint venture, PartsAmerica.com (PA) by acquiring 37 percent of the outstanding equity of PA. The company accounted for its investment in PA under the equity method.

    a. What financial effects did the company record to reflect its investment in PartsAmerica on its financial statements?

    b. During fiscal 2000, the company recognized its proportionate share of PA's net loss and wrote off the remaining investment in the joint venture. What did the company record to reflect these events in its financial statements?

5. CSK Auto reports that included in property and equipment (net) are assets under capital leases (net of accumulated depreciation) of $38.067 million and $35.676 million on February 4, 2001 and January 30, 2000, respectively. Consider the information on leases provided in the financial statements and footnotes.

    a. What cash payment is CSK Auto expecting to make for operating leases for the year ending February 4, 2002?

    b. What financial effects will CSK Auto record for its capital leases for the year ending February 4, 2002?

6. CSK Auto recognizes income taxes based on pretax income.

    a. What financial effects did CSK record to recognize income taxes in 2000?

    b. Has CSK Auto reported more or less income to its shareholders cumulatively through February 4, 2001, than to the tax authorities? How much more or less?

7. On February 4, 2001, CSK Auto's share price closed at $6.10 per share. Using the residual income valuation model, calculate the equity value of the company. Assume that the company's cost of equity is approximately 10.4 percent. Top management thinks the share price should be considerably higher. How would you explain the situation to management?

CSK AUTO CORP. Consolidated Balance Sheet		
($ thousands)	02/04/01	01/30/00
Assets		
Cash and cash equivalents	$ 11,131	$ 11,762
Receivables, net of allowances of $4,236 and $3,294, respectively	79,901	69,129
Inventories	621,814	625,480
Deferred income taxes	3,133	—
Assets held for sale	1,497	4,745
Prepaid expenses and other current assets	19,169	18,471
Total current assets	736,645	729,587
Property and equipment, net	175,358	160,561
Leasehold interests, net	20,244	8,341
Goodwill, net	130,544	124,750
Other assets, net	14,190	12,413
Total assets	$1,076,981	$1,035,652
Liabilities and Stockholders' Equity		
Accounts payable	$ 199,483	$ 168,770
Accrued payroll and related expenses	27,673	38,910
Accrued expenses and other current liabilities	42,448	50,663
Current maturities of amounts due under Senior Credit Facility	54,640	3,340
Current maturities of capital lease obligations	10,878	9,893
Deferred income taxes	—	1,417
Total current liabilities	335,122	272,993
Facility	471,840	505,480
Subordinated Notes	81,250	81,250
Obligations under capital leases	29,273	27,170
Deferred income taxes	10,544	5,801
Other	9,339	8,411
Total noncurrent liabilities	602,246	628,112

(continued)

(continued from previous page)

CSK AUTO CORP. Consolidated Balance Sheet		
($ thousands)	02/04/01	01/30/00
Stockholders' equity		
Common stock, $0.01 par value, 50,000,000 shares authorized, 27,841,178 and 27,834,574 shares issued and outstanding at February 4, 2001, and January 30, 2000, respectively	278	278
Additional paid-in-capital	291,063	291,004
Stockholder receivable	(745)	(584)
Deferred compensation	(156)	(324)
Accumulated deficit	(150,827)	(155,827)
Total stockholders' equity	139,613	134,547
Total liabilities and stockholders' equity	$1,076,981	$1,035,652

CSK AUTO CORP. Consolidated Statements of Income			
($ thousands)	2/4/01	1/30/00	1/31/99
Net sales	$1,452,109	$1,231,455	$1,004,385
Cost of sales	769,043	636,239	531,073
Gross profit	683,066	595,216	473,312
Other costs and expenses	—	—	—
Operating and administrative	568,873	471,340	391,528
Store closing costs	6,060	4,900	335
Legal settlement	8,800	—	—
Transition and integration expenses	23,818	30,187	3,075
Equity in loss of joint venture	3,168	—	—
Goodwill amortization	4,799	1,941	—
Write-off of unamortized management fee	—	—	3,643
Secondary stock offering costs	—	—	770
Operating profit	67,548	86,848	73,961
Interest expense, net	62,355	41,300	30,730
Income before income taxes, extraordinary loss and cumulative effect of change in accounting principle	5,193	45,548	43,231
Income tax expense	193	17,436	15,746
Income before extraordinary loss and cumulative effect of change in accounting principle	5,000	28,112	27,485
Extraordinary loss, net of $4,236 of income taxes	—	—	(6,767)
Income before cumulative effect of change in accounting principle	5,000	28,112	20,718
Cumulative effect of change in accounting principle, net of $468 of income taxes	—	(741)	—
Net income	$ 5,000	$ 27,371	$ 20,718

CSK AUTO CORP. **Consolidated Statements of Cash Flow**			
($ thousands)	**02/04/01**	**01/30/00**	**01/31/99**
Cash flows provided by (used in) operating activities			
Net income	$ 5,000	$ 27,371	$ 20,718
Adjustments to reconcile net income to net cash provided by (used in) operating activities	—	—	—
Depreciation and amortization of property and equipment	33,120	26,066	20,930
Amortization of goodwill.	4,799	1,941	—
Amortization of leasehold interests	1,841	761	919
Amortization of other deferred charges	1,067	607	563
Amortization of deferred financing costs	2,224	1,406	1,016
Tax benefit relating to stock option exercises	—	393	184
Equity in loss of joint venture	3,168	—	—
Extraordinary loss on early retirement of debt, net of income taxes	—	—	6,767
Cumulative effect of change in accounting principle, net of income taxes	—	741	—
Write-off of unamortized deferred charge	—	—	3,643
Deferred income taxes	193	15,637	15,542
Change in operating assets and liabilities, net of effects of acquisitions	—	—	—
Receivables	(11,915)	(5,812)	(21,056)
Inventories	(7,577)	(93,567)	(45,848)
Prepaid expenses and other current assets	(208)	7,240	(200)
Accounts payable	25,172	11,203	7,925
Accrued payroll, accrued expenses and other current liabilities	(23,332)	2,793	(947)
Other operating activities.	(1,083)	(811)	(6,753)
Net cash provided by (used in) operating activities	32,469	(4,031)	3,403
Cash flows provided by (used in) investing activities			
Business acquisitions, net of cash acquired	(1,182)	(218,201)	(892)
Capital expenditures	(32,080)	(41,358)	(37,846)
Expenditures for assets held for sale	(5)	(7,400)	(19,144)
Proceeds from sale of property and equipment and assets held for sale	5,029	8,760	21,650
Investment in joint venture	(3,168)	—	—
Due to affiliate	—	—	(1,000)
Other investing activities	(3,136)	(2,022)	(292)
Net cash used in investing activities	(34,542)	(260,221)	(37,524)
Cash flows provided by (used in) financing activities			
Borrowings under Senior Credit Facility.	309,500	502,000	126,000
Payments under Senior Credit Facility.	(291,840)	(218,340)	(87,065)
Issuance of common stock in initial public offering	—	—	172,482
Underwriter's discount and other IPO costs	—	—	(13,859)
Premiums paid upon early retirement of debt	—	—	(4,875)
Retirement of 11% Senior Subordinated Notes.	—	—	(43,750)
Retirement of 12% Subordinated Notes	—	—	(50,000)
Payment of Senior Credit Facility with public offering proceeds	—	—	(53,825)
Payment of debt issuance costs	(1,815)	(4,730)	—
Payments on capital lease obligations.	(10,934)	(10,905)	(8,634)
Advances to stockholders	(189)	—	—
Recovery of stockholder receivable.	28	434	150
Exercise of options.	59	791	367
Other financing activities	(3,367)	(726)	(232)
Net cash provided by financing activities.	$ 1,442	$268,524	$ 36,759
Net increase (decrease) in cash and cash equivalents	(631)	4,272	2,638
Cash and cash equivalents, beginning of period.	11,762	7,490	4,852
Cash and cash equivalents, end of period.	$ 11,131	$ 11,762	$ 7,490

CSK AUTO CORP.
Consolidated Statements of Stockholders' Equity (Deficit)

($ thousands)	Common Stock Shares	Common Stock Amount	Additional Paid-in Capital	Shareholder Receivable	Deferred Compensation	Accumulated Deficit	Total Equity (Deficit)
Balances at February 1, 1998	19,113,388	$191	$130,513	$(1,168)	$(675)	$(203,916)	$ (75,055)
Amortization of deferred compensation....					182		182
Recovery of stockholder receivable.......				150			150
Issuance of common stock in initial public offering, net of transaction costs	8,625,000	86	158,537				158,623
Stock compensation			220				220
Exercise of options...................	30,444	1	366				367
Tax benefit of options.................			184				184
Net income..........................						20,718	20,718
Balances at January 31, 1999	27,768,832	278	289,820	(1,018)	(493)	(183,198)	105,389
Amortization of deferred compensation....					169		169
Recovery of stockholder receivable.......				434			434
Exercise of options...................	65,742		791				791
Tax benefit of options.................			393				393
Net income..........................						27,371	27,371
Balances at January 30, 2000	27,834,574	278	291,004	(584)	(324)	(155,827)	134,547
Amortization of deferred compensation....					168		168
Recovery of stockholder receivable.......				28			28
Advances to stockholders				(189)			(189)
Exercise of options...................	6,604		59				59
Net income..........................						5,000	5,000
Balances at February 4, 2001	27,841,178	$278	$291,063	$(745)	$(156)	$(150,827)	$139,613

Note 8: The Company leases its office and warehouse facilities, all but three of its retail stores, and a majority of its equipment. Generally, store leases provide for minimum rentals and the payment of utilities, maintenance, insurance and taxes. Certain store leases also provide for contingent rentals based upon a percentage of sales in excess of a stipulated minimum. The majority of lease agreements are for base lease periods ranging from 15 to 20 years, with three to five renewal options of five years each.

Operating lease rental expense is as follows (in thousands):

Fiscal Year	2000	1999	1998
Minimum rentals...	$123,298	$97,748	$75,689
Contingent rentals	945	976	1,088
Sublease rentals...	(6,970)	(5,395)	(5,089)
	$117,273	$93,329	$71,688

Future minimum lease obligations under noncancelable leases at February 4, 2001, follows:

For Fiscal Years ($ thousands)	Operating Leases	Capital Leases
2001	$122,985	$14,800
2002	115,549	13,387
2003	103,244	10,002
2004	87,459	6,496
2005	77,683	1,456
Thereafter..	387,218	3,410
	$894,138	49,551
Less amounts representing interest		9,400
Present value of obligations...............................		40,151
Less: current portion		(10,878)
Long-term obligation		$29,273

P12.36 **Financial Statement Analysis and Firm Value.** Weis Markets, Inc., is a Pennsylvania business founded   TA 6
by Harry and Sigmund Weis in 1912. The company is engaged principally in the retail sale of food and pet
supplies in Pennsylvania and surrounding states. The Weis family currently owns approximately 62 percent
of the outstanding shares. The company's retail food stores sell groceries, dairy products, frozen foods, meats,
seafood, fresh produce, floral, prescriptions, deli/bakery products, prepared foods, fuel and general merchandise items, such as health and beauty care and household products.

Required

1. Was Year 3 a good year or a bad year for Weis? Why?
2. What was the company's interest coverage ratio in Year 3 and Year 2? On July 1, Year 3, Weis considered
   borrowing $100 million of long-term debt at an interest rate of ten percent per year to finance a $100 million investment in additional stores. The new properties would not generate earnings until Year 4. What
   would the company's interest coverage ratio have been for Year 3 if it had completed the borrowing?
3. Evaluate Weis's profitability in Year 2 and Year 3 using the ROE Model discussed in Chapter 4.
4. On March 31, following Year 3, Weis's share price closed at $29.85 per share. Value Line forecasted sales
   of $2,050 million and $2,125 million and EPS of $2.00 and $2.10 per share for fiscal Year 4 and Year 5,
   respectively. The company's cost of equity is approximately nine percent. Using the Residual Income
   valuation model, calculate the equity value of the company. [As a base case, a company whose expected
   ROE is twelve percent (14 percent) per year, whose cost of equity is nine percent, and whose growth in
   book value is expected to be four percent per year for the first ten years and three percent per year thereafter, would have an intrinsic value of 1.54 (1.90) times current book value.] Do you think Weis is worth
   $29.85 per share? Why?

WEIS MARKETS, INC. Consolidated Balance Sheet		
($ thousands, for period ended)	Year 3	Year 2
Assets		
Cash	$ 3,929	$ 3,255
Marketable securities	43,510	28,675
Accounts receivable, net	30,188	26,530
Inventories	182,832	169,952
Prepaid expenses.	3,980	8,294
Income taxes recoverable	—	3,395
Total current assets	264,439	240,101
Property and equipment, net	428,153	439,977
Intangible and other assets	24,107	24,107
	$716,699	$704,185
Liabilities		
Accounts payable.	$101,917	$ 98,382
Accrued expenses	15,704	11,043
Accrued self-insurance.	16,117	15,040
Payable to employee benefit plans	8,950	8,672
Income taxes payable	6,112	—
Deferred income taxes.	702	4,633
Total current liabilities.	149,502	137,770
Deferred income taxes	14,765	16,051
Long-term debt	—	25,000
Shareholders' Equity		
Common stock, no par value, 100,800,000 shares authorized,		
32,986,337 and 32,978,037 shares issued, respectively.	7,882	7,630
Retained earnings	678,294	648,522
Accumulated other comprehensive income.	4,145	6,479
	690,321	662,631
Treasury stock at cost, 5,792,800 and 5,774,830 shares, respectively	(137,889)	(137,267)
Total shareholders' equity	552,432	525,364
	$716,699	$704,185

WEIS MARKETS, INC.
Consolidated Statements of Income

($ thousands except per share amounts, for period ended)	Year 3	Year 2	Year 1
Net sales.	$1,999,364	$1,971,665	$2,042,329
Cost of sales, including warehousing and distribution expenses.	1,471,479	1,457,002	1,518,136
Gross profit on sales	527,885	514,663	524,193
Operating, general and administrative expenses.	448,478	451,723	444,110
Income from operations.	79,407	62,940	80,083
Investment income.	879	9,860	18,557
Interest expense.	(394)	(1,400)	—
Other income	14,794	10,447	18,172
Income before provision for income taxes.	94,686	81,847	116,812
Provision for income taxes.	35,537	31,792	42,989
Net income.	$ 59,149	$ 50,055	$ 73,823
Cash dividends per share.	$1.08	$1.08	$1.06
Basic and diluted earnings per share.	2.17	1.55	1.77

WEIS MARKETS, INC.
Consolidated Statements of Cash Flow

($ thousands, for period ended)	Year 3	Year 2	Year 1
Cash flows from operating activities			
Net income.	$ 59,149	$ 50,055	$ 73,823
Adjustments to reconcile net income to net cash provided by operating activities			
Depreciation.	41,885	43,755	44,169
Amortization.	5,797	7,222	6,682
(Gain) loss on sale of fixed assets	(3,620)	1,629	(5,913)
Gain on sale of marketable securities	—	(570)	(1,279)
Changes in operating assets and liabilities			
Inventories	(12,880)	(1,411)	(1,395)
Accounts receivable and prepaid expenses	656	(2,923)	8,508
Income taxes recoverable	3,395	(251)	1,194
Accounts payable and other liabilities	9,551	14,993	(2,696)
Income taxes payable	6,112	—	—
Deferred income taxes.	(3,561)	1,381	2,472
Net cash provided by operating activities	106,484	113,880	125,565
Cash flows from investing activities			
Purchase of property and equipment.	(46,056)	(48,046)	(56,331)
Proceeds from the sale of property and equipment.	14,520	86	11,714
Purchase of marketable securities.	(21,754)	(299,064)	(259,574)
Proceeds from maturities of marketable securities	2,929	556,141	108,154
Proceeds from sale of marketable securities.	—	123,660	127,043
Increase in intangible and other assets	(702)	(19)	(13,379)
Net cash provided by (used in) investing activities	(51,063)	332,758	(82,373)
Cash flows from financing activities			
Proceeds (payments) of long-term debt, net	(25,000)	25,000	–0–
Proceeds from issuance of common stock	252	36	35
Dividends paid.	(29,377)	(37,202)	(44,191)
Purchase and cancellation of stock.	—	(434,317)	—
Purchase of treasury stock.	(622)	(289)	(199)
Net cash used in financing activities	(54,747)	(446,772)	(44,355)
Net increase (decrease) in cash.	$ 674	$ (134)	$ (1,163)

CORPORATE ANALYSIS

CA12.37 The Procter & Gamble Company. The 2014 annual report of The Procter & Gamble Company (P&G)   TA 1, 4
is available at Procter & Gamble's website. http://www.pginvestor.com/interactive/lookandfeel/4004124/
PG_Annual_Report_2014.pdf.

After reviewing P&G's annual report, respond to the following questions:

a. Prepare pro forma income statements for 2012, 2013, and 2014, using the following assumptions.
Round all amounts to the nearest million. (*Hint:* You will need to access the 2011 annual report for your
historical data accumulation.)
- Sales will grow by 0.4 percent annually.
- Cost of goods sold will remain 51.0 percent of sales.
- Selling, general and administrative expense will amount to 31.0 percent of sales.
- Interest expense will be 2.5 percent times the beginning-of-year "debt due in one year" plus 2.5
percent times the beginning-of-year "long-term debt."
- Other non-operating income will amount to 0.2 percent of sales.
- The effective tax rate will remain 22.0 percent.

b. Prepare pro forma balance sheets for 2012, 2013, and 2014, using the following assumptions:

Assets:
- Total assets will maintain a turnover rate of 0.58 times.
- Cash and cash equivalents will grow at the same rate as sales.
- Accounts receivable will maintain a turnover rate of 13.0 times.
- Inventories (total) will maintain a turnover rate of 5.5 times.
- Deferred income taxes will remain flat each year at the 2011 level.
- Prepaid expenses and other current assets will remain flat each year at the 2011 level.
- Net property, plant and equipment will maintain a fixed asset turnover of 4.5 times.
- Net goodwill and other intangible assets will maintain an intangible assets turnover of 0.92 times.
- Other current assets will remain constant at the 2011 level.

Liabilities:
- Total liabilities and shareholders' equity will equal forecasted total assets.
- Accounts payable will maintain a turnover rate of 5.1 times.
- Accrued and other liabilities will remain constant at the 2011 level.
- Debt due within one year is a plug figure to balance the total liabilities and total shareholders' equity
with total assets.
- Long-term debt will remain constant at the 2011 level.
- Deferred income taxes will remain constant at the 2011 level.
- Other noncurrent liabilities will remain constant at $9,000.

Shareholders' equity:
- Convertible preferred stock, common stock (at par), and additional paid-in-capital will remain
constant at the 2011 level as the company will finance all growth and operating needs using short-
term debt.
- Reserve for ESOP debt retirement and other comprehensive income will remain constant at the 2011
level.
- Treasury stock repurchases remain constant at the 2011 level.
- Non-controlling interest will remain constant at the 2011 level.
- Ending retained earnings equals beginning retained earnings plus net earnings attributable to P&G
less dividends paid.
- P&G is assumed to grow its dividend at the same 0.4% rate as the growth in sales.

2012	$5,790
2013	$5,813
2014	$5,836

c. Using the pro forma income statements from part (a) and pro forma balance sheets from part (b), prepare
pro forma statements of cash flow for 2012, 2013, and 2014.
- Assume that the depreciation and amortization expense equals five percent of the beginning-of-year
balance of net property, plant and equipment plus net goodwill and other intangible assets.

- Assume no gain or loss on sale of assets.

d. Calculate the equity value of Procter & Gamble using the discounted cash flow approach and the following assumptions:
- P&G's cost of equity is 7 percent.
- Assume that the growth rate (g) of free cash flow is 3 percent after 2014.

How does your estimate of firm value compare to P&G's current market capitalization?

e. After completing the pro forma financial statements in part (b) above, return to P&G's website and compare your pro forma results to the company's actual results for the period 2012 through 2014. How well do the pro forma data match up with the company's actual results? Which assumption(s) in part (b) were primarily responsible for any observed variances?

TA 4, 5, 6   **CA12.38 Internet-based Analysis.** Consider a publicly held company whose products you are familiar with. Some examples might include:

Company	Product	Corporate Website
• Johnson & Johnson..............	• Band-Aids	• www.jnj.com
• Microsoft Corporation............	• Windows based software	• www.microsoft.com
• Apple Inc........................	• Cellular phones	• www.apple.com
• Intel Corporation	• Pentium processors	• www.intel.com
• Kimberly-Clark Corporation........	• Kleenex	• www.kimberly-clark.com

Access the company's public website and search for its most recent annual report. (Some companies provide access to their financial data through an "investor relations" link, while others provide a direct link to their "annual reports.") After locating your company's most recent annual report, open the file and review its contents. After reviewing the annual report for your selected company, prepare answers to the following questions:

a. What is the book value of the company? What is the market capitalization of the company? Why are they different?

b. What is the company's current price to book value multiple, price to sales multiple, and price to earnings multiple?

c. Calculate the company's cost of equity, assuming a risk-free rate of 2.0 percent and an equity-risk premium of 7.0 percent. How does the company's cost of equity compare to its ROE? What does the comparison tell you about the company?

d. Calculate the equity value of the company using the residual income model.

SOLUTIONS TO REVIEW PROBLEMS

Solution 12.1

AZUSA COMPANY
Pro Forma Income Statements

	Actual		Forecast		
	2016	**2017**	**2018**	**2019**	**2020**
Sales.....................................	$3,000	$3,120	$3,245	$3,375	$3,510
Cost of goods sold......................	1,200	1,248	1,298	1,350	1,404
Gross profit.............................	1,800	1,872	1,947	2,025	2,106
SG&A expense..........................	300	312	325	338	351
Depreciation............................	1,200	1,200	1,200	1,200	1,200
Interest.................................	250	150	150	150	150
Income before taxes.....................	50	210	272	337	405
Income taxes	15	63	82	101	122
Net income.............................	$ 35	$ 147	$ 190	$ 236	$ 283

AZUSA COMPANY Pro Forma Balance Sheets					
	Actual		**Forecast**		
	2016	**2017**	**2018**	**2019**	**2020**
Cash.	$ 700	$ 750	$ 750	$ 750	$ 750
Other current assets.	1,050	1,125	1,125	1,125	1,125
Total current assets	1,750	1,875	1,875	1,875	1,875
PP&E (net)	12,000	10,800	9,600	8,400	7,200
Total assets.	$13,750	$12,675	$11,475	$10,275	$9,075
Accounts payable.	$ 375	$ 450	$ 450	$ 450	$ 450
Other current liabilities	5,625	4,328	2,938	1,502	19
Total current liabilities.	6,000	4,778	3,388	1,952	469
Long-term debt	5,000	5,000	5,000	5,000	5,000
Total liabilities	11,000	9,778	8,388	6,952	5,469
Common Stock and Paid-in-capital.	1,500	1,500	1,500	1,500	1,500
Retained earnings	1,250	1,397	1,587	1,823	2,106
Total shareholders' equity	2,750	2,897	3,087	3,323	3,606
Total liabilities and shareholders' equity.	$13,750	$12,675	$11,475	$10,275	$9,075

Solution 12.2

1.

Free Cash Flow	2018	2019	2020	2021	2022	Terminal
3 alternative calculations:						
Financing flows:						
Cash dividends.	$350	$350	$350	$400	$400	$400
Net issuance of common stock	—	—	—	—	—	—
	$350	$350	$350	$400	$400	$400
Cash from operations.	$475	$495	$540	$595	$580	$610
Increase in operating cash	(195)	(235)	(290)	(270)	(260)	(295)
Cash from investing	50	70	80	50	55	60
Increase in debt	20	20	20	25	25	25
	$350	$350	$350	$400	$400	$400
Net income.	$500	$505	$525	$575	$600	$612
Increase in common equity	(150)	(155)	(175)	(175)	(200)	(212)
	$350	$350	$350	$400	$400	$400

2.

	2018	2019	2020	2021	2022	Terminal
Free cash flow to common equity	$ 350.00	$350.00	$350.00	$400.00	$400.00	$400.00
Present value of FCF (@ 8%)	$ 324.07	$300.07	$277.84	$294.01	$272.23	
Present value of first 5 years	$1,468.22					
Present value beyond 5 years	4,537.22*					
Value of common equity.	$6,005.44					

$*PV(TV) = [FCF/(r_e - g)]/(1 + 0.08)^5$
$\qquad = [400/ (0.08 - 0.02)]/(1 + 0.08)^5$
$\qquad = \$6,666.67/(1 + 0.08)^5$
$\qquad = \$4,537.22$

Solution 12.3

	2018	2019	2020	2021	2022	Terminal
Common equity at the beginning of the year. . .	$5,500	$5,800	$5,920	$6,100	$6,125	$6,200
Net income.	$ 590	$ 620	$ 635	$ 660	$ 680	$ 710
$r_e CE_t - 1$.	495	522	533	549	551	558
Residual income*	$ 95	$ 98	$ 102	$ 111	$ 129	$ 152
Present value of residual income (@ 9%).	$ 87.16	$ 82.48	$ 78.76	$ 78.64	$ 83.84	
Present value of first 5 years	$ 410.88					
Present value beyond 5 years	1,975.79**					
Beginning common equity as of 2018	$5,500.00					
Value of common equity.	$7,886.67					

$*RI_t = NI_t - r_e CE_{t-1}$
$**PV(TV) = [FCF/(r_e - g)]/(1 + 0.09)^5$
$\qquad = [152/ (0.09 - 0.04)]/(1 + 0.09)^5$
$\qquad = \$3,040/(1 + 0.09)^5$
$\qquad = \$1,975.79$

Solution 12.4

Compute the price-earnings multiples for the three comparable companies (i.e., share price/EPS):

Company	Share Price	EPS	PE
Adams	$31.50	$2.25	14.0
Yosemite.	$11.00	$1.10	10.0
Sequoia	$22.50	$1.50	15.0

The average PE ratio for these comparable companies is $(14 + 10 + 15)/3 = 13.0$

Next, compute Muir & Sons earnings per share: $2,300,000/1,000,000 = \$2.30$

Finally, apply the comparable PE ratio to Muir's EPS (13×2.30):
Estimated IPO price = $29.90

A The Time Value of Money

In this appendix, we illustrate compounding and the time value of money—important concepts that affect your everyday life. We illustrate these concepts using alternative techniques—either with time value of money tables or with electronic tools (i.e., calculators or spreadsheets). Note that whatever technique you use the results should be the same. These points will be emphasized through multiple examples.

To set the stage, consider the following regarding a loan made by Mr. Jacob DeHaven to General George Washington in 1777:

> The U.S. Supreme Court has upheld a refusal to repay a loan that helped save the American Revolution as George Washington's beleaguered army camped in the snow at Valley Forge. Jacob DeHaven of Philadelphia made the loan of gold, food and other supplies with an estimated value of $450,000 in February 1777. The failure of the United States ever to repay the loan obsesses Hershel Weasenforth, one of DeHaven's descendants. Before he died in 1984 at age 79, his daughter, Thelma Lunaas, promised him she would strive to get the U.S. government to settle the debt . . . DeHaven, a wealthy merchant and wine importer, was one of the patriots who responded to a desperate plea for aid for Washington's army at Valley Forge. . . . His descendants have made periodic efforts to get repayment over the past 215 years. (*Houston Chronicle*, January 29, 1992, p. 13A).

The information is not explicit as to whether Mr. DeHaven and General Washington discussed the interest rate on the loan, and if they did, whether they agreed on a specific interest rate. However, if Mr. DeHaven had written a loan agreement with just a five percent annual rate of interest and the U.S. Supreme Court had upheld the claim, Mr. DeHaven's heirs would be owed an astounding $52.2 billion some 239 years later. This case illustrates that even a modest sum of money invested at a low rate of interest for a long period of time can accumulate to a substantial sum as a consequence of the phenomenon of compounding. **Compounding** is a process in which interest is earned not only on an outstanding loan amount but also on any prior unpaid interest.

The key to understanding the concept of compounding is that the value of invested funds grows over time. Another way to think of this is that having $1 now is not the same as having $1 one year from now. If you have $1 now, you can invest it and have more than $1 in a year because your investment can earn interest. This notion—the **time value of money**—is important when evaluating the attractiveness of any investment.

How did we arrive at the $52.2 billion figure owed to Mr. DeHaven by the U.S. government? If Mr. DeHaven had written a loan for one year at five percent interest, he would expect to receive his original investment of $450,000 plus interest of $22,500 (5 percent of $450,000), or a total of $472,500 at the end of year one. If General Washington had wanted to roll the loan over for a second year, Mr. DeHaven could expect to receive $496,125 ($472,500 plus interest of $23,625 [5 percent of $472,500]) at the end of year two. If we repeated the exercise 237 more times (i.e., until 2016), you arrive at $52.2 billion.

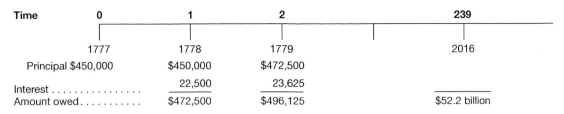

Time	0	1	2	239
	1777	1778	1779	2016
Principal	$450,000	$450,000	$472,500	
Interest		22,500	23,625	
Amount owed		$472,500	$496,125	$52.2 billion

An interesting twist to the story is that Jacob DeHaven's relatives actually sued the U.S. government for $100 billion! What rate of interest would yield that amount? You may be surprised to learn that it would only take an interest rate of 5.286 percent compounded annually over 239 years to grow to $100 billion. In fact, at six percent interest, the amount owed would be over $502 billion! A one percent increase in the rate of interest results in almost a ten-fold increase in the future amount, reflecting the power of compounding.

FUTURE VALUE OF A SINGLE AMOUNT

The DeHaven loan example illustrates the concept of **future value**. The future value of an investment is the amount that an initial investment, or a series of payments, will be worth at some point in the future. In the above example, $52.2 billion is the future value of an initial investment of $450,000 earning five percent interest per year for 239 years. The following formula can be used to compute future values:

$$\text{Future Value} = \text{Present Value} \times (1 + r)^n$$

where the present value is the amount currently invested, r is the prevailing rate of interest, and n is the number of periods (e.g., months, quarters, or years) until the cash inflow occurs. For example, if you can earn eight percent on your investment, how much would an investment of $2,000 today be worth in five years? Using the formula above, we see that the future value of your investment is $2,939, calculated as follows:

$$\text{Future Value} = \$2,000(1+.08)^5 = \$2,939$$

Alternatively, you can use a future value table (see Table 3 at the end of this appendix), which shows that the future value of $1 to be received in 5 years at an interest rate of 8 percent, PV(5, 8%), is equal to 1.46933.[1] Hence,

$$FV = \$2,000 \times PV(5,8\%) = \$2,000 \times 1.46933 = \$2,939$$

What if you want to find the future value of more than one deposit? This is not a problem as you simply add the individual future value computations together using the following formula:

$$FV = \sum_{t=1}^{n} \frac{CF_t(1+r)}{n-t}$$

where CF represents the individual deposits.

To illustrate, suppose you deposit $200 today into a savings account, $150 one year from today, and $300 in three years from today. What will all of this be worth in five years, assuming a six percent rate of interest?

Your first deposit will earn interest for five years and therefore will have a future value of $267.65. The future value of your second and third deposit are $189.37 and $337.08, respectively, for a total future value of $794.10. (You should be certain that you can compute these amounts on your own.)

---

[1] In order to use Tables 1 through 4 at the end of this appendix, you simply find the number, called an interest factor, which is at the intersection of the appropriate interest rate column and the period row. Can you find the interest factor of 1.46933 in Table 3, at the intersection of row n = 5 and the column i = 8%?

FUTURE VALUE OF AN ANNUITY

Rather than investing a single lump sum, or several deposits of differing value, you might invest a fixed amount on a regular basis. To illustrate this, assume that you plan to deposit $100 in a savings account on December 31st of each year for ten years and that you can earn seven percent interest on your deposits. How much would you have at the end of the tenth year? One way to solve this problem would be to use the future value (FV) formula (or Table 3) and compute the sum of the future value of each of the ten deposits. The first $100 deposit will be able to earn interest for nine years so it will be worth $183.85 at the end of ten years. Similarly, the second $100 deposit will earn interest for eight years and be worth $171.82. If we were to do the same calculations for each of the ten deposits and then sum the results, we would have our answer, $1,381.65. Luckily, there is an easier way to solve this type of problem.

An **annuity** is defined as a stream of equal size payments occurring at equal intervals.[2] Fortunately, a formula has been derived that can shorten the computation of the future value of an annuity:

$$\text{Future Value of an Annuity} = \text{Payment} \times FV_a(n, r\%) = \text{Payment} \times [(1+r)^n - 1]/r$$

Using the above formula, we see that $1,381.65 = $100 \times [(1.07^{10} - 1)/0.07]$. To facilitate this calculation, we can use Table 4 and find the interest factor of 13.81645, which when multiplied by the recurring deposit of $100 yields our future value of $1,381.65.

To this point, all of our examples have assumed that the payments and the compounding of interest occur just once per year. This, however, may not be the case in all situations. The only adjustment needed to compute a non-annual compounding is to convert the annual interest rate into a per-period rate of interest and to work with the number of periods rather than the number of years. The per-period interest rate is calculated by dividing the annual interest rate by the number of periods per year (e.g., a twelve percent annual rate would be a one percent monthly rate). In the above example, rather than making one payment per year for ten years, let's compute the future value for ten semiannual payments of $100 with annual interest at eight percent.

We first need to convert the eight percent annual interest rate to a four percent per-period rate. Our formula then becomes $100 \times [(1 + .04)^{10} - 1]/.04 = 1,200.61$. Note that we could also use the interest factor from Table 4 and compute the future value as $100 \times 12.0061 = 1,200.61$.

PRESENT VALUE OF A SINGLE AMOUNT

Thus far, we have been focusing on what an amount will be worth in the future. So, let's reverse our thinking and now consider what an amount to be received in the future is worth today. For example, consider a $100 investment today that will pay back $121.90 in ten years. Intuitively, this doesn't seem like a very good investment. It seems like you could do better just putting your money in a money market account at a bank. A common way to evaluate an investment opportunity like this is to compute the **present value** of the $121.90—that is, the amount that you would have to invest now, at a specified rate of interest, that would grow to $121.90 in ten years. In this case, if we assume that the prevailing interest rate is twelve percent, the present value of $121.90 to be received in ten years is $39.25—that is, if you invested $39.25 now at twelve percent annual interest, in ten years your investment would grow to a future value of $121.90.

The present value (PV) of a single amount is computed like this:

$$\text{Present Value} = \text{Future Amount} \times [1/(1+r)^n]$$

where r is the prevailing rate of interest and n is the number of periods (e.g., months, quarters, or years) until the cash inflow occurs. In the example just shown, the present value of the $121.90 would be computed as follows:

$$\text{Present Value} = \$121.90 \times [1/(1 + 0.12)^{10}] = \$39.25$$

Alternatively, you can use a present value table (see Table 1), which shows that the present value of $1 to be received in 10 years at an interest rate of twelve percent, PV(10, 12%), is equal to 0.32197. Hence,

---

[2] In this appendix we assume that the deposits (often referred to as payments) occur at the end of each period. This type of annuity is called an ordinary annuity or an annuity-in-arrears. An annuity-in-advance is an annuity in which the payments occur at the beginning of each period.

$$PV = \$121.90 \times PV(10,12\%) = \$121.90 \times 0.32197 = \$39.25$$

To help us decide whether to undertake an investment, we can compute the **net present value (NPV)** of the investment as follows:

$$NPV = \text{Present value of cash flows} - \text{Cost of investment}$$

An investment is considered to be a good one if the NPV $\geq$ 0—that is, if the present value of the expected cash inflow is greater than the cost of the investment. Conversely, if the NPV $<$ 0, it is considered to be a bad investment. In our case, the NPV of the $100 investment is equal to negative $60.75 ($39.25 − $100) assuming a prevailing interest rate of twelve percent, and, since the NPV of the investment is less than zero, it would be considered a bad investment.[3]

Let's consider another present value example. Anna Amphlett recently learned that in ten years she would receive $1 million from a trust fund established by her uncle when Anna was born. Given that she could earn about eight percent per year, Anna wondered how much her trust fund was currently worth. Using the present value approach, Anna's trust fund would be currently worth $463,000, calculated as follows:

$$PV = \$1,000,000 \times PV(10, 8\%) \text{ [from Table 1, } PV(10,8\%) \text{ is equal to } 0.46319]$$
$$= \$1,000,000 \times 0.46319$$
$$= \mathbf{\$463,190}$$

In ten years, with an interest rate of eight percent per year, Anna's trust fund will grow to be worth $1 million, its future value.

PRESENT VALUE OF AN ANNUITY

Investments often involve a series of cash flows rather than a single lump-sum cash payment at the end of the investment. For example, consider a $60,000 investment in an MBA degree that is expected to yield an increment to your salary of $5,000 a year for the next 25 years. Is this a good investment? Unlike the previous example, this education investment pays off each year. One way to compute the present value of the incremental cash flows would be to compute the present value of each of the $5,000 annual salary flows and then add the 25 amounts up as follows:

$$\$ 5,000 \times PV(1, 10\%)$$
$$\$ 5,000 \times PV(2, 10\%)$$
$$\vdots$$
$$\underline{\$ 5,000 \times PV(25, 10\%)}$$
$$\$45,385$$

Fortunately, a formula similar to the future value of an annuity has been derived that can shorten the computation of the present value of an annuity:

$$\text{Present Value of an Annuity} = \text{Payment} \times PV_a(n, r\%) = \text{Payment} \times \{1 - [1/(1 + r)^n]\}/r$$

The present value of the 25 years of extra salary, assuming an interest rate of ten percent, is computed as follows:

$$\text{Present Value of an Annuity} = \$5,000 \times \{1 - [1/(1 + 0.10)^{25}]\}/0.10 = \$45,385$$

Alternatively, you can use a present value table (see Table 2), which shows that the present value of $1 to be received every year for 25 years at an interest rate of ten percent, $PV_a(25, 10\%)$, is equal to 9.07704. Hence,

---

[3] You may wonder what interest rate resulted in the deposit of $100.00 growing to $121.90 in ten years. This can be found with the use of Table 1 and the present value formula. Simply rearrange the present value (PV) formula as follows:

$$PV = FV \times PV \text{ factor}$$
$$PV / FV = PV \text{ factor}$$

We can then compute the PV factor as $100.00 / $121.90 = 0.820. We then search for this PV factor in Table 1 by scanning across the ten-period row until we find this a factor of 0.820 in the two percent column.

$$\text{Present Value of an Annuity} = \$5,000 \times 9.07704 = \$45,385$$

But is this a good investment? Using the formula to calculate the net present value of an investment reveals that the NPV of receiving $5,000 per year for 25 years, with a prevailing interest rate of ten percent, is negative $14,615, calculated as follows:

$$
\begin{aligned}
\text{NPV} &= \$5,000 \times \text{PV}_a(12,10\%) - \$60,000 \\
&= \$5,000 \times 9.077 - \$60,000 \\
&= \$45,385 - \$60,000 \\
&= -\$14,615 < 0
\end{aligned}
$$

In this case, since the NPV of the investment is less than zero, the investment in the MBA degree is a bad one from a financial standpoint.

Consider a final example of an annuity. Josie Walsh recently won the lottery, which will pay her $500,000 every year for the next 20 years. Josie's friend, Paul, offered her $3.5 million now if she will give him the winning ticket. Josie figures that she could always put the money in U.S. government bonds earning twelve percent. Should Josie sell her winning ticket for $3.5 million? Calculating the net present value of 20 payments of $500,000 reveals that the NPV of keeping the ticket is $234,720, calculated as follows:

$$
\begin{aligned}
\text{NPV} &= \$500,000 \times \text{PV}_a(20, 12\%) - \$3,500,000 \text{ [from Table 2, PV}_a(20,12\%) \text{ is equal to } 7.46944] \\
&= \$500,000 \times 7.46944 - \$3,500,000 \\
&= \$3,734,720 - \$3,500,000 \\
&= \$234,720 > 0
\end{aligned}
$$

Since the NPV of refusing the offer is $3,734,720, which is greater than zero, Josie should not accept Paul's offer to buy her winning lottery ticket.

TABLE 1	Present Value of $1											
Period	**1%**	**2%**	**3%**	**4%**	**5%**	**6%**	**7%**	**8%**	**9%**	**10%**	**11%**	**12%**
1	0.99010	0.98039	0.97087	0.96154	0.95238	0.94340	0.93458	0.92593	0.91743	0.90909	0.90090	0.89286
2	0.98030	0.96117	0.94260	0.92456	0.90703	0.89000	0.87344	0.85734	0.84168	0.82645	0.81162	0.79719
3	0.97059	0.94232	0.91514	0.88900	0.86384	0.83962	0.81630	0.79383	0.77218	0.75131	0.73119	0.71178
4	0.96098	0.92385	0.88849	0.85480	0.82270	0.79209	0.76290	0.73503	0.70843	0.68301	0.65873	0.63552
5	0.95147	0.90573	0.86261	0.82193	0.78353	0.74726	0.71299	0.68058	0.64993	0.62092	0.59345	0.56743
6	0.94205	0.88797	0.83748	0.79031	0.74622	0.70496	0.66634	0.63017	0.59627	0.56447	0.53464	0.50663
7	0.93272	0.87056	0.81309	0.75992	0.71068	0.66506	0.62275	0.58349	0.54703	0.51316	0.48166	0.45235
8	0.92348	0.85349	0.78941	0.73069	0.67684	0.62741	0.58201	0.54027	0.50187	0.46651	0.43393	0.40388
9	0.91434	0.83676	0.76642	0.70259	0.64461	0.59190	0.54393	0.50025	0.46043	0.42410	0.39092	0.36061
10	0.90529	0.82035	0.74409	0.67556	0.61391	0.55839	0.50835	0.46319	0.42241	0.38554	0.35218	0.32197
11	0.89632	0.80426	0.72242	0.64958	0.58468	0.52679	0.47509	0.42888	0.38753	0.35049	0.31728	0.28748
12	0.88745	0.78849	0.70138	0.62460	0.55684	0.49697	0.44401	0.39711	0.35553	0.31863	0.28584	0.25668
13	0.87866	0.77303	0.68095	0.60057	0.53032	0.46884	0.41496	0.36770	0.32618	0.28966	0.25751	0.22917
14	0.86996	0.75788	0.66112	0.57748	0.50507	0.44230	0.38782	0.34046	0.29925	0.26333	0.23199	0.20462
15	0.86135	0.74301	0.64186	0.55526	0.48102	0.41727	0.36245	0.31524	0.27454	0.23939	0.20900	0.18270
16	0.85282	0.72845	0.62317	0.53391	0.45811	0.39365	0.33873	0.29189	0.25187	0.21763	0.18829	0.16312
17	0.84438	0.71416	0.60502	0.51337	0.43630	0.37136	0.31657	0.27027	0.23107	0.19784	0.16963	0.14564
18	0.83602	0.70016	0.58739	0.49363	0.41552	0.35034	0.29586	0.25025	0.21199	0.17986	0.15282	0.13004
19	0.82774	0.68643	0.57029	0.47464	0.39573	0.33051	0.27651	0.23171	0.19449	0.16351	0.13768	0.11611
20	0.81954	0.67297	0.55368	0.45639	0.37689	0.31180	0.25842	0.21455	0.17843	0.14864	0.12403	0.10367
25	0.77977	0.60953	0.47761	0.37512	0.29530	0.23300	0.18425	0.14602	0.11597	0.09230	0.07361	0.05882
30	0.74192	0.55207	0.41199	0.30832	0.23138	0.17411	0.13137	0.09938	0.07537	0.05731	0.04368	0.03338
35	0.70591	0.50003	0.35538	0.25342	0.18129	0.13011	0.09366	0.06763	0.04899	0.03558	0.02592	0.01894
40	0.67165	0.45289	0.30656	0.20829	0.14205	0.09722	0.06678	0.04603	0.03184	0.02209	0.01538	0.01075
50	0.60804	0.37153	0.22811	0.14071	0.08720	0.05429	0.03395	0.02132	0.01345	0.00852	0.00542	0.00346

TABLE 2	Present Value of an Ordinary Annuity of $1 per Period										
Period	**1%**	**2%**	**3%**	**4%**	**5%**	**6%**	**7%**	**8%**	**9%**	**10%**	**11%**	**12%**
1	0.99010	0.98039	0.97087	0.96154	0.95238	0.94340	0.93458	0.92593	0.91743	0.90909	0.90090	0.89286
2	1.97040	1.94156	1.91347	1.88609	1.85941	1.83339	1.80802	1.78326	1.75911	1.73554	1.71252	1.69005
3	2.94099	2.88388	2.82861	2.77509	2.72325	2.67301	2.62432	2.57710	2.53129	2.48685	2.44371	2.40183
4	3.90197	3.80773	3.71710	3.62990	3.54595	3.46511	3.38721	3.31213	3.23972	3.16987	3.10245	3.03735
5	4.85343	4.71346	4.57971	4.45182	4.32948	4.21236	4.10020	3.99271	3.88965	3.79079	3.69590	3.60478
6	5.79548	5.60143	5.41719	5.24214	5.07569	4.91732	4.76654	4.62288	4.48592	4.35526	4.23054	4.11141
7	6.72819	6.47199	6.23028	6.00205	5.78637	5.58238	5.38929	5.20637	5.03295	4.86842	4.71220	4.56376
8	7.65168	7.32548	7.01969	6.73274	6.46321	6.20979	5.97130	5.74664	5.53482	5.33493	5.14612	4.96764
9	8.56602	8.16224	7.78611	7.43533	7.10782	6.80169	6.51523	6.24689	5.99525	5.75902	5.53705	5.32825
10	9.47130	8.98259	8.53020	8.11090	7.72173	7.36009	7.02358	6.71008	6.41766	6.14457	5.88923	5.65022
11	10.36763	9.78685	9.25262	8.76048	8.30641	7.88687	7.49867	7.13896	6.80519	6.49506	6.20652	5.93770
12	11.25508	10.57534	9.95400	9.38507	8.86325	8.38384	7.94269	7.53608	7.16073	6.81369	6.49236	6.19437
13	12.13374	11.34837	10.63496	9.98565	9.39357	8.85268	8.35765	7.90378	7.48690	7.10336	6.74987	6.42355
14	13.00370	12.10625	11.29607	10.56312	9.89864	9.29498	8.74547	8.24424	7.78615	7.36669	6.98187	6.62817
15	13.86505	12.84926	11.93794	11.11839	10.37966	9.71225	9.10791	8.55948	8.06069	7.60608	7.19087	6.81086
16	14.71787	13.57771	12.56110	11.65230	10.83777	10.10590	9.44665	8.85137	8.31256	7.82371	7.37916	6.97399
17	15.56225	14.29187	13.16612	12.16567	11.27407	10.47726	9.76322	9.12164	8.54363	8.02155	7.54879	7.11963
18	16.39827	14.99203	13.75351	12.65930	11.68959	10.82760	10.05909	9.37189	8.75563	8.20141	7.70162	7.24967
19	17.22601	15.67846	14.32380	13.13394	12.08532	11.15812	10.33560	9.60360	8.95011	8.36492	7.83929	7.36578
20	18.04555	16.35143	14.87747	13.59033	12.46221	11.46992	10.59401	9.81815	9.12855	8.51356	7.96333	7.46944
25	22.02316	19.52346	17.41315	15.62208	14.09394	12.78336	11.65358	10.67478	9.82258	9.07704	8.42174	7.84314
30	25.80771	22.39646	19.60044	17.29203	15.37245	13.76483	12.40904	11.25778	10.27365	9.42691	8.69379	8.05518
35	29.40858	24.99862	21.48722	18.66461	16.37419	14.49825	12.94767	11.65457	10.56682	9.64416	8.85524	8.17550
40	32.83469	27.35548	23.11477	19.79277	17.15909	15.04630	13.33171	11.92461	10.75736	9.77905	8.95105	8.24378
50	39.19612	31.42361	25.72976	21.48218	18.25593	15.76186	13.80075	12.23348	10.96168	9.91481	9.04165	8.30450

TABLE 3	Future Value of $1										
Period	**1%**	**2%**	**3%**	**4%**	**5%**	**6%**	**7%**	**8%**	**9%**	**10%**	**11%**	**12%**
1	1.01000	1.02000	1.03000	1.04000	1.05000	1.06000	1.07000	1.08000	1.09000	1.10000	1.11000	1.12000
2	1.02010	1.04040	1.06090	1.08160	1.10250	1.12360	1.14490	1.16640	1.18810	1.21000	1.23210	1.25440
3	1.03030	1.06121	1.09273	1.12486	1.15763	1.19102	1.22504	1.25971	1.29503	1.33100	1.36763	1.40493
4	1.04060	1.08243	1.12551	1.16986	1.21551	1.26248	1.31080	1.36049	1.41158	1.46410	1.51807	1.57352
5	1.05101	1.10408	1.15927	1.21665	1.27628	1.33823	1.40255	1.46933	1.53862	1.61051	1.68506	1.76234
6	1.06152	1.12616	1.19405	1.26532	1.34010	1.41852	1.50073	1.58687	1.67710	1.77156	1.87041	1.97382
7	1.07214	1.14869	1.22987	1.31593	1.40710	1.50363	1.60578	1.71382	1.82804	1.94872	2.07616	2.21068
8	1.08286	1.17166	1.26677	1.36857	1.47746	1.59385	1.71819	1.85093	1.99256	2.14359	2.30454	2.47596
9	1.09369	1.19509	1.30477	1.42331	1.55133	1.68948	1.83846	1.99900	2.17189	2.35795	2.55804	2.77308
10	1.10462	1.21899	1.34392	1.48024	1.62889	1.79085	1.96715	2.15892	2.36736	2.59374	2.83942	3.10585
11	1.11567	1.24337	1.38423	1.53945	1.71034	1.89830	2.10485	2.33164	2.58043	2.85312	3.15176	3.47855
12	1.12683	1.26824	1.42576	1.60103	1.79586	2.01220	2.25219	2.51817	2.81266	3.13843	3.49845	3.89598
13	1.13809	1.29361	1.46853	1.66507	1.88565	2.13293	2.40985	2.71962	3.06580	3.45227	3.88328	4.36349
14	1.14947	1.31948	1.51259	1.73168	1.97993	2.26090	2.57853	2.93719	3.34173	3.79750	4.31044	4.88711
15	1.16097	1.34587	1.55797	1.80094	2.07893	2.39656	2.75903	3.17217	3.64248	4.17725	4.78459	5.47357
16	1.17258	1.37279	1.60471	1.87298	2.18287	2.54035	2.95216	3.42594	3.97031	4.59497	5.31089	6.13039
17	1.18430	1.40024	1.65285	1.94790	2.29202	2.69277	3.15882	3.70002	4.32763	5.05447	5.89509	6.86604
18	1.19615	1.42825	1.70243	2.02582	2.40662	2.85434	3.37993	3.99602	4.71712	5.55992	6.54355	7.68997
19	1.20811	1.45681	1.75351	2.10685	2.52695	3.02560	3.61653	4.31570	5.14166	6.11591	7.26334	8.61276
20	1.22019	1.48595	1.80611	2.19112	2.65330	3.20714	3.86968	4.66096	5.60441	6.72750	8.06231	9.64629
25	1.28243	1.64061	2.09378	2.66584	3.38635	4.29187	5.42743	6.84848	8.62308	10.83471	13.58546	17.00006

continued

continued from previous page

TABLE 3	Future Value of $1											
Period	1%	2%	3%	4%	5%	6%	7%	8%	9%	10%	11%	12%
30	1.34785	1.81136	2.42726	3.24340	4.32194	5.74349	7.61226	10.06266	13.26768	17.44940	22.89230	29.95992
35	1.41660	1.99989	2.81386	3.94609	5.51602	7.68609	10.67658	14.78534	20.41397	28.10244	38.57485	52.79962
40	1.48886	2.20804	3.26204	4.80102	7.03999	10.28572	14.97446	21.72452	31.40942	45.25926	65.00087	93.05097
50	1.64463	2.69159	4.38391	7.10668	11.46740	18.42015	29.45703	46.90161	74.35752	117.39085	184.56483	289.00219

TABLE 4	Future Value of an Ordinary Annuity of $1 per Period											
Period	1%	2%	3%	4%	5%	6%	7%	8%	9%	10%	11%	12%
1	1.00000	1.00000	1.00000	1.00000	1.00000	1.00000	1.00000	1.00000	1.00000	1.00000	1.00000	1.00000
2	2.01000	2.02000	2.03000	2.04000	2.05000	2.06000	2.07000	2.08000	2.09000	2.10000	2.11000	2.12000
3	3.03010	3.06040	3.09090	3.12160	3.15250	3.18360	3.21490	3.24640	3.27810	3.31000	3.34210	3.37440
4	4.06040	4.12161	4.18363	4.24646	4.31013	4.37462	4.43994	4.50611	4.57313	4.64100	4.70973	4.77933
5	5.10101	5.20404	5.30914	5.41632	5.52563	5.63709	5.75074	5.86660	5.98471	6.10510	6.22780	6.35285
6	6.15202	6.30812	6.46841	6.63298	6.80191	6.97532	7.15329	7.33593	7.52333	7.71561	7.91286	8.11519
7	7.21354	7.43428	7.66246	7.89829	8.14201	8.39384	8.65402	8.92280	9.20043	9.48717	9.78327	10.08901
8	8.28567	8.58297	8.89234	9.21423	9.54911	9.89747	10.25980	10.63663	11.02847	11.43589	11.85943	12.29969
9	9.36853	9.75463	10.15911	10.58280	11.02656	11.49132	11.97799	12.48756	13.02104	13.57948	14.16397	14.77566
10	10.46221	10.94972	11.46388	12.00611	12.57789	13.18079	13.81645	14.48656	15.19293	15.93742	16.72201	17.54874
11	11.56683	12.16872	12.80780	13.48635	14.20679	14.97164	15.78360	16.64549	17.56029	18.53117	19.56143	20.65458
12	12.68250	13.41209	14.19203	15.02581	15.91713	16.86994	17.88845	18.97713	20.14072	21.38428	22.71319	24.13313
13	13.80933	14.68033	15.61779	16.62684	17.71298	18.88214	20.14064	21.49530	22.95338	24.52271	26.21164	28.02911
14	14.94742	15.97394	17.08632	18.29191	19.59863	21.01507	22.55049	24.21492	26.01919	27.97498	30.09492	32.39260
15	16.09690	17.29342	18.59891	20.02359	21.57856	23.27597	25.12902	27.15211	29.36092	31.77248	34.40536	37.27971
16	17.25786	18.63929	20.15688	21.82453	23.65749	25.67253	27.88805	30.32428	33.00340	35.94973	39.18995	42.75328
17	18.43044	20.01207	21.76159	23.69751	25.84037	28.21288	30.84022	33.75023	36.97370	40.54470	44.50084	48.88367
18	19.61475	21.41231	23.41444	25.64541	28.13238	30.90565	33.99903	37.45024	41.30134	45.59917	50.39594	55.74971
19	20.81090	22.84056	25.11687	27.67123	30.53900	33.75999	37.37896	41.44626	46.01846	51.15909	56.93949	63.43968
20	22.01900	24.29737	26.87037	29.77808	33.06595	36.78559	40.99549	45.76196	51.16012	57.27500	64.20283	72.05244
25	28.24320	32.03030	36.45926	41.64591	47.72710	54.86451	63.24904	73.10594	84.70090	98.34706	114.4133	133.3339
30	34.78489	40.56808	47.57542	56.08494	66.43885	79.05819	94.46079	113.2832	136.3075	164.4940	199.0209	241.3327
35	41.66028	49.99448	60.46208	73.65222	90.32031	111.4348	138.2369	172.3168	215.7108	271.0244	341.5896	431.6635
40	48.88637	60.40198	75.40126	95.02552	120.7998	154.7620	199.6351	259.0565	337.8824	442.5926	581.8261	767.0914
50	64.46318	84.57940	112.7969	152.6671	209.3480	290.3359	406.5289	573.7702	815.0836	1163.909	1668.771	2400.018

TIME VALUE CALCULATIONS USING A FINANCIAL CALCULATOR OR AN ELECTRONIC SPREADSHEET

Although time value calculations can be performed as we have done using tables, it is far more common, and more efficient, to perform these calculations using either a financial calculator or an electronic spreadsheet. We will illustrate the use of each in this section. Whatever the method you choose to perform time value of money calculations, all should yield identical results (subject to small rounding errors). Your preference will be a matter of taste.

Financial calculators are both inexpensive and very powerful, providing an easy way to perform time value calculations using only a few specialized keys. While small differences exist among the various calculator brands, all of them include at least the five input keys shown in the following graphic:

N represents the number of periods (e.g., months, quarters or years), I/Yr represents the interest rate per period, PV represents the present value, PMT represents the periodic payment amount in an annuity, and FV represents the future value. To solve a time value problem, you must input four known values, allowing the calculator to then compute the remaining unknown value. By default, each of the input keys is assumed to have a value of zero unless a value is input into its register. Also worth noting, most calculators will treat the annuity value under the PMT key as being an ordinary annuity (i.e., an annuity payment made at the end of a period). You should check the settings in your calculator to be certain of this treatment.

The use of a spreadsheet program such as Microsoft Excel provides another useful method to perform time value calculations.[4] Excel has a tremendous amount of built in functions that aid in the user's computations. For time value of money calculations, similar to a financial calculator, you will need to provide inputs into the spreadsheet program so that it can compute the output you desire. These inputs are entered using a spreadsheet function unique to that program. We will illustrate a few of the financial functions in the following section using Excel 2016 for Windows. Depending on the computer platform you are using and the version of Excel you are running, there may be slight differences from these illustrations in the manner in which you must enter the required inputs. However the basic method to perform these computations tends to remain essentially the same.

Whether one uses a financial calculator or a spreadsheet program, there are a few items that need to be observed while using these devices. First, cash inflows and outflows must be input with opposite signs. This should make sense as inflows and outflows are themselves opposites. For example, if the present value (e.g., an amount received) is input as a positive number, the future value (an amount paid) will be displayed as a negative number. In essence the future value is the amount that can be withdrawn (cash outflow) from an initial deposit (cash inflow). Since most users prefer to see output calculations as positive numbers, inputs tend to be entered as negative values. Second, N, the number of periods, is not the same as the number of years unless the compounding is done on an annual basis. For example, a five-year bond that pays semiannual interest would have ten (two times five) periods. Likewise, the interest rate needs to be input as a period interest rate.[5] Assuming our five-year bond pays a 10 percent annual interest, compounded semiannually, we would need to input the period interest rate of 5 percent (ten divided by two).

Future Value of a Single Amount

Earlier in this appendix we used tables to find the future value of a current $2,000 investment that earns an annual interest rate of 8 percent for five years. To solve this problem with a financial calculator we number input N as 5, I/Yr as 8, PV as −$2,000 (so that our desired future value will be shown as positive), and PMT as 0. We then compute FV to produce a result of $2,939.

Calculator				
N	**I/Yr**	**PV**	**PMT**	**FV**
5	8	2,000	0	**2,939**

There are multiple ways we can solve this same problem using Excel. Excel has a function wizard denoted as *fx* that can greatly simplify these and many other calculations. To access the function wizard either (1) click it directly on the formula bar, or (2) select the Formulas tab and either select the function wizard (2a) or select Financial (2b) for financial formulas.

---

[4] While Microsoft Excel is the most widely used spreadsheet program, other popular spreadsheet programs include Google Sheets and Apple Numbers. Each of the alternate programs solves time value problems in a similar manner as Excel.
[5] Some calculators will assume you have input the interest rate as an annual amount, while others will require you to first specify the periodic rate of compounding.

Regardless of how you access the function wizard, the next step is to choose the appropriate formula to apply. To solve our future value problem we select the function FV from the pull-down menu. This will then open up a dialog box that can be used to input the required variables.

Function Arguments   ?   ✕

FV

Rate	.08	📊	=	0.08
Nper	5	📊	=	5
Pmt		📊	=	number
Pv	-2000	📊	=	-2000
Type		📊	=	number

= 2938.656154

Returns the future value of an investment based on periodic, constant payments and a constant interest rate.

Pv is the present value, or the lump-sum amount that a series of future payments is worth now. If omitted, Pv = 0.

Formula result =   2938.656154

Help on this function   OK   Cancel

After providing the required inputs, the solution appears in the dialog box as well as on the Excel spreadsheet.

	A	B	C	D	E	F	G	H
1	Interest rate	0.08						
2	Number of periods	5						
3	Present value	-2,000						
4	Future value	$2,938.66						
5								
6								
7								
8								
9								
10								

B4 fx =FV(B1,B2,,B3)

An alternate way to use the dialog box is to use cell references as inputs rather than typing numbers directly into the dialog box. Below is a representation of this approach.

Function Arguments

FV

Rate	+B1	=	0.08
Nper	+B2	=	5
Pmt		=	number
Pv	+B3	=	-2000
Type		=	number

= 2938.656154

Returns the future value of an investment based on periodic, constant payments and a constant interest rate.

Pv is the present value, or the lump-sum amount that a series of future payments is worth now. If omitted, Pv = 0.

Formula result = 2938.656154

Help on this function   OK   Cancel

Future Value of an Annuity

Earlier in this appendix we used tables to find the future value of $100 deposited on December 31st of each year for ten years earning an annual interest rate of seven percent on those deposits. To solve this problem with a financial calculator we input N as 10, I/Yr as 7, PV as 0, and PMT as negative $100, and then have the calculator compute FV. A result of $1,381.64 will be produced.[6]

Calculator				
N	**I/Yr**	**PV**	**PMT**	**FV**
10	7	0	−100	**1,381.64**

We would use the same FV dialog box in Excel as we did with the prior future value problem; however our inputs now include the Pmt variable and exclude (leave as zero) the PV variable.

Function Arguments	? ☓

FV

Rate	.07	▦	= 0.07
Nper	10	▦	= 10
Pmt	-100	▦	= -100
Pv		▦	= number
Type		▦	= number

= 1381.644796

Returns the future value of an investment based on periodic, constant payments and a constant interest rate.

Pv is the present value, or the lump-sum amount that a series of future payments is worth now. If omitted, Pv = 0.

Formula result =   1381.644796

Help on this function   OK   Cancel

The future value problems so far have both involved annual compounding. If instead, we wish to know the future value of ten *semiannual* payments of $100 with an annual interest rate of eight percent, we will first need to convert the annual interest rate of eight percent to a semiannual rate of four percent (8 percent for the year divided by two six-month periods). We then input to the dialog box as follows to get a solution of $1,200.61

---

[6] Both the financial calculator and the Excel spreadsheet will lead to a slightly more precise solution than the tables due to rounding in the tables.

Function Arguments		?	✕

FV

Rate	.04|	📊	=	0.04
Nper	10	📊	=	10
Pmt	-100	📊	=	-100
Pv		📊	=	number
Type		📊	=	number

= 1200.610712

Returns the future value of an investment based on periodic, constant payments and a constant interest rate.

Rate is the interest rate per period. For example, use 6%/4 for quarterly payments at 6% APR.

Formula result =   1200.610712

Help on this function   OK   Cancel

Present Value of a Single Amount

Earlier in the appendix we used tables to determine the present value of $1 million dollars received in ten years with annual compounding of eight percent was $436,190. We next solve this same problem with a financial calculator and an Excel spreadsheet.

On a financial calculator we now input values for N, I/Yr, and FV, then compute PV to solve the problem.

Calculator				
N	**I/Yr**	**PV**	**PMT**	**FV**
10	8	**463,193**	0	1,000,000

Using Excel, we now choose the PV formula from the function wizard and input values in the dialog box as follows.

Function Arguments		?	✕

PV

Rate	.08	📊	=	0.08
Nper	10	📊	=	10
Pmt		📊	=	number
Fv	-1000000|	📊	=	-1000000
Type		📊	=	number

= 463193.4881

Returns the present value of an investment: the total amount that a series of future payments is worth now.

Fv is the future value, or a cash balance you want to attain after the last payment is made.

Formula result =   463193.4881

Help on this function   OK   Cancel

Present Value of an Annuity

By now you are seeing the similarity in each of these examples. To solve a present value of an annuity problem we use the same approaches. The below graphic shows the results of inputting values into a financial calculator and into the dialog box in Excel in order to solve the present value of receiving $5,000 each year for 25 years, with annual compounding at 10 percent. The value is computed to be $45,385.

Calculator				
N	**I/Yr**	**PV**	**PMT**	**FV**
25	10	45,385	−5,000	−0

Function Arguments   ?   X

PV

Rate	.10	🔢	=	0.1
Nper	25	🔢	=	25
Pmt	-5000	🔢	=	-5000
Fv		🔢	=	number
Type		🔢	=	number

= 45385.20009

Returns the present value of an investment: the total amount that a series of future payments is worth now.

Pmt   is the payment made each period and cannot change over the life of the investment.

Formula result =   45385.20009

Help on this function   OK   Cancel

Solving More Complex Time Value Problems

In Chapter 9 we introduced valuing bonds using present value tables to determine the issuance price of a bond. In an illustration we valued a ten-year $100 million bond that pays a semiannual coupon payment at four percent per period, and the semiannual compounded discount rate was at five percent per period. To solve this problem using a financial calculator, we would input N as 20, I/Yr as 5, PMT as −4, and FV as +100. A PV can then be computed as $87.54 million. Notice that in this problem we have input both a PMT amount and a FV amount, but all else in the methodology is the same. What should be apparent is regardless of the approach one must be very careful to get the structure and inputs exactly correct.

Calculator				
N	**I/Yr**	**PV**	**PMT**	**FV**
20	5	87.54	−4	−100

Using the PV dialog box in Excel will yield a similar result.

In Chapter 9 we also illustrated the creation of an amortization table for this bond. Excel provides an excellent tool for constructing an amortization table. And we can also use the PV dialog box to find the book value and market value at any point during the life of the bond. For example, if we wished to compute the book value of this bond after 10 periods have passed (one-half of its life) we would fill in the PV dialog box with "Nper" as 10 rather than 20 because there are now 10 periods remaining. This results in a book value of 92.28.

Function Arguments		? ✕
PV		

Rate	.05	▦	= 0.05
Nper	10	▦	= 10
Pmt	-4.0	▦	= -4
Fv	-100	▦	= -100
Type		▦	= number

= 92.27826507

Returns the present value of an investment: the total amount that a series of future payments is worth now.

Nper is the total number of payment periods in an investment.

Formula result = 92.27826507

Help on this function   OK   Cancel

In order to determine the market value at this same point in time all we would need to do is substitute the current market discount rate in the dialog box. Assuming, as we did in Chapter 9, that the market discount rate increased to six percent per period we calculate the market value to be $85.28 million.

Function Arguments		? ✕
PV		

Rate	.06	▦	= 0.06
Nper	10	▦	= 10
Pmt	-4.0	▦	= -4
Fv	-100	▦	= -100
Type		▦	= number

= 85.2798259

Returns the present value of an investment: the total amount that a series of future payments is worth now.

Rate is the interest rate per period. For example, use 6%/4 for quarterly payments at 6% APR.

Formula result = 85.2798259

Help on this function   OK   Cancel

Another useful feature of Excel is the IPMT function, by which we are able to determine the interest expense for any payment on our amortization schedule. For example, the interest expense for the tenth payment is computed by inputting the rate as .05, the period we are trying to determine the interest expense for (Per) as 10, the total number of periods for the bond (Nper) as 20, and the initial present value (PV) that we previously computed as −87.54, and the FV as 100. This results in an interest expense of $4.58 million.

Function Arguments   ?   ✕

IPMT

Rate	.05	🔢	=	0.05
Per	10	🔢	=	10
Nper	20	🔢	=	20
Pv	-87.54	🔢	=	-87.54
Fv	100	🔢	=	100

= 4.584752952

Returns the interest payment for a given period for an investment, based on periodic, constant payments and a constant interest rate.

Fv is the future value, or a cash balance you want to attain after the last payment is made. If omitted, Fv = 0.

Formula result = 4.584752952

Help on this function   OK   Cancel

As a final illustration, note that we can use Excel to find the net present value (NPV) of a series of different values such as the minimum lease payments from the AMR lease disclosure reported in the Business Perspective box near the end of Chapter 9.

The first step in this calculation requires inputting all of the cash flows in a continuous range within the spreadsheet (see cells B1 through B14 below). It is important not to skip any cells and to input a zero if no cash flow is present during a time period. Positive and negative cash flows can be mixed if the problem involves both cash inflows and outflows.

The next step is to select the NPV formula from the function wizard. In this case we assumed the rate was ten percent. The cash flows can either be input as separate values, or as a range that references where the cash flows appear in the spreadsheet. The solution of $6.026 million appears in the lower left hand corner of the dialog box and will appear in cell B16 once we click on OK in the dialog box.

B16   =NPV(.10,B1:B14)

	A	B
1	2012	1.176
2	2013	1.091
3	2014	0.942
4	2015	0.779
5	2016	0.685
6	2017	0.685
7	2018	0.685
8	2019	0.685
9	2020	0.685
10	2021	0.685
11	2022	0.685
12	2023	0.685
13	2024	0.685
14	2025	0.460
15	Total	10.613
16	PV	,B1:B14)
17		

Function Arguments   ?   ✕

NPV

Rate	.10	🔢	=	0.1
Value1	B1:B14	🔢	=	{1.176;1.091;0.942;0.779;0.685;0.685;0.685...
Value2		🔢	=	number

= 6.026123371

Returns the net present value of an investment based on a discount rate and a series of future payments (negative values) and income (positive values).

Value1: value1,value2,... are 1 to 254 payments and income, equally spaced in time and occurring at the end of each period.

Formula result = 6.026123371

Help on this function   OK   Cancel

Our examples above illustrate just a few of the many types of time value problems that can be solved using either a financial calculator or an electronic spreadsheet. You are encouraged to practice, and practice more, as learning to use these powerful tools can prove invaluable.

Assignments with the ⬤ logo in the margin are available in BusinessCourse.
See the Preface of the book for details.

EXERCISES

A.1   Margaret Diver invests $7,000 into her bank account that pays 12 percent, compounded annually. How much will she have if:
  a. She leaves the money in her account for two years?
  b. She leaves the money in her account for three years?
  c. She leaves the money for two years but the bank's 12 percent annual rate is compounded quarterly?

A.2   Jay Stone invested $3,000 he won in a poker match at 8 percent annual interest for 10 years. At the end of the 10 years he took all the money out and went on a spending spree. How much can he spend if:
  a. The interest is compounded annually?
  b. The interest is compounded semiannually?
  c. The interest is compounded quarterly?

A.3   Julie Lynch invests $1,000 annually into her bank at the end of each year for five years. Her bank pays interest at the annual rate of 6 percent. How much will she have at the end of the fifth year?

A.4   Murat Borat just opened an Individual Retirement Account (IRA) and plans to contribute $4,000 per year for 30 years at which time he will retire. Assume he funds his IRA at the end of each of the 30 years and he can earn 12 percent compounded annually. How much will he have at retirement?

A.5   Debra Moore needs $20,000 3 years from now. How much should she invest today in order to reach her goal if:
  a. She can earn 6 percent compounded annually?
  b. She can earn an annual rate of 6 percent compounded semiannually?

A.6   Abe Washington sold some property in Oregon and will receive $40,000 in 5 equal payments of $8,000 at the end of each year from today. What is the present value of these future payments at an interest rate of 9 percent compounded annually?

A.7   Lucky Lewis won a jackpot that offered him the option of receiving $15,000 immediately or $30,000 20 years from now. Assuming Lucky can earn a rate of 8 percent compounded annually, which option should he select?

A.8   You have been offered an investment that will pay you a lump sum of $30,000 25 years from today, along with a payment of $1,000 per year for 25 years starting one year from today. How much are you willing to invest today to have this investment in your portfolio assuming you wish to earn a rate of 6 percent compounded annually?

A.9   Jesse would like to have $1 million dollars in 10 years. Jesse will invest $75,000 in a money market account at the end of each year for the next 10 years. His account will earn an annual rate of 6 percent compounded annually. Will Jesse reach his goal of becoming a millionaire? If not, how much will his mother have to gift him at the end of 10 years?

A.10   Muir would like to have $6 million dollars in 20 years. Muir will invest $150,000 in a money market account at the end of each year for the next 20 years. His account will earn an annual rate of 7 percent compounded annually. Will Muir reach his goal of accumulating $6 million? He told his business partner that if he exceeds his goal he will contribute the excess to charity. How large of a contribution, if any, will he make?

B Financial Statement Ratios and Metrics

The primary purpose of financial statements is to quantify the financial position of a company as of a specific point in time, and the performance of that company over a period of time. A variety of asset, liability, and shareholders' equity accounts are used on the balance sheet. And on the income statement, revenues and various expenses matched against those revenues are reported. In addition, the reasons for changes in the cash and shareholders' equity accounts are detailed on the statement of cash flow and the statement of shareholders' equity, respectively. Because these financial statements provide summary data in aggregate dollar form, their users will often apply a mix of financial ratios and other metrics to help them understand in greater detail critical information about the company. Chapter 4 provides a detailed overview of how financial information is used in investing and credit decisions, and in that chapter key financial ratios were introduced. There are many more, however. This appendix provides a more comprehensive listing of those key ratios and metrics. They are segregated by their common groupings, as related to: (i) asset management and efficiency, (ii) profitability, (iii) cash flow, (iv) liquidity, (v) solvency and capital structure, and (vi) miscellaneous other. For each ratio its most common formula definition is provided along with a brief explanation of its meaning.

Asset Management and Efficiency

Asset management and efficiency ratios, broadly speaking, assess how management has utilized its invested asset base in running the company. You will note that for each ratio there is a balance sheet asset account evaluated relative to an account from the income statement. Together they convey unique information about asset performance, efficiency, and/or utilization.

Ratio	Definition	Explanation
Asset Management		
Receivable turnover	$\dfrac{\text{Net sales}}{\text{Accounts receivable}}$	Number of sales/collection cycles experienced by a firm.
Receivable collection period	$\dfrac{365}{\text{Net sales / Accounts receivable}}$	Number of days required, on average, to collect an outstanding account receivable.
Inventory turnover	$\dfrac{\text{Cost of goods sold}}{\text{Inventory}}$	Number of production/sales cycles experienced by a firm.
Inventory-on-hand period	$\dfrac{365}{\text{Cost of goods sold / Inventory}}$	Number of days, on average, required to sell the inventory currently on hand.
Intangible asset turnover	$\dfrac{\text{Net sales}}{\text{Intangible assets}}$	Ability of intangible assets to generate sales.
Fixed asset turnover	$\dfrac{\text{Net sales}}{\text{Property, plant and equipment, net}}$	Ability to generate sales from fixed asset base.
Asset turnover	$\dfrac{\text{Net sales}}{\text{Total assets}}$	Amount of sales generated from each dollar invested in assets.

Profitability Ratios

Profitability ratios are those that evaluate net income relative to a value deployed to earn that net income. Returns on invested capital (i.e., assets or equity), and marginal returns on net sales are common measures of profitability.

Ratio	Definition	Explanation
Profitability		
Return on shareholders' equity (ROE)	$$\frac{\text{Net income} - \text{Preferred stock dividends}}{\text{Shareholders' equity}}$$	Rate of return generated by a business for its common shareholders.
Return on assets (ROA)	$$\frac{\text{Net income} + [\text{Interest expense} (1 - \text{Tax rate})]}{\text{Total assets}}$$	Rate of return generated on a company's investment in assets from all sources.
Return on sales (ROS)	$$\frac{\text{Net income}}{\text{Net sales}}$$	Percentage of net income remaining from a dollar of sales after subtracting all expenses. Often this ratio is referred to as "net profit margin."
Gross profit margin ratio	$$\frac{\text{Net sales} - \text{Cost of goods sold}}{\text{Net sales}}$$	Percentage of income generated from sales after deducting the cost of goods sold.
Earnings per common share (EPS)	$$\frac{\text{Net income} - \text{preferred dividends}}{\text{Average common shares outstanding}}$$	An earnings measure specified in share units. Shares can be either "basic" or "diluted."
Pro forma earnings per share	$$\frac{\text{Adjusted net income}}{\text{Average common shares outstanding}}$$	EPS, wherein management adjustments are made for items deemed non-descriptive of true economic earnings.

Cash Flow Ratios

Cash flow ratios are those that evaluate the ability of the firm to generate and use cash.

Ratio	Definition	Explanation
Cash Flow		
Cash conversion ratio	$$\frac{\text{Cash from sales}}{\text{Net sales}}$$	Conveys the ability of the firms to convert total sales to cash.
Free cash flow yield	$$\frac{\text{Free cash flow}}{\text{Market capitalization}}$$	The amount of cash flow freely available to shareholders relative to the market equity value.
Operating funds ratio	$$\frac{\text{Cash from operations}}{\text{Net income}}$$	Proportion of earnings supported by cash flow.

Liquidity Ratios

Liquidity ratios reflect the ability of the firms to generate cash and its ability to meet its short-term obligations.

Ratio	Definition	Explanation
Liquidity		
Cash and marketable securities to total assets	$$\frac{(\text{Cash} + \text{Marketable securities})}{\text{Total assets}}$$	Percentage of total assets held as highly liquid assets.
Quick ratio	$$\frac{(\text{Cash} + \text{Marketable securities} + \text{Accounts receivable})}{\text{Current liabilities}}$$	Amount of liquid assets available to pay short-term liabilities.
Current ratio	$$\frac{\text{Current assets}}{\text{Current liabilities}}$$	Amount of current assets available to service current liabilities.
Accounts payable turnover	$$\frac{\text{Cost of goods sold}}{\text{Accounts payable}}$$	Number of account payment cycles experienced by a firm.
Days' payable period	$$\frac{365}{\text{Costs of goods sold} / \text{Accounts payable}}$$	Number of days, on average, required to pay an outstanding account payable.
Cash collection period	Days receivable + Days inventory − Days payable periods	The amount of time, in total days, to sell inventory, receive payment from customers, and pay suppliers.
Operating cash flow to current liabilities	$$\frac{\text{Operating cash flow}}{\text{Current liabilities}}$$	Ability to pay current liabilities with current operating cash flow.

Solvency and Capital Structure Ratios

Solvency refers to the ability of a company to repay its outstanding long-term obligations. Capital structure (i.e., leverage) ratios measure the amount of those long-term obligations relative to another base. The two ratio concepts relate directly to one another, in inverse fashion, as higher leverage implies less solvency, all else equal.

Ratio	Definition	Explanation
Solvency		
Long-term debt to total assets	$\dfrac{\text{(Long-term debt + Current portion of long-term debt)}}{\text{Total assets}}$	Percentage of total assets provided by creditors.
Long-term debt to shareholders' equity	$\dfrac{\text{(Long-term debt + Current portion of long-term debt)}}{\text{Shareholders' equity}}$	Relative investment of long-term creditors versus shareholders in a business.
Financial leverage	$\dfrac{\text{Total assets}}{\text{Total shareholders' equity}}$	The relative size of assets to shareholders' invested capital.
Interest coverage ratio	$\dfrac{\text{Net income before taxes + Interest expense}}{\text{Interest expense}}$	Extent to which current operating income covers current debt service charges.

Miscellaneous Other Ratios

There are numerous other important ratios and metrics used in financial analysis to help better understand the company and its financial reporting. These help in inference about such things as management judgments, asset quality, dividend policy and borrowing costs. Examples of some of those important ratios are provided below.

Ratio	Definition	Explanation
Miscellaneous Other		
Accumulated depreciation to gross fixed assets	$\dfrac{\text{Accumulated depreciation}}{\text{Gross property, plant and equipment}}$	Proportion of investments in fixed assets thus far depreciated.
Allowance for uncollectibles to gross receivables	$\dfrac{\text{Allowance for uncollectibles}}{\text{Gross accounts receivables}}$	Proportion of receivables expected not to be collected.
Capital intensity	$\dfrac{\text{Total assets}}{\text{Net sales}}$	Total capital investment needed to generate sales.
Conservatism ratio	$\dfrac{\text{Net income before taxes}}{\text{Taxable income}}$	A measure of aggressiveness in financial reporting.
Dividend payout	$\dfrac{\text{Dividends}}{\text{Net income}}$	Proportion of net income paid in dividends during the year.
Dividend retention rate (DRR)	$\dfrac{\text{Net income} - \text{Dividends}}{\text{Net income}}$	Proportion of net income not paid in dividends during the year.
Dividend yield	$\dfrac{\text{Dividends per share}}{\text{Stock price per share}}$	Proportion of market stock value distributed in dividend.
Sustainable growth rate	$\text{ROE} \times \text{DRR}$	An estimate of the maximum desired rate of growth for a firm.

C IFRS Illustrated: LVMH Moët Hennessey-Louis Vuitton S.A.

In this appendix, the financial statements of **LVMH Moët Hennessey-Louis Vuitton S.A.** (LVMH hereafter) are presented as an illustration of IFRS-based financial statements. LVMH is a French company that was founded in 1987 with the merger of champagne producer Moët et Chandon and the cognac manufacturer Hennessey. The company is one of the world's largest luxury goods conglomerates, owning more than 60 well-recognized luxury brands of wines and spirits, watches and jewelry, fashion and leather goods, retailing, and perfumes and cosmetics. The company's brands include Dom Pérignon (wines/spirits), TAG Heuer (watches), Givenchy (fashion and leather goods), DFS (retail), and Parfums Christian Dior (perfumes).

LVMH is Paris-based and is a member of the prestigious CAC 40 index on the Euronext Paris Exchange. The company employs 120,000 and operates 3,600 retail stores in 69 countries. The company's shares trade in the United States as an American Depository Receipt on the Over-The-Counter (OTC) exchange under the symbol LVMUY. The company prepares its financial statements using IFRS.

LVMH GROUP
Condensed Consolidated Financial Statements
Consolidated Income Statement

(€ millions, except for earnings per share)	Notes	2014	2013	2012
Revenue	23-24	30,638	29,016	27,970
Cost of sales		(10,801)	(9,997)	(9,863)
Gross margin		19,837	19,019	18,107
Marketing and selling expenses		(11,744)	(10,767)	(10,013)
General and administrative expenses		(2,373)	(2,212)	(2,151)
Income (loss) from joint ventures and associates	7	(5)	(23)	(19)
Profit from recurring operations	23-24	5,715	6,017	5,924
Other operating income and expenses	25	(284)	(119)	(182)
Operating profit		5,431	5,898	5,742
Cost of net financial debt		(115)	(101)	(138)
Other financial income and expenses		3,062	(97)	126
Net financial income (expense)	26	2,947	(198)	(12)
Income taxes	27	(2,273)	(1,753)	(1,821)
Net profit before minority interests		6,105	3,947	3,909
Minority interests	17	(457)	(511)	(484)
Net profit, Group share		5,648	3,436	3,425
Basic Group share of net earnings per share (EUR)	28	11.27	6.87	6.86
Number of shares on which the calculation is based		501,309,369	500,283,414	499,133,643
Diluted Group share of net earnings per share (EUR)	28	11.21	6.83	6.82
Number of shares on which the calculation is based		503,861,733	503,217,497	502,229,952

LVMH GROUP
Condensed Consolidated Financial Statements
Consolidated Balance Sheet

(€ millions)	Notes	2014	2013	2012
ASSETS				
Brands and other intangible fixed assets.	3	13,031	12,596	11,322
Goodwill	4	8,810	9,058	7,709
Property, plant and equipment.	6	10,387	9,621	8,694
Investments in joint ventures and associates.	7	519	480	483
Non-current available for sale financial assets.	8	580	7,080	6,004
Other non-current assets	9	489	457	519
Deferred tax	27	1,436	913	952
Non-current assets		**35,252**	**40,205**	**35,683**
Inventories and work in progress	10	9,475	8,492	7,994
Trade accounts receivable	11	2,274	2,174	1,972
Income taxes		354	223	201
Other current assets.	12	1,916	1,856	1,813
Cash and cash equivalents	14	4,091	3,226	2,187
Current assets		**18,110**	**15,971**	**14,167**
Total assets		**53,362**	**56,176**	**49,850**
LIABILITIES AND EQUITY				
Share capital	15.1	152	152	152
Share premium account.	15.1	2,655	3,849	3,848
Treasury shares and LVMH-share settled derivatives	15.2	(374)	(451)	(414)
Cumulative translation adjustment.	15.4	492	(8)	342
Revaluation reserves		1,019	3,900	2,731
Other reserves		12,171	16,001	14,340
Net profit, Group share.		5,648	3,436	3,425
Equity, Group share		21,763	26,879	24,424
Minority interests	17	1,240	1,028	1,084
Total equity		**23,003**	**27,907**	**25,508**
Long-term borrowings	18	5,054	4,149	3,825
Non-current provisions.	19	2,291	1,797	1,772
Deferred tax	27	4,392	4,280	3,884
Other non-current liabilities	20	6,447	6,404	5,456
Non-current liabilities.		**18,184**	**16,630**	**14,937**
Short-term borrowings.	18	4,189	4,674	2,950
Trade accounts payable.		3,606	3,297	3,118
Income taxes		549	357	442
Current provisions	19	332	324	335
Other current liabilities	21	3,499	2,987	2,560
Current liabilities		**12,175**	**11,639**	**9,405**
Total liabilities and equity		**53,362**	**56,176**	**49,850**

LVMH GROUP
Condensed Consolidated Financial Statements
Consolidated Statement of Changes in Equity

(€ millions)	Number of Shares	Share Capital	Share Premium Account	Treasury Shares and LVMH-Share Settled Derivatives	Cumulative Translation Adjustment	Revaluation Reserves — Available for Sale Financial Assets	Hedges of Future Foreign Currency Cash Flows	Vineyard Land	Employee Benefit Commitments	Net Profit and Other Reserves	Total Equity — Group Share	Minority Interests	Total
As of December 31, 2012	**508,163,349**	**152**	**3,848**	**(414)**	**342**	**1,943**	**118**	**758**	**(88)**	**17,765**	**24,424**	**1,084**	**25,508**
Gains and losses recognized in equity					(350)	912	18	188	51		819	21	840
Net profit										3,436	3,436	511	3,947
Comprehensive income					**(350)**	**912**	**18**	**188**	**51**	**3,436**	**4,255**	**532**	**4,787**
Stock option plan and similar expenses										31	31	3	34
(Acquisition)/disposal of treasury shares and LVMH-share settled derivatives				(103)						(7)	(110)	—	(110)
Exercise of LVMH share subscription options	1,025,418		67								67	—	67
Retirement of LVMH shares	(1,395,106)		(66)	66							—	—	—
Capital increase in subsidiaries											—	8	8
Interim and final dividends paid										(1,500)	(1,500)	(228)	(1,728)
Acquisition of a controlling interest in Loro Piana											—	235	235
Changes in control of consolidated entities										1	1	(1)	—
Acquisition and disposal of minority interests' shares										(73)	(73)	(76)	(149)
Purchase commitments for minority interests' shares										(216)	(216)	(529)	(745)
As of December 31, 2013	**507,793,661**	**152**	**3,849**	**(451)**	**(8)**	**2,855**	**136**	**946**	**(37)**	**19,437**	**26,879**	**1,028**	**27,907**
Gains and losses recognized in equity					500	(2,648)	(122)	(15)	(96)		(2,381)	108	(2,273)
Net profit										5,648	5,648	457	6,105
Comprehensive income					**500**	**(2,648)**	**(122)**	**(15)**	**(96)**	**5,648**	**3,267**	**565**	**3,832**
Stock option plan and similar expenses										37	37	2	39
(Acquisition)/disposal of treasury shares and LVMH-share settled derivatives				27						(17)	10	—	10
Exercise of LVMH share subscription options	980,323		59								59	—	59
Retirement of LVMH shares	(1,062,271)		(50)	50							—	—	—
Capital increase in subsidiaries											—	3	3
Interim and final dividends paid			(1,203)							(1,579)	(1,579)	(328)	(1,907)
Distribution in kind of Hermès shares										(5,652)	(6,855)	—	(6,855)
Changes in control of consolidated entities										(5)	(5)	11	6
Acquisition and disposal of minority interests' shares										(2)	(2)	32	30
Purchase commitments for minority interests' shares										(48)	(48)	(73)	(121)
As of December 31, 2014	**507,711,713**	**152**	**2,655**	**(374)**	**492**	**207**	**14**	**931**	**(133)**	**17,819**	**21,763**	**1,240**	**23,003**

LVMH GROUP
Condensed Consolidated Financial Statements
Consolidated Cash Flow Statement

(€ millions)	Notes	2014	2013	2012
I. OPERATING ACTIVITIES AND OPERATING INVESTMENTS				
Operating profit		5,431	5,898	5,742
Income / (loss) and dividends from joint ventures and associates[a]	7	26	49	37
Net increase in depreciation, amortization and provisions		1,895	1,435	1,289
Other computed expenses		(188)	(29)	(59)
Other adjustments		(84)	(76)	(52)
Cash from operations before changes in working capital		**7,080**	**7,277**	**6,957**
Cost of net financial debt: interest paid		(116)	(111)	(152)
Income taxes paid[a]		(1,639)	(1,832)	(1,880)
Net cash from operating activities before changes in working capital		**5,325**	**5,334**	**4,925**
Change in working capital	14.1	(718)	(620)	(810)
Net cash from operating activities		**4,607**	**4,714**	**4,115**
Operating investments	14.2	(1,775)	(1,657)	(1,694)
Net cash from operating activities and operating investments (free cash flow)		**2,832**	**3,057**	**2,421**
II. FINANCIAL INVESTMENTS				
Purchase of non-current available for sale financial assets	8	(57)	(197)	(131)
Proceeds from sale of non-current available for sale financial assets	8	160	38	36
Dividends received[a]	8	69	71	179
Income tax related to financial investments[a]		(237)	(11)	(21)
Impact of purchase and sale of consolidated investments	2.4	(167)	(2,161)	(59)
Net cash from (used in) financial investments		**(232)**	**(2,260)**	**4**
III. TRANSACTIONS RELATING TO EQUITY				
Capital increases of LVMH SE	15.1	59	66	95
Capital increases of subsidiaries subscribed by minority interests	17	3	7	8
Acquisition and disposals of treasury shares and LVMH-share settled derivatives	15.2	1	(113)	5
Interim and final dividends paid by LVMH SE	15.3	(1,619)[b]	(1,501)	(1,447)
Income taxes paid related to interim and final dividends paid[a]		(79)	(137)	(73)
Interim and final dividends paid to minority interests in consolidated subsidiaries	17	(336)	(220)	(314)
Purchase and proceeds from sale of minority interests	2.4	10	(150)	(206)
Net cash from (used in) transactions relating to equity		**(1,961)**	**(2,048)**	**(1,932)**
Change in cash before financing activities		639	(1,251)	493
IV. FINANCING ACTIVITIES				
Proceeds from borrowings		2,407	3,095	1,028
Repayment of borrowings		(2,100)	(1,057)	(1,494)
Purchase and proceeds from sale of current available for sale financial assets	13	(106)	101	(67)
Net cash from (used in) financing activities		**201**	**2,139**	**(533)**
V. EFFECT OF EXCHANGE RATE CHANGES		**27**	**47**	**(43)**
NET INCREASE (DECREASE) IN CASH AND CASH EQUIVALENTS (I+II+III+IV+V)		**867**	**935**	**(83)**
CASH AND CASH EQUIVALENTS AT BEGINNING OF PERIOD	14	**2,916**	**1,981**	**2,064**
CASH AND CASH EQUIVALENTS AT END OF PERIOD	14	**3,783**	**2,916**	**1,981**
TOTAL INCOME TAXES PAID		**(1,955)**	**(1,980)**	**(1,974)**
Transactions included in the table above, generating no change in cash:				
− acquisition of assets by means of finance leases		5	7	5

(a) Restated to reflect the amended presentation of dividends received and income tax paid starting in 2014. See Note 1.4.
(b) The distribution in kind of Hermès shares had no impact on cash, apart from related income tax effects. See Note 8.
(1) The financial statements as of December 31, 2013 and 2012 have been restated to reflect the retrospective application as of January 1, 2012 of IFRS 11 Joint Arrangements. See Note 1.2.

D Accounting Mechanics: T-Accounts and Journal Entries

CHAPTER 2: TECHNICAL LANGUAGE OF ACCOUNTING— THE DEBIT AND CREDIT PARADIGM

The approach used in Chapter 2 to analyze the effects of various accounting events on the balance sheet equation is intuitive and closely resembles how modern electronic accounting systems process accounting information. Yet financial professionals sometimes still use the technical accounting language of "debit" and "credit" when referring to how transactions impact financial statements. To help you understand this technical language, we revisit the accounting events of the Russian River Valley Winery and process them using the debit/credit mechanism and double-entry bookkeeping. But first—a little history.

Luca Pacioli, an Italian monk, is credited with being the first to describe double-entry bookkeeping in his book, *Summa de Arithmetica, Geometria, Proportioni et Proportionalita,* published in Latin in 1494. Some claim that Luca didn't really invent double-entry bookkeeping; he just took the time to observe what Italian merchants were doing and then documented his observations. Instead of using pluses and minuses, Luca invented the T-account having two sides. The left side was referred to as the **debit** side—often represented as "Dr"—and the right side he called the **credit** side—or "Cr" for short. The T-account Luca devised looked like this:

T-Account

Debit	Credit
(Dr)	(Cr)

Of course, Luca had to decide which side would be a positive and which would be negative. So, he concluded that an increase in assets would be a debit (the left side) and a decrease in assets would be a credit (the right side). Similarly, an increase in a liability must be a credit and a decrease in a liability a debit. And, since shareholders' equity is on the same side of the balance sheet equation as the liabilities, an increase (decrease) in shareholders' equity would be a credit (debit). The reasons why Luca selected this particular convention have been lost with time. But be careful to note that the words debit and credit are not synonymous with increase and decrease. Instead, they merely identify the left or right side of the T-account. They also relate to the conventional balance sheet equation of Assets equal Liabilities plus Shareholders' Equity. The following diagram summarizes the debit/credit convention described by Luca:

Asset		=	Liability		+	Shareholders' Equity	
Debit	Credit		Debit	Credit		Debit	Credit
(+)	(−)		(−)	(+)		(−)	(+)

The Accounting Cycle

The process of analyzing and recording accounting data for a business is often referred to as the **accounting cycle**. The cycle begins when an accounting event involving a business occurs. The event is analyzed and a determination made as to which of the company's accounts are affected. This analysis is then entered into the firm's accounting system by means of a **journal entry**, which will be illustrated shortly. Immediately after the data is entered it is transferred, or **posted**, to the appropriate T-accounts. The preparation of journal entries and posting of data to the T-accounts are daily activities at a business.

At the end of each fiscal period, prior to the preparation of any financial statements, a number of data verification checks are undertaken. First, **adjusting entries** are prepared to update various accounts for any new or previously unreported financial information and to correct any observed data errors. Second, a **trial balance** is prepared to insure that the amount of recorded debits equals the amount of recorded credits. Finally, the financial statements are prepared, typically in the following sequence: income statement, statement of shareholders' equity, balance sheet, and statement of cash flow. The preparation sequence reflects the fact that the basic financial statements are interdependent—that is, they articulate with one another.

Prior to the preparation of the statement of shareholders' equity, **closing entries** are prepared. Closing entries transfer the results of a company's operating activities—that is, its revenues, expenses, and dividends—to retained earnings on the statement of shareholders' equity (and hence, the balance sheet). The accounts appearing on the income statement, along with the dividend account, are referred to as *temporary accounts* because they are closed, or zeroed out, at the end of each accounting period. Each of these accounts will therefore start the next accounting period with a zero balance. This makes intuitive sense since we wish to measure performance over a period of time and thus need to start each period with a blank slate. The accounts appearing on the balance sheet, in contrast, are referred to as *permanent accounts* because they are not closed out at the end of each accounting period. In fact, the temporary accounts are closed to a permanent account, retained earnings. Again, this makes intuitive sense since it is the purpose of the balance sheet to report a business's financial condition at a point in time, rather than for a period of time. Considered a different way, the various accounts such as cash or accounts payable that exist at the end of the period should still exist at the start of the next period unless all cash is paid out and all accounts payable are paid in full. After the closing entries are executed, the remaining financial statements—the statement of shareholders' equity, the balance sheet, and the statement of cash flow—can be prepared.

To summarize, the various steps in the accounting cycle are:

1. Record the daily accounting events using journal entries.
2. Post the journal entry data to the appropriate T-accounts.
3. At the end of the fiscal period, record any needed adjusting entries.
4. Prepare a trial balance.
5. Record the closing entries for the revenue, expense, and dividend accounts.
6. Prepare the financial statements.

The Accounting System

There are three arrows originating from the Trial Balance. Each of these loops represents a different version of the trial balance—(a) pre-adjustment, (b) post-adjustment, and (c) post-closing trial balances. It is the final post-closing trial balance that is used to create the company's financial statements.

To illustrate the accounting cycle, we return to the pre-opening balance sheet for the Russian River Valley Winery presented in Exhibit D.1.

EXHIBIT D.1	
RUSSIAN RIVER VALLEY WINERY, INC. **Balance Sheet**	
($ thousands)	**Pre-Opening**
Assets	
Cash.	$ 4,700
Buildings.	2,000
Land	4,000
Intangible assets	100
Total assets.	$10,800
Liabilities and Shareholders' Equity	
Loan payable	$ 4,800
Shareholders' equity	
Common stock.	6,000
Liabilities and shareholders' equity	$10,800

Step 1—Record the accounting events using journal entries.

The 14 events for the Russian River Valley Winery are recorded below using journal entries and the debit/credit paradigm (see Chapter 2 for a summary of these transactions). The convention is to record the debit portion of a journal entry on top and then to record the credit part of the entry below. Care must be exercised that the total of the debit portion of each entry exactly equals the credit portion.

Event	Accounts	Debit	Credit
1(a)	Inventory	380	
	Accounts payable.............................		380
1(b)	Accounts payable..............................	360	
	Cash..		360
2	Equipment	1,500	
	Cash..		1,500
3	Equipment	2,000	
	Cash..		2,000
4(a)	Cash..	380	
	Accounts receivable...........................	1,520	
	Sales revenue.................................		1,900
4(b)	Cash..	720	
	Accounts receivable...........................		720
5(a)	Wage expense	100	
	Cash..		100
5(b)	Selling & administrative expense	300	
	Cash..		300
6(a)	Loan payable	480	
	Cash..		480
6(b)	Interest expense................................	288	
	Cash..		288
7	Cost of goods sold..............................	380	
	Inventory.......................................		380
8(a)	Depreciation expense—equipment	175	
	Accumulated depreciation		175
8(b)	Depreciation expense—buildings..................	50	
	Accumulated depreciation		50
9	Amortization expense............................	50	
	Intangible asset		50
10	Cash..	400	
	Common stock..................................		400
11	(No event is recorded)		
12	Income tax expense.............................	240	
	Income taxes payable		96
	Cash..		144
13	Inventory.......................................	60	
	Accounts payable.............................		60
14	Retained earnings (dividend declared)..............	260	
	Cash..		260

Step 2—Post the journal entry data to the appropriate T-accounts.

If you examine the T-accounts below, you will see that each of the debits and credits from the journal entries above has been entered into the appropriate T-account. Notice that the ending balance[s] for each of the T-accounts exactly correspond to the ending balances obtained using the approach followed in Chapter 2.

Cash			
Bal	4,700		
4(a)	380	360	1(b)
4(b)	720	1,500	2
		2,000	3
		100	5(a)
		300	5(b)
		480	6(a)
		288	6(b)
10	400	144	12
		260	14
Bal	768		

Accounts Receivable			
Bal	0		
4(a)	1,520		
		720	4(b)
Bal	800		

Inventory			
Bal	0		
1(a)	380		
		380	7
13	60		
Bal	60		

Equipment			
Bal	0		
2	1,500		
3	2,000		
Bal	3,500		

Buildings			
Bal	2,000		

Accumulated Depreciation			
		0	Bal
		175	8(a)
		50	8(b)
		225	Bal

Land			
Bal	4,000		

Intangible Assets			
Bal	100	50	9
Bal	50		

Accounts Payable			
		0	Bal
		380	1(a)
1(b)	360		
		60	13
		80	Bal

Income Taxes Payable			
		0	Bal
		96	12
		96	Bal

Loan Payable			
		4,800	Bal
6(a)	480		
		4,320	Bal

Common Stock			
		6,000	Bal
		400	10
		6,400	Bal

Retained Earnings			
		0	Bal
14	260		
Bal	260	317	17
		57	Bal

Income Summary			
		1,900	15
16	1,583		
17	317		
		0	Bal

Sales Revenue			
		1,900	4(a)
15	1,900		
		0	Bal

Cost of Goods Sold			
7	380		
		380	16
Bal	0		

Wage Expense			
5(a)	100		
		100	16
Bal	0		

Depreciation Expense			
8(a)	175		
8(b)	50		
Bal	225		
		225	16
Bal	0		

Selling & Admin Expense			
5(b)	300		
		300	16
Bal	0		

Interest Expense			
6(b)	288		
		288	16
Bal	0		

Amortization Expense			
9	50		
		50	16
Bal	0		

Income Tax Expense			
12	240		
		240	16
Bal	0		

* Entries 15, 16, and 17 in **blue font** are closing entries from Step 5.

Step 3—At the end of the fiscal period, make any needed adjusting entries.

Accounting events such as the recording of depreciation expense (8(a)) and amortization expense (8(b)) are considered to be adjusting entries. They are often recorded at the end of each fiscal period when a company's accounting staff reviews the company's financial data for completeness. Other examples of adjusting entries include correcting any amounts that were previously incorrectly recorded and estimating and recording the estimated losses associated with any uncollected accounts receivable.

Step 4—Prepare a trial balance.

The trial balance is a listing of the account balances from the company's various T-accounts. Russian River Valley's post-adjustment trial balance is presented in Exhibit D.2. Notice in the winery's post-adjustment trial balance that the total debit balance ($13,021) for the winery's T-accounts equals the total credit balance ($13,021). If the balances were not equal, it would indicate that an error had been made in recording some piece of accounting information.

EXHIBIT D.2		
RUSSIAN RIVER VALLEY WINERY, INC. **Post-Adjustment Trial Balance**		
Account	**Debit**	**Credit**
Cash..	$ 768	
Accounts receivable...........................	800	
Inventory.....................................	60	
Equipment	3,500	
Buildings.....................................	2,000	
Accumulated depreciation......................		$ 225
Land...	4,000	
Intangible assets	50	
Accounts payable.............................		80
Taxes payable................................		96
Loan payable		4,320
Common stock...............................		6,400
Retained earnings	260	
Sales revenue................................		1,900
Cost of goods sold............................	380	
Wages expense	100	
Depreciation expense..........................	225	
Selling & administrative expense	300	
Interest expense..............................	288	
Amortization expense..........................	50	
Tax expense	240	
Totals	$13,021	$13,021

Step 5—Record closing entries for the temporary accounts.

Closing entries (events 15, 16, and 17) transfer the ending balances from the revenue and expense T-accounts to an income summary account, and then ultimately to the retained earnings account on the statement of shareholders' equity, and thus, the balance sheet. Closing entries also serve another function—they set the revenue and expense T-accounts equal to zero at the end of each fiscal period (see the closing balances for the T-accounts from Step 2). By doing so, the revenue and expense T-accounts only contain information from the current period, thus facilitating comparisons of net income from one fiscal period to the next.

Event	Account	Debit	Credit
15	Sales revenue.	1,900	
	Income summary		1,900
16	Income summary	1,583	
	Cost of goods sold		380
	Wage expense.		100
	Depreciation expense		225
	Selling & administrative expense.		300
	Interest expense		288
	Amortization expense		50
	Tax expense.		240
17	Income summary	317	
	Retained earnings		317

Exhibit D.3 presents Russian River Valley's post-closing trial balance, reflecting the closing of the company's temporary accounts—that is, the revenue, expense, and dividend accounts.

EXHIBIT D.3

RUSSIAN RIVER VALLEY WINERY, INC.
Post-Closing Trial Balance

Account	Debit	Credit
Cash.	$ 768	
Accounts receivable.	800	
Inventory.	60	
Equipment	3,500	
Buildings.	2,000	
Accumulated depreciation		$ 225
Land	4,000	
Intangible assets	50	
Accounts payable.		80
Taxes payable.		96
Loan payable		4,320
Common stock.		6,400
Retained earnings		57
Totals	$11,178	$11,178

Step 6—Prepare the financial statements.

The financial statements prepared from data organized using the debit/credit paradigm will be identical to those derived using the spreadsheet approach, as presented in Exhibits 2.2 through 2.5 in the text and reproduced below.

EXHIBIT 2.2	Illustrative Balance Sheets

RUSSIAN RIVER VALLEY WINERY, INC.
Balance Sheets

($ thousands)	Pre-Opening	End of Year 1		Pre-Opening	End of Year 1
Assets			**Liabilities and shareholders' equity**		
Current assets			*Current liabilities*		
Cash..........................	$ 4,700	$ 768	Accounts payable.........	$ 0	$ 80
Accounts receivable............	0	800	Taxes payable............	0	96
Inventory.....................	0	60	Loan payable—current.....	0	480
Total current assets	4,700	1,628	Total current liabilities......	0	656
Noncurrent assets			*Noncurrent liabilities*		
Property, plant & equipment			Loan payable—noncurrent..	4,800	3,840
Equipment	0	3,500	**Total liabilities**...........	**4,800**	**4,496**
Buildings.....................	2,000	2,000	*Shareholders' equity*		
Land.........................	4,000	4,000	Common stock...........	6,000	6,400
	6,000	9,500	Retained earnings	0	57
Accumulated depreciation	0	(225)	**Total shareholders' equity** .	**6,000**	**6,457**
Property, plant & equipment (net). .	6,000	9,275			
Intangible assets	100	50	**Total liabilities &**		
Total noncurrent assets	6,100	9,325	**shareholders' equity**......	**$10,800**	**$10,953**
Total assets..................	**$10,800**	**$10,953**			

EXHIBIT 2.3	An Illustrative Income Statement

RUSSIAN RIVER VALLEY WINERY, INC.
Income Statement

($ thousands)	Year 1
Revenues..	**$1,900**
Cost of goods sold..	380
Gross profit...	**1,520**
Operating expenses	
Wages and salaries	100
Selling & administrative	300
Depreciation...	225
Amortization...	50
Total operating expenses	675
Operating income...	**845**
Interest expense...	288
Income before income taxes	557
Income taxes	240
Net income	**$ 317**

EXHIBIT 2.4	An Illustrative Statement of Shareholders' Equity

RUSSIAN RIVER VALLEY WINERY, INC.
Statement of Shareholders' Equity

($ thousands)	Common Stock	Retained Earnings	Total
Balance at beginning of Year 1.................	$6,000	$ 0	$6,000
Net income......................................		317	317
Dividends paid		(260)	(260)
Sale of common stock	400		400
Balance at end of Year 1	$6,400	$ 57	$6,457

EXHIBIT 2.5	An Illustrative Statement of Cash Flow

RUSSIAN RIVER VALLEY WINERY, INC.
Statement of Cash Flow

($ thousands)	Year 1
Operating activities	
Cash receipts	
Cash sales	$ 380
Cash collections on account	720
Total cash receipts	1,100
Cash disbursements	
Cash payments for inventory..	(360)
Cash payments for interest	(288)
Cash payments for wages & salaries..................................	(100)
Cash payments for selling & administrative...........................	(300)
Cash payments for taxes...	(144)
Total cash disbursements...	(1,192)
Cash flow from operations	**(92)**
Investing activities	
Purchases of property, plant & equipment	(3,500)
Cash flow from investing.......................................	**(3,500)**
Financing activities	
Sale of common stock...	400
Repayment of loan..	(480)
Payment of common stock dividends...................................	(260)
Cash flow from financing.......................................	**(340)**
Change in cash..	(3,932)
Cash balance, beginning of year	4,700
Cash balance, end of year.......................................	**$ 768**

D.1   **Recording Transactions Using the Debit/Credit Paradigm.** Miller & Co. experienced the following six events in its first year of operations:

1.   Shareholders contributed $60,000 cash.
2.   Purchased land for $40,000 cash.
3.   Borrowed $18,000 in cash from a bank.
4.   Provided services for $16,000, which will be paid to Miller & Co. next year.
5.   Paid $11,000 cash for miscellaneous operating expenses.
6.   Paid a $1,000 cash dividend to shareholders.

Required
Prepare journal entries using the debit/credit paradigm to record the above transactions.

D.2   **Recording Transactions Using the Debit/Credit Paradigm.**   The following events occurred for The KMF Corporation during 2016:

1. Sales of products totaled $219,000, of which $15,000 remained uncollected at year-end.
2. The cost of goods sold during the year was $56,000.
3. A cash disbursement of $50,000 was made on July 1, 2016, to pay for a 12-month office equipment lease that expires on June 30, 2017.
4. Depreciation expense for the year on the company's warehouse amounted to $7,500.
5. Employee wages for the year totaled $40,000, of which $2,000 was unpaid at year-end.
6. Selling, general, and administrative expenses amounted to $10,000 for the year and were paid in full.
7. A cash payment of $25,000 was made to reduce the balance of accounts payable.
8. Interest expense on long-term debt was $18,000 for the year, of which $4,500 was unpaid at year-end.
9. The company paid income taxes of $25,000 on its earnings.

Required
Prepare journal entries using the debit/credit paradigm to record the above transactions.

CHAPTER 5: RECORDING OPERATING REVENUE AND RECEIVABLES USING THE DEBIT AND CREDIT PARADIGM

In this appendix, the traditional approach to recording accounting transactions—that is, the debit and credit paradigm—is followed to illustrate how the journal entries for the operating revenue and receivables for ProFlight Inc. and for Pan American Enterprises, Inc. would be recorded by these enterprises. The information used in this appendix is taken directly from the content of Chapter 5. To facilitate your understanding of the transactions, asset accounts are labeled with an (A), liability accounts with an (L), shareholders' equity accounts with an (SE), and revenue or expense accounts with an (R) or an (E), respectively.

Revenue Recognition Transactions: ProFlight Inc.

ProFlight Inc., a manufacturer of private corporate jets, signed a contract to build five jets over a two-year period for TransGlobal Airlines. Under the terms of the contract, ProFlight will receive total revenue of $10 million and anticipates that its cost to build the planes will total $8 million. During 2015, ProFlight completed 20 percent of the work, sent an invoice for $1 million to TransGlobal, and received a cash payment of $500,000. During 2016, ProFlight completed the remaining 80 percent of the work on budget, delivered the five planes, sent an invoice for the remaining $9 million to TransGlobal and received a $4.5 million cash payment. In 2017, after completing flight testing of the aircraft, Trans-Global remitted the final $5 million in cash to ProFlight. Journal entries are presented to reflect ProFlight's accounting transactions under the percentage-of-completion method and the completed contract method of revenue recognition.

Percentage-of-Completion Method.   Under the percentage-of-completion approach to revenue recognition, ProFlight will recognize its operating revenue and expenses on the basis of the amount of work actually completed each fiscal period (20 percent in 2015 and 80 percent in 2016). Consequently, the journal entries for ProFlight for the period 2015 through 2017 would appear as follows:

Date	Accounts	Debit	Credit
2015	No entry is required at contract signing		
	Production-in-progress (A).	2,000,000	
	Accounts payable (L).		2,000,000
	To record the acquisition of production material on credit.		
	Accounts receivable (A)	1,000,000	
	Unbilled accounts receivable (A)	1,000,000	
	Revenue (R).		2,000,000
	To recognize revenue based on a 20 percent work completion: 20% × $10,000,000.		
	Cash (A)	500,000	
	Accounts receivable (A).		500,000
	To record the collection of cash on the billed account receivable.		

continued

continued from previous page

Date	Accounts	Debit	Credit
2015 cont.	Cost of production (E)	1,600,000	
	Production-in-progress (A)		1,600,000
	To record the consumption of production material—that is, cost of goods sold—related to the revenue recognized, 20 percent of $8 million.		
	Accounts payable (L)	2,000,000	
	Cash (A)..		2,000,000
	To record the payment of accounts payable for production materials.		
2016	Production-in-progress (A).......................................	6,000,000	
	Accounts payable (L)..		6,000,000
	To record the acquisition of production material on credit to complete the contract.		
	Accounts receivable (A)	9,000,000	
	Unbilled accounts receivable (A)............................		1,000,000
	Revenue (R)...		8,000,000
	To record the completion of the contract, the remaining revenue and final customer billing.		
	Cash (A)	4,500,000	
	Accounts receivable (A).....................................		4,500,000
	To record the collection of cash on billed accounts receivable.		
	Cost of production (E)	6,400,000	
	Production-in-progress (A)		6,400,000
	To record the consumption of production material—that is, the cost of goods sold—related to the revenue recognized in 2016, 80 percent of $8 million.		
	Accounts payable (L)	6,000,000	
	Cash (A)..		6,000,000
	To record the payment of accounts payable.		
2017	Cash (A)	5,000,000	
	Accounts receivable (A)......................................		5,000,000
	To record the collection of cash on billed accounts receivable.		

Completed Contract Method. Under the completed contract approach, ProFlight will defer the recognition of any operating revenue or expenses until the contract is fully satisfied at the end of 2016. Consequently, the journal entries for ProFlight for the period 2015 through 2017 would appear as follows:

Date	Accounts	Debit	Credit
2015	No entry is required at contract signing		
	Production-in-progress (A).......................................	2,000,000	
	Accounts payable (L)..		2,000,000
	To record the acquisition of production materials on credit.		
	Accounts receivable (A)	1,000,000	
	Deferred revenue (L)		1,000,000
	To record progress billing sent to customer.		
	Cash (A)	500,000	
	Accounts receivable (A).....................................		500,000
	To record cash collected on billed account receivable.		
	Accounts payable (L)	2,000,000	
	Cash (A)..		2,000,000
	To record payment of accounts payable related to production material.		
2016	Production-in-progress (A).......................................	6,000,000	
	Accounts payable (L)..		6,000,000
	To record the acquisition of production material on credit.		

continued

continued from previous page

Date	Accounts	Debit	Credit
2016 cont.	Accounts receivable (A)	9,000,000	
	Deferred revenue (L)		9,000,000
	To record progress billing sent to customer.		
	Cash (A)	4,500,000	
	Accounts receivable (A).		4,500,000
	To record cash collection on billed accounts receivable.		
	Accounts payable (L)	6,000,000	
	Cash (A).		6,000,000
	To record payment of accounts payable related to production material.		
	Deferred revenue (L).	10,000,000	
	Revenue (R).		10,000,000
	To recognize revenue associated with contract completion.		
	Cost of production (E)	8,000,000	
	Production-in-progress (A)		8,000,000
	To recognize the cost of goods sold associated with contract completion.		
2017	Cash (A)	5,000,000	
	Accounts receivable (A).		5,000,000
	To record the collection of cash on billed accounts receivable.		

Accounting for Receivables: Pan American Enterprises, Inc.

Pan American Enterprises, Inc. sells its internationally recognized wine on account to bars and restaurants throughout the United States. The company's credit terms require customers to pay their bills within 30 days of a transaction. During 2016 and 2017, Pan American Enterprises experienced the following accounting events:

Year	Credit Sales	Cash Collections	Estimated Bad Debt	Bad Debt Write-Off
2016	$3,200,000	$2,850,000	$10,925	$ —
2017	5,300,000	4,838,500	22,500	11,500

Using the debit/credit paradigm, Pan American Enterprises would record the following journal entries to reflect this accounting information:

Date	Accounts	Debit	Credit
2016	Accounts receivable (A)	3,200,000	
	Sales (R)		3,200,000
	To record credit sales for 2016.		
	Cash (A)	2,850,000	
	Accounts receivable (A).		2,850,000
	To record collections on credit sales.		
	Bad debt expense (E).	10,925	
	Allowance for uncollectible accounts (CA)		10,925
	To record the estimated bad debt expense and establish the allowance for future account write-offs.		
2017	Allowance for uncollectible accounts (CA).	11,500	
	Accounts receivable (A).		11,500
	To write off uncollected accounts receivable that have proven to be worthless.		

continued

continued from previous page

Date	Accounts	Debit	Credit
2017 *cont.*	Accounts receivable (A)	5,300,000	
	Sales (R)		5,300,000
	To record credit sales for 2017.		
	Cash (A)	4,838,500	
	Accounts receivable (A).		4,838,500
	To record cash collections on credit sales.		
	Bad debt expense (E).	23,075	
	Allowance for uncollectible accounts (CA)		23,075
	To record the estimated bad debt expense of $22,500 for 2017 and to record the underestimated expense of $575 for 2016.		

To validate your understanding of the above journal entries, create T-accounts for each of the accounts, post the journal entry amounts to the appropriate T-accounts, and create account totals. Your T-account balances should reconcile with the balances reported in the chapter.

D.3 **Recording the Bad Debt Expense Using the Debit/Credit Paradigm.** Holcombe Inc. uses the aging method to estimate the company's bad debt expense. Travis Holcombe, president of the company, collected information about the company's outstanding accounts receivable and their probability of collection:

Account Age	Amount	Probability of Non-Collection
0–30 days	$725,000	0.5%
31–60 days	275,000	1.5
61–90 days	170,000	2.5
91–120 days	100,000	4.0
Over 120 days	40,000	20.0

Required

Calculate the expected bad debt expense for Holcombe Inc., and prepare the journal entry to record the estimate using the debit/credit paradigm. Assume that one-half of the estimated bad debts prove to be uncollectible. Prepare the journal entry to write off the uncollectible accounts receivable. If $1,000 of the previously written off uncollectible receivables is found to be collectible, what entry would be needed to reinstate the accounts receivable on the books of Holcombe Inc.?

D.4 **Recording Revenue and Expenses Using the Debit/Credit Paradigm.** RJ Miller Company won a contract to build a shopping center at a price of $240 million. The following schedule details the estimated and actual costs of construction and the actual cash collections under the contract:

	Estimated (Actual) Costs of Construction	Cash Collections From Customer
2016	$ 40,000,000	$ 48,000,000
2017	60,000,000	60,000,000
2018	70,000,000	60,000,000
2019	30,000,000	72,000,000
	$200,000,000	$240,000,000

Required

1. Prepare the journal entries to record the revenue and expenses for RJ Miller Company for 2016 through 2019 assuming that the company recognizes revenue under the completed contract method.
2. Prepare the journal entries to record the revenue and expenses for RJ Miller Company for 2016 through 2019 assuming that the company recognizes revenue under the percentage-of-completion method.

CHAPTER 6: RECORDING COST OF GOODS SOLD AND INVENTORY USING THE DEBIT AND CREDIT PARADIGM

In this appendix, the traditional approach to recording accounting transactions—that is, the debit and credit paradigm—is used to illustrate how the journal entries for the cost of goods sold and inventory for the Arizona Ice Cream Company, Inc., would be recorded. Since the journal entries are similar under FIFO, LIFO, and the weighted-average cost method (only the recorded amounts differ), we assume that the company adopts the FIFO method to value its cost of goods sold and ending inventory (see Exhibit 6.3).

Arizona Ice Cream Company, Inc.: Recording Inventory Transactions

During the year, Arizona Ice Cream Company, Inc. (AICC), made the following cash purchases of ice cream:

Date	Amount	Cost per Bucket	Total Cost
September 5.	1,000	$10	$ 10,000
October 22	2,500	12	30,000
November 15	4,500	13	58,500
December 30	2,000	15	30,000
	10,000		$128,500

AICC also sold 8,000 buckets of ice cream at a retail price of $20 per bucket for total operating revenue of $160,000. All sales were in cash and the sales occurred on the following dates:

Date	Number of Buckets Sold
September 20.	800
November 4	2,600
December 22	3,400
December 31	1,200
	8,000

At year-end, the AICC's CEO determined that the replacement cost of the company's inventory of 2,000 buckets of ice cream was $28,000 ($14 per bucket × 2,000 buckets).

The above financial data would be recorded as follows:

Date	Accounts	Debit	Credit
Sep 5	Inventory (A)	10,000	
	Cash (A)		10,000
	To record the cash purchase of 1,000 buckets.		
Sep 20	Cash (A)	16,000	
	Revenue (R)		16,000
	To record the cash sale of 800 buckets.		
	Cost of Goods Sold (E)	8,000	
	Inventory (A)		8,000
	To record the cost of goods sold on 800 buckets.		
Oct 22	Inventory (A)	30,000	
	Cash (A)		30,000
	To record the cash purchase of 2,500 buckets.		
Nov 4	Cash (A)	52,000	
	Revenue (R)		52,000
	To record the cash sale of 2,600 buckets.		

continued

continued from previous page

Date	Accounts	Debit	Credit
Nov 4 *cont.*	Cost of Goods Sold (E).	30,800	
	Inventory (A).		30,800
	To record the cost of goods sold on 2,600 buckets.		
Nov 15	Inventory (A)	58,500	
	Cash (A).		58,500
	To record the cash purchase of 4,500 buckets.		
Dec 22	Cash (A)	68,000	
	Revenue (R).		68,000
	To record the cash sale of 3,400 buckets.		
	Cost of Goods Sold (E).	44,100	
	Inventory (A).		44,100
	To record the cost of goods sold on 3,400 buckets.		
Dec 30	Inventory (A)	30,000	
	Cash (A).		30,000
	To record the cash purchase of 2,000 buckets.		
Dec 31	Cash (A)	24,000	
	Revenue (R).		24,000
	To record the cash sale of 1,200 buckets.		
	Cost of Goods Sold (E).	15,600	
	Inventory (A).		15,600
	To record the cost of goods sold on 1,200 buckets.		
	Cost of Goods Sold (E).	2,000	
	Inventory (A).		2,000
	To record the lower-of-cost-or-market write-down of inventory.		

D.5 **Recording Inventory and the Cost of Goods Sold Using the Debit/Credit Paradigm.** The following information was disclosed in the 2016 annual report of The Claremont Company.

	2016	2015
Beginning inventory	$20,970	$11,560
Purchase of inventory.	83,300	42,640
Ending inventories	19,310	20,970
Cost of goods sold.	84,960	33,230

Required

Prepare the journal entries to record (1) the purchase of inventory and (2) the cost of goods sold for The Claremont Company for 2015 and 2016.

CHAPTER 7: RECORDING INVESTMENTS IN, AND SALES OF, LONG-LIVED ASSETS USING THE DEBIT AND CREDIT PARADIGM

In this appendix, the traditional approach to recording accounting transactions—that is, the debit and credit paradigm—is used to illustrate the journal entries for the acquisition, depreciation, and retirement of long-lived assets. Data for the current illustration follows the example in the chapter and assumes the use of straight-line depreciation:

A truck having an expected useful life of five years and a resale value of $4,000 upon retirement is purchased for $30,000 cash at the beginning of the year (BOY). At the end of the five-year period, the truck is sold for $4,500. Note: End of the year is represented by (EOY).

Illustrative Journal Entries

Date	Accounts	Debit	Credit
Year 1 (BOY)	Truck (A) . . . . Cash (A). . . . . *To record the cash purchase of an asset.*	30,000	30,000
Year 1 (EOY)	Depreciation Expense (E) . . . . Accumulated Depreciation (CA) . . . . *To record the annual depreciation expense on the truck.*	5,200	5,200
Year 2 (EOY)	Depreciation Expense (E) . . . . Accumulated Depreciation (CA) . . . . *To record the annual depreciation expense on the truck.*	5,200	5,200
Year 3 (EOY)	Depreciation Expense (E) . . . . Accumulated Depreciation (CA) . . . . *To record the annual depreciation expense on the truck.*	5,200	5,200
Year 4 (EOY)	Depreciation Expense (E) . . . . Accumulated Depreciation (CA) . . . . *To record the annual depreciation expense on the truck.*	5,200	5,200
Year 5 (EOY)	Depreciation Expense (E) . . . . Accumulated Depreciation (CA) . . . . *To record the annual depreciation expense on the truck.*	5,200	5,200
	Cash (A) . . . . Accumulated Depreciation (CA) . . . . Gain on Sale of Asset . . . . Truck (A). . . . . *To record the sale of the truck for $4,500, the gain (G) on sale of $500, and the removal of the truck and related accumulated depreciation from the financial records.*	4,500 26,000	500 30,000

D.6 **Recording Investments in, and Sales of, Long-lived Assets Using the Debit/Credit Paradigm.** At the beginning of 2015, The Beall Corporation purchased a warehouse for $10 million and immediately made certain necessary renovations to the facility which cost $2 million. The chief financial officer of the company decided to depreciate the new warehouse using the straight-line method over a 20-year expected useful life, assuming no salvage value at the end of the 20-year period. After two years of use, Beall received an offer to sell the warehouse for $17 million and accepted the offer.

Required

Prepare the journal entries to record (1) the purchase and renovation of the warehouse, (2) the depreciation expense on the warehouse for the first two years, and (3) the sale of the warehouse.

CHAPTER 8: RECORDING INVESTMENTS IN OTHER CORPORATE ENTITIES USING THE DEBIT AND CREDIT PARADIGM

In this appendix, the traditional approach to recording accounting transactions—that is, the debit and credit paradigm—is used to illustrate the journal entries associated with the various investments made by The New South Wales Trading Company, Inc. and by Savanna, Inc. Please refer to the content of Chapter 8 for additional information regarding these transactions (see Exhibits 8.3 through 8.12).

Accounting for Marketable Debt and Equity Securities: The New South Wales Trading Company Inc.

In August, The New South Wales Trading Company, Inc. raised $50 million from an initial public offering (IPO) of its common shares. The company decided to temporarily invest some of its IPO cash in various debt and equity securities having a high degree of liquidity. These events are recorded below:

Date	Accounts	Debit	Credit
August	Cash (A)	50,000,000	
	Common Stock (SE)		50,000,000
	To record the sale of common stock for $50 million.		
September	Investment in Qantas Inc. 10% Notes (A)	10,000,000	
	Cash (A)......................................		10,000,000
	To record the purchase of held-to-maturity debt securities.		
November	Investment in BHP, Inc. Common Stock (A).........................	6,100,000	
	Cash (A)..		6,100,000
	To record the investment in trading equity securities.		
December	Investment in Coles Inc. Common Stock (A)	8,400,000	
	Cash (A).......................................		8,400,000
	To record the investment in available-for-sale equity securities.		

At the end of the year, the CFO of The New South Wales Trading Company, Inc. determined that the Qantas notes were worth $9.8 million, the BHP common shares worth $6.8 million, and the Coles Inc. common shares worth $8.2 million. In addition, the CFO observed that Qantas Inc. had made an interest payment of $1 million on its notes on December 31. This information would be recorded as follows:

Date	Accounts	Debit	Credit
December 31	Cash (A)	1,000,000	
	Interest Income (I)		1,000,000
	To record interest income I on the Qantas notes.		
	Investment in BHP Inc. common stock (A).........................	700,000	
	Unrealized Gain on Trading Securities (G).....................		700,000
	To record the gain of $700,000 on trading equity securities.		
	Unrealized Loss on Available-For-Sale Securities (SE)	200,000	
	Investment in Coles Inc. Common Stocks (A)...................		200,000
	To record the decline in market value on available-for-sale securities.		

To verify your understanding of these transactions, create a series of T-accounts for the affected accounts, post the amounts to the T-accounts, and calculate a year-end balance. Your results should reveal the following balances:

Assets		Shareholders' Equity	
Cash............................	$26,500,000	Common stock......................	$50,000,000
Investments		Retained earnings	1,700,000
Qantas notes	10,000,000	Other Comprehensive Income	
BHP common stock.............	6,800,000	Unrealized loss on available-for-sale	
Coles common stock............	8,200,000	securities	(200,000)
Total	**$51,500,000**	Total	**$51,500,000**

Equity Method and Consolidated Accounting: Savanna, Inc.

Case 1. Savanna Inc. acquires 40 percent of the common shares of Waterloo Inc. for $8 million at the beginning of the year. At year-end, Savanna reports cash earnings of $30 million; Waterloo reports cash earnings of $10 million; and, Waterloo pays its shareholders a cash dividend of $5 million. These transactions would be recorded as follows on Savanna's books:

Date	Accounts	Debit	Credit
January	Investment in Waterloo Inc. (A).......................................	8,000,000	
	Cash (A)...		8,000,000
	To record the initial investment in Waterloo Inc.		
December	Cash (A)	30,000,000	
	Retained Earnings (SE)		30,000,000
	To record Savanna's cash earnings of $30 million.		

continued

Date	Accounts	Debit	Credit
December cont.	Investment in Waterloo Inc. (A).	4,000,000	
	Income From Equity Affiliate (I)		4,000,000
	To record Savanna's 40 percent share of Waterloo's $10 million in earnings.		
	Cash (A)	2,000,000	
	Investment in Waterloo Inc. (A)		2,000,000
	To record Savanna's 40 percent share of Waterloo's $5 million dividend payment.		

Case 2.   Savanna Inc. acquires 80 percent of Waterloo's common shares for $16 million in January; the fair market value of Waterloo's net assets equals their book value of $20 million (no goodwill is implicit in the investment). At year-end, Savanna reports cash earnings of $30 million; Waterloo reports cash earnings of $10 million; and, Waterloo pays its shareholders a cash dividend of $5 million. Because of its majority shareholding, Savanna prepares consolidated financial statements at year-end. These transactions would be recorded as follows on Savanna's books:

Date	Accounts	Debit	Credit
January	Investment in Waterloo Inc. (A).	16,000,000	
	Cash (A).		16,000,000
	To record Savanna's acquisition of an 80 percent shareholding in Waterloo Inc.		
December	Cash (A)	30,000,000	
	Retained Earnings (SE)		30,000,000
	To record Savanna's cash earnings of $30 million.		
	Investment in Waterloo Inc. (A).	8,000,000	
	Income From Equity Affiliate (I)		8,000,000
	To record Savanna's 80 percent ownership interest in Waterloo earnings of $10 million.		
	Cash (A)	4,000,000	
	Investment in Waterloo (A).		4,000,000
	To record Savanna's 80 percent ownership interest in Waterloo's dividend payment of $5 million.		
	Cash (A)	25,000,000	
	Inventory (A)	80,000,000	
	Investment in Waterloo (A).		20,000,000
	Minority Interest (L/SE)		5,000,000
	Long-Term debt (L)		80,000,000
	To consolidate Waterloo's net assets with those of Savanna and to establish the minority interest account.		

(The journal entries for Case 3 are not presented here. You may wish to create these entries using the contents of Exhibits 8.11 and 8.12.)

D.7   **Recording Marketable Equity Securities Transactions Using the Debit/Credit Paradigm.**   **Microsoft Inc.** maintains a large investment in marketable securities (principally fixed income securities) valued at approximately $42 billion as of the beginning of the year. During the year, the securities produced investment income (dividends and interest income) totaling $2 billion. At year-end, the portfolio of marketable securities had appreciated to $43.5 billion.

Required
Using journal entries, record (1) Microsoft's purchase of the securities at the beginning of the year, (2) the receipt of $2 billion in investment income during the year, and (3) the appreciation of the portfolio by $1.5 billion at the end of the year. Assume that the entire portfolio is classified as "trading securities."

D.8   **Recording Equity Method Transactions Using the Debit/Credit Paradigm.**   On January 1, 2016, The Miller Corporation purchased 300,000 shares of The Mayfair Corporation for $5.7 million. The investment represented 25 percent of The Mayfair Corporation's outstanding common shares. During 2016, Mayfair reported net earnings of $2.25 million and paid a cash dividend of $0.15 per share. During 2017, Mayfair reported a net loss of $180,000 and again paid a dividend of $0.15 per share.

Required

Using journal entries, record (1) The Miller Corporation's initial investment in The Mayfair Corporation and (2) the appropriate entries for 2016 and 2017 assuming that The Miller Corporation uses the equity method to account for its investment in Mayfair.

CHAPTER 9: RECORDING DEBT FINANCING TRANSACTIONS USING THE DEBIT AND CREDIT PARADIGM

In this appendix, the traditional approach to recording accounting transactions—that is, the debit and credit paradigm—is used to illustrate how the journal entries associated with the issuance of various debt instruments by Midwestern Airlines, Inc. would be recorded. Specifically, the accounting for interest-bearing notes, zero-coupon notes, and operating and capital leases is illustrated.

Accounting for Notes

On January 1, 2016, Midwestern Airlines, Inc., issued $100 million face value (maturity value) of mortgage notes with an annual coupon rate of eight percent and a maturity of ten years. The notes pay interest on June 30 and December 31 of each year. At the time the notes were issued, the market yield rate on equivalent risk-rated instruments was ten percent. Five years later, on December 31, 2020, the market yield rate on equivalent risk-rated securities had increased to twelve percent. No longer needing the debt financing, Midwestern Airlines decided to retire all of its outstanding debt on December 31, 2020. (Please refer to the chapter for the calculation of the following values.)

Date	Accounts	Debit	Credit
Jan 1, 2016	Cash (A)	87,548,000	
	Note discount (CL)	12,452,000	
	Notes payable (L).		100,000,000
	To record the issuance of $100 million in notes at a discount.		
Jun 30, 2016	Interest expense (E)	4,377,400	
	Cash (A).		4,000,000
	Note discount (CL).		377,400
	To record the payment of interest on the notes.		
Dec 31, 2016	Interest expense (E)	4,396,300	
	Cash (A).		4,000,000
	Note discount (CL).		396,300
	To record the payment of interest on the notes.		

(Interest payment entries similar to those presented above would be recorded for 2017, 2018, 2019, and 2020. Appropriate values for the entries can be obtained from the Note Amortization Table in Exhibit 9.1.)

Dec 31, 2020	Notes payable (L)	100,000,000	
	Cash (A).		85,240,000
	Note discount (CL).		7,720,000
	Gain on early retirement (G).		7,040,000
	To record the early retirement of the notes at a gain.		

Assume now that on January 1, 2016, Midwestern Airlines, Inc., issued $100 million face value of zero-coupon mortgage notes, having a maturity of ten years with semiannual compounding. At the time of issuance, the yield rate on equivalent risk-rated debt securities was twelve percent. (Please refer to the chapter for the calculation of the following values.)

Jan 1, 2016	Cash (A)	31,200,000	
	Note discount (CL)	68,800,000	
	Notes payable (L).		100,000,000
	To record the issuance of $100 million in zero-coupon notes.		
Jun 30, 2016	Interest expense (E)	1,872,000	
	Note discount (CL).		1,872,000
	To record the interest expense implicit in the zero-coupon notes.		
Dec 31, 2016	Interest expense (E)	1,984,000	
	Note discount (CL).		1,984,000
	To record the interest expense implicit in the zero-coupon notes.		

Accounting for Leases

Midwestern Airlines entered into a ten-year lease agreement for flight equipment having a fair market value of $100 million and an implicit interest rate of ten percent per year. Annual lease payments of $16.27 million are paid at the end of each year. The leased equipment had an expected remaining useful life of 13 years.

If the lease is accounted for as an operating lease, the following transactions would be recorded:

Date	Accounts	Debit	Credit
Year 1 (BOY)	No entry is recorded at the time of lease signing.		
Year 1 (EOY)	Lease expense (E)	16,270,000	
	Cash (A).		16,270,000
	To record the annual lease payment and lease expense.		
Year 2 (EOY)	Lease expense (E)	16,270,000	
	Cash (A).		16,270,000
	To record the annual lease payment and lease expense.		

(Equivalent journal entries would be recorded each year until the lease agreement expires at the end of ten years.)

If the lease is accounted for as a capital lease, the following transactions would be recorded:

Year 1 (BOY)	Leased equipment (A)	100,000,000	
	Lease liability (L)		100,000,000
	To record the signing of a capital lease agreement.		
Year 1 (EOY)	Interest expense (E)	10,000,000	
	Lease liability (L).	6,270,000	
	Cash (A).		16,270,000
	To record annual lease payment, debt reduction, and interest expense.		
	Depreciation expense (E)	10,000,000	
	Accumulated depreciation (CA).		10,000,000
	To record the depreciation expense on the leased equipment.		
Year 2 (EOY)	Interest expense (E)	9,370,000	
	Lease liability (L).	6,900,000	
	Cash (A).		16,270,000
	To record annual lease payment, debt reduction, and interest expense.		
	Depreciation expense (E)	10,000,000	
	Accumulated depreciation (CA).		10,000,000
	To record annual depreciation expense on the leased equipment.		

D.9 **Recording Debt Financing Transactions Using the Debit/Credit Paradigm.** During 2016, the Mayfield Corporation issued $100 million of zero-coupon debentures, due in 2026. The proceeds of the bond sale totaled approximately $45.64 million, assuming the bonds were sold to yield 4 percent per period.

Required

Using journal entries, record (1) the proceeds from the sale of the Mayfield bonds in 2016 and (2) the interest expense to be recognized on the bonds at the end of the first six-month period.

D.10 **Recording Lease Financing Transactions Using the Debit/Credit Paradigm.** Maximum Electronics Inc. is a retail chain of discount electronic stores throughout the southwest United States. Maximum leases a fleet of 200 trucks to deliver purchases to its customers. The annual lease payment per truck totals $5,000 and the interest rate implicit in the lease is eight percent. On January 1, 2017, Maximum renewed its truck fleet lease under the same terms for a five-year period.

Required

1. Assume that the fleet lease should be accounted for as a capital lease. Using journal entries, record the leased assets and lease liability on January 1, 2017.
2. Assume that the trucks will be depreciated on a straight-line basis with no salvage value. Using journal entries, record the depreciation expense on the leased assets and the interest expense and debt payment on the lease liability on December 31, 2017.

CHAPTER 11: RECORDING EQUITY FINANCING TRANSACTIONS USING THE DEBIT AND CREDIT PARADIGM

In this appendix, the traditional approach to recording accounting transactions—that is, the debit and credit paradigm—is used to illustrate the journal entries for various equity financing transactions. For purposes of this appendix, the following illustrative transactions are assumed to have occurred during the year.

- Claremont Company incorporated on January 1, and authorized the issuance of 100,000 shares of $1 par value common stock and 50,000 shares of no-par value preferred stock. The preferred stock had a stated dividend of $5 per share.
- On January 10, Claremont Company sold 25,000 shares of common stock for $500,000 cash and 10,000 shares of preferred stock for $100,000 cash.
- On June 30, the Board of Directors of Claremont Company declared and paid a cash dividend of $0.10 per share on each outstanding common share and $2.50 per share on each outstanding preferred share, or a total of $27,500 in cash dividends ($2,500 + $25,000).
- On September 1, Claremont Company repurchased 5,000 shares of common stock at a cost of $15 per share, or a total outlay of $75,000.
- On December 31, the Board of Directors of Claremont Company declared a 2:1 forward stock split on the issued and outstanding common shares.
- On December 31, the Board of Directors of Claremont Company issued 1,000 treasury shares to company executives who exercised stock options at an exercise price of $10 per share.

The following journal entries would be recorded to reflect the above equity transactions.

Date	Accounts	Debit	Credit
Jan 1	No entry is recorded to reflect the authorization to sell equity shares.		
Jan 10	Cash (A)	500,000	
	Common stock, $1 par (SE)		25,000
	Additional paid-in-capital (SE).		475,000
	To record the sale of 25,000 shares of $1 par value common stock.		
	Cash (A)	100,000	
	Preferred stock (SE).		100,000
	To record the sale of 10,000 shares of no-par value preferred stock.		
Jun 30	Dividends (D)	27,500	
	Cash (A).		27,500
	To record the declaration and payment of a cash dividend on the outstanding common and preferred shares.		
Sep 1	Treasury Stock (SE)	75,000	
	Cash (A).		75,000
	To record the repurchase of 5,000 common shares at $15 per share.		

continued

Date	Accounts	Debit	Credit
Dec 31	Common Stock, $1 par value.	25,000	
	Common Stock, $0.50 par value.		25,000
	To record a reduction in the par value on the common shares from $1.00 to $0.50 per share, and to increase the shares issued and outstanding from 25,000 to 50,000 shares.		
	Retained Earnings (SE).	5,000	
	Cash (A)	10,000	
	Treasury Shares (SE)		15,000
	To record the exercise of stock options on 1,000 shares of common stock previously purchased at $15 per share.		

To validate your understanding of the above journal entries, create a set of T-accounts and calculate the value of shareholders' equity for Claremont Company at year-end. Your answer should appear as follows:

Shareholders' Equity

Common stock, $0.50 par value	$ 25,000
Additional paid-in-capital	475,000
Preferred stock, no par value	100,000
Retained earnings	(32,500)
Treasury stock	(60,000)
	$507,500

D.11 **Recording Shareholders' Equity Transactions Using the Debit/Credit Paradigm.** The following transactions occurred during 2017 for The Niagara Company:

1. Sold 10,000 shares of common stock having a par value of $0.01 for $22 per share.
2. Paid a cash dividend of $2 per share to its preferred shareholders when 5,000 shares were outstanding.
3. Issued a ten percent stock dividend on its outstanding common stock when the price was $22 per share.
4. Repurchased 10,000 shares of common stock at $18 per share.
5. Declared a 2-for-1 forward stock split on its common stock.

Required
Using journal entries, record the shareholders' equity transactions for 2017 for The Niagara Company.

D.12 **Recording Shareholders' Equity Transactions Using the Debit/Credit Paradigm.** During 2017, The Mann Corporation, a private entity, decided to go public. A charter of incorporation was constructed which authorized the sale of ten million shares of $1 par value common stock, 100,000 shares of $100 par value eight percent preferred stock, and 200,000 shares of $5 no-par value convertible preferred stock. The following shares were sold as part of the firm's initial public offering:

- 1,000,000 shares of common stock at $10 per share.
- 100,000 shares of $100 par value, eight percent preferred stock at $105 per share.
- 100,000 shares of $5 convertible, no-par preferred stock at $55 per share.

At the end of 2017, the full dividend was declared and paid on both preferred stock offerings.

Required
Using journal entries, record the financial effects of the shareholders' equity transactions for The Mann Corporation for 2017.

E Working Capital Management

In earlier chapters we defined working capital as current assets less current liabilities and stated that analysts often use this metric in the determination of a firm's liquidity. In this appendix we further explore working capital and illustrate its importance for firms in their management of working capital resources.

For purposes of this section we limit our study of working capital to three of its most important components; on the asset side accounts receivable and inventory, and on the liabilities side accounts payable. If you recall from Chapter 4, these three components are those that define a firm's cash collection period:

	Inventory-on-hand period
+	Receivable collection period
−	Days' payable period
=	Cash collection period

Failure to properly manage a firm's cash collection period can lead to financial distress and possibly bankruptcy. We will illustrate key concepts by way of an example for a hypothetical company, Zipped Tunes.[1] It provides an excellent illustration of the dangers of unmanaged growth and failure to properly manage a firm's cash collection period. Even though a hypothetical, the problems encountered by companies such as Zipped Tunes are all too real.

Growth and Working Capital: An Illustration of Risk

Zipped Tunes, founded by Maggie Paul III, was a consumer electronics manufacturer that produced and marketed an MP3 player under the brand name "Zipper." The company sold each Zipper for $85, and the net (off-shore) production costs were $55. In addition to these production costs, the company also incurred $20,000 monthly costs for such things as office building rent and administrative staff. Paul felt that given the high quality and rich feature set of the Zipper she would be able to aggressively grow sales.

By year-end Paul had been producing and selling Zippers for several months. The balance sheet on December 31 was as follows:

---

[1] Zipped Tunes is based on the case DNR Medieval Adventures Company by Robert N. Anthony, Harvard Business School.

	ZIPPED TUNES
	Balance Sheet
	As of December 31

Assets	
Cash........................	$292,500
Accounts receivable............	137,500
Inventory....................	70,000
	$500,000

Stockholders' Equity	
Common stock................	$500,000
Retained earnings	0
	$500,000

Things were going very well for Zipped Tunes. In fact, December proved to be profitable, something rare for such a young company. In addition, sales are growing rapidly – December sales were at 750 units, up from 500 in November. Sales were budgeted to be 1,000 units in January, and expected to increase by 500 units per month thereafter. At that rate May monthly sales were expected to be 3,000 units.

Because Zipped Tunes was such a young and unknown company it was very important for Paul to maintain good vendor and seller relations in order to continue increasing sales and avoid stock-outs. To keep Zipper deliveries prompt, the company produced Zippers 30 days in advance of predicted sales. For example, Zipped Tunes had produced 1,000 Zippers in December for January sales, and would produce 1,500 in January for February's demand. The company billed its customers with stated terms of 30 days, but was a bit loose on enforcing those credit terms. The result was an average receivables collection period of 60 days. In contrast, as part of the effort to maintain good vendor relations, all of the company's costs were paid in cash in the month in which they were incurred.

Zipped Tunes' budget proved accurate and 2,000 Zippers were sold in March. March production was 2,500 units for April's budgeted sales. March year-to-date profit reached $75,000, with March profit alone reaching $40,000. At this point Paul decided that things were going so well that she would reward herself with a mini-vacation to visit friends in the Midwest.

As soon as Paul arrived in St. Louis she received an urgent call from the company accountant. Zipped Tunes was nearly out of cash, meaning necessary materials could not be purchased for production. Paul was forced to return right away and get immediate financing so that Zipped Tunes would not be closed down.

What can be going on? Zipped Tunes was growing at what appears a very healthy pace, and further, it was profitable. In fact, profits were growing every month along with revenue. Yet Zipped Tunes was nearly out of cash.

Exhibit E.1 provides actual financial data through April, along with projected May data.

EXHIBIT E.1	Zipped Tunes Budgeted Financial Statements					
		Dec.	Jan.	Feb.	Mar.	Apr.	**Projected May**

	Dec.	Jan.	Feb.	Mar.	Apr.	Projected May
Cash forward		$292,500	$232,500	$166,250	$ 93,750	$ 36,250
Collection ($85 × sales of 60 days prior)...		$ 42,500	$ 63,750	$ 85,000	$127,500	$170,000
Outflows ($20,000 + $55 × production) ...		102,500	130,000	157,500	185,000	212,500
Operating cash flow		$(60,000)	$(66,250)	$(72,500)	$(57,500)	$(42,500)
Income Statement						
Sales...........................	$ 63,750	$ 85,000	$127,500	$170,000	$212,500	$255,000
Cost of Goods Sold	41,250	55,000	82,500	110,000	137,500	165,000
Gross Profit	22,500	30,000	45,000	60,000	75,000	90,000
Other...........................	20,000	20,000	20,000	20,000	20,000	20,000
Net Income.......................	$ 2,500	$ 10,000	$ 25,000	$ 40,000	$ 55,000	$ 70,000

continued

continued from previous page

EXHIBIT E.1	Zipped Tunes Budgeted Financial Statements					
	Dec.	**Jan.**	**Feb.**	**Mar.**	**Apr.**	**Projected May**
Balance Sheet						
Cash.	$292,500	$232,500	$166,250	$ 93,750	$ 36,250	$ (6,250)
Accounts Receivable	137,500	180,000	243,750	328,750	413,750	498,750
Inventory.	70,000	97,500	125,000	152,500	180,000	207,500
Total assets.	$500,000	$510,000	$535,000	$575,000	$630,000	$700,000
Common Stock	$500,000	$500,000	$500,000	$500,000	$500,000	$500,000
Retained Earnings	0	10,000	35,000	75,000	130,000	200,000
Total	$500,000	$510,000	$535,000	$575,000	$630,000	$700,000
Statement of Cash Flow						
Net income.		$ 10,000	$ 25,000	$ 40,000	$ 55,000	$ 70,000
Increase in Accounts Receivable		(42,500)	(63,750)	(85,000)	(85,000)	(85,000)
Increase in Inventory		(27,500)	(27,500)	(27,500	(27,500)	(27,500)
Cash from Operations		(60,000)	(66,250)	(72,500)	(57,500)	(42,500)
Net cash change		(60,000)	(66,250)	(72,500)	(57,500)	(42,500)
Beg cash		292,500	232,500	166,250	93,750	36,250
End Cash		$232,500	$166,250	$ 93,750	$ 36,250	$ (6,250)

Exhibit E.2 reports some key data pulled from the above financial statements that highlight the situation facing Zipped Tunes. Notice that the company was certainly "profitable" with consistently rising gross profit and net income. However, Exhibit E.2 reveals a very troubling situation. Gross profits may be positive and rising, but cash flows remain negative, leading to a depletion of Zipped Tunes' cash balance. How can this be?

EXHIBIT E.2	Zipped Tunes Key Metrics					
	Dec.	**Jan.**	**Feb.**	**Mar.**	**Apr.**	**Projected May**
Sales.	$ 63,750	$ 85,000	$127,500	$170,000	$212,500	$255,000
COGS.	41,250	55,000	82,500	110,000	137,500	165,000
Gross Profit	22,500	30,000	45,000	60,000	75,000	90,000
Net income.	2,500	10,000	25,000	40,000	55,000	70,000
Cash.	292,500	232,500	166,250	93,750	36,250	(6,250)
Accounts Receivable	137,500	180,000	243,750	328,750	413,750	498,750
Inventory.	70,000	97,500	125,000	152,500	180,000	207,500
Cash Collection		42,500	63,750	85,000	127,500	170,000
Cash Payments		102,500	130,000	157,500	185,000	212,500
Net Cash Flow		(60,000)	(66,250)	(72,500)	(57,500)	(42,500)

The answer lies in the concepts first introduced in Chapter 1. Net income is based on the accrual basis of accounting where revenue is recorded when earned and expenses are then matched against these revenues. The timing of these revenues and expenses is often quite different from the actual receipts and disbursements of cash. This certainly is the situation with Zipped Tunes. Revenues are recorded at the time of the sale, but Zipped Tunes does not receive its cash until 60 days later. Instead, Zipped Tunes simply records an accounts receivable evidencing the amount that is to be received at a later time. A similar timing difference exists with cash disbursements. Zipped Tunes pays for its inventory purchases right away; however, the expense is not recorded until the inventory is later sold.

Chapter 4 introduced the concept of a company's cash collection period. The idea behind this concept is that there is potentially a significant lag between when a company receives cash from its activities and when it must spend cash to keep the business running. A company first purchases inventory for resale (or materials for manufacturing products for later sale). The company now has a physical asset, inventory, but has less liquidity (i.e., cash). Next the company sells the inventory. If the sale is on credit the company has an accounts receivable, but still is lacking cash. The combined amount of time the company holds the inventory and the time needed to collect the accounts receivable is the cash collection period. This period of time also represents a period where the company must find a way to continue operating without this cash. In other words, this working capital of inventory and accounts receivable must be financed. Part of the financing may come from the company's vendors in the form of accounts payable, where the purchase of the inventory is not paid for immediately. Unfortunately for Zipped Tunes, it paid its bills right away and therefore did not utilize an accounts payable balance.

Growing companies like Zipped Tunes must be acutely mindful of their cash collection period and their additional working capital financing period. Note how Zipped Tunes' accounts receivable and inventory must grow in order to support the growth in sales. Also notice how growth in these working capital components results in cash collections lagging behind cash payments, with a resulting negative cash flow. While this situation is often unavoidable for growing companies, especially companies that lack the market power to dictate better collection and payment terms, with proper management the situation facing Zipped Tunes can be avoided. The first step is to properly forecast the need for additional financing.

Cash budgets can help alert management for the need to secure additional financing in time to avert cash shortages. But is there anything Zipped Tunes could have done differently to have maintained a positive cash balance and not be forced to find external financing, and still be able to keep growing? The answer is yes.

Two items are responsible for the majority of Zipped Tunes' cash problems: growing accounts receivables and growing inventory. To see the impact of growing accounts receivable and inventories we first illustrate the current situation graphically in Exhibit E.3 then change the assumptions slightly and illustrate the impact of these changes in Exhibit E.4 and E.5. First, in Exhibit E.3 note that while net income (in green) is positive and increasing, cash flows are negative (in purple), leading to a cash deficit (in red).

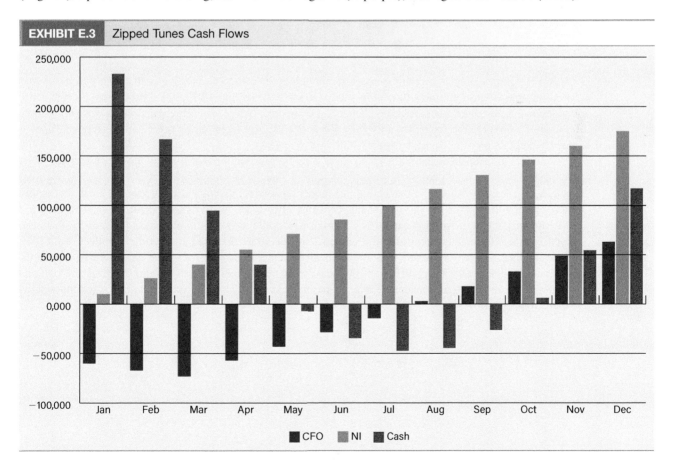

EXHIBIT E.3   Zipped Tunes Cash Flows

Methods to Manage Working Capital Financing Needs

What if we allow Zipped Tunes to speed up its collections by 30 days? Exhibit E.4 depicts this situation graphically. This one change allows the company to maintain a positive cash balance, and notice that while net income is unaltered, operating cash flows turn positive much sooner.

EXHIBIT E.4   Zipped Tunes Cash Flows—Collections in 30 Days

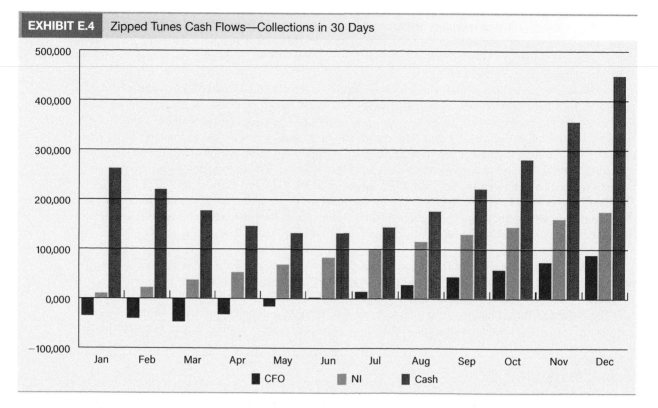

Exhibit E.5 shows another alternative scenario, modeling the effect of returning cash collections to 60 days as in the original case, but now having inventory made to order and a $70,000 constant inventory balance maintained. Again, note that there is no change in net income. Now, however, Zipped Tunes does not require so much cash utilization for inventory levels. Without this large drain on working capital, Zipped Tunes is able to maintain a positive cash balance.[2]

The lesson from this example is quite simple; while revenue growth is a key success factor for many companies and is of high interest to financial statement users, revenue growth includes several hidden costs such as the required increase in assets (e.g., accounts receivable, inventory, and property, plant, and equipment) needed to support the growth. Managers must always be aware of their cash flows. This means a careful management of working capital is essential. And while growth is important, it too must be managed properly. A careful management of working capital means more than just attempting to collect receivables sooner and keep inventory levels reasonable. It also means forecasting working capital financing needs. With a reasonable forecast Zipped Tunes could easily see how revenue growth would impact cash flows and identify the need for interim financing. With proper management, Zipped Tunes could keep growing without the ensuing cash flow crises.

---

[2] One other option that Zipped Tunes could explore is to slow its payments to vendors. Any accounts payable will amount to a form of financing known as vendor financing. Vendor financing is especially desirable because it usually carries no interest cost. In essence, it is the flip side to Zipped Tunes' accounts receivables.

EXHIBIT E.5   Zipped Tunes Cash Flows—Made to Order Inventory

Assignments with the 🔵 logo in the margin are available in BusinessCourse.
See the Preface of the book for details.

EXERCISES

E.1   **Net Income and Cash Flows.**   W.T. Grant was the largest retailer in the United States when it caught nearly everyone by surprise by filing for bankruptcy in 1975. W.T. Grant had been in existence since the turn of the century and had a long history of profitability including regularly paying dividends from 1906 to 1974. How is it possible that a company can report positive net income and yet be forced to seek bankruptcy protection?

E.2   **Working Capital Financing.**   Best Buy Co., Inc. reported the following financial information in a recent financial statement (in $ millions):

Sales.	$50,272
Cost of sales.	$37,611
Inventory.	$5,897
Accounts receivable.	$2,348
Accounts payable.	$4,894

Compute the additional working capital financing period for Best Buy.

E.3   **Working Capital Financing.**   Costco Wholesale reported the following financial information in a recent financial statement (in $ millions):

Sales.	$87,048
Cost of sales.	$77,739
Inventory.	$6,638
Accounts receivable.	$965
Accounts payable.	$6,544

Compute the additional working capital financing period for Costco.

Index

A

Abercrombie & Fitch, 108–109
accelerated depreciation, 266–267, 280
Accenture, 180
account receivable sold with recourse, 381
accounting equation, 8
Accounting Principles Board (APB), 16
Accounting Standards Updates, FASB, 17, 204
accounting. *See* financial accounting
accounts payable
    credit period and, 238
    defined, 9
    in days' payable period, 137, 238, 523
    operating cycle and, 237–240
    pro forma financial statements, 149–150
    working capital management, 554–559
accounts payable turnover, 137, 523
accounts receivable
    aging method, 189–193
    conservatism principle, 187
    defined, 9, 180
    direct write-off method, 187n
    financial analysis, 198–200
    forecasting, 460–462
    in liquidity ratios, 137
    managing investments in, 194–196
    matching principle, 187
    monetizing, 196–197
    operating cash flow management, 196–197
    percentage-of-credit-sales method, 187–189
    pro forma financial statements, 149–150
    in quick ratio, 137, 523
    in receivable collection period, 139, 522
    in receivable turnover, 137, 522
    revenue recognition and, 177–186
    tax perspective, 195
    valuing and reporting, 186–193
    working capital management, 554–559
accreted value, 348–349
accrual accounting
    capital investments analysis, 280–282
    cash-basis accounting vs., 68–70
    defined, 9
    expense matching, 69
    future cash flows, 86
    GAAP and, 9
    going concern assumption, 9
    interest owed, 46
    net income, 102, 556
    revenue recognition principle in, 68–69, 179
accumulated depreciation,52–53, 265, 524
accumulated depreciation contra-asset account, 265
accumulated depreciation to gross fixed assets, 524
accumulated other comprehensive income (AOCI)
    accounting example, 302–304
    fair value adjustments, 347
    financial analysis, 436
    foreign income, 319
    GAAP, 300, 302

shareholder equity disclosure, 423
Ackerlof, G. A., 14n
acquisition costs, 262–264, 269, 546–547
acquisition goodwill, 277
acquisition method, 311
ACSOI (Adjusted Consolidated Segment Operating Income), 200
Actavis, 387
Acxiom Corporation, 100
additional paid-in-capital, 419–420
Adjusted Consolidated Segment Operating Income (ACSOI), 200
adjusting entries, 533–541
Adolph Coors Company, 419
ADT, 315
advertising, 69, 278
affiliate-company earnings, 307–313
affiliated groups, 322
after-tax cost of borrowing, 65n
agency costs/problem, 24–26, 424
aging method, 189–193, 275
AICPA (American Institute of Certified Public Accountants), 16–17, 241
Airbus, 175
Alibaba, 39
all events test, 195
allowance for sales returns account, 196
Allowance for Uncollectible Accounts contra-account, 187, 190–193
allowance for uncollectibles to gross receivables, 524
Altair 8800 computer, 413
Altman, E., 342n
Amazon Fire TV, 3
Amazon
    accounting methods of, 14–16
    company overview, 3
    debt covenants, 26
    executive compensation, 25
    financial statements of, 7–10
    mission statement, 6–7
    stock performance, 10–11
America Online, 69, 70
American Accounting Association, 16–17
American Airlines, 274, 359
American Depository Receipts, 526
American Eagle Airlines, 274, 359
American Institute of Certified Public Accountants (AICPA), 16–17, 241
American International Group, Inc., 431
amortization schedule, 349, 352–353
amortization/amortization expense
    accounting policy changes, 281
    bonds and notes, 345–346, 518–519
    debt securities, 300
    defined, 264
    discounts, 345–346
    financial reporting, 53
    forecasting, 460–462
    goodwill, 277–278
    intangible assets, 277
    leases, 352–353

as noncash expense, 93
    premiums, 345–346
    straight-line method, 345–346. *See also* straight-line method
    statement of cash flow preparation, 93,99
    zero-coupon bonds and notes, 349
amortized cost, defined, 300
AMR Corporation, 274, 277, 359–361
annuity, 508, 509–512, 515–517, 518
annuity-in-advance, 508n
annuity-in-arrears, 352n, 508n
Anthony, Robert N., 554n
antitrust claims, 383, 422
AOCI. *See* accumulated other comprehensive income (AOCI)
AOL, 315
APB (Accounting Principles Board), 17
Apple Inc., 424, 434, 430n
Apple Watch, 424
Arcadia, Inc., 384–387
Arch Coal, 25
Arctic Sea Oil & Gas Company Ltd., 464–467
arms-length transactions, 307
Aronson, Donald H., 415
Arthur Andersen, 15, 21, 322
articulation, financial statements, 60–62
ASC 606, *Revenue from Contracts with Customers*, 177–178, 186, 195, 201, 202–204
asset(s)
    balance sheet equation, 40–42
    conservatism in reporting, 146–147
    defined, 8, 43
    depreciation, 52–53
    in double-entry system, 532
    GAAP definition, 26
    leases and, 350–356
    long-lived. *See* long-lived assets
    management of, 134–135 522
    marketing costs as, 200
    net book value, 52
    overfunded, 392
    pro forma financial statements, 458–464
    statement of cash flow preparation, 87–95
    working capital management, 554–559
    write-offs, 384n
asset revaluation reserve, 274, 277
asset turnover, 65, 137, 139
    in ROE, 65–66, 137, 143–146, 148–149, 523
Association for Investment Management and Research, 16–17
AT&T, 263
audit report, 15
auditors, 14–16, 21, 281, 322
Australia, asset revaluation, 274
authorized shares, 416
available-for-sale securities, 299–300, 301–307, 428–430
average cost method, 223
average life expectancy, 281

560

Note: The letter e indicates an exhibit on that page. The letter n indicates footnote.

B

B.J.'s Wholesale Club Inc., 68–69, 70
backdating, 434
bad debt expense, 186–193, 384
balance sheet
    accounting myths and, 22
    accounts receivable reporting, 193
    aging method, 189–193
    budgeted, 556
    capitalized expenditures, 262–263
    captions and titles in, 57, 90, 436
    common-size, 134, 135
    consolidated. *See* consolidated balance sheet
    contingent liabilities disclosure, 397–398
    debt and equity securities, 299–301
    deferred tax liability, 397
    defined, 8
    discounted cash flow approach, 464–467
    fair value of liabilities, 347
    financial reporting example, 57–58
    financial statement articulation, 60–62
    financial statement link, 319–320
    GAAP elements, 26–27
    IFRS example, 526–530
    indirect method of statement of cash flow
        preparation, 87–95
    leases, 350–356, 361
    LIFO and FIFO, 233–234
    title of, 57
balance sheet equation
    accounting terms in, 42–43
    defined, 42
    operating expenses and, 69
    operating revenues and, 68–69
    overview, 40–42
    statement of cash flow preparation, 89
Bank of America, 198–199, 347
bankruptcy, lease disclosure, 359–361
Barth, M., 9n
basic accounting equation, 8
basic earnings per share, 105–106
BASIC interpreters, 413
benchmarking, financial analysis, 141–143
benefit cost, 394
Berkshire Hathaway, 298, 426
best efforts basis, 414
beta, 151, 469–470
betterment, 263–264
Bezos, Jeff, 3
BHP Billiton, 297
binomial model, 431
Black-Scholes model, 431
"blue sky" laws, 16
board of directors, 24–26, 307
Boeing, 175, 181
Bombardier, 175
bonds
    amortization, 345–346, 518–519
    average return, 19–20
    callable, 341
    century, 349
    commodity-based, 341
    convertible, 341
    defined, 340
    features of, 340–341
    gold, 349
    interest expense, 344–346
    junk, 341, 342
    rating of, 341–342
    repo agreements, 399
    valuation, 342–350, 518–519
    zero-coupon, 348–350
book value
    amortization of bonds and notes, 345–346
    debt, 346
    deconsolidation, 314–315

    market capitalization vs., 101
    securities example, 307–313
    shareholders' equity, 418, 473–475
    zero-coupon bonds and notes, 348–350
Brady, Tom, 129
brand awareness, 129
brand name, financial reporting, 53, 54
Brazil, research and development costs, 277
Bristol-Myers Squibb, 85, 98, 276
budgeted financial statements, 555–556
Buffett, Warren, 426
Burger King, 387
Burlington Northern Santa Fe Corporation, 426
Business Ethics, 457
business events, preparing financial statements from,
        43–63
business life cycle, cash flow and, 97–98
business operating cycle, 176–177
BusinessWeek, 397n
buy-side analysts, 147

C

Cadabra.com, 3
calculators, time value of money calculation,
        512–521
callable bonds and notes, 341
callable preferred shares, 421
CAP (Critical Accounting Policy) disclosure, 269
capital
    going public and, 415
    providers of, management and, 24–26
    supply and demand of, 19
    surplus of, 419
capital asset pricing model (CAPM), 150–151,
        469–470
capital expenditures
    acquisition cost, 261
    allocation of costs to future periods, 264–274
    betterment vs. maintenance expenditures,
        263–264
    defined, 100
    forecasts of, 261
    in free cash flow calculations, 100
    incremental betterment, 100n, 280
    intangible assets, 276–279, 281
    interest, 262–263
    maintenance, 100n, 280
    natural resources, 278–279
    PP&E, 279–280
    revaluation, 273–274
capital in excess of par value, 419
capital intensity, 130, 219, 524
capital-intensive business/industries, 99, 131
capital investments, financial analysis, 280–282
capital leases, 350–356
capital markets, 19–20, 344
Capital Markets Subcommittee, 18
capital structure ratios, 524
capitalization
    acquisition cost, 261
    defined, 263
    expensing vs., 263
    GAAP, 270
    interest costs, 281
    operating expenses and, 281
capitalized interest, 262–263
CAPM (capital asset pricing model), 150–151,
        469–470
cash
    forecasting, 460–462
    GAAP definition of, 101
    IFRS definition of, 101
    in liquidity ratios, 137
    in quick ratio, 137, 139, 523
    from sales, 99, 523
cash and marketable securities to total assets, 137,
        523

cash assets, statement of cash flow preparation,
        87–95
cash-basis accounting, 8, 68–69
cash collection period, 139, 523, 556–557
cash conversion ratio, 99, 198, 523
cash dividends, 421–424
cash equivalents, defined, 139
cash flow. *See also* statement of cash flow
    accounting myths and, 22
    alternative measures of, 99–101
    business life cycle and, 97–98
    data, equity valuation, 464–467
    from financing, 86–95, 96–98, 111–112
    from investing, 86–95, 96–98, 111–112
    from operations, 86–95, 96–98, 111–112
    reporting requirements, 100, 101
    working capital management, 557–559
cash flow ratios, 98–99, 523
cash payments, 343–344, 351n
Caterpillar Inc., 234–235
century bonds, 349
certified public accounting (CPA) certificate, 241
change in the inventory reserve, 233
channel stuffing, 85, 98
charter of incorporation, 416
cherry picking, 305
China, capital markets in, 419
Chubb Corporation, 306
circular references, solving in Excel, 461n
Cisco Systems, Inc, 431
Citigroup, 198–199, 347, 427
Claremont Company, 357, 552–553
Class A shares, 419
classified balance sheet, 58
closing entries, 533–541
Codification Project, FASB, 17, 26
Coles Inc., 301–307
Colonial Downs Racetrack, 199–200
Commercial and Industrial Bank of China, 417
commitments, 379, 380–382
commodities, forward purchase agreements, 399
commodity-based bonds, 341
common equity share of operating earnings (CSOE),
        149
common shareholders' equity, in ROE, 65n
common shares, 341, 416–420, 430–435
common stock, 43, 105–106
common-size balance sheet, 134, 135
common-size financial statements, 132–135
common-size income statement, 133–134
companies. *See* corporations; public companies
comparability, GAAP, 26
compensation contracts, 110
competition, business environment, 176–177
completed contract method, revenue recognition,
        183–186, 384, 542–543
compounding, time value of money and, 506–507
comprehensive income, 27, 428
computer software industry, 277, 413
Conroy, R. M., 427n
consensus earnings forecasts, 476–477
conservatism
    accounts receivable, 187
    financial analysis, 146–147
    GAAP, 26
    gain and loss contingencies, 381–382
    LCM method, 230
    revaluation of long-lived assets, 273–274
    conservatism ratio, 389, 524
consistency principle, 105, 229
consolidated balance sheet
    deferred income tax disclosures, 389–391
    financial analysis, 131–132
    IFRS example, 528
    long-lived fixed asset disclosures, 272
    noncontrolling interest, 310–311
    Waterloo Inc. and Savanna Inc. securities
        example, 307–318
consolidated financial statements, 309, 321–322,
        526–530

consolidated income statement, 9, 109, 131, 307–318, 527
consolidated statement of cash flow, 133, 272, 467, 530
consolidated statement of changes in equity, 529
consolidated tax returns, 322
consolidation accounting method, 299–301, 307–318, 548–550
contingent liabilities, 351, 379, 380–382
continuing value, 468
contra accounts
    allowance for sales returns, 196
    contra-liability accounts, 344
    contra-revenue accounts, 134
    contra-shareholders' equity account, 416
    defined, 52
    uncollectible accounts, 187, 190–193
contract(s)
    executory, 380–382
    fair value and, 17–18
    financial instruments, 399
    lease, 350–356
    percentage of completion method, 175
    prospectus as, 344
    revenue recognition, 181–186
    contracting role, 25
contra-liability accounts, 344
contra-revenue accounts, 134
contra-shareholders' equity account, 416
contributed capital, 43, 418–419
contributory retirement plans, 392–393
conversion ratio, 198, 341, 420
convertible bonds and notes, 341
convertible preferred shares, 106, 420
Cook, Tim, 430n
Cooper, Cynthia, 322
copyrights, 277, 281
Core, J. E., 106n
corporate charter, 24
corporate entities, investments in, 547–550
corporate governance, 24–26
Corporate Social Responsibility movement, 70
corporations. *See also* public companies
    agency costs, 24–26, 110
    evaluating performance/profitability. *See* financial analysis
    family-controlled, 423–424
    financial reporting requirements, 26–27
    forms of, 24–26
    income taxes paid by, 24, 383, 387, 388–399
    investments in, recording transactions, 547–550
    limited liability and, 24–25
    multinational, 388
    regulation of, 21
    separation of management and capital providers, 24–26
    social responsibility, 457
cost allocation, long-lived assets, 264–274
cost method, treasury stock, 420n
cost of common equity, 469–470
cost of debt. *See also* interest expense
    credit rating and, 341–342
    financing, 344–346
    incremental, 352
    weighted average, 352, 356–357
cost of equity, 473–475
cost of goods sold
    in accounts payable turnover, 137, 523
    caption for, 226
    in days' payable period, 137, 238, 523
    financial analysis, 240–241
    forecasting, 460–462
    in gross profit margin ratio, 137, 523
    in inventory-on-hand period, 137, 522
    in inventory turnover, 137, 522
    measurement of, 221–225
    pro forma financial statements, 149–150

recording transactions, 545–546
Costco Wholesale Corp., 422
costs, allocation to future periods, 264–274
costs, capitalized. *See* capitalized expenditures
counterparties, 399
coupon rate, 342–344
covenants, 26. *See also* debt covenants
CPA (certified public accounting) certificate, 241
credit, 47, 134, 532
credit default swaps, 18
credit rating agencies, 341–342
credit ratings, 187, 341–342, 358
credit risk analysis, 141, 357
credit sales, 176–177, 186–193, 237–240
Credit Suisse, 356
credit terms, 194
credits, terminology, 23. *See also* debits and credits system
Critical Accounting Policy (CAP) disclosure, 269
cross-sectional analysis, defined, 141
CSK Auto Corporation, 103, 104–105
CSOE (common equity share of operating earnings), 149
CTA (cumulative foreign currency translation adjustment), 320, 428
cumulative foreign currency translation adjustment (CTA), 320, 428
cumulative preferred shares, 420
cumulative prior period effect, 273
currency exchange rate fluctuations, 319
currency hedges, 318
current assets
    in current ratio, 137
    defined, 58
    financial reporting, 57–58
current liabilities
    in current ratio, 137, 523
    defined, 58
    financial reporting, 57–58
    in operating cash flow to current liabilities ratio, 99, 523
    in quick ratio, 137, 523
    valuation, 342
current maturities of long-term debt, 91
current portion of long-term debt, 137
current rate method, 319–320
current ratio, 137, 139, 523
Curry, Stephen, 129

D

days' inventory turnover, 237n
days' payable period, 137, 139, 238, 523
De Haven, Jacob, 342
debentures, 341
debentures, 100-year, 349
debit and credit system
    accounting cycle, 533–541
    cost of goods sold and inventory, 545–546
    debt financing transactions, 550–552
    equity financing, 552–553
    investments in and sale of long-lived assets, 546–547
    investments in other corporate entities, 547–550
    operating revenue and receivables, 541–544
    recording transactions, 44
    steps of, 533–541
    terminology, 23
debt
    avoiding, 358
    book value of, 346
    cost of. *See* cost of debt
    early retirement of, 346–348
    effect on ROA and ROE, 358
    interest-bearing vs. noninterest-bearing, 348
    reported, management of, 357
    transaction costs, 343
debt and equity securities. *See also* bonds; notes

accounting for, 299–301
amortization, 300
disclosure, 321–322, 344
GAAP, 318
IFRS, 101, 318
managerial discretion in reporting, 321–322
marketable, accounting for, 301–307
recording sale of, 302–304
recording transactions, 547–548
SEC registration, 344
tax-deductibility of interest payments, 349
tax laws, 321–322
valuation adjustments, 302
debt covenants, 20, 25, 342
debt financing
    analysis of leverage use, 358–362
    cost of debt, 341–342, 344–346
    credit ratings, 341–342
    early retirement of, 346–348
    equity vs., 65n, 340–341
    financial analysis, 358–362
    forecasting, 460–462
    managing reported debt, 357
    off-balance-sheet. *See* off-balance-sheet financing
    overview, 340–341
    recording transactions, 550–552
    ROE and ROA and, 66
    valuing bonds and notes, 342–350
    weighted average cost of debt, 356–357
debt instruments, fixed interest rate, 346
debtholders, 20, 25–26
decision usefulness, 13
deconsolidation, 314–315
default, bonds and notes, 342
deferred costs, 69
deferred income tax account, 384
deferred income tax assets, 388, 433
deferred income tax liabilities, 382–392, 397
deferred revenue, 183
defined benefit plans, 392–393
defined contribution plans, 392–393
DeHaven, Jacob, 506–507
delivery and performance, revenue recognition, 202
Dell Computer, 237
Dell, 434
Deloitte & Touche, 15
Delta Air Lines, 188
demand for capital, 19
Demirakos, N., 475n
deontology, 477
depletion, 264
depreciable cost, 265
depreciation
    accelerated methods, 266–267
    accounting policy changes, 271–273, 281
    assets, 52–53
    defined, 264
    double-declining-balance method, 266–267
    financial reporting, 52–53, 271–273
    forecasting, 460–462
    GAAP, 269–271
    leases, 351
    matching concept, 53
    method of *Fortune 1000* companies, 268
    method selection, 269–271, 281
    modified accelerated cost recovery system (MACRS), 270, 384–387
    recording transactions, 546–547
    straight-line method. *See* straight-line method
    sum-of-the-years' digits method, 266n
    temporary differences and, 384–387
    units-of-production method, 267–269
depreciation expense
    accounting standards vs. tax law, 384
    as noncash expense, 93
    capital leases, 352–353

financial reporting, 52–53
pro forma financial statements, 149–150
statement of cash flow preparation, 93, 99
straight-line method vs. MACRS, 384–387
depreciation tax shield, 386
derivative securities, 399
determinable sale price, 202
DFS, 526
Dharam, D., 271n
Dick's Sporting Goods, 129
Dillard's, 224n
diluted earnings per share, 106
dilutive claims, 106
dilutive securities, 106
direct method, statement of cash flow preparation,
    87, 101, 111–112
direct write-off method, accounts receivable, 187n
disclosures and footnotes
    accounting policy summary, 315
    capitalized costs, 262–263
    debt securities, 344
    deferred tax liability, 389–391, 397
    defined, 14
    depreciation method, 269
    due diligence and, 141
    fair value, 305–306
    gain and loss contingencies, 381–382
    intangible assets, 276
    intercompany transactions, 321–322
    leases, 351, 353, 354–355, 359–361
    LIFO reserve, 233–234, 235
    long-lived fixed assets, 272
    managerial discretion in. See managerial
        discretion
    materiality and, 14
    of debt, 357
    parent-company aggregate assets, 311–312
    public companies, 415
    related-party transaction, 307
    requirements for public companies, 88
    retirement benefits, 393, 394–396
    revenue recognition modifications, 203
    shareholders' equity, 423
    special purpose entities (SPEs), 317
discontinued operations, 102, 105, 106
discount amortization, 345–346
discount rate
    leases, 352
    opportunity cost of investment, 469–470
    retirement obligations, 396
discount, bonds and notes, 343–344
discounted cash flow model
    buy, sell, hold recommendations, 471–472
    equity method and, 464–467
    equity valuation, 467–472
    firm value, 467–468
discounts, amortization, 345–346
discretionary cash flow, 99–101
distribution date, dividend, 421
distributions to owners, GAAP definition, 27
dividend payments, in discretionary cash flow, 101
dividend payout ratio, 145n, 422, 524
dividend retention rate, 145, 524
dividend yield, 421, 422, 524
dividend-in-arrears, 420
dividends
    Apple, Inc., 424
    cash, 421–424
    financial reporting, 56
    free share distributions, 424
    GAAP, 101
    IFRS, 101
    interest payments as, 349
    liquidating, 308
    pro forma financial statements, 149–150
    reporting requirements, 101
    stock, 425
    stock repurchases vs., 418

stock splits, 425–428
tax law, 321–322
taxation of, 24
dividends-in-arrears, 435–436
DJIA (Dow Jones Industrial Average), 19
Dom Pérignon, 526
double taxation, 24
double-declining-balance method, 266–267
double-entry accounting, 8n, 44, 532. See also debit
    and credit system
Dow Jones Industrial Average (DJIA), 19
due diligence, 141, 281, 397–398, 471–472
Dun and Bradstreet, 187
DuPont Chemical Company, 142
DuPont Model, 142
duration, 194

E

earnings. See also net income; sustainable earnings
    cost of goods sold and ending inventory,
        222–223
    financial reporting, 68–70
    operating vs. nonoperating, 109
    permanent, 102
    pro forma, 108–110
    transitory, 102
earnings after taxes, P/E multiples, 475–477
earnings before interest and taxes, P/E multiples,
    475–477
earnings before interest, taxes, depreciation and
    amortization (EBITA), 99–101
earnings before interest, taxes, depreciation and
    amortization, P/E multiples, 475–477
earnings forecasts, 475–477
earnings management. See managerial discretion
earnings per common share, 523
earnings per share (EPS), 105–106, 108–109,
    475–477
earnings persistence, 102
earnings reserve, 185
East Asian countries, family-controlled corporations,
    423–424
Eastman Kodak Company, 104
eBay, Inc., 315
Ebbers, Bernard, 263
EBITA (earnings before interest, taxes, depreciation
    and amortization), 99–101
economic entity, GAAP, 26
economic environment, 16–17, 21–22
Economic Value Added (EVA), 457, 473
effective tax rate, taxable, 64–65, 389
efficient market, 20
Einhorn, David, 261
Eli Lilly, 85
Embraer, 175, 178
Emergency Stabilization Act of 2008, 18
employee pension obligations, 91
Employee Retirement Income Securities Act
    (ERISA), 393
employee retirement obligations, 392–397
employee stock options, 10, 430–435
employment compensation contracts, 110
employment contracts, 147
Empresa Brasileira de Aeronáutica S.A., 175
ending inventory, 221–225, 232–236
endorsement, 129
Enron, 5, 16, 17, 21, 24, 70, 141, 241, 316, 317,
    321, 322, 431
entity changes, 271–273
entity principle, 45
equipment purchase, financial reporting, 48
equity, GAAP definition, 26
equity beta, 151
equity capital, 416
equity financing
    calculating cost of, 150–151
    debt vs., 65n, 340–341
    financial analysis, 435–436
    going public, 414–415
    issuances and repurchases of equity, 416–421

recording transactions, 552–553
equity in the earnings (loss) of an unconsolidated
    affiliate account, 301
equity investments, accounting for, 94n
equity method accounting
    debt and equity securities, 299–301
    discounted cash flow approach, 464–467
    fair value, 307–318
    goodwill, 308
    joint ventures, 315–316
    off-balance-sheet financing, 311–312, 321
    recording transactions, 548–550
equity risk premium, 150–151
equity securities. See debt and equity securities
equity valuation
    GAAP, 474
    opportunity cost, 469–470
    pro forma financial statements, 458–464
    time value of money, 469–470
    using cash flow data, 464–467
    using discounted cash flow model, 467–472
    using price-earnings multiples, 475–477
    using residual income model, 473–475
ERISA (Employee Retirement Income Securities
    Act), 393
Ernst & Young, 15, 16
ESOARS, employee stock options, 431
estimate changes, 271–273
ethical issues
    agency costs, 110
    ethics exam, 241
    ethics philosophies, 477
    financial analysts, 147
    financial statement account presentation,
        199–200
    GAAP and rules vs. principles, 22
    lease accounting, 361
    managerial discretion, 70
    off-balance-sheet financing, 361
    shareholder value, 436
    short-term profit focus, 281
    two sets of books, 398
    whistle-blowers, 322
ethics exam, 241
Euronext Paris Exchange, 526
European Union, IFRS and, 18
European Union Committee on Competition, 185,
    422
evaluation. See financial analysis
Excel, time value calculations, 512–520
excess earnings, 473–475
exchange rate fluctuations, 101, 319
ex-dividends, 422
executive compensation, 25, 110
executive stock options, 17
executory contracts, 380–382
exercise price, 430
exit strategy, 414
expected market yield rate, 344
expected rate of return
    credit ratings and, 342
    forecasting, 469–470
    GAAP, 16
    market rate and book value, 346
    pro forma financial statements, 149–150
    retirement obligations, 396
expected useful life, 52
expenses
    GAAP definition, 27
    matching concept, 50, 69
    rear-end loading of, 69n
    relation with revenues and retained earnings,
        49–50
extraordinary items, 103–105
extraordinary losses, 105
Exxon Mobil Corporation, 269

F

face value, 344
Facebook, 39
factor, 381
factoring, 196–197
FAF (Financial Accounting Foundation), 16
fair market value, 306
fair value
  accounting for, 17–18
  accumulated other comprehensive income, 347
  capital investments, 280
  capital leases, 352
  of company, 458
  deconsolidation, 314–315
  FASB, 347
  financial contracts, 17–18
  interest rate swaps, 399
  leases, 351
  liabilities, 347
  market rate and book value, 346
  securities example, 307–318
  stock options, 430, 431, 433–435
Fairfield Communities, Inc., 198
faithful representation, 14, 26
Fannie Mae, 305
FarmVille, 39
FASB. *See* Financial Accounting Standards Board (FASB)
Federal National Mortgage Association, 305
Federal Trade Commission, 6
feedback value, 13
FICO scores, 187
Fidelity Investments, 147
FIFO method. *See* first-in, first-out (FIFO) method
financial accounting. *See also* financial reporting
  accounting cycle, 533–541
  accounting myths, 22–23
  accounting policy changes. *See* financial accounting policy changes
  accrual basis. *See* accrual accounting
  cash-basis, 8, 68–70
  changes in practice, 104–105
  consolidation method, 299–301, 307–318, 548–550
  contracting role of information, 25
  debit and credit system, 532–553
  defined, 5–7
  double-entry accounting, 8n, 44, 532. *See also* debit and credit system
  economic environment, 16–17, 21–22
  equity method. *See* equity method accounting
  fair value. *See* fair value
  fraudulent, 85, 110, 177, 357
  GAAP. *See* generally accepted accounting principles (GAAP)
  intrinsic value method, 430
market-value based, 284, 399
  mark-to-market, 299–301
  methods of, choice in, 68–70, 147
  oversight of, 241
  policy decisions, 62
  receivable valuation policy, 198–199
  relevance of, 4–7
  revenue recognition policy, 198
  role in investment decisions, 19–21
  spreadsheet approach, 44
  terminology, 42–43
Financial Accounting Foundation (FAF), 16–17
financial accounting policy changes
  amortization, 281
  capitalization vs. expensing, 263
  cumulative prior period effect, 273
  depreciation, 271–273
  depreciation, 281
  GAAP, 271–273

principles, change in, 104–105
  voluntary, 273
financial accounting risk, 178–179
Financial Accounting Standards Board (FASB)
  Accounting Standards Updates, 17, 204
  extraordinary items, 104–105
  fair value, 18, 305, 347
  GAAP and, 26
  lease accounting, 351, 356, 361
  overview, 16–17
  pension accounting, 393, 397–398
  revenue recognition, 177–178, 202–204
  stock options, 433
financial accounting standards. *See also* generally accepted accounting principles (GAAP); international accounting standards
  cash flow reporting, 101
  conservatism, 230
  economic landscape, 21–22
  fair value, 17–18
  flexibility and, 14
  global concerns, 18
  historical cost vs. market value, 146
  inventory valuation, 222–223
  overview, 16–19
  politics and, 433
  revenue recognition, 177–178, 186, 201–204
  rule- vs. principle-based, 22
  stock options, 17
  tax law vs., 383–387, 398
financial analysis. *See also* financial ratios
  accounts receivable, 198–200
  AOCI, 436
  bankruptcy prediction, 342
  benchmarking, 141–143
  capital investments, 280–282
  cash flow, 86–102
  common-size financial statements, 132–135
  cost of goods sold, 240–241
  credit risk, 139, 357
  debt financing, 358–362
  deferred income taxes, 387–392
  dividens-in-arrears, 435–436
  equity financing, 435–436
  FIFO methods, 240–241
  financial risk, 67
  fundamentals of, 130–132
  global issues, 139
  inventory, 240–241
  investors and, 9
  LIFO methods, 240–241
  limitations of, 146–147
  off-balance-sheet financing, 358–361, 397–398
  operating revenue, 198–200
  percentage change, 132–135
  performance, 63–67, 130–143
  potential liabilities, 397–398
  profitability, 64–65
  return on equity, 65–66
  ROE model, 143–146
  shareholders' equity, 435–436
  solvency, 357, 398
  statement of cash flow, 96–101
  stock options, 436
  sustainable earnings, 102–110
financial analysts, ethical issues and, 147
financial calculators, time value of money calculations, 512–521
financial crises, 18, 305, 342, 427
financial decisions, 63–67
financial derivatives, 428–430
Financial Executives Institute, 17
financial forecasts, forward-looking, 45
financial instruments, 399

financial leverage, 66, 136 138, 143–146, 149–150, 356–357, 358–362, 524
financial ratios
  accounts payable turnover, 137, 523
  accumulated depreciation to gross fixed assets, 524
  allowance for uncollectibles to gross receivables, 524
  asset management, 137, 522
  asset turnover, 65–66, 137, 139
  benchmarks by industry, 142
  capital intensity, 524
  cash and marketable securities to total assets, 137, 523
  cash collection period, 523
  cash conversion ratio, 99, 198, 523
  cash flow, 98–99, 523
  conservatism ratio, 524
  current ratio, 137, 139, 523
  days' payable period, 137, 139, 238, 523
  debt financing, 361
  defined, 63
  dividend payout ratio, 145n, 524
  dividend retention rate, 524
  dividend yield, 524
  earnings per share, 523
  financial leverage, 524
  financial risk, 136
  free cash flow yield, 523
  GAAP and, 146
  global issues, 139
  gross profit margin ratio, 137, 138, 523
  in performance evaluation, 63
  intangibles turnover, 523
  interest coverage ratio, 67, 137, 141, 398
  inventory turnover, 137, 523
  inventory-on-hand period, 137, 139, 523
  key, table of, 137
  liquidity, 137, 523
  long-term debt to shareholders' equity, 67, 137, 398, 524
  long-term debt to total assets, 137, 398, 524
  operating cash flow to current liabilities, 99, 523
  operating funds, 98–99, 523
  pro forma earnings per share, 523
  profitability, 137, 523
  quick ratio, 137, 139, 523
  receivable collection period, 137, 139, 523
  receivable turnover, 137, 523
  return on assets (ROA), 64, 137, 138, 148–149, 523
  return on sales (ROS), 64–65, 65–66, 137, 138, 148–149, 523
  return on shareholders' equity (ROE), 65–66, 137, 138, 148–149, 523
  role in financial analysis, 136–140
  solvency and capital structure, 137, 524
  sustainable growth rate, 524
  times-interest-earned ratio, 67
  total asset turnover, 523
  uncollectible accounts and gross loans outstanding, 198–199
  unlevering, 148–149
financial reporting
accounts receivable, 186–193
  advertising, 69
  bias in, 147
  business establishment, 45–47
  capitalized expenditures, 262–263
  commitments and contingencies, 379, 380–382
  conservatism and. *See* conservatism
  contingent liabilities, 397–398
  costs of goods sold, 221–225

debt and equity securities, 299–301, 321–322
deferred tax liabilities, 382–392, 397
disclosures. *See* disclosures and footnotes
discontinued operations, 102, 105, 106
dividends, 101
earnings, 68–70
earnings per share, 105–106
employee retirement obligations, 392–397
ending inventory, 221–225
ethical issues, 199–200
extraordinary items, 103–105
financial instruments, 399
footnotes. *See* disclosures and footnotes
forecasted financial statements, 47–56
frequent items, 102
IFRS example, 526–530
income taxes, 103
interest expense, 101, 103
interest income, 103
internal vs. external, 398
joint ventures, 315–316
leases, 350–356
long-term fixed assets, 279–280
managerial discretion. *See* managerial
   discretion
marketing costs, 69, 200
membership fees, 68–69
methods for, 44
natural resources, 278–279
oversight of, 16–19
policy decisions, 62
pro forma earnings, 108–110
revenue recognition, 177–186, 198–200,
   201–204
shareholders' equity, 429
SPEs and SPVs, 316–318
stock dividends, 425
stock options, 433–435
stock splits, 425–428
tax payments, 101
unreported liabilities, 141
usual and unusual items, 102–103
VIEs, 316–318
financial risk, evaluating, 67, 136, 317
financial scandals, 16, 17, 21, 24, 70, 141, 241, 263,
   316, 317, 322, 431, 434
financial statement analysis. *See* financial analysis
financial statements. *See also* specific statements
   accounting myths and, 22–23
   analysis of. *See* financial statement analysis
   articulation of, 60–62
   budgeted, 555–556
   capitalized expenditures, 262–263
   debit and credit system illustration, 533–541
   disclosures. *See* disclosures and footnotes
   fraudulent, 263
   global differences in format, 62
   IFRS example, 526–530
   independent auditing of, 14–16, 281, 322
   information role, 20
   Internet access to, 7
   linkage among, 11–13
   overview, 7–13
   preparation of, 57–62. *See also* financial
      reporting
   preparing from business events, 43–63
   pro forma. *See* pro forma financial statements
   qualitative attributes of, 13–14
   rounding, of, 15
   Sarbanes-Oxley and, 5
financing activities, 59, 101, 351n
financing activities, cash flow from, 86–95, 96–98,
   111–112
finished goods inventory, 220–221
Fire Phone, 3
firm(s). *See* corporations; public companies

firm commitment basis, 414
First Call/ThomsonReuters, 476
first in, first out (FIFO)
   defined, 223
   financial analysis, 240–241
   inventory valuation, 223, 225–232
   LIFO layers and inventory reserve, 232–236
   recording transactions, 545–546
fiscal period, GAAP, 26
fiscal year-end, *Fortune 1000* companies, 13
fixed asset turnover ratio, 263, 522
fixed assets, 264
fixed interest rate debt instruments, 346
fixed rate of return, 346
fixed sales price, 202
Flow International Corp., 194–195
flows, stocks and, 12, 13
footnotes. *See* disclosures and footnotes
Ford Motor Company, 176, 219, 422, 423, 432
Ford, Henry, 219
forecasted financial statements, 45, 47–56, 558. *See
   also* pro forma financial statements
foreign currency translation adjustments, 428
foreign entities, investments in, 318–321
Form 10-K, 11, 26, 88, 147
Form 10-Q, 11, 26, 88
Fortune 1000 companies
   allowance for uncollectible accounts, 191
   balance sheet caption, 90
   balance sheet title, 57
   cost of goods sold caption, 226
   depreciation method, 268
   financial statement rounding, 15
   fiscal year-end, 13
   gain and loss contingencies, 382
   income statement title, 58
   inventory method, 229
   leases of, 352
   other comprehensive income components,
      430
   reporting of cash flow from operations, 93
   revenue recognition method, 183
   shareholders' equity title, 436
   stock splits, 427
Fortune magazine, 5, 339, 457
forward contracts, 399
forward multiple, 476–477
forward purchase agreements, 399
forward stock split, 425
Fox News, 471–472
France, goodwill, 277
Frank, Barney, 18
fraud
   capitalization vs. expensing, 263
   channel stuffing, 85
   compensation contracts, 110
   financial reporting, 70
   net debt reporting, 357
   revenue recognition, 177
   whistle-blowers and, 322
free cash flow, 100, 468–469
free cash flow model, 99–101, 468–469, 471–472
free cash flow to equity, 468
free cash flow yield, 101, 523
free share distributions, 424, 425–428
frequent items, financial reporting, 102–103
front-end loading, revenues, 68n, 198
Frontier Communications, 315
full consolidation, 311
full cost method, 278
funding status, 393
future cash flows, 86
future periods, allocation of costs to, 264–274
future value, 342, 507, 508, 513–517
future value tables, 507, 511–512
futures contracts, 399

G

gains and losses
   asset retirement, 464–467
   contingencies, 381–382
   GAAP definition, 27
   marketable securities, 384
   material vs. immaterial, 348
   one-time, 348
   unrealized. *See* unrealized gains (losses)
Gao, X., 417
General Dynamics Corporation, 181
General Electric (GE), 64, 105, 106, 298, 315,
   388–389, 428–430
General Motors (GM) Corporation, 62, 181, 197,
   230, 396, 419
generally accepted accounting principles (GAAP)
   accounting myths and, 22
   accounting policy changes, 271–273
   accrual basis accounting and, 9
   accumulated other comprehensive income
      (AOCI), 300
   AOCI, 302, 319
   benefit cost, 394, 395–396
   capitalization, 270
   cash basis accounting and, 8
   cash flow reporting, 100, 101
   cash, definition of, 101
   choice in accounting methods, 147
   conservatism, 146–147
   consistency principle, 105
   consolidated financial statements, 321–322
   consolidation accounting, 318
   cost allocation to future periods, 264
   currency exchange rate, 319
   debt and equity investments, 318
   defined, 26
   depreciation methods, 269–271
   direct method, statement of cash flows, 101
   direct write-off method, 187n
   discontinued operations, 102, 105, 106
   dividends, 101
   EBITA and, 100
   elements and concepts of, 26–27
   EPS vs. pro forma EPS, 108–109
   equity valuation, 474
   ethics and, 22
   executory contracts, 381
   extraordinary items, 103–105
   fair value, 305, 347
   Fannie Mae "cherry picking," 305
   financial instruments, 399
   financial ratios, 146
   goodwill value impairment, 277
   HIFO, 232
   historical cost principle, 54, 223n, 299
   IFRS and, 18,21–22, 429
   income statement, 102
   interest payments, 94n, 101
   inventory valuation, 222–223, 229, 230–231,
      232
   LCM method, 23–231, 232
   lease accounting, 354–355, 358
   liabilities valuation, 342
   litigation exposure 380
   long-term debt, 347
   marketable securities, 274
   marketing costs, 278
   matching concept, 388
   mergers and acquisitions, 298
   natural resources, 279
   net income, 383–387
   NIFO, 232
   off-balance sheet financing, 311–312, 381
   other comprehensive income, 428
   overview, 16–19

generally accepted accounting principles (GAAP) *(continued)*
    pension accounting, 428–429
    political influence, 22
    PP&E, 279–280
    present value, 342
    pro forma earnings, 108–109
    purpose of, 26–27
    research and development, 276, 277
    retirement plans, 392
    revenue recognition
    revenue recognition, 177–178, 186, 195, 201–204
    statement of cash flow, 87, 101
    stock options, 433, 436
    tax law vs., 397
    tax payments, 101
    treasury shares, 416, 420
    unrealized gain (loss), 274, 300, 321–322, 428–430
    zero-coupon bonds, 350
Germany, 280, 388
Givenchy, 526
Global Crossing, 16, 17, 21, 24
global issues. *See also* international accounting standards
    accounting standards, 18
    agency problems, 424
    cash flow reporting, 101
    common shares classifications, 419
    depreciation reporting, 279–280
    executory contracts, 381
    financial ratios, 139
    financial statement format, 62
    income tax of multinational corporations, 388
    revenue recognition, 186
    shareholders' equity reporting, 429
    worldwide IPOs, 417
    worldwide tax rate, 387
going concern, 9, 26, 418, 468, 470
going public, 414–415
gold bonds, 349
Golden, Russel, 356
goodwill, 277–278, 308
Google Inc., 431
Grant Thorton, 357
Great Depression, 16
Greenlight Capital, 261, 424
gross loans outstanding, uncollectible accounts and, 198–199
gross profit
    forecasting, 460–462
    FIFO vs. LIFO, 233–234
    inventory valuation method and, 225–232
    LIFO layer liquidation, 235–236
    percentage of completion vs. completed contract method, 184
    pro forma financial statements, 149–150
gross profit margin ratio, 138, 523
gross profit revenues, 58
Groupon, 199–200
growth, working capital management, 554–559
growth companies, 421
Guay, W.R., 106n

H

H.J. Heinz Company, 272
half-year convention, 265
Hall v. Geiger-Jones Co. 1917, 16n
Hap eLoan Corporation, 63, 65
Harris, R. S., 427n
Healy, P. M., 21n
hedge instruments, 399
held-to-maturity debt securities, 299–301, 301–307
Hennessey, 526
highest-in, first-out (HIFO), 232
historical cost convention, GAAP

historical cost principle, 48, 54, 146, 223n, 273–274, 299
Home Depot, 224n
Home Heating Oil Inc., 222–223

I

IASB. *See* International Accounting Standards Board (IASB)
IBM Corporation, 397
IFRS. *See* International Financial Reporting Standards (IFRS)
immaterial gains and losses, 348
impairment loss, 274, 277–278, 279–280
Imperial Government of Russia, 349
incentive stock options (ISOs), 433
income smoothing, 270
income statement
    accounting myths and, 22
    accounting standards vs. tax law, 384
    accounts receivable reporting, 193
    arms-length transactions, 307
    budgeted, 555
    capitalized expenditures, 263
    common-size, 133–134
    consolidated, 9, 109, 131, 307–318, 527
    defined, 9
    discontinued operations, 105, 106
    earnings per share, 105–106
    extraordinary items, 103–105
    financial reporting example, 58–59
    financial statement articulation, 60–62
    financial statement linkages, 11–13, 49–50, 299–300
    IFRS example, 526–530
    GAAP elements, 26–27, 102
    leases, 350–356
    LIFO and FIFO, 233–234
    percentage change, 133–134
    pro forma earnings, 108–110
    SEC reporting requirements, 204n9
    sustainable earnings and, 102–110
    title of, 58
income tax expense, 148, 150, 383–387, 388, 389, 460–462
income taxes. *See also* tax law; taxation/taxes
    corporate, 24, 383, 383, 387, 388–389
    financial reporting, 54–55, 103
    NOL carryforwards/carrybacks, 388
incremental betterment capital expenditures, 280
incremental CapEx, 100n
incremental cost of debt, 352
indenture agreement, 341
independent auditors, 14–16, 281, 322
indirect method, statement of cash flow, 87–95, 96–98, 111–112, 149–150, 464–467
industries, capital intensive, 99
industries, financial ratio benchmarks, 142
inflation rate, 470
information overload, 309
information role, 20
initial public offerings (IPOs), 39, 414, 417
installment method, revenue recognition, 180
Institutional Brokers' Estimate System, 476
intangible assets
    capitalized expenditures, 281
    copyrights, 277
    defined, 46, 264
    disclosures, 276
    forecasting, 460–462
    goodwill, 277–278
    marketing costs, 278
    overview, 276
    patents, 277
    research and development costs, 276, 277
intangible property, MACRS, 270
intangibles turnover, 523
intellectual property rights, 277

intercorporate investments, 321–322
interest
    capitalization, 281
    P/E multiples, 475–477
    ROS, 137, 138n
    time value of money, 506–507
interest-bearing debt, 348
interest cost, pensions, 393
interest coverage ratio, 67, 137, 141, 361, 398, 523
interest expense
    bonds and notes, 342, 344–346, 519–520
    capital leases, 352–353
    debt liabilities, 341
    defined, 344
    in Excel, 519–520
    financial reporting, 103
    as financing activity, 94n
    forecasting, 460–462
    pensions, 393
    in ROA, 64, 137, 148–149
    nonoperating items, 109
    pro forma financial statements, 149–150
    zero-coupon bonds, 350
interest factor, 507n
interest income, financial reporting, 103
interest payments
    GAAP, 94n, 101
    IFRS, 101
    interest rate swaps, 399
    reporting requirements, 101
    tax-deductibility of, 349
interest rate, 342–344
interest rate swaps, 399
Internal Revenue Code, 231, 322, 383–387, 398. *See also* tax law
Internal Revenue Service, 6, 195, 229, 231, 321–322, 350, 354–355, 388, 433, 434
International Accounting Standards (IAS), 18
International Accounting Standards Board (IASB), 18, 177–178, 202–204, 399, 433
International Accounting Standards Committee (IASC), 18
international accounting standards
    cash flow reporting, 101
    consolidated financial statements, 309
    currency exchange rate, 319
    executory contracts, 381
    goodwill, 277–278
    historical cost convention, 223n
    inventory accounting, 232
    inventory valuation, 222–223
    long-term fixed assets, 279–280
    LCM method, 230, 232
    PP&E, 279–280
    research and development, 277
    revenue recognition, 186, 202–204
    rules vs. principles, 22
    shareholders' equity reporting, 429
    stock options, 433
International Business Machines Corporation (IBM), 349
International Financial Reporting Standards (IFRS)
    cash, definition of, 101
    cash flow reporting, 101
    consolidation accounting, 318
    debt and equity investments, 318
    dividends, 101
    executory contracts, 381
    financial statements example, 526–530
    GAAP and, 21–22, 429
    interest payments, 101
    long-term fixed assets, 279–280
    LCM method, 230, 232
    marketing costs, 278
    off-balance sheet financing, 381
    overview, 18
    PP&E, 279–280

research and development, 277
revenue recognition, 186
shareholders' equity reporting, 429
statement of cash flows, 101
tax payments, 101
treasury shares, 416
intrinsic value, 102, 418, 430
inventory
count, 224–225
financial analysis, 240–241
financial reporting, 47–48, 51–52, 55
forecasting, 460–462
international accounting standards, 232
JIT delivery, 237
management systems, 223–224
managing investments in, 237
measurement of, 221–225
pro forma financial statements, 149–150
recording transactions, 545–546
tax law, 231
valuation of, 222–223, 225–232
working capital management, 554–559
inventory-on-hand period, 138, 139, 237, 523
inventory reserves, 233–234
inventory turnover, 138, 523
investing activities, 59, 101, 281, 351n
investing activities, cash flow from, 86–95, 96–98, 111–112
investment decisions, 42
investment in equity affiliate account, 300–301, 307–318
investment-grade credit rating, 341
investment return, 393
investments
in accounts receivable, managing, 194–196
debt and equity securities, 298–321
financial reporting analysis, 130–143, 280–282
foreign entities, 318–321
intercorporate, 321–322
inventory, management of, 237
in long-lived assets, recording transactions, 546–547
net present value, 509
in other corporate entities, recording transactions, 547–550
by owners, GAAP definition, 27
passive, accounting for, 301–307
present and future value of. *See* time value of money
risk and return of, 16, 42n, 393
role of financial accounting in, 19–21
investors, financial statement analysis and, 9
IPOs (initial public offerings), 39, 414, 417
IRC (Internal Revenue Code), 231, 322, 383–387, 398. *See also* tax law
IRS (Internal Revenue Service), 6, 195, 229, 231, 321–322, 350, 354–355, 388, 433, 434
issued shares, 416
Ito Company, 419–420

J

Jaguar, 219, 422
Japan, 280, 388
Jennings, R., 106n
Jimbo de Mexico SA de CV, 319–320
Jimbo Inc., 319–320
JIT (just-in-time) inventory, 237
Jobs, Steve, 424
Johnson & Johnson Inc., 476–477
joint and severable liability, 24
joint ventures, accounting for, 315–316
journal entries, 44, 532–553. *See also* debit and credit system
Julius Company, 425
junk bonds, 341, 342

just-in-time (JIT) inventory, 237
JWS Inc., 301–307

K

Kant, Immanuel, 477
Kershaw, Clayton, 129
Keurig Green Mountain, Inc., 261
Kindle, 3
Kohl's, 106, 109, 389–391
Kothari, S. P., 106n
KPMG, 15, 263

L

Land Rover, 219, 422
Lands' End, 315
Landsman, W., 9n
last-in, first-out (LIFO)
conformity rule, 223, 231
defined, 223
financial analysis, 240–241
at Ford, 219
inventory valuation, 223, 225–232
layers and inventory reserve, 232–236, 240–241
LCM (lower-of-cost-or-market) method, 230–231, 232
LDDS Inc., 263
lease financing, accounting for, 350–356
leases
accounting for, 350–356, 551–552
capital, 350–356
defined, 350
disclosures, 354–355, 359–361
escalation clauses, 351n
ethical issues, 361
FASB, 351, 356, 361
GAAP, 354–355, 358
operating, 350–356
recording transactions for, 551–552
tax law, 354–355
LeClere, M. J., 106n
legislation, Sarbanes-Oxley, 5
lemons problem, 14
lessor, 350
Lev, B., 271n
leverage, 42. *See also* financial leverage
levered free cash flow, 468n
liabilities
balance sheet equation, 40–42
conservatism in reporting, 146–147
contingent, 379, 380–382
deferred income tax, 382–392
defined, 8, 43
double-entry system, 532
fair value, 347
GAAP, 26, 342
potential, 380–382, 397–398
pro forma financial statements, 458–464
statement of cash flow preparation, 87–95
valuation of, 342–350
working capital management, 554–559
Lie, Erik, 434
Lieberman, Joseph, 17
LIFO. *See* last-in, first-out (LIFO)
limited liability, 24
limited liability corporations, 24
limited liability partnerships, 24
limited partnerships, 24
Lincoln, 219
line of credit, 380–382
liquid assets, 139, 357
liquidating dividends, 308
liquidation, LIFO layers, 235–236, 240–241
liquidity, 136–138 415
liquidity ratios, 523
loan applications, 40–42
loan duration, 340

London InterBank Offering Rate (LIBOR), 399
London Stock Exchange, 40
longitudinal analysis, 131
long-lived assets
acquisition costs, 262–264
cost allocation to future periods, 264–274
disclosures, 272
distortion caused by aging, 275
recording transactions, 546–547
revaluation of, 273–274
sale or retirement of, 274–275
tax law, 270
long-term debt, 137, 149–150, 347, 356–357
long-term debt to shareholders' equity ratio, 67, 137, 361, 398, 524
long-term debt to total assets ratio, 137, 361, 398, 524
long-term fixed assets, accounting for, 261, 270, 279–280
long-term liabilities, 345–346
losses. *See* gains and losses
lower-of-cost-or-market (LCM) method, 230–231, 232, 318
Lumia phones, 413
Lundholm, Russel, 468n
LVMH Moet Hennessey-Louis Vuitton S.A., 18, 526–530

M

maintenance expenditures, 100n, 262–264, 280
Mammoth Company, 144
management
bias of, in financial reporting, 147. *See also* managerial discretion
capital providers and, 24–26
conflicts with shareholders, 25
executive compensation, 25, 110
stock option accounting, 17
Management's Discussion and Analysis (MD&A), 269
managerial accounting, 6, 221
managerial discretion
accounting methods, 68–70
conservatism ratio, 389
contingent liabilities, 397–398
debt and equity securities reporting, 321–322
reporting unrealized gain (loss), 305
retirement obligation disclosure, 396–397
stock options, 436
manufacturing companies, 176n, 220–221
mark-to-market accounting, 18, 299–301, 301–307, 384
market-based value, 418
market capitalization, 101, 185, 356
market interest rate, 346
market price per share, P/E multiples, 475–477
market value
accounting example, 301–307
book value of debt, 346
debt and equity securities, 299–301
measurement concerns, 146
stock dividends, 425
market-value model of accounting, 274, 399
market yield rate, 344, 346
marketable securities
accounting for, 301–307
accounting standards vs. tax law, 384
business activity classification of, 91
GAAP, 274
in liquidity ratios, 137
mark-to-market accounting, 299–301
pro forma financial statements, 149–150
in quick ratio, 137
recording transactions, 547–548
unrealized gains (losses), 428–430
marketing costs, 69, 200, 276, 278
Marriott International, 317–318

Martin, Laura, 471–472
matching concept
    accounts receivable, 187
    allocation of costs to future periods, 264–274
    direct write-off method, 187n
    net income, 102
    net operating losses, 388
    plant and equipment, 93
material gains and losses, 348
materiality, 14
maturity date, 342–344
maturity value, 342–344
Mazda, 219
McDonald's Holdings Company (Japan) Ltd., 425
McGuire, William, 434
Medina, D., 472
Medtronic, 387
membership fees, accounting for, 68–69
Mercury, 219
mergers and acquisitions, 263, 276, 277, 297, 298, 422
Merrill Lynch, 147
mezzanine financing, 420
MGM Resorts International, 315
Microsoft Corporation, 185, 383, 413–414, 425–426
MicroStrategy, Inc., 198
Midwestern Airlines, 343–350, 351–356, 550–551
Mill, John Stuart, 477
minority interest, 310
modified accelerated cost recovery system (MACRS), 270, 384–387
Moehrle, S.R., 104n
Moët et Chandon, 526
monetary unit, GAAP, 26
monetization, 196–197
Moody's, 317, 341–342
Morgan Stanley, 147, 347
mortgage backed securities (MBS), 18, 305-306, 342
Mulcahy, Anne, 5
multinational corporations, 388

N

NASDAQ stock exchange, 3, 299, 417
natural resources, 264, 277, 278–279
Needham and Company, 471–472
negative goodwill, 277
net book value, 4, 265, 267, 346
net debt, 357
net income. *See also* earnings
    accrual accounting, 102, 556
    in conservatism ratio, 389
    GAAP, 383–387
    in operating funds ratio, 99
    revenues, 58
    in ROA, 64, 137, 148–149, 523
    in ROE, 65–66, 137, 148–149, 523
    in ROS, 64–65, 134, 137, 138n, 148–149, 523
    statement of cash flow preparation, 93, 94–95
    stock options and, 431
    successful efforts method and, 278n
    sustainable earnings and, 102
net operating loss, 388
net present value, 509, 520
net realizable value, 187, 190
net revenues, 134, 194
net sales
    in asset turnover, 137, 522
    capital intensity and, 130
    in cash conversion ratio, 99, 523
    in gross profit margin ratio, 137, 523
    in receivable collection period, 137, 194, 522
    in receivable turnover, 137, 522
    in ROS, 134, 137, 138n, 148–149, 523
net worth, 41–42
Netflix, 39
New Constructs, 431

New South Wales Trading Company, Inc., 301–307, 547–548
New York Stock Exchange, 40, 299, 417, 426, 427
New Zealand, 274
News Corp, 471–472
News of the World, 471–472
next-in, first-out (NIFO), 232
Nike, 129, 141–143
no-par value shares, 418
Nokia, 413
NOL carrybacks/carryforwards, 388
noncash assets, 87–95
noncash expenses, 93
noncontributory retirement plans, 392–393
noncontrolling interest, 310–311
noncurrent assets, 57–58
noncurrent liabilities, 58
noninterest-bearing debt, 348
nonoperating earnings, vs. operating, 109
nonoperating effects, 94–95
nonqualified stock options, 433
nonrecurring effects, 94–95
non-systematic risk, 151Non-Tax Lease, 354–355
Nordstrom, 224n, 339, 342, 355–356
Nordstrom, John W., 339
normal earnings, 473–475
North American Coffee Partnership, 316
note discount account, 344
notes
    callable, 341
    convertible bonds and, 341
    defined, 340
    features of, 340–341
    interest expense, 344–346
    junk, 341, 342
    rating of, 341–342
    recording transactions for, 550–551
    valuation, 342–350
    zero-coupon, 348–350
notes payable, 238, 4550-551
notes receivable, 180
Novartis AG, 85
Novell, Inc., 383

O

O'Reilly Automotive, Inc., 100
off-balance-sheet financing
    debt disclosure, 357
    defined, 311, 357
    equity method, 312, 321–322
    ethical issues, 361
    executory contracts, 381
    financial analysis, 358–361, 397–398
    GAAP, 311–312, 381
    IFRS, 381
    leases, 351, 356
    SEC, 351, 356
off-balance-sheet liabilities, 43, 141, 147
Office, 413
Office Depot, 356
Office of Federal Housing Enterprises Oversight, 307
oil and gas industry, 277
operating activities, 59, 101, 111–112, 351n
operating activities, cash flow from, 86–95, 96–98, 111–112
operating cash flow, free cash flow, 468
operating cash flow management, 196–197
operating cash flow to current liabilities, 523f
operating earnings, vs. nonoperating, 109
operating expenses
    balance sheet equation and, 69
    capitalization and, 281
    manufacturing companies, 221. *See also* cost of goods sold
    pro forma financial statements, 149–150
operating funds ratio, 98–99, 523
operating income, 58, 67

operating leases, 141, 350–356
operating revenue, 68–69, 198–200, 541–544
operating value of firm, 467–468
opportunity cost, 47, 134, 180, 186–187, 469–470, 473–475
options, 399. *See also* stock options
ordinary annuities, 352n, 508n
organizational forms, 24–25
other comprehensive income, 428–430
outstanding shares, 416, 425–428
overfunded assets, 392
ownership, leases, 350–351, 352, 354
ownership interest, 299–301, 310–311, 340
ownership transferability, 24

P

Pacioli, Luca, 532
Palepu, K. G., 21n
Pan American Enterprises Inc., 189–193, 543–544
par value, 344, 420n, 425
par value shares, 418
Parfums Christian Dior, 526
Parmalat SpA, 357
participating preferred shares, 420
partnerships, 24
passive investments, accounting for, 301–307
patents, 277, 281
PayPal Holdings, 314
payroll expenses, financial reporting, 50
PBGC (Pension Benefit Guarantee Corporation), 393
PBOs (projected benefit obligations), 394
PCAOB (Public Company Accounting Oversight Board), 16, 21, 241
Penman, S., 473n
Pension Benefit Guarantee Corporation (PBGC), 393
pension liability adjustment, 428–429
pension plans, 392–397, 428–429
Pepsi-Cola Company, 316
percentage change, financial analysis, 132–135
percentage-of-completion method, revenue recognition, 175, 181, 184, 384, 541–542
percentage-of-credit-sales method, 187–189
performance, forecasted, 458–464
performance incentives, 25, 110
performance measurement, 63–67, 86–101, 102–110. *See also* financial analysis
periodic system, inventory, 223–224
permanent accounts, 533–541
permanent debt, 349
permanent differences, 383–384
permanent earnings, 102
perpetual system, inventory, 224
perpetuity bonds, 349
perpetuity growth formula, 470
phantom profit, 236
pharmaceutical companies, 277, 278
physical inventory count, 224–225
Pincus, Marc, 39
plan assets at fair value, 394
Plank, Kevin, 129
pledging, 196, 197
plow-back percentage, 145n
policy decisions, financial accounting, 62
political influence, GAAP and, 22
portfolios, repo agreements, 399
posted, journal entries, 533–541
Potash Corp., 297
potential liabilities, 379, 380–382, 397–398
PP&E (property, plant and equipment), 149–150, 279–280, 460–462
predictive value, 13–14
preference shares, 420
preferred shares, 420–421
preliminary statement of cash flow, 464–466
premiums, 344, 345–346
present value
    annuity, 509–512, 518
    capital leases, 352

future value and, 507
GAAP, 342
leases, 351
liabilities, 341, 342–350
long-term liabilities, 345–346
operating value and, 468
residual income model, 473–475
retirement obligations, 396–397
single amount, 508–509, 517
present value table, 345–346, 518–519
price-earnings multiples, 475–477
PricewaterhouseCoopers, 15, 22, 357
principle-based accounting standards, 22
pro forma balance sheet, 149–150, 458–464
pro forma earnings, 108–110
pro forma earnings per share, 523
pro forma financial statements, 45, 149–150, 458–464
Procter & Gamble Company, 394–396
production, revenue recognition, 181–184
production-in-progress, 182
profit margin ratio, 64
profitability, 64–65, 136–138 523
ProFlight Inc., 181–186, 541–542
projected benefit obligations (PBOs), 394
promotional materials, financial reporting for, 69
property, plant and equipment (PP&E), 149–150, 279–280, 460–462
property dividend, 425
prospective basis, accounting changes, 273
prospectus, 344
Prudential, 396
public companies
    advantages and disadvantages of, 415
    capital-intensive, 131
family-controlled, 423–424
    financial reporting requirements, 11,26–27, 88, 415
    goals of, 436
    going public, 414–415
    operating value of, 467–468
    return on investment, 151
    shareholder value maximization, 436
    short-term profit focus, 281
    value, debt and, 358
Public Company Accounting Oversight Board, 16, 21, 241
purchase commitment, 380–382

Q

Qantas Inc., 301–307
qualitative attributes, accounting information, 13–14
quick ratio, 137, 139, 523

R

R&D (research and development), 276, 277
Rankine, G., 425n
rate of return, 150–151
ratios, defined. 136. See also financial ratios
raw material, 220–221
realizable, 177, 201
realized, 177, 201
rear-end loading, 69n, 185, 198
receivable collection period, 137, 139, 194, 523
receivable turnover, 137, 523
receivables, 541–544, 543–544
recognized, 177
record date, dividend, 421
recourse, with vs. without, 196–197
recourse liability, 197n
recurring operations revenues, 59
regular dividend, 421
Regulation G (Reg G), 109
related-party transactions, 321–322
relevance, 13, 26
replacement cost method, 223
repo agreements, 399
reported debt, management of,357

repurchase agreements, 399
repurchased shares, 416–421
research and development (R&D), 276, 277
residual income model, 473–475
residual interest, 416
residual value, 265, 271–273
restructuring, 104, 281
retail companies, 176–177, 224n
retained earnings, 43, 49–50, 93
retirement
    of assets, 274–275, 546–547
    of debt, 346–348
retirement plans, 392–397
retrospective basis, accounting changes, 273
return
    defined, 16
    fixed rate of, 346
    of investments, 42n
    risk and, 342, 469–470
return on assets (ROA), 64, 137, 138, 358, 523
return on equity. See return on shareholders' equity (ROE)
return on investment, 19–20,64–65, 151. See also return on assets (ROA)
return on sales (ROS), 64–65, 134, 137, 138, 523
return on shareholders' equity (ROE), 65–66, 137, 138, 143–146, 148–149, 358, 523
revaluation, long-lived assets, 273–274
Revenue from Contracts with Customers (ASC 606), 177–178, 186, 195, 202–204
revenue recognition
    accrual- vs. cash-basis accounting, 68–70
    airline tickets, 188
    alternative points of, 178
    contracts, 181–186, 541–542
    defined, 49
    disclosure modifications, 203
    FASB, 177–178, 202–204
    financial accounting standards, 177–178, 201–204
    Fortune 1000 companies, 183
    fundamentals of, 177–186
    GAAP, 177–178, 186, 195, 201–204
    IASB, 177–178, 202–204
    installment method, 180
    international accounting standards, 202–204
    manufacturing companies, 176n, 181–186
    recording transactions, 541–542
    retail and service companies, 176–177, 180
    tax perspective, 195
revenue(s)
    accounting standards vs. tax law, 384
    deferral of, 185, 189–193
    defined, 58, 177
    financial reporting, 49
    front-end loading of, 68n, 198
    GAAP definition, 26
    matching concept, 50
    rear-end loading of, 185, 198
    relation with expenses and retained earnings, 49–50
    reverse stock split, 425
risk
    business, financial statement adjustments and. 435–436
    credit ratings and, 341–342
    debt level and, 358
    defined, 16
    equity financing, 150–151
    fair value disclosure and, 306
    financial, 67, 136, 317
    GAAP and, 16
    lease reporting and, 356
    of investments, 42n
    of lenders, compensation for, 341
    preferences, investors, 348
    return and, 342, 469–470

revenue recognition and, 178–179
    working capital management and, 554–559
risk-free rate of return, 150–151, 469–470
risk premium, 469–470
Ritter, J. R., 417
road show, 414
ROA (return on assets), 64, 137, 138, 138, 358, 523
ROE (return on shareholders' equity), 65–66, 137, 138,143–146, 148–149, 358, 523
ROS (return on sales), 64–65, 134, 137, 138, 138, 523
rule-based accounting standards, 22
Russia, 349
Russian River Valley Winery
    debit and credit system illustration, 533–541
    financial statements of, 44–63
    free cash flow, 468–469
    pro forma financial statements, 458–464
    share valuation, 470–471, 474–475
    statement of cash flows, 87–85, 111–112

S

S&P 500, 108, 422
SAB (Staff Accounting Bulletin) 101 (SEC), 177–178, 201–202
sales arrangement, persuasive evidence of, 201
sales discount, 134, 194–195
sales price, fixed or determinable, 202
sales returns, 134
sales revenue
    financial reporting, 49–50
    in ROS, 64–65, 134, 137, 138, 523
    long-lived assets, recording transactions, 274–275, 546–547
    pro forma financial statements, 458–464
salvage value, 265
Sarbanes-Oxley Act, 4, 21–22, 70, 108, 147, 322, 417, 434
Savanna Company, 102, 187–189, 307–313, 548–550
SBC, 263
Schnurr, James, 18
Sears Holdings, 315
SEC. See U.S. Securities and Exchange Commission (SEC)
secured debt, 341
securities. See also debt and equity securities; marketable securities
    average return, 19–20
    derivative, 399
    dilutive, 106
    equity vs. risk-free, 150–151
    prices, 355–356
    purchase agreements, 399
    GAAP and, 16–17
    role of financial accounting, 19–21
Securities and Exchange Commission. See U.S. Securities and Exchange Commission (SEC)
securitization, 197
selling, general, and administrative (SG&A) expenses, forecasting, 460–462
Selling, T., 150n
sell-side analysts, 147
senior debt, 341
service cost, 393
SFAC (Statements of Financial Accounting Concepts), 26
SG&A (selling, general, and administrative) expenses, forecasting, 460–462
Shanghai President Coffee Company, Ltd., 316
share issuance, 54, 416–421
share premium, 419
share price
    Amazon, 10–11
    beta and, 469–470
    de-listing and, 426
    dilutive claims and, 106
    executive compensation and, 25

share price *(continued)*
    exercise price, 430
    financial crises and, 427
    IPOs, 414
    Microsoft, 413
    P/E multiples, 475–477
    stock splits, 425–428
    strike price, 430
share repurchases, 413, 414, 416–421
shareholders
    balance sheet equation and, 40–42
    common stock, 416–420
    conflicts with debtholders, 25–26
    conflicts with managers, 25
    corporate governance and, 24–26
    debt vs. equity financing, 340–341
    deconsolidation distributions, 314–315
    deferred income tax liabilities, 385–387
    preferred stock, 420–421
    property dividends, 425
    return on investment, 19–20, 66n, 150–151
    statement of cash flow and, 61
    stock dividends, 425
    stock splits, 425–428
    value creation and, 435–436
    value for, debt financing and, 361
    voting rights, 341
shareholders' equity
    AOCI. *See* Accumulated Other
        Comprehensive Income (AOCI)
    book value and, 418, 473–475
    deferred income tax liabilities, 385–387
    defined, 8, 43
    disclosures, 423
    double-entry system, 532
    financial analysis, 435–436
    global reporting differences, 429
    in long-term debt-to-equity ratio, 67
    in solvency ratios, 137
    NSWT accounting example, 301–307
    opportunity cost, 473–475
    other comprehensive income, 428–430
    securities example, 307–318
    statement of cash flow preparation, 87–95
    title on balance sheet, 436
shares
    common, 416–420
    initial public offerings, 39, 414, 417
    preferred, 420–421
    on investment, 19–20
    valuation of, 470–471, 474–475. *See also*
        equity valuation
Sharpe, W. F., 150n
short-term debt, 356–357
short-term loans payable, 149–150
SIC (Standard Industrial Classification) code, 141
signaling theory, 273
significant influence, 307
single amount, future and present value, 507, 508–
        509, 513–515, 517
Sloan, Richard, 468n
Small Business Administration, 340, 414
Smith, Adam, 436
social responsibility, 457
solvency, financial analysis, 136–137, 357, 398, 524
South Korea, 423–424
special dividends, 422
special purpose entities (SPEs), 197, 316–318
special purpose vehicles (SPVs), 197, 316–318
specialty items, 103–105
specific identification method, 223
SPEs (special purpose entities), 197, 316–318
Spieth, Jordan, 129
sponsorship, 129
spreadsheet approach, 44
spreadsheet calculations, time value of money,
        512–521

SPVs (special purpose vehicles), 197, 316–318
Squibb Corporation, 85
Staff Accounting Bulletin (SAB) 101 (SEC), 177–
        178, 201–202
stakeholder theory, 436
Standard & Poor's 500 Index (S&P 500), 3, 11, 19,
        317, 341–342, 470
Standard Industrial Classification (SIC) code, 141
Starbucks Coffee Company, 316
stated value method, 418, 420n
statement of cash flow
    accounting myths and, 22
    alternative measures of, 99–101
    analysis of, 996–101
    budgeted, 556
    cash flow ratios and, 98–99
    consolidated, 467, 530
    debt and equity securities, 301
    defined, 9–10
    discounted cash flow approach, 464–467
    financial reporting example, 59–60
    financial statement articulation, 60–62
    financial statement linkages, 11–13
    GAAP, 87
    indirect method of preparing, 87, 88–95,
        96–98, 149–150, 464–467
    overview, 86–87
    preliminary, 91–92
    presentation format, 87–88
    shareholder perspective, 61
statement of retained earnings, 460–462
statement of shareholders' equity
    accounting myths and, 22
    consolidated, 529
    defined, 11
    financial reporting example, 59
    financial statement articulation, 60–62
Statements of Financial Accounting Concepts
        (SFAC), 26
statutory tax rate, worldwide, 387
Stice, K., 425n
Stickney, C., 150n
stock dividends, 425
stock equity securities, prospectus, 344n
stock exchanges, 417, 427
stock market, 16, 470
stock options
    accounting for, 17
    defined, 430
    employee, 430–435
    fair value method, 433–435
    financial analysis, 436
    GAAP, 433, 436
    managerial discretion, 436
    tax law, 433
stock price. *See* share price
stock splits, dividends, 425–428
stockholders' equity. *See* shareholders' equity
stocks, flows and, 12, 13
straight-line method
    bonds and notes, 345–346
    depreciation, 52–53, 264–266, 280, 384–387
    double-declining-balance method vs., 267
    intangible assets, 276, 277
strike price, 430
Strong, N., 475n
structured mortgage backed credit instruments, 342
sub-chapter S corporations, 24
subordinated, 341
successful efforts method, natural resources
        valuation, 278
sum-of-the-years' digits method, depreciation, 266n
supply of capital, 19
sustainable earnings
    discontinued operations, 102, 105, 106
    earnings per share, 105–106
    intercorporate investment reporting and,
        321–322

one-time gains and losses, 348
    overview, 102–103
    pro forma earnings, 108–110
    specialty and extraordinary items, 103–105
sustainable growth, 144–146, 524
Synchrony Financial, 315
systematic risk, 150–151

T

T-accounts, 532–553. *See also* debit and credit
        system
TAG Heuer, 526
takeovers, 297, 298
"taking a bath," 104, 281
tangible assets, 46, 270
tax accounting, 6
tax inversion, 387
tax law
    dividends, 321–322, 349
    GAAP vs., 397
    inventory accounting, 231
    investment accounting, 321–322
    lease accounting, 354–355
    long-term assets, 270
    revenue recognition and accounts receivable,
        195
    stock options, 433
tax rate
    pro forma financial statements, 150
    in ROA, 137, 148–149
    in ROS, 138n, 148–149
    taxable income and, 383
    worldwide, 387
tax shield, 64, 386
taxable income, 383–387, 389
taxation/taxes. *See also* tax law
    of corporations, 24, 383, 387, 388–389
    of dividends, 24
    employee retirement obligations, 392–397
    interest charges, 349
    LIFO conformity rule, 223, 231, 232,
        240–241
    organizational form and, 24
    tax payments, 101
    zero-coupon bonds, 350
temporal method, 319
temporary accounts, 533–541
temporary differences, 384–387
terminal value, 468, 470
terminal year growth rate, 461
terrorist attacks, 274, 277, 427
Texas Instruments, Inc. (TI), 87–88
Thompson, R. B., 106n
Tiffany & Company, 179
time value of money
    calculator calculation of, 512–521
    complex time value problems, solving,
        518–520
    defined, 506
    equity valuation, 469–470
    future value of a single amount, 507,
        513–515
    future value of an annuity, 508, 515–517
    market rate and book value, 346
    opportunity cost, 47, 134, 180, 187
    overview, 506–507
    present value of a single amount, 508–509,
        517
    present value of an annuity, 509–512, 518
    spreadsheet calculation of, 512–521
Time Warner, 315
timeliness, financial analysis, 147
times-interest-earned ratio, 67
Titanium Metals Corporation, 427
Tokyo Stock Exchange, 40
total asset turnover, 523
total assets

in asset turnover, 137, 522
   capital intensity and, 130, 524
   in ROA, 64, 137, 148–149, 523
total debt, net debt and, 357
Toyota, 219
tracking shares, 419
trade credit, 186n
trade terms, 194
trading securities, 299–301, 301–307
trailing multiple, 476–477
transaction costs, bonds and notes, 343
transaction summary
   aging method, 191, 192
   capital lease accounting, 353
   completed contract method, 183–184
   operating lease accounting, 354
   percent of completion method, 182–183
   percentage-of-credit-sales method, 189
   Russian River Valley Winery, 56
transactions, recording, 43–44. *See also* debit and
   credit system
transactions, related-party, 321–322
TransGlobal Airlines, 181, 183
transitory earnings, 102
treasury shares, 416, 419–420
trend analysis, 131
trial balance, 533–541
True Tax Lease, 354–355
trustee, 341, 392
Twentieth Century Fox, 471–472
Tyco International, 315

U

unbilled account receivable, defined, 182
uncollectible accounts, 187, 190–193, 198–199
uncollectible receivables, 186–193
unconsolidated affiliate-company earnings, 310
Under Armour Inc., 129, 130–135, 141–143,
   144–146
unfair competition, 383
uniform cost capitalization rules (UNICAP), 231
United Kingdom, 274, 388, 423–424
UnitedHealthcare, 434
units-of-production method, 267–269, 279
University of Iowa, 434
unlevered financial ratios, 148–149unlevered free
   cash flow, 468n
unlevered return on sales (ROS), 138n
unpaid interest expense, zero-coupon bonds, 350
unrealized gain (loss)
   accounting example, 301–307
   accounting standards vs. tax law, 384
   available-for-sale securities, 274, 428–430
   debt and equity securities, 299–301
   derivative securities, 399
   financial derivatives, 428–430
   foreign currency, 319–320
   GAAP, 274, 300, 321–322, 399, 428–430
   managerial discretion in reporting of,
      306–307
   tax law, 321–322
unsecured debt, 341
unusual items, financial reporting, 103
Urban Outfitters, Inc., 278
U.S. Census Bureau, 141
U.S. Congress, 5, 16, 306–307
U.S. Court of Appeals for the Tenth Circuit, 383

U.S. Department of Justice, 85
U.S. Department of Treasury, 240
U.S. Environmental Protection Agency, 457
U.S. Federal Trade Commission, 422
U.S. Foods, Inc., 236
U.S. GAAP. *See* generally accepted accounting
   principles (GAAP)
U.S. General Accounting Office, 388
U.S. generally accepted auditing standards, 16
U.S. House Capital Markets Subcommittee, 18
U.S. House of Representatives, 433
U.S. Securities and Exchange Commission (SEC)
   capital market registration, 344
   channel stuffing lawsuit, 85
   credit rating agencies and, 342
   establishment of, 16
   financial reporting requirements, 11, 26, 85,
      88, 147, 204n9
   Form 10-K requirements, 11
   Form 10-Q requirements, 11
   GAAP and, 18, 21–22
   IFRS and, 18
   independent auditing, 15
   mark-to-market, 18
   membership fees reporting, 68
   off-balance-sheet financing, 351, 356
   pensions rate of return, 397
   prospectus filing, 39
   Regulation G, 109
   revenue recognition guidelines, 177, 198
   stock options, 431, 434
   WorldCom suit, 263
U.S. Securities Industry Association, 17
U.S. Supreme Court, 383
U.S. Treasury Bonds, 470
U.S. Treasury Department, 349
useful life, 265, 271–273, 281, 281, 384–387
usual items, financial reporting, 103
utilitarianism, 477

V

Valley National Gas, Inc. 273
valuation
   accounting standards, 17–18
   accounts receivable, 186–193
   bonds and notes, 342–350
   debt and equity securities adjustments, 302
   earnings-based, 102
   employee stock options, 431
   equity. *See* equity valuation
   fair value adjustments, 347. *See also* fair
      value
   natural resources, 278–279
   of inventory, 222–223, 225–232
   receivables, 198–199
   special items and, 103–105
Value Investing Conference, 261
ValueLine, 470
Vanguard Group, 147
variable interest entities (VIEs), 197, 316–318
Verizon, 315
virtue-based ethics, 477
voluntary accounting policy changes, 273
Volvo, 219, 422
voting rights, 341, 419

W

wage expenses, financial reporting, 50
Wall Street Journal, 5n, 22, 388n, 434, 471–472
Waller, M., 475n
Wal-Mart, 176, 180, 379–380
Walsh Company, 434–435
warranty expense, 384
Washington, George, 342, 506–507
Waterloo Inc., 307–318
Watermark Company, 224–225
Watkins, Sherron, 322
weighted average cost of capital, 472
weighted-average cost method, 223, 225–232
weighted-average cost of debt, 352, 356–357
Wells Fargo
whistle-blowers, 322
Whole Foods Market, 457
William Wrigley Company, 425
Williams Telecommunications Group Inc., 263
Windows operating system, 413
with recourse, 196–197
without recourse, 197
Words with Friends, 39
working capital accounts, 460–462
working capital management, 554–559
work-in-process inventory, 220–221
World Trade Center, 427
WorldCom, 16, 17, 21, 24, 241, 263, 322, 431
write-downs
   capital investment, 281
   impairment, 281
   inventory, 232
   special items and, 103–105
write-offs
   accounts receivable, 187n
   asset, 384n
   credit sales, 189–193
   long-term fixed assets, 270
   uncollectible accounts, 191–192

X

Xbox, 413
Xerox, 5

Y

Yahoo! Finance, 470
yield rate, 342–344, 346

Z

Zacks Investment Research, 476
zero-coupon bonds and notes, 348–350, 464–467
zero-sum game, 399
Zeta Analysis, 342
Zhu, Z., 417
Zipped Tunes, 554–559
Z-score, 342
Zynga, 39, 54
Zynga Poker, 39